THE SERMONS OF CHARLES WESLEY

THE SERMONS OF CHARLES WESLEY

A Critical Edition, with Introduction and Notes

KENNETH G. C. NEWPORT

OXFORD

UNIVERSITY PRESS

OXFORD

UNIVERSITY PRESS

Great Clarendon Street, Oxford OX2 6DP

Oxford University Press is a department of the University of Oxford.
It furthers the University's objective of excellence in research, scholarship,
and education by publishing worldwide in

Oxford New York

Athens Auckland Bangkok Bogotá Buenos Aires Cape Town
Chennai Dar es Salaam Delhi Florence Hong Kong Istanbul Karachi
Kuala Lumpur Madrid Melbourne Mexico City Mumbai Nairobi
Paris São Paulo Shanghai Singapore Taipei Tokyo Toronto Warsaw

with associated companies in Berlin Ibadan

Oxford is a registered trade mark of Oxford University Press
in the UK and certain other countries

Published in the United States
by Oxford University Press Inc., New York

British Library Cataloguing in Publication Data

Data available

Library of Congress Cataloging in Publication Data

Data applied for

ISBN 0–19–826949–8

1 3 5 7 9 10 8 6 4 2

Typeset by J&L Composition Ltd, Filey, North Yorkshire
Printed in Great Britain
on acid-free paper by
Biddles Ltd,
www.biddles.co.uk

For my mother and father, Jean M. and Dennis W. Newport

Preface

This book brings to publication for the first time a complete collection of the sermons of Charles Wesley (1707–88), the hymn writer and co-founder of the Methodist movement. As such it is part of an attempt now apparent on more than one front to reclaim Charles as a major force in the birth and early history of the Methodist movement and allow more than just his poetic voice to be heard. Charles was, to be sure, a hymn writer of near unparalleled talent, but as a reading of his own journal and letters (and hopefully Chapter 2 of this book) will quickly indicate, his role as a preacher was no less central to his life and ministry.

In contrast to that of his brother John (1703–91), the surviving Charles Wesley sermon corpus is not vast. At the most generous count there are 23 relevant texts, and, as Chapter 4 of this book makes clear, there are significant problems with a number of these. However, in this volume all the texts that have a real claim to being those of sermons that Charles actually preached (even if they may not have come originally from his pen) have been included in an attempt to place them all in the public domain and facilitate further research. Those sermons that have the strongest claim to being by Charles himself are presented first (1–13), arranged in chronological order with any undated but 'certain' Charles Wesley compositions given later in the sequence (11–13). Those that Charles copied from John (or perhaps, on one occasion, from someone else) are presented second, again in chronological order.

The book begins with four introductory chapters dealing with Charles's preaching and the manuscript (MS) evidence that has survived illustrative of it. This sets the general context of the sermons presented in the volume. Short introductions to the individual texts themselves give more specific details on questions of the origin of the sermon, Charles's use of it, the manuscripts (MSS) for the text that have survived, and a summary of its principal points. The notes appended to the texts are largely text-critical, though an attempt has been made to trace all biblical allusions and quotations employed by Charles. Direct quotations, whether enclosed by Charles in quotation marks or not, are given in the footnotes by the relevant biblical reference only. Places where Charles seems dependent upon the biblical text (or the *Book of Common Prayer* form of it) but does not quote directly are preceded by 'cf.' Spelling has been modernized throughout the volume, but punctuation kept as close to the original as modern sensibilities will allow. The main exception here is the replacement of Charles's frequent use of the colon by a period. Charles's use of parentheses, however, has been modernized; the reader may therefore assume that anything in this volume enclosed in square brackets has been added by the editor for the sake of clarity. Such instances have been kept to an absolute minimum.

Acknowledgements

Numerous individuals and organizations have facilitated the production of this book. Special thanks are due in particular to several, chief among whom is my former student and now research assistant Ursula Leahy who, as always, has given willingly of her time and effort over several years in pursuit of what at times seemed an ever-receding goal.

Near one half of the sermon material in this book has been reconstructed from Charles's original shorthand manuscripts and though I have examined every stroke of those at times infuriating texts, I doubt that I would have had either the time or patience to work at them completely from scratch. In this context the pioneering initial work that was carried out on these MSS by Dr Oliver A. Beckerlegge of York, the Revd Tom Albin of Nashville, Tennessee, and Mr and Mrs Douglas G. Lister of Leigh-on-Sea, Essex, needs to be clearly acknowledged at this early juncture. Mr and Mrs Lister have also been exceptionally kind in assisting and advising on several passages of shorthand that appear here in transcribed form for the first time. The contributions of these earlier scholars have in a real sense made this volume possible.

Thanks are due too to Wanda Willard Smith, Methodist Archives Assistant at the Bridwell Library, Southern Methodist University, Dallas, Texas, who has shared with me the fruits of her extensive labours in compiling John Wesley's sermon log. Mrs Jocelyne Rubinetti, Methodist Library Associate at Drew University, was generous in sending material, often by fax, at almost a moment's notice. Gareth Lloyd of the John Rylands University Library of Manchester has also been more than helpful in giving assistance in tracing MSS central to this book; my election to an honorary research fellowship by the Board of the John Rylands Research Institute, University of Manchester, brought with it the provision of very welcome working space and, most importantly, full access to the Methodist collections. All the counter staff at the Rylands have been exceptionally helpful in assisting me to locate material.

Thanks are due also to the Bodleian Library for permission to reproduce the text of Sermon 8. All the remaining sermons are reproduced from manuscript and published sources held in the Methodist Archive at the John Rylands University Library of Manchester. Thanks are due to the Methodist Archives and History Committee for permission to publish this material.

I am particularly indebted to the Arts and Humanities Research Board who funded research leave during part of 1999 to enable me to complete this volume. My institution, Liverpool Hope University College, has generously supported this and other research projects and provided ideal conditions in which such extended work can be carried out. Particular thanks are due to my line manager Professor Ian Markham and to the senior management team, especially Professor Simon Lee and Revd Canon Dr John Elford, for making research in theology and religious studies a priority and clearing the necessary space elsewhere in my contract to allow it to be conducted. The Scouloudi Foundation provided a number of smaller travel grants enabling me to visit archives and libraries in various parts of the country.

Malcolm Bull has throughout encouraged and supported me in this, as he has in several other projects, with his usual patience and positive critical judgement. My wife Rose-Marie and children Matthew, Stephen, and Sarah have lived with Charles Wesley as long as I have. They have supported and encouraged me (and made some good jokes) throughout.

Liverpool   K.G.C.N.
Lent 2000

Abbreviations

BCP	*Book of Common Prayer*
J&D	W. Reginald Ward and Richard P. Heitzenrater (eds.), Journals and Diaries of John Wesley, vols. xviii–xxiii (1988–95) in the Bicentennial Edition of the Works of John Wesley
KJV	King James Version of the Bible
MARC	Methodist Archives and Research Centre
SOSO	*Sermons on Several Occasions*

Contents

PART I
Introduction

CHAPTER 1

CHARLES WESLEY AND
EARLY METHODISM

Charles Wesley (1707–88) was a man of many talents. His most widely known, to be sure, is his poetic ability, where, among religious poets and hymn writers at least,[1] he ranks favourably alongside such greats as Isaac Watts (1674–1748) and John Newton (1725–1807).[2] It was not just in the area of hymn writing and

---

[1] In this context the work of Kenneth Shields is worthy of particular note ('Charles Wesley as Poet', in ST Kimbrough (ed.), *Charles Wesley: Poet and Theologian* (Nashville, TN: Kingswood Books, 1992), 45–67). In this essay Shields argues strongly that Charles himself chose not to enter the world of secular poetry and would not wish to be judged by its standards. Rather, he argues, Charles was a writer of religious verse and that verse was often bound by a number of restrictions—it might be sung, it was largely for non-academic consumption, and commonly Charles was working so close to the biblical 'subtext' that his poetic gift was shackled to it and lacked the liberty which might have allowed it to soar to greater heights. Charles, according to Shields, did have real poetic genius and glimpses of it come occasionally into view. He might, had he chosen so to do, have developed into a great poet of his age. However, he saw his task as altogether different. This cautionary note is a wise one. Charles was a man of faith, of religious zeal, of inner conviction, and, first and foremost, a clergyman of the Church of England. It is in this context, not in a secular-philosophical one, that he needs to be seen.

[2] Studies of Charles's poetical corpus are now many. They include, most recently, that by Richard Watson, who, in his substantial study of the English Hymnic tradition, devotes a chapter and a half, comprising 44 pages, to a study of Charles (J. Richard Watson, *The English Hymn* (Oxford: Clarendon, 1997), 221–64 and bibliography). Other important studies include those J. Ernest Rattenbury, *The Evangelical Doctrine of Charles Wesley's Hymns* (London: Epworth, 1941); id., *The Eucharistic Hymns of John and Charles Wesley to Which is Appended Wesley's Preface Extracted from Brevint's 'Christian Sacrament and Sacrifice', Together with Hymns on the Lord's Supper* (London: Epworth, 1948); R. N. Flew, *The Hymns of Charles Wesley: A Study* (London: Epworth, 1953); Frank Baker, *Charles Wesley's Verse: An Introduction* (London: Epworth, 1964; rev. edn. 1988); id., *Representative Verse of Charles Wesley* (London: Epworth, 1962). There are also several unpublished theses dealing with this area, including James Dale, 'The Theological and Literary Qualities of the Poetry of Charles Wesley in Relation to the Standards of his Age' (Ph.D. thesis, University of Cambridge, 1960); Gilbert Leslie Morris, 'Imagery in the Hymns of Charles Wesley' (Ph.D. thesis, University of Arkansas, 1969); Herbert John Roth, 'A Literary Study of the Calvinistic and Deistic Implications in the Hymns of Isaac Watts, Charles Wesley and William Cowper' (Ph.D. thesis, Texas Christian University, 1978); Richard L. Flemming, 'The Concept of Sacrifice in the Eucharistic Hymns of John and Charles Wesley' (Ph.D. thesis, Southern Methodist University, 1980); E. Hannon, 'The Influence of Paradise Lost on the Hymns of Charles Wesley' (MA thesis, University of Columbia, 1985); Craig Gallaway, 'The Presence of Christ with the Worshipping Community: A Study in the Hymns of John and Charles Wesley' (Ph.D. thesis, Emory University, 1988); Wilma Jean Quantrille, 'The Triune God in the Hymns of Charles Wesley' (Ph.D. thesis, Drew University, 1989). See also more generally Teresa Berger, *Theology in Hymns? A Study of the Relationship of Doxology and Theology according to* 'A Collection of Hymns for the Use of the People Called Methodists' *(1780)*, ET by Timothy Edward Kimbrough (Nashville: Kingswood Books, 1995). There are also a large number of smaller individual studies, including those by John Kirk, *Charles Wesley, the Poet of Methodism: A Lecture* (London: Hamilton, Adams, and Co., 1860); Frederick Bird, *Charles Wesley and Methodist Hymns* (Andover: Warren F. Draper, 1864); Charles Sumner

religious poetry, however, that Charles excelled. He was adept also in writing letters, kept an informative journal, and, as is shown in this present volume, possessed also the homiletic art. Neither were his talents limited to purely intellectual or literary pursuits. As a reading of the primary sources indicates, and as will be seen later in this chapter, he was a strong and determined leader whose strength of character on occasion enabled him to deal firmly with issues to which his more famous brother John (1703–91) seemed either unwilling or unable to attend. All of these qualities are well illustrated in the vast quantity of surviving primary material illustrative of Charles's life and work. Hence the remark seems valid: Charles was a man of many talents, of which the writing of hymns was but one. If he is to be fully appreciated from an historical, literary, and theological perspective, then, attention must be given to more than just his hymns.

Practically speaking Charles has had enormous impact. It was he who formed the Oxford Holy Club, of which his brother John was later to become leader. From this band was to develop the ethos of the Methodist movement and hence Charles, as the founder of that band, was, in this very practical sense at least, the founder of Methodism itself. (This is not of course to dispute the influence of his parents, nor yet to deny that the 'Holy Club' was as much the result of a long Continental and English spiritual tradition in general as the brainchild of Charles. However, in seeking to locate the origins of Methodism there can be little doubt that the 'Holy Club' marked a significant staging-post in the movement's journey to denominational formation.) It was Charles too, rather than John, who first experienced that 'strange warming' (or 'palpitation' as Charles called it) 'of the heart' that comes with the evangelical experience.[3] From 1738 to 1749, the year of his marriage, and for several years thereafter, Charles, like his brother, travelled extensively throughout England, Ireland, and Wales in an effort to establish, sustain, and further the Methodist cause. Even after his withdrawal from the fully itinerant life, he continued to exercise a powerful influence on the direction of Methodism, especially in Bristol and London.

Nutter, 'Charles Wesley as a Hymnist', *Methodist Review* 108 (1925): 341–57; John M. Kellock, 'Charles Wesley and his Hymns', *Methodist Review* 112 (1929): 527–39; John W. Waterhouse, *The Bible in Charles Wesley's Hymns* (London: Epworth, 1954); Mark A. Noll, 'Romanticism and the Hymns of Charles Wesley', *Evangelical Quarterly* 46 (1974): 195–223; Samuel J. Rogal, 'Old Testament Prophecy in Charles Wesley's Paraphrase of Scripture', *Christian Scholar's Review* 13 (1984): 205–16; Barry E. Bryant, 'Trinity and Hymnody: The Doctrine of the Trinity in the Hymns of Charles Wesley', *Wesleyan Theological Journal* 25 (1990): 64–73; Oliver Beckerlegge, 'Charles Wesley's Poetical Corpus', in ST Kimbrough (ed.), *Charles Wesley: Poet and Theologian*, 30–44; and the work by Shields already cited. This body of secondary literature is not surprising given Charles's undoubted abilities in this area and his prodigious output; he wrote about 9,000 poetical compositions in all. Just as important as output and quality, however, is the fact that all the poetic material, unlike the prose works, is available through the work of Osborn and Kimbrough and Beckerlegge (George Osborn (ed.), *The Poetical Works of John and Charles Wesley*, 13 vols. (1868–1872); ST Kimbrough and Oliver A. Beckerlegge (eds.), *The Unpublished Poetry of Charles Wesley*, 3 vols. (Nashville, TN: Kingswood Books, 1988–92).

[3] This aspect of the brothers' lives will be considered more fully below. See especially John Lawson, 'The Conversion of the Wesleys: 1738 Reconsidered', *Asbury Theological Journal* 43 (1988): 7–44.

As one standing at the dawn of Methodism, and as a formative influence upon its early course, Charles was to have significant religious-historical impact. This is so since his influence extends well beyond the history of the Methodist movement and its links with the broader history of the Church of England as a whole, to the part he was to play in the progress of the evangelical revival in general, and indeed in the entire subsequent religious history of Britain.[4] And from Britain, Methodism, and hence Charles's influence, was to spread out across the world, in many parts of which it now has a significance far above that which it enjoys in its mother England. For example, with 8.5 million members the United Methodist Church is the second largest Protestant organization in the USA. To repeat, Charles Wesley had enormous historical impact which extends well beyond the legacy, however important, of his hymns. As an all-round religious-historical figure, no less than as a hymn writer, he cannot be ignored.

PROBLEMS OF HISTORIOGRAPHY

Despite Charles's significance, however, relatively little information regarding his life and works is as yet fully in the public domain and even when attention is given to him, it is most often in his role as the brother of John. Scholars working in Methodist studies have long lamented this situation. Typical are the opening words of the preface to C.W. Flint's work *Charles Wesley and His Colleagues*: 'Charles Wesley', states Flint, 'has been neglected and underestimated . . . Some have unintentionally belittled Charles in magnifying John'.[5] Such sentiments are repeated elsewhere. Frank Baker, for example, notes that 'Charles Wesley is not as well known, even amongst Methodists, as he deserves to be . . . The main reason for the comparative neglect of Charles Wesley is, of course, John Wesley. John has completely overshadowed his brother.'[6] Despite this acknowledgment of the problem, however, little has been done to solve it. There is still a need for a full biography of Charles that does more than summarize uncritically the contents of the only (and defective) edition of his journal.[7] However, the difficulty of the task

---

[4] We leave aside here the important discussion centred upon the nature of Methodism and its possible calming influence on eighteenth-century English society, the so-called 'Halévy thesis', after the French historian Élie Halévy (1870–1937). A summary is found in Stuart Andrews, *Methodism and Society* (London: Longman, 1970), 85–92; see also Ian R. Christie, *Stress and Stability in Late Eighteenth-Century Britain: Reflections on the British Avoidance of Revolution* (Oxford: Clarendon: 1984).

[5] C.W. Flint *Charles Wesley and His Colleagues* (Washington, DC: Public Affairs Press, 1957), vii.

[6] Frank Baker, *Charles Wesley as Revealed by His Letters* (London: Epworth, 1948), 1.

[7] The principal biographical works, in order of date, are John Whitehead, *The Life of the Rev. Charles Wesley: Late Student of the* [sic] *Christ Church, Oxford, Collected from his Private Journal* (1805); Henry Moore, *The Life of the Rev John Wesley and the Rev Charles Wesley*, 2 vols. (New York: Methodist Episcopal Church, 1824–5); Thomas Jackson, *The Life of the Rev Charles Wesley*, 2 vols. (London: John Mason, 1841); Charles Adams, *The Poet Preacher: A Brief Memorial of Charles Wesley, the Eminent Preacher and Poet* (Carlton and Porter, 1859); D. M. Jones, *Charles Wesley: A Study* (London: Epworth, 1919); F. L. Wiseman, *Charles Wesley, Evangelist and Poet* (New York: Abingdon, 1931);

of writing an adequate life of Charles should not be underestimated. Numerous problems must be negotiated. Many of these are common to biographical historiography in general, and can, with some difficulty, be at least partially overcome. Such problems include the nature of the sources available. This is particularly apparent with regard to the secondary material, the bulk of which is distinctly pro-Methodist if not positively hagiographical. (A notable exception here is Brailsford, who does, to her credit, maintain an academic distance and paints a picture of Charles 'warts and all').

Even more serious, however, is the relative unavailability of much of the Charles Wesley literary corpus, for, despite initial appearances, the basic raw material out of which the data for a full study of Charles must be hewn is not widely available to the scholarly guild, at least not in published form. In this context we may note in particular the frequent call for editions of Charles's works. Thomas Albin, for example, voiced the call when he wrote 'There is a very real need for a scholarly edition of Charles Wesley's prose works' and further 'It is time to produce a critical edition of Charles Wesley's prose writings in order to allow this great Christian poet to come to life for current and future generations.'[8] To date little has been done to bring that desired result about, though one finds occasional references to such plans in the literature. The letters are an obvious case in point: in 1948 Baker wrote in his admirable study of the letter material 'In preparation for a collected edition of Charles Wesley's letters the author has made transcripts of about 600, all but about 100 from original manuscripts.'[9] More than fifty years on that 'collected edition' is still awaited. The situation with regard to the journal is equally lamentable.

It is, however, true that a number of substantial volumes of Charles's writings are now available in print and hence a little more needs to be said regarding the potential use to which these volumes may be put by the Charles Wesley researcher. This corpus includes his extensive poetic work. Much of this is available in Osborn's *Poetical Works* (a work difficult to locate outside of specialist Methodist libraries, but generally available at such centres), and this has now been supplemented and brought to probable completion through the work of ST Kimbrough and Oliver A. Beckerlegge.[10] In addition to this poetic material there is a sub-

Mabel R. Brailsford, *A Tale of Two Brothers: John and Charles Wesley* (London: Rupert Hart-Davis, 1954); M. L. Edwards, *Sons to Samuel* (London: Epworth, 1961); E. P. Myers, *Singer of a Thousand Songs: A Life of Charles Wesley* (T. Nelson, 1965); Arnold A. Dallimore, *A Heart Set Free: The Life of Charles Wesley* (Westchester, IL: Crossway Books, 1988); John R. Tyson, *Charles Wesley on Sanctification: A Biographical and Theological Study* (Salem, OH: Schmul Publishing Co. Inc, 1992); T. Crichton Mitchell, *Charles Wesley: Man with the Dancing Heart* (Kansas: Beacon Press, 1994) and the work by Flint already cited.

[8] Thomas R. Albin, 'Charles Wesley's Other Prose Writings', in Kimbrough (ed.), *Charles Wesley: Poet and Theologian*, 85–94.

[9] Baker, *Charles Wesley as Revealed by his Letters*, 4. See also id., 'Charles Wesley's Letters', in Kimbrough (ed.), *Charles Wesley: Poet and Theologian*, 72–84.

[10] Kimbrough and Beckerlegge (eds.), *Unpublished Poetry*.

stantial amount of prose. This includes Charles's journal and some of his letters. There is even a collection of sermons,[11] and, in an early printing, a tract or two.[12] Some of this material is relatively easy to locate, other parts less so.

Such an apparently promising mass of published material, however, conceals a far less valuable reality. The hymns and poems, while absolutely central to the task of seeking a rounded picture of Charles, do not in themselves contain biographical detail either in sufficient quantity or of sufficient kind to enable the biographer properly to ply his or her trade, and with the early material there is always a nagging doubt regarding the authorship of individual compositions.[13] It is true of course that many of the hymns and poems do give an insight into certain aspects of Charles's life. For example much is to be learned regarding his experiences of conversion[14] and falling in love[15] from the hymns and poems he wrote to celebrate them. Similarly some do reflect his life situation, for example his at times stormy relationship with John, his family life,[16] the accidents that befell him,[17] and even the pugilistic abilities of Grimalkin, his pet cat.[18] However, writing a biography of Charles on the basis of the poetic material alone is clearly not possible, though writing one without integrating the material embodied in that corpus would be no less improper. The biographer, then, turns naturally to other genres, and it is here that the problems really begin.

The most obvious place for information on Charles's life is his own journal, but this is fraught with difficulties. The most obvious is that it is so incomplete, for even on the most generous reckoning it really stretches only from 1736 to 1756 (with one or two fragments from outside these dates), that is, less than one-quarter of Charles's life. In fact the entries after 1751 are so sparse and the gaps between them so great as to cut that fraction still further. The brute fact is that

---

[11] *Sermons by the Late Rev. Charles Wesley, A.M. Student of Christ-Church, Oxford. With a Memoir of the Author by the Editor* (London: Baldwin, Cradock, and Joy, 1816). The shortcomings of this edition will be discussed in detail in Chapter 4.

[12] Charles was the author of *A Short account of the Death of Hannah Richardson* (1741). It is quite commonly thought that he was also responsible for the anonymously published twelve-page pamphlet *Strictures on the Substance of a Sermon Preached at Baltimore in the State of Maryland before the General Conference of the Methodist Episcopal Church* (1785). The sermon was delivered by Thomas Coke at the ordination of Francis Asbury. The title page reports the author as 'A Methodist of the Church of England'.   [13] The problem is outlined and discussed in Baker, *Charles Wesley's Verse*, 102–115.

[14] Hence, for example, it is generally argued that the hymn 'Where shall my wond'ring soul begin, How shall I all to heaven aspire' (first published in *Hymns and Sacred Poems*, 1739) was written by Charles to celebrate his own conversion experience, and may hence be able to shed some light on this aspect of his spiritual journey.

[15] See Frank Baker, 'A Poet in Love: The Courtship of Charles Wesley, 1747–1749', *Methodist History* 29 (1991): 235–47.

[16] See Kimbrough and Beckerlegge (eds.), *Unpublished Poetry*, 1. 279–316.

[17] 'And not one single bone is broke / because He keeps them all'. Kimbrough and Beckerlegge (eds.), *Unpublished Poetry*, 3. 170–1.

[18] 'I sing Grimalkin, brave and bold who makes intruders fly': Kimbrough and Beckerlegge (eds.), *Unpublished Poetry*, 1: 280.

Charles's journal does not, so far as is presently known, cover any more than a relatively small, though centrally important, part of his life.

This less than encouraging situation is exacerbated still further by the very deficient nature of the only 'complete' edition of that journal to have been produced to date. This is contained in the two volumes produced by Thomas Jackson, first printed in 1849 and reprinted in 1984.[19] Jackson's work is not to be underestimated. He did seek to make available a text which until that time had gone largely unnoticed, and indeed was nearly lost altogether,[20] but, as is easily seen, his own editorial work leaves much to be desired. This is not the place to enter into a full discussion of all the perceived weaknesses of Jackson's edition of the journal. However, since it is the main source of information on Charles's life currently in published form, a few key observations may be made.

The most obvious problem is the numerous omissions. These are very visible to anyone reading the MS from which Jackson was working, for he himself pencilled through the passages he decided to omit. These include all shorthand passages, some of which are quite extensive, and in addition a number of longhand sections. The reasons for Jackson's omission of the shorthand passages may have been simply that he was ignorant of the shorthand system, but the possibility cannot be ruled out that he knew the shorthand and felt passages in it should remain in the privacy their writer had intended; nor the possibility that he felt the passages to be too sensitive, or too indelicate.

A good example of Jackson's omission of shorthand material will be given below, where it is noted that he decided to omit the section that deals with the various charges made against Charles by a Mrs Welch during Charles's brief sojourn in America. Examples of his omission of longhand material are many, and include the letter that Charles wrote to the bishop of London on 7 February, 1745, which begins with the tantalizing words 'My Lord, I was informed some time ago that your Lordship had received some allegations against me of one E.S. charging me with committing, or offering to commit, lewdness with her.'

It is plain, then, that Jackson's work leaves much to be desired. Some of the problems can be rectified by consulting the later and generally better work of John Telford and/or, for the very early section, Elijah Hoole.[21] In this some, though still not all, of the shorthand sections were deciphered by Nehemiah Curnock, which is an improvement. However, Telford only completed the section of the journal up to August 1739. Similarly, Martin Brose has carried out some work on the journal for the year 1738; his annotation is particularly useful, but is in German.[22] A few

---

[19] Jackson, *The Journal of the Rev. Charles Wesley*; reprint Baker Book House, 1984.

[20] The story of how it was discovered on the floor of a public warehouse is well known. See Jackson, *Journal*, i. v for a brief account.

[21] John Telford (ed.), *The Journal of the Rev. Charles Wesley: The Early Journal 1736–1739* (London: Robert Culley, [1910]); Elijah Hoole, *Oglethorpe and the Wesleys in America* (London: 1863).

[22] Martin E. Brose, *Charles Wesley (1707–1738): Tagebuch 1738* (Stuttgart: Christliches Verlagshaus, 1992).

smaller sections were published by Tyson and Lister.[23] Jackson's is the only edition for the journal after 1739 and hence scholars working in this field have become heavily dependent upon it.

There is also the problem of Jackson's almost total reliance upon one single MS, the bound MS journal now catalogued as DDCW 10/2 in the John Rylands University Library of Manchester.[24] This is by far the most important journal MS, but it is certainly not the only one. For example, the folio DDCW 6 contains some 32 further MS journal fragments (mostly in the form of letters)[25] and the Colman box in the Manchester Archives contains another four. Most of these journal fragments (or 'journal letters') overlap significantly with DDCW 10/2 and almost all cover periods also covered in the bound journal.[26] However, where DDCW 10/2 and the material in DDCW 6 do overlap, it is the latter that is the more extensive. Indeed, what has probably happened is that Charles himself used the material now found in DDCW 6 (and many other such items that seem now to have been lost) in the compilation of his 'Journal Extract', as he himself titles DDCW 10/2. One example will suffice to make the point. Charles's journal extract for 17 May, 1743 is brief, recording simply that he set out for the North with Mr Gurney and on the way preached in Painswick and had a somewhat favourable response. In DDCW 6/3, however, the entry is a good deal longer and records also how Charles travelled back to Brother Wynn's 'rejoicing and singing hosannah to the Son of David'. This was followed by two hours or so of prayer and 'the word of exhortation' and, Charles records, 'the Lord comforted us greatly by each other'. This pattern of partial overlap between DDCW 6 and DDCW 10/2 continues to the end of the entries.

There is more material still dispersed across the surviving corpus. For example the MS now catalogued as DDCW 7/102, though a letter to his wife Sarah, reads very much like a journal entry, giving details of his activities on 12 and 13 February 1759. Similarly, DDCW 5/73, again a letter to Sarah, includes a day-by-day account of Charles's activities from 20 to 23 September 1755. Both sections are absent from DDCW 10/2. In fact, then, the true extent of the surviving Charles Wesley journal will not be known until all folios and other collections of early Methodist materials held at the Rylands and elsewhere have been examined and

[23] Douglas A. Lister and John R. Tyson, 'Charles Wesley, Pastor: A Glimpse inside his Shorthand Journal', *QR: The Methodist Quarterly Review* 4 (1984): 9–21 and John R. Tyson, 'Charles Wesley, Evangelist: The Unpublished Newcastle Journal', *Methodist History* 25 (1986): 41–60.

[24] In this volume references given to Charles's journal are to his 'journal extract', the MS of which is now held at the Methodist Archives and Research Centre (MARC) at the John Rylands University Library of Manchester (MARC DDCW 10/2). References to that MS are here given as 'DDCW 10/2' followed by '*in loc.*' since the page numbering is not consistent. The various editions of this text and associated problems and observations are discussed in more detail later in this chapter.

[25] MARC DDCW 6/1–30, 88a–88b.

[26] As an exception see DDCW 6/1, which contains information relating to Charles's activities from 23 September to 2 October 1742. This material is entirely absent from DDCW 10/2. Tyson's publication, 'Charles Wesley, Evangelist: The Unpublished Newcastle Journal', is a transcription of that MS. The contents of DDCW 6/2 (10 March 1743) are also absent from the extract, though, curiously enough, Charles has left a blank page where they ought perhaps to have been inserted.

compared with DDCW 10/2, the journal extract. This is a painstaking task; it is
under way at the time of writing, but it will be some time yet before a reliable
edition of the journal is finally in print.

The sum of these observations is that Jackson's edition cannot be taken as pro-
viding the scholarly guild with 'Charles Wesley's journal'; the situation is much
more complex. Jackson did not take into account all of the available material and
even cut passages from his main source, DDCW 10/2. Scholars dependent upon
Jackson (even where supplemented by Telford, Hoole, and Brose) are therefore
working with a highly deficient source. Further, as has been noted above, even if
Jackson had collated all the MS material and faithfully reproduced what he found,
we would still have a journal for only 25 per cent of Charles's life. Further
material is needed.

That material comes mainly in the form of the letters. This body of evidence is
in an even worse state of academic repair than the journal. The only substantial
collection of Charles's letters is the 106 items published by Jackson as an appendix
to his edition of the journal.[27] His editorial scissors are again in evidence, though
how widely they were employed is not as yet clear. Baker has published a few more
of the letters in full, and extracts from others, in his *Charles Wesley as Revealed by
his Letters*. Baker has also published Charles's letters to John (to 1755) in his edition of the letters of John Wesley,[28] and some few other items have been published
individually by other scholars.[29] However, even when all this material is added
together it represents only a small fraction of what has actually survived. Already
in 1948 Baker had counted 600 surviving letters by Charles, though no list is provided, a count which seems broadly in line with the holdings of the Rylands. A
small number of other letters are found outside the Rylands. These include a
collection of 27 at Drew University and others at Southern Methodist University,
Duke University and Garrett Theological Seminary. There is even one Charles
Wesley letter in the Dunedin Public Library in New Zealand. Letters coming in
to Charles (the 'in' letters) are even more numerous. These will need to be considered alongside the 'out' letters (letters written by Charles) if the context of the
correspondence is to become apparent.

One other body of evidence also in need of attention is the relatively few reports
and tracts written by Charles, most of which, unlike *A Short Account of the Death
of Mrs Hannah Richardson*, were never actually published. These include the fairly
extensive report on Charles's dealings with the French Prophetess, Mrs Lavington.[30]
There is also an extensive tract on the Lord's Supper, held at the MARC,[31] that
has been catalogued as a Charles Wesley Treatise on the Lord's Supper, though in

---

[27] Jackson, *Journal*, ii. 167–286.

[28] Frank Baker (ed.), *Letters I–II*, vols. xxv and xxvi in the Bicentennial Edition of the Works of John
Wesley (Oxford: Clarendon, 1980–2).

[29] See for example Kenneth G. C. Newport, *Apocalypse and Millennium: Studies in Biblical Eisegesis*
(Cambridge: Cambridge University Press, 2000), ch. 6.

[30] DDCW 8/12; brief details of this episode are found also in the journal.   [31] MARC DDCW 8/16.

fact this item may not be by Charles, and items such as a substantial MS in French held at Wesley College, Bristol.[32] These, together with numerous prayers, short notes, and transcriptions, all need attention before Charles can be appreciated for more than just his undoubted poetic talent. Indeed, there really is little point in seeking to write a biography before this extensive work is done, and the efforts of those who have attempted it are doomed to failure.

This failure is seen, for example, in the work of T. Crichton Mitchell. This is not a book to be dismissed lightly. It is substantial (267 pages including notes) and the writer is clearly well acquainted with the Wesleyan tradition. In the introduction Mitchell states that it is part of his desire 'to coax Charles out from that shadow [of his brother John] insofar as the records allow'.[33] However, the laudable aspiration in this statement of intent is not realized in the work itself. The shortcomings are several, but most seem to stem from the fact that despite Mitchell's implied claim to have examined 'the records' relating to Charles Wesley, he appears to base his entire understanding of Charles on nothing but published sources, mostly Jackson's edition of the journal and the 106 letters, the extracts of the letters in Baker, and the published poetic material. There seems not to be any evidence in the work itself to suggest that Mitchell has accessed any unpublished MS material, and his bibliography does nothing to offset this initial reading. The result is a traditional portrait of Charles that fails to reflect the picture given by the MS materials.

A BRIEF ACCOUNT OF CHARLES'S LIFE

Such problems of availability and deficiencies in the editing of the relevant primary materials have, then, led to an understanding of Charles that is at best patchy, and no attempt can be made to rectify that situation here. However, in an attempt to set the sermons presented in this volume within the broader context of Charles's career, a brief summary of his life follows. Where possible, unpublished materials illustrative of Charles's life have been utilized in an effort to underscore once again the wealth of material that remains as yet untapped.

The precise date of Charles's birth is not altogether clear, though it was in 1707, almost certainly in December, and in all probability on the 18th day of that month.[34] He was the fifteenth or sixteenth[35] child of Samuel Wesley sen.

---

[32] Wesley College D2/9.   [33] Mitchell, *Man with the Dancing Heart*, 11.

[34] See especially Charles's entry for 18 December, 1749, where he writes, 'Mon. Dec. 18. My birthday. FORTY years long have I now grieved and tempted God, proved him, and seen his works. I was more and more sensible of it all day, till I quite sunk under the burden' (DDCW 10/2 *in loc.*). He was actually 42; and see further Frederick C. Gill, *Charles Wesley: The First Methodist* (London: Lutterworth Press, 1964), 17, which discusses the ambiguity surrounding this point in more detail.

[35] The precise number of children in the Wesley household is not absolutely clear. For a very thorough account of the problem and a list of infants see Charles Wallace (ed.), *Susanna Wesley: The Complete Writings* (Oxford: Oxford University Press, 1997), 8. Wallace is drawing on Frank Baker's study of baptismal and burial records.

(1662–1735)[36] rector of Epworth, and Susanna Wesley, née Annesley (1669–1742), a woman whose strong Christian and pedagogic influence Charles was to feel throughout his life.[37] Of his many siblings, only nine survived to maturity,[38] and indeed he himself is said to have been at death's door for the first several weeks of his life. The story of his premature birth and subsequent period wrapped in cotton wool in front of the Epworth fire is commonly reported in the standard biographies and need not be repeated here.[39] At least two of his siblings, his elder brothers John and Samuel, were to play major roles in Charles's life: Samuel as his surrogate father during his years at Westminster school (1716–27) and John as his partner in the often stormy relationship they were later to share as co-founders, shapers, and leaders of the Methodist movement. Maldwyn Edwards has argued that his sister Kezia (Kezzy), too, was important in this context.[40]

The Epworth Rectory of Charles's early years was an intellectually stimulating place. His father was no mean scholar of the classics; his Latin work *Dissertations on Job*,[41] while perhaps not a great work, at least bears witness to a committed pursuit of scholarship and to the generally academic environment in which Charles spent the first years of his life.[42] His mother was clearly a determined pedagogue. Indeed, Susanna's educational and catechetical writings alone occupy some 120 pages of Wallace's edition of her works. These include an essay in the form of a letter 'On Educating my Family' which Wallace suggests 'has become something of a classic statement of evangelical child-rearing practices'.[43] Charles's brothers were intellectually vibrant, though as a result of the age gap Charles's acquaintance with Samuel jnr. in his early years must have been very slight (Samuel had departed for Westminster School three years before Charles's birth). Among his sisters, Mehetabel (Hetty) especially was clearly a woman of outstanding intellectual ability.[44]

After initial education at home Charles entered Westminster School in 1716.[45] He was elected in 1721 as King's Scholar and finally was Captain of the school

[36] There are three Samuel Wesleys to be noted here, Charles's father, elder brother, and son. In this volume they are referred to as Samuel sen., Samuel jun., and Samuel III. Charles's grandson, the great church musician Samuel Sebastian Wesley (1810–76), is not relevant here.

[37] A brief study of Susanna with remarks on her influence on her two more famous sons is found in Maldwyn Edwards, *Family Circle: A Study of the Epworth Household in Relation to John and Charles Wesley* (London: Epworth, 1949), 57–86; more extensive is John A. Newton, *Susanna Wesley and the Puritan Tradition in Methodism* (London: Epworth, 1968).

[38] These were Samuel Jun. (1690–1739), Emilia (1692?–c.1771), Susanna (c.1695–1764), Mary (c.1696–1734), Mehetabel (c.1697/8–1750), Anne (1701–?; she married in 1725), John (1703–91), Martha (1706–91), and Kezia (1709–41).   [39] See for example Gill, *First Methodist*, 17.

[40] Edwards, *Family Circle*, 178–9.   [41] Samuel Wesley, *Dissertationes in Librum Jobi* (1735).

[42] Samuel Wesley sen. also wrote a number of hymns and poems, the most famous of which is surely 'Behold the saviour of mankind / nailed to the wooden tree', which John included in the 1780 'Large Hymn book'. See Franz Hildebrandt and Oliver A. Beckerlegge (eds.), *A Collection of Hymns for the Use of the People Called Methodists*, (vol. vii (1983) in the Bicentennial Edition of the Works of John Wesley; 27 vols, Nashville, TN: Abingdon Press), 107.   [43] Wallace, *Susanna Wesley*, 365–484.

[44] The only work about her is Arthur Quiller-Couch, *Hetty Wesley* (New York and London: Macmillan, 1903), which is actually a novel.

[45] In a letter to Dr Chandler, an Anglican clergyman who was about to set sail for America, Charles himself wrote, 'Rev[d] and dear Sir / As you are setting out for America, and I for a more distant country,

from 1725. Little primary material illustrative of these years is available to the researcher.[46] One detail from the period is, however, reasonably well known and worthy of slightly more generous comment. This concerns Charles's refusal of an offer made by Garrett Wesley, a distant family relation and wealthy childless Irishman, to take Charles on as an adopted son with a view to making him heir to the family estates. The proposal must have been attractive to Charles, as indeed to his father, with the promise of wealth it entailed. It was subsequently taken up by the future grandfather of the first Duke of Wellington. Precisely why Charles refused is unclear, as are the conditions that Garrett Wesley proposed to put in place.[47] The incident represents, however, an early manifestation of Charles's apparent lack of concern for material wealth (though in later life he was fairly well off), a characteristic that was to surface once more in Boston, where he rejected the offer of a comfortable living, and again upon his proposed marriage to Sarah Gwynne. At that time he made it the subject of a written agreement that he was not to benefit financially in any way should his wife die before him. In such an event all potential inheritance was to revert to the Gwynnes and not to himself. [48] Even at this earlier time, however, Charles's mind was clearly set on independence and the pursuit of the academic life.

In 1727 Charles entered Christ Church, Oxford, and it was here, a year later and under his guidance and inspiration, that the 'Holy Club', the spiritual birthplace of organized Methodism, began. That story is well-known and only the briefest of outlines need be provided.

On 22 January 1729,[49] in what is probably the second[50] earliest letter of Charles to have survived, he wrote to John of a new sense of spiritual concern, the awakening

I think it needful to leave you some account of myself and my companions through life. At 8 years old, in 1716, I was sent by my father, Rector of Epworth, to Westminster school and placed under the care of my eldest brother, Samuel, a strict Churchman, who brought me up in his own principles. My brother John, five years older than me, was then at the Charter-house.'
   This letter is dated 28 April, 1785 and is now held at the Rylands (MARC DDWES 1/38). It is printed in full in John R. Tyson, *Charles Wesley: A Reader* (New York: Oxford University Press, 1989), 58–61. Some further extracts from this letter are given below.

[46] Among the few items that have survived is a list of scholars who were admitted to Westminster with Charles (MARC DDCW 4/1). There is also a list of scholars of Westminster awarded scholarships to Christ Church, Oxford (MARC DDCW 4/2). Both these are photographs of the original, which are held at Westminster School.   [47] On this episode see further Gill, *First Methodist*, 33.
   [48] See further Gill, *First Methodist*, 57.
   [49] The letter (MARC DDCW 1/2) is a single folded sheet, written in two parts dated 5 January and 22 January 1729. On the reverse of the MS John Wesley has written 'June 5' and has been followed in this dating by a later annotator. However, Charles's dates of 5 and 22 January seem clear enough in the letter itself. Here, as elsewhere in this volume, the dating system has been modernized. According to the Julian calendar New Year's Day fell on 25 March; according to the Gregorian the year began on 1 January. Hence letters dated by Charles in January, February, and March need to be seen in this context. The letter DDCW 1/1, for further example, is clearly dated by Charles 'January 1727', but for the modern reader this needs adjusting to 1728. The Gregorian calendar was adopted in England in 1752. After that date Charles generally dates letters according to the new way of reckoning.
   [50] The first (MARC DDCW 1/1) was addressed to John and dated January 1727 (= 1728). Baker gives a summary and selections from the letter in Baker, *Charles Wesley as Revealed by his Letters*, 8–10.

of which he put down to the prayers of his mother.[51] This was followed on 5 May by a letter which speaks of a 'coldness' that Charles is experiencing. The coldness is not a surprise: 'one who like me has for almost 13 years', writes Charles, 'been utterly inattentive at public prayers, can't expect to find there that warmth he has never known'.[52] In this same letter Charles refers to 'Bob' (Robert Kirkham)[53] and 'a modest, humble, well-disposed youth' (William Morgan).[54] These three, under Charles's leadership, were the first members of the Holy Club, and it was from this small band, of which John was not yet a member, that the Methodist movement was eventually to grow. The most important details are given by Charles himself, who wrote of these early years in Oxford,

In 1727 I was elected student of Christ-church. My brother John was then fellow of Lincoln. My first year at College I lost in diversions. The next I set myself to study. Diligence led me into serious thinking. I went to the weekly sacrament, and persuaded 2 or 3 young scholars to accompany me, and to observe the method of study prescribed by the statutes of the University. This gained me the harmless nickname of Methodist. In half a year my brother left his curacy at Epworth, and came to our assistance. We then proceeded regularly in our studies, and in doing what good we could to the bodies and souls of men.[55]

Hence the Oxford Holy Club came into existence, though it was not known by this name until a little later.[56] Here was a small group of well-intentioned individuals determined to bring some order and method to the study and practice of religion. Regular communion, regular prayer, and Bible reading formed their staple diet. As Gill observes, there is no hint here of new theology, no suggestion of separation, no radical departure from tradition.[57] Such fitted Charles's temperament, and these non-separatist ideals were ones to which he remained committed to the end of his life.[58] He could not have foreseen then the direction these

---

[51] The relevant passage is quoted by Baker, *Charles Wesley as Revealed by his Letters*, 10–11. It reads, 'I verily think, dear brother, I shall never quarrel with *you* again, till I do with my religion, and that I may never do *that* I am not ashamed to desire your prayers. 'Tis owing in great measure to somebody's (my mother's most likely) that I am come to think as I do, for I can't tell myself how or when I first awoke out of my lethargy—only that 'twas not long after you went away.'

[52] Charles Wesley to John Wesley, 5 May 1729 (MARC DDCW 1/3).

[53] Robert Kirkham (*c*.1708–67) was son of the Revd Lionel Kirkham, rector of Stanton in Gloucestershire. He was a student of Merton College, Oxford (BCL 1735). He later succeeded his father as rector of Stanton, a post he held in 1739–66 (see Donald M. Lewis, *The Blackwell Dictionary of Evangelical Biography 1730–1860*, 2 vols. (Oxford: Blackwell, 1995), ii. 652).

[54] William Morgan (1712?–32) was born in Dublin, the son of Richard Morgan sen. He entered Christ Church in 1728. His poor mental and physical health and early death in August 1732 were by some attributed to his adherence to the strict rules of the Holy Club, a charge rebutted by John Wesley in a letter to Richard Morgan sen. on 19 October, 1732 (Baker, *Letters*, xxv. 335–44). On Morgan see further Samuel Rogal, *A Biographical Dictionary of Eighteenth Century Methodism* (Lewiston, NY: Edwin Mellen Press, 8 vols., 1997–), iv. 276–81; Lewis, *Dictionary of Evangelical Biography*, ii. 792.

[55] Charles Wesley to Dr Chandler (MARC DDWES 1/38).

[56] Richard P. Heitzenrater, *Mirror and Memory: Reflections on Early Methodist History* (Nashville, TN: Kingswood Books, 1989), 65.   [57] Gill, *First Methodist*, 37.

[58] Thus even in the letter to Chandler, written three years before Charles's death, he wrote, 'I never lost my dread of separation, or ceased to guard our societies against it. I frequently told them, "I am

'Methodists' were later to take. Indeed, given his vehement opposition to moves towards the later separation of the Methodist movement from the Church of England (including his stinging attacks on John), had he been able so to foresee the results of his actions he might well have felt constrained to strangle his Holy Club at birth.

As Charles himself notes in the letter quoted above, the group which he had brought together continued much as it was for 'half a year'. After this period, however, John Wesley returned to Oxford, having taken a year's absence from Lincoln College in order to assist his father in the Epworth parish, and he took over the leadership of the fledgling movement. It was also at this time that Charles met George Whitefield, with whom, despite serious theological differences and some tension, he was to have a lifelong friendship.[59] Charles recruited him to the cause. Alongside rigorous observance of the religious life including prayer, fasting, Bible reading, and attendance at the sacrament, the members of the group now extended their efforts beyond themselves and into social concern. The visitation of those held at the Castle (Oxford prison) was a matter of particular concern and Charles visited the condemned regularly.[60]

Life at Oxford continued for Charles much in this manner for the next several years. However, in 1735 Samuel Wesley sen. died and the Epworth household was broken up. Contributing to, and indeed also a probable symptom of, that destabilizing break-up was the decision of John and Charles to leave for America. Their main intention seems to have been the conversion of the Native Americans. Charles, however, was also engaged as secretary to General Oglethorpe, Governor of the Colony. In preparation for work in America Charles was ordained deacon in the Church of England on 21 September, 1735 and priest a week later.[61] According to his later statements this was not a move that he himself felt particularly anxious to make. He later wrote,

I took my degrees; and only thought of spending all my days in Oxford. But my brother, who always had the ascendant over me, persuaded me to accompany him and Mr Oglethorpe to Georgia. I exceedingly dreaded entering into holy orders, but he overruled me here also, and I was ordained Deacon by the Bishop of Oxford, and the next Sunday Priest by the Bishop of London.[62]

your servant as long as you remain members of the Church of England; but no longer. Should you forsake her, you would renounce me"' (MARC DDWES 1/38).

[59] George Whitefield (1714–70), a student of Pembroke College, in 1734 approached Charles, who introduced him to John.

[60] Richard P. Heitzenrater, *Wesley and the People Called Methodists* (Nashville, TN: Abingdon Press, 1995), 42, provides some of the evidence.

[61] Charles's diaconal ordination certificate has survived. It is located in the MARC DDCW 6/37.

[62] Charles Wesley to Dr Chandler (MARC DDWES 1/38).

The two set sail, with two other of the Oxford Methodists, Benjamin Ingham[63] and Charles Delamotte,[64] on 22 October, 1735.

The journey, ill-fated it seems from the beginning, got off to a very slow start. The weather delayed the ship at Cowes on the Isle of Wight until 10 December. It was during this time that Charles is first known for certain to have preached, and one of those very early sermons, on 1 Kings 18: 21, has survived in written form. It is printed below as Sermon 2. If his brother's report is to be believed, this was a successful first outing, an early sign of the homiletic success that was to come.[65] On 9 March, 1736, the day Charles's MS journal extract begins, he finally set foot on St Simon's Island and began his brief sojourn in America.[66]

Life for Charles in America proved difficult, especially when Oglethorpe's opinion of him took a turn for the worse and he found himself without some of even the most basic necessities of life. Why this deterioration in the relationship occurred is not altogether clear. Gill puts it down to the pressures of office and the hardships of colonial life,[67] and there is perhaps an element of truth in that suggestion. More significant than these general administrative pressures, however, was the friction that arose as a result of rumours put around by a Mrs Welch and a Mrs Hawkins. It is extremely difficult to untangle these rumours, since the only evidence available is Charles's report of Mrs Welch's account of her own views and those of Mrs Hawkins. However, from that no doubt distorted evidence it seems that Welch told Charles that Oglethorpe was a 'wicked man and a perfect stranger to religion' who 'kept a mistress in England' and now had designs on both Welch and Hawkins. She claimed further that it was Oglethorpe's view, instilled by reports given him by Hawkins, that John had designs on Hawkins, and Charles on Welch. If this is an accurate account of Oglethorpe's understanding of the situation (the real situation is not actually relevant in this context) there is clearly cause for tension. Oglethorpe has designs on Hawkins but thinks that he has a challenger in the person of John Wesley. He has designs also on Welch, for whose affections Charles is a rival. The account of these charges is written in shorthand in Charles's journal extract and has not to date been brought to publication, or even fully deciphered, a deficiency that has probably led to some misunderstanding of the

[63] On Ingham (1712–72) see especially Richard P. Heitzenrater (ed.), *Diary of an Oxford Methodist: Benjamin Ingham 1733–1734* (Durham, NC: Duke University Press, 1985).

[64] Charles Delamotte (1714?-96), son of Thomas Delamotte, from Bexley, Kent, is mentioned in the first entry of John Wesley's journal. See W. Reginald Ward and Richard P. Heitzenrater (eds.), *Journals and Diaries of John Wesley* (hereafter *J&D*), vols. xviii–xxiii (1988–93) in the Bicentennial Edition of the Works of John Wesley, i. 136. He did not return to England until 1738 (*J&D*, xviii. 136 n. 2) where he became a Moravian.

[65] See *J&D*, xviii. 140; this will be discussed more fully in the Introduction to Sermon 2.

[66] An earlier glimpse into Charles's first experience of life in America is found in a letter to Sally Kirkham dated 5 and 14 February 1736 (MARC DDCW 1/6). This letter has been discussed extensively elsewhere and that work need not be repeated here. See the transcription (Elsie Harrison, 'A Charles Wesley Letter'), and discussion (Frank Baker, 'Charles Wesley to Varanese'), *Proceedings of the Wesley Historical Society* 25 (1945–6): respectively 17–23 and 97–104; Tyson, *Charles Wesley: A Reader*, 61–3; Baker, *Charles Wesley as Revealed by his Letters*, 22–3.   [67] Gill, *First Methodist*, 52.

complexities and frustrations of Charles's life in America on the part of later biographers.

The problems posed by Welch's accusations were not the only ones Charles faced. The journal account suggests also that he faced a certain amount of animosity as a result of the incarceration of the colony's doctor for firing a gun on a Sunday. In outline the doctor blamed Charles for having him confined by a 'priestly order' for the offence. Consequently when a Mrs Lawley miscarried, Oglethorpe placed the blame on Charles, suggesting that she had been denied proper medical treatment due to the doctor's confinement. Charles was probably innocent, but the strain shows in the journal. He was also not really to blame for the dispute that arose regarding the baptism of infants by immersion ('dipping'). Such a practice is assumed in the *BCP* ('Publick Baptism of Infants') and he was following what was there laid down. Nevertheless, a Mrs Germain was unhappy with the idea of the triune baptism of her child by immersion, and, though she was prevailed upon by her husband and finally gave her consent, at the actual service she refused to allow her child to be baptized in this manner. The journal also records a stormy incident between Charles and Mrs Hawkins regarding her treatment of her maid.[68]

Given these problems and tensions, it is perhaps not surprising that Charles's stay in America was short. On 25 July, 1736 he wrote a letter of resignation from the post as secretary, and soon after began what was to be a long journey back to England. After a period in Boston, which was generally pleasant but marred (as was much of Charles's life) by illness, he eventually arrived back in England on 3 December, 1736. During the course of the next year Charles's life was a busy one. Much of the time was spent in visiting family and friends, and reporting on the situation in Georgia to various official bodies, though he also carried out spiritual duties, including preaching and administering the sacrament.[69]

As Gill and others have noted, there were influences at work upon Charles during this time that were soon to bear fruit.[70] Perhaps the most important of these was William Law (1686–1761). 'Mr Law', who was himself heavily influenced by such giants of the mystical tradition as John Tauler (1300–61) and Thomas à Kempis (1379?–1471) looms large in the journal from 1737 and it is clear that Charles is falling under his influence. He wrote a vigorous defence of Law in a letter to an unidentified correspondent in 1739.[71] The words he uses are expressive of a deep emotional experience, both his own and that of those to whom he reads and recommends Law's works. For example, on 16 September 1737 Charles read

---

[68] See DDCW 10/2 *in loc.;* Telford, *Journal*, 9.

[69] Note for example the entry for Sunday 5 June: 'We all went in an hired coach to Warmley; where I preached "Few saved", and was pleased to see the family stay the unexpected sacrament' and for Saturday 2 July: 'I was at the Nunnery; and the next day preached at Hatfield. Slept at Cheshunt' (see also 21 and 25 August; 11 and 18 September; 2, 9 and 30 October; 13 and 20 November). MARC DDCW 10/2 *in loc.*; Telford, *Journal*, 118, 120, 121, 122, 123, 124, 126, 127, 129, 130.

[70] Gill, *First Methodist*, 65.   [71] MARC DDCW 5/1

parts of Law's work to his sister Kezzy: 'She was greatly moved, full of tears and sighs, and eagerness for more.'[72] The content of Law's work, especially his *A Serious Call to a Devout and Holy Life* (1728), had a general appeal to the early eighteenth-century evangelicals.[73] Its emphasis upon the pursuit of holiness through the moral virtues, meditation, and self-denial seems, from what we can tell from the journal accounts, to have been particularly appealing to Charles. The fact that he was still trying to procure and pass on copies of Law's work as late as 1783[74] indicates clearly that this influence was more than a passing fad and went more than skin deep. [75]

Charles was also influenced during this time by the Moravians, and in particular the Moravian bishop Count Nikolaus von Zinzendorf (1700–60). Zinzendorf, a firm believer in and preacher of the 'religion of the heart', had arrived in London some time prior to 19 January 1737, when he had sent for Charles and made him 'promise to call every day'.[76] Again the journal indicates that Charles was in the company of 'the Count' and/or Moravians fairly frequently during the early part of that year.[77] He spoke highly of their example and used it to encourage others.[78] During the latter part of 1738 Charles was still in the habit of spending time listening to John's account of and reading 'Moravian experiences'.[79]

A third important influence was that of the German Moravian Peter Böhler (1712–75). Charles began teaching Böhler English on 20 February 1738,[80] but on 22 February was listening to him (presumably in a language other than English) on the subject of the necessity of prayer and faith.[81] The story of how Böhler came to Charles's bedside and shook his head is well-known, but bears repeating here. Charles wrote,

At six in the evening, an hour after I had taken my electuary, the toothache returned more violently than ever. I smoked tobacco; which set me a-vomiting, and took away my senses and pain together. At eleven I waked in extreme pain, which I thought would quickly separate soul and body. Soon after Peter Böhler came to my bedside. I asked him to pray for me. He seemed unwilling at first, but, beginning very faintly, he raised his voice by degrees, and prayed for my recovery with strange confidence. Then he took me by the hand, and calmly said, 'You will not die now.' I thought within myself, 'I cannot hold out in this pain till morning. If it abates before, I believe I may recover.' He asked me, 'Do you hope to be saved?' 'Yes.' 'For what reason do you hope it?' 'Because I have used my best endeavours to

---

[72] MARC DDCW 10/2 *in loc.*; Telford, *Journal*, 124.

[73] See further A. Brown-Lawson, *John Wesley and the Anglican Evangelicals of the Eighteenth Century* (Edinburgh: Pentland Press, 1994), 14–24.   [74] MARC DDCW 6/43.

[75] On Law and the Wesleys see further E. W. Baker, *A Herald of the Evangelical Revival: A Critical Inquiry into the Relation of William Law to John Wesley and the Beginnings of Methodism* (London: Epworth, 1948).   [76] MARC DDCW 10/2 *in loc.*; Telford, *Journal*, 111.

[77] See 23 January, 1, 2, 5, 7, 12, 18 and 20 February (MARC DDCW 10/2 *in loc.*, Telford, *Journal*, 133, 134).   [78] See MARC DDCW 10/2 *in loc.* 8 February, 1737; Telford, *Journal*, 114.

[79] See 17 September, 1738 (MARC DDCW 10/2 *in loc.*; Telford, *Journal*, 204) and 27 September, 1738 (MARC DDCW 10/2 *in loc.*; Telford, *Journal*, 204–5).

[80] MARC DDCW 10/2 *in loc.*; Telford, *Journal*, 134.

[81] MARC DDCW 10/2 *in loc.*; Telford, *Journal*, 134.

serve God.' He shook his head, and said no more. I thought him very uncharitable, saying in my heart, 'What, are not my endeavours a sufficient ground of hope? Would he rob me of my endeavours? I have nothing else to trust to.'[82]

The 'uncharitable' Böhler had by 19 April become 'that man of God', and Charles was also glad to see him on 28 April, when again he was ill.

In the morning Dr. Cockburn came to see me; and a better physician, Peter Böhler, whom God had detained in England for my good. He stood by my bedside, and prayed over me, that now at least I might see the divine intention in this and my late illness. I immediately thought it might be that I should again consider Böhler's doctrine of faith; examine myself whether I was in *the faith*; and if I was not, never cease seeking and longing after it till I attained it.[83]

Böhler was replaced in his role as Charles's unofficial spiritual director by 'Mr Bray' 'a poor ignorant mechanic, who knows nothing but Christ; yet by knowing Him, knows and discerns all things'.[84] Like Böhler, Bray encouraged Charles to think about the grounds of his salvation and brought him ever closer to the assurance he desired.

It is clear, then, that during this period Charles was seeking and finding answers to his personal religious quest. Despite his unbending allegiance to the Church of England, it was nevertheless to the Moravians, especially Zinzendorf and Böhler, and to the non-juror William Law, that he turned for spiritual instruction.

On 21 May his 'Day of Pentecost' came. The entry in the journal is a lengthy one and worth careful consideration. It ends

I now found myself at peace with God, and rejoiced in hope of loving Christ. My temper for the rest of the day was, mistrust of my own great, but before unknown, weakness. I saw that by faith I stood; by the continual support of faith, which kept me from falling, though of myself I am ever sinking into sin. I went to bed still sensible of my own weakness (I humbly hope to be more and more so), yet confident of Christ's protection.[85]

The accounts we have of the events of the day are a jumble, and there is clearly more to the story than can be found in the journal record. However, whatever the truth of the matter, the day was clearly a psychological breakthrough for Charles and it was, if the sermons themselves are anything to go by, a turning-point in his religious experience.[86] This is considered in greater depth in Chapter 3, where it

---

[82] MARC DDCW 10/2 *in loc.*; Telford, *Journal*, 134–5.
[83] MARC DDCW 10/2 *in loc.*; Telford, *Journal*, 138.
[84] 11 May (MARC DDCW 10/2 *in loc.*; Telford, *Journal*, 139).
[85] MARC DDCW 10/2 *in loc.*; Telford, *Journal*, 149.
[86] As always the hymns are also important. On 23 May Charles records in his journal that 'At nine I began an hymn upon my conversion, but was persuaded to break off, for fear of pride. Mr. Bray coming, encouraged me to proceed in spite of Satan. I prayed Christ to stand by me, and finished the hymn' (MARC DDCW 10/2 *in loc.*; Telford, *Journal*, 151).

What that hymn was has been the subject of considerable debate; see for example Dallimore, *A Heart Set Free*, 61–3 and Mitchell, *Man with the Dancing Heart*, 70–1. Three contenders have emerged for the title of 'Charles Wesley's conversion hymn'. Perhaps the strongest is 'Christ the Friend of Sinners'

is argued that the sermons written before the 'Day of Pentecost' and those written after have generally a quite different feel to them, a feel which is the result of a change in Charles's soteriology and the consequent lifting of at least some of his theological gloom. It is, to be sure, easy to over-stress this point and/or to concentrate too much upon the significance of that one experience. There is also the complicating factor that, as will be discussed in detail, many of the pre-Pentecost sermons preached by Charles were originally written by John, a fact which should not be forgotten, even if these same texts were, as is argued here, edited by Charles in keeping with his own theological views. However, as a reading of the texts presented in this volume will make clear, something did happen in Charles's religious life around the middle of the year 1738.

The next decade, up to his marriage in 1749, Charles spent largely in the saddle. A reading of the journal and letters will fill in the mass of details that have survived from this period. This section of the journal is substantial and records Charles's evangelistic endeavours, first firmly within, and then reluctantly without, the buildings and official structures of the established Church. An important aspect of this evangelism was preaching to mass audiences, preaching that was often carried out in the open air. As the journal makes clear, as a herald of the revival Charles was indefatigable as, no less than John, he rode the muddy roads of England and Wales, and also of Ireland, to which he was the first to bring the Methodist message,[87] seeking to fulfil what he considered to be his divine commission.

The many letters penned by Charles during this period are a rich source of information and ought not to be ignored. As was noted above, most of these remain unpublished, though some of those written to John have been edited by Baker and others may be found as an appendix to Jackson's edition of the journal and in a few other places. In this body of evidence there remains much that is yet to be examined. In the letters to John, for example, some of the developing tension with George Whitefield is evident.[88] In a letter to Thomas Hardwick written from Dublin on 22 December (1747), Charles encourages the recipient to 'sell all—and thou shalt have treasure in heaven'.[89] When seen in context, this remark is evidence that Charles encouraged lay ministry (which runs rather counter to the view that

('Where shall my wondering soul begin / How shall I all to heaven aspire'), but 'Free Grace' (And can it be that I should gain / An interest in the saviour's blood) and 'Hymn for Whitsunday' ('Granted is the saviour's prayer / Sent the gracious Comforter') are also possible. See further Tyson, *Charles Wesley: A Reader*, 101–5, and Hildebrandt and Beckerlegge, *Hymns*, 116 and 322. The hymn, whichever it was, was taken up also by John when on 24 May he and Charles 'sang the hymn with great joy' in celebration of the fact that John too had now followed in Charles's footsteps (MARC DDCW 10/2 *in loc.*; Telford, *Journal*, 153).

[87] Charles made two visits to Ireland, the first from 9 September, 1747 to 20 March 1748 and the second from 13 August to 8 October 1748. See MARC DDCW 10/2 *in loc.*; Jackson, *Journal*, i. 456 to ii. 10, and ii. 18–39.

[88] In MARC DDCW 1/12, for example, printed in Baker, *Charles Wesley as Revealed by his Letters*, 41, Charles writes (in shorthand) 'George Whitefield, you know, has come' and then continues in longhand 'His fair words are not to be trusted; for his actions shew most unfriendly.' The letter is dated 16 March, 1740.   [89] MARC DDCW 1/16a.

he was an Anglican of unbending allegiance to the formal structures of the Church). No attempt even to summarize this wealth of MS evidence can be made here. The fact that it exists, however, should not be missed. Charles wrote much more than hymns.

Charles met his future wife, Sarah (Sally) Gwynne, in 1747. Baker has identified the day as 28 August of that year and his reasoning seems secure.[90] Charles's own later account suggests love at first sight

You have heard me acknowledge that at first sight 'My soul seemed pleased to take acquaintance with thee'. And never have I found such pleasure and nearness to any fellow-creature as to you. O that it may bring us nearer and nearer to God, till we are both swallowed up in the immensity of his love![91]

In a previously undeciphered shorthand note in the journal Charles has given what appear to be the date and words of his proposal of marriage. On Sunday, 3 April 1748, he writes, he asked Sarah if 'she could trust herself with me for life and with a noble simplicity she readily answered me she could'.[92] The following day he records (also in shorthand) the fact that he felt somewhat uneasy about what he had said to Sarah the night before: 'Frightened at what I had said last night I condemned mine rashness and almost wished I had never discovered myself.'[93] In several further shorthand entries in the journal it is plain that Charles is working towards his marriage despite meeting some perceived resistance on John's part. On 16 November, for example, he noted that he consulted his brother on the question of a possible 'provision' in case he married and recorded dissatisfaction with his brother's response that the Church could not afford it.[94] Not to be deterred, however, he then spoke to Mr Perronet on the matter, who, says Charles, 'thought a few of my private friends might subscribe what would be sufficient for my maintenance and offered himself to set the example'.[95]

These previously undeciphered notes in Charles's journal are of potential significance for our understanding of the relationship between Charles and John and the importance of Charles's marriage in its development. As we have seen, Charles proposed to Sarah on 3 April, 1748. However, the evidence is that he did not tell his brother about his marriage plans until 11 November of that year, when he recorded in his journal,

My brother and I having promised each other, (as soon as he came from Georgia,) that we would neither of us marry, or take any step towards it, without the other's knowledge and consent, to-day I fairly and fully communicated every thought of my heart. He had proposed three persons to me, S.P., M.W., and S.G.; and entirely approved my choice of the last. We consulted together about every particular, and were of one heart and mind in all things.[96]

[90] Baker, *Charles Wesley as Revealed by his Letters*, 55.   [91] Ibid.
[92] See MARC DDCW 10/2 *in loc.*   [93] See MARC DDCW 10/2 *in loc.*
[94] See MARC DDCW 10/2 *in loc.*   [95] See MARC DDCW 10/2 *in loc.*
[96] See MARC DDCW 10/2 *in loc.*

This consultation with John, however, came some seven months after his actual proposal and Charles had clearly decided upon marriage to Sarah long before speaking to John on the issue. Such a course of action suggests that Charles was quite capable of keeping his real intentions secret from his brother.

Charles and Sarah were married on 8 April, 1749. The event is recorded in the journal[97] and also in a letter to Ebenezer Blackwell.[98] The volume of surviving letters between Charles and his wife is vast and still to a large extent unexplored, but they tell the tale, as does his journal, of a happy married life and the stability and new responsibilities that his marriage brought are a turning-point in his ministry at least as important as his experience of 21 May, 1738.

In September 1749 Charles and Sarah moved to Bristol to set up home in Charles Street.[99] The Wesley family grew to include Charles junior (born 11 December, 1757), Sarah junior (born April, 1759) and Samuel III (born 24 February, 1766). Charles and Sarah's first child, John, was born August 1752, but died at the age of sixteen months. Sarah also bore Martha Maria (1755), Susanna (1761), Selina (1764), and John James (1768). They too died in infancy and there was also at least one miscarriage (see Charles's journal entry for 3 February, 1750). The family stayed in Bristol until they moved to London in 1771.

During the 22 years based there Charles's life was far from static. In the latter part of 1749, for example, he visited London and, closer to home, Bath and Kingswood. In 1750 he travelled more extensively, leaving from Bristol on 19 February and arriving in Ludlow (now home of the Gwynnes) two days later. There he left Sarah and travelled on to Evesham, Oxford, and London, and then back to Ludlow and Leominster, returning to Bristol on 2 May. A similar trip taking in Ludlow, Worcester, Oxford, Chertsey, Croydon, and London and coming back through Oxford, Worcester, and Ludlow began on 15 May. This pattern continues, and in the latter part of the year he was again in London. In 1751 he set out for the north. On 12 June he was in Bradford, on 10 July in Wednesbury, on 16 July in Sheffield, on 19 July in Leeds, on 8 August in Durham, and on 9 August he arrived in Newcastle. He then went on to Sunderland, and eventually back to London, and finally on 4 December returned to Bristol. Charles's life during this period was not, then, quiet or settled.

During this period Charles sought to spread the Methodist message and further its cause. The vitality and energy he put into his preaching is evident in the jour-

[97] MARC DDCW 10/2 *in loc.*; Jackson, *Journal*, ii. 55.

[98] MARC DDCW 1/19. The letter is actually addressed to 'Mr Blackwall' but the address in 'Change Alley, London' makes it certain that Ebenezer Blackwell (1711–82), long-time friend of the Wesleys, is in mind.

[99] The precise location is a matter of some dispute. Number 4 is the house assumed to have been the residence of Charles and his family, but for an alternative view see Robert W. Brown, 'Charles Wesley, Hymnwriter: Notes on Research Carried out to Establish the Location of his Residence in Bristol during the Period 1749–1771' (unpublished pamphlet, 1993, copies of which are available from the New Room, Bristol).

nal and also in the eye-witness accounts of him during this time.[100] It would be easy to paint a picture of a tireless evangelist beating his way along difficult roads, sometimes through violent storms, to bring the message of God's grace to the poor of England; and to be sure there is a measure of truth in just such a portrait. However, Charles's dealings with Methodists and Methodism during this period make a far from simple story, and one does not have to dig too deeply beneath the surface of popular Methodist legend to discover another side to Charles's relationship with his brother and, more importantly perhaps, the Methodist movement that they had jointly brought into being.

Charles's intervention in John's plans for marriage is the most dramatic instance of the friction which could exist between the brothers, though in the context of religious history perhaps not the most important. The story of how Charles successfully outwitted (and out-rode) John and hence prevented his marriage to Grace Murray (1716–1803) is well-known. In outline Charles, for whatever reason, decided that John's plan to marry was unwise and would bring shame both on John personally and also on Charles and the whole of the Methodist movement. The reasons for this opposition are not altogether clear. Charles put forward the complaint that prior to accepting John's offer of marriage, Grace had been engaged to the Derbyshire lay-preacher John Bennet (1714–59), and his testimony at this point must be taken seriously.[101] Some, however, have wondered whether it was not Charles's sensitivity regarding her lowliness of birth that was the real sticking-point, or at least one of them.[102] Some have suggested possessiveness as another of the complicated and intertwined motives.[103] What is clear is that, for whatever reasons, Charles was set against the proposed marriage, and in his endeavour to prevent it, he rode from Bristol to Newcastle, confronting John at Whitehaven on the way. Finding Grace at Hindley Hall he took her to Newcastle and, within a week, had engineered her marriage to John Bennet.

It is not surprising that John was none too pleased with this course of events, and his displeasure could not have been relieved when, the day after Grace's marriage, a moment at which he might well be expected to be at a low point, Charles burst in upon him and pronounced, 'I renounce all intercourse with you, but what I would have with a heathen man or a publican.'[104]

It argues a strong bond between the brothers that their relationship was not damaged beyond repair by the Grace Murray affair. It was not, although there is a definite sense of unease in the letters to Bennet that Charles wrote in the aftermath of the events.[105] On 2 March 1750 he wrote that he had 'talked with our

---

[100] See further Chapter 2.   [101] Baker, *Charles Wesley as Revealed by his Letters*, 72.

[102] Dallimore, *A Heart Set Free*, 164; Brailsford, *Two Brothers*, 190–1.

[103] Brailsford, *Two Brothers*, 190–1.

[104] See further Dallimore, *A Heart Set Free*, 165; Brailsford, *Two Brothers*, 206.

[105] Baker, *Charles Wesley as Revealed by his Letters*, 73–4 provides several extracts. The letters quoted there are MARC DDCW 1/33a (2 March, 1750); DDCW 1/38 (3 September, 1750); DDCW 1/39 (15 December, 1750).

friend in Oxford, and find him quite willing to bury all past matters',[106] but on 15 December of the same year he appears to have revised his opinion, writing 'It is all over with our friend. Only me he cannot love as before.'[107] Even stronger is a letter dated 15 March, 1751, soon after John's marriage to Mary (Molly) Vazeille, again addressed to Bennet: 'You and your partner must make amends for the loss of my brother, whose love I have small hopes of recovering in this world.'[108] Clearly the wound was still not completely healed. It is possible that further reference is made to this situation in a letter to Bennet dated 23 January, 1752. Here Charles speaks of the one whom he calls 'my friend' (later fairly clearly identified as John), with whom Bennet is now in very obvious conflict. 'But', says Charles,

I greatly fear for my friend, knowing the warmth and rashness of his natural temper. Of this I have lately had too strong a proof (which I mention, not to upbraid but warn you).[109]

What the cause of that 'strong proof' of John Wesley's temper was, is not revealed, but given that the letter is addressed to Bennet, it may well be that Charles is again reflecting on John's reaction to his intervention in the marriage plans.

It is clear, then, that Charles and John did not always see eye to eye and that there was, at this time at least, significant friction between them. The marriage issue was a very personal one, but the brothers also clashed over more overtly theological concerns, and in particular on the question of Methodism's relationship to the Church of England. This is an issue which goes well beyond the 1750s and indeed extends to the end of Charles's life. In essence he was and remained always firmly opposed to any moves towards separation from the established Church.[110] The strength of his opposition can be seen in a number of places; the sections of the poetic corpus dealing with this have already been brought to the attention of those working in the area. Perhaps the best-known examples centre upon John Wesley's 'ordination' in 1784 of Richard Whatcoat (1736–1806), Thomas Vasey (1745–1826), and Dr Thomas Coke (1747–1814), all in preparation for their work in America.[111] The ordination of Coke is particularly significant given that he was already an Anglican priest. Charles was infuriated, for he concurred with a remark by his old school-friend Lord Mansfield: 'ordination is separation'.[112] In response he wrote, among other poems, 'Christ our merciful high priest', which begins with the lines

---

[106] MARC DDCW 1/33a (Baker, *Charles Wesley as Revealed by his Letters*, 73).

[107] MARC DDCW 1/39 (Baker, *Charles Wesley as Revealed by his Letters*, 74).

[108] MARC DDCW 1/41 (Baker, *Charles Wesley as Revealed by his Letters*, 75. Baker transcribes as 'loss of my brother . . . whose love'; however, the ellipsis '. . .' in Baker is found at a point in the MS where there is a somewhat ambiguous stroke of the pen. It is unclear, but appears to be a struck-out letter 's'.

[109] MARC DDCW 1/43.

[110] See Baker, *Charles Wesley as Revealed by his Letters*, 91–103, for a summary of the evidence.

[111] John uses 'appointed' in the Journal, but 'ordained' in the diary (*J&D*, vi. 330, 497). See further Frank Baker, *John Wesley and the Church of England* (Nashville, TN: Abingdon Press, 1970), 256–82.

[112] Charles Wesley to Dr Chandler, MARC DDWES 1/38.

Christ our merciful high priest
With thy people's grief distrest
Help us for our guide to pray
Lost in his mistaken way.[113]

And further in another poem

Wesley himself and friends betrays
By his good sense forsook
When suddenly his hands he lays
On the hot head of Coke.[114]

And when Coke himself ordained Francis Asbury as co-superintendent in America, Charles's response reached its sarcastic zenith. Drawing on the story of Caligula's reported appointment of his horse to the Roman Senate, he wrote

A Roman emperor 'tis said
His favourite horse a consul made
But Coke brings greater things to pass
He makes a bishop of an ass.[115]

These poetic outbursts are known to Methodist historians, and many have been in print since Osborn; the remainder are found in Kimbrough-Beckerlegge. However, Charles's clash with his brother on the question of separation is found also in the former's prose compositions. Note for example Charles's letter to John himself in 1760.[116] Charles summed up the differences between the brothers on this issue succinctly: 'His first object was the Methodists and then the Church; mine was first the Church, and then the Methodists.'[117]

Such controversy seems to have been very much a part of Charles's life from the time following his marriage to the end of his life. However, while he was firmly opposed to the separation of the Methodist people from the Church of England, on the level of the grass-roots Methodist societies, he was very much a key figure. Again, there is a mass of detail that still needs to be properly analysed. Most of this is in the form of the letters written by and to Charles, though some relatively small fragments of journal have also survived.[118] From this material there is still much to be learnt. Thus, for example, it is apparent that it was Charles rather than John who took the lead in dealing with the difficult situation that arose in London as a result of the activities of the French Prophetess, Mary Lavington.[119] It is apparent also that the London Methodists were later very much in hope of Charles's advice

---

[113] Kimbrough and Beckerlegge (eds.), *Unpublished Poetry*, 3. 93.   [114] Ibid., 3. 81.
[115] Ibid., 3. 81.
[116] Baker, *Charles Wesley as Revealed by his Letters*, 98. The letter to which Baker refers is preserved also in a copy made by Charles himself and sent to his wife (MARC DDCW 7/57).
[117] See further Baker, *John Wesley and the Church of England*, 208
[118] For example MARC DDCW 7/32 contains an extract from the journal dated September 1773.
[119] See further Kenneth G. C. Newport, 'The French Prophets and Early Methodism: Some New Evidence', *Proceedings of the Wesley Historical Society* 50 (1996): 127–40.

and action over the activities of George Bell and Thomas Maxfield. Both of these were of the view that it was possible for human beings to reach a state of sinless perfection. The former extended his views by announcing that the end of the world was to occur on 28 February 1763. John's attempts to deal with the issue were weak. The full story of Charles's involvement in the matter is yet to be unfolded, but it is apparent that he was active in soliciting information on Maxfield and Bell, and that there were those in the London Society who looked to him rather than to John for leadership in this time of crisis.[120]

There is a good deal more that could be said regarding Charles's life and his contribution to the growth of Methodism, but this is not the place to launch into a full-scale study of that contribution. What has been said already suggests what is yet to be expounded. Charles was, to repeat, much more than a hymn writer. He was a major figure in terms of the birth of organized Methodism and an active supporter and evangelist for it during the first decade and a half of its life. Thereafter, while less of an itinerant, he remained a key figure, being of major influence in Bristol and later in London. While always afraid of any move towards the separation of the Methodists from the established Church, he was clearly concerned for the vibrancy and spiritual well-being of the societies, and directed a good deal of energy to this end. His disputes with others in the movement, including John, on issues such as lay preaching, and particularly the competence of individual lay preachers,[121] the administration of the sacraments,[122] and ordination, largely stemmed from his unbending loyalty to the established Church. There was perhaps an inevitable tension between that loyalty and his support of what increasingly became the separate movement of 'Methodism', and while he may have attempted to hold that tension, in the end he failed. The movement split off from its mother faith and, after an unpromisingly divided start as a separate denomination,[123] managed to survive and to become a major player on the stage of religious history. Charles would have lamented these later developments, and during the latter part of his life sought actively to head them off. But the momentum of religious development is not so easily stopped and already by the 1750s he was in fact swimming against at least an undercurrent if not the tide.

The last act of Charles as a faithful Anglican was his refusal to be buried in anything other than consecrated ground. Shortly before his death he sent a message

---

[120] See further Kenneth G.C. Newport, 'George Bell, Prophet and Enthusiast', *Methodist History* 35 (1997): 95–105; Kenneth G. C. Newport and Gareth Lloyd, 'George Bell and Early Methodist Enthusiasm: A New Source from the Manchester Archives', *Bulletin of the John Rylands University Library of Manchester* 80 (1998): 89–101.

[121] Charles once famously remarked to John Bennet, 'A friend of ours [John Wesley] (without God's counsel) made a preacher of a tailor. I, with God's help, shall make a tailor of him again.' See further Baker, *Charles Wesley as Revealed by his Letters*, 79–90.

[122] See Baker, *Charles Wesley as Revealed by his Letters*, 97–101, for some of the most pertinent material.

[123] See especially Robert Currie, *Methodism Divided* (London: Faber, 1968); John Kent, *The Age of Disunity* (London: Epworth, 1966).

to the parson of his parish saying 'Sir, whatever the world may have thought of me, I have lived, and I die, in the communion of the Church of England, and I will be buried in the yard of my parish church.'[124] John was not pleased with this decision, arguing that the ground prepared for Charles at City Road was every bit as holy as any that the Church of England had to offer.[125] But Charles was as defiant of John on this issue in death as he had been on some others in life. He was buried in the churchyard of the parish church of Marylebone, where he was later to be joined by his wife (who lived another 34 years) and two sons.

Such, then, in outline, was Charles Wesley's life, a life richly documented in the many thousands of MS pages he left behind, but which as yet have been only poorly researched. In this volume some of that material is presented to the reader in what it is hoped is a useful format. That said, this volume doubtless has flaws. In particular there is much more that could have been said in terms of the context and content of Charles's preaching, and the witness it gives to his contribution to the history of Methodism, and of English and world Christianity. In particular much more space could have been given to commenting historically and theologically upon the individual sermons. However, this volume is first and foremost an edition of the text and not a study of the sermons themselves. Consequently the time, energy, and space invested in this volume have been largely text-critical and every effort has been made to achieve the primary task, which is to secure the texts themselves and to present forms of them which are as reliable as the MS evidence allows and as near as possible to what Charles actually wrote. It is hoped that others will now take up the challenge and analyse the sermons here presented from both an historical and a theological perspective as part of the overall effort of reclaiming Charles for the history of English and world Christianity in general, rather than leaving him in the unassailable, but less challenging, position of 'the sweet singer of Methodism' alone.

---

[124] As quoted in Gill, *First Methodist*, 225.   [125] See further ibid.

CHAPTER 2
CHARLES WESLEY, PREACHER

It is reported that Isaac Watts, himself the author of some truly magnificent hymns, once said of Charles Wesley's 'Wrestling Jacob', that it was worth all the verses that he himself had ever penned.[1] Such high praise for Charles's poetic art is not unusual. More recent scholars have judged him to be Britain's 'greatest hymnographer',[2] and the 1780 Methodist hymn book, to which he was much the most important single contributor,[3] 'a liturgical miracle'.[4] It is not surprising, given such recognition of real hymnographic genius, that it is chiefly for his poetic legacy that Charles has been remembered.

His own brother, however, reportedly spoke of Charles's poetic abilities as his 'least'.[5] This may seem extreme, and perhaps few would concur fully with such a view. It is clear, however, that it was not only in the composition of hymns and poems that Charles's literary abilities excelled. According to John, it was Charles and not he who was best able to express himself in letters: 'I am very sensible', wrote John, 'that writing letters is my brother's talent rather than mine'.[6] Similarly, Charles's journal has a lively prose style which conveys well enough, if generally rather tersely, the sense of excitement and challenge he felt as he went about his early work in America and later as an itinerant Methodist preacher.

There is ample evidence to suggest also that the craft of sermon construction, like the writing of hymns, letters, and a journal, was a form of literary activity to which Charles was able to give full and vibrant expression. Indeed, it was probably in the context of Charles's preaching abilities that John wrote to his brother 'In connexion I beat you; but in strong, pointed sentences, you beat me'.[7] This is a judgement with which one Mary Thomas seems to have agreed. In a letter to

---

[1] The remark is attributed to Watts in the obituary of Charles Wesley inserted into the Minutes of Conference for 1788 (*Minutes of the Methodist Conferences, from the First, Held in London, by the Late Rev. John Wesley, A.M. in the Year 1744*, 4 vols. (1812–18), i.201). The hymn 'Wrestling Jacob' was first published in *Hymns and Sacred Poems* (1742). Twelve verses of it were included in *A Collection of Hymns for the use of the People called the Methodists* (1780). The full text, which runs to fourteen verses, is found in Osborn (ed.), *Poetical Works*, ii. 173–6. The hymn is analysed and the opinions of several scholars concerning it are presented in Glenn Clark, 'Charles Wesley's Greatest Poem', *Methodist History* 26 (1988): 163–71.   [2] Kimbrough and Beckerlegge, (eds.), *Unpublished Poetry*, i. 17.

[3] All but around 40 of the 525 hymns in the 1780 volume can be confidently attributed to Charles. See Hildebrandt and Beckerlegge, (eds.), *A Collection of Hymns for the Use of the People Called Methodists*, 31–8

[4] Flew, *The Hymns of Charles Wesley*, 10. See also Watson, *The English Hymn*, 221–64 and *passim*; Bernard Manning, *The Hymns of Wesley and Watts* (London: Epworth, 1942), 50–77.

[5] See *Minutes of Conference*, i. 201.   [6] Baker, *Charles Wesley as Revealed by his Letters*, 6.

[7] John Wesley to Charles Wesley, 27 June, 1766 (*The Works of John Wesley*, 14 vols. (1872), xii. 130–1).

Charles, Thomas wrote, 'When you came to Bristol I seemed to like you better than your brother and thought your way of delivery was finer than his.'[8] Similarly, according to John Whitehead (1740–1804), John Wesley's first official biographer, and an individual who had heard both John and Charles preach, Charles's sermons were more 'awakening and useful' than John's,[9] which is high praise indeed when set against John's own not insignificant preaching abilities. Whitehead went on to observe regarding Charles,

His discourses from the pulpit were not dry and systematic, but flowed from the present views and feelings of his own mind. He had a remarkable talent of expressing the most important truths with simplicity and energy; and his discourses were sometimes truly apostolic, forcing conviction on his hearers in spite of the most determined opposition.[10]

The reference here to the 'energy' with which Charles evidently preached is worthy of further brief note, for there is other evidence to suggest that Charles may sometimes have put more energy into his sermons than was good for him. Indeed, he once got himself so worked up while delivering a sermon on Psalm 23 that he bled from the nose for some time afterwards.[11]

Whitehead's views are of course those of a sympathetic admirer and must be seen as such. However, he does not stand alone in the view that Charles Wesley was an able and effective preacher. According to another early Methodist, John Nelson (1707–74), Charles's preaching was powerful indeed. Nelson reports in his diary that Charles had passed briefly through Birstall, six miles outside Wakefield, around Michaelmas (29 September) 1742.[12] Charles pressed on quickly to Newcastle, but was later to return, and 'when Mr. Charles Wesley came back from Newcastle', wrote Nelson,

the Lord was with him in such a manner that the pillars of hell seemed to tremble; many that were famous for supporting the devil's kingdom fell to the ground while he was preaching, as if they had been thunderstruck.[13]

---

[8] The letter is uncatalogued, but may be found in the MAB section of the MARC in a folio entitled 'Early Methodist Volume' item number 128.

[9] John Whitehead, *Life of the Rev. John Wesley*, 2 vols. (1793–6), i. 292. I owe this reference to Albert C. Outler, (ed.), *Sermons*, i: 2 n. 6. The comparison is also made by Charles Wesley Flint, who notes that 'Charles was a born preacher; of the three he is rated second to George Whitefield but ahead of his brother John' (Flint, *Charles Wesley and his Colleagues*, 146). No evidence is cited in support of this remark.   [10] Whitehead, *Life*, i. 370.

[11] Charles Wesley to Sarah Wesley, 18 June (1763); MARC DDCW 7/16 and printed in Jackson, *Journal*, ii. 251–2.

[12] Charles's journal from 22 September, 1741 to 2 January, 1743 is missing and so this cannot be checked against it. However, where Nelson can be checked he seems generally trustworthy. He records also that he was visited by John Wesley in May 1742, which is confirmed in John's journal for the period (*J&D*, xix. 266–7).

[13] John Telford, *Wesley's Veterans*, 6 vols. (London: Charles A. Kelly, 1912), iii. 65. The quotation continues, 'One day he had preached four times; and one that had been amongst the people all day said at night twenty-two had received forgiveness of their sins that day.' Nelson then goes on to claim that about 'four-score' of individuals were added to the number of 'true believers' as a result of Charles's and Mr Graves's labours. See further W. L. Doughty, 'Charles Wesley, Preacher', *London Quarterly and Holborn Review*, 182 (1957): 263–7, at p.267.

On 17 October, 1739 Joseph Williams of Kidderminster, who was a Congregationalist and not a Methodist, wrote to Charles asking him to look over a letter which Williams intended to send to the editor of the *Gentleman's Magazine*.[14] The letter was designed as a defence of the Methodists who, Williams stated, had been the object of 'the loud, the ignorant, and malignant clamours' which had been raised up against them. Williams himself had heard many rumours concerning Methodist belief and practice, but it was only after he had read Whitefield's *Discourse upon Generation, or the New Birth* that he had begun to get a clearer view of what the Methodists were really about. Some time later he had visited Bristol on business and had heard that Charles Wesley was to preach in the afternoon. Williams got a guide and went to hear Charles preach. There then follows a lengthy account of what he found which gives a rare first-hand glimpse of Charles Wesley the preacher in action. It is worth quoting here in full.

I found him standing upon a table, in an erect posture, with his hands and eyes lifted up to heaven in prayer, surrounded with (I guess) more than a thousand people; some few of them persons of fashion, both men and women, but most of them of the lower rank of mankind. I know not how long he had been engaged in the duty before I came, but he continued therein, after my coming, scarce a quarter of an hour; during which time he prayed with uncommon fervency, fluency, and variety of proper expression. He then preached about an hour from the five last verses of the fifth chapter of the second Epistle to the Corinthians, in such a manner as I have seldom, if ever, heard any minister preach: i.e. though I have heard many a finer sermon, according to the common taste, or acceptation of sermons, yet I scarce ever heard any minister discover such evident signs of a most vehement desire, or labour so earnestly, to convince his hearers that they were all by nature in a state of enmity against God, consequently in a damnable state, and needed reconciliation to God; that God is willing to be reconciled to all, even the worst of sinners, and for that end laid all our guilt on Christ, hath imputed it to him, and Christ hath fulfilled all righteousness and punishment due to our sins in our nature and stead; that on the other hand the righteousness and merits of Christ are, and shall be, imputed to as many as believe on him; that it is faith alone, exclusive entirely of any works of ours, which applys to us the righteousness of Christ, and justifies us in the light of God; that none are excluded but those who refuse to come to him, as lost, undone, yea as damned sinners, and trust in him alone, i.e. his meritorious righteousness, and atoning sacrifice, for pardon and salvation. These points he backed all along as he went on with a great many texts of scripture, which he explained, and illustrated; and then freely invited all, even the chief of sinners, and used a great variety of the most moving arguments, and expositions, in order to persuade, allure, instigate and, if possible, compel them all to come to Christ, and believe in him for pardon and salvation. Nor did he fail to inform them thoroughly, how ineffectual their faith would be to justify them in the sight

---

[14] The letter which Williams intended to send and the covering letter to Charles Wesley are now held in the MARC DDPr 1/92. It was never published in the *Gentleman's Magazine*, but did appear in *Wesleyan Methodist Magazine* (vol. 57 (1828): 383–5). The letter is an extract made by Williams of part of his own diary, the MS of which is held in Dr Williams's Library, London (ref. 1f 6). A slightly more substantial extract from the diary, which includes the account of Williams's meeting with Charles, was published by Geoffrey F. Nuttall in 1980 ('Charles Wesley in 1739. By Joseph Williams of Kidderminster', *Proceedings of the Wesley Historical Society* 42 (1980): 181–5).

of God, unless it wrought by love, purified their hearts, and reformed their lives: for though he cautioned them with the utmost care not to attribute any merit to their own performances, nor in the least degree rest on any works of their own, yet at the same time he thoroughly apprized them, that their faith is but a dead faith if it be not operative, and productive of good works, even all the good in their power.[15]

This passage has been quoted at such length because of the impressions it gives of Charles's style and of the sermon's content. Clearly, if Williams is to be believed, Charles did not lack either the personal commitment or the technical ability to deliver a good and persuasive sermon. The implied content of the sermon is also worthy of note. Charles's call was to faith, but it was to a faith which expressed itself in works and the reformation of lives. This combination of an intense belief in the efficacy of the blood of Christ as an atonement for past sins with a call for the practice of good works in the present is not at all uncommon in Charles's preaching, as a reading of the sermons presented in this volume will make clear. Sermon 10 on John 8: 1 ff. is a good example of such thinking, as is Sermon 8 on Ephesians 5: 14. For Charles faith was not inactive, but something to be worked out in the day-to-day business of Christian living. Sermon 5 on 'faith and good works' (Titus 3: 8) should also be noted. This attitude is typically 'Arminian', that is it reflects the view that John Wesley and others thought could also be attributed to Jacobus Arminius (1560–1609), that though salvation is gained only by the grace of God, the individual has the power either to reject or accept that offer of salvation (contra Calvin), and thereafter progress towards perfection.

There are a few other fragments of information regarding Charles Wesley the preacher which can be gleaned from the primary sources. These include both the briefest of references and some slightly longer accounts. In early 1745, for example, the MP James Erskine (1679–1754) wrote to the Welsh Calvinistic Methodist Howell Harris (1714–73) that Charles had delivered a sermon with 'much power' at 'the chapel in West Street by the 7 dials' on the subject of suffering.[16] This may have been the sermon on 'these are they that came out of great tribulation' (Revelation 7: 14) which he preached at Seven Dials on 26 (or 27) September 1744, though the journal is terse and incomplete at this point and therefore rather ambiguous. The full content of the sermon which Thomas Illingworth heard Charles preach in October 1756 is unknown, though something can be seen mirrored in the brief report Illingworth gives. He writes 'He spoke much concerning the end of the World, telling us the Signs foretold were so fully accomplish'd as demonstratively shew'd its Dissolution near.[17]

---

[15] MARC DDPr 1/92, 2–3.   [16] MARC DDPr 1/26.

[17] As quoted in Frank Baker, *William Grimshaw 1708–1763* (London: Epworth, 1963), 195. It is apparent that Charles preached frequently on the subject of eschatology and the imminent return of Jesus. Between 7 and 9 October 1756, for example, he appears to have spoken several times to different audiences on Luke 21 (the apocalyptic discourse) and concluded 'I have no doubt but they will be counted worthy to escape, and to stand before the Son of Man' (cf. Luke 21: 36). Later on 9 October he warned his audience of the 'impending storm'. On 10 October, writes Charles, 'between four and

On 14 July 1764 the early Methodist itinerant John Valton (1740–94)[18] 'went to London to hear Mr Charles Wesley preach on the ensuing Sabbath'.

His word was with power; and I thought my Saviour was at hand, never being so sensibly affected under a discourse before. In the evening I heard him again at the Foundery, and all seemed to be comforted or affected by his word.[19]

James Sutcliffe heard Charles preach and reported that

The preacher was an aged gentleman in a plain coat and wig. His voice was clear, his aspect venerable and his manner devout. In his introductory sentences he was very deliberate, and presently made a pause of some moments. This I attributed to his age and infirmities, but in a while he made a second pause, twice as long as before. This to me was painful, but the people took no notice of it. However he helped himself out by quoting three verses of the hymn: 'Five bleeding wounds He bears, Received on Calvary'. And when I was most affected with sympathy for his infirmities, as I then thought, he quoted his text in Greek with remarkable fluency. Coming then to the great salvation, he was on his high horse, age and infirmities were left behind. It was a torrent of doctrine, of exhortation and eloquence bearing down all before him.[20]

A fair number of further references to Charles's preaching are found in letters addressed to him which have survived.[21] On 29 June 1762, for example, the otherwise unidentified 'Mary Madden' wrote to Charles

You came upon the pullpet. I was lockt in a seat or otherwise should have gone out of the Church, but I thought however I wold not listen to anything you said, but when God will work, who shall hinder. I well remember your text was 'ye serpents, ye generation of vipers,

---

five thousand were left to receive my warning from Luke 21' and later he judged those to whom he spoke to be 'like men prepared to meet the Lord'. The remainder of the journal continues in this vein right up to the last few entries. It appears, then, that during October and the first few days of November 1756 Charles was much concerned to warn of an impending crisis. The Lord was about to come. Indeed, part of the last but one entry in the journal (4 November, 1756) reads 'I described the last times to between forty and fifty at our sister Blackmore's; and it was a solemn time of refreshing.' See further Kenneth G. C. Newport, 'Premillennialism in the Early Writings of Charles Wesley', *Wesleyan Theological Journal* 32/1 (Spring 1997): 85–106; id. 'Charles Wesley and the End of the World', *Proceedings of the Charles Wesley Society* 3 (1996): 33–61.

[18] Nolan B. Harmon (ed.), *Encyclopedia of World Methodism*, 2 vols. (Nashville, TN: United Methodist Publishing House, 1974), ii. 2409.

[19] Telford, *Wesley's Veterans*, vi. 19; Doughty, 'Charles Wesley, Preacher', 267.

[20] As quoted in Flint, *Charles Wesley and His Colleagues*, 148. Flint also notes that 'Mr Wright' the plumber (Charles's brother-in-law) and the one for whom Wright worked went to hear Charles preach. Mr Wright's employer wrote, 'I find his business is only with the heart and the affections; as to the understanding, that must shift for itself . . . most of the clergy are in the contrary extreme, and apply themselves only to the head' (p. 147).

[21] No claim here is made to exhaustiveness. However, in one volume of such letters at least (the uncatalogued 'Early Methodist Volume') a number of references to the subject and effect of Charles's preaching are found. Items 1, 3, 6, 8, 10, 12, 13, 16, 18, 41, 56, 86, 105, 106, 112, 115, 126, 129, and 130 in particular are of relevance here. I am indebted to one of my research students, the Revd Charles Ellis, for a number of these references.

how shall ye escape the damnation of hell'. The Lord was pleased to send every word home to my hart. I went away crying out 'what shall I do to be saved'?[22]

And earlier in 1740 and 1742 respectively two otherwise unidentified correspondents, Mary Ramsey and Naomi Thomas, had written

The Thursday following being ascension day I had so much Joy when you was preaching that I thought my soul seemed as if it was ascending into heaven indeed. The joy begun in the morning when Mr Harris was preaching on the words 'thy kingdom come' and it so increased in the evening while you was preaching that methought I saw my saviour in glory.[23]

And

One time in the bowling green you preach'd on these words 'I in them and they in me', which came with such power to my soul, that then I had redemption in the blood of Christ and forgiveness of my sins, and filled with such joy that I cannot express.[24]

The position seems to be clear: Charles was judged by his contemporaries to be a preacher of significant ability whose discourses were powerful and able to affect those to whom they were addressed. Naturally due caution is to be exercised when using these materials, since most, though not all,[25] come from within the Methodist camp and hence probably contain some element of bias. However, this appreciation of Charles in the surviving records is more than surface deep, and comes with one voice from various strata of the archival deposits. The cumulative picture therefore seems fairly secure, even if some of the detail may have been distorted. In particular the witness of Whitehead, who makes a comparative judgement, may again be noted. Here we have the voice of one who, we may suspect, had a vested interest and perhaps bias towards the promotion of John as the champion of the cause. However, as has been seen, it was to Charles that Whitehead attributes the greater preaching skills. Mary Thomas, who similarly makes the comparison in Charles's favour, is also to be noted.[26]

Further, Charles's own journal is replete with references to the effect that his words had upon the often very substantial audiences that had gathered to hear him, frequently as early as five o'clock in the morning. Thus, for example, on 10 September, 1739 Charles stated that he

preached in the brick-yard, where I think there could not be less than four thousand. It rained hard, yet none stirred. I spoke with great freedom and power. A woman cried out,

[22] Mary Madden to Charles Wesley 29 June 1762. The letter is uncatalogued, but may be found in the Early Methodist Volume, item 105.
[23] Mary Ramsey to Charles Wesley 4 June 1740 (Early Methodist Volume, item 13).
[24] Early Methodist Volume, item 129. (No day is indicated on the MS.).
[25] Williams, as has been noted, was a Congregationalist.
[26] See Mary Thomas to Charles Wesley 24 May, 1742 (Early Methodist Volume, item 128). According to the letter Charles's 'way of delivery' was 'finer' than that of John.

and dropped down. I spoke to her at Mrs. Norman's, and found she had sunk under the weight of sin.[27]

Six days later Charles preached at Hanham-Mount.

I expounded the good Samaritan[28] to between three and four thousand, with power. While I was repeating that in Jeremiah, 'Is not my word like a fire, saith the Lord, and like a hammer that breaketh the rock in pieces?' a woman fell down under the stroke of it. I found afterwards, that the good Samaritan had poured in his oil, and made her whole. Another declared He had then bound up her wounds also. I heard on all sides the sighing of them that were in captivity, and trust more than I know of were set at liberty; for the Lord was among us of a truth'[29]

These two examples have been chosen from Charles's journal almost at random and could easily be multiplied. One might note, for example, his account of his preaching at Bristol on 15 September 1739, where he spoke on 'Lazarus, come forth'.[30] He reports that he spoke with 'great weakness', but this notwithstanding, goes on to note his surprise at the positive effects which his words had.[31] On another occasion, in May 1743, reports Charles, 'many sincere souls' assembled to hear the word of God at Barley Hall were 'drownded in tears' and yet 'very happy';[32] and so great was the convulsion that fell upon one member of his audience a week later that she had to be carried out of the room to recover.[33] The list goes on, and the same picture emerges from the letters.[34] Further citation seems unnecessary, for the point has already emerged: according to his own testimony Charles's sermons were able to strike deep into the hearts of his audience. This testimony is confirmed by those who had heard him preach and witnessed its effects.[35]

It appears, then, that Charles was a man of significant homiletic skill, the quality of whose preaching did much to further the early Methodist cause. Even a

---

[27] MARC DDCW 10/2 in loc.; Jackson, Journal, i. 171.

[28] The 'Good Samaritan' was evidently one of Charles's favourite sermon (or 'exposition') texts and he preached on it frequently. In the surviving journal alone it is mentioned twenty-two times (Tyson, Charles Wesley: A Reader, 487). The sermon has not survived. However, as is noted in more detail in the following chapter, Charles's hymn 'Woe to me, what tongue can tell?' may contain in poetical format the substance of it.   [29] MARC DDCW 10/2 in loc.; Jackson, Journal, i.173.

[30] The sermon ('exposition') on 'Lazarus come forth'/John 11 was another firm favourite with Charles, and like his sermon on the Good Samaritan seems not to have survived. There are eight references to Charles preaching on Lazarus/John 11 in the surviving journal (Tyson, Charles Wesley: A Reader, 487).   [31] MARC DDCW 10/2 in loc.; Jackson, Journal, i. 173.

[32] MARC DDCW 10/2 in loc.; Jackson, Journal, i.312.

[33] MARC DDCW 10/2 in loc.; Jackson, Journal, i. 314.

[34] As an example, note the letter written by Charles to his wife on 1 June (1763?) MARC DDCW 7/109. Here he speaks of the encouragement he is increasingly getting to stay on and work in London and cites as an example, 'On Sunday my subject was Isai 61.1. The spirit of the Lord God is upon me &c. He gave testimony to the word as many thanksgiving bills declared'.

[35] Possibly significant also is a reference from John Fletcher, who appears to have Charles's preaching ability in mind when he states. 'I thank you for your kind intention of seeing Madeley once in your life: I welcome you beforehand to my house and pulpit . . . So come round this way; correct my scales and strengthen my soul and rouse my stupid flock.' John Fletcher to Charles Wesley 20 February 1774 (MARC ref. MAW Fl. 36. 1). I am grateful to Peter Forsaith for drawing this reference to my attention.

cursory reading of the journal and letters indicates that preaching was absolutely central to his work, both in the period leading up to his marriage and thereafter. Charles Wesley was a preacher. The extent of his ability is not altogether easy to ascertain or assess since only a small number of sermons appear to have survived. Perhaps even more importantly, there is evidence to suggest, as John Tyson has argued in some detail, that many of Charles's sermons *never* existed in written form.[36] To be sure we do know that Charles often preached completely unprepared material, for in his journal he refers fairly frequently to his practice of opening the Bible and 'expounding' the first words upon which he came. Frank Baker (who is in turn quoted favourably by Tyson)[37] has made this point already[38] and evidence from Charles's journal to support Baker's suggestion is not difficult to find. For example the entry for Monday 3 December 1753 reads

I was at loss for a subject at five, when I opened the Revelation, and, with fear and trembling, began to expound it. Our Lord was with us of a truth, and comforted our hearts with the blessed hope of his coming to reign before his ancients gloriously.[39]

Quite when Charles adopted this policy of *ex tempore* preaching is not absolutely clear. It is Tyson's suggestion (the same basic point was made by Doughty in 1957)[40] that Charles began to develop the method on or about 15 October 1738 when, he writes, '[I] Preached the one thing needful at Islington, and added much extempore.'[41] Five days later Charles wrote (Tyson misquotes him somewhat)[42]

Seeing so few present at St. Antholin's, I thought of preaching extempore: afraid; yet ventured on the promise, 'Lo, I am with you always;' and spake on justification from Rom. 3 for three quarters of an hour, without hesitation. Glory be to God, who keepeth his promise forever.[43]

After this date, argues Tyson, Charles began increasingly to preach *ex tempore* and depended less upon written material.

As far as can be judged from the very limited evidence available, Tyson's basic point seems correct, though he probably overestimates the extent to which 15 October 1738 was the turning-point. Charles had been 'adding much extempore' at least since 11 July of that year, when he 'preached faith in Christ to a vast congregation, with great boldness, adding much extempore'.[44] However, he had clearly developed the method by the time Williams went to hear him preach, presumably in late 1739. One of the things that impressed Williams with Charles's ability as a preacher seems to have been that

---

[36] John R. Tyson, 'Charles Wesley's Theology of the Cross: An Examination of the Theology and Method of Charles Wesley as seen in his Doctrine of the Atonement' (Ph.D. thesis, Drew University, 1983), 26–30.
[37] Tyson, *Charles Wesley: A Reader*, 16.
[38] Baker, *Charles Wesley as Revealed by his Letters*, 38.
[39] Jackson, *Journal*, ii. 98.
[40] Doughty, 'Charles Wesley, Preacher', 264.
[41] MARC DDCW 10/2 *in loc.*; Jackson, *Journal*, i. 132.
[42] *Charles Wesley: A Reader*, 15.
[43] MARC DDCW 10/2 *in loc.*; Jackson, *Journal*, i. 133.
[44] MARC DDCW 10/2 *in loc.*; Jackson, *Journal*, i. 120.

[a]lthough he [Charles] used no Notes, nor had anything in his Hand but a Bible, yet he delivered his Thoughts in a rich, copious Variety of Expressions, & with so much Propriety, that I could not observe anything incoherent, or inaccurate thro' the whole Performance.[45]

Already by 1739, then, according to Williams and the testimony of Charles's own journal, he seems to have been preaching fairly regularly without notes, or, it seems, even mental preparation. By March 1740 the method seems to be well ingrained, so much so that Charles can describe the act of 'premeditating what to preach' as 'unusual'. He wrote

I was greatly distracted by an unusual unnecessary premeditating what to preach upon. My late discourses had worked different effects. Some were wounded, some hardened and scandalized above measure. I hear no neuters. The Word had turned them upside down. In the pulpit, I opened the book and found the place where it is written, 'the Spirit of the Lord is upon me, because He hath anointed me to preach the gospel to the poor, &c.' I explained our Lord's prophetic office, and described the persons on whom alone He could perform it. I found as did others that he owned me.[46]

It is true, as Baker notes,[47] that few knew the Bible as well as Charles, and his knowledge of the scriptures made the business of *ex tempore* preaching less of a hazardous occupation for him than it might have been for most others. However, he did encourage others to adopt the practice. This can be seen in a letter written to him by Walter Shirley (1726–86), an evangelical Anglican who became rector of Loughrea in Ireland.[48] In January 1760 Shirley wrote, 'I have upon my late coming here assumed that resolution which your council [sic] inspired, and no longer making use of a formal written discourse, I only plan out the heads, and so trust to the Lord for the rest.'[49]

Shirley then goes on to discuss in greater detail what he considered to be the chief benefits of this method of preaching. In December of the same year, in another letter to Charles, Shirley thanks God for his gift of 'enabling me to preach ex tempore' since it is a great blessing in his time of sickness not to have to spend time preparing material beforehand.[50]

The length of Charles's sermons is far from uniform; among those for which MSS have survived there is considerable variety. The sermon on Romans 3: 23–5, for example, is *c.*10,000 words; the shorter of the two on 1 Kings 18: 21 only *c.*3,500. The journal and letters have much to say on the length of Charles's preaching. For example the journal entry for 10 September 1739 records that at 'Gloucester-lane' he 'discoursed two hours on John 3'.[51] A letter which he wrote

---

[45] Nuttall, 'Charles Wesley', 184.
[46] Charles Wesley to John Wesley, March 1740 as quoted in Baker, *Charles Wesley as Revealed by his Letters*, 38.   [47] Baker, *Charles Wesley as Revealed by his Letters*, 38–39.
[48] Harmon, (ed.), *Encyclopedia*, ii. 2146.
[49] Walter Shirley to Charles Wesley, 12 January 1760, MARC DDPr 1/69.
[50] Walter Shirley to Charles Wesley, (10 December 1760), MARC DDPr 1/99. The date is taken from a note which Charles has himself made on the letter, which was presumably the date upon which it was received.   [51] MARC DDCW 10/2 *in loc.*; Jackson, *Journal*, i. 171.

to his wife in June 1764 included a reference to Mr Venn whom Charles had apparently chastised for preaching a 'long sermon' and then goes on to note that Charles himself preached at the Foundery 'near an hour and a half long'.[52] He often spoke for more than an hour.[53]

It must be noted also that it is plain from the obvious discrepancy between the text of the surviving written sermons and references in primary sources to the length of Charles's preaching that he did often diverge from what he had prepared. In the one case mentioned that can be checked, Sermon 8 on Ephesians 5: 14 ('Awake thou that Sleepest'), this possibility becomes almost a certainty. It was claimed by a critic, 'Mr Salmon', that the orally delivered form of this sermon lasted two hours. Speaking of St Mary's, Oxford, Salmon wrote

the times of the day the University go to this church, are 10 in the morning, and 2 in the afternoon, on Sunday and holidays, the sermon usually lasting about half an hour. But when I happened to be at Oxford, in 1742, Mr. W. the Methodist, of Christ-Church, entertained his audience 2 hours, and, having insulted and abused all degrees, from the highest to the lowest, was in a manner hissed out of the pulpit by the lads.[54]

Charles rejected this claim, stating that in fact his sermon lasted less than one hour and that he had not been 'hissed' as Salmon charged. Even on Charles's defensive reckoning, however, it is plain that a substantial portion of what he said did not make it into the published form, which takes about half an hour to read aloud at a modest pace. Thus, as Baker notes,[55] Charles must have strayed considerably from his written text. (Alternatively, of course, he may have cut down the text for publication.)

The true spirit and content of Charles's preaching, then, cannot be recaptured simply by printing the few surviving texts of his sermons. The vast majority have not survived in any form, and even those for which there are written texts need to be treated with caution, for the written text and the spoken words seem often to have diverged. That 'much' which Charles 'added extempore' has gone forever. The texts printed here must be seen in this context; any conclusions regarding the style and content of Charles's preaching run the risk of being based upon only the

[52] Charles Wesley to Sarah Wesley, 7 June (1764), MARC DDCW 7/10; Jackson, *Journal*, ii. 242–4; quoted in Baker, *Charles Wesley as Revealed by his Letters*, 37.

[53] See for example MARC DDCW 7/16, Letter of Charles Wesley to Sarah Wesley, 18 June (1763) in which he notes that his sermon on Psalm 23 lasted more than an hour, and then reports that 'I was near two hours speaking of blessed Mr Grimshaw', who had died in April 1763. Charles spoke for at least an hour on 'holiness'—see MARC DDCW 7/31, Letter of Charles Wesley to Sarah Wesley, n.d. He refers also to 'the old days, at the Foundery, where I exhorted the society for above an hour to humility and love' —see MARC DDCW 7/20, Letter of Charles Wesley to Sarah Wesley, n.d.

[54] See Charles's journal for 15 April, 1750 (MARC DDCW 10/2 *in loc.*; Jackson, *Journal*, ii. 70–1) where he reports that he read 'Mr. Salmon's *"Foreigner's Companion through the Universities of Cambridge and Oxford"* printed in 1748' and copies out the passage quoted.

[55] See an unpublished typescript of a two-volume bibliography Baker was preparing, which is held in the John Rylands University Library of Manchester. It is known as the 'Draft Bibliography'. This comment is in i. 142

surviving fragments of what must have been an originally very large body of first-hand and literary evidence. They do, however, give at least the thrust of his message.

Charles's evident fluency in the scriptures and his ability to preach from them *extempore* obviating the need for written MSS is, from the perspective of the later historical researcher, somewhat unfortunate, for it is probably as a result that so little written material has survived. Certainly the lack of surviving material should not be taken as indicating a corresponding lack of activity, for a reading of Charles's journal suggests that for all the period for which it has survived, preaching was very much the life-blood of Charles's work and the focal point of his ministry. During the period from 18 to 25 July 1754, for example, by no means an untypical week, Charles preached no less than thirteen times.[56] Later sources complement this picture in the journal. On Saturday 18 June (1763)[57] Charles wrote to his wife indicating that he had preached a sermon the night before, had spoken in the chapel for over two hours the preceding Wednesday, was due to preach twice the following day, again on Tuesday, and deliver a funeral sermon on Thursday, a total of six speaking appointments in eight days.[58] In late 1764 to early 1765, well after he had given up the life of the itinerant and settled in Bristol, Charles was still preaching very frequently, often twice and sometimes three times a week.[59] In

[56] MARC DDCW 10/2 *in loc.*; Jackson, *Journal*, ii. 102–5.

[57] The date does not include a year, but its contents suggest 1763, the year in which William Grimshaw died. [58] MARC ref. DDCW 7/16.

[59] This information is gained from Anon, 'Texts of sermons preached by Wesley, Oddie, Davis, & Others (at Bristol) 1764–5'. MARC MAB Anonymous Sermons. According to this source, in 1764–5 Charles preached on Sunday 12 August (Isa. 50: 2); Thursday 16 August (Ps. 39: 7); Sunday 19 August (Isa. 55: 1); Thursday 23 August (Deut. 33:26 ff.); Sunday 26 August (Mic. 7: 18–20); Tuesday 28 August (Ps. 40: 16–17); Sunday 2 September (1 John 5: 20); Sunday 14 October (Ps. 106: 4); Sunday 21 October (Heb. 7: 25); Sunday 28 October (Isa. 35: 4); Sunday 4 November (Deut. 6: 5 ff.); Sunday 25 November (Zech. 13: 1); Sunday 2 December (Acts 3: 25–6); Sunday 9 December (Acts 2: 41 ff.); Sunday 23 December ('For the son of man came to save that which was lost'); Tuesday 25 December (Isa. 9: 6–7); Sunday 30 December (1 Sam. 20: 3); Tuesday 1 January (Hag. 2: 19); Sunday 6 January (1 Cor. 1: 21); Sunday 13 January (Luke 11: 2); Tuesday 15 January (no text noted ('I was late')); Sunday 20 January (Heb. 9: 27–8); Tuesday 22 January (no text noted ('I was late')); Sunday 27 January (Acts 13: 38–9); Sunday 3 February (2 Tim 4: 7–8); Tuesday 5 February (no text noted ('I was too late for the text')); Sunday 10 February (Zech 12: 10); Tuesday 12 February (Rev. 22: 20); Sunday 17 February (Isa. (no reference given)); Tuesday 19 February (no text noted ('I was too late for the text')); Sunday 11 March (*sic*); it was 10 March. No text is given; a note at this point reads 'I have been kept for [*sic*] hearing the word preacht near two weeks through my daughter's illness'); Tuesday 19 March (Jer. 8: 22); Tuesday 26 March (Luke 10: 42); Sunday 31 March (Isa. 51: 12); Tuesday 2 April (Isa. 50: 2); Friday 5 April (Good Friday) Isa. 53: 3ff.); Sunday 7 April (Easter day) Acts 17: 18); Tuesday 9 April (Acts 5: 30–2); Sunday 14 April (Gal. 2: 20); Tuesday 16 April (Gen. 32: 26); Tuesday 23 April (no text noted ('I was to [*sic*] late for the text'); Sunday 28 April (1 John (no reference given); Tuesday 30 April (Lam. 3: 22ff.); Sunday 5 May (John 8: 31–2); Tuesday 7 May (John 14: 27); Sunday 12 May (Heb. 12: 1); Tuesday 14 May (Luke 12: 32).

Several of the longer gaps between preaching are the result of John Wesley's presence in Bristol, during which periods it was he rather than Charles (or anyone else) who took the pulpit. See also the letter from John Valton to Charles Wesley, an undated letter which Charles has annotated 'Aug. 14, 1780' (MARC DDPR 2/58). In the letter Valton reminds Charles that John Wesley had indicated that Charles was to preach in the New Room on Tuesday and Thursday. This suggests that even towards the end of his life, Charles still sought to maintain an active preaching schedule.

August 1785, now in the seventy-eighth year of his life, he was still preaching,[60] and in July 1787, less than a year before his death, he was managing to preach twice on Sundays, almost as a way of saying 'farewell'.[61]

One of the more famous aspects of the preaching of the Methodist revivalists, most notably that of John Wesley himself, was the practice of open-air preaching. This practice was early engaged in by George Whitefield and was taken up by both the Wesley brothers. John was preaching in the open air at the latest by April 1739[62] and Charles was not too far behind. Quite precisely when Charles first engaged in the activity is not absolutely clear, but the journal indicates that by 29 May, 1739 he had, somewhat reluctantly, begun to follow in the footsteps of Whitefield. The entry for that day reads 'Franklyn, a farmer, invited me to preach in his field. I did so, to about 500, on, "Repent, for the kingdom of heaven is at hand." Returned to the house rejoicing.'[63]

Gill gives this date as that of Charles's first field-preaching[64], which it may well have been. However, the magnitude of this decision by Charles to preach in the open fields and thereby join himself with the work of Whitefield and the other revival preachers should not be underestimated, and the very terse journal entry does not reflect the extent to which, if this was the first occurrence, it represents a radical break with the tradition to which Charles was wedded. This may in fact have been a spur-of-the-moment decision by Charles, driven as he was by circumstance, although he must have been considering the issue for some time before 29 May since, as his journal indicates, he fairly frequently attended George Whitefield in his open-air preaching.[65] During the next month the necessity of preaching outside walls and indeed outside the official structures of the Church became even more pressing, and Charles was forced to make a decision. As a Methodist he was finding it not always easy to gain access to a pulpit from which to proclaim his message. This is seen at several points. For example, on 1 May, 1739 he reports how churchwardens kept guard over the pulpit-stairs and 'I was not inclined to fight my way through them'. Even earlier, on 21 December, 1738, Charles had been refused the pulpit at St Antholin's and had gained access to it only by refusing to accept the name of 'Methodist'. He wrote

---

[60] MARC DDCW 7/71. The letter is dated 8 August, 1785 and postmarked 15 August. Charles preached his sermon on 'be ye also ready' (which he refers to as 'an old Methodist sermon') on the Thursday, which would have been 11 August. It is evident from the letter that Charles had also preached on the subject 'God be merciful to me a sinner' on Sunday 7 August.

[61] Charles Wesley to Betsy Briggs, 2 July 1787. MARC DDCW 1/80 (Xerox copy of original which is held at Garrett Theological Seminary).

[62] See *J&D*, xix. 46 (2 April, 1739). As Outler notes (*Sermons*, i. 14) John had in fact preached in the 'open air' on board the *Simmonds* beginning 19 October, 1735, but these were exceptional circumstances.   [63] MARC DDCW 10/2, *in loc.*; Telford, *Journal*, 233.

[64] Gill, *First Methodist*, 13.

[65] See for example the entries for 27 April, 1739 (Whitefield is preaching in Islington Church yard); 28 April, 1739.

At St. Antholin's the clerk asked me my name, and said, 'Dr. Venn has forbidden any
Methodist to preach. Do you call yourself a Methodist?' 'I do not: the world may call me
what they please.' 'Well, sir,' said he, 'it is pity the people should go away without preaching. You may preach.' I did so, on good works.[66]

The situation deteriorated further. The entry for 19 June, 1739 reads

At Lambeth with Mr. Piers. His Grace expressly forbad him to let any of us preach in his
church: charged us with breach of the canon. I mentioned the Bishop of London's autho-
rising my forcible exclusion. He would not hear me; said he did not dispute. He asked me
what call I had. I answered, 'A dispensation of the gospel is committed to me.' 'That is, to
St. Paul; but I do not dispute: and will not proceed to excommunication YET.' 'Your Grace
has taught me in your book on Church Government, that a man unjustly excommunicated
is not thereby cut off from communion with Christ.' 'Of that I am the judge.' I asked him,
if Mr. Whitefield's success was not a spiritual sign, and sufficient proof of his call: recommended Gamaliel's advice. He dismissed us; Piers, with kind professions; me, with all the
marks of his displeasure.[67]

As has been shown, Charles had already preached in the open air before this
interview at Lambeth. However, the increasingly difficult situation in which the
Methodist preachers found themselves seems to have led him to consider fully the
advice of Whitefield. Four days later he wrote

Dined at Mr. Stonehouse's. My inward conflict continued. Perceived it was the fear of man;
and that, by preaching in the field next Sunday, as G. Whitefield urges me, I shall break
down the bridge, and become desperate. Retired, and prayed for particular direction; offering up my friends, my liberty, my life, for Christ's sake and the Gospel's. Somewhat less
burthened; yet could not be quite easy, till I gave up all.[68]

It is clear, then, that the decision to preach in the open was one that Charles did
not take lightly. However, after this entry it becomes increasingly common to find
him doing so, and with an apparently easy conscience. He preached to 'near ten
thousand, by computation' at Moorfields on Sunday, 8 July.[69] On the same day, and
again on 7 August, he preached on Kennington Common.[70] By the end of 1739,
then, he was frequently preaching in the open.

Charles wrote to Whitefield that he was 'continually tempted to leave off
preaching, and hide myself like J. Hutchins. I should then be freer from temptation, and at leisure to attend my own improvement'.[71] Despite this 'temptation',
however, all the evidence suggests that preaching occupied a central role in his life
from the time of his ordination in 1735 to very near the time of his death. Some
periods were no doubt busier than others (for example, when he preached 'con-

---

[66] MARC DDCW 10/2 *in loc.*; Telford, *Journal*, 216.
[67] MARC DDCW 10/2 *in loc.*; Telford, *Journal*, 239.
[68] MARC DDCW 10/2 *in loc.*; Telford, *Journal*, 240.
[69] MARC DDCW 10/2 *in loc.*; Telford, *Journal*, 242
[70] MARC DDCW 10/2 *in loc.*; Telford, *Journal*, 242, 243–4.
[71] 10 August, 1739 (MARC DDCW 10/2 *in loc.*; Telford, *Journal*, 245).

stantly' in order to relieve the workload of his brother and thereby conserve the latter's strength),[72] but there can be no doubt that preaching was an activity with which he was consistently and regularly concerned throughout the entire course of his 53-year ministry. It is unfortunate then, given the centrality of preaching to Charles's career, that so little of it is now reconstructible. Whatever he did not commit to paper went with him to the grave and cannot now be resurrected, beyond the attempt to reconstruct its outline form as shadowed in the journal (and perhaps the hymns) and the scant remarks of secondary eye-witnesses.

The situation is not, however, without hope, for although *ex tempore* expositions do seem to have been very much a part of Charles's preaching style throughout most of his ministerial life, he did not always speak completely without notes, and this seems particularly true of his early preaching career before, during, and shortly after the ill-fated trip to America and his later evangelical conversion. It is from this period that almost all that survives has come. Thus, for example, on board the *Simmonds* in October 1735 John noted that his brother Charles 'writ sermons',[73] a reference to which more attention will be given below. Similarly, on Sunday 28 May, 1738, that is a week after his evangelical conversion, Charles entered into his diary the remark 'I then began writing my first sermon in the name of Christ my Prophet'.[74] Later, on Monday 31 July, 1738, Charles entered into his diary 'Began writing a sermon upon Gal. 3.22',[75] one which he was later to 'read' to the society at Stanton-Harcourt. It should be noted also that he published a written sermon in 1742[76] and another in 1750.[77]

It is reasonably clear, therefore, that Charles did commit at least some of the sermons he preached to paper, though as has been noted above his tendency of adding 'much extempore' raises serious questions regarding the relationship between the written form and oral delivery of his texts. However, while the vitality with which he evidently delivered his discourses cannot now be recaptured, at least the substance of some of what he said (even if somewhat stilted and truncated by comparison with the preached sermons) is available. The material presented here is the first attempt to gather together all of the surviving Charles Wesley sermon corpus and as such is a response to the oft-repeated call that such an edition should be produced.[78]

While the presentation of this material is a significant step towards the much bigger task of seeking to bring all of Charles's prose works to publication, it does,

---

[72] Incomplete letter of Charles Wesley (to Sarah Wesley, 30 April 1755). MARC DDCW 5/55.

[73] *J&D*, i. 38.   [74] MARC DDCW 10/2 *in loc.*; Telford, *Journal*, 155.

[75] MARC DDCW 10/2 *in loc.*; Telford, *Journal*, 197.   [76] 'Awake Thou that Sleepest' (Sermon 8).

[77] 'The Cause and Cure of Earthquakes' (Sermon 9).

[78] See for example Teresa Berger, 'Charles Wesley: A Literary Overview', in Kimbrough (ed.), *Charles Wesley: Poet and Theologian*, 21–9; Richard P. Heitzenrater, 'The Present State of Wesley Studies', *Methodist History* 22 (1983–4): 221–33, at p.226; Thomas R. Albin, 'Charles Wesley's other Prose Writings', in Kimbrough, (ed.), *Charles Wesley: Poet and Theologian*, 85–94; Thomas R. Albin and Oliver A. Beckerlegge, *Charles Wesley's Earliest Evangelical Sermons: Six Shorthand Manuscript Sermons Now for the First Time Transcribed from the Original* (Ilford: Wesley Historical Society, 1987), 6.

however, have limitations, and these must be openly stated here and kept clearly in mind by the reader. The most obvious of these is the extent to which it is incomplete, for while every effort has been made to bring together all the surviving material, it must still be recognised that the twenty-three texts here printed represent only a tiny fraction of what Charles actually composed in either written or oral form. Following directly on from this we must note also the obvious chronological imbalance in favour of the earlier part of Charles's preaching career. It would be unwise to assume that what Charles preached at this relatively early stage of his ministerial career was typical of what he thought in later life. Similarly the several sermons written close to the 1738 turning-point in Charles's life might in themselves present a one-sided picture of an individual who was at the time of the composition riding high upon the crest of his religious experience. The sermons in this volume need to be balanced. Unfortunately there is very little material in the same genre from the pen of Charles with which such balance can be attempted.

And there is a further problem: it has been pointed out already that even when Charles was using notes, he strayed quite widely from them. If, as seems probable, the sermons printed in this volume also had *ex tempore* additions made to them by Charles as the occasion required, that layer of material too has been lost. It is possible, then, that in some cases at least all that remains is the bare skeletal outline of what Charles actually said.

The sermons presented here, then, give an incomplete and one-sided view of Charles, and this is certainly a problem. No picture based on so incomplete a body of evidence is likely to prove entirely accurate. As more of the other prose materials, in particular the letters, eventually becomes available, the seriousness of this problem ought proportionately to lessen, but it will not disappear altogether. The journal too will help. The hymns will of course remain central.[79]

CHARLES WESLEY AND THE EIGHTEENTH-CENTURY SERMON

What has been said above provides some insight into the centrality, form, extent, and content of Charles Wesley's preaching and throughout this brief sketch an effort has been made to assess the value of the surviving sources, many of them still fully available in MS form only, which relate to this aspect of Charles's ministerial career. It is in the context of this broader grass-roots evidence that the texts pub-

---

[79] The relationship between the hymns and the sermons and the theological overlap between the two is discussed briefly in the next chapter. The basic argument is that some of the hymns carry in poetical format the theological weight of the now lost sermons. So for example Charles's hymn 'Woe is me, what tongue can tell' (Osborn, (ed.), *Poetical Works*, ii. 156–8) may provide an indication of what his sermon on the Good Samaritan contained. Rattenbury argues the same is true of Charles's sermons on the 'Pool of Bethesda' (MARC DDCW 10/2 *in loc.*; Jackson, *Journal*, i. 292 (6 August, 1741) and cf. Osborn (ed.), *Poetical Works*, ii. 153–5) and the 'Woman at Canaan' (see MARC DDCW 10/2 *in loc.*; Jackson, *Journal*, i. 142 (15 February 1739) and cf. Osborn (ed.), *Poetical Works*, ii.150–2). This may be so, though the difficulties of seeking to extract from a hymn the substance of a sermon should not be underestimated.

lished in this volume need to be seen, for while it is true that Charles did preach before the University of Oxford, this was not the primary focus of his preaching activity. Neither, it seems, did Charles write many sermons for publication. He was, rather, an evangelical preacher whose interest was in conversion and the sustaining of faith as it was practised in the early Methodist societies. His homiletic work should be assessed in this context. Indeed the remarks made by Shields regarding the nature of Charles's poetry[80] are relevant here also: Charles had interests that were not purely 'academic'. He ought not to be seen in the context of the academic establishment of his day, but rather in that of heart-felt revivalist religion.

This given, Charles was a child of his age and something needs to be said here briefly regarding the nature of preaching in the eighteenth century more generally. This is an area in which there has been a fair degree of work already, both in general histories [81] and more specific studies and there is little point in simply summarizing that work here.[82] Indeed, Outler deals with the question in the very specific context of John Wesley's preaching[83] and much of what he says with respect to John is applicable also to Charles. Those studies, particularly that of Outler, could usefully be consulted at this point.

In outline Charles's sermons reflect the 'plain style' preaching that had by the eighteenth century become fairly widespread and was commonly practised by the preachers of the revival. This 'plain style', as Outler observes, was argued for by John Wesley himself in the preface to the very first edition of his *Sermons on Several Occasions* (1746), which contained Charles's sermon 'Awake Thou that Sleepest' (Sermon 8 in this volume). Here John makes it clear that his sermons are '*ad populum*' and should be seen in that light. This reference is, as Outler notes, a well-defined term, for Robert Sanderson, bishop of Lincoln, had previously used it in the context of his breakdown of the four types of preaching. According to Sanderson one may preach 'to learned audiences', 'on civil occasions', 'to the clergy' or 'to the people'. It was this latter concern to which John lays claim and everything in the surviving MS corpus suggests that this was Charles's vision also. Thus when introducing his *Sermons on Several Occasions*, John wrote

---

[80] See Chapter 1, n. 1.

[81] See for examples Charles Smyth, *The Art of Preaching: A Practical Survey of Preaching in the Church of England 1747–1939* (London: SPCK, 1940), 99–166; Edwin Charles Dargan, *A History of Preaching*, 2 vols. (London: Hodder and Stoughton, 1905–12), ii. 186–349; also useful is Lori Anne Ferrell and Peter McCullough, (eds.), *The English Sermon Revised: Religion, Literature and History 1600–1750* (Manchester: Manchester University Press, 2000).

[82] Among the more useful works in this area are James Downey, *The Eighteenth-Century Pulpit: A Study of the Sermons of Butler, Berkeley, Secker, Sterne, Whitefield and Wesley* (Oxford: Clarendon, 1969). A sample collection of some of the relevant texts is found in C. H. Sisson, *The English Sermon Volume II: 1650–1750* (Cheadle Hulme, Cheshire: Carcanet Press Ltd., 1976) and Robert Nye, (ed.), *The English Sermon Volume III: 1750–1850* (Cheadle Hulme, Cheshire: Carcanet Press Ltd., 1976); William Fraser Mitchell, *English Pulpit Oratory from Andrewes to Tillotson*, 2nd edn. (London: Macmillan, 1962). [83] Outler (ed.), *Sermons* iv. 13–29.

But I am thoroughly sensible, these are not proposed, in such a manner as some may expect. Nothing here appears, in an elaborate, elegant, or oratorical dress. If it had been my desire or design to write thus, my leisure would not permit. But in truth I, at present, designed nothing less; for I now write (as I generally speak) *ad populum*: to the bulk of mankind, to those who neither relish nor understand the art of speaking: but who, notwithstanding, are competent judges of those truths, which are necessary to present and future happiness. I mention this, that curious readers may spare themselves the labour, of seeking for what they will not find. I design plain truth for plain people. Therefore of set purpose I abstain from all nice and philosophical speculations, from all perplexed and intricate reasonings; and as far as possible, from even the show of learning, unless in sometimes citing the original Scriptures. I labour to avoid all words which are not easy to be understood, all which are not used in common life: and in particular those kinds of technical terms, that so frequently occur in bodies of divinity, those modes of speaking which men of reading are intimately acquainted with, but which to common people are an unknown tongue.[84]

This 'plain style' of preaching in the English homiletic tradition was more than just a Wesleyan whim and, as again Outler notes,[85] in employing it the Wesleys were taking a particular stand on an issue that was widely debated in eighteenth-century England. On the other side of the divide stood those who followed in the tradition of Lancelot Andrewes (1555–1626), John Donne (1573–1631) and others.[86] The style of this latter school was ornate, depending for its power upon the exquisite use of language and exhibiting a carefully constructed web of conceits and images, internal rhymes and assonances. Dargan summed up Andrewes's sermons as

at times artificial and stilted in tone, and often overloaded with learning and Latin quotations, not free from the whimsical fancies of the age, but weighty in thought, exhaustive in treatment and much occupied with the careful exposition of scripture: but his exposition is sometimes vitiated, both by polemical bias and the play of fancy.[87]

Charles, it must be said, could display some of the same characteristics. In Sermon 13 on Acts 20: 7, for example, he quotes in Greek and at some considerable length from the book of Acts, Justin Martyr and the *Apostolic Constitutions*, as he carefully builds up his case in support of regular communion. Elsewhere in the corpus he directs his audience's attention to 'the original Greek' of the biblical passage under consideration, and we know from the eyewitness account of Sutcliff quoted above that he did quote Greek in the pulpit. He plays to some extent on the meaning of the word 'wiser' in Sermon 14 on Luke 16: 8 ('Wiser than the Children of Light') and, as a reading of the texts below will indicate quickly enough, some of his prose is quite elegant. Even in the later sermons (those after 1738) he is at pains to tie in what he has to say with the Homilies[88] and the

---

[84] *Sermons on Several Occasions* (1746), iv–v.   [85] Outler (ed.), *Sermons*, i. 21.
[86] See further ibid.   [87] Dargan, *History of Preaching*, ii. 150.
[88] As a clergyman Charles was well acquainted with the Homilies of the Church of England and indeed uses them fairly extensively in several of the sermons here printed (such usage is identified in the notes). The production and publication of these Homilies was first agreed in 1542, though they did

Articles of the Church of England from which he again quotes at some length. Anyone listening to Charles would hence probably have to conclude that this was a man of considerable learning and mastery of the English language. That said, it will be apparent to the reader of the sermons presented in this volume that much of what Charles had to say he said in a very direct and uncomplicated manner. Like his brother he was aware that his design was to speak *ad populum* and, it seems, he tailored his style to meet that end. Similarly, the eyewitness accounts to which reference has already been made above, give the impression not of a man delivering sermons weighed down by learning or confined within a carefully constructed form, but of a preacher of the revival who preached with energy and conviction from the heart. It must not be forgotten either that Charles often preached 'without notes', even *ex tempore* from texts selected at random from the Bible.

Perhaps the best example of Charles's departure from the norm is Sermon 10 in this volume, on John 8: 1–11. Here Charles abandons altogether the formal style of preaching under 'heads' in favour of a straightforward verse-by-verse exposition of the text. This is a radical departure not only from the more ornate styles of Andrewes and others, but even from what by the early eighteenth century had in some circles become a much simplified form of the Puritan method of preaching under heads and subheads—the 'plain style' of preaching. The biblical text has now become so central to Charles's concern that it dictates not only the content but even the form of the sermon.

The tradition of this 'plain style' preaching in England was not new even in the eighteenth century, though quite when it began to emerge as a self-conscious reaction to other forms of the homiletic art is a matter of some dispute. To be sure there had always been those who had sought to speak directly to the people in a language that they could understand and even some who sought to do so outside of the established ecclesiastical structures and without the necessary licence. Thus when the Wesleys went into the fields in order to preach directly to the people in a language they would understand, they were not only following in the footsteps of contemporary revivalist preachers such as Whitefield, but also continuing a tradition that stretched back well into the pre-Reformation period.[89] Naturally enough perhaps, this tradition continued in the more radical wing of the Reformation and Outler notes its presence in England among the Puritans, Quakers, Baptists, Levellers and Ranters.[90] However, it was not just those outside of the

---

not appear until 1547. There were originally twelve, but to these were added twenty-one more in *c*.1563, and the collection reached its final form in 1571. See further F. W. Cross and E. A. Livingstone (eds.), *Oxford Dictionary of the Christian Church* (Oxford, Oxford University Press, 1997), 785–6. The form known to Charles would have been one very similar to the 1766 edition held at the John Rylands University Library of Manchester entitled *Certain Sermons or Homilies Appointed to be Read in the Churches in the Time of Queen Elizabeth of Famous Memory. Together with The Thirty-Nine Articles of Religion.*

[89] See further Outler (ed.), *Sermons* i. 18, who is drawing on G.R. Owst, *Preaching in Medieval England* (Cambridge: Cambridge University Press, 1926). [90] Outler (ed.), *Sermons*, i. 20.

established Church who were concerned with such matters, and while by definition unlicensed preaching, whether in fields or elsewhere, was not something with
which the vast majority of established churchmen would have had any sympathy,
the attempt to speak directly and in an uncomplicated manner was a real concern
to some. Outler traces such a concern and the resultant conscious attempt to
develop a 'plain style' back at least as far as Joseph Mede (1586–1638) and especially (with Smyth)[91] to the work of John Wilkins (1614–1672), bishop of Chester,
who put forward a reasoned argument in favour of the style in his *Ecclesiastes: Or,
A Discourse Concerning the Gift of Preaching as it Falls Under the Rules of Art*
(1646).[92] Others have argued that the style is already in evidence in the preaching
of Bishop Lloyd (1627–1717)[93] and, even earlier, that of Archbishop James Ussher
(1581–1656).[94] It was arguably with John Tillotson (1630–94),[95] however, that the
style came to fruition and it is perhaps significant that Charles had at least one volume of Tillotson's sermons in his personal library, suggesting that he had some
interest in his work.[96] Tillotson, who became archbishop of Canterbury in 1691,
used the 'plain style', and exhibited simplicity in both language and plan. His style
was to make a lasting impact on the English homiletic tradition. The 'three point
rule' which he espoused, for example, is still influential today.[97] Its influence can
be seen also in a number of the sermons here printed. In one of Charles's earliest
sermons, Sermon 2 on 1 Kings 18: 21, he states that

In discoursing upon which words I shall first show who they are that come under this censure of halting between two opinions. Secondly, I shall consider the folly and danger of such
a state. And thirdly, conclude with an earnest exhortation to an entire devotion of ourselves
to God.

At this time Charles has only just begun to preach (indeed this sermon is the
earliest indisputable example of his preaching) and he has not yet gained the confidence and apparent freedom he will later exhibit. Already, however, barely two
months into his ministerial career, he is showing in the way that he has structured
this sermon his sympathies for the 'plain style'.

   A somewhat lesser figure than Tillotson, but perhaps of particular importance
in the present context, is Robert South (1634–1716). South, an Anglican clergyman, sometime canon of Christchurch and chaplain to Charles II, similarly

---

[91] Smyth, *The Art of Preaching*, 99.   [92] See further Outler (ed.), *Sermons*, i. 23.
[93] Smyth, *The Art of Preaching*, 99.   [94] ibid.
   [95] On Tillotson see especially Smyth, *The Art of Preaching*, 99–166. A sample sermon is found in
Nye, *The English Sermon*, 193–204.
   [96] John Tillotson, *Of Sincerity and Constancy in the Faith and Profession of True Religion, in Several
Sermons* (1695), MARC MAW.CW25. The MAW.CW collection at the MARC is Charles Wesley's own
library. This volume carries Charles's signature inside the front cover. This material is fairly well catalogued, but to date little research on it has been conducted.
   [97] See W. E. Sangster, *The Craft of Sermon Construction*, reprint edn. (London: Marshall Pickering,
1978), 100 ff. Sangster is actually arguing against what he considers to be a slavish following of the
'three decker' rule. The fact that he here is concerned to argue for departure from it suggests that it is
still very much a part of the norm.

employed the 'plain style' of preaching. Charles had three volumes of South's sermons in his own library.[98] Again, then, a potential direct link is hence established between Charles and his 'plain style' predecessors and contemporaries.

In this chapter the case has again been made that Charles was more than a hymn writer. This is not in any way to deny his abilities in this area or even to question the extent to which Charles himself saw the writing of hymns and sacred poems as central to his ministry; it is simply to balance it. Charles was also a preacher.

Preaching was at the heart of the Methodist work and Charles gave himself wholeheartedly to the task. If the (admittedly sympathetic) accounts of his preaching preserved in the seam of archive material relating to this aspect of his ministry come anywhere close to the truth, his preaching was vibrant and capable of bringing about the end for which it was designed. As an Anglican priest he was well acquainted with the homiletic, including the 'plain style', tradition of the church to which he belonged and, as the sermons presented here show, he was not immune from the influence of the content, style, and structure of that tradition. However, as a Methodist itinerant he adapted his style as the situation required, and was prepared to preach in the open-air, to uncouple his sermons from the lectionary, and to preach 'without notes' and even from unprepared texts on the spur of the moment. This is a brave agenda. He cannot always have succeeded. Indeed, the sermons in this volume are somewhat mixed, and one wonders how well some of them, especially perhaps the very lengthy, would have been received. However, the overwhelming body of MS and contemporary published material is more than sufficient to support the view proposed here, namely that Charles was more than just the 'sweet singer of Methodism'.

[98] Robert South, *Twelve Sermons upon Several Subjects and Occasions* (1698) MARC MAW.CW26; *Twelve Sermons Preached at Several Times, and upon Several Occasions* (1715) MARC ref, MAW.CW27; *Twelve Sermons and Discourses on Several Subjects and Occasions* (1717) M5ARC ref. MAW.CW28. The first and third volumes contain the annotation, in Charles's hand, 'Cha. Wesley Xt. Ch. Oxon'.

CHAPTER 3
THEOLOGICAL CHARACTERISTICS
AND USE OF SOURCES

Charles Wesley has not generally been recognized as a theologian in his own right. Studies in this area can be found, but even when they are taken fully into account, the fact remains that his theological views have been the subject of only a small fraction of the detailed discussion that has been conducted concerning those of his brother John.[1] It is perhaps telling that a substantial number of the studies of Charles's theology that do exist are in the form of unpublished Ph.D. theses.

This situation is unfortunate from both a theological and an historical point of view, for as is seen in the sermons published here no less than in the hymns and poems, Charles was a theologian of not insignificant ability, and his attempts to explain both the plight of the human condition and what he perceived to be the divine answer to it deserve careful attention. His imaginative handling of the biblical text also repays examination. Both the systematic theologian and the biblical interpreter,[2] then, will find much in Charles's writings of value.

Charles is also of significance in the context of the history of theology, from both the Anglican and Methodist perspective, for his work is in part an attempt to bring together the biblical text and what he considered to be the authoritative traditions of the church. He was very much a man of the Bible. His sermons, no less than his hymns, are soaked in biblical allusions and imagery, so much so that it is often difficult to see where the biblical paraphrase ends and Charles's comment begins. It is clear from these same texts, however, that he also drew on ecclesiastical tradi-

---

[1] No attempt is made here to examine either the extent or the nature of the work done on John's theology as opposed to Charles's, which would require a substantial essay. However, even a cursory glance through the standard bibliographies of Jarboe—Betty M. Jarboe, *John and Charles Wesley: A Bibliography* (Metuchen, NJ, and London: Scarecrow Press 1987) and Field—Clive D. Field, in vol. iv of Rupert Davies, A. Raymond George, and Gordon Rupp (eds.), *A History of the Methodist Church in Great Britain* (London: Epworth, 1965–88)—updated annually in the Proceedings of the Wesley Historical Society—will underscore the point. In fact a recent remark by Jürgen Moltmann perhaps highlights it even better than a detailed essay. Commenting upon his time spent with Ted Runyon at Candler school of theology in 1983, Moltmann wrote of how he was introduced 'to John Wesley's theology and Charles Wesley's hymns' (Randy L. Maddox (ed.), *Rethinking John Wesley's Theology for Contemporary Methodism* (Nashville, TN: Kingswood Books, 1998), 11). Such a divide is fairly typical in Methodist scholarship; one studies John's theology, but Charles's hymns. Charles is seen largely as a poet, not as a theologian.

[2] On Charles's biblical interpretation see especially ST Kimbrough, 'Charles Wesley as Biblical Interpreter' in Kimbrough (ed.), *Charles Wesley: Poet and Theologian*, 106–36. This essay is an expansion of Kimbrough's earlier essay 'Charles Wesley as a Biblical Interpreter', *Methodist History* 26 (1988): 139–53.

tion. This includes the substantial extracts made from the Homilies and Articles of religion of the Church of England, and also from the Fathers. Other less authoritative ecclesiastical writers are also significant to the composition of the texts. It was from these raw materials, imbued with his own experience, that Charles attempted to fashion a theology which could survive in the hostile environment of the eighteenth century.

Neither should Charles be ignored by those whose historical interests are outside the discipline of purely theological or even ecclesiastical history. Through his preaching and other pastoral activities (including of course his hymn composition) Charles did much to determine the course of Methodist history in the eighteenth century, and while the precise role of the Methodist movement within eighteenth-century society is, and will probably remain, disputed, that it had *a* role is clear. To understand eighteenth-century English society one will need to understand Methodism, which was a partial cause and/or product of it. To understand Methodism one will need to understand Methodist theology, as a mirror of and/or the determining impetus for early Methodist social engagement. To understand Methodist theology, it is here suggested, one will need to understand not only John but also Charles Wesley, who was certainly the disseminator and probably also the co-creator of some significant part of it.[3] Thus the remark seems valid: from several perspectives, both theological and historical, it is unfortunate that more is not known of Charles's views.

As was indicated previously some progress in this area has been made, though much remains to be done. Perhaps the most ambitious project to date has been that of J. Ernest Rattenbury, who in the works already cited set about conducting a thorough examination of Charles's principal doctrinal views. Rattenbury's work contains a mass of highly informative detail, but his main point is the suggestion that Charles's theology cannot be divorced from his experience of salvation. According to Rattenbury, who has been followed by others,[4] Charles was an 'experiential theologian'; his theology was born of experience and intuition rather than abstract speculation and reason.[5]

---

[3] As is discussed further below, one view of Charles's contribution to Methodist theology is that he was the disseminator of views which had their origin either with John or with the evangelical revival in general. Gill, for example, though he is anxious to make the point that 'nothing could be further from the truth than that Charles was a pale shadow of his brother or that he stands in the background of his brother's work' (Gill, *First Methodist*, 231), nevertheless sees Charles as primarily the communicator rather than the originator of Methodist doctrine. On the symbiotic working relationship of the two brothers Gill writes, 'Their work was indivisible. John organized, Charles provided the impulse. John was the head, Charles was the heart. The latter's contribution was immeasurable: in warmth, fervour and affection. And supremely there are the hymns, without which it is doubtful whether Methodism could have survived . . . Charles gave wings to his brother's work, spreading it with a rapidity and gaining for it a popularity it could never otherwise have known'. (p. 231).

Such a view is put forward with even greater force by Langford (see Thomas A. Langford, 'Charles Wesley as Theologian', in Kimbrough (ed.), *Charles Wesley: Poet and Theologian*, 97–105), who does not see Charles himself as a creative theologian. Rather, states Langford, 'Charles served a supportive, encouraging, and propagandizing role to and for John' (Langford, 'Charles Wesley', 100). That view is challenged here.   [4] For example Tyson, *Charles Wesley: A Reader*, 7.

[5] Rattenbury, *Evangelical Doctrines*, 85–107 *et passim*.

Rattenbury's work is exceptional in its attempt to systematize the very un-systematic corpus of Charles's 9,000 or so hymns and other poetical compositions, and the results are well worth the effort that he has evidently put into the task. His insistence that Charles speaks with an evangelical voice of his experience of salvation is impaired only by the extent to which it is limited, as the titles of the books openly acknowledge, to only the poetic portion of Charles's literary legacy; the same limitation is seen in James Dale's informative thesis.[6] Had the full form of Rattenbury's proposed work on Charles's biography, and his ecclesiological and sacramental views, ever reached completion,[7] Wesley scholars would have been even further indebted to him. However, at best Rattenbury has told only part of the story. The missing chapters can only be written once the necessary primary materials, which include not only the hymns but also the sermons, letters, tracts, and full journal, have been made available to scholars working in this field. Part of that task is accomplished here.

Rattenbury's suggestion that Charles is best understood as an 'experiential theologian' finds expression also in the work of Langford, who, though he questions the usefulness of the word 'experiential', makes the same basic point. Charles's theology (which in Langford's view means the theology which he either took over from John or imbibed through association with the evangelical revival in general) does not conform to the norms expected of that discipline; it is not abstract or an end within itself. Rather, states Langford, Charles's theology is a theology of praise; it is a theology which one can pray and sing and is tied 'inseparably to the worship of God'.[8]

It would be difficult not to conclude that any analysis of Charles's theology based upon an examination of his hymns will inevitably lead to the view that it was a theology which could be sung and one tied inseparably to the worship of God. Neither will it come as a great surprise to learn that an examination of that theology (for which read 'hymns') leads to the conclusion that it was as an artist rather than as an individual of great rational insight that Charles may best be remembered. Charles did, of course, write a great number of hymns, and it has already been accepted that these must remain at the centre of any enquiry into his thought. He was an artist. However, as the appearance of this volume itself indicates (and it must be remembered that what has been collected here is only the surviving tip of a very large homiletic iceberg), it is simply not true that Charles used only the poetic medium through which to present his theology.

---

[6] Dale, 'Theological and Literary Qualities'. There are other studies which fall into this general category. See for example James Ekrut, 'Universal Redemption: Assurance of Salvation, and Christian Perfection in the Hymns of Charles Wesley with a Poetic Analysis and Tune Examples' (MM thesis, South-Western Baptist Theological Seminary, 1978), and the works by Flemming, Gallaway, Roth, and Quantrille cited above.

[7] The project was announced in *Evangelical Doctrines*, 15, but came only partially to fulfilment in *Eucharistic Hymns*.   [8] Langford, 'Charles Wesley as Theologian', 97–105, 97.

Neither is it true that his theology did not conform to the norms expected of that discipline. Obviously the hymns present a distinctively poetical form of the theological task, and allowance must be made for the genre in which this part of Charles's theology was expressed. However, like ought surely to be compared with like, and when Charles's other theological output is examined, it soon becomes apparent that he did in fact conform to at least some methodological expectations. Indeed, contrary to Langford's suggestion, he was quite able to write 'abstract theology', and he could appeal to the head.

One example from the extensive letter corpus will demonstrate this point clearly. In 1754 Charles wrote a very long letter (*c*.3,000 words) in which he explained in great detail, using fairly standard eighteenth-century prophetic-exegetical logic, his thinking regarding the eschatological events which he believed were shortly to come upon the world. The letter repays detailed examination.[9] As one follows Charles along his intricate exegetical pathways one is aware that here is someone well conversant with the thinking of his day. Much of what he says in the letter (for example his view that the Jews would be converted before the end)[10] is standard within the eighteenth century. However, in places his exegesis is highly unusual, perhaps even novel,[11] and his reasoning is tight and mature. Here, as also in several of the sermons, we see Charles the theologian and biblical interpreter working at the biblical text (especially Daniel and the book of Revelation) and doing so using standard eighteenth-century exegetical methodology. This letter, then, suggests that Charles could fashion a theology on his own and that what he had to say was by no means always parasitic upon the views of his brother or those of the wider evangelical revival in general.[12] Neither can the contents of this letter

---

[9] This letter is transcribed and discussed in detail in Kenneth G. C. Newport, *Apocalypse and Millennium* (Cambridge: Cambridge University Press, 2000), and earlier in Newport, 'Charles Wesley's Interpretation of Some Biblical Prophecies'.

[10] See further Christopher Hill, 'Till the Conversion of the Jews' in Richard H. Popkin (ed.), *Millenarianism and Messianism in English Literature and Thought 1650–1800* (Leiden: E. J. Brill, 1988), 12–36.   [11] Cf. Langford, 'Charles Wesley as Theologian', 104.

[12] This is a point that could be argued at considerable further length, though only a summary may be offered here. In the same year as this letter by Charles, John began work on the first edition of his *Notes on the New Testament* (published 1755). In the introduction to the book of Revelation found in the *Notes* John wrote that a correct interpretation of the prophecies had eluded 'many wise and good men' and it had once seemed to him that he too might live and die without understanding Revelation at all (p. 932). John's pessimism apparently lessened somewhat following his reading of the works of Johann Albrecht Bengel (*Apparatus criticus* (1734); *Gnomon Novi Testamenti* (1742); *Erklärte Offenbarung Johannis* (1740)), for these, he states, gave him new hope that he might yet understand the prophecies, or at least a good number of them. Despite this profession of optimism, however, it is clear that when writing the first edition of the *Notes*, he still lacks certainty on very many points. He will not undertake to defend all of what Bengel wrote, and indeed some of the prophecies 'will not be opened but in eternity'. The apparent optimism is therefore limited, and it is all but excised by the last paragraph of his introduction to Revelation, which begins 'Yet I by no means pretend to understand or explain all that is contained in this mysterious book' (Wesley *Notes*, 932). A few years later (and in the context of the George Bell affair) John again voiced uncertainty. He wrote, 'Oh how little do we *know* of this deep book! At least, how little do *I* know! I can barely conjecture, not affirm any one point concerning that part of it which is yet unfulfilled' (J&D, xxi. 400). As has been noted above, this was not Charles's view.

be judged as uncharacteristic of Charles's general approach to the Bible and the exegetical and theological task, for he himself says in it that he has been attempting to understand the prophecies for several years, and has presumably been seeking for an equal length of time to construct the kind of detailed, logical exegetical scheme evident in the letter. In fact there is even a suggestion that he is planning to write a book on the topic of biblical-prophetic interpretation, though the words here are ambiguous and may refer to a work written by someone else.[13]

On the issue of eschatology at least, then, Charles was a creative theologian and not simply the disseminator of the views of others.[14] In his arguments he was able to appeal no less to the head than to the heart. Such a judgement, however, can only be arrived at by taking into account not only the hymns, but also the prose materials; not surprisingly, it is in prose not poetry that Charles is more clearly seen to apply the logician's art. This aspect of his work may not appear with great frequency in his hymns, but this is perhaps at least as likely to be the dictates of the genre as the result of any imagined rational shortcomings on Charles's part.

In this context it is hoped that the texts here presented will provide the opportunity for the picture of Charles that has emerged through the study of his hymns to be balanced. The discourse on Acts 20: 7 (Sermon 13), for example, shows his ability to argue and reason his case, and is evidence of his apparent concern to present authoritative material, both scripture and church tradition, in support of his argument. The other texts are not so obviously the work of an academic, but all show a concern to progress logically and in a reasoned way through the material; several show Charles 'engaging the regnant philosophy of the age',[15] and suggest significant exegetical insight.[16]

Other studies into Charles's theology which deserve at least brief mention here include the work of Tyson, who in a monumental two-volume, 1,000-page Ph.D. thesis examined Charles's theology of the cross.[17] Tyson has at least sought to utilize more than just the hymns, though he too fails to examine all of the available material. (And his later *Reader* is so unreliable in the standard of transcription as

---

Rather, thought Charles, God had explained to him the mystery of the book of Revelation and he now knew what lay ahead. When it came to biblical eschatology and the interpretation of Revelation, then, it is apparent that it was Charles and not John who was the creative theologian and biblical interpreter.

[13] See MARC DDCW 1/51 §15 'What I have now hinted is only a small part of the scripture-evidences relating to the subject, which you must be content with till the book comes out.'

[14] For further details of Charles's eschatological thinking see further Newport, 'Premillennialism in the Early Writings of Charles Wesley'; id. 'Charles Wesley and the End of the World'. These relatively brief studies take into account not only MARC DDCW 1/51, but some other (though certainly not all) of Charles's early letters and hymns, the sermon material, and the references to eschatological preaching in the journal.   [15] Cf. Langford, 'Charles Wesley as Theologian', 104.

[16] Cf. ibid.

[17] Tyson, 'Charles Wesley's Theology of the Cross'. The bulk of the work is reproduced in revised form in *Charles Wesley on Sanctification*. On the topic in general note also John R. Renshaw, 'The Atonement in the Theology of John and Charles Wesley' (Th.D. thesis, Boston University, 1965), and also Neville Shepherd, 'Charles Wesley and the Doctrine of the Atonement' (Ph.D. thesis, University of Bristol, 1999).

to make it of far less use than it might otherwise have been).[18] Tyson's main point is clear enough: Charles was a significant theologian in his own right whose theology of redemption was at the heart of his system (not an unknown centre in the history of theology, it must be said). This conclusion is based largely though not exclusively on an examination of the use of individual words in Charles's literary corpus.

Tyson, then, like Rattenbury,[19] Hildebrandt,[20] and Wiseman,[21], but unlike Langford, views Charles as a theologian in his own right, and the material presented in this volume surely suggests that Tyson is on the right track. Charles did not simply reflect his brother's thoughts, as his views on ordination, lay-preaching, and eschatology, for obvious and easily documented examples, surely prove. Neither did he simply put into poetic format another's thoughts and thereby spread a theology which he was committed to but did not shape.

Despite the work referred to above,[22] however, Charles's theological views remain relatively unknown, and there is much to be done. The deficit cannot be rectified here and no pretence is made that it is. Major studies, monographs in themselves, are needed to supplement the work of Rattenbury and others. However, in an effort to make the case that the sermons deserve such a careful analysis, a brief study of one aspect of the theology of the sermons is now presented. The discussion is primarily focused upon the issue of salvation, and is largely aimed at indicating the general flow of Charles's thinking on this point during the period when the sermons were composed and preached. It cannot give a full account of his thinking over the course of his entire ministry. As the brief notes below on Sermons 9 and 13 will indicate, other areas of Charles's theological enquiry could have been explored through the sermons with equal value. What follows, then, is a limited, though it is hoped useful, attempt to highlight the potential of and need for further research into Charles's theological development. The presentation in this volume of the entire sermon corpus provides at least a substantial portion of the raw prose material necessary to that task, and this, when taken together with the poetic corpus, all of which is now available in the works already cited by Osborn and by Kimbrough and Beckerlegge, represents the bulk of Charles's specifically theological work. This is not to underestimate the potential importance of the letters and journal; indeed, the theological importance of

[18] Examples are numerous. A comparison of the shorthand text of Sermon 10 on John 8: 1 ff. printed here, that found in Albin and Beckerlegge, which was Tyson's source, and the form it takes in Tyson's *Charles Wesley: A Reader* (pp. 172–83) will demonstrate the case plainly.

[19] Such a position is put forward throughout Rattenbury's work and, it can be conjectured, would have been argued further had he completed his other studies into Charles's theological views. See in particular *Evangelical Doctrines*, 61 (quoted by Langford), where he states 'It is certainly true that his, Charles's and not John's, was the most effective and comprehensive statement of Methodist doctrine.'

[20] See Langford, 'Charles Wesley as Theologian', 100.

[21] Wiseman, *Charles Wesley, Evangelist and Poet*, 111–54.

[22] It has obviously not been possible to make reference here to all of the available work relevant to the present discussion. The bibliography included in this volume gives details of further studies.

one letter in particular has been highlighted above. However, letters and journal material seem more likely to prove of central significance to the biographical rather than the theological researcher, though in Charles's case it would be unwise to seek to draw too distinct a dividing line between these two areas.

What follows illustrates this point taking Charles's doctrine of salvation as an example. In particular it is argued that his experience in or about May 1738 set his thinking on new lines. The analysis is divided into two parts, the first considering the early (pre-May 1738) sermons, and the second the later sermons.

THE EARLY SERMONS

In the MS journal for 21 May 1738, the day of Charles's evangelical conversion,[23] the day is headed, in upper case letters, THE DAY OF PENTECOST. While May 21 was indeed Whitsunday in 1738, for Charles it marked not simply a festival of the Church, but a major turning-point in his own religious experience.

The exact chronological relationship between this experience and the composition of the hymn 'And can it be, that I should gain / an interest in the Saviour's blood?' has been debated.[24] However, even if composed later, the hymn is doubtless a reflection upon Charles's experience of 21 May. Verse 4 reads

> Long my imprison'd spirit lay,
> Fast bound in sin and nature's night:
> Thine eye diffused a quickening ray;
> I woke; the dungeon flamed with light;
> My chains fell off, my heart was free,
> I rose, went forth, and follow'd Thee.[25]

As with converts generally, Charles may well have overemphasized the discrepancy between his situation before the experience and that after it, a trap into which some of his commentators may also perhaps have fallen.[26] The imagery of the hymn is dramatic: a soul imprisoned by sin in the darkest dungeonal depths is contrasted with a spirit flying free in the glory of celestial light. The wider corpus of Charles's writings does not support such an absolute and total contrast between his life before May 1738 and that after it.[27] However, the sermons do certainly suggest that his experience of salvation, and his homiletic expression of it, underwent a definite shift somewhere between his leaving America and composing the latest of the sermon texts printed below. That contrast is explored here.

A number of sermons from Charles's period of 'nature's night' have survived in his hand. The ones that are dated as pre-1738 sermons are those on Philippians 3: 14–15; 1 Kings 18: 21 (two versions); Psalm 126: 6–7; Matthew 5: 20; Matthew 6:

---

[23] MARC DDCW 10/2 *in loc.*; Telford, *Journal*, 146.   [24] See Chapter 1, n. 64.
[25] Osborn, *Poetical Works*, i. 105.   [26] See for example Dallimore, *A Heart Set Free*, 62 ff.
[27] A point made by Baker, *Charles Wesley as Revealed by his Letters*, 33.

22–3; Luke 16: 8; John 13: 7; Exodus 20: 8; Proverbs 11: 30; and Psalm 91: 11. These are Sermons 1–3, 15–19, and 22–3 in this collection. In addition there are the sermons on Mark 12: 30 and Luke 10: 42 (Sermons 20 and 21) which Charles preached both before and after the May 1738 watershed.[28] The first three of these have a real claim to being Charles's own compositions. The situation with the next five is not so clear, but at the very least they were sermons which Charles preached and which may therefore be taken as expressing his own views. The remaining four are copies of his brother's material.

The darkness of Charles's dungeon and the gloom of his period in 'nature's night' is seen in Sermon 1, on Philippians 3.14–15. In this Charles sets about explaining the road to salvation and encouraging his hearers never once to take their eyes from it, or stop to rest along the way. God has set before the Christian an ideal, perfection; and unless that ideal is constantly striven for (even if never reached) the believer will not find salvation. As reflected in this sermon, Charles's world is a threatening and uncertain place. God demands that the Christian be ever diligent in seeking to reach the ideal of perfection, which includes, for Charles, the observation of all of God's commands; and how unpleasant it will be for the one caught unawares upon the Lord's return. If this were not enough, Charles also perceives that there are two major forces always seeking to drag the believer down. The first is the devil and his evil agents, a company ever seeking to hinder the believer as he treads his difficult path. The second is human nature itself, which is unwilling to bend to the will of God and by inclination seeks what is evil rather than good. Not surprisingly, then, Christians can 'never be absolutely certain of their crown of reward'. The gaining of that crown is dependent upon the waging of a constant battle, and the ultimate triumph of the believer over self and the devil. One may never reach perfection, but God demands that it is a goal after which the believer is constantly to strive. God, it is true, has promised salvation, 'but it must be remembered that all God's promises are conditional, and that we are bound to fulfil our part of the covenant'. Hence one can never be sure of 'the favour of God', and indeed to be so is a danger in itself, for it may promote a false sense of security and turn one from the difficult path which alone leads to the narrow gate.

The sermon is, then, a rather gloomy one. Charles urges his hearers never to rest from their spiritual labours, that is, keeping the commandments and seeking perfection. Salvation is a 'reward which is given' (Charles has struck out the even stronger remark that it is 'wages' which are 'paid'), and since that reward has not yet been given, the task has not yet been accomplished. Nothing short of perfection is required, and the individual must not stop short of that highest 'pitch of piety'. Stopping is fatal, for he

---

[28] For details see the introductions to the individual sermons.

that would stand still in the paths of piety must not be suprized if he find that he goeth back therein. He not only wasteth his time, but loseth his ground too: and will find, if ever he awakes out of his sleep, that he has not only less time to run his race in, but more of his course to go through than he before imagined. He that doth not constantly and daily strive against the storm of vice and torrent of iniquity, wherewith the world is now overflowed, will be infallibly carried down thereby. There is no resting in the mid way between heaven and hell. We must pursue our way to the former, or we shall infallibly make quick advances toward the latter.

There is, then, no instantaneous salvation. The lot of the Christian is uncertain.

Such thinking is clearly psychologically unhealthy and is perhaps both the partial cause and the result of Charles's pessimistic personality, a characteristic that has been commented on before.[29] The contrast between the tone of this sermon and that of many of the hymns is plain and need not be explored in any great detail here. The atoning blood of Christ, so central (as Tyson and Renshaw point out) to Charles's later theology, makes no appearance in this early sermon. Indeed, Jesus himself is noticeable mainly by his absence, and when he does appear it is as a judge and taskmaster.[30] Christ promises and calls, but he also expects and requires.

This sermon is not untypical. Sermon 2, on 1 Kings 18: 21, is also very likely Charles's own composition and here too we find the same basic ingredients. Charles sets before the audience the basic choice they have to make. No one can serve two masters and individuals must choose God or the world. There is no half-way option. The point is elaborated. God demands total service and nothing short of that will do. Conditions for salvation are set,

And it is to that due fulfilling of these conditions of salvation that the promise of entering into rest is made us. We know by the covenant that God made with us at our creation, sinless obedience was indispensably required of us: and though the rigours of this covenant are now abated and God through his tender mercy, in consideration of the manifold frailties and infirmities of our natures hath been graciously pleased to propose heaven to us on other terms; and to accept of repentance in lieu of perfect obedience, yet should we greatly deceive ourselves, that there was less to do than ever before was required of men in order to their attainment of heaven and happiness.

Sinless obedience is not required, for it is not a possibility for those caught between Eden and heaven. But the quest for it is. It is Charles's position at this point in his experience that Adam was sustained in his Edenic state by his own sinless obedience to the will of God. Once sin entered in the situation changed, for with sin came the corruption of human nature and the consequent impossibility of

---

[29] See for example Baker, *Charles Wesley as Revealed by his Letters*, 21–3, 33; Mitchell, *Man with the Dancing Heart*, 72–3 (who appears to be drawing on Dallimore, *A Heart Set Free*, 68).

[30] Note for example Charles's words, 'Has not our Blessed Lord himself expressly required us to be perfect as our father which is in heaven is perfect? Are not we exhorted to be holy as the lord our God is holy? To be pure as he is pure? And to offer our spirits, souls and bodies a holy and perfect, or unspotted sacrifice acceptable to God?'

sinless perfection. However, God is a just God and the level of difficulty with which the human side of the covenant can be kept is no less or more now than it was for Adam. Adam was perfect, and sinless perfection was required of him. Adam's children are imperfect and perfect obedience, though not sinless perfection, is required of them. Charles writes

Were we able, we should be obliged to be spotless and without sin. And though, through the corruption of our nature, a state of perfection is not to be expected in this world, yet are we commanded to aim at it with all our might: and whosoever voluntarily stops short of it, for ought he knows to the contrary, stops short of the mercy of God.

One must, then, do what one can and if one has done that (and only if) the shortfall is made up by the merits of Christ. Again Christ is noticeable mainly by his absence, and again the contrast with the later material is plain enough. In this as in Sermon 1, Charles sets out a difficult path of constant self-examination and the requirement of continual progression from bad to better.

In Sermon 3, on Psalm 126: 6–7, however, there is a sign of what is later to come. Overall it still exudes the basic gloomy air which seems characteristic of these early texts. The opening paragraph sets the general tone

Experience shows us, that even they who are Christians indeed, who serve God with all their strength may go on their way weeping perhaps for many years, perhaps to the end of their lives. They are followers of him who was a man of sorrows and acquainted with grief. And if any man will come after him, he must suffer with his master more or less; being like him to be made perfect through sufferings.

However, the sermon is not as extreme as the two so far discussed when it comes to soteriological pessimism. It is still Charles's view that it is the lot of the Christian to travel the hard road towards final happiness, but it seems far more possible that it is a goal that can be reached. The blood of Christ begins to take on the significance with which Charles will later invest it.

Humility cannot but lead to faith: a sight of our disease makes us soon fly to the cure of it. Who can feel himself sick and not long to be made whole? What contrite sinner is not glad of a saviour? And he is the more glad, the more firmly he believes, that he is able and willing to save to the uttermost: able to save all that believe, for he is God! And willing, for he is man. Here is joy! Joy which none can divide from faith! Joy unspeakable and full of glory! God the Lord God, Jehovah, God over all, the God to whom all things are possible hath undertaken the cause of lost man! He hath promised, he hath sworn to save them. Nay he hath done more than this: he hath bowed the heavens and come down: he hath been made man! He hath lived, suffered, nay died to save them! Yea tell it out in all the lands! ~~God~~ Christ hath died! He hath died to save man! Let the heavens rejoice, and let the earth be glad. Publish ye, praise ye, and say, this is the victory which overcometh the world, even our faith. If we can believe all things are possible to him that believeth: to him it is easy, 'to rejoice evermore'! Yea, he cannot but rejoice in thy strength, O Lord Christ, and be exceeding glad of thy salvation!

This is a message which Charles preached as early as 18 April 1736 and at least twice more that year. It is, to be sure, only a break in the otherwise gloomy clouds that seem to hang over his work during this time. However, it does give a hint of what is later to come.

With Sermon 15 on Matthew 5: 20 we are back on familiar territory. This may well have been copied from John, though the general tone, format, and style seem to fit well enough Charles's perceived state of mind and the thrust of his theology during this period. Charles notes that Jesus instructed his followers to seek a righteousness which is greater than that of the scribes and Pharisees. According to Charles there are two basic ways in which such greater righteousness can be obtained. The first is the performance of a greater number of good deeds than those done by the scribes and Pharisees, and especially the performance of good deeds not only in a distinctly religious (i.e. worship) context, but also in everyday life; more deeds, more righteousness. Secondly, deeds should be done from good motives. The scribes and the Pharisees do deeds to be seen by men, says Charles (drawing on Matthew 6: 5), but the Christian does them to please the Father. Salvation, described here again as a 'reward', is rooted in what is done. The Pharisees do too few deeds for the wrong motives and will not enter the kingdom. The successful Christian, however, does more good deeds and for the right motives (to please God and not man) and will get into the kingdom as his just reward.

The other five sermons that have survived from this pre-conversion period are all copies made from John's MSS and allowance must be made for this fact. However, the central message of such sermons as Sermon 16, 'The Single Intention' is simple enough, and Charles must at the very least have agreed with it. God has brought the people safely to the place in which they now reside (he first preached the sermon on American soil, on 14 March 1736) and it is now their duty to choose whom they will serve. Once this intention is clear, it will direct their actions. The intention of the Christian must be single and not divided between two ends, for God will not be served by halves. There is then an obvious overlap between this and Sermons 1 and 2, and it shares with them a sense of soteriological uncertainty. The religious life and the quest for salvation are not an easy road. Every aspect of one's life should be geared towards a single intention. If the 'eye' wanders, that is, if the individual looks anywhere else other than to God, the consequences will be terrible indeed, for

no sooner shalt thou divide thy heart, and aim at anything beside holiness, than the light from which thou turnest away being withdrawn, thou shalt not know whither thou goest. Ignorance, sin, and misery shall overspread thee, till thou fall headlong into utter darkness.

This sermon also links very clearly with Sermon 17 on Luke 16: 8 ('Wiser than the children of light'). Again we find Charles appealing to his audience to serve only one master. The sermon hinges on the observation that 'the children of this world are . . . wiser than the children of light', in that they know who it is they serve, and serve him with all their heart. This can be contrasted with the position of the Christian, who all too often offers only a half-service to his master. Thus while the 'children of this generation' are not absolutely wise, they are nevertheless wiser than the children of light who, though they know where they want to be, do not pursue their goal with proper, single-minded diligence. A sense of the real effort required to achieve salvation is, then, as obvious in this sermon as in the others sketched in above.

All of these relatively early sermons, from Charles's period in 'nature's night', seem to pull in the same general direction. They do, it is true, touch upon some other issues, but all are predominantly concerned with the question of salvation and how it is attained. In Sermon 3 there is a break in the clouds, but the general picture which emerges in these early documents is of an individual weighed down by feelings of sinfulness and soteriological uncertainty. In the face of this comes Charles's appeal to a more determined approach to religion and the call of God. Jesus said 'be perfect', and it is to such a state that the individual must aspire. He may never reach perfection, but the quest for it (human nature and the devil notwithstanding) is nevertheless a divine imperative.

As a study of the later sermons indicates, Charles never lost this insistence that the Christian must strive to be perfect or that it is the duty of the believer to seek out and do God's will, and it would be inaccurate to suggest simply that a works-based righteousness was replaced by a Christ-based righteousness following the events of 21 May 1738. In particular it must be remembered that two of the 'pre-Pentecost' sermons were used by Charles even after his experience. Conversely we have noted above that the insistence upon the sufficiency and centrality of Christ's death in the plan of salvation, the aspect of Charles's theology which was to become so central in his later work, appears clearly, if briefly, in the early Sermon 3. However, even allowing for these blurred edges, it does seem plain that following his experience in May 1738 a change did occur. As Baker has noted

Henceforth . . . Whitsuntide was always to be a peculiar time of blessing for him. Underlying the choppy surface of his Christian experience were the calm deeps of his new certainty of God's love for him.[31]

The later sermons reflect that certainty.[32]

---

[31] Baker, *Charles Wesley as Revealed by his Letters*, 33.

[32] The three pre-'Pentecost' sermons not discussed here are Sermons 18, 19, and 23, on John 13: 7, Exodus 20: 8, and Psalm 91: 11 respectively. All three were copies from John's MSS and none deals very directly with the question of salvation. The first addresses the question of human understanding (John had originally preached it at Oxford in 1730). Human ability to 'know' through the application of the mind is limited, especially so in the context of religious knowledge. God, for a time, has allowed a 'cloud' to settle upon the human mind, from which many things are kept hidden. By so doing God reminds human beings of their own imperfection and inability to search out divine ways. The proper recognition of ignorance leads to humility. As can be seen in the case of Lucifer, on the other hand, intellectual pride leads to manifest evil. Only in heaven will the veil be drawn back and in that 'hereafter' will all be revealed. This sermon, then, does follow the same basic pattern as those referred to more fully above; what is available now is imperfection, perfection will be achieved only in the hereafter. However, in this case it is intellectual rather than moral perfection that is in focus. Sermon 19

THE LATER SERMONS

The first sermon to have survived from the period after 21 May 1738 is Sermon 4 on 1 John 3: 14, the first of the six 'shorthand sermons' whose provenance will be discussed in Chapter 4. It is divided into two parts, and Charles did not generally preach both parts on the same occasion.[33] It is important not to overemphasize the extent to which this differs from the early sermons. However, that they are different seems unmistakable. In this earliest post-'Pentecost' sermon, Charles still finds a place for good works. They are 'the necessary effects or fruits or signs of a living faith'. They are necessary 'not to make, but to show us acceptable'.

On the question of how one achieves that acceptance in the first place, however, there seems a fair distance between this sermon and the view put forward in the earlier texts. As has been noted, Charles's general position in the earlier material seems to be that God accepts only those who are daily involved in the difficult task of drawing ever closer to that (always elusive) state of perfection. Sins, and sin itself, must be overcome, progress must be made, devotion must be complete and single-minded. All must do whatever is possible, assured only that Christ will make up the deficit when, and only when, the individual has done his very best.[34] In this later sermon, however, the conditions seem easier to fulfil.

Oh that any one of you would even now arise and go to his Father and say unto him, 'Father, I have sinned against heaven and before Thee, and am no more worthy to be called thy Son!' He sees you now, while you are a great way off, and has compassion, and only awaits your turning towards him, that he may run and fall on your neck and kiss you. Then he will say, 'Bring forth the best robe (even the robe of Christ's righteousness) and put it upon him, for this my son was dead and is alive again; he was lost and is found.'

This sermon may even be read as a spiritual autobiography. There are, says Charles, three types of person in the world: those who are wicked and seek not God, those who are wicked and do seek God, and those who are righteous. Those in the first state are without hope so long as they remain in it. Unless they seek God, God can do nothing for them. The second group seems to resemble quite distinctly Charles himself during the period leading up to May 1738. Those in the second group are those who are wicked, who know they are wicked, and seek to

deals with the proper Christian observation of the Sabbath commandment. The position put forward there is that the Sabbath (which of course for the Wesleys means the Lord's Day, Sunday) remains a sacred time and must be put to proper use. Work, other than that dictated by mercy or absolute necessity, should be avoided and the day given over to prayer, worship, and reflection. Sermon 23 deals with the role of guardian angels and their role in human affairs.

[33] See the introduction to the sermon for full details.

[34] Note for example, 'For though God will in consideration of the merits of Christ and upon our own free repentance pardon all those sins, which through the frailty and corruption of our nature we have committed, yet will he never pardon those omissions of duty and commissions of sin which men wilfully live in, through a fond and vain persuasion that it is not required of them to be as holy as possibly they can.'

become righteous; 'the love of Christ seems to constrain them, and they want to do great things for him'. For a while the world seems to have lost its hold upon them; 'the devil, that roaring lion, is chained; and the flesh but rarely troubles them'. However, temptation comes once more and 'their own wickedness makes head against them' and from this time such a person

treads the same dreadful round of sin, repenting and sinning again. His comfort is withdrawn, his peace is lost; he prayed,[35] resolves and strives, but all in vain; the more he labours, the less he prevails; the more he struggles, the faster he is bound: so that after a thousand thousand repeated defeats he finds at last that sin is irresistible. Then does he take up that sad complaint (Romans 7) which he feels the apostle wrote of him, 'That which I do I allow not: for what I would that I do not; but what I hate, that do I . . . Oh wretched man that I am, who shall deliver me from the body of this death!'

It is at this point, according to Charles, that righteousness comes. It is instantaneous. The robe is thrown around the sinner. He has come home.

There is an obvious sense, then, in which this sermon differs from those that have gone before it. The gloomy soul-searching seems largely to have gone and in its place has come a conviction that God in Christ has done in a moment what Charles had thought would take a lifetime. This is not to say, however, that the pilgrim has landed so safely on the other shore that he need never fear a return to his former state. In fact, says Charles, the belief that the justified sinner might never fall from the state of grace is nothing short of an 'arrogant doctrine of devils'. However, Charles assures his audience that no one may fear that he will (as opposed to may) fall from grace so long as he remembers that it is a real possibility. Even in this sermon, then, there is a sense in which salvation is uncertain (one may detect an anti-Calvinist slant here). There is also a place for good works. Neither of these aspects of Charles's post-'Pentecost' theology, however, seems to occupy the central position in his thinking as it did in the earlier corpus.

The other shorthand sermons express similar thoughts. In Sermon 5 on 'faith and good works' (Titus 3: 8), for example, Charles returns to the question of the relationship between the two and again puts forward the view that works come after faith and are the consequence and not the cause of divine acceptance.

First we are to insist that a man is justified, that is, forgiven, and accounted righteous by grace only through faith, exclusive of all good works and righteousness of his own; then, that he is to evidence this justification by universal obedience; by continually exercising himself unto godliness; by expressing the whole mind that was in Christ Jesus.

The sermon continues this general line of argument throughout, but one should not underestimate the continued insistence on the necessity of good works as a part of religious life. Indeed, at one point Charles makes the remark 'His [Christ's] righteousness is not imputed to me unless I manifest it by righteousness inherent

---

[35] The tense seems odd in this context. It may be a simple error on Charles's part, or perhaps even a slip brought about as a result of his remembering his own experience.

in me', which, though its intention may have been simply anti-Calvinistic, surely verges on the synergistic. Drawing on the epistle of James and the Homilies of the Church of England,[36] Charles points out that a faith that is not manifest in works is a dead and worthless faith. Similarly in Sermon 10 on John 8: 1 ff Charles presses home the point that Christ said to the woman go *and sin no more*.

Thus in these sermons the basic framework of a thoroughly Arminian soteriological system seems already firmly in place. Works are still important. They are the signs of justification, but more than that they are still, in Charles's thinking, necessary to it. Thus Charles asks with St James 'For what doth it profit, my brethren, that a man say he hath faith, and hath not works? Can a faith which is without works save him? Can an idle, dead and devilish faith avail for his salvation?' To which comes in effect the answer 'no', although the reply is partially hidden behind a logical smoke-screen (faith that does not manifest itself in works is not true faith, therefore the absence of works indicates an absence of (true) faith; hence the individual who has not works cannot be saved since it is evident from his lack of works that he also lacks (true) faith, which is the requirement of salvation). This being said, however, it seems clear that these early post-'Pentecost' sermons exude a soteriological confidence absent from the texts previously surveyed. While it may be possible to put the material under sufficient logical pressure to reveal inherent theological cracks, this is perhaps to miss the real power of the sermons, which is their appeal to experience and revelation. According to Charles God can, does, and will save sinners. That same God also requires a certain standard of behaviour from those whom he has justified on the basis of their faith. Such assertions make popular religious sense, even if to the theologian they seem to require significant further explication.

The remainder of the shorthand sermons, and Sermon 8 on Ephesians 5: 14 ('Awake thou that sleepest'), continue in the same general vein and need not be discussed here. With all these texts the one overriding concern is salvation and how it is achieved, and the one consistent answer given is that it is by faith in Christ, who has paid the price of human sin. Charles is, as we would expect, thoroughly Anselmian on this point, as a reading of the materials will show.[37]

Not all the sermons presented here, however, centre on the issue of salvation. In Sermon 9, 'On the cause and cure of earthquakes', for example, Charles addresses the theme of eschatology, with which he seems to have been increasingly concerned in the period of the 1750s, though evidence exists in the sources of his

---

[36] Charles draws particularly upon Homilies 4, 'A Short Declaration of the True, Lively, and Christian Faith', and 5, 'Of Good Works Annexed unto Faith'.

[37] The 'Anselmian' view of atonement is that which was espoused by Anselm of Canterbury (*c*.1033–1109), who suggested that through sin mankind had effectively wronged God whose justice now demanded recompense. So great was the extent of this wrong that nothing short of the perfect sacrifice of Christ could satisfy it. Charles's acceptance of this 'satisfaction' theory of the atonement comes across very strongly in the two sermons on Romans 3, where, even allowing for the fact that much of the terminology is taken from the Homilies, Charles's own underlying theology is plain.

interest in this area from 1735 on. This is a point that has been discussed in detail elsewhere[38] and the results of those studies are clear. In the later part of the 1740s and throughout the 1750s Charles had a great interest in things eschatological. (The wider evidence of his eschatological views is important, for it would clearly be unwise to take this one sermon as necessarily typical of his thinking as a whole.) The earthquakes which hit London in 1750[39] gave rise to a general upsurge in warnings of impending apocalyptic doom, and Charles was not alone in seeing in them the hand of God.[40] He also wrote at least eighteen hymns on the same subject.[41]

Perhaps the most obvious aspect of this sermon is its theological pessimism, which here takes on a new and dramatic form. This world, thinks Charles, is destined not to get better, but worse. And then the end will come. Humankind and society at large will not be transformed into the image of God through the general and gradual spread of the gospel, but through the drama of the eschaton. Charles's pessimism thus comes through in this sermon as it does in many others. Mankind is fundamentally wicked and as a consequence things are set to get worse not better. Society will continue to slide downwards into a moral and spiritual abyss until the great eschaton, the coming of Christ, sets all things right. The wicked are finally destroyed and the good rewarded. Neither is man able on his own to come to repentance or even see the danger he is in. Rather, thinks Charles, the gracious God has sent now (and the present earthquake is but one in a sequence) a sign of what is to come in an effort to awaken the sleeping sinner. Earthquakes are a 'call to repentance'.

In the name of the Lord Jesus, I warn thee once more, as a watchman over the house of Israel, to flee from the wrath to come! I put thee in remembrance (if thou hast so soon forgotten it) of the late awful judgement, whereby God shook thee over the mouth of hell!

Such predictions of woe run throughout the course of the sermon. The present earthquakes are but a timely reminder of more awful things to come. Some might be saved, but the outlook for many is grim indeed.[42]

---

[38] See Newport, 'Premillennialism in Charles Wesley's Early Writings'; id. 'Charles Wesley and the End of the World'.

[39] An account of the stronger earthquake is found in John Wesley's journal for 8 March 1750 (*J&D*, xx. 323–4) with a briefer note on the earlier shake on 8 February (*J&D*, xx. 320). Charles records on 8 February simply that 'there was an earthquake in London' (MARC DDCW 10/2 *in loc.*; Jackson, *Journal*, ii. 67). The journal has no entry for 8 March, but the entry for 10 March records how Charles preached on Isa. 24 'a chapter I had not taken much notice of, till this awful providence explained it'. MARC DDCW 10/2 *in loc.*; Jackson, *Journal*, ii. 68. See also Tyerman's account of the events and its effect on the Wesleys (Luke Tyerman, *The Life and Times of the Rev. John Wesley, M.A.*, 3 vols. (1870–1), ii. 71–4) and that of Thomas Jackson (Thomas Jackson, *The Life of the Rev. Charles Wesley, M.A.*, 2 vols. (1841), i. 549–56).

[40] Brief details of this eighteenth-century interest are found in Outler (ed.), *Sermons*, i. 357 n. 6.

[41] Charles Wesley, *Hymns Occasioned by the Earthquake March 8, 1750*, Parts I and II (1750); reprinted in Osborn (ed.), *Poetical Works*, vi. 17–52.

[42] Note further the hymn 'Tremendous Lord of earth, and skies' (Osborn (ed.), *Poetical Works*, vi. 21–3), the sixth verse of which begins 'If earth its mouth *must* open wide, / To swallow up its prey, / Jesu, Thy faithful people hide / In that vindictive day'.

He hath spared thee for this very thing; that thine eyes might see his salvation. Whatever judgements come in these latter days, yet whosoever shall call on the name of the Lord Jesus shall be delivered.

Charles's doubts seem thus to have become more general, and while he may by now be more confident with respect to his own salvation than appears to have been the case in the early sermons, he is not at all confident that this is a blessing which will be extended to all. Just as in the early sermons he is plagued by a sense of his own wickedness, so in this he is plagued by a sense of the general wickedness of humankind and human society as a whole.

Sermon 13, on Acts 20: 7, is the most measured. Indeed, it reads less like a sermon than a tract. That it was intended for use as a sermon, however, seems fairly certain. It has a structure similar to the others, and it uses the expression 'my brethren', apparently to address presupposed hearers.[43] Its point is plain: it is the duty of all Christians to communicate regularly. It is unfinished, which is unfortunate given the fact that Charles himself indicates that he is planning to discuss the three main points, but in fact discusses only one. The second and third sections ought to have been an argument that the practices of the ancient Church are incumbent upon modern believers and 'a practical application of what is said in the 2 foregoing heads'. The sermon is thus truncated and able to yield only a proportion of what it might had it been completed. From it, however, one can deduce something of Charles's churchmanship, in, for example, his criticisms of Luther and Calvin and appeal to the *Apostolic Constitutions*, Justin Martyr, and Tertullian, and something of the reverence in which he held the sacrament and its frequent administration. One is reminded of the practices of Charles's Oxford 'Holy Club', and the use of the name 'sacramentarian' as an alternative to 'Methodist' by those to whom they appeared extreme.[44]

There is, then, much in the sermons that could usefully be explored theologically, and here only some brief indication of that richness has been given. Charles often found that pessimism and depression dogged his steps and this mood is reflected in many of the sermons. However, while caution has properly been urged on this point, it is nevertheless surely true that in the sermons one can see mirrored a distinct change. Charles's heart may on occasions have been recaptured, the chains refastened and the flaming light partially extinguished. But that he did go through a moving experience somewhere in the latter part of the 1730s is certain. The sermons which come after the 1738 watershed display a new-found confidence, which, while it was sometimes prone to assaults from Charles's congenital depressive personality, was never lost. Baker has put it well: even after 1738 the surface of Charles's Christian experience was choppy, but it reached great depths.

---

[43] See Chapter 4 for a slightly fuller analysis of its genre.
[44] See Heitzenrater, *Mirror and Memory*, 72.

It would be of great interest at this point to seek to compare the apparent development in Charles's soteriology from 1735–42 as it is found in the sermons with the content of his hymns. This would, however, be a major study requiring far more space and detailed discussion than there is room for in this present volume. In particular the problem of the authorship of the hymns published jointly under the names of John and Charles Wesley would need to be addressed.[45] So would the issue of the extent to which John may have edited Charles's material; that he was in the practice of editing his brother's work is certain. The problem of reconstructing Charles's early theological views as expressed in the hymns would be accentuated by the total lack of any published or MS poetical work from him prior to 1739.[46] (The 'Charlestown' hymnbook of 1737[47], the first Methodist hymnbook and the first hymnbook to be published in the United States, does not contain material from Charles himself.) Thus, while the overlap between the sermons and the hymns certainly deserves further exploration, the difficulties in the way of such a task are not to be underestimated. Clearly this present volume cannot be the place to engage in such a wide-ranging discussion.

It is worth noting in passing, however, that it is quite possible, as Rattenbury has suggested, that some of Charles's hymns carry in poetic form the theological weight of his (now lost) expositions and sermons. In this context Rattenbury writes

He [Charles Wesley] preached much more on the miracles and parables that Whitefield or John Wesley did; he may indeed have been said to revel in them. His favourite sermons as his *Journal* shows, in the earliest years of the Revival, besides one on 'Wrestling Jacob', were about 'the woman of Canaan', the Pool of Bethesda, and the Good Samaritan. My guess that his hymns on these subjects were verse expressions of the sermons, since they were written at the same period, is not merely plausible, but also almost certainly accurate.[48]

Tyson makes a similar remark. According to him

The parable of the Prodigal Son became one of Wesley's favourite analogies for describing the process of reconciliation. The text was one of his favourite sermon topics (*C.W. Journal*, 1: 174, 188, 319), but unfortunately none of his homilies based on that passage is extant. Yet many of his hymns based on Luke 15: 20 have survived, and they give a sense of the direction his sermons must have taken.[49]

Such arguments seem entirely plausible (perhaps even 'almost certainly accurate', as Rattenbury claims). The early 1740s were a productive time for Charles and one

---

[45] See Hildebrandt and Beckerlegge, *Hymns*, vii. 55–61.

[46] The first, one-volume, edition of *Hymns and Sacred Poems* (1739) was published under the names of both John and Charles and disentangling the contributions of the brothers is a perennial problem in Methodist scholarship. See further Baker, *Charles Wesley's Verse*, 102–15.

[47] The only complete copy known to be extant is that held at the MARC, ref. MAB BOHI/G6.

[48] Rattenbury, *Evangelical Doctrines*, 160–1.   [49] Tyson, *Charles Wesley on Sanctification*, 108.

during which he preached a great deal. For example, frequent reference is found in the *Journal*[50] to his preaching on the Good Samaritan, the first being on 1 April 1739.[51] Charles's hymn on the theme 'Woe is me! what tongue can tell'[52] first appeared in the 1742 edition of *Hymns and Sacred Poems*,[53] a collection which was in fact completed in late 1741.[54] He thus presumably composed 'Woe is me!' during the very early part of the 1740s, and no later than November 1741. It is evident, then, that the period during which he composed the hymn also saw him preach several times on the same text. It must therefore be highly probable that the hymn provides a skeletal outline of the sermon, and by using this hymn, and the others which he composed on the same topic,[55] some basic understanding of what the sermon most probably contained could be gained.

There are other hymns and sermons which may equally well overlap. In addition to that on the Prodigal Son (a sermon which Charles preached at least fourteen times)[56], we might add also those on the Woman of Canaan,[57] the Pool of Bethesda,[58] Acts 16: 30 ('What shall I do'),[59] and of course 'Wrestling Jacob'.[60] This list is indicative rather than exhaustive. More work needs to be done on this potentially fruitful area, and in particular the new materials presented in Kimbrough and Beckerlegge (eds.), *The Unpublished Poetry of Charles Wesley* will need to be taken into account.

[50] In 1739 Charles preached the Good Samaritan on no less than five occasions (1 April, 12, 16, 25 August, 16 September). In 1740 he preached the sermon at least three times (30 March, 7 July, 11 November) and in 1741 at least once (17 July). Tyson counts a total of eighteen occurrences, which puts this text in second place on his chart of Charles's favourite sermon texts (Tyson, *Charles Wesley: A Reader*, 487).   [51] MARC DDCW 10/2 *in loc.*; Jackson, *Journal*, i. 146.

[52] Baker has noted that it is probable that the 'vast majority' of the hymns and poems in the 1742 edition were by Charles and refers to MS evidence to support this suggestion (information taken from p. 54 of vol. 2 of a 3-vol. draft of a proposed bibliography of the works of John and Charles Wesley prepared by Frank Baker. A copy of this volume is held at the MARC, MAR 218F.44).

[53] Osborn (ed.), *Poetical Works*, ii. 156–8.   [54] Baker, *Draft Bibliography*, ii. 54.

[55] See further Kimbrough and Beckerlegge (eds.), *Unpublished Poetry*, ii. 120–3.

[56] Tyson, *Charles Wesley: A Reader*, 487.

[57] Charles preached on this topic on 3 October 1739. A hymn on the same appeared in *Hymns and Sacred Poems* (1742; (Osborn (ed.), *Poetical Works*, ii. 150–2)).

[58] Charles preached on this topic no less than six times (Tyson, *Charles Wesley: A Reader*, 487). A hymn on the same topic appeared in *Hymns and Sacred Poems* (1742; (Osborn (ed.), *Poetical Works*, ii. 153–5)); see also Kimbrough and Beckerlegge (eds.), *Unpublished Poetry*, ii. 234–5.

[59] Charles preached on this text at least three times (Tyson, *Charles Wesley: A Reader*, 488). A hymn on Acts 16: 31, which begins with the very question posed in Acts 16: 30, appeared in *Hymns and Sacred Poems* (1742; (Osborn (ed.), *Poetical Works*, ii. 148–50)); see also Kimbrough and Beckerlegge (eds.), *Unpublished Poetry*, ii. 373–7.

[60] Charles preached on this topic several times (24 May, 16 July 1741; 6 October 1743; 12 June 1744; 7 February, 7 March, 20 May 1748). A hymn on the same topic appeared in *Hymns and Sacred Poems* (1742; (Osborn (ed.), *Poetical Works*, ii. 173–6)); see also Kimbrough and Beckerlegge (eds.), *Unpublished Poetry*, ii. 439.

CHARLES'S USE OF SOURCES

What has been sketched in above is a brief outline of Charles's views (or perhaps one might say 'experience') of salvation as it is found in the surviving sermon corpus. Charles, it is argued here throughout, was a highly imaginative and creative individual and his sermons show evidence of that creativity. However, like most other writers, he drew extensively on source material. Some brief account of that material is now given.

It has often been remarked that Charles's hymns are saturated in scripture references, a remark which is well able to stand critical evaluation.[61] Such references come both in the form of direct quotations, and also in less precise allusions; indeed some of the poetical compositions seem best described as poetical reworkings of biblical passages. Quotations and allusions are woven together to form a seamless whole which presents in memorable, and often singable, format the letter and spirit of the sources. This is a well-ploughed field and need not here be reworked.

As one would expect, the sermons also show heavy dependence upon scripture. This is not merely to state the obvious, that Charles preached on biblical themes, but rather to highlight the fact that much of the linguistic fabric of the sermons is drawn directly from the Bible. One example, from among the countless possible, will suffice. In the sermon on Romans 3: 23–5 we read

The sum of all this is this: they that be whole need not a physician, but they that be sick. Christ came not to call the righteous but sinners to repentance. He is the friend and saviour of sinners; not indeed of those who continue in sin, but of those who feel the weight of it, and groan to him for deliverance. Whosoever is saved by him, is saved as a sinner. His mouth is first stopped, he becomes guilty before God, and submits to be justified freely by his grace through the redemption that is in Jesus Christ. He counts all things but loss that he may win Christ, and be found in him, not having his own righteousness which is of the law, but that which is through the faith of Christ, the redemption which is of God by faith.

This entire passage has been woven from biblical passages, as a comparison of it with Matthew 9: 12; Luke 5: 32; Matthew 11: 19; Romans 6: 1; Romans 3: 24 and Philippians 3: 8 will show. Charles has, to be sure, used the material creatively and has brought together the texts to form a pastiche reflective of his own thoughts; biblical scholars may wish to dwell upon the intertextuality apparent. But almost all the words themselves have been taken from the Bible, a book which, as any reading of his work will show, Charles knew very well indeed. In the sermons printed below an attempt has been made to identify every point at which he has touched upon the biblical text (in either the KJV or the *BCP* form of it). It will quickly become apparent just how extensively he made use of it. How much of this was conscious is unclear; what seems certain is that the biblical language was

---

[61] See for example Baker, *Charles Wesley's Verse: An Introduction*, 34, 121 n. 12; Rattenbury, *Evangelical Doctrines*, 47–52; Waterhouse, *The Bible in Charles Wesley's Hymns*.

natural with him and his mind was quick to settle on passages supporting his point. To fail to see Charles in the context of the biblical text is to fail to see him in context at all.

It is clear also that Charles made significant use of the Homilies of the Church of England in the composition of his own sermons. In several he has made extensive use of these texts, even quoting from them at length verbatim. Thus for example in Sermon 5 on Titus 3: 8 ('Faith and good works') material taken from the Homilies accounts for close to 30 per cent of the entire text, and in Sermon 6 on Romans 3: 23–4 the figure is close to 40 per cent. This is of course hardly surprising. Charles was and remained first and foremost a clergyman of the Church of England whose loyalty to the doctrines, creeds, and traditions of that ecclesiastical body never wavered. As such he drew on the standard Homilies of the Church, which had been prepared 'to move the people to honour and worship Almighty God, and diligently to serve him'.[62] This is not to say, however, that he always copied verbatim from his source, though often he did. Rather, it seems, he has edited in the process of transcription (as he may well have done with his brother's sermons, a point which will be considered in Chapter 4). He has woven the passages from the Homilies into his own material and through that creative process brought into existence a text with which he presumably felt happy. One method for the exploration of the theology of the sermons therefore suggests itself, namely that which in biblical studies is known as redaction criticism. We have the basic source material (the Homilies), and we have also the finished product (the sermon). Comparison of one with the other, then, and the identification of changes, additions, expansions, and deletions, may well reveal the mind of the redactor-composer. There is no space to explore such possibilities here. However, in the texts printed below an attempt has been made to suggest places where the influence of the Homilies seems highly likely.

Charles is also able to quote from other sources he views as authoritative. This is most obvious in Sermon 13 on Acts 20: 7 (The weekly sacrament), which after beginning with a quotation in Greek from the Acts of the Apostles then goes on to quote, also in Greek, from Justin Martyr and the *Apostolic Constitutions*. In Sermon 6 on Romans 3: 23–4 (Justification by faith) he similarly refers to 'Greeks and Latins' (viz. St Hilary, St Basil, and St Ambrose) in support of his view that one is made righteous by faith. He also makes use of the work of the Anglican Platonist philosopher and theologian John Norris (1657–1711) in Sermon 4 on 1 John 3: 14.[63]

It is clear, then, that in the composition of his sermons Charles was dependent upon materials extracted from more than one source. His indebtedness to the

---

[62] *Certain Sermons or Homilies Appointed to be Read in Churches in the Time of Queen Elizabeth of Famous Memory. Together with the Thirty-Nine Articles of Religion* (1766), p. iv.

[63] Charles's source is John Norris's *Practical Discourses on Several Divine Subjects*, 4 vols. (London: 1690). I am indebted to the Albin-Beckerlegge edition of the shorthand sermons for this information.

Bible is no less properly remarked on here than with regard to the composition of his hymns. His extensive use of the Homilies and Articles and his less frequent quotation from and allusion to other written sources is also worthy of careful note. However, it must be emphasized again that he has done far more than simply copy these materials out. In the overall act of composition and arrangement and in the more specific additions, expansions, explications, deletions, and alterations he has made to individual passages he can be seen to be involved in a process which is, from both a literary and a theological perspective, creative. It has already been pointed out that the written form of the sermon texts and the form actually preached must have differed quite significantly, for it was not only to his brother's sermons that he 'added much extempore'. That layer of final redaction at the point of delivery has now been lost. However, some insight into Charles's use of materials can nevertheless be gained by careful attention to the extent of source material in his work and the use he has made of it.

CONCLUSION

The theology of Charles Wesley is relatively under-explored. Part of the reason for this is the inaccessibility of much of his work, and in this area, no less than in research into his life, the presentation to the scholarly guild of critical editions of his work is a *sine qua non* of further progress. Beckerlegge's and Kimbrough's efforts have resulted in most of the poetical material being available in one form or another, though even here there is more to be done, especially with regard to making Osborn's earlier work more accessible and more useful to the researcher. Charles's letters also need to be brought to the surface, and a critical edition of the journal prepared. However, with the production of the present volume one major step has at least been taken. For the first time all of the surviving sermons Charles is known to have preached, most of which are original compositions, are available together in a textually reliable form for further research.

According to John Wesley, his brother's poetical abilities were his 'least talent'. This seems high praise indeed of one who wrote what are without question some of the greatest hymns found in the Christian tradition, and not all will share John's view on this point of the relative merits of poetry and prose in Charles's works. However, that Charles was a preacher of very significant ability is clearly suggested by his own journal and also by secondary eye-witnesses, and this suggestion is not undermined by a reading of the texts presented here. As the remarks cited in Chapter 1 have indicated, Charles was able to speak with a clear voice to persons of all ranks of society, both 'persons of fashion' and 'them of the lower rank of mankind', as Williams put it. It further appears from the sermons presented here that Charles was an able biblical interpreter, and a theologian who could bring together in various formats and mixtures text, tradition, reason, and experience to construct arguments designed to appeal to the professor and the priest no less than to the miner or mill worker. The sermons echo this range of Charles's oratorical ability: he can on the one hand expound with great simplicity the story of the woman caught in adultery, but on the other launch into a tightly argued discourse on the necessity of regular communion drawing on the Greek of Acts, Justin Martyr's *Apology*, and the *Apostolic Constitutions*. He was a man with a message, and with the ability to put his message across. And as he was influential in his day, he has through his hymns remained influential down to the present. This is so not only in the obvious case of the development of Wesleyanism, but much more widely, in that of the whole of the Christian tradition, both Protestant and Catholic.[64] Charles's theology, then, deserves to be studied no less by the historian of theology than by the theologian.

---

[64] See further Teresa Berger, 'Charles Wesley and Roman Catholicism', in Kimbrough (ed.), *Charles Wesley Poet and Theologian*, 205–21; David Butler, *Methodists and Papists* (London: Darton, Longman and Todd, 1993).

CHAPTER 4
CHARLES WESLEY'S SERMON CORPUS

In the three previous chapters attention has been given to the style, extent, and theological content of Charles Wesley's preaching. It has been argued that he was an able preacher who did much to further the early Methodist cause and had an impact not only on the form, but also on the content of early Methodism. Most of the remainder of this book is taken up with a presentation of all of the relevant texts. However, before they can be presented, it is necessary to outline the reasons for their selection. This is particularly important in the context of the ongoing debate regarding which texts are in fact illustrative of Charles's own preaching style. Not all will agree, for example, with the decision made here to include in a volume of Charles's sermons material found in the 1816 edition. In the present chapter the case is argued that all of the sermons in that edition, with the exception of one, sermon XIII, which is clearly labelled as John's, do illustrate Charles's own preaching style, and are 'his', at least to the extent that he has edited them from his brother's MSS (although in three cases it seems probable that the sermons are in fact straightforwardly Charles's own compositions). All other possible MSS and early printed sermons are also examined in an attempt to draw up a definitive list of surviving texts. The result is that twenty-three sermons are identified as being Charles's; most were written by him, though some are the result of his copying and editing his brother's MSS (or in one case, it seems, someone else's). Details of the MS and recension history of those twenty-three now follow. They are grouped into sections for clarity of discussion—sermons published in Charles's lifetime (two); shorthand sermons (six); sermons printed in the 1816 edition (twelve, all but one of which exist in MS form also); and three sermons requiring individual comment.

SERMONS BY CHARLES WESLEY PUBLISHED DURING HIS LIFETIME

Two sermons were published during Charles's lifetime, both of which eventually found their way into editions of John Wesley's works. No controversy surrounds their authorship since early editions of both carry the name of Charles as the author. The MS for neither has survived.

a. A Sermon Preach'd on Sunday April 4, 1742

The first of Charles's sermons to be published was that on Ephesians 5: 14, Sermon 8 in this volume, delivered before the University of Oxford on 4 April

1742. It was published individually with Charles named as the author in 1742[1] and reprinted frequently thereafter.[2] Indeed, it was destined to become the most frequently published Methodist tract during the lifetime of either of the Wesleys,[3] a fact which itself bears adequate witness to the appeal of Charles's sermons to a wide audience. It was included as sermon 3 in John Wesley's *Sermons on Several Occasions* from the 1746 edition of volume 1 onwards[4] and has more recently been reprinted by Albert Outler (with, of course, an acknowledgement that it is a sermon by Charles) in his critical edition of John's sermons.[5] Copies of the first edition are located at the Bodleian Library, Oxford, Yale University Divinity School, Duke University, NC, The Methodist Publishing House in Nashville, TN, and at the Victoria University, Toronto, Ontario.

b. On the Cause and Cure of Earthquakes (1750)

The second sermon to be published by Charles was 'On the cause and cure of earthquakes', Sermon 9 in this volume, first published anonymously in 1750 and reprinted under Charles's name in 1756.[6] Hence, despite the fact that it appears rather confusingly in the works of John Wesley, no dispute surrounds its authorship.

As already mentioned in Chapter 3, the sermon was composed in the wake of the earthquakes which hit London in February and March 1750, and is the latest by Charles for which a text has survived.[7] A copy of the first edition is held at the John Rylands University Library and it is from that text that the sermon is reproduced here.[8]

---

[1] 'A Sermon preached on Sunday, April 4th, 1742, before the University of Oxford. By Charles Wesley, M.A., Student of Christ Church' (London: n.d.). The second edition indicates that it was printed by W. Strahan in 1742.

[2] Precisely how often is not entirely clear, especially since it appears in the various editions and collections of John Wesley's sermons. It was also published together with John Wesley's *The Character of a Methodist* (first published in 1742) under the title *Character of a Methodist: Together with a Call to Those who are Asleep in Sin, to Awake to A Life of Righteousness* (1808).

[3] Tyson, *Charles Wesley: A Reader*, 13; Baker, *Charles Wesley as Revealed by his Letters*, 35–6. The twenty-sixth edition appeared in 1782 and the thirty-third in 1865 (see further Frank Baker, 'The Prose Writings of Charles Wesley' *London Quarterly and Holborn Review* 182 (1957): 268–74, 269). Outler, (ed.), *Sermons*, iv. 437–9, has details of editions and a stemma of them.

[4] *Sermons on Several Occasions. In Three Volumes. By John Wesley M.A., Fellow of Lincoln College, Oxford*, 1, 20–31 (London: 1746).   [5] Outler, (ed.), *Sermons*, 1.142–58.

[6] 'The Cause and Cure of Earthquakes. A Sermon preached from Psalm xlvi. 8. Occasioned by the Earthquake on March 8th, 1750', (London: 1750). The second edition (1756) gives the name of the author as Charles.

[7] Cf. Tyson, *Charles Wesley: A Reader*, 16, who is in error when he notes, 'Wesley committed few of his later sermons to paper, so it is scarcely surprising that so few of them appeared in print. Apart from his formally prepared "Awake, Thou That Sleepest," which he wrote in 1742 and preached "before the University of Oxford" on April 4 of that year, the recently discovered shorthand manuscript sermons are the only extant examples of his mature homiletical work.'

[8] MARC MAB Lawson Collection 133.

THE SHORTHAND SERMONS

In 1987 a major step was taken in the task of bringing Charles's sermon materials to publication when six sermons in shorthand, transcribed by Thomas Albin and Oliver Beckerlegge, were published as an occasional publication of the Wesley Historical Society.[9] The centrality of this material to the task cannot be overestimated. There is no dispute regarding their authorship, they are of substantial length (the longer sermon on Romans 3, for example, is over 10,000 words), they are the texts of preached sermons rather than ones written for publication, and they all stem from the formative few years following Charles's religious awakening in 1738.[10] Consequently they are vibrant and give unmistakable voice to his own evangelical experience. These six sermons, then, have a real claim to being the heart of the surviving homiletic corpus.

The texts are in Byrom's shorthand[11] and the difficulty of transcribing does present something of a problem in bringing the material to publication for the use of other researchers. However, since Byrom's shorthand manual is available,[12] it is possible for present-day researchers to gain a fair insight into the method used by Charles.

The system is consistent and neat and had Charles applied it carefully and without major deviation there would be relatively little problem in deciphering the texts. The situation is not, however, so simple, for Charles's application of the method was, as might be expected, idiosyncratic and tailored to suit his individual needs. This is of course both desirable and inevitable in the use of shorthand by anyone, for while it may be used between two parties wishing to carry on a private correspondence (John and Charles used it in just this way),[13] shorthand scripts are more effectively used as a means of communicating with one self. Shorthand is then a system of placing on paper the basic framework of a written message, to be reread by the one who wrote it. In such circumstances whole words may be

[9] Albin and Beckerlegge, *Charles Wesley's Earliest Evangelical Sermons*. I am indebted to the Wesley Historical Society for permission to make use of the transcribed text of these six shorthand sermons here, though in preparation of this volume all the shorthand texts have been re-read and a number of changes to the Albin-Beckerlegge edition have been made.

[10] Four of the sermons are dated, and two are not, but all seem to have been composed and preached before 1742. Those which are dated stem from July 1738 to July 1739. On the dating of each of the sermons see the individual introductions.

[11] John Byrom (1692–1763) was born in Manchester and educated at Cambridge, being elected a fellow of Trinity in 1714. In the early 1720s he began teaching a method of shorthand which he had earlier devised. Although he issued proposals for publishing his system as early as 1723, his work *The Universal English Short-Hand* was not in fact published until 1767. Charles made extensive use of Byrom's method of shorthand in all forms of his literary output. See further Oliver A. Beckerlegge, 'Charles Wesley's Shorthand', *Methodist History* 29 (1991): 225–34.

[12] A copy is located in the John Rylands University Library, MARC MAB M68.

[13] As for example in a letter written to Charles by John on 23 December 1762 (MARC DDWES 3.19). The letter deals with the problem which has flared up regarding the teachings of Thomas Maxfield and George Bell. It is written mostly in longhand, but at one point uses shorthand to conceal John's expression of his great wish at this time which is that he 'could set Thomas Maxfield right'.

reduced to one letter, then written as the appropriate shorthand stroke, and whole phrases to just a few, then combined into a composite shorthand sign. The memory of the reader will be prompted and the expansion seem obvious. It will not be as obvious, however, to those seeking to read the text without the benefit of having written it in the first place.

The six sermons currently under discussion fall into this general category. They are shorthand texts written by Charles for his own use. Consequently, anyone who wishes to decipher the shorthand will need to overcome not only the idiosyncratic differences between what is in Byrom's manual and the system Charles himself used, but also the problem of extreme abbreviation; to Charles the shorthand signs for 'mfth'[14] might quite obviously mean 'in the midst of that'. However, those reading the text for the first time will hardly be as quick to make the necessary expansion.

There is also the problem of inaccuracy in the formation of the shorthand strokes, and the basic similarity between some of the strokes themselves. For example one of the signs for 'th' and the sign for 'd' share a basic similarity, though they can be distinguished easily enough in Byrom's printed manual. It is often the case, however, that in Charles's text the two signs appear in forms which are scarcely different from one another. Similarly the sign for 't' and the sign for 'f' or 'v' are very obviously different in the printed text of the manual and in most places where they are employed by Charles. However, the possibility for confusion is real, since the only difference between these two signs is the extent to which the 't' is a straight vertical stroke and the 'f' an inclined one. In a hurriedly written shorthand text the two can, and do, become confused.[15] The same is true of other pairs of signs such as that for 'g' and the compound sign for 'gn'.[16] In the manual the signs for 'k' and 'w' are easily distinguished. Both take the form of a line with a loop on the end; the 'k' is a horizontal line, the 'w' a vertical. In Charles's text, however, the two can be less obviously distinct, and when joined to certain other strokes barely distinguishable from one another.[17] Such examples could be multiplied.[18]

Most of the problems identified above can be overcome through careful and painstaking analysis of the shorthand texts, and Albin and Beckerlegge (with assistance also from Douglas Lister) are to be recognized for the time and effort they have put into deciphering the texts. Some problems remain to be solved and there are places where further work needs to be done in an effort to tighten up the text. However, complete certainty on many passages seems likely never to be attainable; in the light of this it would be unwise to postpone an edition of Charles's sermons until that desirable but elusive, perhaps unrealistic, goal can be reached. Rather,

---

[14] Sermon 10 (MS A), page 2, line 23.   [15] Sermon 10 (MS A), page 5, line 21.
[16] Sermon 10 (MS A), page 6, line 20.   [17] Sermon 10 (MS A), page 5, line 14.
[18] Beckerlegge, 'Charles Wesley's Shorthand' discusses these and other such problems at greater length.

this edition includes the texts transcribed by Albin and Beckerlegge, with notation indicating problematic passages which warrant further attention. In preparing the texts for this edition all the shorthand texts have been examined and suggestions have been made in the notes regarding possible alternative readings to those produced by Albin and Beckerlegge. In places where an alternative reading seems warranted, the text has been emended accordingly. All differences between the texts printed here and those in the Albin-Beckerlegge volume have been indicated and the reader is invited to exercise critical judgement.

Manuscripts have survived for earlier drafts of two of the sermons in the Albin-Beckerlegge edition, namely those on John 8: 1 and Luke 18: 9, Sermons 10 and 12 in this volume respectively. Only a small portion of the latter survives in this alternative form, and this precludes any extended investigation into the differences, although all are noted. However, for Sermon 10 there is a second complete MS. One is slightly longer than the other; for convenience they are referred to hereafter as MS A (the longer) and MS B (the shorter.)

The question of the order in which these two MSS came into existence needs to be considered. Close comparison of the two MSS suggests that it is MS A rather than B which has the stronger claim to being the earlier.[19] In particular it is very noticeable that corrections and deletions in MS A are incorporated and smoothed out in MS B. Examples are numerous and we note just one: on lines 19–22 on page 5 of MS A we read

These scribes and Pharisees, we know, were noted for their holiness; they went beyond even our good sort of people, and in all outward appearances were most exemplary saints; but God's ~~justice is not as a man's justice~~ his thoughts are not as our thoughts. These are they that justify themselves before men, but God knoweth their hearts, ~~and searcheth them out to~~ for that which is highly esteemed among men is abominable with him.

The several corrections here are quite obvious. In MS B the words are simply

These scribes and Pharisees we know, were noted for their holiness; they went beyond even our good sort of people, and in all outward appearances were most exemplary saints; but God's thoughts are not as our thoughts. These are they that justify themselves before men, but God knoweth their hearts, for that which is highly esteemed among men is abominable with him.

Now it may be that Charles was copying MS B to create MS A, and in copying decided to add to it, then reversed his decision and deleted the additions he had made. It seems much more likely, however, that he was copying from MS A and in

---

[19] The most significant evidence against the view that MS A is the earlier of the two is the fact that Charles has made a shorthand note upon it which reads 'tcrbd nv 24 1758' ('transcribed 24 November 1758'). One might assume this to be the date upon which Charles copied the material contained in the other MS into this new booklet. It is a question of balance. All of the other evidence points in the opposite direction and hence on the hypothesis presented here 24 November was the date upon which he copied the material from this booklet to form MS B.

the copy smoothed out the deletions and corrections he had made in the earlier MS.

Perhaps the most telling evidence is found on pages 9 and 8 of MS A and MS B respectively. The reading in MS A at this point is

Divided she is, but not equally between hope and fear, and now while she trembles in expectation of a sentence, she hears, (Woman, where are those thine accusers?). We do not hear him railing on her, or reviling her; he doth not say, Thou vile creature, thou execrable adulteress, thou shameless strumpet, but (Woman, where are those thine accusers?). Those who but now so importunately demanded justice against thee . . .

The same section in MS B reads

Divided she is, but not equally between hope and fear, and now while she trembles in expectation of a sentence, she hears, (Woman, where are those thine accusers?). Those who but now so importunately demanded justice against thee . . .

What seems to have happened is plain. We have a case of homeoteleuton. Charles is copying from MS A and his eye has slipped from the first occurrence 'Woman, where are those thine accusers?' to the second. The alternative, that he has here added a new section between the two occurrences of this phrase, is of course possible, but seems relatively unlikely. It is assumed here, then, that the longer MS, MS A, is the earlier and that the shorter, MS B, is the later,[20] and the text of the sermon printed below is based on MS A with all major variation on MS B noted.

The value of these shorthand texts deserves stressing again. They are certainly by Charles and they give more than a glimpse into the style and content of his preaching in the religiously heady days of 1738–42. It is worth noting that these six sermons share a basic similarity in style and content, and give a picture of a man with an overriding message: Christ and him crucified. In keeping with the Arminianism of Charles himself, and of Wesleyan Methodism, there is a stress also on the importance of the upright life and the need for good works on the part of the justified believer. The reader of these sermons must be struck by the obvious difference between them and the sermons Charles preached during his troublesome trip to America. It is also worth noting the differences between these sermons and the two Charles prepared for publication. These latter are considerably more formal, and much more in the style of the Anglican homily, with which, of course, Charles was fully acquainted. The shorthand sermons are better described as 'expositions', the description which Charles himself frequently uses in his journal references. The texts give a picture of his grass-roots preaching which is quite different from the formal appearance of his published materials. With these sermons, then, we may tap into the vibrancy which seems to have been so much a part of Charles's early day-to-day preaching.

[20] This assumption is the opposite to that made by Albin and Beckerlegge, who refer to an 'earlier' and a 'later' draft. These are the MSS labelled in this volume 'B' and 'A' respectively.

THE 1816 EDITION

In 1816 a small volume of sermons appeared under the title *Sermons by the Late Charles Wesley A.M. Student of Christ-Church, Oxford. With a Memoir of the Author by the Editor*. The title of this volume suggests that its contents ought to be reproduced here verbatim, but it poses major problems. It must therefore be dealt with at some length. Twelve of the thirteen sermons in the 1816 edition have in fact been included here. However, only one (sermon 14, on Luke 16.10, for which no MS has been found) appears in exactly the same form; all the others have been freshly prepared for publication from the MSS.

The editor of the 1816 edition is not named, but is quite commonly thought to have been Charles's wife Sarah. Such a view is put forward, for example, by Outler, who when commenting on the sermon on Psalm 91:11 observed 'For the 1816 edition of her husband's sermons, Mrs. Sarah Wesley chose to publish a heavily edited version of the original'.[21] W. L. Doughty had earlier made the same basic claim when he wrote 'In 1816 Mrs Charles Wesley published a short *Memoir* of her husband with twelve of his sermons',[22] a view expressed also by Charles Wesley Flint.[23] The view is probably based upon the last sentence of the introduction to the 1816 edition which states that '[the sermons] are presented to the public by his widow'.[24]

It is, however, quite unlikely that Sarah Wesley was the physical editor of the edition or even that she took any major role in its production, other than expressing her desire to see it accomplished, and agreeing to the sale and use of her husband's MSS. (By virtue of this fact, of course, they could quite properly be described as being 'presented to the public by his wife'.) She would have been ninety-one in the year that the sermons were published and it seems improbable that she would have been either able or willing to undertake the task of editing them at such an advanced age. Perhaps even more significant is the fact that in 1807 she wrote in a letter to Thomas Roberts, who had taken charge of some of the hymn MSS, that she would not wish the sermons to be published unless there were a firm undertaking that they reflect precisely what her husband actually wrote and would not be 'altered from his sentiments'.[25] However, as is pointed out further below, the sermons in the 1816 edition do show major variations from their MS form, and indicate fairly significant editorial redaction, the very thing that Sarah was apparently so anxious to avoid.

It is evident also that the editor of the 1816 edition was not able to decipher Charles's shorthand, for a shorthand note reading 'transcribed from my brother's copies' appears in the 1816 edition as 'preached', which seems to be a sheer guess.

[21] Outler, (ed.), *Sermons* iv. 224.   [22] Doughty, 'Charles Wesley, Preacher', 263.
[23] Flint, *Charles Wesley and His Colleagues*, 146.   [24] *Sermons*, p. xxxiv.
[25] Sarah Wesley to Thomas Roberts, 27 June 1807. MARC DDWF 21/22.

Sarah, on the other hand, is known to have made a study of Byrom's method.[26] How proficient she became is not clear, but any acquaintance at all with it would have guarded the editor from making so major an error as reading 'transcribed from my brother's copies' as 'preached'.

Still further evidence against the possibility that the sermons were edited by Sarah is found in two letters written in 1814 to Joseph Benson, who was at that time on the Board of the Methodist Book Room, On 18 July Sarah Wesley jun. wrote to him[27] expressing her mother's pleasure that an intention had been expressed by the Methodists (as opposed to some other religious group that seemed to be showing an interest) to take the sermon MSS and publish them.[28] On 12 November she wrote again to Benson enquiring when Mrs Wesley might expect any emolument 'from the sermons which the conference agreed to keep'.[29] It appears, then, that the sermons were purchased by the conference, that the editor was someone at the Book Room, and that it was this person who, against the wishes of Charles's wife, edited the material significantly and misread 'transcribed from my brother's copies' as 'preached'.

The question of who that person was is not easy to answer, but there are a few clues. On all of the MSS there appears the notation 'Ex^d WP', which presumably means 'Examined [by] W.P.' and on that for Philippians 3: 13–14 there is noted, in what seems to be the same hand, 'copied April 22, 1816'. A few other notes regarding where and when the sermons were preached are added on the covers of some of the sermons, in what also appears to be 'W.P.'s hand. This suggests that 'W.P.' was the one involved in the production of the 1816 edition. It was perhaps he (or she, but only a man would have been in an official position in the Book Room at that time), who made fair copies of the MSS for the printer.[30] In any case the sermons, as edited by, it seems, 'W.P.' went to the press and *The Sermons of the Late Charles Wesley A.M.* was published. As has been noted, however, the material in this small volume must be used cautiously and with proper critical awareness. The editorial activity of W.P. is only one of a number of problems. The sermons in it will now be examined, in three groups.

The Seven Sermons Copied from John's MSS

It is now clear that at least seven of the sermons in the 1816 edition were not composed by Charles, but were copies made by him from his brother's MSS. This was first pointed out by Richard Heitzenrater in 1969, and his remarks seem entirely

---

[26] See MARC DDCW 5/68, a letter written in April 1750, in which Sarah is enjoined not to neglect her shorthand.

[27] See the 'Minutes of the Book Room Committee 1797–1817' entries for 1 Jan 1813 and 16 February 1815 MARC MAW M5640.

[28] Sarah Wesley jun. to Joseph Benson, 18 July 1814. MARC DDWES 7/103.

[29] Sarah Wesley jun. to Joseph Benson 12 November 1814. MARC DDWES 7/7c.

[30] Despite extensive efforts to identify 'W.P.' no obvious contender has to date emerged. Even a close examination of the minutes of the book room for the period, which are held in the MARC (MAW MS640), gives no clue to the identity.

accurate.[31] Four of them (Sermon 20 'The love of God' (Mark 12: 30), Sermon 21 'The one thing needful' (Luke 10: 42), Sermon 22 'The wisdom of winning souls' (Proverbs 11: 30), and Sermon 23 'Guardian angels' (Psalm 91: 11) are found in MS form in a bound folio[32] at the front of which Charles has written, in shorthand, 'tcrbed f mi brtrs cps', which surely means 'transcribed from my brother's copies', and then in longhand 'on board the London Galley Captain Indivine between Charles-town & Boston 1 Sept, 1736'.[33] On the MSS of three others printed in the 1816 edition Charles has written similar words, again stating that he has copied the sermons from his brother's MSS.[34] These are Sermons 16, 18, and 19 here: 'A single intention' (Matthew 6: 22–3), 'What I do thou knowest not now' (John 13: 7) and 'Remember the Sabbath day' (Exodus 20: 8). What this means is that sermons I, II, V, VI, VIII, IX, and X in the 1816 edition are, by Charles's own very clear, if ciphered, statement copies of sermons from his brother's MSS.

It might thus be suggested that these sermons ought not to be taken as reflecting the mind of Charles. The line of such reasoning would be clear enough: these are not Charles's own work, and therefore may not be taken as evidence of his own theological development or homiletic skill. Albin, for example, although he does not make this statement outright, seems to be working with such an hypothesis in mind, for after suggesting that three further sermons in addition to the seven[35] referred to above are unlikely to be by Charles, he goes on to comment

If one did not accept the sermons from Luke 16.10 and Psalm 126.6,[36] this would certainly avoid a number of difficulties for defining the parameters of the Charles Wesley sermon material. By limiting the corpus to the six shorthand manuscript sermons and the two sermons published during his lifetime, one could be certain that all these texts were composed by Charles.[37]

But Albin goes on to say

On the other hand, to exclude the five questionable texts from a future volume would deny historians, scholars and other readers access to texts that were preached by at least one of the Wesley brothers during the period prior to their evangelical experiences in 1738.[38]

Albin, then, seems inclined to allow for at least the possibility that the five sermons in question are in a limited sense at least Charles's and ought, perhaps, to be included in a volume of his sermons. They may be, though at least three, according

---

[31] See Richard P. Heitzenrater, 'John Wesley's Earliest Sermons', *Proceedings of the Wesley Historical Society* 37 (1969–70): 112–13.   [32] MARC DDCW 8/13.

[33] As was pointed out above, this shorthand note was clearly not understood by the editor; it appears as 'Preached on board the London Galley, between Charles Town and Boston'.

[34] MARC CW Box 5.

[35] Albin actually says that 'at least six of the twelve sermons attributed to Charles in this volume were actually written by John Wesley' ('Charles Wesley's Other Prose Writings', 89).

[36] Charles actually gives the reference as '126.7' indicating that he was using the *BCP* version. The editor of the 1816 edition corrects this to the KJV reference '126.6', which is picked up by Albin here and Heitzenrater below.   [37] Albin, 'Charles Wesley's Other Prose Writings', 90.

[38] ibid.

to Albin, probably are not, original compositions and thus may be used as a source of information on Charles's own theological development. The other side of this particular coin, however, though this is not spelt out by Albin himself, is that the seven sermons which are clearly copies are not to be taken as indicative of Charles's own theological development.

Such a view is, however, too simplistic by far and there is an obvious counter argument which needs to be made. It is certainly true that Charles copied at least seven of the sermons printed in the 1816 edition from his brother's MSS. However, this is not to say that none of these materials is of any use at all in assessing Charles's theological persuasion, homiletic ability, or literary achievement. After all, as can be seen from the individual introductions, he did preach each of the sermons he copied from his brother, some of them several times, and thus presumably felt happy with their content. He was no fool and, as we know from his later dealings and disputes with his brother, he did not feel obliged to agree with all that John had to say.[39] Thus the idea that he preached a sermon, even one composed by his brother, without first vetting its content and even perhaps its style seems unreasonable. The sermons may not have originated with Charles, but the very fact that he took them over and used them does make them, in a limited sense, his. Thus while the seven sermons he copied from his brother's MSS may not be as significant to the task of seeking to reconstruct his sermon corpus as those he wrote himself, it would seem unwise to ignore them altogether. These are sermons which Charles preached, and unless one is willing to argue that he preached sermons with which he did not agree, they must be allowed some place in an edition of his works. They reflect, even if at second hand, his own views. Indeed, the very fact that he chose to transcribe these particular sermons, when many others must have been available, suggests that he may have had a particular affinity with what they contained. Such arguments are made repeatedly in connection with biblical passages (why, for example, has Luke kept some sections of Mark and yet discarded others?) and the logic seems applicable here also.

It is unfortunate that none of these sermons in Charles's hand have survived also in John's, for this means that we are unable to check the extent to which Charles may have edited his brother's sermons in the process of transcription. The suggestion that he did so edit his source therefore remains an unproved hypothesis. It is not, however, an unreasonable one, and indeed has some (admittedly slight) MS support.[40]

---

[39] A point which, as was noted in Chapter 1, comes across in Charles's poetical compositions 'Christ Our Merciful High Priest' and 'Your Little Sketch, and Sage Advice' which are stinging attacks on John's decision to ordain Coke (see Kimbrough and Beckerlegge (eds.), *Unpublished Poetry*, iii. 93–101).

[40] In particular we might note the case of the sermon on John 13: 7. In that sermon there is a peculiar discord in the numbering of four consecutive paragraphs: paragraph 1 in this sequence is numbered by Charles as 'III.1', paragraphs 2 and 3 in the sequence have no number, while paragraph 4 is numbered '3'. This may just be a mistake. However, if it is assumed that in the text from which Charles was copying the paragraphs were numbered consistently and consecutively, it is apparent that something has happened to the text between the form it had in John's copy and that form we find in the present

All seven of these sermons are therefore included in this edition. It is important, of course, that the reader keep clearly in mind the fact that they did originate with John, and make due allowance for this when seeking to explore and analyse their theological content. If they are to be used to reconstruct Charles's thought, a proper critical argument will need to be advanced to support this approach.[41] Since he did take the sermon over from another's MS, he will not have been completely free to develop his thoughts in ways which he might otherwise have done. The basic structure of the sermon was in place, even if, as seems entirely possible, some of the detail was altered by Charles himself. These seven are therefore of limited use. They are not, however, of no use at all.

Manuscripts for all seven are held in the MARC; they are reproduced here directly from those sources.[42]

The Other Five Sermons from the 1816 Edition

There are five further relevant sermons in the 1816 edition, any of which may have been composed by Charles, though again caution must be exercised in their use. For one of them, on Luke 16: 10 (sermon III in the 1816 edition, Sermon 14 here), no MS has survived and thus it is not possible to check whether it was copied from elsewhere. It should however be noted that there is no evidence to suggest that this was a sermon text on which John preached, though John's sermon registers are very fragmented.

This sermon, then, must be treated with caution by the Charles Wesley scholar and proper allowance made for the possibility that it is a copy which Charles has

MS. Either Charles has split a paragraph in two (the original III.2 becoming 2a and 2b), or he has added one paragraph, or else he has deleted one paragraph (the original III.2) and added two new ones in its place. Whichever is the case, such evidence is suggestive of Charles's own creative input into the sermon text. We might note also the sermon on Luke 16: 8. There are several places in the MS of that text where a number of words, and sometimes fairly lengthy sections, are inserted in square brackets. However, if all the material enclosed in the brackets is omitted, the text still reads well and without any obvious hiatus. It might quite reasonably be conjectured, then, that the words enclosed in square brackets are those that Charles himself has added to his brother's MS. Similar remarks could be made regarding a number of the other sermons which Charles copied from John. These have been included in the discussion of the texts themselves.

[41] It is worth noting in this context Tyson's rather confusing remark regarding the sermon on 'The one thing needful (Luke 10: 42)'. As Tyson knows (Tyson, *Charles Wesley: A Reader*, 81) this sermon was one of John's (Tyson's 'probably composed by John Wesley' seems rather more hesitant than Charles's shorthand note 'transcribed from my brother's copies' would imply). Nevertheless, Tyson goes on to introduce the sermon on 'The one thing needful' with the following words: "'The One thing Needful" gives further elaboration to Charles's conception of Christian Perfection, emphasizing the symmetry and unqualified character of it; both these elements would later distinguish his conception of sanctification from that of his brother John' (*Charles Wesley: A Reader*, 85). It may well be, as is argued here, that the sermon does indeed provide an insight into Charles's (as opposed to John's) theological development. However, in Tyson one is left wondering at the obvious discrepancy between the remark that the sermon is probably by John and the suggestion that it nevertheless 'gives further elaboration to Charles's conception of Christian Perfection'.

[42] I am also indebted to the work of Albert Outler, who transcribed afresh each of these seven texts for inclusion in his edition of John's sermons. The texts presented here are, however, my own transcriptions; where appropriate corrections to Outler's texts have been indicated.

made from another's MS. Of course, if he did take this text from some other
source, then the arguments made above in connection with the seven he clearly did
copy apply in this case also. This sermon is, then, problematic, but this does not
mean that it ought to be totally ignored. It must be assumed that the editor of the
1816 edition had access to a MS in the hand of Charles Wesley and that this is the
text of a sermon which Charles did preach. It is apparent from the other sermons
in the edition that the editor felt free to alter his source in places, and the probability must be that the same process took place during the transcription of the present sermon. The text as published will not be exactly the text of the now lost MS,
but since no other source is available, it is from that published edition that the
present text has been prepared.

For the remaining four sermons in the 1816 edition (viz. sermons IV, VII, XI,
and XII of that edition, Sermons 15, 3, 1, and 2 here) MSS have survived and all
are in the John Rylands University Library of Manchester.[43] None carries any evidence of being copied from any source. This is a fact that should not too hastily be
overlooked. We know that Charles did indicate on several MSS the fact that he had
copied the material they contain. There is no such indication on these four. While
it may be that Charles was inconsistent on this point, and either forgot or deliber-
ately failed to record the fact that the material in these sermons had been extracted
from elsewhere, that is not the most obvious explanation. Rather it might be
argued that the four sermons should be taken as being by Charles unless firm evidence can be marshalled for the opposite case.

Albin has in fact brought some such evidence to bear in relation to the sermon
on Matthew 5: 20 (sermon IV in the 1816 edition, Sermon 15 here). He notes that
John Wesley preached on this text on 5 January 1735[44] and that the MS has upon
it the same date (in shorthand, so not noted in the 1816 edition). The date
precedes Charles's own ordination by several months. Consequently, unless
Charles wrote the sermon for John (not impossible), it must be by John. It appears,
then, that this is at the very least based upon a sermon on the same text by John.
The question must therefore be asked why, if it is a copy, has Charles not made a
note of this fact as he has done in the cases of the seven others discussed above?
Again it is possible that he simply forgot to mention it, or felt the information
unimportant. However, such reasoning is not entirely satisfactory; the fact remains
that Charles chose to note on seven MSS the fact that he copied the material they
contained from his brother. There is no such note on this text.

The situation with regard to this sermon is, then, unclear, and due caution will
need to be exercised in using it in assessing Charles's theological views. However,
the scholar is not faced with an abundance of evidence relating to Charles's sermon corpus and consequently all that is available, including this text with its
uncertainties, must be investigated.

---

[43] MARC CW Box 5.   [44] Albin, 'Charles Wesley's Other Prose Writings', 89.

The text in this volume has been prepared from the MS. Comparison with the form in the 1816 edition reveals many differences, as with all those for which the comparison is possible. This being so, the text as given here is the first printing of the original form. In particular the shorthand section found on pages 13 and 14 of the MS has been here transcribed for the first time.

The other three sermons are of rather more certain potential. They are those on Psalm 126: 6 (sermon VII), Philippians 3: 13–14 (sermon XI), and 1 Kings 18: 21 (sermon XII), Sermons 3, 1, and 2 here. Again, scholars will probably be left with a nagging doubt about their authenticity, athough it is important to note that there is nothing at all to suggest that they were copies. Heitzenrater for one thinks that the sermon on Psalm 126: 6 is perhaps Charles's own composition.[45] Albin's claim that the case for the authenticity of the sermons on Philippians 3: 13–14 and 1 Kings 18: 21 is 'exceedingly weak' seems to be based on the rather odd argument that the only evidence to support the case for their authenticity is that the MSS are in Charles's own handwriting.[46] Albin has, as has been noted, made a much more convincing argument with respect to the sermon on Matthew 5: 20, and does seem to have tipped the balance of probability. On these two, however, he has not really made a case at all.

The burden of proof must surely lie with those disputing the authenticity of all the texts in the 1816 edition. Heitzenrater has presented indisputable evidence on seven of them, and Albin has made a strong case against one more. Insufficient evidence can be brought to bear either way for the sermon on Luke 16: 10, and what evidence once existed now seems to be lost to scholarship. Three sermons remain standing, and the case against them is far from proven. Even if they were copies, for which there is no evidence, these texts also were preached by Charles and were in this sense 'his'. The arguments presented with regard to the seven undoubtedly copied sermons are applicable here also.

With the sermon on 1 Kings 18: 21 (sermon XII in the 1816 edition, Sermon 2 here), there is good evidence to suggest that it is in a very definite, even if not authorial, sense, Charles's. This evidence deserves further discussion, especially so since it is among those for which Albin has judged the case for authenticity 'exceedingly weak'.[47]

The textual history of this sermon seems quite complex, but in that complexity there is real information to be gained. As it appears in the 1816 edition it is an edited form of a MS held in the John Rylands University Library of Manchester. What is significant, however, is that in fact two MSS of this sermon have survived, and these show considerable differences. The longer form is annotated that it was preached at Cowes in November 1735, and the shorter that it was preached in America in 1736. The later form is about 25 per cent shorter than the earlier one, and is the one used in the 1816 edition.

---

[45] Heitzenrater, *Mirror and Memory*, 155.
[46] Albin, 'Charles Wesley's Other Prose Writings', 89.   [47] ibid.

Both MSS are clearly in Charles's own hand, and thus we know for certain that he did edit this text himself. To a large extent this editing took the form of a drastic cutting of the material. Nevertheless, the fact remains: Charles revised a sermon. He changed it, cut it, and added to it and in that editorial process had ample opportunity to make any changes he thought fit. What he felt less important could be cut and what he thought more significant could be kept and even highlighted. The end product, then, must have been to his liking, and may without any reserve be taken as indicating his own views. The later, shorter form may thus be taken as a Charles Wesley sermon, even if it started life with someone else, though there is no evidence whatsoever to suggest that it did so. Charles has changed the sermon and has presumably done so thoughtfully and creatively. He has done more than simply copy it out.

But the textual history of this sermon is in fact even more complex than has so far been indicated. Careful study of the earlier, longer form, which has never been printed prior to this volume, suggests strongly that it is itself an edited text. A reasonably clear indication of this is the fact that on page 4 of the MS Charles stops writing half-way down the page; the words with which this truncated page finish are the same as the first words on the top of page five, which is where the sermon continues. Pages 1–4 of the MS are physically separable from the rest of the sermon. This suggests that there once existed a sermon which had a longer introductory section, and that the material on pages 1–3 and half-way down page 4 has been written to replace material which originally filled four full pages. If so then we are left with the conclusion that Charles has edited an even earlier sermon to arrive at the one he preached in late 1735. The sermon MS of even the earlier form is thus an edited text, and the editor was Charles. The text he edited was also his own, and pages 5 and following of that earlier form have remained intact. This form of the sermon may therefore also be taken fairly confidently as indicative of Charles's own views. There is doubtless more work to be done on its textual history, but initial findings give cause for optimism. Here at least we may be reasonably confident in placing a sermon text alongside the two sermons printed in Charles's lifetime, the six shorthand sermons, and a sermon on John 4: 41 which will be discussed below, as a text reflecting Charles's own views. There is no evidence to suggest that the sermon is a copy. However, even if we were to accept this hypothesis for the sake of erring on the side of caution, the textual history indicates that it is a text which Charles himself edited more than once. The creative process can be seen at work.

Both the longer and the shorter forms of the sermon are represented in this volume. The text printed is that of the longer form; the critical notes provide information on the ways in which the shorter version differs from it, which scholars will wish to note. The longer form is printed here for the first time. The shorter form is also a new text, since it has been freshly transcribed from the MS and has thus been stripped of the significant editorial emendations made for the 1816 edition.

All the sermons in the 1816 edition have now been discussed and the situation seems reasonably hopeful. Three have a real claim to absolute authenticity, the evidence for one more is not available, and even if the other eight are copies, they may yet reveal something of the content and style of Charles's preaching. All twelve thus seem of potential use, though not all will have equal value. Consequently, the 1816 edition should not (contrary to Albin's apparent inclination) be written off by the Charles Wesley scholar. There are significant problems with the material it contains and these problems must be handled cautiously and carefully. However, simply to dismiss all of the sermons it contains as being of no real use in assessing Charles's theological development would be to err unduly on the side of caution. If more texts had survived the situation might have been less crucial, but given the scarcity of material all avenues must be explored, including the rather poorly lit one of the 1816 edition.

SERMON 17, LUKE 16: 8[48]

In the John Rylands University Library of Manchester there is a MS sermon in the hand of Charles on Luke 16: 8. It can be dealt with here very briefly. Like the seven discussed above, it bears a note indicating that Charles has copied it from another's MS. He does not indicate his source, but Outler prints it as a sermon which *may* have been by John. Heitzenrater is less cautious, referring to it simply as a sermon which Charles has copied from his brother.[49] It is not in the 1816 edition. It is included here, since the arguments made above with regard to the seven copied sermons and their use in assessing Charles's theology are equally applicable.

SERMON 13, ACTS 20: 7

It is not altogether clear that this text on the weekly sacrament is in fact a sermon, and hence not certain that it is proper to print it in this volume. In Homer L. Calkin's *Catalog of Methodist Archival and Manuscript Collections* (1985) it is listed as a 'Treatise on the Weekly Sacrament'.[50] The John Rylands University Library

---

[48] In the MARC this text is located in cw Box 5 and not, as Outler states, among the Colman collection.

[49] Heitzenrater, 'Early Sermons of John and Charles Wesley', in *Mirror and Memory*, 155, refers to this sermon as one that Charles 'transcribed from his brother's copy on 6 May 1736 and preached that following Sunday at Frederica, then again on 25 July in Savannah'. However, although this sermon was copied by Charles, his source is not named. Rather Charles notes in shorthand at the conclusion of the MS 'transcribed May 6, 1736 at Frederica'. The probability is of course that the source was John, especially so since the text appears on John's list of sermon texts (Heitzenrater, 'Early Sermons of John and Charles Wesley', 160). John preached from this text at least three times (See further Outler, *Sermons,* iv. 360).

[50] Homer L. Calkin, *Catalog of Methodist Archival and Manuscript Collections* (World Methodist Historical Society, 1985), A 9.

catalogue, however, lists it as a 'Sermon/article in the hand of Charles Wesley regarding the nature of the Eucharist'.[51] It begins with quotations in Greek, which, one might well imagine, would not be the kind of opening designed to appeal to the average prospective Methodist convert or society member. It remains rigorously academic in its mode of argumentation, appealing not only to the Bible but also to Pliny the Younger, Tertullian, the *Apostolic Constitutions*, Justin Martyr, and Dr Hammond.[52] However, as it develops, it does begin to take on more of the appearance of a sermon. There are some basic formal similarities between this and the other sermons by Charles. It begins, as do all the others, with a text of scripture, which it is Charles's intention to explain and apply to his audience (or readers). It exhibits the same division into 'heads', that is, principal divisions, of which in this case there are three, though only the first is in fact covered. It uses the term 'my brethren' to refer to the presumed audience, and has a concern for the practical consequences and application of the text as well as for its more formal academic significance. Indeed, it is Charles's (apparently unfulfilled) intention to 'conclude with a practical application of what is said'. It also carries the number '12', which may be an indication that it was placed by Charles among his sermon papers, which show evidence of a similar numbering system. Thus while there must be some doubt as to whether it was a sermon text designed by Charles for actual preaching, there is at least sufficient ambiguity on this point to warrant its inclusion. There is nothing to suggest that it is anything other than Charles's own composition.

The text was printed for the first time by John Bowmer in *The Sacrament of the Lord's Supper in Early Methodism*.[53] The text printed here has been prepared from the MSS,[54] and the more significant differences from Bowmer's version are indicated in the notes.

SERMON 11, JOHN 4: 41

There is one further sermon that needs mention here. It is the only one which has never been published in any form before and for that reason alone deserves particular attention. It seems to have gone largely unrecognized by scholars heretofore, though Albin refers in passing to its existence, as does Heitzenrater.[55] The MS is in the hand of Charles.

---

[51] *Catalogue of the Charles Wesley Papers ref.* DDCW, 2 vols. (John Rylands University Library of Manchester, Methodist Archives and Research Centre, 1994), ii. 109.

[52] The reference is to Dr Henry Hammond (1605–60).

[53] John C. Bowmer, *The Sacrament of the Lord's Supper in Early Methodism* (London: Dacre Press, 1951), 223–32.   [54] MARC DDCW 9/14.

[55] Albin, 'Charles Wesley's Other Prose Writings', 93; Heitzenrater, 'Early Sermons of John and Charles Wesley', 161.

It seems that 'W.P. 'looked at it, for the words 'undated and not finished' are written in what appears to be his hand on page 1. The MS is certainly undated,[56] but it is not at all clear that it is 'unfinished', though it is in poor condition and part of the final section is missing. The final paragraph is in shorthand and is written on the back of page 16. All the other pages are written recto only. This suggests that Charles was in fact trying to round off the sermon within the confines of the physical space left and to facilitate this wrote the final section in shorthand.

It appears, however, that one leaf of the sermon has now been lost. The final words on leaf 16 verso are 'Not but this kind of R[eligion]' and the first words on the recto 'and slow, high and low'. These plainly do not run on naturally. It can be noted also that in this section Charles is drawing things to a close and making his summary points, to which he assigns numbers. Point 1 is found on leaf 16 verso. Point 2 also appears there, but is not completed. Point 3 is not mentioned, but it is presumably the last few words of this point that are found on leaf 16 recto. Point 4 is on leaf 16 recto, beginning in longhand, but completed in shorthand. This evidence indicates clearly that a final leaf or leaves have come astray. The surviving text of the sermon is not particularly long by Charles's sermon standards, running to about 3,000 words.

There is no evidence to suggest that the sermon was copied by Charles from another source, though the cover is also missing and is the place where such a notation might have been written. The possibility therefore cannot be ruled out. There is also no evidence to suggest that John ever preached on this text, though our knowledge of his sermon corpus may well be wanting.

Perhaps even more persuasive evidence of Charles's own authorship of the sermon, however, is the fact that examination of the MS reveals numerous corrections, additions, and deletions. Thus, for example, on the very first page Charles changes the word 'containing' to 'contained', replaces the phrase 'first of these' with the word 'former', deletes the word 'acts' and replaces it with 'it', deletes completely the phrase 'and the soul in which it is seated' and finally apparently adds and then deletes the word 'people'. Such corrective editing suggests that the author is composing rather than copying. He is 'making it up as he goes along', not transcribing a text which he has before him. As a part of this creative exercise Charles frequently has to backtrack, and alter what he has just written to facilitate the transition to what he has just thought. The obvious test is of course to compare the tidiness of this MS with that of those he 'transcribed' from his brother's copies. The result of such comparison is in keeping with the argument advanced here. Where Charles is, by his own statement, copying the work of someone else, the resultant MS is neat and precise with few corrections or deletions. A good

---

[56] Charles 'expounded the woman of Samaria' several times, the first being 27 August 1739, but the content of the MS sermon seems not really to fit this description. It is not an 'exposition' in the genre of the shorthand 'expositions' discussed above and it is not centred upon the woman of Samaria.

example is Sermon 19, on Exodus 20: 8, a longer text than this, where there are no changes of substance at all.[57]

It appears, then, that this sermon may be of central importance to the task of seeking to provide as complete an edition as possible of the surviving Charles Wesley sermons. A full transcription, including the shorthand passage with which it ends, has therefore been prepared.

SERMON OUTLINES

The John Rylands University Library holds the Colman collection of Wesleyana. Among this there is a packet of 130 sermons and sermon outlines written partially in Byrom's shorthand and partially in longhand. The outlines are in an envelope, upon which there appear the words '130 Sermons and Outlines [by] Charles Wesley'.

In 1948 Frank Baker referred to these MSS without raising any question regarding their authenticity. After noting that Charles set great store by spontaneity, with the result that his surviving sermon MSS are comparatively few, Baker added a note which says '130 sermons and outlines are preserved in the Colman Collection at the Methodist Book Room'.[58] In Calkin's *Catalog* they are listed as being among 'A collection of Wesley manuscripts, including letters written by or to John Wesley, papers written by Charles Wesley, and miscellaneous papers belonging to John Wesley'.[59] It is this same collection of sermons and outlines to which W. L. Doughty was probably referring when he remarked '[i]n the strong-room of the Epworth there is a bundle of Charles Wesley's sermons in manuscript'.[60] They surface once again in a brief remark made by Albin, who noted that the MSS were referred to by Baker and need scrutiny.[61] Thomas Langford also referred to them (again on the basis of the Baker note) and urged that 'these [130 MSS] must be examined carefully in order to determine more clearly the nature of Charles Wesley's homiletic style, content, and practice'.[62]

Should these MSS have proved to be by Charles, they would obviously be of central significance, and it is surprising given the several references to them, two as late as 1992, that so little attention appears to have been paid to them. If there really are 130 sermons and sermon outlines by Charles Wesley among the Colman collection, why has not more work been done on them? The MSS are not,

---

[57] In the whole MS there are only eight corrections, all of which are very minor. On page 15, for example, Charles copies the words 'who will not' twice and then crosses out the first; on page 9 he corrects 'lest' to 'least' and on page 11 'of' to 'on'. Similar minor changes occur on pages 4, 6, 13, and 14. The same pattern of neatness and precision is found also in the other copied MS sermons.

[58] Baker, *Charles Wesley as Revealed by his Letters*, 38 n. 1.   [59] Calkin, *Catalog*, A 10.

[60] Doughty, 'Charles Wesley, Preacher', 266.

[61] Albin, 'Charles Wesley's Other Prose Writings', 236 n. 30.

[62] Langford, 'Charles Wesley as Theologian', 236 n. 4.

however, by Charles, a fact noted in 1960 by Baker himself, who slipped into the envelope containing the sermons a typed note indicating his doubts regarding their authenticity. This note states 'although these sermons from the Colman Collection are described as by the Revd. C. Wesley . . . they are not in his hand'.[63] In one case Baker is not entirely confident of this, but in the 129 others he is.

Baker's later conclusions seem correct. The longhand writing is clearly not that of Charles Wesley, and the same seems true of the shorthand sections. Even more persuasive, perhaps, as Baker noted, is the fact that one of the sermons is signed 'J. H.' and that the sermon so signed seems clearly to be from the same hand as all the others. Even the one sermon that Baker is prepared, possibly, to allow, seems doubtful on these grounds.

More recently Charles Ellis has conducted an extensive study of these materials and his conclusions seem sound.[64] Most of the sermon outlines in the Colman collection carry a date; Ellis has shown that none of these dates corresponds directly to Charles's known preaching schedule, and several directly contradict it. It is an important finding of Ellis, though one that goes beyond the concerns of the present volume, that one of the sermon outlines is clearly an outline of a John Wesley sermon and that at least one other seems likely also to be a summary of a sermon that John preached. (What will be done with regard to this apparently new John Wesley sermon material remains to be seen.)

For several reasons, then, the most conclusive being the ones presented by Ellis, it now seems certain that the Colman MSS do not provide any further material for an edition of Charles Wesley's sermons. Consequently the call for these MSS to be examined as a route to understanding the theology of Charles Wesley can now be ignored.

In the Colman collection there is a further packet of forty loose sheets which seem quite clearly to be the work of the same individual who was responsible for the collection of the 130 sermon and outlines. (Colman A 10). Again it is clear that these are not the work of Charles Wesley.

CONCLUSION

In 1987 Albin and Beckerlegge expressed the wish that the sermons of Charles Wesley, together with a proper introduction and annotation, might one day be produced. They did much to make such an edition possible, but the full task has only now been undertaken. In this Charles has been done a serious injustice, for there can be no doubt that his sermons were central to his religious mission and his

[63] See the note that Baker has inserted into the envelope in which the 130 sermons and outlines of the Colman Collection are kept. The Colman Collection is itself housed in a trunk in the MAB section of the Methodist Archives at the John Rylands University Library of Manchester.

[64] Charles Ellis, 'Charles Wesley's Prose Works: A Theological Study', (Ph.D. thesis, University of Liverpool, in process).

quest to propagate what he considered to be true religion. The previous lack of such an edition is symptomatic of the malaise which has afflicted scholarship into Charles's life and work. The present volume fills one substantial gap, but even more serious is the lack of any critical edition of Charles's letters or a full critical edition of his journal.

This edition, it is true, contains only twenty-three items, and some might argue that eight, or even twelve, of these do not actually deserve their place. This is indeed a small collection when compared to the very much larger number of John's sermons which are now in print. However, paucity should not be equated with insignificance, nor the comparative lack of material with its uselessness. Not much has survived, but this fact alone ought to encourage historians and theologians alike to make the most of what has.

Part II
The Sermons

SERMON 1
PHILIPPIANS 3: 13–14

INTRODUCTORY COMMENT

Charles's MS of this sermon is dated 21 October, 1735 and carries the further inscription 'on board the Simmonds'. In the 1816 edition there is an editorial note prefixed which reads 'Preached on board the Simmonds',[1] but there is no independent evidence that Charles preached this sermon on that day. No section of the journal covering that period is extant. It was on this same day, however, that John Wesley described in his journal the way in which he, his brother, Mr Delamotte, and Mr Ingham spent their time on board the ship. During the hours from nine to twelve, said John, 'my brother writ sermons'.[2] How many of the days of the journey Charles spent in this way cannot be ascertained. On this particular day, however, he clearly did engage in this activity; it may be that 21 October was the date of Charles's composition (or transcription) rather than delivery. Possibly significant for the date is the fact that the sermon closes with the Collect for the second Sunday after Trinity, though Charles's use of this Collect probably has more to do with the content of the sermon than with the Church calendar.

There is no indication on the MS to suggest that the sermon was copied from John. Indeed, though John preached from Philippians 3: 13–14 three times, there is no record of his doing so before 1741.[3] This fact and other indications of the sermon's originating with Charles have already been discussed in Chapter 4. The conclusion of that discussion was that in this sermon we have an early, probably the earliest surviving[4], example of a complete sermon by Charles.

The MS is located at the John Rylands University Library of Manchester.[5] It comprises 14 leaves (7 folded sheets) which have been stitch-bound into booklet form. Leaf 1 comprises the cover and is written recto only. The sermon itself is found on leaves 2–14; 2–13 are written recto and verso and leaf 14 recto only. With one minor exception,[6] the sermon is written in longhand throughout.

It was published as sermon XI in the 1816 edition, though as with all of the texts in that volume there are major differences between the MS form and what was published. Thus, for example, the words '*Christian Perfection* is the goal of our religious race; the stand whereon our crown of reward is placed', found on page 14 of the MS, appear in the 1816 edition as 'Christian perfection, or universal holiness, is the goal of our religious course', where both the addition of 'or universal holiness' and the omission of 'the stand whereon

---

[1] *Sermons*, 186.   [2] *J&D*, xviii. 138

[3] The occurrences are: the New Room in Bristol, 4 January, 1741; Kingswood on the same date; and Newcastle upon Tyne on 21 November, 1743. I am grateful to Wanda Smith for help with this question.

[4] This judgement seems secure, with the proviso that Sermon 15 on Matthew 5: 20 is dated even earlier (5 January, 1735). As was discussed in Chapter 4, however, that sermon is in all probability one of John's.   [5] MARC CW Box 5.

[6] As noted in the text, there is one possible shorthand sign in the margin on p. 12.

our crown of reward is placed' are of obvious theological significance. Such examples could be multiplied, though the editorial policy adopted in the 1816 edition is not of concern here. On the front of the MS appear the words 'Ex^d W.P. ' and also the note 'Copied April 22, 1816', which is probably an indication of the date that a fair copy was made in preparation for the 1816 volume.

Whatever the precise date of the preaching of this sermon it seems clear that it comes from the period prior to the experience of 1738. While it was emphasized in the discussion in Chapter 3 above that this date should not be taken as marking a total turn-around in Charles's understanding of the process of salvation, it is nevertheless true that an examination of what have here been called the 'pre-' and 'post-Pentecost' sermons does reveal that somewhere between his days in America and the composition of the early shorthand texts a substantial change took place in Charles's soteriological convictions. This very early sermon illuminates the earlier period well enough. Throughout it Charles is insistent upon the need for good works and sheer human effort, for it is upon the basis of those that the 'crown of reward' is given. Salvation is uncertain and the Christian life one of constant struggle. Thus, for example, on page 7 we read

> Were the crown of glory already in our hands, our labours must needs be at an end; as men are always supposed to have finished their work, before they receive their reward for it. But we are expressly told that our life must be a constant labour, that we must daily strive against sin and regularly watch against all assaults of our enemy; and therefore it may be concluded, that we have not apprehended or attained either the reward of our labour or the pitch of grace and Christian perfection from which we can never be shaken or removed.

This sermon is, then, very significant. Its claim to being Charles's own composition (as opposed to a creatively edited form of one of his brother's) is strong. It is early and gives a clear indication of Charles's views regarding the path to salvation prior to his evangelical experience. It hence helps place the power of his later conversion hymns in the broader context of his theological development.

Oct. 21 1735
On board the Simmonds $\Sigma.\Theta.$[1]

———

Phil. 3.13,[2] 14

Brethren I count not myself to have apprehended, but this one thing I do forgetting those things which are behind, and reaching forth unto those things which are ~~behind~~ before, I press towards the mark of the high calling of God in Christ Jesus.

It is observed that the several inspired writers of Holy Scripture who have professedly treated of our progress in religion, and pointed out the several steps in the scale of perfection, have always represented their sentiments of the matter by obvious allegories and familiar allusions. Thus we find Christianity sometimes compared to a race,[3] at others to a wrestling match,[4] and at others to a warfare.[5] And the passage of sacred scripture now before us is no way to be understood without this metaphorical way of interpretation: the phrases used in it, being in a great measure borrowed from the circus, and the diversion of racing therein represented. Thus when the apostle tells his Philippians that he counteth not himself to have apprehended, in order to understand him it must be remarked that the word we translate 'apprehended' is in the original Greek[6] almost always applied in a technical sense to him that wins the race and carries off the prize. It being the custom to hang a crown which was to be the victor's reward over the goal which he was looked upon as entitled to who came in first of the competitors, and reached the prize and carried it off with him. So that when the apostle saith, he counteth

---

[1] Presumably '$\sigma\acute{\upsilon}\nu\ \theta\epsilon\tilde{\omega}$' 'with God'.

[2] It is worth comparing this sermon with the poetical composition on Phil. 3: 13 which Charles published (Osborn, *Poetical Works*, xiii. 80–1). The composition reads

No; not after twenty years | Of labouring in the word! | After all his fights, and fears, | And sufferings for his Lord, | *Paul* hath not attain'd the prize | Though caught up to the heavenly hill: | Daily still th'apostle dies, | And lives imperfect still!

'But we now, the prize t'attain, | An easier method see, | Save ourselves the toil and pain, | And lingering agony, | Reach at once the ladder's top, | While standing on its lowest round | Instantaneously spring up, | With pure perfection crown'd'

Such the credulous dotard's dream, | And *such* his shorter road, | Thus he makes the world blaspheme, | And shames the church of God, | Staggers thus the most sincere, | Till from the gospel-hope they move, | Holiness as error fear, | And start at perfect love.

Lord, Thy real work revive, | The counterfeit to end. | That we lawfully may strive, | And truly apprehend, | Humbly still Thy servant trace, | Who least of saints himself did call, | Till we gain the height of grace | And into nothing fall.

[3] Charles may have 1 Cor. 9: 24; 2 Tim. 4: 7 and/or Heb. 12: 1 in mind here.

[4] The verb 'to wrestle' is not common in the KJV. It appears in Gen. 32: 24–5 (and Charles's poetical composition 'Wrestling Jacob' is worth noting in this context) and in Eph. 6: 12. Charles may of course have in mind other passages such as 2 Tim. 4: 7, which, though the verb 'to wrestle' is not used, speaks of the 'good fight' of faith (cf. also 1 Tim. 6: 12).

[5] Charles may have in mind such passages as 1 Cor. 9: 7; 2 Cor. 10: 4; and 1 Tim. 1: 18, all of which use 'warfare' in this metaphorical sense. Eph. 6: 11–18 is probably also in his mind.

[6] i.e. $\kappa\alpha\tau\epsilon\iota\lambda\eta\phi\acute{\epsilon}\nu\alpha\iota$ ($\kappa\alpha\tau\alpha\lambda\alpha\mu\beta\acute{\alpha}\nu\omega$) which, as Charles notes, has the meaning of 'to win' 'to attain' or 'to make one's own' (cf. 1 Cor. 9: 24).

not himself to have apprehended, his meaning is that he does not think himself already possessed of his crown, nor yet that he is so secure of it as not to be exposed to some danger of losing it. He imagineth not that he hath yet attained the reward of his labours, nor sufficiently ascertained himself of victory in the contention wherein he is engaged; and therefore as he elegantly goes on 'this one thing I do', or this is my only care 'forgetting those things which are behind and reaching forth unto those things which are before, I press toward the mark for the prize of the high calling of God in Christ.' And here again are two terms borrowed from the races to be explained. The phrase which we have rendered 'forgetting those things which are behind' is in the original 'not looking behind me',[7] and the term 'reaching forward' is something stronger in the Greek, being expressed by a word that signifieth vehemently to stretch forward.[8] Now these are plain allusions to the Olympic[9] racers' customs, who stand not idly looking back, and examining either how how far their antagonists are or how much of the course they have passed over; but set ardently to their business and endeavour to overtake, and outrun all that are behind them behind them before them, and to get through the remainder of the race and arrive at the goal as soon as possible.

So that the sense of the words may be thus paraphrased:

My brethren, I count not myself to have attained my crown, nor do I think that I am so sure of it as that I can't miss it: but this one thing I do without marking or considering how much of my race I have got through or how many of my competitors I have overcome, I stretch as hard as I can to get to the end of that which is unfinished; and so having alway [sic] in my mind the goal, and keeping my eye fixed upon the way marked out for me to run to it, I make all possible speed, that so I may in good time gain the crown which God in Christ Jesus hath proposed to me. The words thus explained will furnish us with these several topics of discourse.

First to show that in this world, Christians are never absolutely certain of their crown of[10] reward.

Secondly that it is never to be attained by resting contented with any pitch of piety short of the highest.

Thirdly that a constant progress towards Christian perfection is therefore the indispensable duty of all Christians.

I am first etc.

We know this world is a state of trial and probation wherein we are placed by providence to work the works of God,[11] to conquer and subdue the enemies of our

---

[7] i.e. τὰ μὲν ὀπίσω ἐπιλανθανόμενος (ἐπιλανθάνομαι).   [8] i.e. ἐπεκτεινόμενος (ἐπεκτείνομαι).

[9] The word 'Olympic' has been inserted above the line in the MS and is somewhat unclear. It is followed by a second word, which is unreadable.

[10] The MS is problematic at this point. Charles probably wrote 'or' rather than 'of'. The word 'or' was then changed to 'of' by someone else, who then struck it out (the form of the strike-out is quite dissimilar to Charles's horizontal line). In the 1816 edition the words 'crown of' are omitted altogether.

[11] John 6: 28

salvation and to do penance for those manifold sins and iniquities, whereby our nature is wholly corrupted and depraved. Now a state of trial always supposeth a state of danger and whilst we are only in our probation for heaven[12] we may not think ourselves secured from all possibility of losing it. True it is we are inheritors of God's kingdom, and we have his gracious promise to secure us of our title to this inheritance;[13] but then it must be remembered that all God's promises are con-ditional, and that we are bound to fulfill our part of the covenant, or else have no right to expect that he should stand to his. Our covenant with God we know partly consists in a vow of perpetual enmity and war against the world, the flesh and the devil.[14] Those are our spiritual foes which can never be entirely vanquished whilst we continue in this life. So long as we live in the world and carry the flesh about us, so long must we be unavoidably exposed as well to their temptations, as to the attacks of that powerful, that invisible enemy who in Holy Scripture is represented as going to and fro in the earth and walking about in it seeking whom he may devour.[15] We know the great abilities of this our[16] spiritual adversary, nor are we ignorant of his devices,[17] and of his many cunning wiles, whereby he lieth in wait to deceive.[18] And cunning and powerful as he is, will he, do we think, propose temptations, which have no strength nor are attended with any possibility of success? No—he knoweth our weak side, and understandeth where to make the most successful attacks upon us. And so strong, so irresistible I had almost said, are his temptations, that happy, thrice happy, is he who is not sometimes ensnared by them. He is the prince of the power of the air,[19] and therefore wanteth not strength to assault us; he is the old serpent that deceiveth the world,[20] and there-fore wanteth not cunning sometimes to circumvent us. Indeed so great is his power, so ensnaring his wiles,[21] that of ourselves we can by no means be a match for him; and all the hopes we have of success against him are founded upon our belief of that great truth of the gospel, that greater is he that is[22] with us, than he that is against us:[23] and that God is on our side, who will not suffer us to be tempted above that we are able, but will with the temptation make a way to escape, that we may be able to bear it.[24]

But further we are exhorted in holy scripture to be constantly upon our guard to take to ourselves the whole armour of God that we may be able to stand in the day of temptation and having done all to stand.[25] Again we are *advised*, that he that *thinketh he standeth should take heed lest he fall*[26] and commanded to work out our salvation with fear and trembling.[27] Now to what end is all this caution; what

---

[12] The words 'for heaven' have been inserted above the line.
[13] Charles may be alluding to Matt. 25: 34 at this point.
[14] Cf. *BCP* Collect for 18th Sunday after Trinity. The words also appear in the *BCP* form of the baptismal service, though in the order 'devil, world and flesh'.   [15] Cf. Job 1: 7; 2: 2; 1 Pet. 5: 8.
[16] The word 'our' is not clear in the MS.   [17] Cf. 2 Cor. 2: 11.   [18] Cf. Eph. 4: 14.
[19] Eph. 2: 2.   [20] Cf. Rev. 12: 9.   [21] Cf. Eph. 6: 11.
[22] The words 'that is' are inserted above the line.   [23] Cf. Rom. 8: 31.   [24] Cf. 1 Cor. 10: 13.
[25] Cf. Eph. 6: 11–13.   [26] Cf. 1 Cor. 10: 12.   [27] Phil. 2: 12.

occasion for all this carefulness and fear unless there be some mighty danger in the case? Why should we take to ourselves the armour of God, were there no difficulty in conquering the enemies that attack us? Or wherefore should we be bid to look to our steps were there no danger in the snares that are laid for us? Were the crown of glory[28] already in our hands, our labours must needs[29] be at an end; as men are always supposed to have finished their work, before they receive their reward for it. But we are expressly told that our life must be a   constant[30] labour, that we must daily strive against sin and regularly watch against all assaults of our enemy; and therefore it ~~must~~ may[31] be concluded, that we have not apprehended or attained either the reward of our labour or the pitch of grace and Christian perfection from which we can never be shaken or removed.[32]

The great apostle Saint Paul had reason to think that he had not yet attained, neither was already perfect, and found himself obliged still to press forward toward the mark of the high calling of God in ~~Christ~~ Jesus.[33] And great presumption would it be in us to think that we had attained either to a pitch of perfection, or a height of security, which a divinely inspired apostle fell short of.[34] Now if there was danger of *his* miscarrying, much greater reason have we not to *build* ourselves up with fancied security. If notwithstanding the abundance of the revelations[35] given to him, St Paul still thought himself bound to work out his salvation with fear and trembling,[36] much stronger ground have we to follow his advice, and not to be high-minded but fear.[37] God knows the best among us must content himself as with acting in a much lower sphere, so with fulfilling the duties of his station, in a manner infinitely inferior to what this great apostle did, and therefore all the caution and watchfulness, that vigour and resolution, that labour and industry, that fear and trembling, which became him do ~~as~~ more immediately *belong* to us.

I know there is a sect of people in England who have received it as an unquestionable tenet of religion that grace once received, can never be forfeited and that he who has attained to a given degree of faith and holiness can never fall off from it. But this is a mistake which has arisen from mixing metaphysics with divinity, and making everyone's private opinion his rule of faith. When people ~~begin~~ began to dispute about grace and free will without understanding wherein either the one or the other consisted, no wonder that difficulties were raised, which none of them could solve, and that schism and heresy were brought into the church, by turning points of philosophy into religious disputes and making the quirks and quibbles of

---

[28] 'Crown of glory' appears in 1 Pet. 5: 4 and in several places in the OT (e.g. Prov. 4: 9; Isa. 62: 3).
[29] 'Need' has been corrected to 'needs' at this point in the MS.
[30] Before the word 'constant' a gap of approximately 5 letter spaces has been left in the MS.
[31] The word 'must' is corrected to 'may' above the line. It is not clear if this is the work of Charles himself.   [32] Charles may be alluding here to Heb. 12: 27.
[33] '~~Christ~~ Jesus' appears in the MS as 'X J'. It does appear as though the 'X' has been struck through, though the resulting use of 'Jesus' alone (that is without 'Christ') is unusual in Charles's sermons.
[34] See the poetical composition 'No; not after twenty years / Of labouring in the word!' (quoted above), which gives expression to the same sentiment.   [35] 2 Cor. 12: 7.
[36] Phil. 2: 12.   [37] Rom. 11: 20.

the schoolmen upon them of as much consequence as if they had been so many articles of faith. Holy scripture, I am sure, has taught us no such doctrine: but on the contrary has assured us that as the wicked man may turn from his wickedness, so likewise the righteous man may turn from his righteousness.[38] Nay, moreover we are told that we may apostatise so far as to commit things worthy of death, and to be guilty of sins in which ~~he~~ we shall surely die.[39] And the catholic church of Christ, always thought that all Christians were in this world constantly exposed to temptation, and of consequence constantly in danger of falling. We need not multiply quotations to prove this; it appears plainly enough from their solemn form of addressing almighty God in behalf of the penitents as it is recorded in the apostolic[40] constitutions, wherein every Christian is bound to acknowledge his own obnoxiousness to sin, and to pray to God for his preventing and restraining, as well as assisting, grace, to preserve him from falling. And when the penitent is restored, the congregation are moved by the deacon to pray, and afterward by the mouth of the priest or bishop do pray for the reconciled penitent that God ~~that~~ would keep him steadfast and unmovable in the way of righteousness, and would grant he might never fall nor be shaken more.[41] Now their prayers would be superfluous were it not allowed that the most perfect estate[42] in the world is but a state of trial and probation, and that the highest pitch of perfection attainable in this life is not sufficient to exempt us from all danger of falling. We know even the Son of God himself did not escape being tempted by the devil;[43] and therefore his disciples and followers must expect to be more nearly beset with them. That grand enemy of our souls knows full well that the crown of glory is not in this life given us[44] and therefore is never without hopes of preventing us from attaining it. And if his temptations be backed by any fancied security of our own, and his assaults come upon us unawares, and catch us unprovided for them; greater, far greater, hazard is there of their prevailing, and working their designed effect upon us.

Thus have I at large insisted upon the first doctrinal point, contained in my text, and sufficiently proved that no Christian is in this life absolutely secured of attaining his crown of reward or can pretend to have advanced so high in the school of Christ, as to be free from all danger of falling from his station and forfeiting that portion of God's grace he has now attained. The order laid down at the beginning for my discourse now leads to the consideration of my second point, but as the time will not permit me perfectly to discuss it at present, I choose rather to waive entering upon it now and instead thereof,[45] ~~insisting upon it~~ shall conclude with a practical inference, drawn from what has been already said.

---

[38] Cf. Ezek. 18: 21–8; 33: 29.   [39] Cf. Ezek 3: 20; 2 Pet. 2: 21.
[40] Charles wrote 'apost' at this point. This has been expanded to 'apostolic' in another hand.
[41] *Apostolic Constitutions*, Book 8: 8–9.
[42] The word is not entirely clear in the MS; 'state' is also possible.
[43] Cf. Mark 1: 13 and parallels.   [44] Cf. 1 Pet. 5: 4.
[45] At this point in the MS Charles has altered 'of' to 'thereof' by inserting 'there' above the line.

My inference is this: that since we are not so secured of our reward, as to be excluded from all possibility of losing it, we are not at liberty to indulge ourselves in a state of ease and security. We may easily perceive and know that since our ~~wages are~~ reward is not yet ~~paid~~ given our work is not as yet perfectly performed. Instead therefore of enjoying ourselves in peace, and indulging ~~ourselves~~ hearts in an imaginary certainty of attaining our inheritance in heaven, vigour and industry[46] and perseverance become the necessary duties of Christians. We[47] must watch and pray that we enter not into temptation,[48] or that we may have power to overcome, those which we can't escape from. We must be continually striving to enter in at the strait gate,[49] and be constantly fighting against our spiritual enemies, the world, the flesh and the devil. When we are upon our guard, we are always safe, but if we trust to ~~the merit of~~ our best performances, and think them sufficient to secure us, I need not tell you how grievously we shall find ourselves mistaken. There is not perhaps a more dangerous piece of self-deceit, than for a man to think himself beyond the power of temptation, or out of the reach of danger. It makes us careless in our duty and negligent in our *station*; and when we are so, we greatly impose upon ourselves, if we are secure either of the favour of God, or from the assaults of the devil.

Caution and watchfulness is a necessary characteristic of a true Christian. It is enjoined by our blessed Lord himself frequently to his disciples and by them the obligation to it extended to all mankind, 'what I say unto you I say unto all, watch'.[50] None you see is excepted from the duty, no excuse can be urged for not performing it. Watch therefore for the coming of your Lord, for you know neither the day nor hour of his coming.[51] 'Let your loins be girded, your lamps burning and ye yourselves like unto men that watch for their Lord that they may be ready to enter in with him when he cometh. For blessed are those servants whom his Lord when he cometh shall find so doing.'[52] Stand fast therefore in the faith, be strong and quit yourselves like men,[53] that so in God's good time ye may at length apprehend or attain that crown of glory,[54] which is laid up for those that unfeignedly love God,[55] that faithfully ~~strive~~ serve, honour, and humbly obey him.

---

[46] Before the word 'industry' a short blank has been left in the text. In the left hand margin Charles has written a shorthand sign (which has been struck out in pencil by a later hand), perhaps the word he intended to insert at this point. The sign appears to read 'crf/ving'. Why this word is thus written is not clear and its expansion equally problematic.

[47] In the left hand margin of the line that reads 'We must watch and pray that we enter' there appears the shorthand mark for 'y' which has beneath it the dot that suggests that it is representing an entire word. The intention of this stroke or at what point in the text the word was to be added is unclear.

[48] Cf. Mark 14: 38 and parallels.   [49] Matt. 7: 14.   [50] Mark 13: 37.
[51] Cf. Mark 13: 32 and parallels.   [52] Cf. Luke 12: 35–6.   [53] Cf. 1 Cor. 16: 13.
[54] Cf. 1 Pet. 5: 4.   [55] Cf. 2 Tim. 4: 8.

II

I now proceed to my second general head, wherein I am to show that our crown of reward is never to be attained by resting contented with any pitch of piety, short of the highest.

Christian Perfection is the goal of our religious race; the stand whereon our crown of reward is placed. Hitherto therefore must all our desires be bent; hitherto must all our endeavours tend. To this are all the promises of the gospel made. *This* therefore is the only title we can pretend to have to them. We know that in a race, the prize is never to be obtained, without arriving at the end of it. And we are plainly taught in scripture that our religion bears a near resemblance to this exercise: and therefore to carry on the allusion, if we stop in our Christian course, and strive not to reach the end of it, we must be contented to sit down without our reward. The idle racer who spends his time in viewing the space he hath run through, and fancies he hath gone far enough to deserve[56] the prize, and therefore sits down in the middle of his course, must expect both to lose the reward and to suffer the scorn and insultings of his brethren. Just so the lazy inactive Christian who judges that he has already full[57] cups merited heaven by his performances, and therefore seeks not of for higher[58] degrees of perfection in religion, must not wonder to hear himself condemned to lose the prize and to see himself the contempt and derision of men and angels.[59] Our wages should not be scanty and deficient and therefore neither should our labour be so.[60] The highest pitch of happiness is proposed to us, and therefore it deserves the[61] utmost pains and industry to attain it. The gates of heaven are wide opened to us, and we are invited by God himself *thither* to come,[62] and their [sic] to take up our constant, our eternal, residence. And does not such a reward more than[63] deserve the labours of life? Are not fourscore years well spent if eternity is gained thereby? Or can anyone think a it hard bargain to be obliged to spend all his days upon the earth, which at best are but few and evil,[64] in the service of God, when by so doing, he secureth to himself an everlasting inheritance? See we not the tradesman toiling and [?][65] in his business, regular and constant in his employment and zealous in the prosecution

---

[56] The word 'deserve' has been struck out in the text and replaced with 'obtain'. The hand is not Charles's.

[57] The word here taken as 'full' has been heavily struck out in the MS. The 'f' is relatively clear; 'ull' is not.   [58] Charles originally wrote 'highest' at this point, but has changed it to 'higher'.

[59] Charles perhaps has 1 Cor. 4: 9 in mind.

[60] The words 'Our wages should not be scanty and deficient and therefore neither should our labour be so' have been struck out in the MS. However, the strike-out is in pencil and does not appear to be Charles's own. In the 1816 edition these words are missing. In fact the editor of that edition has cut a substantial section here beginning with the words 'this therefore is the only title' and running to 'utmost pains and industry to attain it'.

[61] The words 'it deserves the' are struck out in the text and replaced by 'we ought to use the'. The hand is not that of Charles.

[62] It is possible that Charles is here influenced in his wording by Rev. 4: 1.

[63] The words 'more than' are inserted above the line.   [64] Gen. 47: 9.

[65] The word in the text is so heavily struck out as to make it unreadable.

and attainment of every thing which may make him eminent in his profession and all to gain a competence in the world, an estate to supply him with necessaries and conveniences whilst he lives. Is a treasure in the kingdom of heaven[66] of less value than the fading riches of the world? No, no! Heaven is a matter of such consequence, that nothing else is worthy our seeking besides it. And does not the Christian's prospect deserve the same eagerness and ap intense application of his business, as the trading doth?[67] And therefore it must bespeak the same ardour and diligence in working out our salvation, as the children of this world use to attain the pleasures, riches and honours of this present life.[68] And as a man must[69] be a master of his trade, that would get an estate by his business, so must he be a perfect Christian, who would secure to himself these invaluable riches by his Christianity.[70]

Again all our pretensions to heaven we know are only founded upon the promises of God; we have no manner of reason[71] therefore to hope for it except we fulfil the conditions upon which it is promised. Now I would desire to know whether Christian perfection is not the only way which the gospel proposeth to us to obtain salvation by Christ. Has not our blessed Lord himself expressly required us to be perfect as our father which is in heaven is perfect?[72] Are we not exhorted to be holy as the Lord our God is holy?[73] To be pure as he is pure?[74] And to offer our b spirits, souls and bodies a holy and perfect, or unspotted sacrifice acceptable to God?[75] Now if this be so (and what Christian dares to say it is not) we must by[76] of necessity conclude, that he that wilfully stoppeth short of Christian perfection for ought he knows to the contrary stops short of the mercy of God.

But here it may be urged that in God's house are many mansions[77] and that the stations of the kingdom of heaven shall differ in glory.[78] The consequence[79] therefore all mankind are not expected to attain to an equal pitch of piety, or to be

---

[66] cf. Mark 10: 21 and parallels; Matt. 13: 44–52; Luke 12: 21.

[67] Several of the words in the sentence 'And does not the Christian's prospect deserve the same eagerness and intense application of his business, as the trading doth?' are not entirely clear in the text. They have been inserted at the bottom of the page, continuing in the left hand margin and are difficult to read due to their small and compacted form.

[68] This comparison between those Christians who do not seek their estate with the same vigour as 'the children of this world' seek theirs is the subject of Sermon 17.

[69] Charles originally wrote 'may', which he changed to 'must'.

[70] The words 'And as a man must be a master of his trade, that would get an estate by his business, so must he be a perfect Christian, who would secure to himself these invaluable riches by his Christianity' have been struck out in the MS, but the strike-out is in pencil and is not the work of Charles himself. They are omitted from the 1816 edition.

[71] 'Reason' has been inserted above the line; the correction is in Charles's hand.

[72] Matt. 5: 48.   [73] Cf. 1 Pet. 1: 15.   [74] 1 John 3: 3.

[75] Cf. Rom. 12: 1.   [76] The word 'by' is not clear in the MS.   [77] John 14: 2.

[78] Charles perhaps has in mind here the words of Matt. 5: 19: 'Whosoever therefore shall break one of these least commandments, and shall teach men so, he shall be called the least in the kingdom of heaven: but whosoever shall do and teach them, the same shall be called great in the kingdom of heaven.'

[79] In an effort to correct this apparent grammatical slip, the MS has been altered at this point to read 'glory and of consequence'. The change appears not to be Charles's own.

entitled to an equal degree of glory. In answer to which I must observe that though there be different degrees of glory in God's kingdom, yet that he who aspireth not after the highest is not worthy of[80] the lowest. The man that doth not ~~his~~ endeavour to become a perfect Christian, deceives himself if he thinks he is any Christian at all. True it is, God knoweth our frame[81] and constitution, he understandeth the weakness of our nature and is acquainted with the strength and number of those temptations to which we are exposed. And therefore of his infinite mercy and goodness he vouchsafeth, not to exclude us absolutely from his favour for every crime that we commit.[82] But still it can't be shown that he doth not require perfection at our hands. I mean that he doth not require us to aim at it. The terms of his new covenant with man is [sic] that he should do the very best he can for his maker and observe all God's commands to the utmost of our [sic] power. And therefore however his mercy may prevail upon him to overlook those sins which through his own infirmities and his adversary's power man daily commiteth, yet will not his justice permit him to pass by those defects and imperfections which are wilful and voluntary, or to pardon those sins which through neglect and stubbornness we run into. The infirmities of nature are therefore ~~as~~ so far from being an argument against aiming at Christian perfection that they ought to be the strongest incitement to it. Because a sense of our many unavoidable defects should teach us great caution and diligence not to add to the account of our trespasses by sins of wilful negligence or careless indifference.

Thus have I fully evinced the truth of my II general proposition and sufficiently proved that our crown of reward is never to be secured or attained by resting contented with any pitch of piety short of the highest and most perfect that we are capable of in this world.

I therefore proceed to my III general head. Wherein I am to show that a constant progress in Christianity is the necessary indispensable duty of all ranks and degrees of Christians.

They that would hope in ~~the~~ *time* to attain to perfection, must as the royal psalmist expresses it, 'go on from strength to strength'.[83] Whilst we can be better than we are, we are not to think of ourselves as perfect. And he that thinketh he is so good as that it is impossible for him to be better would do well to follow the apostle's advice and 'not think of himself more highly than he ought to think'.[84] Alas! whilst we are in the world we are surrounded with snares and beset with temptations by some of which the best among us daily falls.[85] We

[80] The words 'worthy of' have been struck out and replaced with 'prepared for' in the MS. However, this change seems not to have been effected by Charles.

[81] This word, which has been partially struck out and corrected, is unclear in the text, though 'frame' looks probable; see Ps. 103: 14.

[82] The words 'every crime that we commit' have been changed in the MS to 'every sin of which we may be guilty'. The hand is not that of Charles.   [83] Cf. Ps. 84: 7.

[84] Rom. 12: 3.

[85] The words 'daily falls' are changed in the MS to 'are sometimes overcome'. The hand appears not to be that of Charles.

often[86] repent and often sin again. And therefore sure may we be that 'we have not yet attained neither are already perfect'.[87] Our crown is not yet put into our hands, nor the victory over our spiritual enemies perfectly gained. Still therefore must we fight and strive against them, still must we press forward toward the mark of the high calling of God in Christ Jesus.[88] Whilst we are in the world we are but in the road to heaven, and therefore must keep marching on, would we hope ever to get thither. Life is our pilgrimage, heaven is our home: and as here we have no abiding city,[89] so neither have we any end of our labours. Death will put an end to all our ~~trials~~ toils, but whilst life lasts our work will never have an end. We may sit down and please ourselves with thinking what we have already done; but be assured that such a thought does only make us lose our time and hinder us from finishing what yet is left undone. When we have done all that we can, our Saviour directs us to look upon ourselves but as unprofitable servants.[90] And whilst we are so, it can never be a time to rest contented with our state, but rather to aim at more exalted holiness and aspire after higher degrees of perfection.

He that has often done his duty to God, and laboured earnestly to do good to his brethren, has no right to sit down contented with what he has done and to think no more is required of him. No! such a thought would taint his piety, tarnish the lustre of his virtue and spoil the merit of[91] his best performances. When we have done all the good we can, we are still to seek for opportunities of doing more. And though we have been ever so charitable to our brethren, yet if charity increaseth not, if we do not seek out for farther objects of it and farther means of assisting and relieving them, it is but an imaginary virtue, and has no manner of title to the name of Christian charity. And what is true of charity may likewise be said of all the virtues of the gospel: their very essence consisteth in the improvement we make of them; and their nature is wholly changed whenever we think we are far enough advanced in the practice of them.

2. But farther: it is a maxim universally true and established by the general consent of all mankind that he that maketh no progress is sure to go backward in the world. Now this maxim is infallibly certain when applied to religion as to all other any things.[92] He therefore that would stand still in the paths of virtue[93] must not be surprised if he find that he goeth back therein. He not only wasteth his time,

---

[86] The words 'we often' have been changed to the rhetorical 'do we not often' in the MS. However, the change appears not to have been effected by Charles himself.   [87] Cf. Phil. 3: 12.

[88] Phil. 3: 14.   [89] Cf. 1 Cor. 4: 11.

[90] Luke 17: 10. One is reminded here of John Wesley's self-written and premature (1753) epitaph, the last line of which read 'God be merciful to me, an unprofitable servant'.

[91] The words 'the merit of' have been struck out in the MS. However, the hand is not that of Charles himself.

[92] Charles originally wrote 'as to other things'. A number of changes to this have been made in his hand. The first amendment probably resulted in 'to all other things' which was changed to 'to any thing'. However, 'all' and 'other' have been left in to give the rather confused reading printed above.

[93] The word 'virtue' has been changed to 'piety' in the MS. However, the hand appears not to be that of Charles himself.

but loseth his ground too: and will find, if ever he awakes out of his sleep,[94] that he has not only less time to run his race in, but more of his course to go through than he before imagined. He that doth not constantly and daily strive against the storm of vice and torrent of iniquity, wherewith the world is now overflowed,[95] will be infallibly carried down thereby. There is no resting in the mid way between heaven and hell. We must pursue our way to the former, or we shall infallibly make quick advances toward the latter.

3. All virtue consisteth in habit: and habits, we know, are only to be obtained by constant and repeated acts. He therefore that would be truly pious must be always exercised in piety; and he that would attain to real Christian charity must never cool in his labour of love.[96] If we keep continually labouring in the task our great master has given us to do, we must of consequence continually increase in our ability to perform it. But if we ever abate of our zeal, we must not wonder if our habit of virtue begins to fail us. Besides in order to attain a habit, constant repeated acts are not only necessary, but we must likewise take care that every act of piety be proportionally better than the last. He that contenteth himself with a bare[97] plodding at the rudiments of learning will never make a scholar; and he that aspires no higher than the first steps in the scale of perfection will never make a Christian. It is St Paul's advice to the Hebrews that they should leave the principles of the doctrine of Christ, and go on to perfection; not resting satisfied with laying the foundations of Christianity, but endeavouring to raise a proportionable superstructure thereupon.[98] And were this advice regularly complied with, Christianity would be in another condition than at present can be boasted of. Men would not be babes[99] in Christianity all the days of their life, nor would a hoary head and an ignorant heart be such frequent companions as God knows at present they are. Did people daily aspire after improving themselves in Christianity we should see youth more sober and old age more venerable. The longer men lived, the wiser would they grow, and the wiser they were, the more holy would they be.

Thus have I shown by these unanswerable arguments that people of all ranks and conditions are indispensably obliged to make a constant progress and proficiency both in the knowledge and practice of true Christianity. The doctrines of this discourse are so plain and evident that they need no application and so necessary and indispensable that they will sufficiently commend themselves to the serious consideration and practice of all that hear me. Instead therefore of an exhortation to them I choose rather to require you to join with me in prayer to God that he would graciously assist us in the performance of them. For which purpose I shall conclude with an excellent collect of our Church.

---

[94] Cf. Eph. 5: 14, the text treated at length in Sermon 8.
[95] There is a possible allusion here to Rev. 12: 16.   [96] Cf. 1 Thess. 1: 3; Heb. 6: 10.
[97] Or 'base'; the word is unclear in the MS.   [98] Cf. Heb. 6: 1 ff.
[99] An allusion perhaps to 1 Cor. 3: 1.

Col[lect] for 2 Sun after Trinity

O God who declarest thy mighty power, most chiefly in showing mercy and pity, mercifully grant unto us such a measure of thy grace that we running of thy commandments, may obtain thy gracious promises and be made partakers of thy heavenly treasure through Jesus Christ our Lord. Amen.

SERMON 2
1 KINGS 18: 21

INTRODUCTORY COMMENT

Two MSS of Charles's sermon on 1 Kings 18: 21 have survived. Both are held at the John Rylands University Library of Manchester,[1] and both are written in longhand. The first MS comprises 14 leaves (including covers). The leaves of this MS, here referred to as 'MS A' are written both verso and recto. The second MS, which is shorter and later, comprises 20 leaves (including covers), written almost exclusively recto only. The exception is the front cover, on the verso of which is the sermon register. This second MS is here cited as 'MS B'.

The sermon was originally published in the 1816 edition (pp. 207–24) and for that edition the editor has utilized the shorter, later MS, to which numerous editorial changes have been made by the editor him- or herself. The fuller, longer sermon (MS A) has not before been published and it is from that MS that the sermon printed below has been transcribed. All differences between the two MSS are indicated in the notes.

Charles first preached this sermon in Cowes on the Isle of Wight in 1735 during the very early stages of his crossing to America, where he was to take up the post of secretary to General Oglethorpe. He had set out on this journey from Gravesend together with his brother John on 21 October 1735, but had been delayed off the Isle of Wight due to unfavourable sailing conditions, and the journey did not restart until 10 December.[2] According to the information found on the recto of leaf 1 of MS A Charles preached from 1 Kings 18: 21 (using MS A) on 30 November. It is regrettable that Charles's journal does not begin until after that date, so no cross-reference from that source is available. However, in his entry for 20 November 1735, John Wesley records that

> The continuance of the contrary winds gave my brother an opportunity of complying with the desire of the minister of Cowes, and preaching there three or four times. The poor people flocked together in great numbers.[3]

It is evident, then, that not all of Charles's preaching on the Isle of Wight has survived. Indeed, this MS on 1 Kings 18: 21 is the only one still extant. This MS sermon hence gives a valuable glimpse of Charles's preaching in its infancy (Charles was ordained priest on 29 September 1735, only a little over two weeks before setting out for Georgia).[4]

It is apparent from the very slender evidence that has survived that Charles's preaching at Cowes, including, presumably, this sermon, was a success. John's reference to the 'flocking' of the people has been noted already. Further, John wrote to his elder brother Samuel on 1 February 1736 and included a report on Charles's preaching, though unfortunately

---

[1] MARC CW Box 5.   [2] *J&D*, xviii.139–40.   [3] *J&D*, xviii.140.
[4] The journey had begun on 14 October with a boat journey to Gravesend, where the company embarked the *Simmonds*. The *Simmonds* itself did not depart for Georgia until 21 October (see further *J&D* xviii. 136–8).

that letter itself has not survived.[5] However, Samuel's response to John's letter has, and the response is suggestive of the earlier letter's contents. Samuel writes

> I know of no other part of yours that requires any remark, except perhaps that of my brother Charles's preaching in Cowes—I hope by the behaviour of those poor people he is fully convinced that he needed not have gone to Georgia in order to do good by his ministry.[6]

Whether Charles preached this longer form of the sermon again during the crossing or in America itself is unknown. However, by 20 June, 1736 he had evidently cut it down and refined it somewhat to form the sermon as it is found in MS B. According to information on the MS itself,[7] Charles preached this shorter form of the sermon at least four times during that year (20 June; 12 September; 17 October twice). None of these references can be confirmed from the journal.

The sermon deals with one reasonably simple point: that devotion to God must not be half-hearted. At one point in the sermon Charles refers to the message to the Laodiceans as found in the book of Revelation 3: 14 ff. Here, Charles notes, the Spirit instructs the angel of the Church to condemn unequivocally the half-hearted nature of their devotion to God. Better would it be for them if they were either hot or cold, a theme which Charles picks up and upon which he comments

> O dreadful doom of the lukewarm and indifferent in religion! See we not here that the indifferent man is debased even below him that has no religion at all. 'I wish thou wert either cold or hot'.

A choice must be made: if God be God then follow him, but if Baal be the Lord, then follow him. There is no place for indecision and no place for a half-devotion.

As with Sermon 1 on Philippians 3: 13–14, though perhaps to a lesser extent, a distinct note of works-righteousness runs through this text. Some of this material has been discussed already in Chapter 3. Charles's basic point is that although the merits of Christ will make up the deficiency brought about by the change in human nature wrought by the fall of Adam, this does not mean that human beings are free from the requirements of the law. Were it possible, writes Charles, sinless perfection would be required. However, that is not, on account of the fall, possible and God has a plan to make up the deficiency. However, human beings must do all they can, be as holy as it is possible for them to be. Charles writes

> For though God will in consideration of the merits of Christ and upon our own true repentance pardons all those sins, which through the frailty and corruption of our nature we have committed, yet will he never pardon those omissions of duty and commissions of sin which men wilfully live in, through a fond and vain persuasion that it is not required of them to be as holy as possibly they can.

The terminology employed is significant. The terms of the covenant are 'no less rigorous' than those of the covenant made with Adam and it would be self-deception to think that 'there was less to do than ever before was required of men in order to their attainment of

---

[5] See further Baker, (ed.), *Letters*, xxv. 740. [6] Baker (ed.), *Letters*, xxv. 459.
[7] See the notes to the text for details.

heaven'. The business of salvation requires 'the utmost labour the greatest pains and most constant diligence' and even that 'will be but barely sufficient to entitle us to the reward of good soldiers of Christ, and faithful servants of God'. This sermon, then, does not exude the evangelical air that Charles's later sermons (as of course his hymns) were to acquire.

And[1] Elijah came unto all the people and said ~~why~~ how long ~~halt ye~~ will ye halt between two opinions? If the Lord be God follow him; but if Baal follow him.[2]

When the people of God the Jews had by their manifold transgressions provoked the Lord to anger and called down for [*sic*] his heavy judgments upon them; when their iniquities were increased and their wickedness multiplied; it pleased the good God to send the scourges of his vengeance upon them that so by the severity of his chastisement he might recall those to the right way who had despised his mercy and rejected his counsel. Thus when King Ahab by his abominable impiety had filled up the measure of his father's iniquities; when he had led the people with him into idolatry[3] and like his predecessor Jeroboam had made Israel to sin,[4] God was pleased in mercy to visit his people with the judgment of famine; which was so remarkably great that the heaven is said to be shut up for 3 years so that there was neither rain nor dew upon the earth; the effects of which were so terrible, that all the brooks and fountains of water were dried up and there remained not any longer food for man or beast. Amidst the miseries of this severe calamity it pleased the Lord still to remember mercy[5] and to send his prophet Elijah to Ahab and to his people to see whether they were yet humbled by the things they had suffered and whether the hand of vengeance which had lain so long upon them had at all ~~suf~~[6] disposed them to turn from the evil of their ways and to serve the true and living God,[7] with all their mind, with all their soul and with all their strength.[8] Accordingly the prophet requesteth the king to gather all Israel to him unto Mount Carmel together with Baal's 450 prophets and all the prophets of the groves; that he might show the people the absurdity as well as abomination of that idol worship whereof they were guilty and persuade them to follow the Lord their God ~~with~~ in word and deed, and in uprightness and integrity. God's judgments had indeed softened their hearts so far as to make them seek to him for a redress of them; but yet their hearts was not sound, neither walked they steadfastly in his way but while they worshipped the true God Jehovah with their lips, in their minds they went after idols.[9] And though they sometimes poured out their prayer to the God of heaven and earth; yet did they also sometimes do sacrifice to Baal. The prophet therefore begins his exhortation with this pathetical ~~exhort~~ exclamation 'How long will ye halt between two opinions? If the Lord be God, follow him, but if Baal, then follow him.' An[10]

[1] Inside the front cover of MS A Charles has written 'Preached at Cows in the Isle of Wight, Nov. 30. 1735'. On this see further the introduction to this sermon.
[2] The corrections are smoothed out in MS B.
[3] Cf. 1 Kgs. 16: 32–3; the story of King Ahab, the famine, and the challenge to the prophets of Baal to which Charles here makes reference, is found in 1 Kgs. 17–18.   [4] Cf. 1 Kgs. 14: 16.
[5] Cf. Hab. 3: 22.   [6] These letters are unclear in the text.   [7] Cf. 1 Thess. 1: 9.
[8] Cf. Deut. 6: 5.   [9] *BCP*, General Thanksgiving.
[10] The shorter sermon ('B', the version printed in the 1816 edition) begins at this point. As noted above Charles preached this shorter version four times. This information is given on the inside of the front cover, which reads 'Preached at Savanna in Georgia in the M[orning] June 20, 1736' and goes on

exclamation this wherein[11] Christians are no less concerned than those Jews to whom it it was immediately spoken, for do we not most of us halt between two opinions? Do we not endeavour to do service to two masters?[12] And is it not the constant care of the generality of Christians, to compound matters between God and the world? To contrive how to serve God without renouncing the service of the world, the flesh, and the devil?[13] Do we not see many Christians who make loud professions of zeal for religion, still anxious for the good things of this life? In short may we not truly say, that while we all pretend to be true worshippers of God, we do every one in particular, set up his idol in his heart[14] and divide his religious worship between the God of heaven and earth and the idolator's *God* to whom he hath devoted himself in a most special and extraordinary manner?[15] To you therefore is this scripture given: and every one is still concerned in this expostulation of the prophet, 'how long will ye halt between two opinions? If the Lord be God then follow him, but if Baal, then follow him'.

In discoursing upon which words I shall first show who they are that come under this censure of halting between two opinions.

Secondly, I shall consider the folly and danger of such a state.[16] And

Thirdly, conclude with an earnest exhortation to an entire devotion of ourselves to God.

I am first to show etc.[17]

And here I doubt upon a serious and impartial examination of ourselves, we shall most of us find that we stand self-condemned on this point, and when we enquire who they are that halt between two opinions our conscience will reply to each of us, 'thou art the man'.[18] For judge I pray you, and judge impartially every-one of himself; hath God the entire possession of your souls? Are ye in heart and mind solely and wholly devoted to him? Have ~~we~~ you no other end of all your actions? No other design in all your undertakings but to perform the will of God and finish that work which he hath given you to do?[19] Who among us can stand so

to record that Charles preached the sermon also 'on board the London-Galley, Sept. 12. 1736'; at 'Dr Cutler's Church in Boston N.E. Oct. 17, 1736' and at 'Mr Price's in Boston N.E Oct. 17, 1736'. On the front cover of B, Charles has copied out the text. Several other notes appear on the front cover, but these are not in Charles's hand. These notes read 'Cows (*sic*) in the Isle of Wight', 'Preached Nov. 30 1735', 'Preached in Georgia & Boston, June 20, Oct. 17 1736', and 'Preached Nov 30 17 (*sic*)'. The familiar 'Ex^d W.P.' also appears at this point on B. Before the words 'An exclamation this' Charles has given his text. The MS reads. 'In the 18th chapter of the 1st book of Kings at the 21 verse it is thus written "And Elijah came unto all the people and said, how long will ye halt between two opinions? If the Lord be God follow him, but if Baal follow him." '

[11] For 'wherein' B has 'in which'.   [12] cf. Matt. 6: 24 and parallel.

[13] *BCP*, Collect for 18th Sunday after Trinity.   [14] Cf. Ezek. 14: 3.

[15] In place of 'and divide his religious worship between the God of heaven and earth and the idola-tor's *God* to whom he hath devoted himself in a most special and extraordinary manner', B has 'and divide his religious worship between that and the God of heaven and earth'.

[16] In B this word has been struck out and replaced with 'conduct'.

[17] In B the words 'Who they are that come under this censure of halting between two opinions' appear at this point.   [18] 'Thou art the man' is underlined in B. The words are from 2 Sam. 12: 7.

[19] Perhaps John 4: 34.

severe a test as this? Or whom will not conscience condemn[20] upon so strict a trial? Well may we say with the royal psalmist, that mankind are all corrupted and gone out of the way; that there is none that doth good, no not one.[21] For[22] who is there among us that may be termed holy in the strict sense of the word as it implies a total renunciation of the world, the flesh, and the devil;[23] an entire and absolute devotion of ourselves to God? Alas we have all of us private views, and secret ends of our own. God may perhaps have the chief place in some of our hearts, but I doubt he can't be said to have them wholly at his disposal, or to reign solely in them. There are, God knows,[24] many rivals, who will dispute with him his right to absolute and entire dominion. The world with her pomps and vanities,[25] pleasures and delights, entertainments and diversions, has monopolized a large share of our affections. The flesh too ruleth with almost uncontrolled sway in most of our souls. Nor is the devil without his share of power, and influence over us.

Now whilst none any of these things can be said and proved[26] of us, whilst we set our hearts upon the flesh and its gratifications, or fix our affections at[27] all upon the world or the things thereof; it must be said[28] if God has any place at all in our hearts, that his empire is disputed, his claim to our obedience contested ques- tioned, and his supreme[29] authority oftentimes neglected. We are not in propriety of speaking his servants, since we have offered a part of our service to other masters, nor can we be said to be listed under his banners, since we suffer ourselves to be led at all by others.[30]

Thus then may they be said to halt between two opinions who are divided between God and the world: who serve suffer the creator and the creature to share their affections between them[31] and who allow only a portion of their heart and mind to the service of him that made them. Where God by his grace has taken root in any man's heart so far as to engage him to set himself in some degree about his service; and yet the cares of this world, the lust of the flesh,[32] and temptations of

---

[20] This point in A is reached approximately half-way down page 4. Charles stops writing on this page and continues on the top of page 5. To make the transition he writes 'etc' and repeats the words 'con- science condemn' on the top of the new page. As discussed previously, this suggests the material to this point has replaced a more original section.   [21] Cf. Pss. 14: 1, 3; 53: 1, 3 (quoted also in Rom. 3: 10).
    [22] The words 'Well may we say with the royal psalmist, that mankind are all corrupted and gone out of the way; that there is none that doth good, no not one. For' are absent from B.
    [23] *BCP*, Collect for 18th Sunday after Trinity.   [24] The words 'God knows' are absent from B.
    [25] See *BCP*, 'A Catechism [before Confirmation]'.
    [26] The words 'and proved' are absent from B.
    [27] At this point in B, Charles has written 'at all upon the flesh and its gratifications or set our hearts' and then struck the words out. It is clearly an error in copying A.
    [28] B has 'owned' in place of 'said'.
    [29] Spelt 'supream' in both A and B, but corrected in another hand to supreme in B (which was the MS used by the editor of the 1816 edition).
    [30] The words 'We are not in propriety of speaking his servants . . . nor can we be said to be listed under his banner, since we suffer ourselves to be led at all by others' are replaced by 'We are not strictly speaking his servants . . . nor can we be said called his faithful soldiers, since we are likewise listed under the banner of his enemy' in B.   [31] The words 'between them' are absent from B.
    [32] Cf. 1 John 2: 16; cf. *BCP*, 'A Catechism [before Confirmation]'.

the devil, have still their share of influence over him; truly may that man be said to halt between two opinions, and happy it is for him, if he do not stumble upon the worst of them.[33]

The man of the world is oftentimes[34] found to profess himself a strict and serious Christian. He will tell you gravely[35] that he looks upon religion to be a matter of the utmost importance and which next to the main chance, the making of a fortune he means, is[36] by all men to be carefully ~~minded and~~ regarded. Such a man we see constant in all the external duties of religion, and abounding in all outward works of piety. He dares not omit the public service of the church, and scruples even to turn his back upon the altar. He is constant in his private prayers, frequent in giving alms, and regular in observing the church's fasts. And yet with all this seeming zeal, it may perhaps be found that the world has made a deeper impression upon him than religion; and that he taketh[37] more pains to get an estate in the world, than to lay up for himself a treasure in heaven.[38] Else how should we see the same man conscientious in church and knavish behind his counter?[39] How otherwise could we account for the public piety and secret villainy of this halting Christian? He has two principles of all his actions, the love of God and love of the world: and from this contrariety of his principles arises the inconsistency which is visible in his practice.[40] He halteth between two opinions and therefore is sometimes found adoring and praising God, and at others paying ~~their~~ his worship to mammon.[41]

We know it ~~is~~ was because the cares of this world and the desires of riches were not rooted out of the hearts of those that heard the gospel, but suffered to grow up with the good seed of the word which was sown in their hearts, that good seed brought forth no ~~seed~~ fruit to perfection.[42] And indeed no wonder; for the same ground can't produce thorns and grapes, figs and thistles.[43] Indeed this part of the parable of the sower[44] doth seem to have an immediate relation to the case in hand, and particularly to respect those who halt between two opinions, who are divided between God and the world. We there see that the good seed took root and sprung up in the hearts of them that heard it. God had gained some footing in their souls, and was in possession of a part of their affections. But yet as the cares of the world and the desires of riches, those spiritual thorns and briars, were not rooted out, but

---

[33] The words 'and happy it is for him, if he do not stumble upon the worst of them' are written but then struck out in B.   [34] 'Oftentimes' appears simply as 'often' in B.

[35] The words 'gravely that' are absent from B.

[36] The words 'which next to the main chance, the making of a fortune he means, is' are missing in B. The resultant hiatus is smoothed by Charles by changing 'which' to 'what' and the insertion of 'ought' between 'man' and 'to be'.   [37] The words 'and that he taketh' appear as 'and he takes' in B.

[38] Matt. 6: 19–20.   [39] The words 'behind his counter' are underlined in B.

[40] The words 'He has two principles of all his actions, the love of God and love of the world: and from this contrariety of his principles arises the inconsistency which is visible in his practice' have been altered to 'he has two principles the love of God and the love of the world, from whence arises the inconsistency visible in his practice' in B and then struck out.   [41] Cf. Matt. 6: 24 and parallel.

[42] Cf. Mark 4: 3ff. and parallels.   [43] Cf. Matt. 7: 16.

[44] The remainder of this paragraph is a reflection on Mark 4: 3ff. and parallels.

still suffered to keep their ground in the heart, they sprung up together with good seed; the consequence of which was that at last they choked it and hindered it from ever bringing forth any fruit to perfection.

There are still other *characters* of persons whom the text accuseth of halting between two opinions. There are men, that will renounce their vices if they may do it with the reserve of one favourite sin. There is some darling iniquity generally left behind after the strictest reformation; ~~some spice of the old leaven is often suffered to remain, after the severest repentance~~. Now this is a plain *instance* of double-mindedness and insincerity of heart. It is a manifest indication, that we halt between two opinions; that we are averse from sin in general, whilst we countenance and encourage ourselves in the practice of some particular ones.[45]

The sum of the matter is this: all they are concerned in this expostulation in the text, and stand condemned by the censure of it, who are not wholly devoted to God; who have not absolutely and entirely dedicated themselves to his service; who have not renounced the world, the flesh and the devil,[46] who do not abstract themselves as much as possible, from the consideration of every thing but God and divine things, in order to enable them the more perfectly to perform that duty, and service to him, which they are convinced in their hearts, they owe him. All they may be said to halt between two opinions who preserve any of that respect for any creature which is due only to God, whosoever loveth anything, feareth anything, or hopeth for anything but God, he hath set up his idol in his heart: [47] he is divided in himself; and therefore can't love, serve and fear God as he ought.[48] It is on this account that the blessed apostle[49] St Paul calleth the covetous man an idolater;[50] because such a one permitteth his gold to share in the love which is due only to God, and[51] alloweth his desire of gain to share a part of ~~this~~ those affections which God and religion ought wholly to engross. And as the covetous man is an idolater so also is the epicure,[52] the sensualist, the proud, the passionate,[53] and ambitious

---

[45] The paragraph beginning 'We know it was because the cares of this world' in A has been changed significantly in B. In B the text reads,
'And thus it must be with all who are divided between God and the world. The good seed may even take root and spring up in their hearts, God may gain some footing in their souls and be in possession of part of their affections; but if the cares of the world and the desire of riches, those spiritual thorns and briars be not rooted out, but still suffered to keep their ground in the heart, and spring up together with the good seed, the consequence will be that at last they will choke it, and hinder its ever bringing forth any fruit to perfection.'
'There are still other sorts of persons whom the text accuseth of halting between two opinions. These are men that will renounce their vices if they may do it with the *reserve* of one *favourite* sin. Now this is a plain instance of *insincerity*, while we are averse from sin in general and countenance and encourage ourselves in the practice of some particular ones.'

[46] *BCP*, Collect for 18th Sunday after Trinity.   [47] Cf. Ezek. 14: 3.

[48] The words 'as he ought' are absent from B.

[49] The words 'the blessed apostle' are absent from B.   [50] Cf. Eph. 5:5.

[51] In B the words 'such a one permitteth his gold to share in the love which is due only to God, and' are absent. The resultant hiatus has been smoothed over by Charles by changing 'alloweth' to 'he allows'.   [52] The word 'epicure' is absent from B.

[53] In B the words 'proud' and 'passionate' are transposed.

man. Each of them having some other ultimate[54] end of all[55] their actions, beside God and religion.[56] In short, whosoever pretendeth to be a Christian and yet at the same time[57] suffers himself to be guided by anything but God, he is doubtless guilty of halting between two opinions; of owning the Lord to be God, and[58] yet not paying him that worship and obedience which is only due unto him.[59] The folly and danger of this state comes now to be considered in the

II General Head.

Now the dangerousness of such a state as this may sufficiently[60] appear from the following considerations. First, that it is a state which God has nowhere promised to reward. And secondly, that it is a state against which he has threatened the most severe[61] punishments.

First, heaven is the free gift of God, and therefore not to be attained but upon such terms ~~but up~~[62] only as he has appointed. Now where has he promised to reward such a half piety as we have before described? Can it be shown that he has anywhere bound himself to accept of any ——[63] service which falls short of all that lies in our power to offer him? Hath he ever capitulated with us and bought the dominion over us upon conditions that the empire[64] should be divided between him and his creatures? No, this can never be shown. The promises[65] of heaven are only made to those who take the utmost pains to attain it. It is a holy violence, which is preached in the gospel as necessary to introduce us into the peaceable possession of the kingdom of God.[66] The utmost labour, the greatest pains and most constant diligence will be but barely sufficient to entitle us to the reward of good soldiers of Christ, and faithful servants of God.[67] The gospel informs us that to be disciples of Christ we must forsake father and mother, houses and land, and every thing else which the world counts dear to us.[68] And it is to the due fulfilling of these conditions of salvation that the promise of entering into rest is made us.[69]

---

[54] In B the words 'other ultimate' are absent.   [55] The word 'all' is absent from B.

[56] In B Charles began to write 'and religion', but having written 'and reli' struck the words out.

[57] 'At the same time' is absent from B.   [58] The word 'and' is absent from B.

[59] In the place of 'which is only due unto him', B reads 'due to him alone'.

[60] In place of 'Now the dangerousness of such a state as this may sufficiently', B has 'Now the danger may sufficiently'.   [61] B has 'severest' in place of 'most severe'.

[62] Here, in all probability, is an example of homeoarchon, and an indication that Charles is copying.

[63] At this point in A (but not in B) a horizontal line appears between the words 'any' and 'service'. The purpose of that line is not clear.   [64] B has 'it' in the place of 'the empire'.

[65] B has 'promise' and the verb 'is'.   [66] Cf. Matt. 11: 12.

[67] Cf. Matt. 25: 21 and parallel. The remainder of this paragraph is greatly reduced in B, which reads, 'And though through ~~our~~ the corruption of our nature, a state of perfection is not to be expected in this life, yet are we commanded to aim at it with all our might; and whosoever wilfully stops short of it, stops short of the mercy of God. For though God will, upon our true repentance, for Christ's sake pardon all those sins which through the frailty of our nature we have committed, yet will he never pardon those commissions of sin and omissions of duty which men wilfully live in through a fond and vain persuasion that it is not required of them to be as holy as possibly they can.'

[68] Cf. Mark 10: 29 and parallels.

[69] The term 'enter into rest' is used several times in this soteriological sense in the third and fourth chapter of the Letter to the Hebrews.

—[70] We know by the covenant that God made with us at our creation, sinless obedience was indispensably required of us: and though the rigours of this covenant are now abated and God through his tender mercy, in consideration of the manifold frailties and infirmities of our natures, hath been graciously pleased to propose heaven to us on other terms; and to accept of repentance in lieu of perfect obedience, yet should we greatly deceive ourselves did we imagine that there was less to do than ever before was required of men in order to their attainment of heaven and ~~heaven~~[71] happiness. No—the case is far otherwise with us. For ~~the~~ though God hath been pleased to enter into a new and more gracious covenant with his children, yet the terms of it are no less rigorous, considering the change of nature that was wrought in us by the fall, than those of the first covenant were. For as absolute sinless obedience was required then, so is it absolute obedience to the utmost of our power required of us now. Were we able, we should be obliged to be spotless and without sin. And though, through the corruption of our nature, a state of perfection is ~~hardly~~ not to be expected in this world, yet are we commanded to aim at it with all our might: and whosoever voluntarily stops short of it, for ought he knows to the contrary, stops short of the mercy of God.[72] For though God will in consideration of the merits of Christ and upon our own true repentance pardons all those sins, which through the frailty and corruption of our nature we have committed, yet will he never pardon those omissions of duty and commissions of sin which men wilfully live in, through a fond and vain persuasion that it is not required of them to be as holy as possibly they can.

We say then that a state of voluntary imperfection, a half *course*[73] of piety, a life divided between God and the world, is a state which God has nowhere promised to accept nor yet assured us of a reward for it.[74] And this alone is sufficient to show the dangerousness of such a state; since as was before observed, heaven is the free gift of God, and therefore may only be expected upon such terms as he has proposed it to us upon. But there is still another argument whereby we may prove the danger of this state, and that is

2ndly, the severe punishment which God hath threatened against it.

Many and obvious are the texts of scripture wherein God threateneth the pains of hell to all those who fullfil not his will; and how God's will may be fulfilled without this entire devotion of ourselves to his service is more than in holy scriptures God hath thought proper to teach[75] us. We are therein taught to love the Lord our God with all our heart and with all our mind, and to do him service with all our

---

[70] At this point in A there appears a short dash. The purpose of that dash is not clear, but it may represent a pause in the spoken form of the sermon.

[71] Here, perhaps, is a case of homeoarchon and an indication of the fact that Charles was copying.

[72] Cf. 'we must of necessity conclude, that he that willfully stoppeth short of Christian perfection for ought he knows to the contrary stops short of the mercy of God', in Sermon 1.

[73] The word 'course' is not underlined in B.

[74] In B the remainder of this paragraph reads,
'But there is still another argument for the danger of it, namely 2. the severe punishment which God has threatened against it.'   [75] 'Thought proper to teach' is replaced by 'taught' in B.

soul and all[76] our strength.[77] And the sanction annexed to this divine law is the penalty of being utterly excluded from the sweetest comforts of God's presence if we fail in the performance of it.[78]

We are expressly told [in] Luke 14.33 that whosoever he be that forsaketh not all that he hath, he cannot be Christ's disciple. Now what can be possibly[79] more plain than this text, the sense of which is clearly this, that unless we renounce everything in the world so far as that our affections may be placed wholly and solely upon[80] God and religion[81] we cannot be disciples of Christ. And if we be not his disciples what will become of our claim to salvation by him? Certainly being[82] excluded from the name of a disciple of Christ is an exclusion from that heaven which he died to purchase for us, [83]and therefore a severer threat against this divided piety can't ~~perhaps~~ possibly be conceived, than what the doctrine of this text plainly sets before us.

But whosoever[84] desires to see the terrible condemnation which awaiteth this state more fully represented, let him hear what the spirit of God saith to the angel of the church of the Laodiceans in the 3rd ch. Rev v. 15. 16[85] 'I know thy works that thou art neither cold nor hot.[86] I would thou wert cold or hot. So then because thou art lukewarm and neither cold nor hot I will spew thee out of my mouth.' O dreadful doom of the lukewarm and indifferent in religion! See we not here that the indifferent man[87] is debased even below him that has no religion at all? 'I wish thou wert either cold or hot';[88] so saith the spirit, showing that coldness or an absolute negligence of religion was a more eligible[89] state, than lukewarmness or indifferency. Add to all which the dreadful doom that attendeth[90] this state 'because thou art neither hot nor cold, saith[91] God, I will spew thee out of my mouth'. I will

---

[76] B inserts 'with' before 'all'.   [77] Cf. Deut. 6: 4–5.

[78] The words 'And the sanction annexed to this divine law is the penalty of being utterly excluded from the sweetest comforts of God's presence if we fail in the performance of it' are replaced by 'and that under pain of being utterly excluded from God's presence, if we fail in the performance of it' in B.

[79] B has 'possibly be' rather than 'be possibly' at this point in the MS.

[80] The words 'everything in the world so far as that our affections may be placed wholly and solely upon' are inserted above the line in A. This is clearly a slip since without the inserted words the MS reads 'that unless we renounce God and religion'. In B Charles wrote 'unless we renounce God and R'; he then struck out 'God and R' and inserted 'every' and continued on the next page 'thing in this world . . .' Perhaps as Charles was copying A into B he realized his slip in A and inserted the words placed above the line.   [81] The words 'and religion' are absent from B.

[82] B adds 'the' before 'being' at this point.

[83] In B the remainder of this paragraph reads, 'And therefore a severer threatening against this divided piety cannot be conceived than that of this text.' Square brackets appear around these words, suggesting that they may have been omitted in the spoken form of the sermon.

[84] The word 'whosoever' is replaced by 'who' in B.

[85] In B the reference is given as 'Rev 3 v. 15, 16'. The reference is enclosed in square brackets.

[86] The words 'cold nor hot' are reversed to 'hot or cold' in B (cf. Rev. 3: 15).

[87] In B the words 'indifferent man' are replaced by 'luke-warm Christian (if we will call him such)'.

[88] Charles has written '2' and '1' beneath 'cold' and 'hot' respectively, indicating that he reversed the order in the spoken form of the sermon (cf. Rev. 3: 15).

[89] 'Eligible' is replaced by 'desirable' in B.

[90] The words 'that attendeth' are changed to 'which attends' in B.

[91] Before 'saith' in B there appears '~~but~~'.

cast thee from me with zeal and indignation; and withdraw my grace from every one that maketh no better a[92] use of it than the lukewarm and indifferent man doth.

I[93] need not add farther proofs to shew you the dangerousness of pretending to be a Christian and yet not being wholly devoted to God; I have fully proved it to be a state which God has nowhere promised to reward; and likewise a state against which he has denounced the severest woes and judgments; and this proof to a Christian congregation must be acknowledged with a sufficient demonstration of the *point*.

I therefore proceed farther to consider the folly of such a state.

The folly of living in such a state as this,[94] of dividing our hearts between God and the world, may be easily collected from the danger attending such a state.[95] For is it not the greatest madness in nature to continue in such a course of life as we are sure we shall never be rewarded for? Doth not reason plainly teach us that[96] the service of God is the most honourable, easy and profitable that we can possibly[97] be engaged in? The consequence of which must be that it is the highest folly for any one to quit that service,[98] and take up with a more[99] stern master, and that too upon more severe terms.[100] But thus[101] does every one, who seeks to compound matters between God and the world, and[102] to divide his service between religion and pleasure. For no man can serve two masters,[103] we must therefore of necessity either renounce the service of mammon or of God.[104] The blessed apostle[105] St James saith expressly (Jam 4.4)[106] that[107] the friendship of the world is enmity with God; and whosoever will be a friend of the world is an enemy to of God. Here we see that there is no such thing as dividing our love. The love of the world is absolutely inconsistent with the love of God. So that if we afford the world, or anything[108] besides God any part of our love, in such proportion do we become the enemies of God.

And can there be a greater instance of folly than this, to lose the favour of God, and the recompense of all the[109] services we do him,[110] for the sake of a little self-

---

[92] The word 'a' has been written and then struck out in B.

[93] The next two paragraphs, ending 'the folly of such a state', are absent from B.

[94] The words 'as this' are absent from B.

[95] The words 'attending such a state' are replaced by 'of it' in B.

[96] The words from 'For is it not' to 'Doth not reason plainly teach us that' are absent from B.

[97] The word 'possibly' is absent from B.

[98] The words 'The consequence of which must be that it is the highest folly for any one to quit that service' are replaced with 'it must therefore be the greatest folly to quit that service' in B.

[99] The word 'more' is absent from B.

[100] The words 'and that too upon more severe terms' are replaced with 'upon the severest terms' in B.

[101] The word 'thus' is replaced by 'so' in B.   [102] The word 'and' is absent from B.

[103] Cf. Matt. 6: 24 and parallel.

[104] The words 'we must therefore of necessity either renounce the service of mammon or of God' are replaced by 'we must of necessity renounce the service either of God or of mammon' in B.

[105] The words 'The blessed apostle' are absent from B.   [106] The reference is absent from B.

[107] The word 'that' is absent from B.   [108] The word 'else' is inserted at this point in B.

[109] In B Charles wrote 'the', but struck it out and replaced it with 'our'.

[110] The words 'we do him' are absent from B.

love, a small proportion of affection for the world and the ~~good~~ God thereof.[111] For shame! follow the prophet's advice in my text:[112] if the Lord be God serve him and him alone;[113] but if not serve whomsoever you do serve heartily; that so ye may have the reward of your services. For the man that is religious by halves, that dares not totally[114] renounce the service of God, and yet will not entirely devote himself to him; has taken the ready way wholly[115] to divest himself both of the pleasures of religion and of the world. He has just got religion enough[116] to make ~~himself~~[117] uneasy. He has got so much of the fear of God, as will serve[118] to poison all his delights, to give him qualms amidst his entertainments[119] and to[120] hinder his soul from the enjoyment of whatsoever it lusteth after. Thus he suffereth all the pains, nay ten times more, than the truly religious man endures, and yet at the same time has none of those pleasures which virtue bringeth along with her[121] whereby ample retribution is made for those worldly ~~pleasures~~ delights which are given up.[122]

And[123] how there can be a greater pitch of folly and madness than this is more than I am able to determine. Nor doth the point need farther illustration, it being sufficiently plain that the man who halteth between two opinions, who endeavors to serve God and mammon,[124] who ~~will~~ divides his heart between the creator and the creature, liveth in a state of utmost danger and utmost folly that can well be imagined. I therefore proceed

III and lastly[125]

To conclude with an earnest exhortation to an entire devotion of yourselves[126] to God. —[127] Ye have seen, brethren, the true nature of the crime of halting between two opinions, exclaimed against in my text;[128] which has been shown to consist in dividing our affections between God and the things he hath made and placing only

[111] The words 'for the sake of a little self-love, a small proportion of affection for the world and the God thereof' are replaced by 'for a small proportion of this world's good' in B. The expression 'the god of this world' is found in 2 Cor. 4: 4.   [112] The words 'in my text' are absent from B.

[113] The word 'alone' is replaced by 'only' in B.

[114] The word 'totally' has been replaced by 'wholly' in B.

[115] The word 'wholly' is absent from B.

[116] The words 'He has just got religion enough' are replaced by 'He has just enough of religion' in B.

[117] Written as 'himself' in B.

[118] The words 'He has got so much of the fear of God, as will serve' are absent from B (though Charles began by writing 'he has g' which he then struck out). The resultant hiatus has then been smoothed out by changing the period after 'uneasy' to a semicolon.

[119] The words 'to give him qualms amidst his entertainments' are absent from B.

[120] The word 'to' is absent from B.

[121] The words 'which virtue bringeth along with her' have been struck out in another hand and replaced in the margin with 'which always accompany genuine piety' in B.

[122] The words 'whereby ample retribution is made for those worldly delights which are given up' are absent from B.   [123] This entire paragraph is absent from B.

[124] Cf. Matt. 6: 24 and parallel.

[125] In B these words are replaced by 'I proceed thirdly and lastly'.

[126] 'Yourselves' has been changed to 'ourselves' in B.

[127] There is a short dash at this point in MS A. In MS B the words 'Ye have seen' begin a new paragraph.   [128] The words 'exclaimed against in my text' are absent from B.

such a part of our[129] love upon our creator as we can well spare from his creatures.[130] Ye have likewise been shown how full such a course of life ~~is~~ of folly and
impertinence,[131] of weakness and contempt. Nay,[132] moreover ye have been told of
the many and great dangers wherewith it is attended: that it is a state of life which
God[133] hath nowhere promised to reward; nay farther,[134] that he hath expressly[135]
denounced his vengeance upon it. Now surely all this will be abundantly sufficient
to persuade you totally to renounce the world and to set your affections on things
above not on things that are below.[136] Ye have seen that no less a degree of religion
than this will profit you. That whosoever wittingly falls short of this does, for
ought he knows, fall short of the mercy of God.[137] Be strong therefore and quit
yourselves like men.[138] Be bold to assert your liberty; to vindicate the dignity of
your nature;[139] to shake off the bondage of corruption;[140] and to behave yourselves
as becometh the children of God, and inheritors of the kingdom of heaven.[141] God,
be assured, is infinitely worthy of our highest love, abundantly deserving of our
best services. He has done far more for our salvation, than ever we shall be able to
~~pay~~ [142] make sufficient returns for.[143] He hath created and preserved us, and therefore has a right to all that we can do in return for such blessings. Nay moreover, he
has redeemed us from sin and delivered us from the bondage of corruption;[144] and
therefore were it possible he has a just demand to more than we are able to pay.[145]
But his mercy is pleased in consideration of our weakness, and of[146] the poor corrupted state of our nature, to content himself with such services as we are able to
do for him. And since we have nothing else to return for all those favours and

---

[129] The word 'our' is absent from B.   [130] Cf. Rom. 1: 25.

[131] The word 'impertinence' is underlined in the MS. However, Charles seems then to have struck
out the underline by marking it through with three short vertical strokes.

[132] The word 'Nay' is underlined in the MS. However, Charles seems then to have struck out the
underline by marking it through with three short vertical strokes.

[133] The words 'Ye have likewise been shown how full such a course of life is of folly and impertinence,
of weakness and contempt. Nay, moreover ye have been told of the many and great dangers wherewith
it is attended: that it is a state of life which God hath nowhere promised to reward' are replaced in B
with 'Ye have likewise been shown the folly and danger of such a state; that God has nowhere promised
to reward it'.   [134] The word 'farther' is absent from B.

[135] The word 'expressly' is absent from B.

[136] Cf. Col. 3: 2; the words 'not on things which are below' are absent from B.

[137] The words 'That whosoever wittingly falls short of this does, for ought he knows, fall short of the
mercy of God' are replaced by 'That whoever wilfully falls short of this, falls short of the mercy of God'
in B.   [138] Cf. 1 Sam. 4: 9; 1 Cor. 16:13.

[139] In B the words 'to vindicate the dignity of your nature' have been written, but then struck out.

[140] Rom. 8: 21.   [141] Charles may be reflecting here on 1 Cor. 6: 9–10; Gal. 5: 21.

[142] At this point in the MS there appears the mark '†' indicating that a section is to be added. That
section, also marked with '†', appears at the end of the MS. It runs from 'to make sufficient returns
for' to 'than we are able to pay'.

[143] The words 'He has done far more for our salvation, than ever we shall be able to make sufficient
returns for' are absent from B.   [144] Rom. 8: 21.

[145] The fact that this inserted passage ends with the word 'pay', the word struck out immediately
before the passage was inserted, suggests the error of homeoteleuton. This perhaps adds further weight
to the hypothesis that this MS of Charles's sermon on 1 Kgs. 18: 21 was not the earliest he composed.
See the discussion in Chapter 4.   [146] The word 'of' is absent from B.

mercies he hath vouchsafed to confer upon us[147] he is pleased graciously to accept[148] the poor and beggarly oblation of ourselves. Less than this, he will not accept, had we the conscience to offer it: [149] and this sure no man will think too ~~much for~~ great a return for all the mighty obligations which[150] he hath received from God. For even whilst we serve God, we dignify our nature, augment[151] the perfection of our being and partake of his honour and glory. To be admitted to worship his God is doubtless the highest honour wherewith a creature can be p blest and to devote ourselves entirely to his service is only to be secured of our title to this dignity and prominence which the king of heaven and earth allows[152] us. There may be other fancied happiness, honour[153] and renown:[154] but in truth and[155] reality there is no happiness, no honour, no glory, but in the service of God. All the happiness that[156] the world can afford ~~them~~ us[157] at the[158] best is[159] but a suspension of misery. What can riches do for us but only keep us from the evil of want, we can enjoy no more than we want and a very little is sufficient to supply us with that. All beyond this[160] is nothing to us, mere superfluity which bringeth neither pleasure nor profit. And who, for such a reward as this, would forfeit those exalted pleasures, those refined delights[161] which flow so plentifully from the service of God. Delights[162] they are which fade not in the enjoyment,[163] which do not pall upon our senses nor destroy our palate, which[164] increase the more[165] we partake of them! Pleasures which extend our faculties of enjoyment, which furnish us with new senses as they bring us new matter of fruition. Such a season[166] of delights is his life who lives wholly devoted to God,[167] who suffers not the world to take any hold upon him, whose heart is fixed on heaven alone and whose soul is void of all cares but that of serving and pleasing God.[168] O glorious task, O blissful employment![169] It is the delight of angels, a forestalling of the joys of

---

[147] The words 'for all those favours and mercies he hath vouchsafed to confer upon us' are absent from B.

[148] The words 'he is pleased graciously to accept' are replaced by 'he graciously accepts' in B.

[149] The words 'had we the conscience to offer it' are absent from B.

[150] The word 'which' is absent from in B.

[151] The word 'augment' is replaced by 'increase' in B.

[152] The word 'allows' is replaced by 'vouchsafed' in B.

[153] The words 'happiness' and 'honour' are found in B, but Charles has indicated that they are to be transposed in the spoken form of the sermon.   [154] The word 'renown' is absent from B.

[155] The words 'truth and' are absent from B.   [156] The word 'that' is absent from B.

[157] The word 'is' is inserted at this point in B.   [158] The word 'the' is absent from B.

[159] The word 'is' is absent from B.   [160] The word 'this' is replaced by 'that' in B.

[161] The words 'those refined delights' are absent from B.

[162] The word 'delights' is replaced by 'pleasures' in B.   [163] Cf. Matt. 6: 19–20 and parallel.

[164] The word 'which' is replaced by 'but' in B.   [165] The words 'the more' are written twice in B.

[166] The word 'season' is replaced by 'scene' in B.

[167] At this point in the MS there appears the mark '†' indicating that a section is to be added. That section, also marked with '†', appears at the end of the MS. It runs from 'who suffers not the world' to 'but that of serving and pleasing God'.

[168] See the note immediately above. The fact that this inserted passage ends with the word 'God', the word struck out immediately before the passage was inserted, again suggests the error of homeoteleuton.

[169] Charles originally wrote 'enjoyment' and amended it to 'employment'.

futurity[170] and[171] a foretaste of the blessedness of heaven. Cast away from you therefore every thing but this love of God. Divest yourselves of every ~~thing~~ pleasure but that of serving him. Halt no longer between two opinions, but since ye own the Lord to be God, follow him and him alone. Serve him truly and faithfully with all your strength: love him with all your heart and mind.[172] Worship him in your body and in your ~~heart~~ spirit. Be perfect in the love and fear of God, that so your happiness may be perfected in the enjoyment of his heavenly kingdom throughout all ages; world without end.

[170] The word 'futurity' has been replaced by 'eternity' in B.
[171] The word 'and' is absent from B.   [172] Cf. Deut. 6: 4–5.

SERMON 3
PSALM 126: 7

INTRODUCTORY COMMENT

Charles preached this sermon at least three times in 1736 (18 April,[1] 6 June,[2] 10 October[3]), again in 1737 (14 August)[4] and again on 28 August of an unspecified year. Those occasions are noted on the front cover of the MS. This is therefore a sermon that Charles preached both during his time in America and back in England.

There is no indication on the MS that this is anything other than Charles's composition, and positive evidence for its authenticity has been outlined in Chapter 4. The conclusion reached there (which is in accordance with that of Heitzenrater) is that this sermon was by Charles and may therefore be taken as fully illustrative of his own views.

The MS is held at the John Rylands University Library of Manchester,[5] and comprises 10 leaves, five folded sheets which have been stitch-bound to form a booklet. The leaves are mostly written recto only. However, leaves 8 and 10 have some material verso. The first of these is clearly an addition by Charles himself and the point at which he intended it to be inserted into the text is indicated. The second section of verso material is written in short-hand and comprises a prayer and a blessing with which the sermon ends. All else is written in longhand.

The sermon was published as sermon VII in the 1816 edition, where, as always, there are numerous changes. For example, on page 1 of the MS we read that sufferings are 'sent' to lead to a higher perfection; in the 1816 edition the sufferings are not 'sent' but 'permitted'.[6] On page 6 of the MS we read that 'God hath died'; Charles's editor, aware no doubt of the possible theological implications of this statement, omits it.[7] (Patripassianism, the view that the Father suffered on the cross, was early rejected by the Christian church.) Such examples could be multiplied easily, though to do so seems unnecessary. The front of the MS carries the normal 'Ex^d W.P.' together with the additional words also, it seems, in W.P.'s hand, 'an excellent discourse'.

The central thrust of this sermon is plain enough: the lot of the Christian is not a particularly happy one. The followers of Christ are the followers of 'him who was a man of sorrows' and like him will be called upon to suffer, perhaps to the end of life. However, though the present lot of the Christian is not happy, the reward will be great for those who stay the course. This, then, like Sermon 1 on Philippians 3: 13–14, though to a lesser extent,

---

[1] Part of the journal entry reads 'I preached in the afternoon on "He that now goeth on his way weeping, and beareth forth good seed, shall doubtless come again with joy, and bring his sheaves with him"'. See MARC DDCW 10/2 *in loc.*; Telford, *Journal*, 39.
[2] Charles makes an entry for this day in the journal, but no reference to the sermon.
[3] 'Recovered a little strength in the sacrament but my body was extremely weakened by preaching twice' (MARC DDCW *in loc.*; Telford, *Journal*, 83).   [4] There is no entry in the journal for this day.
[5] MARC DDCW Box 5.   [6] *Sermons*, 114.   [7] Cf. *Sermons*, 121.

speaks of rewards for duties done.[8] That said, however, this sermon is in a generally lighter tone than the others from this period, and as one reads it one does not get the same sense of Charles's depressive personality struggling with its own wickedness. Indeed, there are clear signs and precursors here of Charles's later evangelical experience and proclamations of the standard evangelical themes of the all-sufficiency of the blood of Christ and the assurance of salvation that comes with the act of belief.

In this sermon Charles also presents his view on the nature, origin, purpose, and end of human virtues. The context in which this is worked out is that of an inaugurated eschatological scheme; the eschatology itself is of a traditional linear-apocalyptic kind. The moment one believes and places Christ in his proper place in one's life, argues Charles, one begins to live in the 'Kingdom of Heaven'. The joy that this brings is the same in kind, though not in degree, as that which is enjoyed in eternity, for 'heaven is begun upon earth'. That joy is the fruit of small seeds, and the seeds are human virtues. Virtues themselves spring from the graces of humility, faith, hope, and love. Supposed virtues that are not based upon these graces are in fact no virtues at all. The followers of Christ are hence living in the kingdom already. They already experience a measure of joy. 'But' writes Charles

> the hour is at hand, when that which is perfect shall come and that which is in part be done away. Yet a little while and he shall come again with fullness of joy to reap his entire harvest.

This, then, is an important text. It has every claim to being an original composition by Charles and witnesses his movement towards the kind of assurance of salvation in the blood of Christ that was later to be the hallmark of many of his hymns (and indeed was a characteristic of the evangelical revival in general). If the other sermons from this period are anything to go by, it is plain that this assurance did not stay with him. The text presents, however, a window on Charles's thought world during this period, a period during which, it seems, the clouds of self-doubt and soteriological uncertainty at least occasionally dissipated.

---

[8] Thus for example on p. 1 of the MS Charles writes, 'As sure as God is, and as he is a rewarder of them that diligently seek him, so sure no one virtue of any follower of Christ shall in any wise lose its reward. Only let him bear forth this good seed unto the end and though he may now go on his way weeping he shall doubtless come again with joy and bring his sheaves with him.'

I.N.D[1]

Psalm 126: 7[2]

He that now goeth on his way weeping, and bearing[3] forth good seed, shall doubtless come again with joy, and bring his sheaves with him.

1. Experience shows us, that even they who are Christians indeed, who serve God with all their strength,[4] may go on their way weeping, perhaps for many years, perhaps to the end of their lives. They are followers of him who was a man of sorrows and acquainted with grief.[5] And if any man will come after him, he must deny himself and take up his cross.[6] He must suffer with his master more or less; being, like him, to be made perfect through sufferings.[7]

2. Indeed for this very cause are those sufferings sent to lead them to higher perfection. They go on their way weeping, that the good seed they bear forth may yield them the more fruit.[8] And that good seed, even all those Christian virtues, which are perfected by affliction shall in due time grow up into a plentiful harvest of rest and joy and life eternal.

3. The certainty of this great truth is pointed out to us by the very manner wherein it is revealed. Heaven and earth may, nay they must pass away; but not one tittle of this shall pass.[9] As sure as God is, and as he is a rewarder of them that diligently seek him,[10] so sure no one virtue of any follower of Christ shall in any wise lose its reward.[11] Only let him bear forth this good seed unto the end and though he may now go on his way weeping he shall doubtless come again with joy and bring his sheaves with him.

What I intend at present is briefly to explain, how every virtue is the seed of joy eternal: a great truth! such as deserves your frequent thoughts and deepest consideration. The time indeed will not suffer me to consider now every particular Christian virtue, but only those general graces which we can never consider

---

[1] '*In Nomine Dei*'; this invocation is used also in Sermons 4, 5, 6, 16, and 22, those on 1 John 3: 14; Titus 3: 8; Rom. 3: 23–4; Prov. 11.30; and Matt. 6.22–3. On the use of this invocation see further Outler, *Sermons*, iv. 268 n. 1. These are the first words of the sermon itself, however on the front cover Charles has written out his text: 'Psalm 126.7. He that now goeth on his way weeping and beareth forth good seed, shall doubtless come again with joy, and bring his sheaves with him.' This is from the *BCP*. He records also a register, which reads
Preached at Frederica, April 18. 1736 in the afternoon
at Savannah June 6. 1736 in the Morning
at Christ-Church in Boston N[ew] E[ngland] October 10, 1736 Morning
Duke-Street Chapel August 14, 1737
St John's August 28
Also on the front cover are the words '1736 April 18 at Frederica—June 6 at Savannah', 'Ex^d W.P.', and 'An excellent discourse', though they have been written in another hand, probably that of W.P.
[2] As was noted above, the verse number is taken from the *BCP*.
[3] *Sic*; the word is 'beareth' in the *BCP*.   [4] There is an echo here of Deut. 6: 5.
[5] Isa. 53: 3.   [6] Cf. Mark 8: 34 and parallels; 10: 21.   [7] Cf. Heb. 2: 10.
[8] Cf. Mark 4: 8 and parallel.   [9] Cf. Matt. 5: 18.   [10] Cf. Heb. 11: 6
[11] Cf. Matt. 10: 42.

enough: humility and faith and hope and love. Yet this is almost the same thing; since these are the common root of all the particular virtues: none of which has any worth nor in truth any being unless it spring from these. It will therefore suffice, to show in few words, that each of these is the seed of joy; that every one of these graces, although when first sown it may be small as a grain of mustard seed yet as it groweth up shooteth out great branches[12] full of delight and blessedness.

2.[13] This joy I therefore called eternal, because the holy scriptures assure us, that it is the same in kind, though not in degree, with that we shall enjoy to eternity. For it should be well observed and always remembered, that heaven is begun upon earth. And accordingly our saviour often means by 'the kingdom of heaven' that temper of mind which a Christian now enjoys. He begins to enjoy it when he begins to be a Christian, when Christ begins to reign in his soul. And the more absolutely he reigns there, the more happiness he enjoys. For as all the poor in spirit,[14] all that believe in God, all that trust in him, all that love him, are blessed; so the greater their humility, faith, hope and love, the greater is their blessedness. And thus as they go on from strength to strength,[15] they go on from one measure of joy to another, till what was sown on earth, be removed into a better soil, and grow up to perfection in heaven.[16]

But before this is explained farther, it may be proper to consider an objection which almost every one is ready to make. And this is; that this doctrine, 'every Christian is happy,' is contrary to experience, there being many good Christians who scarce know what joy means. I answer 1. is that mind which was in Christ[17] in these they call Christians? Have they those tempers which he requires? Are they renewed in humble faith, and hope and love? Else they are no Christians at all; and however unhappy they are it is nothing to the present question. 2. Supposing they have some degree of these Christian tempers, have they such a degree of them as they might have? Have they so much of them as the first Christians had? Have they so much as God would give them too, if they would receive it? If not let none wonder that a little holiness gives, if any, but a little, happiness. 3. If they have a deep humility, a strong faith, a lively hope, and a fervent love sometimes, do they not at other times droop, and so faint in their minds as to become like common men? If they do, no one can expect their joy should reach farther than the cause of it; they cannot be always happy till they are always holy. When they are always heavenly-minded, they shall then rejoice evermore!

3. Yet 'tis most true as was before observed that till that happy hour, when God shall wipe away all tears from their eyes,[18] even they who bear forth this seed of joy may go on their way weeping. They may, nay they must, endure affliction, for so did the captain of their salvation.[19] But 'tis as true that a Christian knows to rejoice

[12] Cf. Mark 4: 31–2 and parallels.
[13] *Sic*; the numbering of the paragraphs is not consistent.   [14] Cf. Matt. 5: 3.
[15] Psa. 84: 7.   [16] Cf. 1 Cor. 15, esp. v. 42.   [17] Phi. 2: 5.
[18] Rev. 7: 17; 21: 4.   [19] Cf. Heb. 2: 10.

not only after but even in tribulation. As in the laughter of the wicked, the heart is sorrowful,[20] so in the tears of the righteous there is joy.[21] He does not stay till his afflictions are overpassed, but in everything giveth thanks. Though he cannot but feel when he is in pain, yet in the midst of it, he can 'rejoice in the Lord'.[22]

Let us now consider this great truth a little more particularly. The first of all Christian graces and the foundation of all is humility: a deep sense of our spiritual poverty, a feeling knowledge that we are nothing but sin and deserve nothing but shame. And a clear sight that we have nothing and can do nothing no, not so much as think a good thought. And is such a virtue as this the seed of joy? Yea, as surely as it is the seed of all other virtues. As surely as it is contrary to pride which is the seed of all torment. No sooner does humility enter a soul, which before was all storm and tempest, but[23] it says to that sea 'Peace, be still', and there is a great calm.[24] There is indeed in every branch of humility a sweetness which cannot be uttered. There is pain, 'tis true, in the entrance into it, but that very pain is full of pleasure. There is mourning joined with it; but even that mourning is blessedness; it is health to the soul, and marrow to the bones.[25] It heals even while it wounds;[26] it delights at the same time and in the same degree wherein it softens the heart. Humility not only removes all that pain and anguish with which pride drinks up the blood and spirits; it not only plants peace wherever it comes, and brings rest to the weary soul; but joy too and such joy as together with it increases more and more unto the perfect day.[27]

5. Humility cannot but lead to faith: a sight of our disease makes us soon fly to the cure of it. Who can feel himself sick and not long to be made whole? What contrite sinner is not glad of a saviour? And he is the more glad, the more firmly he believes, that he is able and willing to save to the uttermost; able to save all that believe, for he is God! And willing, for he is man! Here is joy! Joy which none can divide from faith! Joy unspeakable and full of glory![28] God, the Lord God, Jehovah, God over all,[29] the God to whom all things are possible,[30] hath undertaken the cause of lost man! He hath promised, he hath sworn to save them! Nay, he hath done more than this: he hath bowed the heavens and come down:[31] he hath been made man! He hath lived, suffered, died[32] to save them! Yea, tell it out in all lands! God[33] hath died! He hath died to save man! Let the heavens rejoice, and let the earth be glad.[34] Publish ye, praise ye, and say, this is the victory which

[20] Cf. Prov. 14: 13.   [21] Cf. Ps. 126: 6 (*BCP*).   [22] Cf. *inter alia* Zech. 10.7; Phil. 3: 1; 4: 4.

[23] The word 'but' has been struck out and the word 'than' inserted above it. However, the hand does not appear to be that of Charles himself.   [24] Cf. Mark 4: 39 and parallels.

[25] Cf. Prov. 3: 8.   [26] Cf. Deut. 32: 39.   [27] Prov. 4: 18.

[28] 1 Pet. 1: 8.   [29] Cf. Ps. 83: 18.   [30] Mark 10: 27 and parallel.

[31] Cf. Ps. 144: 5.

[32] The word 'nay' has been inserted above the line before 'died'. However, the hand appears not to be that of Charles himself.

[33] The word 'God' has been struck out and the word 'Christ' written in the margin. However, the hand appears not to be that of Charles himself.   [34] Cf. 1 Chr. 16: 31; Ps. 96: 11.

overcometh the world, even our faith.[35] If we can believe, all things are possible to him that believeth:[36] to him it is easy, 'to rejoice evermore'![37] Yea, he cannot but rejoice in thy strength, O Lord Christ, and be exceeding glad of thy salvation![38]

6. Now if it be so joyful a thing to believe that Christ died to save sinners, what must it be to add to our faith hope? To be assured that he died to save us? If the knowing that a ransom[39] is paid for lost man, and a new covenant of mercy given him, be the source of a peace which passeth all understanding,[40] yea, of joy unspeakable, and full of glory,[41] how does he rejoice, who feels within his own soul, that this ransom is paid for him? Whose heart assures him, that he is within that covenant and shall find mercy even in the day of vengeance? If the belief, that all who are faithful servants of their great master have an house eternal in the heavens, be a continual spring of gladness of heart; how shall not his heart sing for joy, with whom the spirit of God bears witness[42] that he is faithful? Who can lay hold of those great and precious promises,[43] and lay them close to his own soul! Whose eye God hath opened to look into eternity, and to take a view of those mansions of glory, into which he knows his blessed Lord is gone before, to prepare a place for him.[44]

7. Such joy have all they that hope in God, and the stronger their hope the greater their joy. But this is not all: for hope leads to love; and in the love of God joy is perfected. Very excellent things are spoken of the happiness that flows from loving God. But whosoever has this love shed abroad in his heart,[45] feels more than can ever be spoken, yea though he spake with the tongue of men and angels,[46] he could not utter the joy of charity.[47] It is the hidden manna,[48] the inexpressible sweetness, whereof none can know, but he that tastes it. But some little imperfect knowledge thereof may be had from what appears in outward exercises of it. Not to insist on the joy, with which one that loves God shows all love to his neighbour for God's sake; how is he rejoiced, whenever he has an opportunity of pouring out his heart before him? How is his soul satisfied as it were with marrow and fatness, when his mouth praiseth him with joyful lips![49] How does his joy still increase when he joins with the congregation of the faithful in prayer and praise and thanksgiving. ~~And how does it overflow all bounds, when in memory of him whom his soul loveth, he eateth the living bread which came down from heaven, and drinketh of the cup of salvation!~~[50] He[51] needeth not the exhortations of man, no, nor even the *command* of God to drag him to the house of prayer. He needeth not

---

[35] 1 John 5: 4.   [36] Mark 9: 23.   [37] 1 Thess. 5: 16.

[38] Cf. Ps. 21: 1.   [39] Cf. Mark 10: 45 and parallel; 1 Tim. 2: 6.   [40] Phil. 4: 7.

[41] 1 Pet. 1: 8.   [42] Rom. 8: 16.   [43] 2 Pet. 1: 4.

[44] Cf. John 14: 1–3.   [45] Cf. Rom. 5: 5.   [46] Cf. 1 Cor. 13: 1.

[47] Cf. 1 Cor. 13: 1.   [48] Rev. 2: 17.   [49] Cf. Ps. 63: 5.

[50] The words that have here been struck out appear in slightly modified form at the end of the paragraph.

[51] The words from this point to 'cup of salvation' have been written on the verso of the preceeding page and a mark made in the text indicating the point at which they were to be inserted. This emendation is the work of Charles.

to be assured that if [he]⁵² does forbear assembling himself with the people of God, as the manner of *most* is, he thereforeby breaks the communion of saints, he renounces the privileges of his baptism, he casts himself out of the congregation of faithful people; he excommunicates, or cuts himself off from the body of Christ, and that consequently Christ shall profit him nothing.⁵³ No,—on the contrary he is glad when they say unto him, let us go unto the house of the Lord;⁵⁴ but his joy overflows all bounds, when in memory of him,⁵⁵ whom his soul loveth,⁵⁶ he eateth the living bread which came down from heaven⁵⁷, and drinketh the cup of salvation.⁵⁸

8. Lo thus is the man blest that feareth the Lord!⁵⁹ That beareth forth good seed! These sheaves shall he bring home in this life, however he may now⁶⁰ go on his way weeping! These are the first fruits which he shall receive even here: but the harvest is not yet. He as yet knows and loves God only in part, therefore he as yet enjoys him in part only. But the hour is at hand, when that which is perfect shall come and that which is in part be done away.⁶¹ Yet a little while and he shall come again with fullness of joy to reap his entire harvest. Behold, one standeth at the door,⁶² who will complete what he hath begun, who shall ripen the seeds of grace into glory; and instead of that dew of heaven which now refreshes his soul, shall give him rivers of pleasures⁶³ evermore!⁶⁴

---

⁵² The word 'he', which is clearly needed in this context, has been added above the line. However, the hand appears not to be that of Charles himself   ⁵³ Gal. 5: 2.
⁵⁴ Ps. 122: 1.   ⁵⁵ Cf. Luke 22: 19; 1 Cor. 11: 25.   ⁵⁶ Cf. Song of Songs 3: 1–4.
⁵⁷ Cf. John 6: 33, 41, 50, 51, 58.   ⁵⁸ Cf. Ps. 116: 13.   ⁵⁹ Cf. Ps. 128: 4.
⁶⁰ The word 'now' has been inserted above the line. The addition appears to be in the hand of Charles.   ⁶¹ Cf. 1 Cor. 13: 10.
⁶² Cf. Rev. 3: 20; Mark 13: 29 and parallel. If Charles has in mind the latter, which seems more probable in the context, it indicates his expectation of the return of Jesus soon.   ⁶³ Cf. Ps. 36: 8.
⁶⁴ Charle.s has written 4 lines of shorthand on the back cover of the booklet. That shorthand reads, 'Grant we beseech thee Almighty God that the words which we have heard this day with outward ears may through thy grace be so grafted inwardly in our hearts that they may bring forth in us the fruit for good living to the honour and praise of thy holy name through Jesus Christ our Lord' (lines 1–2; this is the one of the Collects which may be said after the Offertory in the *BCP*). 'The peace of God which passeth all understanding, keep your hearts and minds in the knowledge and love of God and of his son Jesus Christ our Lord; and the blessing of God almighty, the Father, Son and Holy Ghost, be amongst you, and remain with you always' (lines 3–4; this is the *BCP* post-communion blessing).

SERMON 4
1 JOHN 3: 14

INTRODUCTORY COMMENT

Charles preached from his sermon on 1 John 3: 14 at least twenty-one times during 1738 and 1739. The dates and places are recorded on the MS itself and almost all can be confirmed in the journal. These were almost certainly not the only occasions on which he preached from this scripture text, though just how frequently he made use of this particular written sermon cannot be ascertained. However, there is strong evidence for at least one further use.[1] The sermon itself is divided into two very unequal parts; part one is approximately 6,700 words, part two 1,600 words. It appears from the register that during July and August 1738 Charles preached both halves on the same day (even if not back to back); from September 1738, however, he began to preach only one part per visit. On 3 September 1738, for example, he preached part one at St Botolph's, returning the following week (10 September) to preach part two.

There is no reason to think that this is anything other than a Charles Wesley composition. It is written entirely in Charles's idiosyncratic form of Byrom's shorthand, with the exception of the sermon register on the verso of leaf 1, which is in longhand. The MS, now held at the John Rylands University Library of Manchester,[2] comprises 14 separate leaves which have been stitch-bound to form a booklet. Leaves 13–14 are completely blank, perhaps indicating that Charles proposed to add to the sermon at a later stage, which would have balanced the unequal parts somewhat. Leaves 2–12 contain the sermon itself; 2–11 are written recto and verso, leaf 12 recto only. The verso of leaf 1 to the recto of leaf 12 are numbered by Charles as pages 2–21. The first leaf forms a front cover. The recto is blank while the verso contains the sermon register. As is clear from the transcription here produced, the text of the MS is fairly neat, though there are in places minor additions and deletions, all of which appear to be in Charles's own hand. They have been indicated in the notes.

In 1987 a transcription of this sermon was produced by Albin and Beckerlegge and published by the Wesley Historical Society; extensive use of that transcription has been made here. Proper credit for that ground-breaking work must be given, and it is a pleasure to acknowledge my indebtedness to those earlier scholars. However, in preparing this text for publication the original shorthand MS has been thoroughly re-examined, and numerous alterations have been made or suggested to the Albin-Beckerlegge edition. The more significant differences between this form of the text and that presented by Albin and Beckerlegge are indicated in the notes, as are the places where, although the Albin-Beckerlegge reading seems probable, the shorthand itself is insufficiently clear to make the reading certain. In these places a literal, unexpanded form of the shorthand has been given in the notes for the reader's further consideration.

---

[1] See note 1 on the text itself.　　[2] MARC DDCW Box 5.

Throughout the MS Charles has indicated by the use of quotation marks the fact that he has borrowed material from other sources. The first major example comes on the recto of leaf 2 (implicitly Charles's page 1, although not numbered by him) and runs onto the recto of leaf 3 (Charles's page 3). This section, as Albin and Beckerlegge note, is taken from John Norris's *Practical Discourses on Several Divine Subjects*. The extensive quotations in the rest of the sermon are composites of passages from the Bible.[3] For example, with the exception of the first half-line or so, Charles's page 15 is made up entirely of quotations from passages such as Isaiah 49, 51, and 61.

The main theological point that Charles makes in this sermon is plain enough. There are three types of persons in the world. They are those who know not God and do not seek him, those who know not God and do seek him, and those who know God. The first are in the state of natural man who, as a son of Adam, is born in a state of sin and death. Baptism temporarily corrects this situation and restores to the individual the image of God. But this is soon marred once again: ''Tis happened unto them according to the true proverb, the dog is turned to his own vomit again, and the sow that was washed to her wallowing in the mire.' The second state is that represented by the gaoler in Acts 16: 29–30 who cries out 'what must I do to be saved?' God draws such people on and preserves them from the onslaughts of the enemy. They have a brief period free from spiritual warfare, have peace with God and can momentarily at least experience a 'joy unspeakable'. However, this is not to last. War breaks out in their members and the enemy assaults. This is a difficult time, for the individual seeks God and yet finds himself fast bound by sin and 'the more he struggles, the faster he is bound'. He now finds himself convicted not only of sin (which was his experience as he emerged from the first state), but also of his own inability to escape from it. He still serves sin, though now (contrary to what was operative in the first state) only reluctantly. Like Paul in Romans 7 he cries out in anguish 'Oh, wretched man that I am, who shall deliver me from the body of this death?' It is now that the real conversion can take place. (It should be remembered that this sermon was first preached only two months after Charles's own 'strange palpitation of the heart'.) Into this situation comes the spirit of God with the offer of justification on the basis of faith and faith alone. The third state results.

This, then, is an interesting and important text. There is no question but that it is Charles's own work; even those who dispute (unconvincingly, it has been argued) Charles's authorship of sermons 1, 2, and 3, on Philippians 3: 13–14, 1 Kings 18: 21, and Psalm 126: 7, do not quarrel with the view that this is Charles's own (see Chapter 4). Further, because this is such an extensive text (in excess of 8,000 words in total) it provides far more than just a passing glimpse of Charles's theological views and his rhetorical, homiletic, and theological method in general. The text is important also in that it is almost certainly the earliest of Charles's 'post-Pentecost' sermons to have survived; as such it provides, along with the journal, the first[4] clear insight into Charles's state of mind during those heady days of the summer of 1738.

---

[3] There is also one quotation from Pascal, noted in the text.

[4] This is not of course to deny the potential importance of the 'conversion hymn', but merely to draw attention to the fact that the prose works of Charles, where they exist, must be taken into consideration in any attempt to reconstruct his theology. Assuming that the 'conversion hymn' was 'Where shall my wondering soul begin', which is itself open to some question (see Tyson, *Charles Wesley: A Reader*, 101–5), it is plain that there is much in this sermon, as in the journal, that can be added to that poetic account of his experiences.

Sermon Register[1]

July 16, 1738	S. George Martyr, Queen's Square Black-friars[2]	
July 23, ——	All-hallows, Thames-Street at[3] twice[4]	
Aug. 13, ——	Islington at twice[5]	
Aug. 26,[6] ——	S. John Zackary near Bloomsbury at 2[ce7]	
Aug. 29, ——	Castle, Oxford[8]	
Sept. 3, ——	S. Botolph's, little Britain	1 pt.[9]
Sept. 10, ——	S. Botolph's, little Britain	2d pt.[10]
Oct. 1,[11] ——	S. Margaret's, Westminster	1 pt.[12]
Oct. 29, ——	S. George's, Bloomsbury	1 pt.
	~~Sir G[eorge] Wheeler Chapel~~	
	Ironmonger's Almshouse	1 pt.[13]
Nov. 5, ——	Shadwell	1 pt.
	S. Alban's, Wood Street	1 pt.[14]
Nov. 19, ——	Bishopsgate	1 pt.
	S. George's, Bloomsbury	2d pt.[15]

[1] This extensive record of Charles's preaching is located on the verso of leaf 1. To this record should be added also 28 January, 1739 Bexley ('I preached on the 3 states at Bexley', MARC DDCW 10/2 *in loc.*; Telford, *Journal*, 219). Also to be noted is a letter from Martha Jones to Charles Wesley dated 1 June, 1740 in which she states, 'When you came amongst us then I blessed my dear Lord who out of his tender love did not in this sense leave us comfortless. Your sermon of the threefold state which I often heard with tears showed me I was one of those that was seeking God, but as yet had not found him.' It is not clear from this when precisely she heard Charles preach, but it may be that it relates to an occasion in 1740 itself. This letter is uncatalogued, but may be found in the MAB section of the archive in a folio entitled 'Early Methodist Volume', item number 3.

[2] Cf. MARC DDCW 10/2 *in loc.*; Telford, *Journal*, 190.

[3] Albin and Beckerlegge have simply 'a' at this point. There is a crease in the MS, which would not have been clear in a photocopy. The 't' of 'at' is concealed by that crease.

[4] The words 'at twice' are clear in the MS. The meaning is probably 'on two occasions', i.e. that Charles preached the whole of this sermon at All Hallows, and later at Islington and Bloomsbury, where he also records he preached 'at twice', but did so in two parts and at two different times of the day (see further *OED* on this phrase). I am indebted to an anonymous copy-editor at Oxford University Press for alerting me to this probability.

[5] Cf. MARC DDCW 10/2 *in loc.*; Telford, *Journal*, 198. 'Preached at Islington; gave the sacrament'. Again the words 'at twice' are clear in the MS.

[6] This appears to be an error. The date should be 27 August, when Charles entered into his journal 'Preached at S. John's the 3 fold state, and helped administer the sacrament to a very large congregation' (MARC DDCW 10/2 *in loc.*; Telford, *Journal*, 201).

[7] The words 'at 2[ce]' ('at twice') are clear in the MS.

[8] Cf. MARC DDCW 10/2 *in loc.*; Telford, *Journal*, 201; 'Preached to the poor prisoners in the Castle'. 'The Castle' was a prison on the outskirts of Oxford whose occupants had long been of concern to Charles.   [9] MARC DDCW 10/2 *in loc.*; Telford, *Journal*, 203.

[10] Ibid.

[11] There is a further vertical stroke of the pen at this point in the MS, whose meaning is unclear.

[12] MARC DDCW 10/2 *in loc.*; Telford, *Journal*, 206.

[13] MARC DDCW 10/2 *in loc.*; Telford, *Journal*, 210.

[14] Ibid.; 'and preached threefold state at St. Alban's, Wood Street'.

[15] MARC DDCW 10/2 *in loc.*; Telford, *Journal*, 213.

Nov. 26, ———	Coggs	1 pt.[16]
Jan. 7, 1739	Alphage	1 pt.
Mar. 18, ———	S. Catherine's	1 pt.
April 1, ———	S. Catherine's	2 pt.[17]

I. N. D.[18]

1 John 3, the former part of the 14th verse, 'We know that we have passed from death unto life'.

In these words of the beloved disciple,[19] we have discussed the two opposite states of nature and grace, into the former of which our first birth introduced us, into the latter, our second birth in Christ Jesus.[20] But between these two is, as it were,[21] a middle state, which we are equally concerned to understand aright, lest we deceive ourselves by an ill-grounded hope, and forever stop short of the glory of God.[22]

I trust there is no one here, who will not seriously attend, while in the name of our great prophet[23] and teacher, now present among and with us, I endeavour

I. to explain these three states; and

II. to apply myself particularly to the persons under each.

I begin with explaining these three states, and this I shall first do in general and chiefly in the words of an excellent divine of our own church;[24] 'Who reduces all the men in the world, and every particular man in the several periods of his life, to one of these three orders. Either he is one of those, who do not apprehend sin as an evil, who either ~~through want of understanding and reflexion~~ have not awakened to any sense of its malignity, or through debauchery and habitual viciousness have lost it, and so will and choose sin purely and entirely with unity of consent, and without any mixture of reluctancy (which is the most exalted pitch of wickedness that a creature is capable of): or else he is one of those who do indeed look upon sin as evil, and as such refuse, and are averse to it; but not looking upon it

---

[16] MARC DDCW 10/2 *in loc.;* Telford, *Journal*, 214; 'preached the threefold state at Coggs' [near Witney, Oxon].   [17] MARC DDCW 10/2 *in loc.;* Telford, *Journal*, 227.

[18] On the use of I.N.D see the note on Sermon 3.

[19] Charles is assuming, of course, that the author of the gospel is the author of the epistle, and that that person is to be identified with the 'beloved disciple' or 'other disciple' of John's gospel (Cf. John 13: 23; 18: 16; 20: 2 *et passim*).   [20] Cf. John 3: 3 ff.

[21] The words 'as it were' have been inserted by Charles above the line.

[22] Cf. Rom. 3: 23 and Sermon 1 (Phil. 3: 13–14) above.   [23] Luke 7: 16.

[24] As Albin and Beckerlegge note, and I have used their information here, the remainder of this paragraph and the three which follow are extracted from John Norris's *Practical Discourses on Several Divine Subjects*, 4 vols. (London: 1690, and republished frequently thereafter). The paragraphs here come from the first volume, 'Christian Blessedness: Or, Discourses on the Beatitudes', discourse 4 on Matthew 5: 6, (pp. 81 f. in the 1707 edn.). This volume by Norris was a standard part of the Oxford Methodist reading programme, as is made clear in Ingham's diary. See Heitzenrater (ed.), *Diary of an Oxford Methodist*, 23–42, where Ingham notes that on 15 July 1734 he 'began Norris' Beatitudes and Discourses'.

always as the greatest, nay as the only evil, do often refuse it only imperfectly, so that in effect they do choose it by yielding to, and choosing it sometimes: or else lastly, he is one of those[25] who looking upon sin not only under the notion of evil, but as the greatest, nay as the only evil, refuse it not only in some certain respects, but truly and absolutely so as not by any means to be persuaded to commit it.'

'These three degrees take in all mankind: and accordingly the scriptures make mention of a threefold law; the first is the law of sin, which is in the members (Rom 7.23), the second is the law of the mind or conscience (Rom 7.23), the third is the law of the Spirit of life (Rom 8.2). These three laws answer exactly to the three moral states of human nature. Under the first law, the law of sin, are those who will and embrace sin purely and entirely: under the second law, the law of the mind, are those who refuse, and stand averse to sin in some certain respects as evil, but yet do in effect will and choose it, by choosing it sometimes: under the third law, the law of the Spirit of life, are those who absolutely and thoroughly[26] refuse to commit sin'.

'The first of these states is a state of mere sin and death, and those of this order are they who are said to be dead in trespasses and sins (Eph 2.1). The second is a state of imperfect life, the third is a state of a ~~true~~ health and vigour. The first is a state of rest and acquiescence in sin; the second is a state of contention; the third is a state of victory. In the first state, the mind is laid fast in a deep sleep; in the second she is between sleeping and waking; in the third she is broad awake and will come to herself. He that is in the first state is born only of the flesh, and has no higher principle in him; he is that natural man who perceiveth not the things of the Spirit of God (1 Cor 2.14). He that is in the second, has as it were some quickening motions, some ineffectual stirrings and endeavours towards the divine life; but he that is in the third is born of the Spirit and of God, and doth not commit sin because his seed remaineth in him.'

'The first of these states makes no pretensions to salvation; and the second, though it seem to have something of life and righteousness in it, is yet such as is consistent with the final and absolute prevalency and dominion of sin, and consequently such as cannot qualify a man for pardon, or put him into a state of grace and salvation. Whereas in the last, the principle of divine life is so strong, as not only to resist, but to overcome sin; and he that is thus spiritually alive is alive indeed; alive to himself and alive to God; and if he abide in this life, shall live forever.'[27]

---

[25] The words 'of those' have been added by Charles above the line.

[26] Albin and Beckerlegge suggest that one might read 'truly' for 'thoroughly' at this point. The ambiguity arises because the initial vertical stroke may be taken as either 't' or 'th'. However, while the sign for 'th' is the same as that for 't', they are distinguished in the shorthand system by the relative size of the attached strokes which follow; where 'th' is meant the attached stokes are written half size. As is reflected in Albin and Beckerlegge's note, the combined sign is not entirely clear in the MS. On balance, however, 'thrli' seems more probable than 'trli'.

[27] At this point the extract from Norris's *Practical Discourses* comes to an end.

From this general discussion, any person may easily perceive his true state; for to one of these three every one of us, and of all mankind, must belong. 'Three sorts of men there are in the world and no more: those who, having found God, resign themselves up entirely to his service; those who having not yet found him, do indefatigably search after him; and lastly those who have neither found him, nor are inclined to seek him. The first are happy and wise; the third are unhappy and fools; the second must be owned to be wise, as they own themselves to be unhappy' (Pascal's *Thoughts*).[28]

Having spoken of these states in general, I shall endeavour to discuss them more particularly. And first as to those who are dead in trespasses and sins;[29] whom the Lord[30] of life points out under the same character, 'Let the dead bury their dead.'[31] In the midst of life these are in death, even that spiritual death which Adam tasted together with the forbidden fruit. God, who cannot lie,[32] had plainly told him, 'in the day that thou eatest thereof, thou shalt surely die'.[33] The sentence was accordingly executed. The union of his soul with God (in which his spiritual life consisted, like as the natural life stands in the conjunction of the soul with the body) this union, I say, was dissolved. His soul was separated from God, and in the day that he ate, he spiritually died.[34]

Thus Adam died and all in him. By one man sin entered into the world, and death by sin, and so death passed upon all men.[35] Adam begat a son in his own likeness, after his image,[36] not that of his Creator, in which he himself was made,[37] but from which he fell through sin, and we in him.[38] It is true, at the moment of our baptism, our second birth, that image was restored to us, a principle of divine life infused, and the child of wrath[39] became the child of God. But alas, the soul of most of us soon lost that second life: again was that image wholly impaired and diffused; and the image of the world so strongly graven on it, that God's is no more discernible there. The seed of immortality is trodden down and the fowls of the air have devoured it.[40] Our spark[41] is put out, our principle lost, our life extinguished. Pride and self-will have recovered their ground: the strong man armed[42] has made his re-entrance, and again keeps possession of our soul.[43] Sin has revived and we have died.[44] Walking after the flesh, we are made subject to the law of sin and

---

[28] Blaise Pascal, *Pensées*, ed. Louis Lafuma, trans. John Warrington (London: Dent, 1973), 257.

[29] Eph. 2: 1.

[30] Albin and Beckerlegge have 'law' at this point. The shorthand reads simply 'l' with a point so positioned as to indicate a contraction. The context suggests 'Lord'.   [31] Matt. 8: 22.

[32] Titus 1: 2.   [33] Gen. 2: 17.

[34] Here Charles is reflecting a widely held eighteenth-century view that the 'death' which Adam was to suffer on the very day that he ate the fruit was spiritual and not literal. This was in part to solve the problem of the precise wording of Gen. 2: 17, 'in the day that thou eatest thereof, thou shalt surely die'.

[35] Rom. 5: 12.   [36] Gen. 5: 3.   [37] Cf. Gen. 1: 26–7.

[38] Cf. 1 Cor. 15: 22.   [39] Cf. Eph. 2: 3.   [40] Cf. Mark 4: 4 and parallels.

[41] This may be based on Job 18: 5.   [42] Luke 11: 21 and parallels.

[43] Charles is perhaps alluding here to Matt. 12: 45 and parallel.   [44] Cf. Rom. 7: 9.

death,[45] living after the flesh, we are again dead. For to be carnally minded is death, as to be spiritually minded is life and peace.[46]

Here then you see the cause why ~~those~~[47] many who had put on Christ in baptism,[48] are stripped of him, their imputed righteousness,[49] and clothed again in their own shame and sin and misery. They now appear the genuine children of their father the devil,[50] they bear his image, and do his works. They fulfil the lusts of the flesh,[51] living without hope and without God in the world.[52] 'Tis happened unto them according to the true proverb, the dog is turned to his own vomit again, and the sow that was washed to her wallowing in the mire.'[53]

But are these, who live in gross and open sins, sins against the second table,[54] are these I say the only baptised heathens? So the prince of this world[55] would persuade his subjects. While they do no harm, that is, are guilty of no notorious vice, he tells them they are safe enough. A little outward religion, added occasionally to a worldly life is abundantly sufficient to denominate them good Christians; but if over and above all this, they are tolerably constant in the means of grace (which 'tis surely all our bounden duty to be) and sometimes reach out their hands to the poor, this sets them even above our good sort of[56] people, and makes them great saints ~~indeed~~![57]

But alas, what shall it profit them to have a form of godliness while they deny the power of it?[58] They still live in all worldly tempers, making provision for the flesh to fulfil the lusts thereof,[59] the desires, the mere unregenerate nature. Self-will is the principle of all their actions. They think themselves at full liberty to please themselves, though Christ pleased not himself;[60] nay they scruple not to avow it. With them it is a sufficient reason for doing anything, that they have a mind to it. Tell them from our Lord, 'that except a man forsake all that he hath, he cannot be Christ's disciple,'[61] and you bring strange things to their ears.[62] Jesus said unto his disciples, 'If any man will come after me let him deny himself, and take up his cross, and follow me.'[63] Why, this they have often read, but never

---

[45] Cf. Rom. 8: 1–2.   [46] Rom. 8: 6.

[47] The word 'those' does not appear in the Albin-Beckerlegge text. The struck-out shorthand sign is reasonably clear in the MS.   [48] Gal. 3: 27.

[49] Cf. Rom. 4: 22.   [50] Cf. John 8: 44.   [51] Cf. *inter alia* Rom. 13: 14; Eph. 2: 3.

[52] Cf. Eph. 2: 12.   [53] 2 Pet. 2: 22.

[54] The meaning here is not absolutely clear. The shorthand reads '2ᵈ tb', which Albin and Beckerlegge expand, probably correctly, to 'second table', i.e the second table of the law, containing commandments 5–10.

[55] The title 'prince of this world' is used of the devil in John 12: 31; 14: 30; 16: 11.

[56] The shorthand at this point reads 'gd sf ppl' which Albin and Beckerlegge expand to 'good safe people'. The phrase 'good sort of people' appears also in the sermons on John 8: 1 and in Luke 18: 9.

[57] The word 'indeed' does not appear in Albin and Beckerlegge's text. The sign 'ndd' is relatively clear in the MS, though it has been struck through making it partially unreadable. The word 'great' has been written above the line. It appears, then, that Charles originally wrote 'and makes them saints indeed!', which he then changed to 'and makes them great saints!'   [58] 2 Tim. 3: 5.

[59] Rom. 13: 14.   [60] Rom. 15: 3.   [61] Cf. Luke 14: 33.

[62] Cf. Acts 17: 20.   [63] Matt. 16: 24 and parallel.

thought it concerned them; this[64] he meant only of his apostles, nay, but he turned to the multitude[65] and said unto them, 'Whosoever doth not bear his cross and come after me, cannot be my disciple.'[66]

These words demonstrate the utter impossibility of any man's becoming a Christian till he is thoroughly[67] convinced that he is not his own, he is not the proprietor of himself, or any thing he enjoys, he has no right to dispose of his goods, body, soul, or any of the actions or possessions of him; and till, agreeable to this conviction, he does endeavour to live, not to himself, not to pursue his own desires, not to please himself, or to suffer his own will to be any principle of action to him.

Till he has thus renounced himself, he has no share in Christ, but is as truly dead to God as if he lived in all manner of sins and wickedness. For 'he that liveth in pleasure is dead while he liveth.'[68] He has no more appreciation of spiritual things than a dead body has of natural; no more will or inclination to the creator than a dead body has to the creature; no more taste or relish for his only true happiness, than a dead body has for music and dancing. 'Having his understanding darkened, being alienated from the life of God through the ignorance that is in him, because of the blindness of his heart, he receiveth not the things of the Spirit of God, for they are foolishness unto him'.[69] So speaks the great apostle concerning the natural man; and as if this were not sufficient to express his miserable condition, he adds, 'Neither indeed can he know them, because they are spiritually discerned.'[70]

As to the will of man in his natural state, the same apostle assures us that it is not subject to the law of God; and adds, neither indeed can it be.[71] So dead is he to God, so without all faculties for apprehending him! He has such a mind as neither understands, nor can understand, the things of God, he has such a will as neither is, nor can be subject to the law of God.

In his affections he is most vile, alienated from the law of God. Here he is dead indeed! Twice dead![72] So far is he from having set[73] his affections on things above, that his very soul cleaveth to the dust.[74] So far is he from having his senses exercised to discern both good and evil,[75] that he counts all spiritual sensation madness. Bid him taste and see that the Lord is[76] gracious,[77] and you only place a banquet before the dead. Tell him religion is situated in the heart and must therefore be felt wheresoever it is, and it will all appear delusion to him. Saint Paul in his epistle to the Philippians, 1.9, prays for all those 'that are partakers of his grace, that their love may abound yet more and more in knowledge and in all judgment

---

[64] The word 'this' is absent from the Albin and Beckerlegge text.   [65] Cf. Luke 14: 25.

[66] Luke 14: 27.

[67] As Albin and Beckerlegge note, one might read 'truly' for 'thoroughly' at this point. Thoroughly seems more probable.   [68] Cf. 1 Tim. 5: 6.

[69] Eph. 4: 18; 1 Cor. 2: 14.   [70] 1 Cor. 2: 14.   [71] Cf. Rom. 8: 7.

[72] Cf. Jude 12.   [73] The word 'set' has been inserted above the line.   [74] Ps. 119: 25.

[75] Heb. 5: 14.   [76] The words 'that the Lord is' are inserted above the line.

[77] Cf. 1 Pet. 2: 3.

(αἰσθήσει)', in all sense or feeling, as it is in the original and in our margin. But of this the natural man has no cause for apprehension; nay, he presumes to give God himself the lie in blasphemously saying all feeling in religion is enthusiasm!   Him we must own to be past feeling either God[78] or sin, and leave him to that mercy which he denies.[79]

I proceed to those who, having renounced themselves, are striving to enter in at the strait gate;[80] in whom the divine principle received in baptism, but buried ever since and seemingly extinct, begins to move and extort the cry of the trembling gaoler, 'What must I do to be saved!'[81] They have now turned their faces towards heaven and stirred themselves up to take hold on the Lord. The work of repentance is begun, and by it they endeavour to break off their sins. They use all the means of grace, do all good works, and labour after the renewal of their souls in all heavenly tempers, even the whole mind that was in Christ Jesus.[82] In a word, they are in earnest. They own and pursue the one thing needful,[83] even a participation of the divine nature, the life of God in the soul of man.[84]

In the beginning of this state, they are generally full of delight; God does not let them serve him for nought,[85] but draws them on with sensible comforts, and leads them in the ways of pleasantness.[86] They seem to taste the good word of God and the powers of the world to come[87] in the witness of sensible devotion. Nor is there any temper of a real inward Christian which they do not in some sort anticipate. They will often have peace with God, even the peace which passes all understanding,[88] and sometimes rejoice with joy unspeakable.[89] Nay, the love of Christ seems to constrain them,[90] and they long to do great things for him.[91]

The world seems now to have quite lost its hold upon them; the devil, that roaring lion,[92] is chained; and the flesh but very rarely troubles them. God does not immediately lead them through the land of their enemies, 'lest peradventure the people repent when they see war, and return to Egypt!'[93] No! The sons of Anak[94]

---

[78] One might read 'good' for 'God'.

[79] The MS is not entirely straightforward at this point, though the transcription given above seems to represent Charles's intended reading fairly. After the words 'all feeling is enthusiasm' Charles has left a short gap, perhaps indicating a pause in the spoken form of the sermon. The words 'Him we must own to be past' are found in the same line, after the gap, and are clear enough. However, the next line begins with a gap followed by a comma. The words 'feeling either God or sin' are inserted in the left hand margin of the same line (not in the gap) and after 'sin' there is another sign that has been so heavily struck out as to make it unreadable. Following the comma, the words 'and leave him to that mercy' appear followed by another gap in the MS. Finally, on the same line as 'and leave him to that mercy', but after the gap which follows, the words 'which he denies' have been written. This rather unclear composition suggests uncertainty on Charles's part, and perhaps later redactional activity (in his hand). However, the precise composition and editorial history of this section seems unreconstructible from the evidence that has survived.   [80] Matt. 7: 13–14 and parallel.

[81] Acts 16: 29–30.   [82] Phil. 2: 5.   [83] Luke 10: 42, the subject of Sermon 21.

[84] The phrase is taken from the title of Henry Scougal's *The Life of God in the Soul of Man* (1677), an abridged version of which was published by John Wesley in 1744.   [85] Cf. Job 1: 9.

[86] Prov. 3: 17.   [87] Heb. 6: 5.   [88] Phil. 4: 7.

[89] 1 Pet. 1: 8.   [90] Cf. 2 Cor. 5: 14.   [91] Cf. Mark 5: 20.

[92] Cf. 1 Pet. 5: 8.   [93] Exod. 13: 17.   [94] Num. 13: 33.

are kept out of sight, and peace is in all their borders.[95] They seem altogether translated into the glorious liberty of the sons of God,[96] and abound in thanksgiving to him for what they call their conversion.

When the divine goodness hath thus retained them in his service, and by these arts allured them as it were to follow him, then the war in the members[97] breaks out. Having prepared their soul to meet temptation, he now suffers it to assault them. Their own wickedness, which they seemed long since to have eschewed, makes head against them, even the sin which did so easily beset them.[98] For sin, taking occasion by the commandment, works in them now all manner of concupiscence. Without the law indeed it was dead: it had no force or malignity, comparatively speaking, while they were ignorant of their duty. They were alive, or seemed so to be, without the law once, but now the commandment comes, sin revives, and they die. And the commandment which was ordained to life, they find to be unto death. For sin, taking occasion by the commandment, deceives them, and by it slays them. Thus sin, that it may, to them, appear sin, works death in them by that which is good, that sin by the commandment may become exceeding sinful.[99]

From the time that any man knows that the law is spiritual, he knows that he himself is carnal, sold under sin:[100] and from this time he treads the same dreadful round of sin, repenting and sinning again. His comfort is withdrawn, his peace is lost: he prayed,[101] resolves and strives, but all in vain; the more he labours, the less he prevails; the more he struggles, the faster is he bound: so that after a thousand thousand repeated ~~conflicts~~ defeats he finds at last that sin is irresistible. Then does he take up that sad complaint (Romans 7) which he feels the apostle wrote of him, 'That which I do, I allow not: for what I would that do I not; but what I hate, that do I. (If then I do that which I would not, I consent unto the law that it is good). Now then, it is no more I that do it, but sin that[102] dwelleth in me. For I know that in me, that is, in my flesh, in my nature, dwelleth no good thing: for to will is present with me, but how to perform that which is good, I find not. For the good that I would, I do not; but the evil which I would not, that I do. (Now if I do that I would not, it is no more I that do it, but sin that dwelleth in me.) I find then a law, that when I would do good, evil is present with me. For I delight in the law of God, after the inner man. For I see another law in my members, warring against the law of my mind, and bringing me into captivity to the law of sin, which is in my members. Oh wretched man that I am, who shall deliver me from the body of this death!'

---

[95] Cf. Ps. 147: 14.   [96] Cf. Rom. 8: 21.   [97] Cf. Jas. 4: 1.
[98] Cf. Heb. 12: 1.
[99] Much of the above paragraph is a loose paraphrase of Rom. 7, which is so much in evidence here that no attempt has been made to disentangle the strands.   [100] Rom. 7: 14.
[101] 'Prays' rather than 'prayed' might have been expected here. The MS is somewhat untidy at this point. The words 'prayed, resolves and strives, but all in vain' have been written in the right hand margin and the word 'the' before 'more' in the left.
[102] The word 'that' has been added above the line (cf. Rom. 7: 17).

Such is the language of one whom the Holy Spirit has reproved of sin, but not rescued from it. Being dead in sin, he once served it willingly: it is now with the utmost reluctance; yet still he serves it, and so he must do till, being justified by faith,[103] the law of the spirit of life makes him free from the law of sin and death.[104] But where the Spirit of the Lord is, there is liberty,[105] and whomsoever the Son makes free, that man is free indeed.[106] Being risen with Christ, death ~~and sin~~ hath no more dominion over him.[107] Being born of God, he doth not commit sin.[108] Believing in him, he hath everlasting life,[109] even that life which is hid with Christ in God: [110] a life which is not to be expressed but felt; nor could we fully describe it though we speak with the tongues of men and of angels.[111] He only comprehends and lives[112] it, who hath Christ's righteousness imputed to him;[113] for the just shall live by faith;[114] and from the moment any one believes with the heart,[115] he can truly say, 'I am crucified with Christ; nevertheless I live; yet not I, but Christ liveth in me. And the life which I now live in the flesh, I live by the faith of the Son of God, who loved me and gave himself for me.'[116] He knows the 'mystery which hath been hid from ages and from generations, but now is made manifest to his saints; to whom God would make known what is the riches of this mystery among the Gentiles, which is Christ in you, the hope of glory; Christ who is our life,'[117] as verily and indeed living in the believing soul as in the third heaven.[118]

This I know, to you who feel it not, is the very foolishness of folly, it is presumption, it is blasphemy, it is what the world the flesh and the devil[119] please to have it. 'For no man can receive this saying unless it be given him from above: but wisdom is justified of her children, and he that hath an ear let him hear what the spirit saith unto the churches'.[120] 'To him that overcometh will I give to eat of the hidden manna; and will give him a white stone and in the stone a new name written, which no man knoweth, saving he that receiveth it'.[121]

I am secondly to apply myself particularly to the persons under each of the three states. And first to you who are dead in sin, though now through accident or curiosity or custom you have strayed into the house of God. To you I speak who knowingly allow yourselves in open or secret sins, and securely sleep in the shadow of death, in the very confines of hell. Whether your lives are stained with outward visible ~~vice~~ enormities, or less observable abominations, it makes no great difference. Whether lust or pride, adultery or worldly mindedness, theft or covetousness, revenge or pleasure, fleshly or spiritual sins, keep you unconcerned in the great business of salvation; you are equally dead to God, and liable to his just

---

[103] The words 'being justified by faith' have been written in above the line.   [104] Rom. 8: 2.
[105] 2 Cor. 3: 17.   [106] Cf. John 8: 36.   [107] Rom. 6: 9.
[108] The words 'Being born of God, he doth not commit sin' have been written in above the line. They are based on 1 John 3: 9.   [109] Cf. John 6: 47.
[110] Col. 3: 3.   [111] 1 Cor. 13: 1.   [112] The words 'and lives' have been written in above the line.
[113] Cf. Rom. 4: 22.   [114] Hab. 2: 4; Rom. 1: 17; Gal. 3: 11; Heb. 10: 38.   [115] Cf. Rom. 10: 9.
[116] Gal. 2: 20.   [117] Cf. Col. 1: 26–7; 3: 4.   [118] Cf. 2 Cor. 12: 2.
[119] *BCP*, Collect for 18th Sunday after Trinity.
[120] Cf. John 3: 27; Luke 7: 35; Rev. 2: 7, 11, 17, 29; 3: 6, 13, 22.   [121] Rev. 2: 17.

judgments, to feel 'the worm that never dies, and the fire that never shall be quenched';[122] 'for as the wicked shall be turned into hell, so shall all the people that forget God'.[123] The careless and the debauched, the scandalous and the reputable sinner, the filthy and the ignorant thoughtless one, are held in equal abomination with God. Nay, he seems to loathe the lukewarm person even worse than him that is cold, and threatens with a peculiar abhorrence to spew him out of his mouth.[124]

Indeed while ye live to please yourselves, it matters not much in what particular way; be it in the grossest issues of self-love, or the most refined, in all uncleanness or in all diversions, in vice or pleasure, the playhouse or the brothel. 'Hear ye this, and tremble, ye that are at ease! Be troubled, ye careless ones, for to you am I sent to cry aloud and spare not, to lift up my voice like a trumpet, and show you your transgressions and your sins'.[125] Mean you to continue in this spirit of slumber till the everlasting flames awake you? Ye serpents, ye generation of vipers, how can ye escape the damnation of hell?[126] 'God is not a man that he should lie'?[127] 'The soul that sinneth, it shall die'.[128] 'Hath he said and shall he not do it? Or hath he spoken and shall he not make it good?'[129] It is he hath pronounced your doom. 'Depart from me, ye cursed, into everlasting fire, prepared for the devil and his angels!'[130] For we know him that hath said, 'Vengeance belongeth unto me, I will recompense, saith the Lord.'[131] And again, 'The Lord shall judge his people. It is a fearful thing to fall into the hands of the living God!'[132]

I would gladly hope there are some here present, who, having never before entertained a serious thought about their salvation, are now pricked in their heart, and ready to ask, What shall we do?[133] To these I answer in the words of my Master, 'If he hath warned you to flee from the wrath to come, bring forth fruits meet for repentance.'[134] Repentance is the indispensable preparation[135] for mercy, and 'except ye repent ye shall all likewise perish.'[136] 'But when the wicked man turneth away from his wickedness that he hath committed, and doth that which is lawful and right, he shall save his soul alive. All his transgressions that he hath committed, they shall not be mentioned unto him, because he considereth and turneth away from all his transgressions, he shall surely live, he shall not die.'[137]

These and a thousand other gracious invitations, God makes to bring back sinners to himself. He not only threatens but promises; and courts you with the most importunate entreaties. He draws you with the cords of a man,[138] and leaves no way untried to win you to your own happiness. 'Wash you, make you clean, put away the evil of your doings from before mine eyes: cease to do evil, learn to do well.

---

[122] Cf. Isa. 66: 24; Mark 9: 43–8.   [123] Cf. Ps. 9: 17.   [124] Cf. Rev. 3: 16.

[125] Cf. Isa. 32: 11; 58: 1.   [126] Cf. Matt. 3: 7 and parallel; 12: 34; 23: 33.

[127] Cf. Num. 23: 19; the question mark, omitted by Albin and Beckerlegge, is present in the MS. Its force must have been dependent upon intonation.   [128] Ezek. 18: 4, 20.

[129] Num. 23: 19.   [130] Cf. Matt. 25: 41.   [131] Heb. 10: 30, citing Deut. 32: 35.

[132] Heb. 10: 30–1, citing Deut. 32: 36.   [133] Acts 2: 37.   [134] Cf. Matt. 3: 8 and parallel.

[135] As Albin and Beckerlegge note, the context requires 'preparation' or a similar word, but the usual symbol for 'tion' is lacking in the MS.   [136] Luke 13: 3, 5.

[137] Cf. Ezek. 18: 22–3 and 27–8. (Charles has conflated the two.)   [138] Hos. 11: 4.

Come now, and let us reason together, saith the Lord. Though your sins be as scarlet, they shall be as white as snow; though they be red like crimson, they shall be as wool.[139] As I live, saith the Lord, I have no pleasure in the death of the wicked, but that the wicked turn from his way[140] and live. Turn ye, turn ye from your evil ways, for why will ye die, oh house of Israel!'[141]

Is any of you so senseless, as not to feel some relentings for such amazing condescension and love? Surely that man's heart is harder than the nether millstone.[142] May God who made it soften it; and to this end hear ye him!'[143] Hear him in that vehement expression of his unutterable[144] tenderness toward the most obstinate offenders, 'How shall I give thee up, O Ephraim? How shall I deliver thee, Israel? How shall I make thee as Admah? How shall I set thee as Zeboim? Mine heart is turned within me; my repentings are kindled together. I will not execute the fierceness of mine anger, I will not return to destroy Ephraim, for I am God, and not man, the Holy One in the midst of thee.'[145]

Here you see the strong reluctance there is in God to punish: such lingering backwardness, such sweet delay! As if the Father of compassions could not put so great a force upon his nature, as to give up the most hardened sinner. Still his mercy triumphs over his justice; it will be heard: it binds the hands of the Almighty, and will not let him alone to destroy.

'Therefore also now, saith the Lord, turn ye even to me with all your heart, and with fasting and with weeping, and with mourning. And rend[146] your hearts and not your garments, and turn unto the Lord your God; for he is gracious and merciful, slow to anger and of great kindness, and repenteth him of the evil.'[147] Oh that this infinite goodness of God might lead you to repentance! Oh that any one of you would even now arise and go to his Father and say unto him, 'Father, I have sinned against heaven and before thee, and am no more worthy to be called thy son!' He sees you now, while you are a great way off, and has compassion, and only awaits your turning towards him, that he may run and fall on your neck and kiss you. Then will he say, 'Bring forth the best robe (even the robe of Christ's righteousness) and put it upon him, for this my son was dead and is alive again; he was lost and is found.'[148]

---

[139] The quotation to this point is from Isa. 1: 16–18.

[140] As Albin and Beckerlegge note, the word 'way' is clear in the MS (p. 11, line 10). They suggest that 'one would expect Charles to use 'wickedness' in this context'. The reasons for that expectation are unclear, since 'way' is found in the passage from which the quotation is taken (Ezek. 33: 11).

[141] The second part of this composite quotation is from Ezek. 33: 11.   [142] Cf. Job 41: 24.

[143] Matt. 17: 5.

[144] Before 'unutterable' there appears another sign in the MS that has been struck out. The sign is faint, but appears to be an 'm', perhaps the beginnings of 'most'.   [145] Hos. 11: 8–9.

[146] As Albin and Beckerlegge note, the MS actually reads 'rent' (rnt) at this point. However, Charles almost certainly would have read 'rend' (see Joel 2: 13).   [147] Joel 2: 12–13.

[148] See the parable of the Prodigal Son (Luke 15: 11–32).

2.[149] To you whom God hath wrought for this selfsame thing[150] I am next to speak, and show the way of peace and salvation. God is not far from every one of you. For you there [is] about to be joy in heaven,[151] and the angels are tuning their harps. I shall therefore warn you of the one obstacle, which earth or hell can throw in your way to happiness;[152] and that is your listening to those miserable comforters, who would persuade you, you are already in possession of it; of the greatest happiness which God hath promised to his children below. If ye will hearken unto God more than unto man,[153] and take the scriptural promises in their plain, obvious meaning, ye will find a happiness unutterably inconceivable which God hath prepared for them that love him,[154] even before the Son of Man.[155] Some foretaste of this happiness he gave you, when first you turned from those dumb idols,[156] honour, riches, and pleasure, to serve the living God: [157] nor hath he since that [day][158] left you comfortless,[159] but oft refreshed you with the dew of heaven, and fed you with the fruits of Canaan. [160] But will ye therefore set up your rest on this side Jordan?[161] Because the Holy Spirit hath visited you, will ye not suffer him to make his abode with you?[162] Ye have indeed received the Holy Ghost and so had the apostles when Jesus breathed upon them,[163] yet was he not fully come till till [sic][164] Christ was glorified.[165] 'Ye likewise know him now, for he dwelleth with you, and shall be in you',[166] unless you do despite unto him,[167] by not desiring, or not expecting him. But whosoever, trusting to his past attainments, to anything he has

[149] The number '2' is written in the left hand margin of page 12. It marks the point at which Charles has concluded his first point ('to explain these three states') and picks up his second ('to apply myself particularly to the persons under each').   [150] Cf. 2 Cor. 5: 5.

[151] Cf. Luke 15: 7.

[152] As Albin and Beckerlegge note, it is possible in some of the occurrences within this paragraph that 'happiness' should read 'heaven'. The shorthand symbol in the MS is simply 'h'. However, when the substantive mark is placed under the 'h' it would appear that Charles has in mind 'happiness'. When the same mark is placed over the 'h', however, 'heaven' seems most appropriate.

[153] Cf. Acts 4: 19.   [154] 1 Cor. 2: 9.

[155] Albin and Beckerlegge suggest 'sons of men' at this point, though the meaning of the resultant sentence is unclear. The shorthand reads simply 'sm', with a point so positioned as to suggest that two words are to be read. The same sign appears on line 1 of page 17 of the MS with the clear meaning of 'Son of Man' (it is in a quotation from John 5: 25). If the reading 'Son of Man' is adopted here, the meaning of the sentence is still somewhat unclear. However, Charles may be alluding to Matt. 25: 31 ff. An alternative plausible, but still not totally convincing, solution would be that Charles here meant to read 'sun and moon'. If so he might have had in mind, in addition to 1 Cor. 2: 9, such texts as Jas. 1: 12, and 2: 5, and Matt. 25: 34 which, when combined, speak of the great happiness that God has prepared for those that love him, a happiness and a kingdom prepared 'before the foundation of the world'. Even, that is, before the sun and the moon on the fourth day of creation (Gen. 1: 14–19).

[156] Cf. 1 Cor. 12: 2.   [157] 1 Thess. 1: 9.

[158] The word 'day' is not found in the MS. It has been added here for the sake of clarity.

[159] Cf. John 14: 18.   [160] Cf. Gen. 27: 28; Josh. 5: 12.

[161] Cf. Josh. 22: 24. The shorthand here is rather unclear. The words which have been expanded above as 'on this side Jordan' are given only as 'onis sd jrdn'.   [162] Cf. John 14: 23.

[163] Cf. John 20: 22.

[164] The first sign for 'till' is found at the end of line 2 on page 13. The second 'till' is found at the beginning of line 3.   [165] Cf. John 7: 39.

[166] Cf. John 14: 17.   [167] Cf. Heb. 10: 29.

either done or felt, sits down contented without the seal of his redemption, the earnest of his inheritance,[168] the witness of the spirit, that man has turned[169] God's favours[170] against himself; he is yet in his sins[171] and in his blood, and to him I testify, Christ shall profit him nothing.[172]

But beloved I am persuaded better things concerning you, and things that accompany salvation.[173] You will not forfeit your own privileges by denying them. You will not plead for a perpetuity of bondage, a necessity of living and dying under the law. You own, that if the Son shall make you free, you shall be free indeed![174] And where the Spirit of the Lord is, there is liberty.[175] You claim this Spirit and this liberty, which are by promise yours; and know that as soon as ye are justified by faith, the law of the Spirit of life shall make you free from the law of sin and death.[176] For this is the very end of our Lord's coming, as he himself declares, 'The Spirit of the Lord is upon me, because he hath anointed me to preach the gospel to the poor, he hath sent me to heal the broken hearted, to preach deliverance to the captives, and recovering of sight to the blind, to set at liberty them that are bruised;'[177] or, as it is in the evangelical prophet, 'to preach good tidings unto the meek, to bind up the broken hearted, to proclaim liberty to the captives, and the opening of the prison to them that are bound.'[178] 'Turn thou then to the stronghold, thou prisoner of hope, even to thee does he declare, that he will render double unto thee.'[179] He can translate thee this moment out of darkness into his marvellous light,[180] out of bondage into the glorious liberty of the sons[181] of God. Believest thou that he is able to do this; I know that thou believest![182] 'Be it unto thee according to thy faith!'[183]

You who have not yet attained to that vehemence of importunity, that unutterable sense of your own emptiness, which is the voice of one crying in the wilderness, Prepare![184] You, I would earnestly[185] exhort to labour after it and never rest satisfied with anything less than Christ in you, the hope of glory.[186] Seek him in all the means he hath appointed, yet not trusting or resting in any. Hunger and thirst after him.[187] Pray without ceasing,[188] till he is formed in your hearts by faith,[189] and refuse to be comforted because he is in you all, despite your refusing to be comforted. You must despair before you can hope. Out of the deep must you call upon him, for it is from thence only that he will hear your voice: [190] out of the depth of

---

[168] Cf. Eph. 1: 13–14.   [169] The word 'turned' has been inserted in the right hand margin.

[170] The shorthand here is unclear, but it appears to read 'f/v/f/vrs'. However, the initial 'f/v' is very unclear.   [171] Cf. 1 Cor. 15: 17.

[172] Cf. Gal. 5: 2.   [173] Cf. Heb. 6: 9.   [174] Cf. John 8: 36.

[175] 2 Cor. 3: 17.   [176] Cf. Rom. 8: 2.   [177] Luke 4: 18.

[178] Isa. 61: 1.   [179] Cf. Zech. 9: 12.   [180] 1 Pet. 2: 9.

[181] Rom. 8: 21.   [182] Cf. Acts 26: 27.   [183] Cf. Matt. 9: 28–9.

[184] Mark 1: 3 and parallels.

[185] The word 'earnestly' is not clear in the text, but seems probable. The shorthand reads simply 'er' with a dot so positioned below the sign as to indicate that an adverb is intended.   [186] Col. 1: 27.

[187] Cf. Matt. 5: 6.   [188] 1 Thess. 5: 17.

[189] This appears to be a conflation of Eph. 3: 17 and Gal. 4: 19.

[190] Cf. Ps. 130: 1–2; there is perhaps also a loose reference to the story of Jonah.

invincible sin and remorseful misery. You must own and feel yourselves to be utterly lost without Christ, to be lost, undone and damned forever. But from the moment you discern this, there is nothing can pluck you out of his hand;[191] for (as an excellent author speaks), 'no soul can be lost that can truly humble itself before God, and pray to his mercy to be helped, saved and redeemed in such a manner as it shall please him. Let it be hid or buried or imprisoned where it will, hell and earth, death and darkness, and everything must give way to the soul thus converted to God; that has no confidence of its own; that sees nothing of its own but sin, and that desires and calls upon God to save it by some miracle of his own mercy and goodness. By this sensibility of the want of a Saviour, and by this humble conversion and application to God for him, all chains are broken off, all wounds are healed, and the soul must infallibly find, if it continues to seek, its salvation in the unknown depth and riches of the divine mercy.'

To a soul by Christ thus disposed for Christ, I need not point out any particular promises.[192] All the promises in scripture are made to him, and as sure as God is true[193], he shall find they are. Yet forasmuch as you know faith cometh by hearing, and hearing by the word of God,[194] I shall mention some of those exceeding precious promises[195], and if now is his time, the Spirit of truth[196] shall now apply them.

And first I would ask you in the name and words of God, 'Hath he brought to the birth, and shall he not cause to bring forth? Hath he begun a good work in you, and shall he not perform it until the day of his coming? Nay, but faithful is he that hath promised, who also will do it.'[197] 'The Lord thy God in the midst of thee is mighty; he will save, he will rejoice over thee with joy, he will rest in his love, he will joy over thee with singing. I will gather them that are sorrowful.'[198]

'The Lord hath sent me,' saith our great deliverer, 'to comfort all that mourn: to appoint unto them that mourn in Zion, to give unto them beauty for ashes, the oil of joy for mourning, the garment of praise for the spirit of heaviness, that they may be called trees of righteousness, the planting of the Lord, that he may be glorified.[199] (*I[200] will never leave thee nor forsake thee.[201] Can a woman forget her sucking child, that she should not have compassion on the son of her womb? Yea, they may forget, yet will not I forget thee. Behold, I have graven thee on the palms of my hands.*

---

[191] Cf. John 10: 28–9.

[192] The shorthand sign for 'promises' appears to have been expanded from 'promise' since the horizonal stroke for 's' extends well into the right hand margin.   [193] Cf. 2 Cor. 1: 18.

[194] Rom. 10: 17.   [195] 2 Pet. 1: 4.   [196] John 14: 17.

[197] This composite quotation draws on Isa. 66: 9; Phil. 1: 6 and 1 Thess. 5: 24.

[198] Cf. Zeph. 3: 17–18.   [199] To this point the quotation is from Isa. 61: 2–3.

[200] The words here underlined are underlined in the MS.

[201] After 'thee' there appears in the text another sign that has been so heavily struck out as to make it difficult to read. However it would appear to be ')', that is the close of the brackets begun before 'I' eight words before. These words are taken from Heb. 13: 5. Charles may have originally intended to stop at that point, but then changed his mind and continued (after striking out the now redundant ')') with a quotation from Isa. 49: 15–16; 51: 11.

Therefore the redeemed of the Lord shall return and come with singing unto Zion, and everlasting joy shall be upon their head; they shall obtain gladness and joy, and sorrow and mourning shall[202] flee away).[203]

I, even I, am he that comforteth you![204] And to us, whom he hath sent forth in his name, Comfort ye, comfort ye, my people, saith our God. Speak ye comfortably to Jerusalem, and say unto her, that her warfare is accomplished, that her iniquity is pardoned, for she hath received of the Lord's hand double for all her sins.[205] He hath sent us to lay open these mysteries of his love, and to preach the Gospel unto every creature.[206] He[207] grant that it may now come unto you, not in word only, but in power and in the Holy Ghost, and in much assurance.[208]

He it is that now[209] speaks to you and calls you[210] . . . 'Ho, everyone that thirsteth, come ye to the waters, and he that hath no money; come ye, buy and eat; yea come; buy wine and milk without money and without price. I will pour water upon him that is thirsty, and floods on the dry ground!'[211] The same gracious promise he afterwards repeats, when in the likeness of our sinful flesh, 'Jesus stood and cried saying, If any man thirst, let him come unto me and drink! He that believeth on me, as the scripture saith, out of his belly shall flow rivers of living water.'[212] Or, as he expresses it to the woman of Samaria, 'Whosoever drinketh of the water that I shall give him, shall never thirst, but the water that I shall give him shall be in him a well of water, springing up unto everlasting life. But this he spoke of the Spirit, which they that believe on him should receive.'[213] And that all who will, may receive this faith he assures us in those words, 'He that cometh to me I will in no wise cast out.'[214] And again to us who have obeyed his call (as every man upon earth may) he said, 'Fear not, little flock, for it is your Father's pleasure to give you the kingdom; even that kingdom of God which is within, which is righteousness and peace and joy in the Holy Ghost.'[215]

Oh numberless are the scriptures wherein he promises this Holy Spirit to all that ask him, especially in that last discourse to his church,[216] which the chil-

---

[202] This is the last word to be underlined in the MS. It comes at the end of a line (line 13, page 15).
[203] Near the beginning of this composite quotation (see above for references) there appears in the margin the words (in shorthand) 'seek and ye shall find, saith your gracious Master, seek and . . . etc. Blessed are the poor in spirit . . . etc. Blessed are they that mourn, for . . . etc. Blessed are they that hunger and thirst . . . etc.' It is not clear, however, where Charles would have inserted these words in the spoken form of the text.   [204] Isa. 51: 12.
[205] Isa. 40: 1–2.   [206] Mark 16: 15.
[207] The shorthand at this point is clear enough in the MS. However, there appears to be a word missing, perhaps 'may' before 'he' was intended.   [208] 1 Thess. 1: 5.
[209] The word 'now' has been squeezed in between 'that' and 'speaks', presumably at a later time as an editorial correction.   [210] The words 'to you and calls' have been inserted in the margin.
[211] Isa. 55: 1; 44: 3.   [212] John 7: 37–8.   [213] John 4: 13–14; 7: 39.
[214] John 6: 37.   [215] Cf. Luke 12: 32; 17: 21; Rom. 14: 17.
[216] Albin and Beckerlegge suggest 'children' here. However, the compound shorthand sign here is 'tisch', which might be read as 'to his church'. This reading seems more probable in context since Charles has in mind here Jesus's farewell discourse found in John 13–17, where, in chapters 14 and 16 especially, Jesus promises to send the Spirit upon his followers as a collective unit who will be left behind following his return to the Father.

dren[217] of this generation, no less blasphemously than absurdly ~~would fain~~ appropriate to his apostles. But ye will not so easily quit your title to the legacy of your Lord, even that blessed Spirit, which not only St. Peter or St. John, but you and I and every baptised person may claim as his heritage forever.[218] For to you our Lord had respect when he said, 'I will pray the Father, and he shall give you another Comforter, that he may abide with you for ever. I will not leave you comfortless, I will come unto you. (*Ye*[219] *now have sorrow, but I will see you again, and your heart shall rejoice, and your joy no man taketh from you. Yet a little while, and the world seeth me not* [sic] *more, but ye see me; because I live, ye shall live also.*')[220]

This life and Comforter and joy ye have in believing, and ~~from the first moment that ye do believe with the heart~~, for so saith the author and finisher of our faith,[221] 'Verily, verily, I say unto you, he that heareth my word and believeth on him that sent me hath everlasting life, and shall not come into condemnation, but is passed from death unto life.'[222] And this you may see belongs only to them that believe with a living, saving, justifying faith, which you have not[223] as yet. Therefore is this life or faith promised in the following verse to those that are now spiritually dead. 'Verily, verily, I say unto you, the hour is coming and now is, when the dead shall hear the voice of the Son of Man,[224] and they that hear shall live.'[225] In these words here God, willing more abundantly to show unto the heirs of promise the immutability of his counsel, confirmed it by an oath: that by two immutable things, in which it was impossible for God to lie, we might have a strong consolation, who have fled for refuge to lay hold upon the hope set before us.[226]

I trust there is more than one here present who finds that he hath laid hold of the hope set before him,[227] that believing he hath everlasting life and rejoices in God through our Lord Jesus Christ by whom he hath now received the atonement,[228] the Spirit also bearing witness with his spirit that he is a child of God.[229] To you, who still wait for the promise of his coming,[230] I shall conclude in his own words, 'Behold I come quickly! I, Jesus, have sent mine angel to testify unto you these things in the churches. I am the root and the offspring of David, and the bright morning star.' 'And the Spirit and the bride say, come. And let him that heareth say, come; and let him that is athirst come; and whosoever will, let him

---

[217] The shorthand here is 'ch'; see note above. Again the context is important. 'The children of this generation' (Luke 16: 8) are the subject of Sermon 17.   [218] Ps. 119: 111.

[219] The words here underlined are underlined in the MS.

[220] The closing bracket is not found in the MS. It has been added here for the sake of clarity. This composite quotation draws upon, in order, John 14: 16, 18; 16: 22; 14: 19.   [221] Heb. 12: 2.

[222] John 5: 24.

[223] The word 'not' is somewhat unclear in the text, for the shorthand appears to read 'nti/o' (the 'i' or 'o' is indicated by a small dot positioned next to the vertical line for 't'). However, given the context 'not' seems intended.

[224] John 5: 25 actually reads 'Son of God' at this point. Charles is probably quoting from memory.

[225] Cf. John 5: 25.   [226] Heb. 6: 17–18.   [227] Cf. Heb. 6: 18.

[228] Cf. Rom. 5: 11.   [229] Rom. 8: 16.

[230] Charles may have in mind 2 Pet. 3: 4, though the 'coming' there awaited seems to be one of a different order to that here anticipated.

take of the water of life freely.' He which testifieth these things saith, 'Surely I come quickly. Amen! Even so; come, Lord Jesus!'[231]

'The grace of our Lord Jesus Christ be with you all. Amen!'[232]

(Begun July 8, finished July 15, 1738)[233]

[Part Two][234]

1. I am thirdly and lastly to address myself to you whom God, who is rich in mercy, of his great love wherewith he loved you, hath quickened together with Christ, even when ye were dead in sin, and hath raised you up together, and made you sit together in heavenly places in Christ Jesus.[235] Thanks be to God for his unspeakable gift![236] My first and almost needless advice is 'Be thankful.'[237] Ye cannot but say both now and ever, 'Blessed be the God and Father of our Lord Jesus Christ, who according to his abundant mercy hath begotten us again unto a lively hope by the resurrection of Jesus Christ from the dead, to an inheritance incorruptible and undefiled, and that fadeth not away, reserved in heaven for you who are kept by the power of God through[238] faith unto salvation!'[239]

2. My next advice (if[240] it be not the same) I shall give you in the words of the prophet Isaiah: 'And in that day shalt thou say, O Lord, I will praise thee. Though thou wast angry with me, thine anger is turned away, and thou comfortest me. Behold, God is my salvation: I will trust and not be afraid, for the Lord Jehovah is my strength and my song: he also is become my salvation. Therefore with joy shall ye draw water out of the wells of salvation.'[241] He again repeats and enforces his exhortation to an outward experience of our inward joy: 'And in that day shall ye say, Praise the Lord, call upon his name, declare his doings among the people, make mention that his name is exalted. Sing unto the Lord, for he hath done excellent things; this is known in all the earth. Cry out and shout, thou inhabitant of Zion, for great is the Holy One of Israel in the midst of thee.'[242]

What I mean to press upon you is, that you would not hide Christ's righteousness within your heart, but let your talk be of his truth and of his salvation. Hereby you set to your seal that God is true.[243] Return then and show what great things Jesus hath done for you.[244] What he ~~saith to you, in secret, that~~ told you in darkness, that speak ye in light, and what ye hear in the ear, that preach ye[245] upon the

---

[231] The latter part of this paragraph is heavily dependent upon Rev. 22.

[232] Cf. Rom. 16: 24; Phil. 4: 23; 2 Thess. 3: 18; Rev. 22: 21.

[233] The year '1738' is written below 'July 8'. It may have been added by Charles at a later point.

[234] Part two of the sermon begins on page 18 of the same booklet. As the sermon register makes clear, Charles did view the two parts of the sermon as distinct.   [235] Cf. Eph. 2: 4–6.

[236] 2 Cor. 9: 15.   [237] Col. 3: 15.

[238] The words 'God through' have been added by Charles above the line.   [239] 1 Pet. 1: 3–5.

[240] The word 'if' has been inserted above the line.   [241] Isa. 12: 1–3.

[242] Isa. 12: 4–6.   [243] Cf. John 3: 33.   [244] Cf. Mark 5: 19.

[245] The word 'ye' has been added above the line.

housetops.[246] He hath put a new song in your mouth, even a thanksgiving unto our God; many shall see it and fear,[247] and shall put their trust in the Lord.[248]

Let not Satan deceive you through a false humility. We are not ignorant of his devices,[249] ~~but let~~ whereby he would get that advantage over us which he has got over many sincere souls, by persuading them to keep back glory from God. Beware of him when transformed into an angel of light,[250] a preacher of humility. He never fails preaching it upon one occasion, that is, when our speaking would endanger his congregation or advance that of Christ's. Then he most tenderly cautions you against pride; especially if you presume to mention your own experiences. When you have, notwithstanding all his dissuasives, broke through in the power of faith and testified Christ's triumphant entry into your soul, you must then expect to be rebuked by the righteous Pharisees that you should hold your peace; and do you cry out so much the more,[251] Hosannah to the Son of David! Blessed is he that cometh in the name of the Lord; hosannah in the highest!'[252]

3. My third and most important direction is, 'Be not high minded, but fear.'[253] I mean not to recommend a servile, tormenting fear, for that ye are incapable of,[254] but a humble, filial fear which is perfectly consistent with the most assured confidence in God. You need never fear that you in particular shall fall from grace, while you fear and abhor that arrogant doctrine of devils that it is impossible! The holiest man upon earth is in a possibility of so falling as never to rise again. For so saith the scripture, 'Now the just shall live by faith, but if any man draw back, my soul shall have no pleasure in him.'[255] The words 'any man' are not in the original, for the literal translation is 'Now the just man shall live by faith; but if he draw back,' which evidently proves the possibility of his drawing back, as do the numberless scriptures cautioning us against relapsing, and exhorting us to persevere.

To those who would avoid these scriptures by vainly imagining they may fall away, but not finally, let the great apostle answer: 'It is impossible for those who were once enlightened, and have tasted of the heavenly gift, and were made partakers of the Holy Ghost, and have tasted the good word of God, and the powers of the world to come; if they shall fall away, to renew them again unto repentance; seeing they crucify to themselves the Son of God afresh and put him to an open shame.'[256]

The persons here described are real inward Christians; of whom it is affirmed that if they shall fall away, that is, if they shall totally apostatise, it is impossible to renew them again unto repentance. It is not only said that they can fall away, but

---

[246] Cf. Luke 12: 3.
[247] The shorthand here has been amended. It would seem that Charles originally wrote 'hear' which he changed to 'fear'.   [248] Cf. Ps. 40: 3.
[249] 2 Cor. 2: 11.   [250] 2 Cor. 11: 14.   [251] Cf. Mark 10: 48.
[252] Matt. 21: 9.   [253] Rom. 11: 20.
[254] The words 'incapable of' are not clear in the text. The shorthand reads only 'incf'. However, 'incapable of' seems to fit the context well enough here and other expansions are not obvious.
[255] Heb. 10: 38.   [256] Heb. 6: 4–6.

that they can so fall away as never, never more to return. Not that every wilful sin after conversion is such a falling away, but only absolute apostasy. Mark well what I say, you that seek occasion of offence, and you who receive the words sincerely. I do not say that one who is a Christian indeed can never recover if he sin wilfully; for David sinned most grievously and recovered:[257] so did St. Peter, ~~who~~[258] after he had dissembled the truth and carried away others with his dissimulation: [259] God suffering his most faithful servants to relapse into gross sin, to show them that they were but men, and guard them from this very presumption, this dangerous downfall this horrid delusion—that they could not fully fall from grace.[260]

This then is what I have divine authority for saying, 'The Christian most spiritual[261] may sin wilfully and recover; the most spiritual[262] Christian may likewise so sin as never to recover, so fall as never to lift up eyes again, till he lift them up in torments.'[263]

4. That you may not be of them that draw back to perdition,[264] let me recommend to you[265] in the fourth a constant use of all the means of grace. He that thinketh he can stand without them, is on the brink of falling.[266] Indeed, a man must suppose himself not a whit behind the very chiefest of the apostles, before he can fancy himself above the use of means. Nay, he must be holier than St. Paul, for 'he still kept his body under, and brought it into subjection, lest ~~than~~ that by any means, after he had preached to others, he himself should be a castaway.'[267] I shall only observe upon these words, that they prove it possible for the holiest man upon earth to fall fully from grace, and that the surest forerunner[268] of such apostasy is the discontinuance of the means of grace.

5. A fifth advice I would give you is, to show your faith by your works.[269] Without these all pretensions to faith are false. These are the necessary effects or fruits or signs of a living faith. Necessary they are, not to justify us before God, but to justify us before man; or rather, not to make, but to show us acceptable; not as the cause but as the evidence of our new birth; not as conditions, but consequents

---

[257] Charles presumably has in mind the story of David and Bathsheba in 2 Sam. 11.

[258] The word 'who' appears to have been partially deleted in the MS. If this deletion is accepted, that would allow the sentence to read as it was written without the deletion of 'and' seven words on. The deletion of this 'and' is conjectured by Albin and Beckerlegge, but has no support in the text.

[259] Cf. Gal. 2: 12–13.

[260] The argument of this paragraph is identical to that of John Norris's 'Discourse Concerning Perseverance in Holiness' in his *Collection of Miscellanies*, 4th edn. (London, 1706), 201. Norris was a personal friend of Charles's father, Samuel, and, as already observed (see note 24 above) was an early source for Methodist theology and hymnody.

[261] The words 'most spiritual' appear to have been inserted into the text; 'spiritual' runs out into the right hand margin and the word 'most' has apparently been squeezed in between 'spiritual' and 'Christian'.   [262] The words 'the most spiritual' have been inserted above the line.

[263] Cf. Luke 16: 23.   [264] Heb. 10: 39.

[265] The words 'to you' have been inserted above the line.   [266] Cf. 1 Cor. 10: 12.

[267] Cf. 1 Cor. 9: 27.

[268] Albin and Beckerlegge mark this word as unclear in the text. The shorthand reads 'fornr'.

[269] Cf. Jas. 2: 18. This whole paragraph draws heavily on Jas. 2.

and tokens of our salvation.[270] The faith which worketh not by love,[271] is an idle, barren, dead faith; that is, no faith at all. So St. James describes it in his golden epistle which I would earnestly recommend to your frequent meditation.

'He that abideth in me, and I in him,' saith our blessed Lord, 'the same bringeth forth much fruit.'[272] He, therefore, that doth not bring forth much fruit is not in Christ. Whosoever finds in his heart that Christ is his righteousness, shows in his life that Christ is his sanctification; his works testify of him. He walks worthy of the Lord unto all well-pleasing, being fruitful in every good work and ~~possessed~~ increasing in[273] of [sic] every holy and heavenly temper. Good works are natural emanations of the divine life, and flow from it, as the stream from the fountain. Hereby is the Father glorified, that ye bring forth much fruit.[274] By this shall all men know that ye are Christ's disciples.[275] Wherefore, my beloved brethren, be ye steadfast, unmovable, always abounding in the work of the Lord, forasmuch as ye now know that your labour is not in vain in the Lord.[276] Being made partakers of the divine nature,[277] express and manifest it by all good works and all holiness: 'giving all diligence to add to your faith virtue, and to virtue knowledge, and to knowledge temperance, and to temperance patience, and to patience brotherly kindness, and to brotherly kindness charity. For if these things be in you, and abound, they shall make you that ye shall neither be barren (idle, it is in the original)[278] nor unfruitful in the knowledge of our Lord Jesus Christ.'[279]

---

[270] Cf. Phil. 1: 28.   [271] Gal. 5: 6.   [272] Cf. John 15: 5.
[273] Cf. Col. 1: 10.   [274] Cf. John 15: 8.
[275] The words 'By this shall all men know that ye are Christ's disciples' have been inserted above the line. They are taken from John 13: 35.   [276] 1 Cor. 15: 58.
[277] 2 Pet. 1: 4.
[278] The Greek word is ἀργούς, which can, as Charles notes, have the meaning of 'idle'.
[279] 2 Pet. 1: 5–8.

SERMON 5

TITUS 3: 8

INTRODUCTORY COMMENT

The MS of this sermon is held at the John Rylands University Library of Manchester,[1] and, with the exception of the brief sermon register, is written entirely in shorthand. The MS comprises sixteen leaves, eight folded sheets, and it is upon the recto of leaves 3–13 that the bulk of the sermon is found. On the verso of leaf 12 Charles has written a passage intended for insertion into material written on the recto of leaf 13. The sermon register is written on the verso of leaf 1, which forms the front cover.

The shorthand is reasonably neat, though a number of changes, additions, and deletions are evident, and it is hence unlikely to be a transcription of a previous text. The text was first published by Albin and Beckerlegge, and their transcription has been invaluable in the preparation of the text printed here. However, the shorthand MS has been examined again, and a number of changes have been made to the Albin-Beckerlegge text. The more significant of these are indicated in the notes. The critical notes provided by Albin and Beckerlegge have mostly been kept, though a small number which seem either irrelevant or inaccurate[2] have been discarded or edited.

Charles first preached his sermon on 'Faith and good works' on 21 December 1738 at 'S. Anthony's, Islington'[3], and at least twice thereafter (Kensington, 14 January 1739; St Katherine's (Islington), 4 March 1739).[4] The content suggests also that the sermon on 'Love and good works' which Charles preached on 23 June 1743 at Epworth ('my native place'),[5] if it was not this very one, may at least have overlapped significantly with it.[6] This, however, cannot be proved.

The preaching of this particular sermon at 'St Anthony's' (St Antholin's) is worthy of further brief note. The rector of St Antholin's at the time was Dr Richard Venn (1691-1740),

---

[1] MARC cw Box 5.

[2] See for example Albin's and Beckerlegge's note 18, which states that the word they have transcribed as 'at your hands' might equally be read as 'here'. The shorthand reads 'aturh', from which it is difficult to see how the reading 'here' might result. This is a minor point, however, and does not detract from the exceptional work that Albin and Beckerlegge have carried out on this text.

[3] It is possible that Charles preached this sermon not once but twice on 21 December 1738, though the register is rather unclear. The MS suggests that he first wrote 'S. Anthony's' and then on the line below 'Islington' with the date 'Dec. 21, 1738' to the right of the note of place. It appears that he then added a definite period point after 'S. Anthony's' (the point is in a darker ink) and then added (also in the darker ink) the word 'at' to the left of Islington with '2^{ce}' to the right of it. This all suggests that he was seeking to correct the first entry from 'S. Anthony's, Islington' to 'S. Anthony's [and] at Islington'. The entry is, however, ambiguous. [4] This information is given on the verso of leaf 1 of the MS.

[5] MARC DDCW 10/2 in loc.; Jackson, Journal, i. 319.

[6] See also 17 June 1746 'The Society were now so exceeding urgent with me, that I could not refuse praying with them in their room, and provoking them to love, and to good works' (MARC DDCW 10/2 in loc.; Jackson, Journal, i. 417).

whose rule that no Methodist should preach in his church was noted by Charles himself in the journal.[7] Venn was a staunch high churchman who spent a great deal of energy disputing with those who held alternative views. Given his churchmanship, he may well have looked upon the Methodists as potential if not actual sectarians and hence imposed the ban. The topic chosen by Charles for his sermon, and especially the extensive quotation from the Homilies, may well have been designed to allay the rector's fears.

The sermon deals with an issue that seems to have been of particular concern to Charles, and indeed to the whole Wesleyan-Arminian tradition of which he was both a co-founder and an integral part: the relationship between faith and good works, and the absolute need for the latter. Throughout it Charles presses upon his audience his view that faith, while being the only way through which the righteousness of Christ is made available to the individual, is not in and of itself a sufficient response to God's grace. In this context one is reminded of Williams's comment[8]

> though he [Charles] cautioned them with the utmost care not to attribute any merit to their own performances, nor in the least degree rest on any works of their own, yet at the same time he thoroughly apprized them, that their faith is but a dead faith if it be not operative, and productive of good works, even all the good in their power.

It is of course of no surprise that Charles, an Anglican clergyman concerned to his dying day to remain aboard 'the old ship' (the Church of England), should here promote the necessity for both faith and good works. Such a conjunction is found even in the articles of religion (Article 12), according to which good works on the part of the justified believer, though they cannot counterbalance sins, are nevertheless 'pleasing and acceptable to God in Christ' and 'spring out necessarily of a true and lively faith'. This is precisely the point of this sermon. In support of his views Charles is able to draw upon not only his sermon text, but also the Epistle of James and the Homilies of the Church of England. He has here borrowed from Homily 4 ('A Short Declaration of the True, Lively, and Christian Faith'), from Homily 3 ('Of Good Works'), and also, though less extensively, from Homily 23 ('Of Alms-Deeds'). His use of these sources is indicated in the notes.

The sermon illustrates well, then, the balance of Charles's 'post-Pentecost' position. As has been seen already, even in the pre-1738 sermons there are signs of Charles's later focus on the all-sufficient blood of Christ. However, the period he spent 'fast bound in sin and nature's night' was dark and unfriendly, and one which, as the pre-1738 sermons also suggest, he sought to escape through his own good works and sincerity. (One is reminded further of his famous response to Böhler regarding the grounds of his hoped-for salvation[9].) There is a noticeable shift in emphasis between the early ('pre-Pentecost') sermons, and the later ones. The differences should not, however, be overestimated. Here Charles continues to give voice to his view that works do matter, if not for justification, then at least because of it.

---

[7] See note 2 to the sermon text itself.   [8] See Chapter 2.

[9] See MARC DDCW 10/2 for 24 February 1738; Telford, *Journal*, 134–5

'Soon after Peter Böhler came to my bedside . . . He asked me, "Do you hope to be saved?" "Yes." "For what reason do you hope it?" "Because I have used my best endeavours to serve God." He shook his head, and said no more. I thought him very uncharitable, saying in my heart, "What, are not my endeavours a sufficient ground of hope? Would he rob me of my endeavours? I have nothing else to trust to."' See further Chapter 2.

Sermon Register[1]

St. Anthony's.	Dec. 21, 1738[2]
at Islington, 2^{ce}[3]	
Kensington	Jan. 14, 1739[4]
S. Katherine's	Mar. 4, 1739[5]

I. N. D.[6]

Titus 3: 38 This is a faithful saying, and these things I will that thou affirm constantly, that they which have believed in God might be careful to maintain good works.

St. Paul in this, as in all his other epistles, having first laid the foundation of faith in Christ Jesus, goes on to build the superstructure of good works. He first preaches justification by faith only, and then presses the consequence, namely, of holiness and a good life. 'After that the kindness [7] and love of God our Saviour towards us appeared, not by works of righteousness which we have done, but according to his mercy he saved us . . . . . .[8] that being justified by his grace, we might be made heirs according to the hope of eternal life.'[9] Then he proceeds, 'This is a faithful saying, and these things I will that thou affirm constantly, that they which have believed in God might be careful to maintain good works.'[10] This is the method he prescribes to Titus, and in him, to every preacher of the gospel. First we are to insist that a man is justified, that is, forgiven, and accounted righteous by grace only through faith, exclusive[11] of all works and righteousness of his

---

[1] This register of Charles's preaching is found on the verso of leaf 1.

[2] See Charles's journal entry for 21 December 1738 (MARC DDCW 10/2 *in loc.*; Telford, *Journal*, 216): 'At St. Antholin's the clerk asked me my name, and said, "Dr. Venn has forbidden any Methodist to preach. Do you call yourself a Methodist?" "I do not: the world may call me what they please." "Well, sir," said he, "it is pity the people should go away without preaching. You may preach." I did so, on good works.' In the MS journal this entry appears under 'Thurs. Dec. 20', which is an error on Charles's part. He correctly enters 'Tues. Dec. 19' above it, but seems to have made a slip at this point. (The next entry is very strangely dated 'Sat. July 23' and the one after that 'Christmas day'.)

[3] On this rather ambiguous entry, and the possibility that Charles preached this sermon twice on 21 December 1738, see the discussion in the introduction to this sermon.

[4] There is no entry in Charles's journal for this date.

[5] See Charles's MS journal entry for 4 March 1739 (MARC DDCW 10/2 *in loc.*; Telford, *Journal*, 224 f.): 'Read prayers, and preached, and administered the sacrament at S. Catherine's; at Islington from John 3.; then expounded with much life at Mr. Sims's; and lastly at Mr. Bell's. Concluded the labour of the day with prayer among the bands.'   [6] '*In Nomine Dei*'; see the note on Sermon 3.

[7] The shorthand symbol for this word is somewhat ambiguous. The first symbol appears to be 'k', but may be the compound sign for 'gn'. The rest of the symbol is clearly 'd' followed by 'n' which has been so written as to suggest 'ness'. The resultant possible readings are therefore 'goodness' and 'kindness'. The KJV verse uses 'kindness', and the same symbol occurs below where the context can only read 'kindness', thus making it the more probable reading here.

[8] The sequence of six dots in the MS reflects an ellipsis in the quotation.   [9] Titus 3: 4–7.

[10] Titus 3: 8.

[11] The symbol for 'exclusive' has been rather untidily amended from 'xclv' to 'xclsv', but Charles's intention seems plain enough.

own; then, that he is to evidence this justification ~~sanctified, or made righteous~~ by universal obedience;[12] by continually exercising himself unto godliness; by ~~aqr~~[13] ~~attaining~~ expressing the whole mind that was in Christ Jesus.[14]

In my present discourse I shall endeavour to follow the apostle's direction, and having explained the nature of faith and works, shall exhort you first to believe in God, and then to be careful to maintain good works.

What the true Christian faith is, and what the works that spring from it[15] ~~what is meant by faith and works~~ I shall declare in the words of our own excellent church who thus expresses herself in ~~the~~ her homilies.[16]

'Faith is taken in scripture two ways. There is one faith which is called a dead faith, which bringeth not forth good works, but is dead, barren, and unfruitful. And this faith is a persuasion in man's heart whereby he knoweth there is a God, and agreeth to all truths maintained in holy scripture. And this is not properly called faith. Forasmuch as faith without works is dead[17], it is not now faith, as a dead body is not a man. This faith, therefore, is not the sure and substantial faith which saveth sinners.'

'Another faith there is in scripture which is not idle, unfruitful, and dead, but worketh by love;[18] and[19] as the other vain faith is called dead, so may this be called a quick and lively faith. And this is not only the common belief of the Articles of our faith, but it is also a sure trust and confidence of the mercy of God through our Lord Jesus Christ, and a steadfast hope of all good things to be received at God's hand. This is the true, lively, and unfeigned Christian faith, and is not in the mouth and outward profession only, but it liveth and stirreth inwardly in the heart. And this faith is not without hope and trust in God; nor without the love of God and of our neighbour; nor without the fear of God; nor without the desire to hear God's word and to follow the same in eschewing evil and doing gladly all good works.'

'This faith is the sure ground and foundation of the benefits we ought to look for, and trust to receive of God; a certificate and sure looking for them. And nothing so commendeth good men unto God as this assured faith and trust in him.'

[12] The form and position of the corrections at this point in the MS indicate that Charles originally wrote 'he is sanctified, or made righteous by universal obedience' which he then changed to 'he is to evidence this justification by universal obedience'. The change is of course theologically significant.

[13] The shorthand symbol here struck out is very unclear. Albin-Beckerlegge (p. 26) suggest 'excer'. The symbol is, however, more probably 'aqr' (or 'eqr'), perhaps the truncated form of 'acquiring' (cf. 'acquire' below, where the shorthand symbol in the text is similar to that here).

[14] Cf. Phil. 2: 5.

[15] The words at the beginning of this paragraph have been inserted in place of the struckout words which immediately follow.

[16] The remainder of this paragraph and the three which follow are largely extracted (though there are numerous deletions, alterations, and additions) from part one of Homily 4 'A Short Declaration of the True, Lively, and Christian Faith' ('Of Faith').   [17] Cf. Jas. 2: 20.

[18] Gal. 5: 6. Charles substituted 'love' for 'charity' in the original and omitted the scripture reference.

[19] The remainder of this paragraph has been bracketed by Charles in the right hand margin, perhaps suggesting that it might be omitted or highlighted in the spoken form of the sermon.

'This faith doth not lie dead in the heart, but is lively and fruitful in bringing forth good works, (but without it can no good works be done that shall be acceptable and pleasing to God). As the light cannot be hid,[20] but will show itself, so a true faith cannot be kept secret, but when occasion is offered, it will break out and show itself by good works.[21]

It is no dead, vain, or unfruitful thing; but a thing of perfect virtue, of wonderful operation or working and strength, bringing forth all good motions and good works.'[22]

'A man may easily deceive himself and fancy that he by faith knoweth God, loveth him, feareth him, and belongeth to him, when in very deed he doth nothing less. For the trial of all this thing is a godly and Christian life. He that feeleth in his heart set to seek God's honour, and studieth to know the will and commandments of God, and to frame himself thereunto; and leadeth not his life after the desires of his own flesh,[23] but setteth his mind to serve God for his own sake; and for his sake also to love and to do good to every man; such a man may well rejoice in God, perceiving by his life that he unfeignedly hath the right knowledge of God, a lively faith, a steadfast hope,[24] a true and unfeigned love and fear of God. But he that giveth himself to live after his own sensual mind and pleasure clearly deceives himself, and seeth not his own heart, if he thinketh that he either knoweth God, loveth him, feareth him, or trusteth in him.'

'Christ himself saith, The tree is known by the fruit.[25] Therefore let us do good works and thereby declare our faith to be the lively Christian faith; adding to our faith virtue, and to virtue knowledge, and to knowledge temperance, and to temperance patience, and to patience godliness, and to godliness brotherly kindness, and to brotherly kindness charity.[26] So shall we show indeed that we have the very lively Christian faith, and may so both certify our conscience the better that we be in the right faith, and confirm other men.'

'If these fruits do not follow, we do but mock God, and deceive ourselves and others. We may bear the name of Christians but we do lack the true faith that doth belong thereunto, for the true faith doth ever bring forth good works, as St. James saith, Show me thy faith by thy works[27]. Thy deeds and works must be an open testimonial of thy faith: otherwise thy faith, being without good works, is but the devil's faith,[28] the faith of the wicked, a phantasy of faith, and not the true Christian faith. And like as the devils and evil men be nothing the better for counterfeit faith, but it is unto them the more cause of damnation; so they that be Christians and have received the knowledge of God and of Christ's merits, and yet live idly without good works, thinking the name of a naked faith to be either sufficient for them, or else setting their minds upon vain pleasures of this world, do live

---

[20] Cf. Matt. 5: 15.
[21] The sentence which follows is taken from part two of the Homily 'Of Faith'.
[22] The next three paragraphs are extracted from part three of the Homily 'Of Faith'.
[23] Cf. Eph. 2: 3.   [24] Cf. Heb. 6: 19.   [25] Cf. Matt. 7: 20.
[26] Cf. 2 Pet. 1: 5–7.   [27] Jas. 2: 18.   [28] Cf. Jas. 2: 19.

in sin, not bringing forth the fruits that belong to such an high profession. Upon such presumptuous persons must needs remain the great vengeance of God, and eternal punishment in hell. Therefore as you profess the name of Christ, let no such phantasy or imagination of faith at any time beguile you; but be sure of your faith; try it by your living; look upon the fruits that come of it; mark the increase of love and charity by it towards God and your neighbour, and so shall you perceive it to be a true and lively faith. If you feel and perceive such a faith in you, rejoice in it, and be diligent to maintain it, and keep it still in you. Let it be daily increasing, more and more by well working, and so shall you be sure that you please God by this faith, and at length come to him and receive the end of your faith, even the salvation of your soul.'[29]

Our Church's doctrine concerning works is as follows: [30]

'Without faith can no good work be done, acceptable and pleasing to God. For as a branch cannot bear fruit of itself, saith our Saviour Christ, except it abide in the vine, so cannot you except you abide in Me. I am the vine, and you are the branches. He that abideth in Me, and I in him, he bringeth forth much fruit; for without Me ye can do nothing.'[31] And St. Paul ~~saith~~ in his epistle to the Romans saith, 'Whatsoever work is done without faith, it is sin.'[32] Faith giveth life to the soul; and they be as much dead to God that lack faith, as they be to the world whose bodies lack souls. Without faith all that is done of us is but dead before God, although the work seem never so gay and glorious before man. Even as the picture is but a dead representation of the thing itself, so are the works of all unfaithful persons before God. They be but shadows and shows of lively good things, and not good and lively things indeed. For true faith doth give life to the works; and out of such faith come good works that be very good indeed; but without faith no work is good before God.'

'We must set no good work before faith, nor think that before faith a man may do any good works. For such works, although they seem unto men to be praiseworthy, yet indeed they be but vain and not allowed before God. They be as the course of a horse that runneth out of the way, which taketh great pains, but to no purpose. Let no man, therefore, reckon upon his good works before his faith: whereas faith was not, good works were not. Where faith is not the foundation there is no good work, what building soever we make. There is one good work, in the which be all good works, that is faith which worketh by love.[33] If thou hast it thou hast the ground of all good works. But without this faith he that hath the virtues hath them not, but only the names and shadows of them. All the life of them that lack the true faith is sin; and nothing is good without him who is the

---

[29] 1 Pet. 1: 9.
[30] The following three paragraphs are extracted from part one of Homily 5 'Of Good Works Annexed unto Faith' ('Of Good Works').   [31] Cf. John 15: 4–5.
[32] This is a loose paraphrase of parts of Rom. 3, not a direct quotation.   [33] Gal. 5: 6.

author of goodness: where he is not, there is only feigned virtue, although it be in the best works.'

'You shall find indeed many which have not the true faith, and yet as it appeareth, they flourish in good works of mercy. You shall find them full of pity, compassion, and given to justice; and yet for all that, they have no fruit of their works, because the chief work lacketh. For when the Jews asked of Christ what they should do to work good works, he answered, This is the work of God, to believe in him whom he sent;[34] so that he called faith the work of God. And as soon as a man hath faith, immediately he shall flourish in good works; for faith of itself is full of good works, and nothing is good without faith. Faith may not be naked without good works, for then it is no true faith; and when it is adjoined to works, yet it is above the works. For as men, that be very men indeed, first have life and after be nourished; so must our faith in Christ go before, and after that be nourished with good works. And life may be without nourishment, but nourishment cannot be without life. ~~I can show~~ A man must needs be nourished by good works; but first he must have faith. He that doth good deeds, yet without faith, he hath no life. I can show a man that by faith without works lived and came to heaven. The thief which was hanged when Christ suffered, did believe only, and the most merciful God justified him.[35] And because no man shall say again, that he lacked time to do good works, for else he would have done them: truth it is, and I will not contend therein, but this I will surely affirm, that faith only saved him. If he had lived and not regarded faith and the works thereof, he should have lost his salvation again. But this is what I say, that faith by itself saved him, but works ~~by themselves~~ never justified any man.'

'What manner of works they be which spring out of true faith,[36] and lead faithful men unto everlasting life, cannot be known so well as by our Saviour Christ himself, who being asked by the ruler, 'What good thing shall I do that I may have eternal life?' answered, 'If thou wilt enter into life, keep the commandments.'[37] By which words Christ declared that the laws of God be the very way[38] that doth lead to everlasting life. So that this is to be taken for a most true lesson, taught by Christ's own mouth, that the works of the moral commandments of God be the very true works of faith, which lead to the blessed life to come.'[39]

Such is the doctrine of our excellent and truly apostolical church; and you cannot now but own the infinite importance of being well assured that you have the true faith, even that sure and substantial faith which saveth sinners, and is (to repeat the words of the homily)[40] not only the common belief of the Articles of our

---

[34] John 6: 29.   [35] Cf. Luke 23: 40–3.

[36] This paragraph is extracted from part two of the Homily 'Of Good Works'.

[37] Matt. 19: 16–17 and parallel.

[38] A final 's' has been poorly blotted in the MS so that at first glance the text appears to read 'ways.'

[39] At this point the material which Charles has extracted from the Homilies ends.

[40] Here, as elsewhere, Charles uses [] rather than (). However, the latter are used in the text to avoid modern confusion as to their significance.

faith, but also a true trust and confidence of the mercy of God through our Lord Jesus Christ; and a steadfast hope[41] of all good things to be received at God's hand, a certificate and sure looking for them.

Examine yourselves, my brethren, whether ye be in this faith. If you are not, all your good works are vain, and like a building without a foundation. And you may easily deceive yourselves herein, as I, and thousands besides have done. It is easy to say and think that you believe; but you must feel it. The true faith is to be felt 'and is not in the mouth and outward profession only, but liveth and stirreth inwardly in the heart.'[42] So saith the Church, and saith not the scripture the same: 'If thou shalt believe in thine heart, thou shalt be saved, for with the heart man believeth unto righteousness.'[43]

Hence it evidently appears that the faith which is unto righteousness,[44] or true justifying faith, is of the heart, not of the head; and he who can deny, much more he who can ridicule a faith which is to be felt, demonstrates that his faith is false, as sure as the word of God is true.

Further, if you think the apostle's advice unnecessary, that you need not examine yourself whether you be in the faith, but take it for granted and make no doubt of it but you are; this too is an infallible proof that you are not. He that never doubted never believed, but the god of this world hath blinded[45] his eyes, and deluded him with a faith, false and counterfeit and diabolical like his own. The reason whereof is this:[46] no man's faith is perfect at first, but accompanied, or rather assaulted and tried by many doubts and fears springing from the evil heart of unbelief; which doubts are not wholly dissipated and chased away till the believer is come to a perfect man, to the measure of the stature of the fulness of Christ.[47] Whosoever then hath not experienced these doubtings, he hath never begun to fight the good fight of faith;[48] but he is easy and satisfied about his state; he doubts not of his having faith, or rather he thinks not at all about it; his goods are therefore in peace, because the strong man armed[49] still keeps possession.

You[50] were not born with faith; where then and when and how did you come by it? Learned you it from books or men; by reasoning upon what you have read or heard? hereby you might acquire a human but not a divine faith. You can demonstrate, as

---

[41] Cf. Heb. 6: 19.   [42] Homily 'Of Faith'; book one, sermon four.   [43] Cf. Rom. 10: 9–10.

[44] Rom. 10: 10.   [45] 2 Cor. 4: 4.

[46] The words 'the reason whereof is this' have been added by Charles above the line.

[47] Eph. 4: 13.

[48] In the phrase 'he hath never begun to fight the good fight of faith', the words 'he' and 'begun to' have been inserted by Charles above the line. The shorthand symbol here transcribed as 'fight' (in the infinitive verbal form 'to fight'), in fact has a vowel point in the position of 'o' rather than 'i' (as comparison with the noun 'fight' three words later indicates). It appears, then, that Charles originally wrote 'hath never fought the good fight' which he changed to 'hath never begun to fight the good fight'. The difference is slight, but may be theologically significant. 'Fight the good fight' is from 1 Tim. 6: 12.

[49] Luke 11: 21.

[50] This whole paragraph has been bracketed by Charles in the right hand margin, perhaps suggesting either that it is an extract from some other source or that it might be omitted in the spoken form of the sermon.

may every thinking man, that Christianity must be of God, but if you think you therefore believe, you deceive your own souls, and the truth is not in you.[51] 'The natural man receiveth not the things of the spirit of God: faith is the gift of God; no man can call Jesus the Lord but by the Holy Ghost;[52] flesh and blood cannot reveal it unto him.[53] Faith standeth not in the wisdom of man, but in the power of God.[54] It must be wrought by a stroke of omnipotence. It is the Holy Ghost alone who purifies the heart by faith.'[55]

If this seems strange or new to any of you, that faith is the effect of almighty power; if any among you does even assent to this divine truth, 'faith is the gift of God,'[56] but as to a truth he had not heard or considered before; oh let not that man think he hath faith. He may most surely have it, if, being convinced of unbelief, and utterly renouncing his own works [and] righteousness,[57] both what he hath done and what he is, he humbly and meekly waits to receive this unspeakable gift[58] at the hands of God. But he hath it not yet, unless he is sensible and conscious of its having been wrought in his soul by him who made it.

That you may the better prove your own self, and examine whether you be in the faith,[59] I shall mention the marks or effects of true faith as plainly laid down in scripture; and beseech you by the mercies of God,[60] by the concern you ought to have of your own heart, to consider and[61] try whether these effects of faith be in you.

The first of these is reconciliation with God attested by an inward peace of conscience, even the peace of God which passeth all understanding,[62] bequeathed unto us by our parting Lord.[63] This immediately springs from a sense of forgiveness; faith, pardon and peace being so linked together and intermingled that neither men nor devils can separate them: 'Being justified by faith we have peace with God through our Lord Jesus Christ' (Rom 5.1) 'by whom we have now received the atonement' (verse 11). We have now received it, and by faith the first moment we believed in Jesus 'in whom we have redemption through his blood, the forgiveness of sins' (Eph 1.7). The scripture everywhere speaks of forgiveness as a present grace (not as something to be looked for at the hour of death only) and describes it as the inseparable effect of faith; so that whosoever hath faith hath forgiveness; whosoever hath not forgiveness, hath not faith.

---

[51] At this point in the MS there is a mark indicating an insertion, but what Charles intended it to be is not obvious. 'The truth is not in us/him' is found in 1 John 1: 8; 2: 4.   [52] Cf. 1 Cor. 12: 3.

[53] Cf. Matt. 16: 17.   [54] Cf. 1 Cor. 2: 5.   [55] Cf. Acts 15: 8–9.

[56] Cf. Eph. 2: 8.

[57] The words here transcribed as 'works and righteousness' appear as the symbol 'wr' only in the text. There is no sign for 'and', though there is a dot over the 'w' which probably indicates that it is to be read as a separate whole word and not the first consonant of a word that also includes 'r'. An alternative reading would be works-righteousness (i.e. a righteousness which is based upon works) but given the dual nature of the next clause this seems less likely.   [58] 2 Cor. 9: 15.

[59] Cf. 2 Cor. 13: 5.   [60] Cf. Rom. 12: 1.

[61] The words 'consider and' have been added by Charles above the line.   [62] Phil. 4: 7.

[63] Cf. John 14: 27.

A second effect of faith is joy; for so saith the apostle speaking in the person of all believers, 'Being justified by faith we have peace with God through our Lord Jesus Christ, by whom also we have access by faith into this grace wherein we stand, and rejoice in hope of the glory of God; and not only so, but we glory in tribulations also.'[64] Thus again verse ten, 'When we were enemies we were reconciled to God through the death of his son; and not only so, but we also joy in God through our Lord Jesus Christ.' This joy we have in believing; and he who contradicts the scripture by denying it only proves himself to be without that faith from which it flows. He is that stranger who intermeddleth not with his joy[65]; not being born of God, he cannot see the that kingdom of God, which is righteousness and peace and joy in the Holy Ghost.[66]

A third effect of faith is liberty, not only from the guilt, but likewise from the power of sin. The language of every true believer is this: 'There is therefore now no condemnation to them which are in Christ Jesus. For the law of the spirit of life in Christ Jesus hath made me free from the law of sin and death.'[67] This glorious effect of faith, liberty from sin, is fully and strongly asserted throughout Romans six: 'Sin shall not have dominion over you; for ye are not under the law but under grace. Ye were the servants of sin, but ye have obeyed from the heart that form of doctrine which was delivered you. Being then (namely, when you did first believe with the heart) made free from sin, ye became the servants of righteousness.'[68]

Hereby, my brethren, ye may try yourselves whether you be in the faith. If the son hath made you free, then are you free indeed.[69] Where the spirit of the Lord is, there is liberty;[70] and this spirit is received by the hearing of faith. If Jesus is by faith your Jesus, then hath he saved you from your sins. He that believeth is born of God, and whosoever is born of God doth not commit sin, for his seed remaineth in him, and he cannot sin because he is born of God.[71]

A fourth effect of true saving faith is love. These two are inseparable. Faith works by love, and he that loveth not knoweth not God, for God is love[72]: but whosoever truly believes, has the love of God shed abroad in his heart by the Holy Ghost which is given unto him (Rom 5.5). Having not seen the Lord Jesus, he loves him; in whom, though now he sees him not, yet believing, he rejoices with joy unspeakable and full of glory.[73]

This love to God he expresses and evidences by his love to man; seeing everyone that loveth ~~God loveth~~ him that begat, loveth him also that is begotten of him, (1 John 5.1); and hereby we know that we are passed from death unto life, because we love the brethren.[74] We love them as Christ loved us, and are ready to lay down our lives for them.[75]

---

[64] Rom. 5: 1–3.   [65] Cf. Prov. 14: 10.   [66] Rom. 14: 17.
[67] Rom. 8: 1–2.
[68] Rom. 6: 14, 17–18. The parenthesis denotes Charles's interpolation into an otherwise verbatim quotation.   [69] Cf. John 8: 36.
[70] 2 Cor. 3: 17.   [71] 1 John 3: 9.   [72] 1 John 4: 8.
[73] Cf. 1 Pet. 1: 8.   [74] 1 John 3: 14.   [75] Cf. 1 John 3: 16; John 15: 13.

My brethren, have you this genuine fruit of faith? Do you love the Lord Jesus in sincerity? Does the love of Christ constrain you[76] so that you desire only to spend and to be spent for him and for your brethren? Unless you find your hearts drawn out after Christ by an affection infinitely stronger . . .[77] you have not that faith which works by love, you do not yet believe in Christ.

I shall give you a fifth mark of faith in the words of the beloved disciple. 'He that believeth on the son of God hath the witness in himself,' (1 John 5.10), 'and hereby know we that we dwell in him and he in us, because he hath given us of his spirit' (4.13). So testifies the great apostle speaking to those for whom there is no condemnation, who are in Christ Jesus;[78] that is, who have the true ~~justifying~~ [79] saving faith. 'Ye have not received the spirit of bondage again unto fear, but ye have received the spirit of adoption, whereby we cry "Abba, Father." '[80] The spirit itself beareth witness with our spirit, that we are the children of God.[81] And in the same eighth chapter to the Romans, he speaks no less than 15 times of this spirit as the common privilege of all believers; and they that explain away these texts explain away the whole scripture; and may as well cast off all revelation at once. Whatsoever they be, it maketh no matter to them: they be blind leaders of the blind,[82] and give God the lie no less than his Church, who deny the Holy Ghost to be the common privilege of all believers to the end of the world.

But I trust, my brethren, ye are not of those who thus grieve the spirit of God,[83] contradicting and blaspheming. I trust that many of you have received not the spirit of the world, but the spirit of God; that you might know the things which are freely given to you of God, being sealed with the holy spirit of promise[84] which is the earnest of your inheritance.—But if any man hath not the spirit of Christ, he is none of his; for as many as are led by the spirit of God, they and they only are the sons of God.[85] Are you thus led, not by your own, not by the spirit of the world, but by the spirit of God in all things? Hath God sent the spirit of his son into your hearts? Doth he or hath he borne witness with your spirit that ye are the children of God? [86] Do you live in the spirit and walk in the spirit? Or do these scriptures appear foolishness unto you? Or do you imagine them not to be to you? You may

---

[76] Cf. 2 Cor. 5: 14.

[77] The MS is confusing at this point since the remainder of this line is left blank and the words 'you have not that faith . . .' are written on the line below. It is possible that Charles was intending to return to this section at a later point, perhaps after having reflected on the best words to use to get his message across. If so he has failed to do so. The reference to a 'source document' in Albin and Beckerlegge (32 n. 14) is no more than a justifiable guess at the possible reason for this strange omission. Other speculations (for example that Charles was intending to add at this point in the spoken discourse a reference to some actual person or persons to whom the words seemed particularly to apply) are possible, but no less impossible to prove.   [78] Rom. 8: 1.

[79] The symbol here transcribed as 'justifying' (apparently missed by Albin and Beckerlegge) is unclear in the text and has been poorly formed. The stroke for 'f' crosses the stroke for 'j' and then both are struck through and replaced with 'sv/ing' above the line.   [80] Rom. 8: 15.

[81] Rom. 8: 16.   [82] Matt. 15.14 and parallel.   [83] Cf. Eph. 4: 30.

[84] Eph. 1: 13.   [85] Cf. Rom. 8: 14.   [86] Cf. Rom. 8: 14–15.

[receive][87] this blessed spirit, if as yet you know him not. May he now fall upon you, at least in his convincing power, and reprove you of sin;[88] because not having received him, ye believe not on the name of the only begotten son of God![89]

I should only mention one more mark of faith, without which all the others are fallacious and wrought by that lying spirit of delusion who continually opposes the work of God. This great and outward and visible mark of faith is obedience or an holy life, as appears from the whole tenor of scripture. I shall first allege that place of St. John in his first epistle, chapter two, verse two etc. 'hereby we know that we know him (that is, believe in him) if we keep his commandments. He that saith, I know him, and keepeth not his commandments, is a liar, and the truth is not in him. But he that keepeth his commandments, in him verily is the love of God perfected. Hereby know we that we are in him.'

It is evident from hence, that without obedience, all our pretensions to faith are vain. Without obedience, the inward marks of faith are mere phantasm, or the effect of diabolical illusion: as on the contrary, where the inward marks are not, such as peace, love, joy in the Holy Ghost,[90] all outward obedience is merely formal and Pharisaical. Holiness is the test and evidence, no less than the end of faith. We are God's workmanship created through faith in Christ Jesus unto good works; which God hath before ordained that we should walk in them (Eph 2.10). The very design of our Lord's coming was to purify to himself a peculiar[91] people zealous of good works;[92] to make us holy in all manner of conversation;[93] and to set us an example that we should tread in his steps[94] who went about doing good.

He therefore that saith he abideth in him, ought himself also to walk as he walked.[95] This is a faithful saying, and these things his apostles affirmed constantly, that they which have believed in God might be careful to maintain good works. This was the second thing I proposed exhorting you to, namely, that you might be careful to maintain, or as it ~~ought rather to be~~ should rather be translated, to excel in good works.[96] I have done already it[97] in some measure, but it can never be pressed upon you too much; seeing by this alone you can declare, and evidence to yourselves and others,[98] that you have the true faith. 'For what doth it profit, my brethren, that a man say he hath faith, and hath not works? Can a faith which is without works save him? Can an idle, dead and devilish faith avail for his salvation?

---

[87] The words here are somewhat confusing. The word 'receive' added by Albin and Beckerlegge and retained here does not appear in any form in the MS, but seems required by the context; 'you may' and 'this blessed spirit' are clear enough. Charles may simply have made a slip here and accidentally omitted the required verb.   [88] Cf. John 16: 8.

[89] John 3: 18.   [90] Cf. Gal. 5: 22; Rom. 14: 17.

[91] This word has been inserted by Charles above the line.   [92] Titus 2: 14.   [93] 1 Pet. 1: 15.

[94] Cf. 1 Pet. 2: 21.   [95] 1 John 2: 6.

[96] Titus 3: 14; Charles has in mind the Greek word 'προΐστασθαι'.

[97] In the MS 'already' has been added above the line and the insertion mark is placed between 'done' and 'it'. The order in Albin and Beckerlegge is a probably correct reordering of the words as Charles meant them rather than wrote them.

[98] Charles has inserted 'to yourselves and others' above the line.

Of the true faith he hath none at all. He only says he has it; for unless he shows it by his works, he has certainly no faith to show.

In the sight of God we are justified by faith only without works; but in the sight of men we are justified by works and not by faith only. By faith alone we are counted righteous before God, but by works alone we are declared righteous before men. This very faith we are taught[99] by the great asserter of justification by faith only, Saint Paul, who in the midst of his discourse upon this head, inserts the necessity of holiness and good works, 'What shall we say then, shall we continue in sin that grace may abound? God forbid! How shall we that are dead to sin live any longer therein?'[100] So the sixth chapter of his epistle to the Romans, which is all an exhortation to an holy life. So in the eighth chapter, he several times points out those which are in Christ Jesus, and of whom there is therefore no condemnation, by this mark, 'who walk[101] not after the flesh but after the spirit.'[102]

The same he strongly insists upon in all his epistles, spending the last chapters always in exhortations to all manner of virtuous actions. The sum of all is this: 'As ye have therefore received Christ Jesus so walk ye[103] in him; rooted and built up in him; and established in the faith' (Col 2.6, 7). These two, receiving Christ and walking in him, or faith and obedience, comprehend the whole duty of a Christian and are, and must continue for ever, inseparable. Christ is the author of eternal salvation to all them that obey him; and to none beside, saying, 'Whosoever doth not righteousness is not of God, and without holiness no man shall see the Lord. But if we walk in the light as he is in the light, we have fellowship one with another, and the blood of Jesus Christ cleanseth us from all sin.'[104]

If Christ be given for us, he is likewise given to us; he is formed in our hearts by faith,[105] and lives and reigns in our souls. If Christ is made unto me righteousness, he is, he must be, made unto me sanctification also.[106] His righteousness is not imputed to me[107] unless I manifest it by righteousness inherent in me. Whom he justifies, them he also sanctifies.[108] Having put off the old man they put on the new, which is created unto righteousness and true holiness.[109] They are good that do good, being conformed both outwardly and inwardly to Christ Jesus;[110] in whom

---

[99] There is significant ambiguity in the text at this point. Albin and Beckerlegge have 'this w e/ir[?] verily we are taught' and add a note indicating that the phrase they transcribe as 'we are taught' might read 'were throughout', though quite how this alternative reading would fit in the context is not clear. The shorthand seems to read 'this wer f/vrif wr tt' and a dot beneath the second 'f' on f/vriꜰ probably indicates that it is to read as a separate word. The word 'this' is clear enough and the 'wer' is commonly 'we are' in Charles's shorthand (as it is two lines above in the phrase 'In the sight of God we are justified . . .'). The sign which has been taken here as 'very faith' has a rather odd formation in the MS and 'very faith' is questionable ('very' less so than 'faith'). The 'wr' is most problematic and has here been excluded as an erroneous repetition of 'wer' two signs before, a suggestion that is less than satisfactory. The sign 'tt' has the meaning of 'taught' in page 5 line 13 of the same sermon MS.   [100] Rom. 6: 1–2.

[101] The shorthand here appears to be 'mrk'. Albin and Beckerlegge suggest that here is an example of 'a writer's error', which seems likely; Rom. 8: 4 has 'walk'.   [102] Rom. 8: 1.

[103] 'Ye' has been inserted above the line.   [104] 1 John 1: 7.   [105] Cf. Eph. 3: 17.

[106] Cf. 1 Cor. 1: 30.   [107] Cf. Rom. 4: 22.   [108] Cf. Rom. 8: 30.

[109] Eph. 4: 22–4.   [110] Cf. Rom. 8: 29.

neither circumcision availeth anything, nor uncircumcision,[111] but a new creature. And as many as walk according to this rule, peace be upon them, and mercy, and upon the Israel of God.[112]

By this rule, my brethren, I trust you are resolved to walk, from a full conviction of the absolute, indispensable, eternal need of holiness and a good life. You who do believe, I ~~am persuaded when~~ would more especially exhort that you would not be barren or unfruitful in the knowledge of the Lord Jesus, but ~~will to~~ abound yet more and more in knowledge and in all judgment; being filled with the fruits of righteousness which are by Christ Jesus unto the glory and praise of God.[113] God rewardeth every man according to his works,[114] that the ~~greater~~ more our works, the ~~greater~~ more will be our reward. May you therefore improve every talent to the utmost; having obtained mercy, may you labour more abundantly. Let it be your meat to do the will of your Father.[115] Let it be your constant employment to serve and relieve your Saviour in his poor[116] distressed members.

He[117] gives you now a blessed opportunity. For inasmuch as you do it to one of ~~these his little ones~~ the least of these his children, you do it unto him.[118] He himself has assured you that whosoever shall give a cup of cold water to one of these little ones in the name of a disciple,[119] he shall in no[120] wise lose its [*sic*] reward. Above all give charity because this is the noblest, as taking in both the body and soul. What you give them is given toward training up so many candidates for eternity, and the lover of little children is now waiting to receive it at your hands.

Indeed whenever you do ~~herein[?] or to the poor~~ an alms, you should do it unto the Lord and not unto man. You should see and revere your Saviour in every poor man you ease, and be as ready to relieve him as you would to relieve Christ himself.[121]

Is Christ,[122] is he, an hungered? Give him meat. Is he thirsty? Give him drink. Is he a stranger? Take ye him in. Clothe him when he is naked; visit him when he is sick. When he is in prison, come ye unto him. So shall he say unto you when he comes in his glory, and all the holy angels with him, 'Come ye blessed

---

[111] Gal. 5: 6.   [112] Gal. 6: 16.   [113] Phil. 1: 11.

[114] Cf. Prov. 24: 12.   [115] Cf. John 4: 34.

[116] The word 'poor' has been inserted above the line.

[117] The whole of this paragraph has been written by Charles on the opposite page (i.e. on the verso of leaf 12) and a mark inserted in the text indicating the point at which it was intended to be read.   [118] Matt. 25: 40.

[119] Matt. 10: 42.

[120] Before 'no' there is another sign which has been struck out in the MS. The meaning of this sign is unclear.

[121] This section is similar to part one of Homily 23 'Of Alms-Deeds, and Mercifulness towards the Poor and Needy' ('Of Alms-Deeds').

[122] These words mark the end of the insertion. The MS continues on leaf 13.

of my Father, inherit the kingdom prepared for you from the foundation of the world.'[123] Which God grant us all, for the alone merits of his son Christ Jesus; to whom, with the Father and the Holy Ghost, be ascribed all honour and glory, adoration and praise, now, henceforth, and evermore. Amen.

[123] Cf. Matt. 25: 34–40.

SERMON 6
ROMANS 3: 23–4

INTRODUCTORY COMMENT

Charles's sermon on Romans 3: 23–4 carries three notes regarding the date and location of its delivery. These are 21 January 1739 at Islington, 25 February 1739 at Bexley, and 11 March 1739 at St Catherine's. All three dates can be confirmed from the journal and all are according to the 'new style'. The response to the sermon on these occasions appears to have been mixed. At Bexley some twenty of the congregation left the church.[1] In all three places Charles refers to this sermon as being on 'justification' (or 'justification by faith' in the case of Islington and Bexley). In this context it is worth noting that he records in his journal that he discoursed on this topic on several other occasions during that year, though it is not clear whether he made use of this sermon text.[2] (The 'sermon on justification' which Charles preached before the University (of Oxford) on 1 July 1739 is Sermon 7, the longer sermon on Romans 3: 23–5.) No dispute surrounds the authenticity of this sermon. There is nothing on the MS suggesting anything other than its composition by Charles.

The MS is held in the MARC.[3] It comprises eighteen leaves formed from nine folded sheets which have been stitch-bound into a booklet. Leaves 2–15 are written recto only and leaves 16–17 are entirely blank. Leaf 1, which, together with leaf 18, forms the front and back cover, is written verso only and contains a sermon register (three entries) and a section of shorthand at the bottom which is upside-down (see text for details). The final leaf is also written verso only; here we find a few notes, unrelated it seems to the sermon, on the formation of shorthand signs.[4] The handwriting appears to be that of Charles.

The sermon was first published in 1987 by Albin and Beckerlegge in their edition of the shorthand sermons and that transcription has proven invaluable in the preparation of this edition. However, on a number of points the text as printed here differs from that in Albin and Beckerlegge and the more significant of those differences have been indicated in the notes. Similarly, though in many places the reading given by Albin and Beckerlegge seems to be the most likely, there are occasions when it is perhaps less certain than they indicate. Again, such instances are indicated in the notes and a literal, unexpanded transcription of the shorthand is provided for the reader's further consideration.

This is one sermon where Charles draws fairly extensively on sources other than the Bible. The most important and obvious of these are the Articles of the Faith and the Homilies, particularly the homilies 'Of The Misery of Man' and 'Of the Salvation of all

---

[1] MARC DDCW 10/2 *in loc.*; Telford, *Journal*, 224.   [2] See for example 6 and 22 September.
[3] MARC CW Box 5.
[4] The words are 'substantive dot just under the last letter; adjective dot on the left hand of it; adverb dot on the right'. These rules are then illustrated with the shorthand stroke for 'r' with the words 'religion' 'religious' and 'religiously' written against the appropriate stroke.

Mankind'. Charles's general use of such sources has been discussed in Chapter 2 above. This sermon then itself became a major source for Charles's expanded treatment of Romans 3: 23–5 in the longer sermon on justification, Sermon 7.

This sermon puts forward Charles's 'post-Pentecost' views on the process of justification, and the text exudes an air of soteriological optimism that seems characteristic not just of the 'post-Pentecost' Charles, but of the Wesleyan revival and indeed the evangelical revival in general. As such it fits well with the previous two sermons in this volume. Throughout there is an uncompromising plea for what Charles considers to be the Pauline doctrine of justification by faith. Like Paul in the letter to the Romans, Charles first seeks to show from scripture and tradition that all have sinned and come short of the glory of God and that there is nothing that the individual can do to improve this situation. Even good works performed will not avail, for good works done by wicked sinners are nothing but vain attempts to justify themselves and seek to avert the coming wrath. (It should be noted, however, that Charles quotes with apparent approval the views put forward in Article XII to the effect that good works done by the justified believer are the proper and necessary response to God's act of saving grace.) But God in his mercy has provided an escape route: faith in the blood of Christ. As one would expect of a revivalist preacher, this determined presentation of the efficacy of the sacrifice of Christ dominates the soteriology of the sermon.

Jan. 21, 1739   Islington[2]
Feb. 25, ——   Bexley[3]
Mar. 11, ——   St Catherine's[4]

I. N. D.[5]

Romans 3: 23, 24 All have sinned, and come short of the glory of God; being justified freely by his grace, through the redemption that is in Christ Jesus

Of all the questions which ever did or can employ the minds of men, the most important is that of Bildad's, 'How can man be justified with God?' (Job. 25:4). We are all by nature sold under sin,[6] and enemies to God; and consequently children of wrath[7] and heirs of hell. This our church shows at large from Scripture, in her Homily of the Misery of Man, and of his condemnation to death everlasting by his own sin. Some of her words are these:[8] 'God, who knoweth us best, thus setteth us forth by his faithful apostle Saint Paul, "All men, both Jews and Gentiles, are under sin. There is none righteous, no, not one.[9] They are all gone out of the way, they are altogether become abominable, there is none that doeth good, no, not one."[10] God hath concluded all in unbelief.[11] We cannot think a good thought of ourselves, much less can we say well or do well of ourselves.'

Saint John in the name of himself and all other holy men, be they never so just, makes this open confession, 'If we say we have no sin, we deceive ourselves and the truth is not in us. If we say we have not sinned, we make God a liar, and his Word is not in us.'[12] So the wise man: 'There is not a just man upon earth that doeth good, and sinneth not.'[13] And David is ashamed of his sin, but not to confess it.

---

[1] This record of Charles's preaching is found on the inside of the front cover. At the bottom of this page the following words appear: 'him that cometh to me I will in no wise cast out [cf. John 6: 37]. Come unto me, all that labour and are heavy laden, and I will refresh you [cf. Matt. 11: 28]. He that hath ears to hear, let him hear [cf. Mark 4: 9 and parallels; Luke 14: 35]. He to whom his sins are a burden, let him come and lay them down at [the] foot of the cross. If any man thirst let him come unto Christ and drink, and the water which he shall give him shall be in him a well of water springing up unto everlasting life [cf. John 7: 37; 4: 14].' These words (in shorthand) are written upside-down and there appears on this page, also upside-down, the number '17'.

[2] 'I was much affected under Mr St[onehouse]'s sermon. Preached myself in the afternoon, to a crowded church , on justification by faith.' MARC DDCW 10/2 *in loc.;* Telford, *Journal*, 218.

[3] 'Preached justification by faith at Bexley. In the beginning of my discourse about 20 went out of church. They were better pleased with (or at least more patient of) me in the afternoon, while I preached on the woman at our Saviour's feet.' MARC DDCW 10/2 *in loc.*; Telford, *Journal*, 224.

[4] 'Preached justification at S. Catherine's.' MARC DDCW 10/2 *in loc.*; Telford, *Journal*, 225.

[5] *In Nomine Dei*. For the use of this invocation see the note on Sermon 3.

[6] Rom. 7: 14.   [7] Eph. 2: 3.

[8] As Albin and Beckerlegge note, the remainder of this paragraph and all of the next two are condensed from Homily 2 on 'The Misery of Man'.   [9] Cf. Rom. 3: 9–10.

[10] Cf. Rom. 3:12.   [11] Cf. Rom. 11: 32.   [12] Cf. 1 John 1: 8, 10.

[13] Cf. Eccl. 7: 20.

How oft, how earnestly and lamentably doth he desire God's mercy for his great offences, and that God would not enter into judgment with him.[14] And again, how well weigheth this holy man his sins, which he confesses, that they be so many in number, and so hid, and hard to understand, that it is in a manner impossible to know, utter, or number them. Wherefore, not yet coming to the bottom of them, he maketh supplication to God to cleanse him from his[15] secret faults.[16] He weigheth rightly his sins from the original root and springhead, and saith, 'Behold, I was conceived in sin!'[17]

Our Saviour Christ saith, 'There is none[18] good but God;[19] and without him we can do nothing,[20] nor can any man come to the Father but by him'.[21] He commandeth us also to say that we are unprofitable servants when we have done all that we can do.[22] He preferreth the penitent publican before the holy Pharisee.[23] He calleth himself a physician, but not to them that be whole, but to them that be sick and have need of him.[24] He teacheth us in our prayers to acknowledge ourselves sinners and to ask righteousness and deliverance at our heavenly Father's hands.[25] He declareth that the sins of our own hearts do defile our own selves.[26] He teacheth that an evil thought or word deserveth condemnation.[27] He saith he came to save only the sheep that were utterly lost and cast away.[28] Therefore few of the proud, just, learned, wise, perfect and holy Pharisees were saved by him, because they justified themselves by their counterfeit holiness before men.

Thus have we heard how evil we be of ourselves, how of ourselves and by ourselves we have no goodness, help or salvation; but contrariwise, sin, damnation and death everlasting. Of ourselves we are very sinful, wretched and damnable; not able either to think a good thought, or work a good deed, so that we can find in ourselves no hope of salvation, but rather whatsoever maketh unto our destruction.[29]

It is thus our church, before she treats of the salvation of man, describes [the] misery of man his misery, because before till we are deeply sensible of this, the all attempts to remove it must prove vain and ineffectual. Before we can take one step towards our divine physician, we must go and confess and groan under our disease.[30]

---

[14] Cf. Ps. 143: 2.

[15] The shorthand here reads simply 'f/vis', which Albin and Beckerlegge transcribe as 'of his'. However, the words seem dependent upon Ps. 19: 12 and hence 'from his' seems more probable.

[16] 'Secret faults' is not clear in the text. The shorthand reads 'sf' with a contraction point beneath the 'f'. One might suggest 'sins and failings'. However, in context 'secret faults' would be appropriate, for the words seem dependent upon Ps. 19: 12.   [17] Cf. Ps. 51: 5.

[18] The shorthand here reads 'nn', which Albin and Beckerlegge expand to 'no one'. However, the words are clearly dependent upon Matt. 19: 17 and hence 'none' seems certain.

[19] Cf. Mark 10: 18 and parallels.   [20] Cf. John 15: 5.   [21] Cf. John 14: 6.

[22] Cf. Luke 17: 10.   [23] Cf. Luke 18: 10 ff.; this is the subject of Sermon 13.

[24] Cf. Mark 2: 17 and parallels.   [25] Cf. Matt. 6: 9 ff. and parallel.   [26] Cf. Matt. 15: 18.

[27] Cf. Matt. 5: 22, 27–8.   [28] Cf. Luke 15: 4 ff.

[29] As Albin and Beckerlegge note, this paragraph is extracted verbatim from Homily 2 'The Misery of Man'.

[30] Charles may have in mind Mark 1: 40 and parallel at this point, and/or Matt. 9: 27.

We must own it is by us incurable,[31] and in a holy despair go out of ourselves for a remedy. But to you who truly feel yourselves sick, do I show the way of peace and salvation. Come unto me, saith the author of it, all ye that are weary and heavy laden.[32] He calls none but only the weary and heavy laden,[33] because he knows none else will come. Such only do I invite in his name, such as are not startled at being told they deserve, not one, but ten thousand hells, even as many as their own infinite sins and transgressions.

To you therefore my fellow sinners and fellow prisoners, who are in the same condemnation with me, do I declare the way, the only way whereby we may flee from the wrath to come;[34] and this I shall show in the words of our own excellent church, as they are plainly set forth in the homilies of salvation, which are perhaps the noblest compositions now upon earth, excepting only the inspired writings.[35]

'Because all men be sinners and offenders against God, and breakers of his law and commandments, therefore can no man by his own acts, works or deeds, seem they never so good, be justified or made righteous before God; but every man of necessity is constrained to seek for another righteousness or justification to be received at God's own hands, that is to say, the forgiveness of his sins and trespasses. And this justification or righteousness, which we so receive of God's mercy and Christ's merits, embraced by faith, is taken, accepted and allowed of God for our perfect and full justification.

For the more full understanding hereof, it is our duty ever to remember the great mercy of God, how that (all the world being wrapped in sin by breaking of the law) God sent his only Son[36] our Saviour Christ into this world, to fulfil the law for us,[37] and by the shedding of his most precious blood, to make a sacrifice[38] and satisfaction or amends to his Father for our sins, and assuage his wrath and indignation conceived against us for the same.

Insomuch that infants being baptised, and dying in their infancy, are by his sacrifice washed from their sins, brought to God's favour, and made his children, and inheritors of his kingdom of heaven. And they which in act or deed do sin after

---

[31] Before 'incurable' there is another sign in the text which has been struck out. The sign appears to be 'ncncr' and probably represents Charles's first attempt at writing 'incurable'. If so he appears to have realized that he had written the compound sign for 'nc' twice, struck it out and started again.

[32] Cf. Matt. 11: 28.

[33] 'He calls only the weary and heavy laden' are written above the line and Charles has indicated by an insertion point the place at which they are to be read. These words themselves have had 'none but' added to them, again with an insertion point to make their intended position plain.

[34] Matt. 3: 7 and parallel.

[35] As Albin and Beckerlegge note, the following eight paragraphs are extracted from part one of Homily 3 'Of Salvation'.   [36] Cf. 1 John 4: 9.

[37] Cf. Matt. 5: 17.

[38] There are several places in the New Testament where the death of Jesus is described as a 'sacrifice' (either propitiatory or expiatory). Outside the Letter to the Hebrews, the main occurrences are Rom. 3: 25; 1 John 2: 2; 4: 10 (all given as 'propitiation' in the KJV); Mark 10: 45 and parallel; 1 Tim. 2: 6 (both given as 'ransom' in the KJV).

their baptism,[39] when they turn again to God unfeignedly, they are likewise washed by his sacrifice from their sins in such sort that there remaineth not any spot of sin that shall be imputed to their damnation. This is that justification which St. Paul speaketh of, when he saith, 'No man is justified by the works of the law, but freely by faith in Christ Jesus.'[40] And again he saith, 'We believe in Christ Jesus, that we be justified freely by the faith of Christ, and not by the works of the law, because that no man shall be justified by the works of the law.'[41]

God, in the mystery of our redemption, hath so tempered his justice and mercy together, that he would neither by his justice condemn us unto the everlasting captivity of the devil and his prison of hell, remediless,[42] forever without mercy; nor by his mercy deliver us clearly without justice or payment of a just ransom. And whereas it lay not in us to pay[43] it, he paid a ransom for us; which was the most precious body and blood of his most dear and best beloved Son Jesus Christ; who besides this ransom, fulfilled the law for us perfectly.[44] And so the justice of God and his mercy did embrace together and fulfilled the mystery of our redemption.

Of this justice and mercy of God knit together, speaketh St. Paul (Rom 3), 'All have sinned, and come short of the glory of God, being justified freely by his grace, through the redemption that is in Jesus Christ: whom God hath set forth to be a propitiation through faith in his blood, to declare his righteousness'.[45] And chapter ten, 'Christ is the end of the law for righteousness to every one that believeth.'[46] And chapter eight, 'For what the law could not do in that it was weak through the flesh, God sending his own Son in the likeness of sinful flesh, and for sin, condemned sin in the flesh'; that the righteousness of the law might be fulfilled in us who walk not after the flesh but after the Spirit.[47]

In these places the apostle touches three things, which must go together in our justification. Upon God's part, his great mercy and grace; upon Christ's part, justice, that is the satisfaction of God's justice, or the price of our redemption, by the offering of his body and shedding of his blood,[48] with fulfilling the law[49] perfectly and thoroughly; and upon our part, true and lively faith[50] in the merits of Jesus Christ, which yet is not ours, but by God's working in us.

---

[39] 'After their baptism' is not entirely clear in the text, where the shorthand appears to read simply 'aftrb'. This may be 'after baptism', the reading found in Albin and Beckerlegge.

[40] Cf. Gal. 2: 16.

[41] This paragraph was taken verbatim from Homily 3 'Of Salvation'. The composite quotation draws on Gal. 2: 16; Rom 3: 24; Gal. 3: 11.

[42] 'Remediless' is not clear in the text. The shorthand reads 'rm'.

[43] Albin and Beckerlegge have 'do' rather than 'pay' at this point; however, 'pay' seems clear enough in the MS.   [44] Cf. Matt 5: 17.

[45] Rom. 3: 23–5.   [46] Rom. 10: 4.

[47] Rom. 8: 3–4. As Albin and Beckerlegge note, here as generally Charles replaced the older scriptural quotations in the Homilies with passages from the KJV.   [48] Cf. Mark 14: 22 ff. and parallels.

[49] Cf. Matt. 5: 17.

[50] The phrase 'true and lively faith', which recurs througout this sermon, is found in Article XII of the Articles of Religion.

St. Paul declareth here nothing upon behalf of man concerning his justification but only a true and lively faith which nevertheless is the gift of God.[51] And yet this faith doth not shut out repentance, hope, love, and the fear of God, to be joined with faith in every man that is justified, but it shutteth them out from the office of justifying. So that although they be all present together in him that is justified, yet they justify not all together.

Neither doth faith shut out our own good works, necessarily to be done after-wards of duty towards God (for we are most bounden to serve God, in doing good deeds commanded by him all the days of our life) but it excludeth them, so that we may not do them with this intent, to be made just by doing them. For all the good works that we can do be imperfect, and therefore not able to deserve our justifica-tion; but our justification doth come freely by the mercy of God; and of so great and free mercy, that whereas all the world was not able of themselves to pay any part towards their ransom, it pleased our heavenly Father, of his infinite mercy, without any our deserving, to prepare for us the most precious jewels of Christ's body and blood, whereby our ransom might be fully paid, the law fulfilled,[52] and his justice fully satisfied. So that Christ is now the righteousness of all them that truly do believe in him. He for them paid their ransom by his death;[53] he for them fulfilled the law in his life.'

In her second homily on salvation, our church proceeds thus:

Ye have heard of whom all men ought to seek their justification or righteousness; and how also this righteousness cometh unto men by Christ's death and merits. Ye have heard also how that three things are required to the obtaining of this righ-teousness; God's mercy, Christ's justice, and a true and lively faith, out of which spring good works. Also before was declared at large, that no man can be justified by his own good works, that no man fulfilleth the law according to the strict rigour of the law.

And St. Paul in his epistle to the Galatians, proveth the same, saying thus, 'If there had been any law given which could have justified, verily righteousness should have been by the law.'[54] And again he saith, 'If righteousness come by the law then Christ is dead in vain.'[55] And again, 'You that are justified by the law are fallen from grace.'[56] And furthermore he writeth to the Ephesians on this wise, 'By grace ye are saved through faith, and that not of yourselves, it is the gift of God; not of works lest any man should boast.'[57] And to be short, the sum of all Paul's disputation is this, that if righteousness come of works, then it cometh not of grace; and if it come of grace, then it cometh not of works. And to this end tend all the prophets, as St. Peter saith (Acts 10), 'To him give all the prophets witness, that through his name whosoever believeth in him shall receive remis-sion of sins.'[58]

[51] Cf. Eph. 2: 8.   [52] Cf. Matt. 5: 17.   [53] See note 38 above.
[54] Cf. Gal. 3: 21.   [55] Gal. 2: 21.   [56] Cf. Gal. 5: 4.
[57] Eph. 2: 8–9.   [58] Acts 10: 43.

And after this wise, to be justified only by this true and lively faith in Christ, speak all the ancient authors, both Greeks and Latins. St. Hilary saith these words plainly, 'Faith only justifieth.' St. Basil, 'This is a perfect and full rejoicing in God, when a man advanceth not himself for his own righteousness, but acknowledgeth himself to lack true righteousness, and to be justified by the only faith in Christ. And Paul, saith he, doth glory in the contempt of his own righteousness and looketh for the righteousness of God by faith.'[59]

St. Ambrose saith these words, 'This is the ordinance of God, that they which believe in Christ should be saved without works, by faith only, freely receiving remission of their sins.'[60] Consider diligently these words, 'Without works, by faith only, freely we receive remission of our sins.' Nevertheless, this sentence is not so meant of them, that the said justifying faith is alone in man, without true repentance, hope, charity and the fear of God, at any time or season. Nor do they mean that we are so justified without[61] works that we might be idle, and that nothing should be required on our part afterward; but this saying 'we be justified by faith only, freely, and without works'[62] is spoken to take away clearly all merit of our good works, and thereby most plainly to express the weakness of man and the goodness of God; the great infirmity of ourselves, and the might and power of God; the imperfection of our own works, and the most abundant grace of our saviour Christ, and therefore wholly to ascribe our justification unto Christ only, and his most precious blood-shedding.

This faith, the Holy Scripture teacheth us, is the strong rock and foundation of the Christian religion.[63] This doctrine all ancient authors of Christ's church do approve, this doctrine advanceth and setteth forth the true glory of Christ, and beateth down the vainglory of man; this whosoever denieth, is not to be accounted for a Christian man, nor for a setter-forth of Christ's glory, but for an adversary to Christ and his gospel, and for a setter-forth of men's vainglory.[64]

Justification is not the office of man, but of God; for man cannot make himself righteous by his own works, neither in whole nor in part; for that were the greatest arrogancy and presumption of man that Antichrist could set up against God, to affirm that a man might by his own works take away and purge his own sins, and so justify himself. But justification is the office of God only, and is not a thing which we render unto him, but which we receive of him. By his free mercy, and by the only merits of his most dearly beloved Son, our only Redeemer, Saviour,

[59] Cf. Phil. 3: 9; Charles has taken the quotations from the Fathers from Homily 3 'Of Salvation', part 2.   [60] Charles has taken this quotation from Homily 3 'Of Salvation', part 2.

[61] Before 'without' there is another word in the text which is unclear and, it seems, incomplete. Charles has struck it out. The sign appears to be a 'b' (or perhaps a 'p') with the vowel point for 'i' after it. This would suggest 'by'. In fact this is probably an example of homeoteleuton since in the next line of Charles's text we have the same two words, 'justified by', appearing together.

[62] The quotation marks are not present in the MS. They have been added here for the sake of clarity.   [63] Cf. 1 Cor 3: 11.

[64] In the margin next to this paragraph Charles placed a 'q'. He has quoted verbatim from Homily 3 'Of Salvation', part 2.

and Justifier, Jesus Christ. So that the true understanding of this doctrine—that we be justified freely by faith without works, or, we be justified by faith in Christ only[65]—is not that this our own act to believe in Christ, or this our faith in Christ, which is within us, doth justify us and deserve our justification unto us, (for that were to account ourselves justified by some act or virtue that is within ourselves) but the true meaning is ~~this~~ that although we hear God's word and believe it, although we have faith, hope, repentance, and the fear of God within us, and do never so many works thereunto, yet we must renounce the merit of all our said virtues and good deeds which we either have done, shall do, or can do, as things that be far too weak and insufficient to deserve remission of our sins, and our justification. And therefore we must trust only in God's mercy, and the sacrifice which our High Priest and Saviour Jesus Christ the Son of God, once offered for us upon the cross,[66] to obtain thereby God's grace and remission as well of our original sin in baptism, as of all actual sins committed by us after our baptism, if we truly repent, and turn unfeignedly to him again. So that as St. John [the] Baptist, although he were never so virtuous and godly a man, yet in this matter of forgiveness of sin, he did put the people from him, and appointed them to Christ, saying thus unto them, 'Behold, yonder is the Lamb of God which taketh away the sins of the world';[67] even so, as great and godly a virtue as the lively faith is, yet it putteth us from itself, and remitteth or appointeth us unto Christ, to have only by him remission of our sins or justification. So that our faith in Christ, as it were, saith unto us thus, 'it is not I that take away your sins, but it is Christ only; and to him only I send you for that purpose, forsaking therein all your good virtues, words, thoughts, and works, and only putting your trust in Christ'.

In the third homily upon salvation you have these words,[68]

'It hath been manifestly declared unto you that no man can fulfil the law of God, and therefore by the law all men are condemned: whereby it followeth necessarily that some other thing should be required for our salvation than the law, and that is a true and a lively faith in Christ, bringing forth good works, and a life according to God's commandments. And also you see the mind of this saying—we be justified by faith only[69]—is this: 'We put our faith in Christ, that we be justified by him only, and by no virtue or good works of our own that is in us, or that we can be able to have, or to do, to deserve the same, Christ himself only being the cause meritorious thereof.'

'Truth it is, that our works do not make us, for[70] unjust, just before God, but God of his own mercy through the only merits of his Son Jesus Christ doth justify

---

[65] Dashes have been added here for the sake of clarity.   [66] Cf. Heb. 7: 27.

[67] Cf. John 1: 29.

[68] As Albin and Beckerlegge note, the remainder of this paragraph and the three that follow are extracted from Homily 3 'Of Salvation'.   [69] Dashes have been added here for the sake of clarity.

[70] The text here clearly reads 'f/v uj' where in context 'uj' must mean 'unjust'. The meaning of the 'f/v' is less clear. Albin and Beckerlegge (p. 43) suggest 'of'; however, this results in the rather strange reading 'Truth it is, that our works do not make us, of unjust, just before God'. The reading suggested

us. Nevertheless, because faith doth directly send us to Christ for remission of our sins, and that by faith given us of God, we embrace the promise of God's mercy, and of remission of our sins (which thing none other of our works or virtues properly doth) therefore the Scripture useth to say, that faith without works doth justify.

'Yet that faith which bringeth forth either evil works, or no good works, is not a right, pure and lively faith, but a dead, devilish counterfeit, and feigned faith. For even the devils know and believe[71] all the Articles of our creed, and yet, for all this, they be but devils, remaining still in their damnable estate. For the right and true Christian faith is not only to believe the holy Scripture to be true, but also to have a sure trust and confidence in God's merciful promises to be saved from everlasting damnation by Christ: whereof doth follow a loving heart to obey his commandments.

'Therefore to conclude, these great and merciful benefits of God do not minister unto us occasion to be idle, and to live without doing any good work, neither yet stir us up by any means to do evil things, but contrariwise, if we be not desperate, they move us to render ourselves wholly unto God with all our will, hearts, might, and power to serve him in all good deeds, obeying his commandments during our lives; to seek in all things his honour and glory, not our own sensual pleasures and vainglory, evermore dreading willingly to offend such a merciful God and loving Redeemer in word, thought or deed. And the said benefits of God, deeply considered, move us for his sake also to be ever ready to give ourselves to our neighbours, ~~and as much as lieth in us~~ to study with all our endeavour, to do good to every man. These be the fruits of true faith, to do good as much as lieth in us to every man, and above all things, and in all things, to advance the glory of God, of whom only we have our sanctification, justification, salvation and redemption.'

This is our church's doctrine concerning justification which she thus sums up in her article, 'We are accounted righteous before God, only for the merit of our Lord and Saviour Jesus Christ by faith, and not for our own works or deservings. Wherefore, that we are justified by faith only, is a most wholesome doctrine, and very full of comfort, as more largely is expressed in the Homily of Justification.'[72]

In her Article of good works our church thus teaches:

Albeit that good works, which are the fruits of faith, and follow after justification, cannot put away our sins, and endure the severity of God's judgment, yet are they pleasing and acceptable to God in Christ, and do spring out necessarily of a true and lively faith, insomuch that by them a lively faith may be as evidently known as a tree discerned by the fruit.[73]

---

here is perhaps a slight improvement ('for' in the sense of 'in the place of'), but the situation is, to be sure, unclear.

[71] Cf. Jas. 2: 19.   [72] Article XI, 'Of the Justification of Man', is reproduced verbatim.
[73] Article XII, 'Of Good Works', is reproduced verbatim.
[74] Article XIII, 'Of Works before Justification', is reproduced verbatim.   [75] Rev. 13: 8.

Of works done before justification her judgment is this:

Works done before ~~the grace of God~~ the grace of Christ, and the inspiration of his Spirit, are not pleasing to God, forasmuch as they spring not of faith in Jesus Christ neither do they make men meet to receive grace, or as the school authors say, to deserve grace of congruity: yea rather, for that they are not done as God hath willed and commanded them to be done, we doubt not but they have the nature of sin.[74]

Having now laid before you the full doctrine of justification by faith only, as plainly proved from Scripture by our own Church, I shall first apply myself to those that deny this truth, and secondly to you who receive it.

And first as to those who deny this doctrine, and ignorantly call it new and the preachers of it schismatics. Would they look into their Bibles, they would find it as old as Christianity; they would find it as old as the fall of man, and his redemption in Christ Jesus, who was the Lamb slain from the foundation of the world[75] to take away the sin of the world.[76] But they do therefore err because they know not the Scriptures, neither the power of faith.[77] They find no such efficacy in their own historical, lifeless, shadowy faith, and so cannot conceive how faith only should justify. That their faith cannot justify, we readily grant; for if it could, the devils having the very same[78] would be justified ~~by it~~ too. But what must they do then in order to be[79] justified? Why, they will take in outward good works to their assistance, and then the business is done. The works of a heathen, and the faith of a devil will, in their judgment, make a man [a] complete Christian, and fully justify him in the sight of God.

Thus mighty are these men in the Scriptures; and as deeply skilled are they in the doctrines of our church. Tell me, you that are of the church, do ye not hear the Church?[80] I know ye do; and to you I therefore appeal. Judge you which are the schismatics, ~~??????~~[81] we who maintain, or they who deny, justification by faith only. Indeed, they are worse than schismatics who deny it; for if they have ever subscribed to our Articles, they are perjured schismatics. God forbid that I, or any of my brethren the clergy, should preach another gospel,[82] or bring any other doctrine than this. For we have solemnly declared upon oath our belief of this everlasting truth, 'We are justified by faith only'; and for us to teach any other doctrine would be wicked[83] flat inexcusable perjury.

---

[76] Cf. John 1: 29.   [77] Cf. Matt. 22: 29.   [78] Cf. Jas. 2: 19.

[79] The shorthand is rather unclear at this point. The strokes from 'dtb' are present, but not in the form one might have expected (Charles generally joins 't' and 'b' together when expressing the verbal form 'to be'). The situation is confused further by the alternative form as it appears in the longer Oxford sermon on justification; cf. further Sermon 7 below.

[80] Charles appears here to be playing on the wording of Gal. 4: 21.

[81] The shorthand signs that have been here struck out are now unreadable.   [82] Cf. Gal. 1: 6–8.

[83] 'Wicked' is not clear in the text. The shorthand reads 'w' with a point indicating that an adjective is signified. Albin and Beckerlegge (p. 45) suggest 'widely', though this seems unlikely as an adjective and not an adverb seems intended.

[84] 'Repugnant' is not clear in the text. The shorthand reads 'rpg' with a dot so positioned as to

One infamous evasion I know there is, but hope we all have it in equal abhorrence, namely that every man may subscribe the Articles in his own sense. We
grant that the seventeenth Article is purposely so worded as to take in people of
different sentiments, yet without giving the least sanction to the horrid doctrine
and decree of reprobation. But what is this to those Articles where the sense is
plain, precise and distinct, as it is in that of justification, for the full understanding of which, the Church refers us to her homilies, and thereby ties us down to the
one sense therein delivered. Nor is it in the power of words more fully and plainly
to express any truth, than she has there expressed that everlasting truth: 'We are
justified by faith only without works.'

What then, my brethren, can we think of those, if any such there be, who swear
to this Article in a sense altogether repugnant[84] and contrary to the true? Who
declare upon oath their belief that 'we are justified by faith only'? That is, say they
in their hearts, we are not justified by faith only, but by a popish[85] jumble of faith
and works. What horrid mockery is this of God and man? Can charity itself suppose ~~such a~~ that their mental reservation acquits them of perjury? Or does it not
rather wholly aggravate it? I shall say no more of this wicked subterfuge, but that
it was found out by our modern Arius,[86] that hereby he subscribed our Article
though he denied the Lord that bought him, ~~and that~~ as might ~~his~~ the elder
~~brother~~ Arius likewise, or any other heretic old or new.

Let not those, therefore, who deny this doctrine, any longer call themselves of
the Church of England. They may be of the Church of Rome, but cannot be of
ours, who allow works any share in our justification. Papists indeed they are,
though they may not know it; for they lay the wood, hay, stubble of their own
works, not as the superstructure, but as the very foundation of their acceptance
with God. Pharisees are they, for they justify themselves. Perjured are they likewise, as many of them as have sworn to the truth of what they deny. In short, they

suggest a substantive.

[85] Before the word 'popish' there appears another word that has been heavily struck out. That word
is difficult to read, but appears to be 'pssh', possibly a mistake for 'ppssh', to which Charles has
corrected it in the next sign.

[86] See Albin and Beckerlegge, 46 n. 16, for the possible reference to Samuel Clarke here. They write,
'Undoubtedly Charles had Dr. Samuel Clarke (1675–1757) in mind here. The subscription controversy
had occupied the attention of the Established Church in the latter part of the 17th century and the early
part of the 18th. The introduction to Clarke's work on *The Scripture Doctrine of the Trinity* (1712)
added fuel to these fires, particularly his statement, "that every person may reasonably agree to such
forms, whenever he can in any sense at all reconcile them with Scripture". Whiston immediately
opposed this proposition and Robert Nelson, Stephen Nye, Henry Stebbing and others soon followed.
In 1721 Dr. Waterland also entered the dispute with his tract entitled *The Case of Arian Subscription
Considered*. Charles's reference to Tillotson below may well have originated from Clarke's own use of
the Archbishop's works to defend his position.'

The subscription issue was never resolved in the 18th century as Francis Blackburne's anonymous
work entitled *The Confessional* (1766) and the Feathers Tavern petition of 1772 demonstrate. It was not
until an Act of Parliament in 1865 that the direction Clarke had begun reached the status of official
church policy.

[87] The sign for 'him' appears to have been inserted into the text at a later time. The sign is in a darker

may call themselves anything but Christians and Church of England men, for such we can never allow them to be; since, to repeat the words of the Church, 'Whosoever denieth this doctrine of justification by faith only, is not to be counted for a Christian man, nor for a setter-forth of Christ's glory, but for a setter-forth of men's vainglory, an adversary to Christ and his gospel.'

I am secondly to apply myself to you who receive this doctrine, as must everyone who receives the testimony of God and his Church. If it appears new to any of you, that a man is justified by faith only without the deeds of the law, let that man be assured that he trusteth in his own righteousness, and consequently is not justified, he hath not faith. Whosoever trusts not on the merits of Christ alone for justification, him[87] we must account to trust in something else: and he that does so cannot be justified by faith only, because he does not desire or expect it. This you own, my brethren, but see that you do not trust in your own righteousness. I hope you do not; but no man thinks he does: and of all instances of[88] self-deceit this is the most common. There is no one of us all who hath not trusted to his own righteousness more or less, and yet who of us will acknowledge it?

That you may know whether you still trust in it, let me persuade you to make this experiment. Suppose you see before you a scandalous and filthy sinner stained[89] with the most abominable, gross, and notorious vices, ~~with~~ guilty of[90] fornication, adultery, theft, perjury, covetousness, and murder; one who has lived in these and every other vice; who has done no good in his whole life, and all sorts of evil. Ask yourselves, what has this man to trust to? Nothing but the very grace of God, the infinite mercy of Christ Jesus. This you will readily ~~great~~ answer. But do you see that you have no more to trust to than he? That he has just as much to trust to as you have? The same physician[91] of souls, the same friend of sinners,[92] the same Saviour of that which was lost.[93] Do you now depend upon the blood of Christ[94] as fully, entirely, and solely as you would do were you this sinner? Do you rely on his death as the one sufficient satisfaction, oblation and sacrifice[95] for your sins, and on nothing else? On, nothing you either are, or have done? If you think

---

ink and extends a little into the right hand margin.

[88] The shorthand is very brief here; the MS reads only 'inf/v'. Albin and Beckerlegge suggest 'infamous'.

[89] Albin and Beckerlegge suggest 'stand' at this point (p. 47); 'stained' seems more probable in context. The shorthand reads 'stand' or, less probably, 's' followed by contraction point followed in the same compound sign with 'tnd'.

[90] The word 'with' has been struck out and replaced with the sign here transcribed as 'guilty of', which has been written to the left of the struck-out sign. The sign 'guilty of' is not entirely clear in the MS. The stroke here taken as a 'g' may in fact be an 'n', which would give the alternative reading 'envy', a reading found in Albin and Beckerlegge.   [91] Cf. Mark 2: 17 and parallels.

[92] Cf. Matt. 11: 19 and parallel.   [93] Cf. Matt. 18: 11 and parallel.

[94] 'Blood of Christ' is simply 'bc' in the MS with a dot so positioned as to indicated that two words are meant. Albin and Beckerlegge suggest 'benefits of Christ'.

[95] The words 'satisfaction, oblation and sacrifice' have here been expanded from a single sign 'sobs' in the MS. A dot placed before the horizontal stroke for the initial 's' indicates that more than one word is indicated by the composite sign. The words are taken from the *BCP* Prayer of Consecration.

[96] The sign here transcribed as 'justified' is 'jed' in the MS. Albin and Beckerlegge suggest 'judged'.

you have more to trust to than this murderer, thief, adulterer, then do you most infallibly trust, not to the merits of Christ only, but to something of your own, your own works or righteousness. If you cannot herein put yourself upon a level with this sinner, in that you look, like him, to receive a free pardon from the mere mercy of God in Christ Jesus; if you cannot submit to be justified[96] as ungodly; then are you of those that justify themselves; then are you further from ~~the kingdom of heaven~~ the kingdom of God[97] than the publicans and harlots;[98] then will even this thief, adulterer, and murderer enter into the kingdom of heaven before you.[99]

My brethren, let me press this matter something farther: why are you offended at being told you have just as much ~~more~~ to trust to, just as much merit, as a thief or common prostitute? Is it not because you really think you have more? But while you think you have any at all, [the] merits of Christ can never avail you; they can never be made yours till you renounce your own. If you have the least unwillingness to part with all the merits of all your best actions, it is plain to a demonstration[100] that you fancy there is some merit in them, or in other words, that you trust in them. If you imagine God cannot forgive a sinner because he has done no good works, you make good works into justification, and evidently show what you depend upon. You do trust to your own righteousness, unless in the matter of justification you utterly renounce it as filthy rags,[101] unless you count it but as dung and dross[102] that you may win Christ and be found in him, not having your own righteousness which is of the law, but the righteousness which is of God by faith.[103]

Turn your eyes once more to the wretch[104] above mentioned and behold him full of all filthiness both of flesh and spirit,[105] guilty of all the sins that ever were committed. Can anyone be in a worse condition than him? Yes; the man who thinks himself in a better, without Christ. Does anyone more need the merits of Christ? The man who imagines he needs them less. Is anyone at a greater distance from God? Yes, the virtuous, holy, self-justifying Pharisee. The greatest sin upon earth

[97] Cf. Mark 12: 34.

[98] The sign expanded here to 'publicans and harlots' is 'ph' only in the MS. A dot placed before the stroke for 'p' indicates that more than one word is indicated by the composite sign. Albin and Beckerlegge suggest 'prince of hell'. The words may be dependent upon Matt. 21: 31.

[99] Cf. Matt. 21: 31.

[100] The stroke indicating 'tion' is not present in the MS. The shorthand reads 'dmn' with a dot so placed as to suggest a substantive is to be understood.   [101] Cf. Isa. 64: 6.

[102] 'Dung and dross' is not clear in the text. The shorthand reads 'dd' with a dot so positioned as to suggest that two words are indicated. 'Dung' seems reasonably certain given the obvious influence of Phil. 3: 8–9 at this point; 'dross' is less clear.   [103] Cf. Phil. 3: 8–9.

[104] Albin and Beckerlegge suggest 'example' rather than 'wretch' and supply a footnote explaining their reasoning (p. 48 n. 18). However, the shorthand seems clear enough. It is, as Albin and Beckerlegge note, just possible that 'rch' (here expanded to 'wretch') could be read 'xm', but this would have involved Charles in an uncharacteristic slip in the formation of the shorthand sign and seems improbable.

[105] Albin and Beckerlegge indicate some uncertainty on 'spirit'. The shorthand reads 'fs' with a dot so positioned as to suggest that two words are indicated (demanded in context anyway by the preceding 'both').

[106] The shorthand reads 'q/knt' with a dot so positioned as to indicate that a substantive is intended.

is self-righteousness, and what God hates with the most perfect hatred. It is the quintessence[106] of that pride which cast Satan out of heaven and man out of Paradise; and though Christ hath died that we might receive mercy,[107] yet till we are purged of this abomination, Christ with regard to us, is dead in vain.[108]

The sum of all is this: ' ~~he filleth the hungry with good things and the rich he hath sent empty away~~. They that be whole need not a physician, but they that be sick. Christ came not to call the righteous but sinners to repentance.[109] He is the friend[110] and Saviour of sinners: not indeed of those who wilfully[111] continue in sin, but of those who feel the weight of it, and groan to him for deliverance. Whosoever is saved by him is saved as a sinner. His mouth is first stopped; he becomes guilty before God and submits to be justified freely by his grace through the redemption that is in Jesus Christ.'[112]

Which of you, my brethren, will consent to these conditions,[113] and suffer God to save him in his own way? You have often told him in the words of the church, that the remembrance of your sins was grievous unto you, the burden of them intolerable.[114] Was it so indeed, or did you only mock God when you told him so? Can you from your heart join in this prayer now? Would to God you could, for then you might be healed, you might believe unto righteousness[115] and ~~then would you~~ most assuredly know that the gospel is the power of God unto salvation to everyone that believeth.[116]

Blessed are the poor in spirit for theirs is the kingdom of heaven,[117] even that kingdom of God within which is righteousness and peace and joy in the Holy Ghost.[118] What hinders its being just now set up in your souls? Nothing but your not knowing yourselves sinners. To him that feelingly[119] knows it, our Lord himself hath said, 'him that cometh to me I will in no wise cast out.[120] Come unto me all that labour and are heavy laden and I will refresh you.[121] If any man thirst, let him come unto me and drink,[122] and the water that I shall give him shall be in him a well of water springing up into everlasting life.[123] He that hath ears to hear let him hear!'[124] He that hath a heart to ~~feel~~ believe, let him come. Whosoever thou art

---

Albin and Beckerlegge suggest 'counterpart'.

[107] The shorthand reads 'rem'; Albin and Beckerlegge suggest 'receive them'.   [108] Gal. 2: 21.

[109] Cf. Mark 2: 17.   [110] Cf. Matt 11: 19 and parallel.

[111] The shorthand reads 'w' only at this point with a dot so positioned as to indicate that an adverb is intended. Albin and Beckerlegge suggest 'wholly'.   [112] Rom. 3: 24.

[113] Albin and Beckerlegge suggest 'this condition'. However, the position of the medial vowel in the stroke for 'this/these' suggests 'e' rather than 'i' and the horizontal stroke for 'tion' appears to have been extended to 'tions' (the suffix 'tion' and the consonant 's' are both indicated by a horizontal stroke).   [114] *BCP*, Holy Communion, General Confession.

[115] Before the word 'righteousness' there appears another stroke in the text. It has been struck out and is evidently incomplete. After 'righteousness' there appears to be a full stop which has also been struck out.   [116] Rom. 1: 16.

[117] Matt. 5: 3.   [118] Rom. 14: 17.

[119] The sign here expanded to 'feelingly' is 'f/vling' with a dot so positioned as to suggest an adverb.

[120] John 6: 37.   [121] Cf. Matt. 11: 28.   [122] John 7: 37.

[123] John 4: 14.   [124] Mark 4: 9 and parallels.

[125] Luke 15: 2.   [126] The words 'not the righteous but' have been inserted above the line.

to whom thy sins are a burden, come even now and lay them down at the feet of Jesus. This man receiveth sinners, and eateth with them.[125] He justifies not the righteous[126] but the ungodly. He quickens those that are dead in trespasses and sins.[127] Hast thou faith to be healed, oh thou poor, infirm, helpless sinner? Believest thou that he is able to do this; to speak peace to thy soul at this very instant, and seal thy pardon by his promised Spirit? If thou canst believe, all things are possible to him that believeth.[128] It is possible for thee to know this moment that all thy sins are forgiven thee: and if thou dost believe, thou dost this moment know it. Thou feelest I have divine commission for speaking comfortably to thee and crying, 'Thy legal[129] warfare is accomplished, thy iniquity is pardoned, for thou hast received of the Lord's hand double for all thy sins!'[130]

---

[127] Cf. Eph. 2: 1.   [128] Mark 9: 23.   [129] The word 'legal' has been inserted above the line.
[130] Cf. Isa. 40: 2.

SERMON 7
ROMANS 3: 23–5

INTRODUCTORY COMMENT

On Sunday 1 July 1739, Charles records in his journal, 'I preached my sermon on justification before the University, with great boldness. All were very attentive. One could not help weeping.'[1] Even though there is no record of the place or date of preaching on the MS itself, it is plain that the sermon he preached on this occasion was the longer form of his sermon on justification, that is, the sermon on Romans 3: 23–5 which is reproduced here. The link is established by the bidding prayer, written in longhand at the beginning, which makes reference to those 'here in Oxford' including 'the Right Honourable Charles, Earl of Arran, our Honoured Lord and Chancellor'. This information, when combined with Charles's use of the term 'sermon on justification [by faith]' to refer to his shorter sermon on Romans 3: 23–4, printed here as Sermon 6, makes it certain that this was the text he preached before the university.

As was shown in the introduction to Sermon 6, Charles spoke fairly frequently on 'justification by faith' during the course of the next several months; it is not clear whether he used this or the shorter sermon text as the basis of his delivery. It is quite possible of course that he used neither.

This sermon is the longest to have survived, and one wonders how long it must have taken him to deliver it. The text as printed below amounts to close on 10,000 words, which if read at a reasonable speed and without 'adding much extempore' (as we know he was wont to do) would still take a good hour to preach.

The MS is held at the John Rylands University Library of Manchester[2] and is in a generally good state of repair. It comprises twenty-one leaves, twenty formed from ten folded sheets, one of which forms the front and back cover. The odd sheet is the one upon which the bidding prayer has been written, which raises the possibility that it may have been a later addition. All sheets are now stitch-bound to make a booklet. The leaves are written recto only, with the exception of two short additions on the verso of leaves 16 and 18. The places where these are to be inserted are clearly indicated in the text on the recto facing.

This sermon was first published by Albin and Beckerlegge as part of their edition of the shorthand sermons, and their original transcription has been invaluable in the preparation of this volume. However, as with the other sermons in the Albin-Beckerlegge edition, this has been thoroughly re-examined and numerous changes made and suggested. The more significant of these have been indicated in the notes.

This sermon draws fairly extensively upon Sermon 6, the shorter sermon on Romans 3: 23–4. It seems certain that the influence is this way round, since the shorter pre-dates this by more than six months. However, as Albin and Beckerlegge note,[3] Charles's use of the

---

[1] MARC DDCW 10/2 *in loc.*; Telford, *Journal*, 241.   [2] MARC CW Box 5.
[3] Albin and Beckerlegge, *Sermons*, 39 n. 6.

Homilies is less exact and less extensive in this sermon than in the shorter one. The quotations from the Homilies are identified in the notes to the text.

Charles here presents a vigorous account of his doctrine of justification by faith. As with the shorter sermon, he begins by following St Paul in first making the case that all indeed have sinned and fallen short of the glory of God. No one is exempt from this condition. There is a universal problem that needs a universal answer. In this context Charles puts forward the traditional Christian view regarding original sin. A corrupt tree can bring forth only corrupt fruit, therefore all the children of Adam are tainted by the sin of their forefather. They naturally incline towards the evil, which is itself evidence of corruption, and in addition attain that to which they incline. Nothing that human beings in this state do is in any way pleasing to God. Rather it is the blood of Christ that cleanses from sin and brings righteousness. This emphasis upon the total sufficiency of the blood of Christ to be applied in each individual case is characteristic of the preaching of the revival in general, and of these 'post-Pentecost' sermons of Charles in particular.

Let[1] us pray for all mankind, for the catholic Church; especially that part of it established in these kingdoms; for our gracious Sovereign Lord, GEORGE of Great Britain, France, and Ireland, King, Defender of the Faith; for their Royal Highnesses, Frederick, Prince of Wales, the Princess of Wales, the Duke, the Princesses, and all the Royal Family. For His Majesty's most honourable Privy Council, the Nobility, Clergy, Gentry, and Commons of this land; for all schools and nurseries of true religion and useful learning; particularly the two Universities. And here in Oxford, for the Right Honourable Charles, Earl of Arran, our honoured Lord and Chancellor;[2] for the very worthy the Vice-Chancellor;[3] for all the Doctors, both the Proctors, all heads and governors of Colleges and Halls with their respective societies; and (as I am more especially obliged) for the good estate of Christ-church; and therein for the Reverend the Dean, the Rt. Reverend, and Reverend the Canons, the students, chaplains, commoners, and all other members of that society.

Let us bless GOD unfeignedly for all his mercies in Christ Jesus, spiritual and temporal; particularly for the liberality of our founders and benefactors, among whom was Henry VIII, the munificent founder of Christ-church. Let us commend to his fatherly compassion the afflicted, and conclude our prayers saying:

Our[4] Father which art in heaven, hallowed be thy name. Thy kingdom come. Thy will be done in earth as it is in heaven. Give us this day our daily bread; and forgive us our trespasses, as we forgive them that trespass against us. And lead us not into temptation, but deliver us from evil. For thine is the kingdom, the power and the glory, for ever and ever. Amen.

---

[1] The bidding prayer is written in longhand. The fact that this is written in longhand may be significant. As is well known, the Wesleys were frequently suspected of Jacobite sympathies. On one occasion, it was alleged that Charles prayed for the Pretender. Part of the journal entry for Thursday 15 March, 1744 reads, 'Justice Burton said, he was informed that we constantly prayed for the Pretender in all our Societies, or *nocturnal meetings*, as Mr. Zouch called them. I answered, "The very reverse is true. We constantly pray for His Majesty K. George by name. These are such hymns as we sing in our Societies, a sermon I preached before the University, another my brother preached there, his Appeals, and a few more treatises, containing our principles and practice". Here I gave them our books, and was bold to say, "I am as true a Church-of-England man, and as loyal a subject, as any man in the kingdom"'. Charles may, then, have written the prayer in longhand in order to provide evidence when needed of his prayer for King George.

[2] As Albin and Beckerlegge note, the reference here is to Charles Butler, Earl of Arran, DCL, who was Chancellor from 1715 to 1758.

[3] As Albin and Beckerlegge note, the reference here is to Theophilus Leigh, DD, Master of Balliol and Vice-Chancellor from 1738 to 1740.   [4] The Lord's Prayer is written in shorthand.

†

I. N. I.⁵

Rom. 3: 23, 24, 25

All have sinned and come short of the glory of God, being justified freely by his grace,
through the redemption that is in Jesus Christ; whom God hath set forth to be a propitiation
through faith in his blood.

In⁶ this epistle the spirit of God⁷ by the mouth of his apostle, first convinces the
world of sin and then of righteousness.⁸ Herein is the wrath of God revealed from
heaven against all ungodliness and unrighteousness of men who hold the truth in
unrighteousness:⁹ as the heathen are first proved to do, because they lived not up
to the light of nature, or that knowledge of himself which God had showed unto
them. God therefore for their unthankfulness and idolatry¹⁰ gave them over to
uncleanness, to vile affections, to a reprobate mind: he severed¹¹ the best in them
to chastise the vile¹²; unnatural lust to punish learned pride.¹³

Next¹⁴ he proves the Jews to hold the truth in unrighteousness, and declares
them inexcusable and self-condemned for judging others, because they did the
same things which they condemned. They were called Jews indeed, and rested in
the law, and made their boast of God. But they did not keep the law they gloried
in, but dishonoured God by transgressing it. They broke it in its spiritual meaning. In heart they were thieves, adulterous, sacrilegious, and were all concluded
under sin by 'he is not a Jew which is one outwardly; neither is that circumcision
which is outward in the flesh: but he is a Jew which is one inwardly, and circum-

---

⁵ '*In Nomine Iesu*', 'In the name of Jesus'. See note on Sermon 3.

⁶ This paragraph is a summary of Rom. 1.

⁷ The shorthand sign for 'the spirit of God' is simply 'sog' ('son of God' is also possible, though less
likely in context). The definite article has been added here (as elsewhere in similar situations in this
sermon) in keeping with the grammatical demands of the context.   ⁸ Cf. John 16: 8.

⁹ Rom. 1: 18.

¹⁰ Albin and Beckerlegge suggest 'adultery' rather than 'idolatry. However, the intial 'i' seems fairly
clear in the text and idolatry seems better to fit in context.

¹¹ The word 'severed' is unclear in the MS. Albin and Beckerlegge suggest 'stirred', though it is at
least equally probable that the sign they have taken for a 't' is in fact an 'f/v'. If so the compound sign
is 'svrd' and not 'strd'. This seems in keeping with the logic of the remainder of the paragraph, which
is clearly based on Paul's argument in Rom. 1. According to Paul, the wicked slipped so far into sin
that 'God gave them up unto vile affections' (Rom. 1: 26) and 'gave them over to a reprobate mind'
(Rom. 1: 28). Sin punishes sin. It is perhaps this point that Charles is making, for he states explicitly
that 'unnatural lust' was used by God to punish the heathen's 'learned pride'. Similarly, perhaps, it is
Charles's view that God 'severed the best in them', i.e. he gave them over completely to sin, overruling
even that faint image of God that remained, as a way of chastising the vile.

¹² The MS is unclear at this point. It is possible that the shorthand transcribed here as 'vile' in fact
reads 'dvl', which would give 'devil'. However, the 'd', if it is there at all, is very indistinct.

¹³ In Albin and Beckerlegge the words 'unnatural', 'lust' 'punish', and 'learned' are marked as being
uncertain. The adjustment above of 'stirred' to 'severed' perhaps makes them less so. The shorthand
for the final six words in this paragraph reads 'untrl lst to pnsh lrnd prid'.

¹⁴ This paragraph is Charles's summary of Paul's argument in Rom. 2.

cision is that of the heart; in the spirit not in the letter, whose praise is not of men but of God'.[15]

To convince them that they[16] were in no wise better by nature than the heathen, he shows from Scripture that there is no one righteous, no, not one;[17] and then observes 'Now we know that what things soever the law saith, it saith to them that are under the law; that every mouth may be stopped, and all the world become guilty before God'.[18]

Therefore by the deeds of the law shall no flesh be justified in his sight.[19] The consequence is inevitable. Because all men without exception are breakers of the law, therefore by his obedience to the law shall no man living be justified with God.[20] For by[21] the law (the moral law) is the knowledge of sin[22] (only, but no deliverance from it). But now (that all men are condemned and proved to have no sufficient righteousness of their own) the righteousness of God without the law (that is as contradistinguished ~~from our own morals obedience~~ from legal right-eousness)[23] is manifested, being witnessed by the law and the prophets; even the righteousness of God (not of men) which is by faith of Jesus Christ (which by faith as the instrument of receiving it) is (imputed) unto all, and (bestowed or put) upon all them that believe: for there is no (natural) difference, for (as it follows in the words of my text) all have sinned, and come short of the glory of God: being justified freely by his grace through the redemption that is in Jesus Christ; whom God hath set forth to be a propitiation[24] through faith in his blood.[25]

In discoursing upon each word I shall first show that all have sinned and come short of the glory of God. Secondly, that we are justified freely by his grace through the redemption that is in Jesus Christ. Thirdly, I shall show what that faith is through which we receive the atonement *applied to our soul in particular*; and fourthly I shall conclude with a particular application.[26]

I am first to show that all have sinned and come short of the glory of God, 'ὑστεροῦνται τῆς δόξης τοῦ θεοῦ', are deprived of the glory of God, the glorious image of him that created them.[27] This is the cause of all actual ~~transgression~~ sin, our having lost the ~~moral~~ perfection of the divine nature. First then I shall show that we have sinned originally and then actually.

---

[15] Rom. 2: 28–9.

[16] Charles here began to write some word other than 'they', but struck it out at a very early stage of its formation.   [17] Rom. 3: 10.

[18] Rom. 3: 19.   [19] Rom. 3: 20.   [20] Ps. 143: 2.

[21] In place of 'by' Charles first wrote some other word. That original word is so heavily struck out that it is now unreadable in the MS.   [22] Rom. 3: 20.

[23] In the MS another word appears before 'righteousness', but has been so heavily struck out as to make it unreadable.

[24] As is clear elsewhere in the sermons generally, Charles is able to work with the Greek and fre-quently does so (see for example his quotation of ὑστεροῦνται τῆς δόξης τοῦ θεοῦ two paragraphs below). The fact that he keeps the KJV reading of 'propitiation' here (ἱλαστήριον) is hence potentially significant in the context of his view of the death of Christ.   [25] Cf. Rom. 3: 21–5.

[26] In the right margin Charles has placed the Roman numerals I–IV by the appropriate line.

[27] Cf. Gen. 1: 27.

God created man in his own image, after his likeness.[28] He made him perfect, but a little lower than the angels,[29] one in heart and mind[30] with himself, a real partaker of[31] the divine nature. But man soon fell from that original dignity. He sinned by eating of the forbidden fruit, and in the day that he ate he spiritually died. The life of his soul, consisting in its union with God (like as the natural life consists in the union of soul and body) his spiritual life, I say, was extinguished. The glory immediately departed[32] from him, and he knew that he was naked;[33] naked of[34] God, stripped of the divine image; a motley mixture of beast and devil.[35]

In the moment that he was thus alienated from the life of God, his understanding was darkened through the ignorance that was then in him. Then also, he first felt the torment of self-will, and hell of pride. His heart was turned within him, from good to evil, from the creator to the creature:[36] his very soul clave to the dust,[37] and all his affections became earthly, sensual, devilish.[38]

In him we see the type and father of us all. We all inherit from him a miserable, corrupt and sinful nature. We are a race of fallen spirits. We are all by nature children of wrath,[39] ignorant of good, and haters of God.[40] For the natural man (that is, every man without exception while in a state of nature) receiveth not the things of the Spirit of God: for they are foolishness unto him, neither can he know them because they are spiritually discerned.[41] The carnal mind is enmity against God;[42] for it is not[43] [subject] to the law of God, neither indeed can be. All the powers of man are totally depraved. The whole head is sick, and the whole heart faint.[44] From the sole of the foot even unto the head there is no soundness in him, but wounds and bruises and putrefying sores:[45] his understanding is darkened, his will perverse, his affections set on earthly things.[46] Pride and concupiscence make up his wretched composition; and if you take away that spark of God which was restored to him at his redemption, there remains in him nothing but pure beast and devil.[47]

---

[28] Cf. Gen. 1: 26–7.	[29] Cf. Ps. 8: 5; Heb. 2: 7.

[30] The shorthand here is simply 'ham' and is hence ambiguous. However, 'heart and mind' seems probable in context.

[31] The shorthand sign which has here been rendered 'partaker of' is simply 'pf' in the MS. One might suggest 'partner' or 'participant' in place of 'partaker'.

[32] There is a probable echo here of 1 Sam. 4: 21–2.	[33] Cf. Gen. 3: 7.

[34] The shorthand is ambiguous at this point. The sign here rendered 'naked of' is in the MS simply 'nf/v'. Albin and Beckerlegge suggest 'in the view of'.

[35] As Albin and Beckerlegge note (p. 52 n. 6), this phrase was originally coined by William Law. The phrase is used by Charles again in his sermon on Luke 18: 9, Sermon 12.	[36] Cf. Rom. 1: 25.

[37] Cf. Ps. 119: 25.	[38] Jas. 3: 15.

[39] The sign here rendered as 'children of wrath' is 'chr' in the MS (with contraction point beneath the ch). The reading seems certain on the basis of Eph. 2: 3.	[40] Rom. 1: 30.

[41] 1 Cor. 2: 14.	[42] Rom. 8: 7.

[43] Albin and Beckerlegge mark 'not' as uncertain at this point in the MS. However, the influence from Rom. 8: 7 is plain. The addition of 'subject' as the following word is also justified on the basis of that biblical text.	[44] Isa. 1: 5.

[45] Isa. 1: 6.	[46] Cf. Phil. 3: 19.	[47] On this phrase see above n. 35.

Such are we all through original sin, or 'that fault and corruption of the nature
of every man, whereby man is very far gone from original righteousness, and is of
his own nature inclined to evil, so that the flesh lusteth always contrary to the
Spirit'.[48] That this infection is, and remains, both in the unregenerate and regener-
ate, our own church teaches us[49] agreeable to Scripture and experience: and those
unhappy men ~~thus together~~[50] who deny this corruption, are themselves the
strongest proof of it. How else were it possible for one pretending to reason to
imagine such a creature as man could[51] in his present state come out of the hands
of a pure and wise and mighty God? As is the workman, such must be the workmanship. A powerful, perfect, happy being could make nothing weak, imperfect or
miserable. Man therefore must have undergone a change since his first creation. Of
this every thinking person has sensible demonstration in those astonishing contra-
rieties he finds within himself.[52] He finds two opposite principles, inclining him to
good and evil,[53] which nothing can account for but the scriptural doctrine of a
fallen race.[54]

But I now speak to those who acknowledge all Scripture to be given by inspiration of God:[55] and while we receive his testimony we must own that we are literally born in sin, and consequently children of wrath[56] and heirs of hell. We are
naturally engendered of the offspring of Adam. A corrupt tree can bring forth only
corrupt fruit;[57] and such as is the fountain, such must be the stream. Whence every
man must say with David 'Behold, I was shapen in wickedness, and in sin did my
mother conceive me';[58] or with Eliphaz 'What is man that he should be clean, and
he that is born of a woman that he should be righteous?'[59] (How then can man be
justified with God, or how can he be clean that is born of woman?) Alas, in him
dwelleth no good thing;[60] but sin dwelleth in him:[61] his inward parts are very
wickedness;[62] his heart is deceitful above all, and desperately wicked;[63] nay, every
imagination of the thoughts of his heart is only evil continually.[64]

How truly then does our church teach us that this infection of nature in every
person born into the world deserveth God's wrath and damnation;[65] for saith not
the Scripture so? By one single man's disobedience many are made sinners;[66] by

---

[48] Cf. Gal. 5: 17.   [49] See the ninth Article of Religion 'Of Original or Birth-sin'.
[50] The words here struck out are not clear in the MS.
[51] In the MS there is a word before 'could' which has been so heavily struck out as to make it
unreadable.
[52] Compare Albin and Beckerlegge, 53, for an alternative transcription. I am indebted to Mr Douglas
and Mrs Esther Lister for helpful suggestions regarding this sentence in particular.
[53] There is a probable echo here of Rom. 7: 23.
[54] 'A fallen race' is unclear in the text. The shorthand reads simply 'fr' with a contraction point over
the 'f'. However, 'a fallen race' seems to fit within the general context of the argument which Charles
is here developing.   [55] Cf. 2 Tim. 3: 16.
[56] On the phrase 'children of wrath' see above n. 39.   [57] Cf. Matt. 7: 17–18.   [58] Ps. 51: 5.
[59] Job 15: 14.   [60] Rom. 7: 18.   [61] Rom. 7: 17.
[62] Cf. Ps. 5: 9.   [63] Cf. Jer. 17: 9.   [64] Gen. 6: 5.
[65] See the ninth Article of Religion 'On Original or Birth-sin'.   [66] Cf. Rom. 5: 19.

the offence of one, judgment is come upon all men to condemnation.[67] In Adam all died.[68] Sin by him entered into the world, and death by sin, and so death passed upon all men for that all have sinned in him.[69] Death reigns by one, even spiritual,[70] temporal and eternal death. In the midst of life we are in spiritual death;[71] a few posseting[72] hours[73] brings on our trouble;[74] and that consigns us to the death that never dies, the fire that never shall be quenched.[75]

Such is the portion of our natural inheritance. We are all involved in the guilt of original sin,[76] which like the ancient flood has overspread the face of the earth, and sweeps all before it into a miserable eternity. The Scripture hath concluded all under sin;[77] and that not only original, but also actual. This the great apostle shows at large in the words preceding my text, where speaking of Jews and Gentiles he asks 'Are we better than they'? (are we in ourselves better than the most profligate sinners?) 'No, in no wise. For we have before proved both Jews and Gentiles that they are all under sin. As it is written '[78]There is none righteous, no, not one.[79] They are all gone out of the way, they are together become unprofitable, there is none that doeth good, no, not one.'[80] Now we know that what things soever the law saith, it saith to them that are under the law, that every mouth may be stopped and all the world become guilty before God.[81] There is no difference. All have sinned and come short of the glory of God'.[82] There is not a just man upon earth, said[83] the preacher, that doeth good and sinneth not':[84] and we have therefore the greatest reason, every one of us, to say with the man after God's own heart, 'Enter not into judgment with thy servant, Oh Lord, for in Thy sight shall no man living be justified.[85] If thou, Lord, wilt be extreme to mark what is done amiss, O Lord, who may abide it?'[86]

---

[67] Rom. 5: 18.   [68] Cf. 1 Cor. 15: 22.   [69] Rom. 5: 12.

[70] Before 'spiritual' there is another word in the MS which has been so heavily struck out as to make it unreadable.

[71] The shorthand in the MS is very much abbreviated at this point and hence uncertain. The words here rendered 'spiritual death' are in the MS simply 'sd'.

[72] The word 'posseting' (i.e. self-pampering) is not clear in the MS. The shorthand has 'psting' or possibly 'pssting'.

[73] This word is far from clear in the MS. The shorthand appears to be 'hrs', though the 'h' may be an 'x'. Albin and Beckerlegge have 'a foolish boasting exercise' in place of 'a few posseting hours'.

[74] 'Trouble' is not clear in the MS, which has simply 't' at this point. However, there may be a loose reference here to Job 14: 1.   [75] Mark 9: 43 ff.

[76] Albin and Beckerlegge (p. 54) have 'g[uilt?] of ours' rather than 'guilt of original sin'. These words are unclear in the text, but the transcription suggested above seems probable. The shorthand reads 'gf ors'. The single shorthand sign here rendered 'guilt of' appears with the meaning 'ignorant of' on page 5 of the MS, at line 10. It is just possible, though unlikely, that Charles used the one sign 'ors' to mean 'our sin', in which case the words 'guilt of ours' might be rendered 'ignorance of our sin' or perhaps better 'guilt of our sin'.   [77] Gal. 3: 22.

[78] The quotation marks are not in the MS. They have been added here for the sake of clarity.

[79] Rom. 3: 10.   [80] Rom. 3: 12.   [81] Rom. 3: 19.

[82] Rom. 3: 23.

[83] The signs for 'said' and 'saith' are difficult to distinguish in the shorthand, though some attempt has been made here to do so.   [84] Eccl. 7: 20.

[85] Cf. Ps. 143: 2.   [86] Cf. Ps. 130: 3.

From these and many other Scriptures, it is evident that if we say we have no sin, we deceive ourselves and the truth is not in us:[87] if we say we have not actually sinned, we make God a liar and his word is not in us.[88] We have offended and in many things do still offend all.[89]

This will appear still plainer to us, if we consider the nature and extent of that law in the transgressing of which sin consists. Indeed while we look upon it as did the carnal Jews, as do the generality of Christians, to be merely an outward fence or restraint, we may flatter ourselves[90] that we keep the law, because we abstain from the outward act of sin. But this is the least[91] part of the law. It does indeed condemn every one[92] of gross sin, and he that so committeth sin is of the devil; but it no less condemns every idle word and every unholy thought.[93] He breaks the law who breaks it outwardly and in the letter; but not he only. The law is spiritual,[94] that is, it has a meaning infinitely[95] broader, higher and deeper than we can at first sight perceive, richer indeed than we can ever perceive till God hath opened our eyes by that Spirit which he hath promised to send that he may reprove the world of sin.[96] Without his operation it is impossible to discern the full sense and spirituality of the law, though our Lord himself came down from heaven to discover it. Of this we need no stronger proof than those Christians, as they are called, who read his sermon upon the mount, and yet continue utterly ignorant of what spiritual righteousness means.

Throughout that excellent discourse, our Lord sets himself to rescue the law from those softening, polluting,[97] gross interpretations the scribes and Pharisees[98] had put upon it, who had purged it of all its spiritual meaning and taught[99] that whoso observed it outwardly fulfilled it effectually.[100] In opposition to this our divine teacher explains that law which he only could fulfil. He begins with discussing those holy tempers without which all outward obedience is formal and

---

[87] 1 John 1: 8.   [88] Cf. 1 John 1: 10.   [89] Cf. Jas. 3: 2.

[90] 'Fool ourselves' is not clear in the text. Albin and Beckerlegge have 'feel of ourselves', but this seems less probable. The shorthand is 'f/vors', where the 's' is formed in such a way as to suggest that '-tion' (or -esion) or 'selves' is meant. An alternative reading would be 'fool ourselves'.

[91] There is a possible echo here of Matt. 5: 19.

[92] The shorthand sign here transcribed as 'one of' is simply 'nf/v' in the MS with a vowel point indicating either an 'o' or an 'i' before the 'n'. Consequently one might read 'instance of' rather than 'one of' at this point.   [93] Charles may have the six antitheses in Matt. 5: 21–48 in mind here.

[94] Cf. Rom. 7: 14.   [95] Written 'infinite' in the MS.   [96] Cf. John 16: 8.

[97] 'Polluting' is unclear in the text. The composite shorthand sign clearly includes the consonants 'plt' and has the termination 'ing'. The vowel between 'p' and 'l' is indicated and appears most probably to be an 'e'. This would give 'pelting' as the basic frame of the word and not 'polting'. However, allowing for some slight inaccuracy in the positioning of the vowel point 'polluting' seems probable in context.

[98] 'Scribes and Pharisees' is 'sf/v' in the shorthand. However, the expansion to 'scribes and Pharisees' seems clear enough, and is confirmed by the frequent use of 'sf/v' to mean 'scribes and Pharisees' in Sermon 10 on John 8: 1 ff.

[99] The shorthand reads only 'tt' at this point in the MS. Albin and Beckerlegge suggest 'truth' rather than 'taught'.

[100] 'Effectually' is not clear in the text. The shorthand is simply 'ef/v' with a point so positioned as to indicate that an adverb is to be formed.

pharisaical. For all our pretensions to righteousness are vain till we taste that poverty of spirit, to which alone belongs the kingdom of heaven;[101] till we not only see but feel our misery, and go mourning all the day long,[102] refusing to be comforted by any created good, and looking for the Holy Ghost the Comforter.[103] To this must be added a meekness which no injuries can overcome, no affronts or indignities can exasperate;[104] a hunger and thirst after divine righteousness[105] as much stronger than the natural appetite, as spiritual food is better than bodily; a purity of heart which sees God and only God in everything. Merciful we must likewise be as our Father which is in heaven is merciful;[106] and lastly peacemakers,[107] like unto him when he was in Christ reconciling the world to himself.[108] After all, the world, or they that will not be reconciled to him, must set to their seal that we belong to Christ, by reviling and persecuting[109] and saying all manner of evil against us falsely for his sake,[110] while we rejoice and are exceeding glad, in nothing terrified by our adversaries, which is to them an evident token of perdition, but to us of salvation, and that of God.[111]

Such are the tempers required of every Christian as abounding[112] unto salvation.[113] Herein must our righteousness exceed the righteousness of the Scribes and Pharisees, or we shall in no wise enter into the kingdom of heaven.[114] God is a Spirit, and they that worship him must worship him in spirit and in truth.[115] He requires the heart; a spiritual not a mere literal obedience, the power of godliness not the bare form.[116] Wherefore if we allow him to be a true interpreter of the law, we must acknowledge ourselves to be transgressors of it. Two instances in the 6th commandment: concerning which our Lord himself assures us that not only he that sheddeth man's blood transgresses it, but that whosoever is angry with his brother without a cause, whoso expresses that anger in an opprobrious name or slighting word is guilty of murder.[117]

The seventh[118] commandment he explains in like manner, extending it to the first wandering of the desire: as that a[119] single thought, a secret motion of the heart makes a man in the sight of God a murderer or an adulterer.[120] And here he may justly say to every one of us, Thou art the man![121] Thou art a murderer, thou

---

[101] Cf. Matt. 5: 3.   [102] Ps. 38: 6.   [103] Cf. John 14: 16, 26; 15: 26; 16: 7.

[104] Cf. Matt. 5: 39.   [105] Cf. Matt. 5: 6.   [106] Cf. Matt. 5: 48.

[107] Cf. Matt. 5: 9.   [108] 2 Cor. 5: 19.

[109] Albin and Beckerlegge (p. 55) have 'being' in place of 'persecuting' at this point. However, the influence of Matt. 5: 11–12 is plain, and while the shorthand sign might just be a poorly written 'b' it is much more probably a 'p'. The extreme contraction to one letter is the result of Charles's familiarity with the text.   [110] Cf. Matt. 5: 11.

[111] Phil. 1: 28.   [112] This word is not clear in the text. The shorthand gives only 'ab'.

[113] The word 'salvation' is unclear in the text. The shorthand gives only 's' with a contraction point.

[114] Cf. Matt. 5: 20.   [115] John 4: 24.   [116] Cf. 2 Tim. 3: 5.

[117] Cf. Matt. 5: 21–2.

[118] A now unreadable word has been struck out above '7' (which is written in Arabic numerals).

[119] The word 'a' has replaced some other word that has now been so heavily struck out as to make it unreadable.   [120] Cf. Matt. 5: 27–8.

[121] 2 Sam. 12: 7.

art an adulterer! For which of us can say he never felt any touch of causeless anger against his brother? He that hath ever felt the least degree of hatred against another whether valid or not,[122] he stands convicted of murder: for he that hateth his brother is a murderer.

With respect[123] to the adulterer, likewise we may mark[124] our Lord's charge,[125] he that is without sin amongst you, let him first cast a stone at her.[126] But suppose our hearts could acquit us of having ever known one impure thought throughout our lives, are we hereby justified of this charge? No, in no wise. The apostle informs[127] us of a spiritual adultery. Ye adulterers and adulteresses, said he, know ye not that the friendship of the world is enmity with God?[128] Know ye not that the whole course of your life[129] is one continued ~~act~~ habit of rebellion, treachery, and unfaithfulness to that one husband to whom ye were espoused in baptism . . . unless you have indeed renounced that world which ye then so solemnly promised and vowed to renounce. If you have now any share[130] in its pursuits after riches, honour and pleasures, any conformity to its fashions,[131] any hope of keeping fair[132] with it, that is with those who are not led by the Spirit of God in love, then do you live in an habit of spiritual[133] adultery, then are you friends to the world and enemies to God.

To those among us[134] who are thus of the world, that is who either love or are loved by it, it may hence appear that they have not so much as the Pharisee's plea, 'I thank God that I am not as other men are, extortioners, unjust, adulterers!'[135] But suppose we had; does righteousness stand in negatives only? Does it not require good to be done as well as evil to be left undone? Yes[136] doubtless, we may

---

[122] 'Valid or not' is unclear in the text. The shorthand gives only 'f/vn'. The word 'whether' is however clear enough, and hence the presence of 'or' is required between 'f/v' and 'n'.

[123] The word 'respect' is unclear in the text. The shorthand reads simply 'r' at this point.

[124] Albin and Beckerlegge suggest 'make' rather than 'mark'. The shorthand reads only 'mk'.

[125] Albin and Beckerlegge suggest 'commandment' rather than 'charge'. However, the shorthand sign in the MS is reasonably clear and reads 'ch' with a dot so positioned as to suggest a contracted substantive.   [126] John 8: 7; and see Sermon 10.

[127] In context this seems the most probable meaning of the shorthand sign. However, it should be noted that the 'f' in 'infrms' has been formed in such a way as to look more like a 't' than an 'f'.

[128] Jas. 4: 4.

[129] 'Course of your life' is not clear in the MS, which reads only 'cf/vrl' with either a 'u' or an 'o' before the 'r'. Albin and Beckerlegge suggest 'conversation of our life'.

[130] Written as 'ashr' in the MS, but 'share' seems intended.

[131] The shorthand stroke here expanded to 'fashions' is 'f/vss' in the MS so written as to suggest that the suffix '-tions' is intended. Albin and Beckerlegge suggest 'affections'.

[132] 'Fair' is not clear in the text. The 'f/v' is plain as is the 'a'. However, the stroke here taken as 'r' might in fact be 'th', which might be read as 'faith', the reading suggested by Albin and Beckerlegge.

[133] The sign here transcribed as 'spiritual' is 's' only in the MS. Albin and Beckerlegge suggest 'secret'.

[134] The sign for 'among us' has been squeezed in, presumably at a later stage in the development of the MS, between 'those' and 'who'.

[135] Cf. Luke 18: 11. (The closing quotation mark does not appear in the MS.)

[136] The word 'yes' is not clear in the text. The sign appears to be 'hs' rather than 'ys'. However, 'yes' seems required by the context and it may be that Charles has been less than accurate in the formation of the 'y' (which is distinguished from the 'h' only by the former's inclination and the latter's perpendicularity).

answer, and go on with our boasting Pharisee, 'I fast twice a week, I give tithes of all that I possess,'[137] or to put it in other words, 'I use[138] all the means of grace, I do much good'. It is well: he is no fulfiller of the law that does not; but neither is he that does,[139] unless all these actions proceed from a heart entirely devoted to God; unless they are fruits of that perfect love required by the first and great commandment, 'Thou shalt love the Lord thy God with all thy heart and mind and soul and[140] strength'.[141] Who among us is there that can say, This have I done: I have so loved God; with my entire affection, with the utmost extent of my understanding, with all[142] and every degree of all my powers and feelings,[143] with the whole capacity and propensity[144] of my soul. Who of all the sons of Adam could ever say it? Alas we must confess, with man this is impossible:[145] here every mouth is stopped indeed, and all the world become guilty before God.[146]

As evil doers[147] are we concluded under sin[148] by almost every part[149] of the gospel. 'Pray without ceasing; in everything give thanks;[150] rejoice evermore;[151] whether ye eat or drink or whatsoever ye do, do all to the glory of God'.[152] But these Scriptures, some one will say, are not to be taken literally. I ask that person, who told you so? The world, the flesh, and the devil[153] did, I grant you; but not Christ: and their authority will never bear you out in your contempt of this: no, not though you could confront him (which God forbid you ever should) with ten thousand of his own almighty scriptures![154] Yea, let God be true, but every man a liar.[155] He hath assured us the law is spiritual,[156] and the commandment holy and just

---

[137] Cf. Luke 18: 12.

[138] In the manuscript the letter 'h' appears above the word 'use' and may have been intended to read 'habitually use'.   [139] A line, presumably indicating a pause, is placed here in the text.

[140] Albin and Beckerlegge omit 'and soul'. However the MS seems quite clearly to have an extended horizontal line at this point, indicating 'ss' rather than 's'. The influence of the biblical text seems apparent.

[141] Mark 12: 30 (the subject of Sermon 20) and parallels; Deut. 6: 5. The quotation mark at the beginning of the quotation has been supplied; the closing quotation mark is present in the MS.

[142] Another word appears between 'with' and 'all' but has been so heavily struck out as to make it unreadable.

[143] The words 'powers and feelings' are unclear in the text. the shorthand reads only 'pf', with a contraction point placed over the sign. In the context 'powers and feelings' seems plausible since Charles is here referring back to the words of the Shemaᶜ (Deut. 6: 5) which have been quoted a few lines above.

[144] 'Propensity' is not clear in the MS. Albin and Beckerlegge suggest 'possibility'. The shorthand reads 'pst', with the 't' being formed in such a way as to indicate that the suffix 'ity' is meant.

[145] Cf. Mark 10.27 and parallel.   [146] Cf. Rom 3.19

[147] 'Evil doers' is not clear in the text. The shorthand reads 'ef/vd' with a contraction point beneath the composite sign. In context 'evil doers' seems quite plausible.   [148] Cf. Gal. 3: 22.

[149] One might read 'precept' rather than 'part' at this point.   [150] 1 Thess. 5: 17–18.

[151] 1 Thess. 5: 16.

[152] 1 Cor. 10: 31. The quotation mark at the beginning of the quotation has been supplied; the closing quotation mark is present in the MS.   [153] BCP, Collect for 18th Sunday after Trinity.

[154] 'Almighty scriptures' is very uncertain. The shorthand reads simply 'ams' with what would appear to be a contraction point beneath the 'm', though it may be that the point is the sign of the vowel 'a' following the 's' (which would give 'amsa' as the basic framework of the word or words signified). Albin and Beckerlegge suggest 'amens' as another possible reading of this sign.   [155] Rom. 3: 4.

[156] Rom. 7: 14.

and good.[157] He hath likewise shown us a way whereby the righteousness of the law may be filled[158] in us without our bringing it down to the practice of modern Christians. If we will hearken unto him more than unto man,[159] we cannot but acknowledge that[160] the law does in the rigour[161] require perfection, or universal unsinning[162] obedience, to which we must therefore come up, or own ourselves transgressors. For whosoever shall keep[163] the whole law, and yet offend in one point, he is guilty of all:[164] and cursed is every one that continueth not in all things which are written in the book of the law to do them.[165]

Nor is the doing them outwardly the doing them at all. God requireth truth in the inward parts:[166] and he that is in Christ is a new creature in the strictest sense; old things are passed away in him and all things are become new.[167] He has a new heart, a right spirit created in him,[168] and has undergone an entire change. He is as different from what he was as light from darkness, life from death, the kingdom of God from that of Satan. But except a man be thus born again, he cannot see the kingdom of God;[169] he cannot so much as discern there is any such thing as that kingdom of God within,[170] which is righteousness and peace and joy in the Holy Ghost.[171] But till he knows this expressly, he knows nothing yet as he ought to know. So far is he from not offending in any, that he offends in every point of the law; so far is he from keeping the whole, that he does not fulfil the least part of it. Nor can he fulfil it in any, nor can he help breaking it in every particular, till he is renewed in the image of his maker,[172] and so born of God as not to commit sin;[173] till Christ, the end of the law for righteousness unto every one that believeth,[174] be of God made unto him wisdom and righteousness and sanctification and redemption.[175]

[157] Rom. 7: 12.

[158] The shorthand here is 'fld'; Albin and Beckerlegge have '[ful]filled', which seems more appropriate in context. However, at the bottom of page 7 of the MS and again on page 8, Charles has 'flfl' for 'fulfil' which suggests that had he meant 'fulfilled' here, he would have written the shorthand 'flfld'.

[159] There is a word in the MS before 'man' that has been struck out. It is difficult to read, but 'gd' or 'God' looks probable. If so it was a slip on Charles's part which he corrects with 'man' (or 'men').

[160] The words 'but acknowledge that' are unclear in the text. The 'b' is clear as is the 'a'. However, the 'k' may in fact be a 'q' and the final 'th' a 't'. Albin and Beckerlegge suggest 'be acquitted'.

[161] The word 'rigour' is unclear in the MS. The shorthand reads 'rgr' which could be 'righteousness of God revealed' or perhaps even 'revelation [of] God's righteousness' (Cf. Rom. 1: 17).

[162] The word 'unsinning' is not absolutely clear in the text, which is unfortunate given the potential significance of it to the task of assessing the views of Charles on 'perfection'. The shorthand strokes 'unsning' are reasonably plain, but the expansion more problematic.

[163] 'Shall' has been inserted into the text at this point and a correction made to the sign for 'keep'. It would appear that the text originally read 'for whosoever keepeth the whole law'.   [164] Jas. 2: 10.

[165] Gal. 3: 10.   [166] Ps. 51: 6.   [167] Cf. 2 Cor. 5: 17.

[168] Cf. Ps. 51: 10.   [169] Cf. John 3: 3.   [170] Cf. Luke 17: 21.

[171] Rom. 14: 17.

[172] Cf. Col. 3: 10. The shorthand here is brief in the extreme. It reads only 'ifism', which Albin and Beckerlegge take to mean 'imagination of his mind', though it is difficult to see what this phrase might mean in context. They suggest that 'spirit' rather than 'image' would be a more appropriate reading.

[173] Cf. 1 John 3: 9; 5: 18.   [174] Rom. 10: 4.

[175] The shorthand here is 'wrsr'; however 'wisdom, righteousness, sanctification and redemption' seems appropriate in view of the wording of 1 Cor. 1: 30.

This brings me to my second head, 'We are justified freely by his grace through the redemption that is in Jesus Christ'. A most important truth, as that on which alone depends the salvation of all men; but which no child of Adam can receive till he is thoroughly[176] convinced of sin; till he receives the sentence of death in himself, that he may not trust in himself; till, in a word, he owns and feels that all his desert is hell.

Before a man is thus deeply sensible of his misery, all attempts to remove it must prove vain and unfruitful.[177] Before he can take one step towards his divine physician, he must know and confess and groan under his disease.[178] He must acknowledge it is by him incurable, and in a just despair go out of himself for a remedy. 'Come unto me, says the God of our health, all ye that labour and are heavy laden, and I will give you rest'.[179] He calls none but the weary and heavy, because he knows none else will come. Such only do I invite in his name; such as are not startled or offended at being told they deserve not one, but ten thousand hells, even as many as their own infinite sins and transgressions.

Every sinner deserves to be damned, every man is a sinner, therefore every man deserves to be damned. Which of the premises[180] can be denied without denying the Scriptures? 'The wages of sin are death; the wrath of God is revealed against all unrighteousness of men, and there is none righteous, no, not one'.[181] The Scripture hath concluded all under sin.[182] To convince the world of this, is the first office of the Holy Spirit:[183] and when a man is truly convinced[184] of sin, then and not till then, may he be convinced[185] of righteousness also; even the righteousness of God which is by faith of Jesus Christ unto all and upon all them that believe; for there is no difference; for all have sinned and come short of the glory of God, being justified freely by his grace, through the redemption that is in Jesus Christ.

I shall deliver this foundation[186] doctrine[187] of justification by faith only, in the words of our own excellent church as they are plainly set forth in the homily 'Of Salvation'.[188]

Because all men be sinners and offenders against God, and breakers of his law and commandments, therefore can no man by his own acts, works and deeds, seem they never so good, be justified or made righteous before God; but every man of

---

[176] Albin and Beckerlegge suggest 'truly'. However, the initial 'th' seems probable.

[177] This paragraph, and the quotations which follow, also appear in Sermon 6 on Rom. 3: 23–4. 'Unfruitful' might be read as 'ineffectual'.

[178] Charles may have in mind Mark 1: 40 and parallel at this point.   [179] Cf. Matt. 11: 28.

[180] Albin and Beckerlegge (p. 58) transcribe this word 'promises' rather than 'premises'.

[181] Cf. Rom. 6: 23; 1: 18; 3: 10.   [182] Gal. 3: 22.   [183] Cf. John 16: 8.

[184] In the MS there is a word before 'convinced', but it is so faint as to make it almost unreadable.

[185] Before 'convinced' in the MS there is another shorthand mark, most probably an 'r', but this has now been struck out.

[186] 'Foundation' is not clear in the text. Albin and Beckerlegge suggest 'offending'.

[187] In the MS there is another shorthand sign before that for 'doctrine'. It is however faint and unreadable.

[188] The following nine paragraphs are taken by Charles from Homily 3, book one, 'Of Salvation'. Charles's use of quotation marks in this section has here been modernized.

necessity is constrained to seek for another righteousness or justification to be received at God's own hand, that is to say, the forgiveness of his sins and trespasses. And this justification or righteousness which we so receive of God's mercy and Christ's merits embraced by faith, is taken, accepted and allowed of God for our perfect and full justification.

For the more full understanding hereof, it is our duty ever to remember the great mercy of God, how that all the world being wrapped in sin by breaking of the law, God sent his only Son our saviour Christ into this world to fulfil the law for us, and by the shedding of his most precious blood, to make a sacrifice and satisfaction or amends to his Father for our sins, and assuage his wrath and indignation conceived against us for the same.

This is that justification which St. Paul speaketh of when he saith 'No man can be justified by the works of the law, but freely by faith in Christ Jesus'.[189] And again, we believe in Christ that we be justified freely by the faith of Christ and not by the works of the law, because that no man shall be justified by the works of the law.[190]

God in the mystery of our redemption hath so tempered his mercy and justice together, that he would neither by his justice condemn us without mercy, nor by his mercy deliver us clearly without justice or payment of a just ransom. And whereas it lay not in us to pay it, he provided a ransom for us which was the most precious body and blood of his most dear and best beloved Son Jesus Christ; who besides this ransom filled[191] the law for us perfectly; and so the justice of God and his mercy did embrace together and filled the mystery of our redemption.

Of this justice and mercy knit together speaketh St. Paul [in] Romans 3, all have sinned and come short of the glory of God, being justified freely by his grace, through the redemption that is in Jesus Christ. And chapter 10, Christ is the end of the law for righteousness to every one that believeth.[192] And chapter 8, for what the law could not do in that it was weak through the flesh, God, sending his own Son in the likeness of sinful flesh, and for sin, condemned sin in the flesh, that the righteousness of the law might be filled in us, who walk not after the flesh but after the Spirit.[193]

In these places the apostle touches three things which must go together in our justification. Upon God's part, his great mercy and grace; upon Christ's part justice, that is the satisfaction of God's justice, or the price of our redemption by the offering of his body and shedding of his blood with fulfilling of the law perfectly and thoroughly; and upon our part, true and lively faith in the merits of Jesus Christ, which yet is not ours but by God's working in us.

St. Paul declareth here nothing upon the behalf of man concerning his justification, but only a true and lively faith, which nevertheless is the gift of God. And

[189] Cf. Gal. 2: 16.   [190] Cf. ibid.

[191] Or 'fulfilled'; see above n. 158; and similarly for the other occurrences in this and the next paragraph.

[192] Rom. 10: 4.   [193] Rom. 8: 3–4.

yet this faith doth not shut out repentance, hope, love, and the fear of God in every believer that is justified, but it shutteth them out from the office of justifying. So that although they be all present in him that is justified, yet they justify not all together.

Neither doth faith shut out our own good works necessarily to be done afterwards of duty towards God, but it excludeth them so that we may not do them with this intent, to be made just by doing them. For all good works that we can do be imperfect, and therefore not able to deserve our justification: but our justification doth come freely by the mercy of God; and of so great and free mercy, that whereas all the world was not able of themselves to pay any part towards their ransom, it pleased our heavenly Father of his infinite mercy, without any our deserving, to prepare for us the most precious jewels of Christ's body and blood, whereby our ransom might be fully paid, the law filled, and his justice satisfied. So that Christ is now the righteousness of all them that do believe in him.[194]

That no man can be justified by his own good works, that no man filled[195] the law according to the strict rigour of the law, St. Paul proveth in his epistle to the Galatians, saying thus: 'If there had been any law given which could have given life, verily righteousness should have been by the law'.[196] And again he saith, 'If righteousness come by the law, then Christ is dead in vain'.[197] And again, 'You that are justified by the law are fallen from grace'.[198] And to the Ephesians, 'By grace ye are saved through faith, and that not of yourselves; it is the gift of God; not of works, lest any man should boast'.[199] And to be short, the sum of all Paul's disputation is this: that if righteousness come by works, then it cometh not by grace; and if it come of grace, then it cometh not of works. And to this end tend all the prophets as St. Peter saith, 'To him give all the prophets witness, that through his name whosoever believeth in him shall receive remission of sins'.[200]

This faith, holy scripture teacheth us, is the strong rock and foundation of the Christian religion. This doctrine all ancient authors of Christ's Church do approve. This doctrine advanceth and setteth forth the true glory of Christ, and beateth down the vainglory of man; this doctrine whosoever denieth is not to be accounted for a Christian man, nor for a setter-forth of Christ's glory, but for an adversary to Christ and his gospel, and for a setter-forth of man's vainglory.

Justification is not the office of man but of God, for man cannot make himself righteous by his own works, neither in whole nor in part: for that were the greatest arrogancy and presumption of man that Antichrist could set up against God, to affirm that a man might by his own works take away and purge his own sins, and so justify himself. But justification is the office of God only, and is not a thing which we render unto him, but which we receive of him, by his own free mercy

---

[194] The three paragraphs which follow are extracted from the second part of Homily 3 'Of Salvation'.
[195] Albin and Beckerlegge (p. 60) suggest 'fulfilleth'; however, the shorthand sign seems clearly to be 'fld'.   [196] Cf. Gal. 3: 21.
[197] Gal. 2: 21.   [198] Cf. Gal. 5: 4.   [199] Eph. 2: 8–9.
[200] Acts 10: 43.

and by the only merit of his most dearly beloved Son, our only Redeemer, Saviour and Justifier, Jesus Christ.[201]

This is the doctrine of Scripture and our own Church concerning justification which she thus sums up in her Articles:[202] 'We are accounted righteous before God, only for the merit of our Lord Jesus Christ through faith, and not for our own works or deservings. Wherefore, that we are justified by faith only, is a most wholesome doctrine, and very full of comfort, as more largely is expressed in the Homily of Justification'.

Of works done before justification, her judgment is this:[203] 'Works done before the grace of Christ, and inspiration of his Spirit, are not pleasant to God, forasmuch as they spring not of faith in Jesus Christ, neither do they make men meet to receive grace, or, as the school authors say, to deserve grace of congruity: yea rather, because they are not done as God hath willed and commanded them to be done, we doubt not but they have the nature of sin'.

Neither can those[204] good works which are the fruits of faith, and follow after justification, put away our sins and endure the severity of God's judgments. It cost more to redeem a soul; more than all good works of all men, so that man must let that alone forever.[205] That we must leave to God. It is God that justifieth. It is the blood of Christ that cleanses from all sin.[206] It is the Lamb of God that taketh away the sin of the world.[207] And he that doth not acknowledge this, and doth not utterly renounce his own righteousness as filthy rags,[208] and seek to be justified freely by grace through faith, that man is in his sins and in his bondage[209] to this hour. Unless he relies, not on anything he is or does, but on the death of Christ alone, as the one sufficient sacrifice, oblation and satisfaction for the sins of the whole world, unless in the matter of[210] justification he puts himself upon a level with vilest sinners, looking like them to receive a free pardon from the mere mercy of God in Christ Jesus, unless he can submit to be justified as ungodly, he never can be justified at all. For he is of those who justify themselves; of those who, following after the law of righteousness, have not attained to the law of righteousness, because they sought it not by faith, but as it were by works of the law,[211] while gross but self-condemned and believing sinners, who followed not after righteousness, attain to righteousness, even the righteousness which is of faith.[212] They are accepted while the self-righteous one is cast out: verily, verily, Christ saith unto him, the publicans and the harlots go into the kingdom of God before you![213]

---

[201] This concludes Charles's extract from Homily 3 'Of Salvation'.
[202] Charles here quotes Article XI, from which he makes some minor omissions.
[203] Charles here quotes Article XIII, with some minor verbal alterations.
[204] As Albin and Beckerlegge note, the remainder of this sentence follows Article XII.
[205] Cf. Ps. 49: 7–8, *BCP*.   [206] Cf. 1 John 1: 7.   [207] Cf. John 1: 29.
[208] Cf. Isa. 64: 6.
[209] The shorthand reads 'b' with a point indicating contraction. Albin and Beckerlegge suggest 'blood', but it is difficult to see quite how this fits the context.
[210] 'Matter of' is unclear in the text. The shorthand reads 'mf'.   [211] Cf. Rom. 9: 31–2.
[212] Cf. Rom. 9: 30.   [213] Matt. 21: 31.

The sum of all is this: they that be whole need not a physician, but they that be sick.[214] Christ came not to call the righteous but sinners to repentance.[215] He is the friend[216] and Saviour of sinners; not indeed of those who continue in sin, but of those who feel the weight of it, and groan to him for deliverance. Whosoever is saved by him, is saved as a sinner. His mouth is first stopped, he becomes guilty before God, and submits to be justified freely by his grace through the redemption that is in Jesus Christ. He counts all things but loss that he may win Christ, and be found in him, not having his own righteousness which is of the law, but that which is through the faith of Christ, the redemption which is of God by faith.[217]

Whoso is justified is justified by a simple act of faith in Christ Jesus, without any reference to works past, present or to come. Indeed till a sinner does exert[218] this act of faith he is in a state of condemnation. He that believeth on him is not condemned, but he that believeth not is condemned already, because he hath not believed on the name of the only begotten Son of God.[219] He that believeth on the Son hath everlasting life, but he that believeth not the Son shall not see life, but the wrath of God abideth on him.[220] Verily, verily, Christ saith unto you, he that heareth my word and believeth on him that sent me hath everlasting life, and shall not come into condemnation, but is passed from death unto life.[221] In the moment wherein a self-despairing sinner looks up with faith to Christ Jesus, in that self-same moment the power of the Lord is present to heal him; his sins are forgiven, his person[222] is accepted, his faith hath made him whole.[223] He was a sinner, but he is washed, but he is justified in the name of the Lord Jesus, and by the Spirit of our God.

What the faith is, through which we thus receive the atonement and apply Christ and all his merits to our soul in particular, was the third thing I proposed discoursing upon. Our Church describes it thus:[224] The true, lively and converting faith, the sure and substantial faith which saveth sinners, is not only a common belief of the Articles of our creed, but it is also a true trust and confidence of the mercy of God through our Lord Jesus Christ, and a steadfast hope of all good things to be received at God's hand. It is not in the mouth and outward profession only, but liveth and stirreth inwardly in the heart. It is the sure ground and foundation of the benefits which we trust to receive of God, a certificate and sure looking for them. It is no dead, vain or unfruitful thing, but a thing of perfect virtue, of wonderful operation or working and strength, bringing forth all good motions and good works.[225]

---

[214] Cf. Mark 2: 17 and parallels.   [215] Mark 2: 17.   [216] Cf. Matt. 11: 19 and parallel.
[217] Cf. Phil. 3: 9.   [218] 'Exert' is not clear in the text. The shorthand reads 'xt'.
[219] John 3: 18.   [220] John 3: 36.   [221] John 5: 24.
[222] Albin and Beckerlegge indicate some doubt regarding the expansion of this word. However, their 'person' seems reasonably well suited to the context and the shorthand 'prsn' is relatively clear.
[223] Cf. Mark 5: 34 and parallels.   [224] Extracted from part one of Homily 4 'Of Faith'.
[225] This final sentence is from part two of the same Homily.

The faith which justifies is not purely an assent to things credible as known;[226] it is not that speculative, notional, airy shadow which floats in the heads of some learned men; it is not a lifeless, cold, historical faith, common to devils[227] and nominal Christians; it is not learnt of books or men; it is not a human thing, but a divine energy. We believe according to the working of the mighty power of God. ~~By grace ye are~~ The faith by which we are saved is not of ourselves; it is the gift of God; not of works lest any man should boast.[228] We can as well reach heaven with our hands,[229] as believe by any act or power or strength of our own. ~~For effecting faith~~ There is required a stroke of omnipotence. It can only be wrought in the soul by him who made it. ~~We believe according to the working of the mighty power of God~~. God who commanded the light to shine out of darkness, must shine[230] in our hearts to give the knowledge of the glory of God in the face of Jesus Christ.[231] Faith does not stand in the wisdom of men but in the power of God. No man can call Jesus the Lord but by the Holy Ghost.[232]

When Peter made that confession of faith, Thou art the Christ, the Son of the living God, Jesus answered and said unto him, Blessed art thou, Simon Peter, for flesh and blood hath not revealed it unto thee, but my Father which is in heaven.[233] So our Lord himself assures us no man can come unto the Son[234] except the Father draw him.[235] No man cometh to the Father, but by the Son.[236] They only believe, to whom it is given to know the mind of Christ. Eye hath not seen, nor ear heard, neither have entered into the heart of man, the things which God hath prepared for them that love him.[237] But God hath revealed them unto us by his Spirit, for the Spirit searcheth all things, yea, the deep things of God. For what man knoweth the things of a man but the spirit of man which is in him? Even so the things of God knoweth no man but the Spirit of God. But the natural man receiveth not the things of the Spirit of God, for they are foolishness unto him; neither can he know them because they are spiritually discerned.[238] God hath hid these things from the wise and prudent, and revealed them unto babes.[239] No man knoweth the Son but the Father, neither knoweth any man the Father save the Son, and he to whomsoever the Son will reveal him.[240]

---

[226] 'Known' is not clear in the text. Albin and Beckerlegge have 'certain', but this seems unlikely as the shorthand sign is 'k' (a sign also used for the hard 'c'). Had Charles had 'certain' in mind he would have used the shorthand sign for 's' not 'c'. We might note for example the word 'certifying' used in the previous paragraph where the shorthand reads 'srtf'.   [227] Cf. Jas 2: 19.

[228] Eph. 2: 9.

[229] 'Hands' is not clear in the text. The composite shorthand sign here rendered 'with our hands' is 'worh'.

[230] It is apparent in the text that Charles has changed a sign which originally read 'shines' to the 'must shine' which now stands in the MS.   [231] Cf. 2 Cor. 4: 6.

[232] Cf. 1 Cor. 12: 3.   [233] Matt. 16: 17.

[234] There is a word before 'Son' that has been so heavily struck out that it is now unreadable.

[235] Cf. John 6: 44.   [236] Cf. John 14: 6.

[237] This and the next three sentences quote 1 Cor. 2: 9–11.   [238] 2 Cor. 2: 14.

[239] Cf. Luke 10: 21.   [240] Matt. 11: 27 and parallel.

These and numberless other Scriptures demonstrate the impossibility of believing till God hath given us the spirit of revelation.[241] We can never know the things of God till he hath revealed them by his Spirit, till we have received the Son of God[242] that we should know the things which are freely given us of God. For this cause Jesus is called the author of our faith:[243] and we are said to receive the Spirit by the hearing of faith,[244] because we receive in one and the same moment, power to believe and the Holy Ghost, who is therefore called the Spirit of faith. And a true faith we cannot have till God gives unto us the Holy Ghost purifying our hearts by faith.[245]

We need no further testimony to prove that faith is wrought by him from whom every good and perfect gift cometh.[246] God is plainly the cause of faith: what are its effects? They are briefly[247] these: peace, love, joy, victory over the world, the flesh and the devil,[248] fellowship with God, the indwelling of his Spirit, present salvation and everlasting life.

Being justified by faith we have peace with God[249] (attested by that inward peace which passes all understanding):[250] and not only so, but we also joy in God through our Lord Jesus Christ by whom we have now received the atonement.[251] In whom we have redemption through his blood, the forgiveness of sins.[252] Whom having not seen we love; in whom, though now we see him not, yet believing, we rejoice with joy unspeakable and full of glory,[253] receiving the end of our faith, even the salvation of our souls.[254] Receiving it now in part, for by grace ye are saved through faith,[255] and he that believeth hath everlasting life.[256]

Faith works by love.[257] The love of God is shed abroad in all believers' hearts by the Holy Ghost which is given unto them.[258] This love they show by keeping his commandments;[259] which none except believers can keep. But they are delivered not only from the guilt but also from the power of sin.[260] The law of the spirit of life which is in Christ Jesus hath made them free from the law of sin and death.[261] Sin shall not have dominion over them, for they are not under the law but under grace.[262] They were the servants of sin, but they have obeyed from the heart that form of doctrine which was delivered them.[263] Being then made free from sin, they became the servants of righteousness.[264] Jesus is their Jesus[265] ~~by having~~ for he

[241] 'Spirit of revelation' is not clear in the text. The shorthand reads only 'sr'. In place of 'spirit of revelation' Albin and Beckerlegge (p. 64) have 'spirit of r[egeneration?]'.
[242] Or 'Spirit of God'; the sign is simply 'sog'.   [243] Cf. Heb. 12: 2.
[244] Cf. Gal. 3: 2.   [245] Cf. Acts 15: 9.   [246] Cf. Jas 1: 17.
[247] Albin and Beckerlegge suggest 'spiritually' rather than 'briefly'. However, though the text is not absolutely clear the initial 'b' rather than 'sp' seems highly probable.
[248] BCP, Collect for the 18th Sunday after Trinity.   [249] Rom. 5: 1.
[250] Cf. Phil. 4: 7.   [251] Rom. 5: 11.   [252] Eph. 1: 7.
[253] Cf. 1 Pet. 1: 8.   [254] Cf. 1 Pet. 1: 9.   [255] Eph. 2: 8.
[256] Cf. John 6: 47.   [257] Cf. Gal. 5: 6.   [258] Cf. Rom. 5: 5.
[259] Cf. John 14: 15.   [260] Charles may here be reflecting upon Paul's argument in Rom. 6.
[261] Cf. Rom. 8: 2.   [262] Cf. Rom. 6: 14.   [263] Cf. Rom. 6: 17.
[264] Cf. Rom. 6: 18.
[265] Charles is presumably playing here on the meaning of 'Jesus', which, according to Matthew, is linked to the office of saviour (Matt. 1: 21). Matthew is himself playing not on the Greek form 'Jesus'

hath saved them from their sins. He that believeth is born of God;[266] and whosoever is born of God doth not commit sin, for his seed remaineth in him, and he
cannot sin because he is born of God.[267]

Whatsoever is born of God overcometh the world also. And this is the victory
that overcometh the world, even our faith.[268] Who is he that overcometh the world
but he that believeth that Jesus is the Son of God?[269] Nor can the prince of this
world[270] stand before him. He takes unto him the shield of faith, and thereby
quenches all the fiery darts of the devil.[271] He resists him steadfast in the faith,[272]
and the devil flees from him. The seed of the woman continually bruises the serpent's head,[273] and he is more than conqueror through Christ that loveth him[274]
and dwelleth in his heart by faith.

This is the greatest and most glorious privilege of the true believer:[275] whosoever shall confess that Jesus is the Son of God, God dwelleth in him and he in
God:[276] and hereby knoweth[277] he that God abideth in him, by the Spirit which he
hath given him.[278] He that believeth hath the witness in himself,[279] even the
Spirit[280] of God bearing witness with his spirit that he is a child of God. Christ is
formed[281] in his heart by faith. He is one with Christ and Christ with him. He is a
real partaker of the divine nature.[282] Truly his fellowship is with the Father and the
Son.[283] The Father and the Son are come unto him and make their abode with
him,[284] and his very body is the temple of the Holy Ghost.[285]

Such are the privileges of all true believers. But alas where shall we find them?
How are the faithful minished from among the children of men! When the Son of
man cometh shall he find faith upon earth![286] We have lost the very notion of it,
and denied it its first and peculiar office, namely that of justifying[287] us before God.
A preacher of justification by faith only is now looked upon as a setter-forth of new
doctrines, and his audience are ready to cry out, 'thou bringest strange things to

---

($I\eta\sigma o\hat{u}s$) but rather on the Hebrew/Aramaic 'Joshua/Jesuah', which means 'the Lord is salvation'.
Charles must have felt confident, given the audience before him, that the puns and allusions (now twice
removed by the use of English for the Greek for the Hebrew/Aramaic) would have been understood.

[266] Cf. 1 John 5: 1.   [267] 1 John 3: 9.   [268] 1 John 5: 4.

[269] 1 John 5: 5.   [270] 'Prince of this world' is a phrase used in John 12: 31; 14: 30; 16: 11.

[271] Cf. Eph. 6: 16.   [272] 1 Pet. 5: 9.

[273] Cf. Gen. 3: 15. In place of 'the seed of the woman continually bruises the serpent's head' Albin
and Beckerlegge suggest 'the spirit of the world continually oppresses the spirit of holiness'. The shorthand reads 't sw cntnli brss [possibly 'prss'] sh'.   [274] Cf. Rom. 8: 37.

[275] In the MS there is a opening quotation mark at this point, but no closing quotation mark. What
follows is in fact a mixture of several texts which Charles has sewn together to make his point.

[276] 1 John 4: 15.

[277] In the MS there is a word before 'knoweth'. However, it has been so heavily struck out as to make
it unreadable.   [278] Cf. 1 John 3: 24; 4: 13.

[279] 1 John 5: 10.

[280] Albin and Beckerlegge (p. 65) have 'Son' rather than 'Spirit'. However 'Spirit' seems certain on
the basis of Rom. 8: 16.   [281] Cf. Gal. 4: 19.

[282] Cf. 2 Pet. 1: 4.   [283] Cf. 1 John 1: 3.   [284] Cf. John 14: 23.

[285] Cf. 1 Cor. 6: 19.   [286] Luke 18: 8.

[287] Albin and Beckerlegge suggest 'judging' rather than 'justifying'.

our ears'.[288] It is therefore wholly seasonable that I should therefore apply myself (as I proposed in the IV part) first to them who deny this doctrine, and secondly to you who receive it.

And firstly, as to those that deny this doctrine, and ignorantly call it new, and pronounce the preachers of it schismatics. Would they look into their Bibles they would find it as old as Christianity; as old as the fall of man and his redemption in Christ Jesus, who was the lamb slain from the foundation of the world[289] to take away the sins of the world.[290] But they do therefore err because they know not the Scriptures, neither the power of faith.[291] They find no such mighty efficacy in their own hearsay[292] faith, and so cannot conceive how faith only should justify. That their faith cannot we readily grant; for if it could, the devils having the very same would be justified too.[293] But what must they do then in order to earn[294] their justification? Why, they will take in good works to their cause (outwardly good I mean) and the business is done. The works of a heathen, and the faith of a devil, will, in their judgment, make a man a complete Christian, and fully justify him in the sight of God.

Thus mighty are these men in the Scriptures; and as deeply skilled are they in the doctrines of our own church. Tell me, you that are of the church, do ye not hear the church?[295] I know ye do; and to you I therefore appeal. Judge you, which are the schismatics, we who maintain or they who deny, justification by faith only? Indeed they are worse than schismatics who deny; for if they have ever subscribed[296] our Articles, they are perjured schismatics. God forbid that I, or any of my brethren, should preach another gospel;[297] for we have solemnly[298] declared upon oath our belief of justification by faith only, and for us to hold any other doctrine would be wicked[299] flat inexcusable perjury.

One infamous evasion I know there is, but hope we all have it in equal abhorrence, namely that every man may subscribe the Articles in his own sense. Suppose it granted that the 17th Article[300] is purposely so worded as to take in persons of differing sentiments, what is this to those Articles where the sense is

[288] Cf. Acts 17: 20.   [289] Rev. 13: 8.   [290] Cf. John 1: 29.
[291] Cf. Mark 12: 24.

[292] The word 'hearsay' is not clear in the text. The shorthand reads 'hrs' with what is most probably the sign of an 'e' after the 's'. This point could, however, be an 'a' which would then give 'hrsa'.

[293] Cf. Jas. 2: 19.

[294] The shorthand here is somewhat unclear. It appears to read 'dter', which Albin and Beckerlegge take as 'to their justification', though the resultant 'what must they do then in order to their justification' seems rather awkward (and had the 't' been intended as 'th' the stroke for 'r' in the conjectured 'their' would have been half size). 'Justification' is clear enough. In Sermon 6 on Rom. 3: 23–4, which is quoted here, the shorthand appears to read 'rto b' followed by 'justified', which may be taken as 'in order to be justified'.   [295] Charles is here playing on Gal. 4: 21.

[296] 'Subscribed' here, like 'subscribe' and 'subscribed' below, appears here without a preposition.

[297] Cf. Gal. 1: 6.

[298] Albin and Beckerlegge suggest 'so' rather than 'solemnly' at this point. The shorthand reads 'so' with a dot so positioned as to suggest that the suffix 'ly' should be added.

[299] 'Wicked' is not clear in the text. The shorthand reads 'w' with a point indicating that an adjective is signified.   [300] 'Of Predestination and Election'.

plain, precise and distinct? As it is in that of justification; for the full understanding of which the church refers us to her homilies and thereby ties us down to the
one sense therein delivered. Nor is it in the power of words more fully and plainly
to express any truth, than she has there expressed that everlasting truth, 'We are
justified by faith only without works'.[301]

What then, my brethren, can we think of those who swear to those Articles in a
sense altogether repugnant to the true intended one? Who declare upon oath their
belief that we are justified by faith only: that is, say they in their hearts, not by faith
only, but by a popish[302] jumble of faith and works. What horrid mockery is this of
God and man! Can charity itself suppose that their mental reservation acquits
them of perjury? Or does it not rather wholly aggravate it? I shall say no more of
this wicked subterfuge, than that it was taught by our modern Arius: that hereby
he subscribed[303] our Articles though he denied the Lord that bought him; as might
his elder brother have done, or any other heretic old or new.

Let not those therefore who deny this doctrine any longer call themselves of the
Church of England. They may be of the Church of Rome, but cannot be of ours,
who allow works any share in our justification with God. Papists indeed they are,
though they may not know it, for they lay the wood, hay, stubble of their own
works, not as the superstructure, but as the very foundation, of their acceptance
with God. Pharisees are they, for they justify themselves; perjured are they likewise, as many of them as have sworn to the truth of what they disbelieved. In short,
they may call themselves anything but Church of England men and Christians; for
such[304] we can never allow them to be; since, to repeat the words of our own
church, 'Whosoever denieth this doctrine, is not to be counted for a Christian
man, nor for a setter-forth of Christ's glory, but for a setter-forth of men's vainglory, an adversary to Christ and his gospel'.[305]

This is our Church's censure of all that bring[306] any other doctrine than justification by faith only; she calls them antichrists ~~and professes them such~~ who presume to say ~~we~~ they can by ~~our~~ their own works justify ~~ourselves~~ themselves.[307]
But alas! how are these antichrists multiplied upon earth! Our pulpits speak a quite

---

[301] See Article XI 'Of the Justification of Man'.

[302] 'Popish' is unclear in the text. Albin and Beckerlegge suggest 'papistic'. However, the shorthand
reads 'ppssh' where the final 'sh' (one stroke in Charles's shorthand) is clear enough.

[303] 'Subscribed' is not clear in the text. The shorthand reads 'ssd', where the initial 's' is clearly
meant as the prefix 'sub'. It appears here without the preposition.

[304] Before 'for such' (one sign in the shorthand) there appear two signs (one a correction of the other)
which have both been struck out. Neither is now readable.

[305] The words are from Homily 3 'Of Salvation', part 2.

[306] In the MS there is a word before 'bring' which has been so heavily stuck out as to make it
unreadable.

[307] The phrase 'who presume to say we can by our own works justify ourselves' is written above the
words '~~and profess them such~~'. All but the first two of the words in this new phrase have then themselves been struck out and the phrase rewritten on the opposite page as 'who presume to say they can
by their own works justify themselves', though this phrase has itself been changed from what appears
to be 'who presume to say we can by our own works justify ourselves'.

different language from our Articles and homilies: the writings of our most celebrated divines are full of justification by faith *and*[308] works. The religion of Christ is utterly[309] denied, exploded, and blasphemed. It were needless to name all these Judaising Christians (if I may so call them whom[310] our church denies to be any Christians at all),[311] but as God shall give me strength, I mean to name them, and that upon the housetop,[312] and to warn the people of God to beware of false prophets.[313]

This is not justifying faith, says one of them, to lay hold on the righteousness and merits of Christ for the pardon of our sins, that is to trust and confide only in that as the meritorious cause of our pardon.[314] He goes on (this angel of the church of God) to do the devil's work, pulling down that church of which he is a pillar, and labouring to overturn what she calls the strong root and foundation of the Christian religion, justification by faith only. I tremble to think (and so should all his admirers) of that terrible sentence pronounced by the great apostle, 'Though we or an angel from heaven preach any other gospel unto you than that which we have preached unto you, let him be accursed'.[315] To preach justification by faith and works, is, if may we may[316] believe an inspired apostle,[317] to preach another gospel; and he repeats the doom of all such preachers, 'As we said before, so say I now again, if any man preach any other gospel unto you than that ye have received, let him be accursed'.[318]

So speaks the great asserter[319] of justification by faith only, who as a wise master builder, laid this sure ~~lays this only~~ foundation of all good works and holiness, and ~~assures tells~~ assures us, other foundation can no man lay than that is laid, which is Christ Jesus. On this very doctrine our church was founded and flourished for 100 years. But alas, was the father of the Reformation to rise again and visit us, how would he take up the apostle's words: 'I marvel that ye are so soon removed from him that called you into the grace of Christ unto another gospel!'[320] Oh foolish

[308] The sign for 'and' is written slightly larger in the MS, which suggests emphasis.

[309] Before the word 'utterly' there appear two signs in the MS which have been heavily struck out. The first is unreadable. The second appears to be incomplete and reads 'crs', presumably the beginning of the word 'Christian/s'.

[310] Before 'whom' there appear several other words in the MS that have been so heavily struck out as to make them unreadable (though the first of these appears to begin with 'crs' (= Christian/s)).

[311] The words 'any Christians at all' are a correction for a word that is now struck out and unreadable.

[312] Before 'housetop' there appears another word in the MS that has been struck out. This word appears to be 'housetop' as well, though it may have been rather clumsily formed by Charles who then struck it out and wrote it again.   [313] Cf. Matt. 7: 15.

[314] Charles wrote in the margin: '173 sermon on justifying faith, page 460, 3rd volume, Tillotson'. The reference is to John Tillotson, the archbishop of Canterbury at the end of the seventeenth century; see further Chapter 2.   [315] Gal. 1: 8.

[316] The MS reads 'if may we' and Charles has inserted a second 'may' above the line after 'we' without striking out the former.

[317] The words 'an inspired apostle' have been written above the line and replace a word that has been heavily struck out. The word is largely unreadable, but appears to begin with an 's', perhaps 'scripture'.

[318] Gal. 1: 9.   [319] 'Asserter of' is not clear in the text. The shorthand reads only 'af/v'.

[320] Gal. 1: 6.

Galatians, who hath bewitched you, that you should not obey the truth!³²¹ I am afraid for you, lest I have bestowed upon you labour in vain.³²² Christ is become of none effect unto you, whoso of you are justified by the law, ye are fallen from grace.³²³ Ye did run well; who ~~hath bewitched~~ did hinder you, that ye should not obey the truth. This persuasion cometh not of him that calleth you. A little leaven leaveneth the whole lump'.³²⁴

Would to God, my brethren, the following words were applicable to us all, 'I have confidence in you through the Lord that ye will be none otherwise minded!'³²⁵ Would to God that everyone who hath not made shipwreck of the faith³²⁶ would avow and preach and publish it upon the housetop. Suffer ye the word of exhortation from the least and meanest of your brethren. O consider, I beseech you, by the mercies of God, whether this be not the cause of all our vice and infidelity, our not holding the head³²⁷ (I speak of the generality), our not laying the foundation, our not adhering to our own principles.

We may date our apostasy from the time of the Grand Rebellion: unto which many were drawn who maintained justification by faith only. For no better a reason than this we renounced the doctrine (though it still confronts us in our Articles and homilies) ~~and ran headstrong unto works, popery and deism.~~³²⁸ ~~But~~³²⁹ ~~woe unto the men who first dared preach justification by faith and works; who laid this stumbling block in our way. Good had it been for them had they never been born. Woe unto the man who stumbled upon the doctrine [and] first dared preach justification by faith and works.~~³³⁰ ~~Or if as soon as born, they had had a millstone tied about their necks, and been cast into the depth of the sea! But let not us, my breathren, deny the truth because some hold it in unrighteousness.~~

But woe unto the men by whom the offence came. It had been better for them that a millstone had been hanged about their neck and they cast into the sea. ³³¹ Woe unto them who stumbled at this rock of offence,³³² and first dared teach justification by faith and works. Good had it been for those men had they never been born.³³³ But let not us, my brethren, increase the unhappy number. Let not us deny the truth because some held it in unrighteousness,³³⁴ professing to know God, while in works they denied him.³³⁵ Oh what an advantage did Satan then get over

---

³²¹ Gal. 3: 1.   ³²² Cf. Gal. 4: 11.   ³²³ Gal. 5: 4.
³²⁴ Gal. 5: 7–9.   ³²⁵ Gal. 5: 10.   ³²⁶ Cf. 1 Tim. 1: 19.
³²⁷ 'Head' is not clear in the text. The shorthand reads 'hd'.
³²⁸ 'Deism' is unclear in the text. The shorthand reads 'dsm'. Albin and Becker Legge suggest 'dissimulation'. One might also read 'doctrines of men', though this too seems very uncertain.
³²⁹ Before 'but' Charles inserts a square bracket in the text. No corresponding closing bracket is found.
³³⁰ This sentence was written between the lines and then marked through. The words 'faith and works' are uncertain in the text. Beckerlegge and Albin suggest 'faith only', but this seems not to fit the context. The words are more probably the same as those in the following paragraph, which seems to be a corrected form of the paragraph here struck out.   ³³¹ Cf. Mark 9: 42 and parallels.
³³² 1 Pet. 2: 8.   ³³³ Cf. Mark 14: 21.   ³³⁴ Cf. Rom. 1: 18.
³³⁵ Cf. Titus 1: 16.

us! By filling the mouths of his children with faith in Christ; saving faith, justifying faith, he hath driven and kept it out of the hearts of almost all this nation.

But be not ye ignorant of his devices.[336] This place was always a bulwark against his inroads,[337] a rampart against vice and infidelity. Ye are the salt of the earth. But if the salt hath lost its savour, wherewith shall it be seasoned?[338] ~~You~~ Ye are the eyes of this people: but if the light which is in us[339] be darkness, how great is that darkness![340] Here is the fountain: and if that be pure, the river of the flood thereof shall make glad the city of our God.[341] Oh that our glorious title might be[342] ever be that of true Church of England men! Oh let not the enemies of our church ~~any longer~~ triumph in our having fallen from the doctrine of redemption![343] Let it not be said concerning ~~her~~ our desolate mother, there is none to guide her, of all the sons which she hath brought up.[344] Never will she lift up her drooping head again, till we preach not ourselves but Christ Jesus the Lord: the Lord our righteousness: Christ made unto us of God wisdom, righteousness, sanctification, and redemption.[345] Righteousness first and then immediately sanctification. First let us insist that we are justified freely, that is forgiven and accepted for Christ's sake, not our own; justified in our sins and in our blood; justified as ungodly by faith only without works. And then upon this sure foundation let us build the gold, silver, precious stones of good works, and inward holiness. Oh let us not corrupt the gospel of Christ by allowing works the least share in our justification with God. Corrupt it, said I? Rather let us not overthrow it. For by not acknowledging ~~him~~ Christ to be the sole ground of our acceptance, we tread under foot the Son of God and count the blood of the covenant, wherewith we were sanctified, an unholy thing, and do despite to the spirit of grace.

God hath much against us because we have left our first love,[346] even that pure love which is wrought by faith. Let us remember therefore from whence we are fallen, and repent and do the first works, or else he will come unto us quickly, and will remove our candlestick out of this place, except we repent.[347] Year after year hath he come to this barren fig tree, seeking fruit and finding none.[348] And[349] behold,[350] even now the word is gone forth, 'cut it down, why cumbereth it the

---

[336] Cf. 2 Cor. 2: 11.

[337] 'Inroads' is unclear in the text. The shorthand reads 'in rds', where 'in' is most probably meant as a prefix.   [338] Cf. Matt. 5: 13.

[339] 'Us' is clear in the text, though the antecedent 'ye' requires 'you' at this point.

[340] Cf. Matt. 6: 23.   [341] Cf. Ps. 46: 4, *BCP*.

[342] This 'be' appears to be a mistake. Albin and Beckerlegge suggest the reading 'but' at this point.

[343] 'Doctrine of redemption' is not clear in the text. the shorthand reads 'dr' with a clear contraction point beneath the 'd'.   [344] Cf. Isa. 51: 18.

[345] See above n. 175.   [346] Cf. Rev. 2: 4.   [347] Cf. Rev. 2: 5.

[348] Cf. Luke 13: 6 ff. and, perhaps, Mark 11: 13 ff.

[349] 'And' is written above the line. It would appear that Charles intended to insert the word at this point in the sermon.

[350] The shorthand reads only 'b' at this point. Albin and Beckerlegge suggest 'brethren'.

~~earth~~ ground?'[351] Behold,[352] even now he is going to take away the kingdom of God from us, and to give it to another nation bringing forth the fruits thereof.[353] Oh, who will stand before him in the gap to turn away his wrathful indignation lest he should destroy us?[354] ~~Who will stand, rise up, with me against the wicked, who will take~~ Who will become protecting angels to a guilty land? Unless that iniquity is come in like a flood, who is there to lift up a standard against it?[355] Who will rise up with ~~me~~ God against the wicked, who will take his part against the evil doers?

Members of the brotherhood of faith[356] upon you I call that ye come to the help of the Lord, to help the Lord[357] against the self-righteous. Ye[358] masters[359] in Israel, lead the way. Be determined not to know or preach anything save Jesus Christ and him crucified.[360] Preach the gospel in simplicity. Insist on justification by faith only, even by faith in the blood of Jesus, that only name given under heaven whereby we may be saved[361] else I call holy writ[362] to record against you this day! As many of you as bring any other doctrine, I call the ~~whole~~ Church of God in all ages, the noble army of martyrs, especially those of our own nation who have sealed this truth with their blood, these and the whole church militant and triumphant I call to testify against you that ye have erred from the faith and trampled upon the everlasting gospel. Behold,[363] I am now free from the blood of every man; look ye to that! I have declared the truth, I have borne my testimony, I have delivered my own soul![364]

[351] Luke 13: 7; the quotation marks are not present in the MS but have been added here for the sake of clarity.

[352] The shorthand reads only 'b' at this point. Albin and Beckerlegge suggest 'brethren'.

[353] Cf. Matt. 21: 43.   [354] Cf. Ezek. 22: 30–1.

[355] This sentence is not present in Albin and Beckerlegge's text. It is written on the back of page 16 of the MS and an insertion mark on page 17 indicates where Charles intended it to be read.

[356] 'Members of the brotherhood of faith' is far from clear in the text. The shorthand reads 'mbf' with a contraction point beneath the 'm'. Albin and Beckerlegge suggest 'my brethren in the faith', which is perhaps an equally plausible expansion. However, the fact that Charles has placed the expansion point beneath the 'm' possibly suggests that by it more than a short pronoun is expressed.

[357] 'Help the Lord' is unclear in the text. The shorthand reads 'hl'. However, beneath the 'h' (which is joined to the 'l' in the shorthand) there appears to be a contraction point, which perhaps suggests that two words 'h' and 'l' are meant.

[358] Before 'ye' there appears in the text a further sign which has been struck out. The sign is more extensive than the 'w' which has been expanded to 'would' in Albin and Beckerlegge. It is far from clear, but the strokes for 'nsw', possibly 'nspw' (though if so the formation of the 'p' is uncharacteristic of Charles), are visible.

[359] 'Masters' is unclear in the text. The shorthand reads 'mstr'. If, as seems entirely probable, this is to be taken as a noun, it will be in apposition to 'ye' and will therefore be in the plural form. Hence 'masters' seems probable.   [360] Cf. 1 Cor. 2: 2.

[361] Cf. Acts 4: 12.

[362] 'Holy writ' is unclear in the text. The shorthand reads 'hr' with what would appear to be a contraction mark above the 'h'. Two separate words may therefore be signified. Albin and Beckerlegge leave it as 'h#r' in the text. 'Holy writ' seems at the very least possible in context: Charles here calls the Church, the martyrs and 'h[oly] [w]r[it]' to testify against those who preach a doctrine other than justification by faith only.

[363] The shorthand reads only 'b' at this point. Albin and Beckerlegge suggest 'brethren'.

[364] At this point the sermon ends. As Albin and Beckerlegge note, the following benediction was written at a later time and/or with a different pen.

Now to God the Father, who first loved us and made us accepted in the Beloved; to God the Son who loved us and washed us from our sins in his own blood, to God the Holy Ghost who sheddeth abroad the love of God in our hearts, be all praise and all glory in time and in eternity!

SERMON 8
EPHESIANS 5: 14

INTRODUCTORY COMMENT

Charles preached his sermon on Ephesians 5:14 before the University of Oxford on Sunday 4 April 1742, which was not the first time that he had addressed that congregation.[1] This date falls in the middle of one of the larger gaps in the MS journal extract, and no other record appears to have survived of Charles's movements during the early part of 1742.[2] However, the date is clearly recorded on the first edition of the sermon itself and, as was noted in Chapter 4, John's journal entry for that day records how 'about two in the afternoon, being the time my brother was preaching at Oxford before the University, I desired a few persons to meet with me and join in prayer'.[3] Given the clear attestation of authorship, then, it is not surprising that there is no dispute regarding the origin of the sermon with Charles. This despite the fact that it has been consistently printed in collections of sermons by John Wesley from the edition of 1746 on (though unlike 'The Cause and Cure of Earthquakes', it has always been identified as the work of Charles). Outler included it in the bicentennial edition.[4]

No MS is known. Numerous copies of the various pamphlet editions are scattered widely across Methodist archives,[5] but only four copies of the first edition have to date been traced. These are at the Bodleian in Oxford (a copy of which is held at Duke), Yale, Toronto, and at the Methodist Publishing House in Nashville, Tennessee. The Oxford copy has been used as the basis for the text printed here. However, comparison of the Bodleian and Toronto texts indicates that they are not identical. Certainly they have been typeset differently and there are some minor changes in wording. The earliest edition that has been traced to date in the MARC is the sixth (1744). The more significant differences between the first edition and the form that this sermon has in *Sermons on Several Occasions* have been indicated in the notes.

The main outline and purpose of this sermon is not difficult to discern. Drawing on the words of his text 'Awake, thou that sleepest, and arise from the dead, and Christ shall give thee light', Charles seeks to call those he considers to be in a state of spiritual somnolence from their slumbers. This 'sleep' is, says Charles, the natural state of the human soul until

---

[1] His 'sermon on justification', Sermon 7 on Rom. 3: 23–5, was preached before the university on 1 July 1739.

[2] The journal extract ends on 22 September 1741 and does not restart until 2 January 1743. In the MARC folio DDCW 6 there are several items which relate to periods during this gap, but nothing from April 1742.   [3] *J&D*, xix. 258.

[4] Outler (ed.), *Sermons*, i. 142–58.

[5] See especially Outler (ed.), *Sermons* iv. 437–41 for an account of the various editions through which this sermon went. Outler also has a stemma of it. It was also included in *Character of a Methodist: Together with a Call to those who are Asleep in Sin to Awake to a Life of Righteousness* (1808).

it is awoken by the call of God. However, once this call comes the sleeper has a chance to come to a knowledge of his or her true state and awakens as out of dream into a new reality.

It is plain from the second section that Charles thought it was his particular task to issue such a call, and that the preaching of this sermon itself (and, one may presume, its subsequent publication) was a part of the very 'calling' to the sleeper that he here describes. In the third section he seeks to comment upon the promise to the awakened sleeper, namely that 'Christ will give you light'. This 'light' comes through the working of the spirit. The sermon ends on what appears to be a fairly raw eschatological note.

My brethren, it is high time for us to awake out of sleep; before 'the great trumpet of the Lord be blown', and our land become a field of blood. O may we speedily see the things that make for our peace, before they are hid from our eyes! 'Turn thou us, O good Lord, and let thine anger cease from us.' 'O Lord, look down from heaven, behold and visit this vine'; and cause us to know the time of our visitation.

As was seen in Chapter 2, it was the view of 'Mr Salmon' that when Charles preached this sermon in St Mary's in 1742 he went on for over two hours. Charles says it was less than one. Even on Charles's reckoning it is obvious that he must have said far more than has survived into print. Thus the true spirit and some of the content of the spoken form of this sermon have quite definitely been lost. However, the text doubtless shows Charles in his role as a lively and energetic preacher of the 'awakening'.

A Sermon Preach'd on Sunday, April 4, 1742;
before the university of Oxford.
By Charles Wesley, M.A.,
Student of Christ-Church.[1]

Eph 5.14
'Awake, thou that sleepest, and arise from the dead,
and Christ shall give thee light.'[2]

In discoursing on these words I shall, with the help of God,

First, describe the sleepers to whom they are spoken,

Secondly, enforce the exhortation, 'Awake thou that sleepest, and arise from the dead'; and

Thirdly, explain the promise made to such as do 'awake' and 'arise, Christ shall give thee light'.

1.1. And first, as to the sleepers here spoken to. By sleep is signified the natural state of man: that deep sleep of the soul into which the son[3] of *Adam* hath cast all who spring from his loins; that supineness, indolence and stupidity, that insensibility of its[4] real condition, wherein every man comes into the world, and continues till the voice of God awakes him.

2. Now 'they that sleep, sleep in the night'.[5] The state of nature is a state of utter darkness, a state wherein 'darkness covers the earth, and gross darkness the people'.[6] The poor unawakened sinner, how much knowledge soever he may have as to other things, has no knowledge of himself. In this respect 'he knoweth nothing yet as he ought to know'.[7] He knows not that he is a fallen spirit, whose holy[8] business in the present world is to recover from his fall, to regain that image of God wherein he was created. He sees *no necessity* for the 'one thing needful'[9] even that inward universal change, that 'birth from above'[10] (figured out by Baptism) which is the beginning of that total renovation, that sanctification of spirit, soul, and body, 'without which no man shall see the Lord'.[11]

3. Full of all diseases as he is, he fancies himself in perfect health. Fast bound in misery and iron, he dreams that he is happy and at liberty. He says 'Peace,

---

[1] In addition to this title, the front page of the first edition includes the words: 'London: Printed by W. Strahan, and sold by Thomas Harris, at the *Looking Glass* and *Bible*, on *London-Bridge*; by Tho. Trye, at *Gray's-Inn-Gate, Holborn*; and at the *Foundery*, near *Upper Moorfields*. MDCCXLII [Price Two-pence].'

[2] In the first edition of the sermon (and in *SOSO*) italics are used both for emphasis and for quotations. In this transcription, as in Outler, italics have been kept in places where emphasis seems intended, but quotation marks are used for quotations (the two are not of course necessarily mutually exclusive).   [3] This is corrected to 'sin' in *SOSO*.

[4] So the first edition. *SOSO* gives 'his', which appears to be a correction, but 'its' seems defensible as applying to the soul.   [5] Cf. 1 Thess. 5: 7.

[6] Cf. Isa. 60: 2.   [7] Cf. 1 Cor. 8: 2.   [8] This word is 'only' in the Toronto text.

[9] Luke 10: 42; this is the text of Sermon 21.   [10] Cf. John 3: 3.   [11] Heb. 12: 14.

peace,'[12] while the devil as 'a strong man armed'[13] is in full possession of his soul. He sleeps on still, and takes his rest,[14] though hell is moved from beneath to meet him;[15] though the pit, from whence there is no return[16], hath opened its mouth to swallow him up[17]. A fire is kindled around him, yet he knoweth it not; yea, it burns him, yet he lays it not to heart.

4. By one who sleeps we are therefore to understand (and would to God we might all understand it!) a sinner satisfied in his sins, contented to remain in his fallen state, to live and die without the image of God: one who is ignorant both of his disease and of the only remedy for it; one who never was warned, or never regarded the warning voice of God 'to flee from the wrath to come'[18]; one that never yet saw he was in danger of hell-fire, or cried out in the earnestness of his soul, 'what must I do to be saved?'[19]

5. If this sleeper be not outwardly vicious, his sleep is usually the deepest of all: whether he be of the *Laodicean* spirit, 'neither cold nor hot',[20] but a quiet, rational, inoffensive, good natured professor of the religion of his fathers; or whether he be zealous and orthodox, and 'after the most straitest sect of our religion live a Pharisee';[21] that is, according to the scriptural account, one that 'justifies himself',[22] one that labours 'to establish his own righteousness'[23] as the ground of his acceptance with God.

6. This is he who 'having a form of godliness, denies the power thereof';[24] yea, and probably reviles it, wheresoever it is found, as mere extravagance and delusion. Meanwhile the wretched self-deceiver thanks God that he 'is not as other men are, adulterers, unjust, extortioners.'[25] No, he doth no wrong to any man. He 'fasts twice in the week',[26] uses all the means of grace, is constant at church and sacrament; yea, and 'gives tithes of all that he has',[27] does all the good that he can. 'Touching the righteousness of the law', he is 'blameless':[28] he wants nothing of godliness but the power; nothing of religion but the spirit; nothing of Christianity but the truth and the life.[29]

7. But know ye not that however highly esteemed among men *such a Christian* as this may be, he is an abomination in the sight of God,[30] and an heir of every woe which the Son of God yesterday, today, and forever denounces against 'scribes and Pharisees, hypocrites'?[31] He hath 'made clean the outside of the cup and the platter',

---

[12] The quotation marks are not present in the text; they have been added here for the sake of clarity.
[13] Luke 11: 21.   [14] Mark 14: 41 and parallel.   [15] Cf. Isa. 14: 9.
[16] Cf. Job 10: 21; 16: 22.   [17] Cf. Num. 16: 30.   [18] Matt. 3: 7.
[19] Acts 16: 30.   [20] Rev. 3: 15.   [21] Cf. Acts 26: 5.
[22] The first edition, and *SOSO*, have this in italics, which could denote either a quotation or emphasis. Later editions of *SOSO* have it in normal type, and Outler italicizes it, indicating emphasis. However, it could well be a quotation—the echo of Luke 16: 15 ('Ye [= the Pharisees] are they which justify yourselves before men') is strong.   [23] Cf. Rom. 10: 3.
[24] Cf. 2 Tim. 3: 5.
[25] Cf. Luke 18: 11; the three nouns are quoted in the reverse order from the text.
[26] Cf. Luke 18: 12.   [27] Cf. ibid.   [28] Cf. Phil. 3: 6.
[29] Cf. John 14: 6.   [30] Luke 16: 15.   [31] Matt. 23: 13, 14, 15, 23, 25, 27, 29.

but within is full of all filthiness.[32] 'An evil disease cleaveth' still 'unto him',[33] so that 'his inward parts are very wickedness'.[34] Our Lord fitly compares him to a 'painted sepulchre', which 'appears beautiful without', but nevertheless is 'full of dead men's bones and of all uncleanness'.[35] The bones indeed are no longer dry; 'the sinews and flesh are come up upon them, and the skin covers them above': but 'there is no breath'[36] in them, no Spirit of the living God. And 'if any man have not the Spirit of Christ, he is none of his.'[37] 'Ye are Christ's',[38] 'if so be that the Spirit of God dwell in you.'[39] But if not, God knoweth that ye abide in death, even until now.

8. This is another character of the sleeper here spoken to. He abides in death, though he knows it not. He is dead unto God, 'dead in trespasses and sins'.[40] For 'to be carnally minded is death.'[41] Even as it is written, 'By one man sin entered into the world, and death by sin; and so death passed upon all men'[42]—not only temporal death, but likewise spiritual and eternal. 'In that day that thou eatest' (said God to Adam) 'thou shalt surely die.'[43] Not bodily (unless as he then became mortal) but spiritually; thou shalt lose the life of thy soul, thou shalt die to God, shalt be separated from him, thy essential life and happiness.

9. Thus first was dissolved the vital union of our soul with God, insomuch that 'in the midst of' natural 'life we are' now 'in' spiritual 'death'.[44] And herein we remain till the second Adam becomes a quickening spirit to us, till he raises the dead, the dead in sin, in pleasure, riches, or honours. But before any dead soul can live, he 'hears' (hearkens to) 'the voice of the Son of God':[45] he is made sensible of his lost estate, and receives the sentence of death in himself. He knows himself to be 'dead while he liveth'[46] dead to God and all the things of God; having no more power to perform the actions of a living Christian than a dead body to perform the functions of a living man.

10. And most certain it is that one dead in sin has not 'senses exercised to discern' spiritual 'good and evil'.[47] 'Having eyes, he sees not; he hath ears, and hears not.'[48] He doth not 'taste and see that the Lord is gracious'.[49] He 'hath not seen God at any time',[50] nor 'heard his voice',[51] nor 'handled the Word of life'.[52] In vain is the name of Jesus 'like ointment poured forth',[53] and 'all his garments smell of myrrh, aloes, and cassia'.[54] The soul that sleepeth in death hath no perception of

---

[32] Cf. Matt. 23: 25.   [33] Cf. Ps. 41: 8.   [34] Cf. Ps. 5: 9.

[35] Cf. Matt. 23: 27.

[36] Cf. Ezek. 37: 8. Both the 'but' in the middle of the quotation and the 'in them' following are in the KJV, but are not italicized in the first edition.   [37] Rom. 8: 9.

[38] 1 Cor. 3: 23.   [39] Rom. 8: 9.   [40] Eph. 2: 1.

[41] Rom. 8: 6.   [42] Rom. 5: 12.   [43] Gen. 2: 17.

[44] *BCP*, Burial Service—'in the midst of life, we are in death'.   [45] John 5: 25.

[46] Cf. 1 Tim. 5: 6.   [47] Heb. 5: 14.   [48] Cf. Mark 8: 18.

[49] Cf. Ps. 34: 8; this is actually a conflation of the KJV and *BCP* versions, and is not exactly either.

[50] Cf. John 1: 18; 1 John 4: 12.   [51] Cf. John 5: 37.   [52] Cf. 1 John 1: 1.

[53] Cf. Song of Songs 1: 3.   [54] Cf. Ps. 45: 8.

any objects of this kind. His heart is 'past feeling',[55] and understandeth none of these things.

11. And hence, having no spiritual senses, no inlets of spiritual knowledge, the natural man receiveth not the things of the Spirit of God; nay, he is so far from receiving them that whatsoever is spiritually discerned is mere foolishness unto him.[56] He is not content with being utterly ignorant of spiritual things, but he denies the very existence of them. And spiritual sensation itself is to him the foolishness of folly.[57] 'How', saith he, 'can these things be?'[58] How can any man know that he is alive to God? Even as you know that your body is now alive?[59] Faith is the life of the soul: and if ye have this life abiding in you, ye want no marks to evidence it *to yourself*, but that '*elenchos pneumatos*'[60] divine consciousness, that 'witness of God',[61] which is more and greater than ten thousand human witnesses.

12. If he doth not now bear witness with thy spirit that thou art a child of God,[62] O that he might convince thee, thou poor unawakened sinner, by his demonstration and power, that thou art a child of the devil! O that as I prophesy there might now be 'a noise and a shaking', and may 'the bones come together, bone to his bone'.[63] Then 'come from the four winds, O breath, and breathe on these slain that they may live!'[64] And do not ye harden your hearts[65] and resist the Holy Ghost, who even now is come to 'convince *you* of sin',[66] 'because you believe not on the name of the only-begotten Son of God'.[67]

II.1. Wherefore, 'Awake thou that sleepest, and arise from the dead.' God calleth thee now by my mouth; and bids thee know thyself, thou fallen spirit, thy true state and only concern below: 'what meanest thou, O sleeper? Arise! Call upon thy God, if so be thy God will think upon thee, that thou perish not.'[68] A mighty tempest is stirred up round about thee, and thou art sinking into the depths of perdition, the gulf of God's judgements. If thou would escape them, cast thyself into them. 'Judge thyself' and thou shalt 'not be judged of the Lord.'[69]

2. Awake, awake! Stand up this moment, lest thou 'drink at the Lord's hand the cup of his fury'.[70] Stir up thyself 'to lay hold on the Lord',[71] 'the Lord thy righteousness, mighty to save!'[72] 'Shake thyself from the dust.'[73] At least, let the earth-

---

[55] Eph. 4: 19.   [56] Cf. 1 Cor. 2: 14.   [57] Cf. Prov. 14: 24.
[58] John 3: 9.   [59] *SOSO* omits the question-mark.
[60] Heb. 11: 1 gives πραγμαάτων ἔλεγχος. See Outler (ed.), *Sermons*, i. 146 n. 55 for the context of Charles's use of this term.   [61] 1 John 5: 9.
[62] Cf. Rom. 8: 16.   [63] Cf. Ezek. 37: 7.   [64] Ezek. 37: 9.
[65] Cf. Ps. 95: 8.
[66] Cf. John 8: 46. In the first edition 'you' is printed in normal font in the middle of italicized text. This presumably reflects a MS which had an underlining for emphasis set within text enclosed in quotation marks.   [67] Cf. John 3: 18.
[68] Cf. Jonah 1: 6.   [69] Cf. 1 Cor. 11: 31.
[70] Cf. Isa. 51: 17. The entire sentence follows the text closely but not verbatim, although only the latter part is italicized in the first edition.
[71] Cf. Heb. 6: 18 and 1 Tim. 6: 12, 19; although the texts refer to laying hold of 'the hope' (Heb.) or 'eternal life' (Tim.), rather than the Lord.   [72] Cf. Jer. 23: 6; Isa. 63: 1.
[73] Isa. 52: 2.

quake of God's threatenings shake thee. Awake and cry out with the trembling
gaoler, 'what must I do to be saved?'[74] And never rest till thou believest on the
Lord Jesus, with a faith which is his gift, by the operation of his spirit.

3. If I speak to any one of you more than to another it is to thee who thinkest
thyself unconcerned in this exhortation. I have a message from God unto thee.[75]
In his name I 'warn *thee* to flee from the wrath to come'.[76] Thou unholy soul, see
thy picture in condemned Peter, lying in the dark dungeon between the soldiers,
bound with two chains, the keepers before the door keeping the prison.[77] The
night is far spent, the morning is at hand[78] when thou art to be brought forth to
execution. And in these dreadful circumstances thou art fast asleep; thou art fast
asleep in the devil's arm,[79] on the brink of the pit, in the jaws of everlasting
destruction.[80]

4. O may 'the angel of the Lord come upon thee', and 'the light shine into thy
prison'![81] And mayst thou feel the stroke of an almighty hand raising thee with,
'arise up quickly, gird thyself, and bind on thy sandal[s],[82] cast thy garment about
thee, and follow me.'[83]

5. Awake, thou everlasting spirit, out of thy dream of worldly happiness. Did
not God create thee for himself? Then thou canst not rest till thou restest in him.[84]
Return, thou wanderer. Fly back to thy ark.[85] 'This is not thy home.'[86] Think not
of building tabernacles here.[87] Thou art but 'a stranger, a sojourner upon earth';[88]
a creature of a day but just launching out into an unchangeable state. Make haste;
eternity is at hand. Eternity depends on this moment: an eternity of happiness, or
an eternity of misery!

6. In what state is thy soul? Was God, while I am yet speaking, to require it of
thee,[89] art thou ready to meet death and judgement? Canst thou stand in his sight,
'who is of purer eyes than to behold iniquity'?[90] Art thou 'meet to be partaker of
the inheritance of the saints in light'?[91] Hast thou 'fought a good fight and kept the
faith'?[92] Hast thou secured 'the one thing needful'?[93] Hast thou recovered the
image of God, even 'righteousness and true holiness'?[94] Hast thou 'put off the old
man and put on the new'?[95] Art thou 'clothed upon with Christ'?[96]

---

[74] Acts 16: 30.

[75] Judg. 3: 20. *SOSO* italicizes the sentence, but it is not italicized in the first edition.

[76] Cf. Matt. 3: 7 and parallel.   [77] Cf. Acts 12: 6.   [78] Cf. Rom. 13: 12.

[79] So the first edition. *SOSO* gives 'arms' rather than 'arm', which may be a correction, and seems
probable.   [80] 2 Thess. 1: 9.

[81] Cf. Acts 12:7.

[82] The first edition has sandal; the plural is in the KJV, and is clearly required. *SOSO* gives the plural.

[83] Cf. Acts 12: 7–8.   [84] Augustine, *Confessions*, 1: 1.   [85] Cf. Gen. 8: 9.

[86] The first edition italicizes the sentence, although if it is a quotation the exact source has not been
traced. There is an echo of Heb. 13:14 ('we have here no continuing city').

[87] Cf. Matt. 17: 4 and parallel.   [88] Cf. 1 Chron. 29: 15.   [89] Cf. Luke 12: 20.

[90] Cf. Hab. 1: 13.   [91] Col. 1: 12.   [92] Cf. 2 Tim. 4: 7.

[93] Luke 10: 42. This text is the subject of Sermon 21.   [94] Eph. 4: 24.

[95] Cf. Eph. 4: 22, 24; Col. 3: 9, 10.

[96] Cf. 2 Cor. 5: 2, although the passage speaks of being 'clothed upon with Heaven' rather than Christ.

7. Hast thou oil in thy lamp?[97] Grace in thy heart? Dost thou 'love the Lord thy God with all thy heart and with all thy mind, and with all thy soul, and with all thy strength'?[98] Is 'that mind in thee which was also in Christ Jesus'?[99] Art thou a Christian indeed? That is, a new creature? Are 'old things past away, and all things become new'?[100]

8. Art thou 'partaker of the divine nature'?[101] 'Knowest thou not that Christ is in thee, except thou be reprobate?'[102] Knowest thou that 'God dwelleth in thee, and thou in God, by his Spirit which he hath given thee'?[103] Knowest thou not that 'thy body is a temple of the Holy Ghost, which thou hast of God'?[104] Hast thou the 'witness in thyself',[105] 'the earnest of thine inheritance'?[106] Art thou 'sealed by that Spirit of promise unto the day of redemption'?[107] Hast thou 'received the Holy Ghost?'[108] Or dost thou start at the question, not knowing whether there be any Holy Ghost?

9. If it offends thee, be thou assured that thou neither art a Christian nor desirest to be one. Nay, thy very 'prayer is turned into sin';[109] and thou hast solemnly mocked God this very day by praying for 'the inspiration of his Holy Spirit',[110] when thou didst not believe there was any such thing to be received.[111]

10. Yet on the authority of God's Word and our own Church I must repeat the question, 'Hast thou received the Holy Ghost?' If thou hast not thou art not yet a Christian; for a Christian is a man that is 'anointed with the Holy Ghost and with power'.[112] Thou art not yet made a partaker of pure religion and undefiled.[113] Dost thou know what religion is? That it is a participation of the divine nature,[114] the life of God in the soul of man: 'Christ in thee, the hope of glory';[115] 'Christ formed in thy[116] heart',[117] happiness and holiness; heaven begun upon earth; a 'kingdom of God within thee',[118] 'not meat and drink', no outward thing, 'but righteousness, and peace, and joy in the Holy Ghost';[119] an everlasting kingdom brought into thy soul, a 'peace of God that passeth all understanding';[120] a 'joy unspeakable and full of glory'?[121]

11. Knowest thou that 'in Jesus Christ neither circumcision availeth anything, nor uncircumcision; but faith that worketh by love;'[122] but a new creation?[123] Seest

---

[97] Cf. Matt. 25: 4.

[98] Mark 12: 30 and parallels, citing Deut. 6: 5. This text is the subject of Sermon 20.

[99] Cf. Phil. 2: 5.   [100] Cf. 2 Cor. 5: 17.   [101] Cf. 2 Pet. 1: 4.

[102] Cf. 2 Cor. 13: 5.   [103] Cf. 1 John 3: 24; 4: 12, 13.   [104] Cf. 1 Cor. 6: 19.

[105] Cf. 1 John 5: 10.   [106] Cf. Eph. 1: 14.   [107] Cf. Eph. 1: 13; 4: 30.

[108] Acts 19: 2.

[109] Cf. Ps. 109: 7. *SOSO* includes the 'very' within the quotation marks, but it is not italicized in the first edition.

[110] See the first Collect in the Order for Holy Communion, *BCP* ('Cleanse the thoughts of our hearts by the inspiration of thy Holy Spirit').

[111] The first edition has a question-mark here, which seems an error. *SOSO* omits it.

[112] Acts 10: 38.   [113] Jas. 1: 27.   [114] Cf. 2 Pet. 1: 4.

[115] Cf. Col. 1: 27. *SOSO* reverses the order of this and the next quotation.

[116] *SOSO* has 'the' rather than 'thy'.   [117] Cf. Gal. 4: 19.   [118] Cf. Luke 17: 21.

[119] Rom. 14: 17.   [120] Cf. Phil. 4: 7.   [121] Cf. 1 Pet. 1: 8.

[122] Gal. 5: 6.   [123] Cf. Gal. 6: 15.

thou the necessity of that inward change, that spiritual birth, that life from the dead, that holiness? And art thou thoroughly convinced that 'without it no man shall see the Lord'? [124] Art thou labouring after it? 'Giving all diligence to make thy calling and election sure'?[125] 'Working out thy salvation with fear and trembling'?[126] 'Agonising to enter in at the strait gate'?[127] Art thou in earnest about thy soul? And canst thou tell the Searcher of hearts,[128] 'Thou, O God, art the thing that I long for!'[129] Lord, thou knowest all things! Thou knowest that I *would* love thee![130]

12. Thou hopest to be saved. But what reason hast thou to give of the hope that is in thee?[131] Is it because thou hast done no harm? Or because thou hast done much good? Or because thou art not like other men,[132] but wise, or learned, or honest, and morally good? Esteemed of men, and of a fair reputation? Alas, all this will never bring thee to God. It is in his account lighter than vanity.[133] Dost thou 'know Jesus Christ whom he hath sent'?[134] Hath he taught thee that 'by grace we are saved through faith? And that not of ourselves: it is the gift of God; not of works, lest any man should boast.'[135] Hast thou received the faithful saying as the whole foundation of thy hope, 'that Jesus Christ came into the world to save sinners'?[136] Hast thou learned what that meaneth, 'I came not to call the righteous, but sinners to repentance'?[137] 'I am not sent but to the lost sheep'?[138] Art thou (he that heareth, let him understand!) lost, dead, *damned already*? Dost thou know thy deserts? Dost thou feel thy wants? Art thou 'poor in spirit'?[139] *Mourning* for God and refusing to be comforted? Is the prodigal 'come to himself'[140], and well content to be therefore thought 'beside himself'[141] by those who are still feeding upon the husks which he hath left?[142] Art thou willing to 'live godly in Christ Jesus'?[143] And dost thou therefore 'suffer persecution'?[144] Do 'men say all manner of evil against thee falsely, for the Son of Man's sake'?[145]

13. O that in all these questions ye may hear the voice that wakes the dead, and feel that hammer of the Word which 'breaketh the rock in pieces'![146] 'If ye will hear his voice today, while it is hardly called today, harden not your hearts.'[147] Now awake thou that sleepest in spiritual death, that thou sleep not in death eternal! Feel thy lost estate, and 'arise from the dead.' Leave thine old companions in sin and death. Follow thou Jesus, and 'let the dead bury their dead.'[148] 'Save thyself from this untoward generation.'[149] 'Come out from among them, and be thou separate, and touch not the unclean thing; and the Lord shall receive thee.'[150] 'Christ shall give thee light.'

[124] Cf. Heb. 12: 14.   [125] Cf. 2 Pet. 1: 10.   [126] Cf. Phil. 2: 12.
[127] Cf. Luke 13: 24.   [128] Cf. Rom. 8: 27.   [129] Cf. Job 6: 8.
[130] Cf. John 21: 17.   [131] Cf. 1 Pet. 3: 15.   [132] Cf. Luke 18: 11.
[133] Ps. 62: 9.   [134] Cf. John 17: 3.   [135] Cf. Eph. 2: 8–9.
[136] Cf. 1 Tim. 1: 15.   [137] Mark 2: 17.   [138] Matt. 15: 24.
[139] Matt. 5: 3.   [140] Cf. Luke 15: 17.   [141] Mark 3: 21.
[142] Cf. Luke 15: 16–17.   [143] 2 Tim. 3: 12.   [144] ibid.
[145] Cf. Matt. 5: 11.   [146] Jer. 23: 29.   [147] Cf. Heb. 3: 7–8.
[148] Matt. 8: 22.   [149] Acts 2: 40.   [150] Cf. 2 Cor. 6: 17.

III.1   This promise I come, lastly, to explain. And how encouraging a consideration is this, that whosoever thou art who obeyest his call, thou canst not seek his
face in vain. If thou even now 'awakest and arisest from the dead', he hath bound
himself to 'give thee light'. 'The Lord shall give thee grace and glory;'¹⁵¹ the light
of his grace here, and the light of his glory when thou receivest the 'crown that
fadeth not away.'¹⁵² Thy light shall 'break forth as the morning,'¹⁵³ and thy darkness be as the noonday.¹⁵⁴ 'God, who commanded the light to shine out of
darkness', shall 'shine in thy heart, to give the knowledge of the glory of God in
the face of Jesus Christ.'¹⁵⁵ 'On them that fear the Lord shall the Sun of righteousness arise with healing in his wings.'¹⁵⁶ And 'in that day it shall be said unto
thee',¹⁵⁷ 'Arise, shine; for thy light is come, and the glory of the Lord is risen upon
thee.'¹⁵⁸ For Christ shall reveal himself in thee. And he is the 'true light'.¹⁵⁹

2.   God is light,¹⁶⁰ and will give himself to every awakened sinner that waiteth
for him. And thou shalt then be a temple of the living God,¹⁶¹ and Christ shall
'dwell in thy heart by faith'.¹⁶² And, 'being rooted and grounded in love, thou shalt
be able to comprehend with all saints what is the breadth, and length, and depth,
and height of that love of Christ which passeth knowledge, that thou mayest be
filled with all the fullness of God.'¹⁶³

3.   Ye see your calling, brethren.¹⁶⁴ We are called to be 'an habitation of God
through his Spirit';¹⁶⁵ and through his Spirit dwelling in us 'to be saints'¹⁶⁶ here,
and 'partakers of the inheritance of the saints in light'.¹⁶⁷ 'So exceeding great' are
the 'promises which are given unto us',¹⁶⁸ actually given unto us who believe. For
by faith 'we receive, not the spirit of the world, but the Spirit which is [of]¹⁶⁹ God',
the sum of all the promises, 'that we may know the things that are freely given to
us of God.'¹⁷⁰

4.   The Spirit of Christ is that great gift of God which at sundry times and in
divers manners¹⁷¹ he hath promised to man, and hath fully bestowed since the time
that Christ was glorified. Those promises before made to the fathers he hath thus
fulfilled: 'I will put my Spirit within you, and cause you to walk in my statutes.'¹⁷²
'I will pour water upon him that is thirsty, and floods upon the dry ground: I will
pour my Spirit upon thy seed, and my blessing upon thine offspring.'¹⁷³

---

¹⁵¹ Cf. Ps. 84: 11.   ¹⁵² Cf. 1 Pet. 5: 4.   ¹⁵³ Isa. 58: 8.
¹⁵⁴ Isa. 58: 10.   ¹⁵⁵ Cf. 2 Cor. 4: 6.   ¹⁵⁶ Cf. Mal. 4: 2.
¹⁵⁷ Cf. Zeph. 3: 16.   ¹⁵⁸ Isa. 60: 1.   ¹⁵⁹ John 1: 9; 1 John 2: 8.
¹⁶⁰ 1 John 1: 5.   ¹⁶¹ 2 Cor. 6: 16.   ¹⁶² Eph. 3: 17.
¹⁶³ Cf. Eph. 3: 17–19.   ¹⁶⁴ 1 Cor. 1: 26.   ¹⁶⁵ Cf. Eph. 2: 22.
¹⁶⁶ Rom. 1: 7; 1 Cor. 1: 2.   ¹⁶⁷ Col. 1: 12.

¹⁶⁸ See 2 Pet. 1: 4. *SOSO* carries the quotation through the words 'are the'. The italicizing in the first
edition is somewhat arbitrary; the KJV actually reads 'Whereby are given unto us exceeding great and
precious promises ...'.

¹⁶⁹ The first edition omits the 'of', which is presumably an error. *SOSO* gives it.

¹⁷⁰ Cf. 1 Cor. 2: 12.   ¹⁷¹ Heb. 1: 1.

¹⁷² This quotation is footnoted in the first edition as being from Ezek. 36: 27.

¹⁷³ This quotation is footnoted in the first edition as being from Isa. 44: 3.

5. Ye may all be living witnesses of these things, of remission of sins, and the gift of the Holy Ghost.[174] 'If thou canst believe, all things are possible to him that believeth.'[175] 'Who among you is there that feareth the Lord', and yet 'walketh on in darkness, and hath no light?'[176] I ask thee in the name of Jesus, believest thou that 'his arm is not shortened at all'?[177] That he is still 'mighty to save'?[178] That he is the 'same yesterday, today and for ever'?[179] That he hath 'now *power*[180] on earth'[181] to forgive sins? 'Son, be of good cheer; thy sins are forgiven.'[182] God, for Christ's sake, hath forgiven thee. Receive this, 'not as the word of man; but as it is indeed, the word of God';[183] and thou art 'justified freely through faith'.[184] Thou shalt be sanctified also through faith which is in Jesus,[185] and shalt set to thy seal,[186] even thine, that 'God hath *given unto us*[187] eternal life, and this life is in his Son.'[188]

6. Men and brethren, let me freely speak unto you,[189] and 'suffer ye the word of exhortation',[190] even from one the least esteemed in the church. Your conscience beareth you witness in the Holy Ghost[191] that these things are so, 'if so be ye have tasted that the Lord is gracious'.[192] 'This is eternal life, to know the only true God, and Jesus Christ whom he hath sent.'[193] This experimental knowledge, and this alone, is true Christianity. He is a Christian who hath received the Spirit of Christ. He is not a Christian who hath not received him. Neither is it possible to have received him and not know it. For 'at that day' (when he cometh, saith our Lord) 'ye shall know that I am in my Father, and you in me, and I in you.'[194] This is that 'Spirit of Truth, whom the world cannot receive, because it seeth him not, neither knoweth him. But ye know him; for he dwelleth with you, and shall be in you.'[195]

7. The world cannot receive him, but utterly reject[eth][196] the promise of the Father, contradicting and blaspheming. But every spirit which confesseth not this

---

[174] Cf. Acts 2: 38; 10: 43.   [175] Mark 9: 23.   [176] Cf. Isa. 50: 10.

[177] Cf. Isa. 50: 2; 59: 1.   [178] Isa. 63: 1.   [179] Heb. 13: 8.

[180] It is difficult to deduce what Charles or the printer were doing here. The first edition has normal type until 'now', which is italicized; normal type again for 'power', then italics for 'on earth'. The KJV, in the Matthean version which Charles appears to have been using at this point, has 'that the Son of man hath power on earth to forgive sins'. The likeliest hypothesis is that Charles, marking quotations with quotation marks or parentheses in the MS, placed the marks either as shown or more widely, and underlined 'power' for emphasis, and that the printer then made the best of this, using normal type for 'power' to denote emphasis within the italicized portion. *SOSO* does the same.

[181] Cf. Matt. 9: 6 (and parallels, but as stated in the previous note it appears to be the Matthean version which Charles was using).   [182] Matt. 9: 2.

[183] Cf. 1 Thess. 2: 13.   [184] Cf. Rom. 3: 24. This text is the subject of Sermon 6.

[185] Cf. Acts 26: 18.   [186] Cf. John 3: 33.

[187] A similar crux arises here to that discussed above. The first edition, followed by *SOSO*, has 'God' in the usual small capitals, 'hath' in italics, 'given unto us' in normal type, and italics to the end. There seems relatively little need to emphasize the 'given unto us' phrase, but even less reason to simply take it out of the quotation, which is the only other significance that the type usage can have. (It may of course simply be an error, on Charles's part or the printer's.) The punctuation here given has accordingly been adopted. Later editions of *SOSO* simply begin the quotation marks at 'that' and take them to the end.   [188] Cf. 1 John 5: 11.

[189] Acts 2: 29.   [190] Cf. Heb. 13: 22.   [191] Cf. Rom. 9: 1.

[192] 1 Pet. 2: 3.   [193] Cf. John 17: 3.

[194] This quotation is footnoted in the first edition as being from John 14: 20.   [195] John 14: 17.

[196] The first edition, and the first edition of *SOSO*, have 'reject', which is plainly an error. Later editions of *SOSO* correct to 'rejecteth'.

is not of God.[197] Yea, 'this is that spirit of Antichrist, whereof ye have heard that it should come into the world; and even now it is in the world.'[198] He is Antichrist whoever[199] denies the inspiration of the Holy Ghost, or that the indwelling Spirit of God is the common privilege of all believers, the blessing of the gospel, the unspeakable gift, the universal promise, the criterion of a real Christian.

8. It nothing helps them to say,[200] 'We do not deny the *assistance* of God's Spirit, but only this *inspiration*, this "receiving the Holy Ghost" and being *sensible* of it. It is only this *feeling of the* Spirit, this being *moved* by the Spirit, or *filled* with it, which we deny to have any place in sound religion.' But in 'only denying this' you deny the whole scriptures, the whole truth and promise and testimony of God.

9. Our own excellent Church knows nothing of this devilish distinction; but speaks plainly of[201] 'feeling the Spirit of Christ'; of being[202] 'moved by the Holy Ghost', and knowing and[203] 'feeling there is no other name than that of Jesus' whereby we can receive life and salvation.[204] She teaches us all to pray for the[205] 'inspiration of the Holy Spirit', yea, that we may be 'filled with the Holy Ghost'[206] Nay, and every presbyter of hers professes to 'receive the Holy Ghost by the imposition of hands'.[207] Therefore to deny any of these is in effect to renounce the Church of England, as well as the whole Christian revelation.

10. But 'the wisdom of God' was always 'foolishness with men'.[208] No marvel, then, that the great mystery of the gospel should be now also 'hid from the wise and prudent',[209] as well as in the days of old; that it should be almost universally denied, ridiculed, and exploded as mere frenzy, and all who dare avow it still branded with the names of madmen and enthusiasts. This is 'that falling away'[210] which was to come—that general apostasy of all orders and degrees of men which we even now find to have overspread the earth. 'Run to and fro in the streets of Jerusalem, and see if ye can find a man,'[211] a man that loveth the Lord his God with all his heart, and serveth him with all his strength.[212] How does our own land mourn (that we look no farther) under the overflowings of ungodliness?[213] What

---

[197] Cf. 1 John 4: 3.   [198] Cf. 1 John 2: 18; 4: 3.   [199] *SOSO* has 'whosoever'.

[200] The first edition, and *SOSO*, have quotation marks from this point until 'sound religion'.

[201] The reference which follows is footnoted at this point in the first edition as being from Article XVII of the Articles of Religion.

[202] The reference which follows is footnoted at this point in the first edition as being from the Office of Consecrating Priests (*BCP*).

[203] The reference which follows is footnoted at this point in the first edition as being from the Visitation of Sick (*BCP*).   [204] The prayer actually refers to 'health and salvation'. Cf. Acts 4: 12.

[205] The reference which follows is footnoted at this point in the first edition as being from the Collect before Holy Communion (*BCP*).

[206] There is an oddity here. In *SOSO* as in the Toronto MS this reference is footnoted as being from the *BCP* Order of Confirmation. However, as Outler notes (*Sermons* iv: 156 n. h), the words are not found there but in the *BCP* Collect for St Stephen's Day. However, in the Oxford MS the reference in the footnote is given as being from the Collect for St Stephen's Day.

[207] See *BCP*, Ordering of Priests.   [208] Cf. 1 Cor. 1: 21–5.   [209] Matt. 11: 25.

[210] Cf. 2 Thess. 2: 3.   [211] Cf. Jer. 5: 1.   [212] Cf. Mark 12: 30 and parallels.

[213] Ps. 18: 4. The first edition, and the first editon of *SOSO*, have the question-mark. Later editions of *SOSO* replace it with an exclamation mark, which the sense and context seem to call for.

villanies of every kind are committed day by day; yea, too often with impunity by those who sin with a high hand, and glory in their shame![214] Who can reckon up the oaths, curses, profaneness, blasphemies; the lying, slandering, evil speaking; the sabbath-breaking, gluttony, drunkenness, revenge; the whoredoms, adulteries, and various uncleanness; the frauds, injustice, oppression, extortion, which over-spread our land as a flood?[215]

11. And even among those who have kept themselves pure from those grosser abominations, how much anger and pride, how much sloth and idleness, how much softness and effeminacy, how much luxury and self-indulgence, how much covetousness and ambition, how much thirst of praise, how much love of the world, how much fear of man is to be found! Meanwhile, how little of true religion?[216] For where is he that loveth either God or his neighbour, as he hath given us commandment[?][217] On the one hand are those who have not so much as the form of godliness; on the other, those who have the form only:[218] there stands the *open*, there the *painted* sepulchre.[219] So that, in very deed, whosoever were earnestly to behold any public gathering together of the people (I fear those in our churches are not to be excepted) might easily perceive 'that the one part were Sadducees, and the other Pharisees':[220] the one having almost as little concern about religion as if there were 'no resurrection, neither angel nor spirit';[221] and the other making it a mere lifeless form, a dull round of external performances without either true faith, or the love of God, or joy in the Holy Ghost.[222]

12. Would to God I could except us of this place. 'Brethren, my heart's desire and prayer to God for you is that ye may be saved'[223] from this overflowing of ungodliness,[224] and that here may its proud waves be stayed![225] But is it so indeed? God knoweth, yea, and our own conscience, it is not. We have not kept ourselves pure.[226] Corrupt are we also and abominable; and few are there that understand any more, few that worship God in spirit and truth.[227] We too are 'a generation that set not our hearts aright, and whose spirit cleaveth not steadfastly unto God'.[228] He hath appointed us indeed to be 'the salt of the earth. But if the salt have lost its savour, it is thenceforth good for nothing but to be cast out, and to be trodden under foot of man.'[229]

13. And 'shall I not visit for these things? saith the Lord. Shall not my soul be avenged on such a nation as this?'[230] Yea, we know not how soon he may say to the sword, 'Sword, go through this land!'[231] He hath given us long space to repent. He lets us alone this year also.[232] But he warns and awakens us by thunder. His judgments

---

[214] Phil. 3: 19.   [215] Cf. Jer. 47: 2; and Rom. 1: 18–32.
[216] The first edition, and the first editon of *SOSO*, have the question-mark. Later editions of *SOSO* replace it with an exclamation mark, which the sense and context seem to call for.
[217] The first edition ends with a colon rather than the question-mark, which *SOSO* supplies.
[218] Cf. 2 Tim. 3: 5.   [219] Cf. Matt. 23: 27.   [220] Acts 23: 6.
[221] Acts 23: 8.   [222] Cf. Rom. 14: 17.   [223] Cf. Rom. 10: 1.
[224] Ps. 18: 4.   [225] Cf. Job 38: 11.   [226] Cf. 1 Tim. 5: 22.
[227] John 4: 24.   [228] Cf. Ps. 78: 9 (*BCP*).   [229] Matt. 5: 13.
[230] Jer. 5: 9, 29.   [231] Cf. Ezek. 14: 17.   [232] Cf. Luke 13: 8.

are abroad in the earth.[233] And we have all reason to expect that heaviest of all even 'that he should come unto us quickly, and remove our candlestick out of its place, except we repent and do the first works';[234] unless we return to the principles of the Reformation, the truth and simplicity of the gospel. Perhaps we are now resisting the last effort of divine grace to save us. Perhaps we have wellnigh 'filled up the measure of our iniquities'[235] by rejecting the counsel of God against ourselves, and casting out his messengers.

14. O God, 'in the midst of wrath remember mercy'![236] Be glorified in our reformation, not in our destruction. Let us 'hear the rod, and him that appointed it'.[237] Now that 'thy judgments are abroad in the earth',[238] let the 'inhabitants of the world learn righteousness'.[239]

15. My brethren, it is high time for us to awake out of sleep; before the 'great trumpet of the Lord be blown',[240] and our land become a field of blood.[241] O may we speedily see the things that make for our peace, before they are hid from our eyes![242] 'Turn thou us, O good Lord, and let thine anger cease from us.'[243] 'O Lord, look down from heaven, behold and visit this vine';[244] and cause us to know the time of our visitation.[245] 'Help us, O God of our salvation, for the glory of thy name; O deliver us, and be merciful to our sins, for thy name's sake.'[246] 'And so we will not go back from thee: O let us live, and we shall call upon thy name. Turn us again, O Lord God of hosts, show the light of thy countenance, and we shall be whole.'[247]

'Now unto him that is able to do exceeding abundantly above all that we can ask or think, according to the power that worketh in us, unto him be glory in the church by Christ Jesus throughout all ages, world without end.' Amen.[248]

---

[233] Cf. Ps. 105: 7.   [234] Cf. Rev. 2: 5.

[235] The only text which relates to this is Matt. 23: 32, and the context fits. The text actually says (to the Scribes and Pharisees) 'fill ye up then the measure of your fathers'.   [236] Hab. 3: 2.

[237] Cf. Mic. 6: 9.   [238] Cf. 1 Chron. 16: 14; Ps. 105: 7.   [239] Isa. 26: 9.

[240] Isa. 27: 13.   [241] Matt. 27: 8.   [242] Cf. Luke 19: 42.

[243] Ps. 85: 4 (BCP).   [244] Cf. Ps. 80: 14.   [245] Luke 19: 44; cf. also Jer. 8: 12.

[246] Ps. 79: 9.   [247] Ps. 80: 18–19.   [248] Eph. 3: 20–1.

SERMON 9
PSALM 46: 8

INTRODUCTORY COMMENT

This sermon was written in response to the several earthquakes that hit London in February and March 1750. The most significant appears to have been that on 8 March.[1] There is no entry in Charles's journal for this day, but the entry for 10 March records how he preached on Isaiah 24 'a chapter I had not taken much notice of, till this awful providence explained it'. Quite what the content of that sermon was is unknown, but a reading of the chapter clearly suggests what Charles might have said given the 'awful providence' he had just experienced.[2] By 4 April, 1750 he had constructed a written text of a sermon on the subject of earthquakes. His journal entry for that day reads

> Fear filled our chapel, occasioned by a prophecy of the earthquake's return this night. I preached my written sermon on the subject, with great effect, and gave out several suitable hymns. It was a glorious night for the disciples of Jesus.[3]

It must be a very real probability that the 'written sermon' here referred to is the *Cause and Cure of Earthquakes* published the same year. Charles's specific reference to his 'written' sermon may suggest that by this date he was no longer in the regular habit of committing his sermons to paper. This is conjecture, but in the light of the evidence presented in Chapter 2, not at all unreasonable. In any case, this sermon is the latest for which any literary evidence has survived. The 'suitable hymns' referred to in the journal entry may have been taken from those which he composed specifically to mark these startling events, later published by him under the title *Hymns Occasioned by the Earthquake March 8, 1750*.[4]

There is no dispute concerning the authenticity of this sermon, though it was printed in the major 1872 edition of the works of John Wesley without any qualifying note.[5] This has led to some confusion. However, the second edition (1756) clearly gives the name of Charles Wesley as the author. No MS has survived. The text reproduced below is that which has been reconstructed from the first edition, a copy of which is held in the John Rylands University Library of Manchester.[6]

---

[1] An account of the earthquake is found in John Wesley's journal for 8 March, 1750 (*J&D* xx. 323–4) with a briefer note on the earlier shake on 8 February (*J&D* xx. 320). Charles records on 8 February simply that 'there was an earthquake in London' (MARC DDCW 10/2 *in loc.*; Jackson, *Journal*, ii. 67). See also Tyerman's account of the events and its effect on the Wesleys (*Life* ii. 71–4) and that of Jackson (*Life*, i. 549–56).

[2] In this context also the hymns that Charles wrote on this chapter might be informative. There are at least two: 'Sure the word which God doth say' (Osborn, *Poetical Works*, ix. 389–90) and 'Come, eternal King surrounded' (Osborn, *Poetical Works*, ix. 390).

[3] MARC DDCW 10/2 *in loc.* (Jackson, *Journal*, ii. 69).

[4] Charles Wesley, *Hymns Occasioned by the Earthquake March 8, 1750*, Parts I and II (1750); reprinted in Osborn, *Poetical Works*, vi. 17–52.   [5] *Works of John Wesley*, vii. 386–99.

[6] The text is as yet uncatalogued but can be found in the MAB section of the MARC.

The sermon makes lively reading, especially if one tries to imagine its impact upon those hearing it for the first time in the wake of the London earthquakes. Charles here paints a terrifying picture of God's anger, anger that has already begun to spill over into judgement and destruction. Note the first line of the sermon itself, which reads 'Of all the judgments which the righteous God inflicts on sinners here, the most dreadful and destructive is an earthquake.' God's wrath and anger have been stirred up and, as in the past, he is poised to act. According to Charles, the destructive action of God is clearly seen in the numerous earthquakes that have come upon the world prior to those which are now being experienced in London. The graphic accounts he gives of those earlier earthquakes must surely have had considerable impact upon those who heard him as he sought to convince his audience that in the London earthquakes one could hear the fast approaching footsteps of an angry God. However, according to Charles, earthquakes are not just punishments, but also warnings, and through them God gives sinners a chance to repent. This is an urgent matter, for, he asks, 'What but national repentance can prevent national destruction?' But repentance will provide an escape route and those who repent 'shall not be hewn down, and cast into the fire'. According to Charles the cause of earthquakes is sin and the cure repentance.

This, then, is an anguished sermon, firmly rooted in the historical situation in which it was written. Through it one catches a glimpse of Charles's world-view as he seeks to make sense of what must have been very frightening events. One catches a glimpse also of Charles the preacher as he sought to heed, and to encourage others to heed, what he perceived to be God's final warnings to a guilty human race.

Psalm XLVI. 8[1]

'O come hither, and behold the works of the Lord, what destruction
he hath brought upon the earth!'

Of all the judgments which the righteous God inflicts on sinners here, the most
dreadful and destructive is an earthquake. This he has lately brought on our part
of the earth, and thereby alarmed our fears, and bid us 'prepare to meet our God'![2]
The shocks which have been felt in divers places since that which made this city
tremble, may convince us that the danger is not over, and ought to keep us still in
awe; seeing 'his anger is not turned away, but his hand is stretched out still'. (Isa.
10. 4.).[3]

That I may fall in with the design of providence at this awful crisis, I shall take
occasion from the words of my text,

I.   To show that earthquakes are the works of the Lord, and he only bringeth
       this destruction upon the earth.[4]

II.   Call you to behold the works of the Lord, in two or three terrible instances.
       And

III   Give you some directions suitable to the occasion.

I   I am to show you that earthquakes are the works of the Lord, and he only
bringeth this destruction upon the earth. Now, that God is himself the author, and
sin the *moral* cause, of earthquakes, (whatever the natural cause may be) cannot be
denied by any who believe the scriptures; for these are they which testify of him,
that 'it is God who removeth the mountains, and overturneth them' in his anger;
'who shaketh the earth out of her place, and the pillars thereof tremble' (Job 9.5,
6). 'He looketh on the earth and it trembleth, he toucheth the hills and they smoke'
(Psalm 104. 32). 'The hills melted like wax at the presence of the Lord, at the presence of the Lord of the whole earth' (Psalm 97. 5). 'The mountains quake at him,
and the hills melt.—Who can stand before his indignation? and who can abide in
the fierceness of his anger? His fury is poured out like fire, and the rocks are
thrown down by him' (Nahum 1. 5,6).

Earthquakes are set forth by the inspired writers as God's proper judicial act, or
the punishment of sin; sin is the cause, earthquakes the effect of his anger. So the
Psalmist: 'The earth trembled and quaked, the very foundations also of the hills

---

[1] On the front cover of the first edition: 'The Cause and Cure of Earthquakes. A Sermon Preach'd
from Psalm xlvi.8 London: Printed in the Year MDCCL'. Charles is not named as the author. The
second edition (1756) gives Charles as the author.

[2] Cf. Amos 4: 12. In the first edition of the sermon italics are used both for emphasis (corresponding
of course to underlining in the original manuscript) and for quotations. In this transcription, italics
have been kept in those places where emphasis seems intended, but quotation marks have been inserted
where quotations were italicized.

[3] Throughout the 1750 printed edition of this sermon the scripture references were placed in footnotes and marked in the text using signs such as *, †, and ‡ . Those references have been raised here
to the text for the sake of clarity. There are a number of places where scripture passages are quoted,
either verbatim or loosely, but neither referenced nor printed in italics. The references for these are
simply supplied in a footnote.   [4] Cf. Jer. 4: 6.

shook, and were removed,' because he was wroth (Psalm 18. 7).[5] So the prophet Isaiah, 'I will punish the world for their evil—and will lay low the haughtiness of the terrible,—therefore I will shake the heavens, and the earth shall remove out of her place', in the wrath of the Lord of hosts, and in the day of his fierce anger (Isai. 13. 11, 13i [*sic*]).[6] And again, 'Behold the Lord maketh the earth empty, and maketh it waste, and turneth it upside down' (in the original, perverteth the face therof) 'and scattereth abroad the inhabitants thereof:—For the windows from on high are open, and the foundations of the earth do shake. The earth is utterly broken down, the earth is clean dissolved, the earth is moved exceedingly. The earth shall reel to and fro like a drunkard, and be removed like a cottage, and the transgression thereof shall be heavy upon it, and it shall fall and not rise again' (Isai. 24. 1,18, 19, 20). 'Tremble thou earth at the presence of the Lord, at the presence of the God of Jacob' (Psalm 114. 7). 'Thou shalt be visited of the Lord of hosts with thunder, and with earthquake, and great noise' (Isaiah 29. 6).

Nothing can be more express than these scripture testimonies, which determine both the cause and author of this terrible calamity. But reason, as well as faith, doth sufficiently assure us it must be the punishment of sin, and the effect of that curse which was brought upon the earth by the original transgression. Steadfastness must be no longer looked for in the world, since innocency is banished thence. But we cannot conceive that the universe would have been disturbed by these furious accidents during the state of original righteousness. Wherefore should God's anger have armed the elements against his faithful subjects? Wherefore should he have overthrown all his works to destroy innocent men? Or why overwhelmed the inhabitants of the earth with the ruins thereof, if they had not been sinful? Why buried those in the bowels of the earth who were not to die? Let us then conclude, both from Scripture and reason, that earthquakes are God's 'strange works'[7] of judgment, the proper effect and punishment of sin. I proceed,

II   To set before you these works of the Lord in two or three terrible instances.

In the year 1692 there happened in Sicily one of the most dreadful earthquakes in all history; it shook the whole island, and not only that, but Naples and Malta shared in the shock. It was impossible for any one to keep on their legs on the dancing earth; nay, those who lay on the ground were tossed from side to side, as on a rolling billow. High walls leaped from their foundations several paces.

The mischief it did is amazing; fifty-four cities and towns, besides an incredible number of villages, were almost entirely destroyed. Catania, one of the most famous, ancient, and flourishing cities in the kingdom, the residence of several monarchs, and an university, had the greatest share in the judgment. Fath. Anth. Serrvoita, being on his way thither, a few miles from the city, observed a black cloud like night hovering over it; and there arose from the mouth of Etna great

---

[5] The last four words are part of the scripture passage but were not italicized in the printed edition.

[6] The words from 'in' to 'anger' are part of the text but were not italicized in the printed edition.

[7] The reference in Isa. 28: 21 to God's 'strange act', cited later, may have been in Charles's mind.

spires of flame, which spread all around. The sea all on a sudden began to roar, and rise in billows; the birds flew about astonished; the cattle ran crying in the fields; and there was a blow as if all the artillery in the world had been discharged at once!

His and his companions' horses stopped short, trembling, so that they were forced to alight. They were no sooner off, but they were lifted from the ground above two palms. When casting his eyes towards Catania, he was astonished to see nothing but a thick cloud of dust in the air. This was the scene of their calamity, for of the magnificent Catania there is not the least footstep to be seen. Of eighteen thousand nine hundred and fourteen inhabitants, eighteen thousand perished therein. In the several cities and towns sixty thousand were destroyed out of two hundred and fifty-four thousand nine hundred.

In the same year, 1692, on June 7, was the earthquake in Jamaica. It threw down most of the houses, churches, sugar-works, mills and bridges, throughout the island; tore the rocks and mountains, reducing some of them to plains; destroyed whole plantations, and threw them into the sea; and, in two minutes' time, shook down and destroyed nine-tenths of the town of Port-Royal; the houses sunk outright thirty or forty fathom deep.

The earth opening swallowed up people, and they rose in other streets, some in the midst of the harbour (being driven up again by the sea which rose in those breaches) and so wonderfully escaped.

Of all wells, from one fathom to six or seven, the water flew out of the top with a vehement motion. While the houses on one side of the street were swallowed up, on the other they were thrown into heaps. The sand in the street rose like waves of the sea, lifting up every body that stood on it, and immediately dropping down into pits, and at the same instant, a flood of water, breaking in, rolled them over and over, while catching hold of beams and rafters to save themselves.

Ships and sloops in the harbour were overset and lost. A vessel, by the motion of the sea and sinking of the wharf, was driven over the tops of many houses, and sunk there.

The earthquake was attended with a hollow rumbling sound like that of thunder. In less than a minute three quarters of the houses, and the ground they stood on, with the inhabitants, were quite sunk under water, and the little part left behind was no better than a heap of rubbish.

The shock was so violent that it threw people down on their knees or their faces, as they were running about for shelter; the ground heaved and swelled like a rolling sea; and several houses, still standing, were shuffled and moved some yards out of their places; a whole street is said to be twice as broad now as before.

In many places the earth would crack, and open and shut quick and fast, of which openings, two or three hundred might be seen at a time; in some whereof the people were swallowed up; others the closing earth caught by the middle, and squeezed to death; and in that manner they were left buried with only their heads above ground; some heads the dogs eat [sic].

The Minister of the place in his account saith, that such was the desperate wickedness of the people, that he was afraid to continue among them. That on the day of the earthquake some sailors and others fell to breaking open and rifling warehouses, and houses deserted, while the earth trembled under them, and the houses fell upon them in the act; that he met many swearing and blaspheming; and that the common harlots, who remained still upon the place, were as drunken and impudent as ever.

While he was running towards the Fort, a wide open place, to save himself, he saw the earth open and swallow up a multitude of people; and the sea mounting in upon them over the fortifications, it likewise destroyed their large burying-place, and washed away the carcases out of their graves, dashing their tombs to pieces. The whole harbour was covered with dead bodies, floating up and down without burial.

As soon as the violent shock was over, he desired all people to join with him in prayer. Among them were several Jews, who kneeled and answered as they did, and were heard even to call upon Jesus Christ. After he had spent an hour and an half with them in prayer, and exhortations to repentance, he was desired to retire to some ship in the harbour, and passing over the tops of some houses which lay level with the water, got first into a canoe, and then into a long-boat, which put him on board a ship.

The larger openings swallowed up houses, and out of some would issue whole rivers of water, spouted up a great height into the air, and threatening a deluge to that part which the earthquake spared. The whole was attended with offensive smells, and the noise of falling mountains. The sky in a minute's time was turned dull and red, like a glowing oven. Scarce a planting-house or sugar-work was left standing in all Jamaica. A great part of them was swallowed up, houses, trees, people, and all at one gape; in the place of which afterwards appeared great pools of water, which when dried up left nothing but sand, without any mark that ever tree or plant had been thereon.

About 12 miles from the sea, the earth gaped and spouted out with a prodigious force vast quantities of water into the air. But the greatest violence was among the mountains and rocks. Most of the rivers were stopped for 24 hours, by the falling of the mountains, till swelling up they made themselves new channels, tearing up trees and all they met with in their passage.

A great mountain split, and fell into the level ground, and covered several settlements, and destroyed the people there. Another mountain having made several leaps or moves, overwhelmed great part of a plantation lying a mile off. Another large high mountain, near a day's journey over, was was [*sic*] quite swallowed up, and where it stood is now a great lake some leagues over.

After the great shake, those who escaped got on board ships in the harbour, where many continued above two months; the shakes all that time being so violent, and coming so thick, sometimes two or three in an hour, accompanied with frightful noises, like a ruffling wind, or an hollow rumbling thunder, with brimstone blasts, that they durst not come ashore. The consequence of the earthquake was, a general sickness from noisome vapours, which swept away above three thousand persons.

On the 28th of October, 1746, half an hour past ten at night, Lima, the capital city of Peru, was destroyed by an earthquake, which extended an hundred leagues northward, and as many more to the south, all along the sea-coast. The destruction did not so much as give time for fright; for at one and the same instant the noise, the shock, and the ruin were perceived. In the space of four minutes, during which the greatest force of the earthquake lasted, some found themselves buried under the ruins of the falling houses; and other crushed to death in the streets by the tumbling of the walls, which fell upon them as they ran here and there.

Nevertheless, the greater part of the inhabitants (who were computed near sixty thousand) were providentially preserved, either in the hollow places which the ruins left, or on the top of the very ruins themselves, without knowing how they got up thither. For no person, at such a season, had time for deliberation; and supposing he had, there was no place of retreat, for the parts which seemed most firm, sometimes proved the weakest; on the contrary, the weakest, at intervals, made the greatest resistance; and the consternation was such, that no one thought himself secure, till he had made his escape out of the city.

The earth struck against the buildings with such violence, that every shock beat down the greatest part of them; and these tearing along with them vast weights in their fall (especially the churches and high houses) completed the destruction of everything they encountered with, even of what the earthquake had spared. The shocks, although instantaneous, were yet successive; and at intervals men were transported from one place to another, which was the means of safety to some, while the utter impossibility of moving preserved others.

There were seventy-four churches, besides chapels, and fourteen monasteries, with as many more hospitals and infirmaries, which were in an instant reduced to a ruinous heap, and their immense riches buried in the earth. But though scarce twenty houses were left standing, yet it does not appear that the number of the dead amounted to much more than one thousand one hundred and forty-one persons, seventy of whom were patients in an hospital, who were buried by the roof falling upon them as they lay in their beds, no person being able to give them any assistance.

Callao, a sea-port town, two leagues distant from Lima, was swallowed up by the sea in the same earthquake. It vanished out of sight in a moment; so that not the least sight of it now appears.

Some few towers, indeed, and the strength of its walls, for a time, endured the whole force of the earthquake. But scarcely had its poor inhabitants begun to recover their first fright, which the dreadful ruin had occasioned, when suddenly the sea began to swell, and rising to a prodigious height, rushed furiously forward, and overflowed, with so vast a deluge of water, its ancient bounds, that, foundering most of the ships which were at anchor in the port, and lifting the rest above the height of the walls and towers, it drove them on, and left them on dry ground far beyond the town. At the same time, it tore up from the foundations everything therein of houses and buildings, excepting the two gates, and here and there some small fragments of the walls themselves, which, as registers of the calamity, are still to be seen among the ruins and the waters, a dreadful monument of what they were!

In this raging flood were drowned all the inhabitants of the place, about five thousand persons. Such as could lay hold on any pieces of timber, floated about for a considerable time, but those fragments, for want of room, were continually striking against each other, and so beat off those who had clung to them.

About two hundred, mostly fishermen and sailors, saved themselves. They declared that the waves in their retreat surrounded the whole town, without leaving any means for preservation, and that in the intervals, when the violence of the inundation was a little abated, they heard the most mournful cries and shrieks of those who perished. Those likewise who were on board the ships, which by the elevation of the sea were carried quite over the town, had the opportunity of escaping. Of twenty-three ships in the port at the time of the earthquake, four were stranded, and all the rest foundered. The few persons who saved themselves upon planks were several times driven about as far as the island of St. Lawrence, more than two leagues from the port. At last some of them were cast upon the sea-shore, others upon the island, and so were preserved.

In these instances we may behold and see the works of the Lord, and how terrible he is in his doings towards the children of men (Psalm 66. 5)? Indeed, nothing can be so affecting as this judgment of earthquakes when it comes unexpectedly as a thief in the night,[8] 'when hell enlarges itself, and opens her mouth without measure; and their glory, and their multitude, and their pomp, and he that rejoiceth, descends into it' (Isa 5. 14). When there is no time to flee, or method to escape, or possibility to resist;—when no sanctuary or refuge remains; no shelter is to be found in the highest towers or lowest caverns; when the earth opens on a sudden, and becomes the grave of whole families, streets, and cities; and effects this in less time than you are able to tell the story of it; either sending out a flood of waters to drown, or vomiting out flames of fire to consume them, or closing again upon them, that they die by suffocation or famine, if not by the ruins of their own dwelling. When parents and children, husbands and wives, masters and servants, magistrates, ministers, and people, without distinction, in the midst of health, and peace, and business, are buried in a common ruin, and pass all together into the eternal world; and there is only the difference of a few hours or minutes between a famous city and none at all.

Now, if war be a terrible evil, how much more an earthquake, which in the midst of peace, brings a worse evil than the extremity of war. If a raging pestilence be dreadful, which sweeps away thousands in a day, and ten thousands in a night; if a

---

[8] 2 Pet. 3: 10.

consuming fire be an amazing judgment; how much more astonishing is this, whereby houses, and inhabitants, towns, and cities, and countries, are all destroyed at one stroke in a few minutes! Death is the only presage of such a judgment, without giving leisure to prepare for another world, or opportunity to look for any shelter in this.

For a man to feel the earth, which hangeth upon nothing (but as some vast ball in the midst of a thin yielding air) totter under him, must fill him with secret fright and confusion. History informs us of the fearful effects of earthquakes in all ages; where you may see rocks torn in pieces; mountains not cast down only, but removed; hills raised, not out of valleys only, but out of seas; fires breaking out of waters; stones and cinders belched up; rivers changed; seas dislodged; earth opening; towns swallowed up; and many such-like hideous events.

Of all divine animadversions, there is none more horrid, more inevitable, than this. For where can we think to escape danger, if the most solid thing in all the world shakes? If that which sustains all other things threaten us with sinking under our feet, what sanctuary shall we find from an evil that encompasses us about? And whither can we withdraw, if the gulfs which open themselves shut up our passages on every side?

With what horror are men struck when they hear the earth groan, when her trembling succeeds her complaints, when houses are loosened from their foundations, when the roofs fall upon their heads, and the pavement sinks under their feet! What hope, when fear cannot be fenced by flight! In other evils there is some way to escape; but an earthquake encloses what it overthrows, and wages war with whole provinces; and sometimes leaves nothing behind it to inform posterity of its outrages. More insolent than fire, which spares rocks; more cruel than the conqueror, who leaves walls; more greedy than the sea, which vomits up shipwrecks; it swallows and devours whatsoever it overturns. The sea itself is subject to its empire, and the most dangerous storms are those occasioned by earthquakes.

I come, in the third and last place, to give you some directions suitable to the occasion. And this is the more needful, because ye know not how soon the late earthquake, wherewith God hath visited us, may return, or whether he may not enlarge as well as repeat its commission. Once, yea twice,[9] hath the Lord warned us, that he is arisen to shake terribly the earth. Wherefore, I. Fear God, even that God who can in a moment cast both body and soul into hell.[10] 'Enter into the rock, and hide thee in the dust for fear of the Lord, and for the glory of his majesty' (Isai 2. 10). Ought we not all to cry out, 'Great and marvellous are thy works, O Lord God Almighty! Who shall not fear thee, and glorify thy name, for thy judgments are made manifest!' (Rev. 4.3, 4).[11]

---

[9] Job 33: 14.   [10] Cf. Matt. 10: 28.
[11] The reference is corrected to Rev. 15: 3–4 in later editions.

God speaks to your hearts as in subterranean thunder. 'The Lord's voice crieth unto the city, hear the rod, and who hath appointed it' (Micah 6. 1, 12).[12] He commands you to take notice of his power and justice. 'Come and see!' (Jer 5. 22)[13] while a fresh seal is opening; yea, 'come and see the works of God, he is terrible in his doings towards the children of men' (Psal 11. 7).[14]

When he makes the mountains tremble, and the earth shake, shall not our hearts be moved? 'Fear ye not me? saith the Lord; and will ye not tremble at my presence?' (Amos 3.6, 8).[15] Will ye not fear me, who can open the windows of heaven above, or break up the fountains of the great deep below,[16] and pour forth whole floods of vengeance when I please! Who can rain upon the wicked 'snares, fire and brimstone, and tempest' (Job 36.22, 24);[17] or kindle those steams and exhalations in the bowels and caverns of the earth, and make them force their way to the destruction of towns, cities, and countries! Who can thus suddenly turn a fruitful land into a barren wilderness;[18] an amazing spectacle of desolation and ruin!

'Shall a trumpet be blown in the city, and the people not be afraid? Shall there be evil in a city, and the Lord hath not done it?'[19] 'The lion hath roared; who will not fear?'[20] 'With God is terrible majesty; men do therefore fear him'.[21] Some *do*; and all *ought*. O that his fear might this moment fall upon all you who hear these words, constraining every one of you to cry out, 'My flesh trembleth for fear of thee, and I am afraid of thy judgments!' (Psalm 119. 120). O that all might see, now his hand is lifted up, as in act to strike, is stretched out still, and shakes his rod over a guilty land, a people fitted for destruction. For is not this the nation to be visited? 'And shall not I visit for these things, saith the Lord, and shall not my soul be avenged on such a nation as this!' (Jer. 5. 9). What but national repentance can prevent national destruction.

'O consider this, ye that forget God, lest he pluck you away, and there be none to deliver you!' (Psalm 100).[22] That iniquity may not be your ruin, repent! This is the second advice I would offer you; or, rather, the first enforced upon you farther, and explained. Fear God, and depart from evil; repent, and bring forth fruits meet for repentance;[23] break off your sins[24] this moment. 'Wash ye, make you clean, put away the evil of your doings from before mine eyes, saith the Lord, cease to do evil, learn to do well'.[25] (Isaiah 1. 16, 17).

---

[12] The reference is corrected to Mic. 6: 9 in later editions.
[13] The reference is corrected to Rev. 6: 5 in later editions.
[14] The reference is corrected to Ps. 66: 5 in later editions.
[15] The reference is corrected to Jer. 5: 22 in later editions.   [16] Cf. Gen. 7.11.
[17] The reference is corrected to Ps. 11: 6 in later editions and the words 'an horrible' added before 'tempest', as in the KJV.   [18] Cf. Psa 107: 34.
[19] Amos 3: 6.   [20] Amos 3: 8.   [21] Job 37: 22, 24.
[22] The reference is corrected to Ps. 50: 22 in later editions; it is the *BCP* version which is here quoted.   [23] Matt. 3: 8.
[24] Dan. 4: 27.   [25] The precise form of the quotation is altered slightly in later editions.

'Except ye repent, ye shall all likewise perish.' (Luke 13. 3) 'Therefore now, saith the Lord (who is not willing any should perish),[26] turn ye unto me with all your heart, and with fasting, and with weeping, and with mourning; and rend your hearts, and not your garments, and turn unto the Lord your God; for he is gracious and merciful, slow to anger, and of great kindness, and repenteth him of the evil. Who knoweth if he will return and repent, and leave a blessing behind him?' (Exod 23.5–6).[27]

Who knoweth? A question which should make you tremble. God is weighing you in the balance,[28] and, as it were, considering whether to save or to destroy. 'Say unto the children of Israel, Ye are a stiff-necked people: I will come up into the midst of thee, and consume thee; therefore now put off thy ornaments from thee, that I may know what to do unto thee.' Hos 11.8).[29]

God waits to see what effect his warnings will have upon you. He pauses on the point of executing judgment, and cries, 'How shall I give thee up?'(Isa 1.5)[30] Or, 'Why should ye be stricken any more.' (Ezek 18.31)[31] He hath no pleasure in the death of him that dieth.[32] He would not bring to pass his *strange act*,[33] unless your obstinate impenitence compel him.

'Why will you die, O house of Israel?.'[34] God warns you of the approaching judgment, that ye may take warning, and escape it by timely repentance. He lifts up his hand, and shakes it over you, that ye may see it, and prevent the stroke. He tells you, 'Now is the axe laid unto the root of the tree.'[35] Therefore repent; bring forth good fruit; and ye shall not be hewn down, and cast into the fire.[36] 'O do not despise the riches of his mercy, but let it lead you to repentance! Account that the longsuffering of the Lord is salvation' (2 Pet 3.15).[37] Harden not your hearts,[38] but turn to him that smites you; or, rather, threatens to smite, that ye may turn and be spared.

How slow is the Lord to anger![39] How unwilling to punish! By what leisurely steps does he come to take vengeance! How many lighter afflictions before the final blow!

Should he beckon the man on the red horse[40] to return, and say, Sword, go through this land[41] can we complain he gave us no warning? Did not the sword first bereave abroad?[42] And did we not then see it within our borders? Yet the merciful

---

[26] The words 'who is not willing any should perish' are not in the passage from Joel. Charles has added them on the basis of 2 Pet 3: 9; the parentheses are in the printed edition.

[27] The quotation is corrected to Joel 2: 12–14 in later editions.   [28] Cf. Dan. 5: 27.

[29] The reference is corrected to Exod 33: 5 in later editions.

[30] The reference is corrected to Hos. 11: 8 in later editions.

[31] The reference is corrected to Isa. 1: 5 in later editions.   [32] Cf. Ezek. 18: 32.

[33] Isa. 28: 21.   [34] Cf. Ezek. 18: 31 (noted in later editions).   [35] Cf. Matt 3: 10.

[36] Cf. John 15: 2.

[37] The words here placed in quotation marks are italicized in the text. However, only 'account that the longsuffering of the Lord is salvation' are from 2 Pet. 3: 15. The remainder of the quotation appears to be based on Rom. 2: 4.   [38] Ps. 95: 8.

[39] Cf. Neh. 9: 17, and others.   [40] Cf. Rev. 6: 4.   [41] Cf. Ezek. 14:17.

[42] Cf. Lam. 1: 20.

God said, Hitherto shalt thou come, and no further.[43] He stopped the invaders in the midst of our land, and turned them back again, and destroyed them.

Should he send the man on the pale horse whose name is Death,[44] and the pestilence destroy thousands and ten thousands of us; can we deny that first he warned us by the raging mortality among our cattle?

So, if we provoke him to lay waste our earth, and turn it upside down, and overthrow us, as he overthrew Sodom and Gomorrah; shall we not have procured this unto ourselves? Had we no reason to expect any such calamity; no previous notice; no trembling of the earth before it clave; no shock before it opened its mouth? Did he set no examples of so terrible a judgment before our eyes? Had we never heard of the destruction of Jamaica, or Catania, or that of Lima, which happened but yesterday? If we perish at last, we perish without excuse; for what could have been done more to save us?

Yes; thou hast now another call to repentance, another offer of mercy, whosoever thou art that hearest these words? In the name of the Lord Jesus, I warn thee once more, as a watchman over the house of Israel,[45] to flee from the wrath to come![46] I put thee in remembrance (if thou hast so soon forgotten it) of the late awful judgment, whereby God shook thee over the mouth of hell. Thy body he probably awoke by it, but did he awake thy soul? The Lord was in the earthquake, and put a solemn question to thy conscience: Art thou ready to die? Is thy peace made with God? Was the earth just now to open its mouth, and swallow thee up, what would become of thee? Where wouldst thou be? In Abraham's bosom, or lifting up thine eyes in torment?[47] Hadst thou perished by the late earthquake, wouldst thou not have died in thy sins, or rather gone down quick into hell?[48] Who prevented thy damnation? It was the Son of God! O fall down, and worship him! Give him the glory of thy deliverance; and devote the residue of thy days to his service.

This is the third advice I would give you: Repent *and* believe the gospel. Believe on the Lord Jesus, and ye shall yet be saved.[49] Kiss the Son, lest he be angry, and ye perish.[50] Repentance *alone* will profit you nothing; neither do ye repent, unless ye confess with broken hearts the most damnable of all your sins, your unbelief; your having rejected, or not accepted, Jesus Christ as your *only* Saviour. Neither *can* ye repent unless he himself gives the power; unless his Spirit convince you of sin, because ye believe not in him.

Till ye repent of your unbelief, all your good desires and promises are vain, and will pass away as a morning cloud.[51] The vows which ye make in a time of trouble, ye will forget and break as soon as the trouble is over and the danger past.

But shall ye escape for your wickedness, suppose the earthquake should not return? God will never want ways and means to punish impenitent sinners. He

---

[43] Job 38: 11.   [44] Cf. Rev. 6: 8.   [45] Cf. Ezek. 3: 17.
[46] Matt. 3: 7.   [47] Cf. Luke 16: 22, 23.   [48] Cf. Ps. 55: 15.
[49] Cf. Acts 16: 31.   [50] Ps. 2: 12.   [51] Cf. Hos. 6: 4.

hath a thousand other judgments in reserve; and if the earth should not open its mouth, yet ye shall surely at last be swallowed up in the bottomless pit of hell.

Wouldest thou yet escape that eternal death? Then receive the sentence of death in thyself, thou miserable self-destroyed sinner! Know thy want of living, saving, divine faith. Groan under thy burden of unbelief, and refuse to be comforted till thou hear him of his own mouth say, Be of good cheer, thy sins be forgiven thee.[52]

I cannot take it for granted, that all men have faith; or speak to the sinners of this land as to believers in Jesus Christ. For where are the fruits of faith? Faith worketh by love;[53] faith overcometh the world;[54] faith purifieth the heart;[55] faith, in the smallest measure, removeth mountains.[56] If thou canst believe, all things are possible to thee.[57] If thou art justified by faith, thou hast peace with God,[58] and rejoicest in hope of his glorious appearing.[59]

He that believeth hath the witness in himself;[60] hath the earnest of heaven in his heart;[61] hath love stronger than death.[62] Death to a believer has lost its sting;[63] 'therefore will he not fear, though the earth be removed, and though the mountains be carried into the midst of the sea' (Psalm 46. 2) For he knows in whom he has believed;[64] and that neither life nor death shall be able to separate him from the love of God, which is in Christ Jesus his Lord.[65]

Dost thou *so* believe? Prove thy own self by the infallible word of God. If thou hast not the fruits, effects, or inseparable properties of faith, thou hast not faith. Come, then, to the Author and Finisher of faith, confessing thy sins, and the root of all thy unbelief,[66] till he forgive thee thy sins, and cleanse thee from all unrighteousness. Come to the Friend of sinners, weary and heavy laden, and he will give thee pardon.[67] Cast thy poor desperate soul on his dying love. Enter into the rock—the ark—the city of refuge. Ask, and thou shalt receive faith and forgiveness together. He waited to be gracious. He hath spared thee for this very thing; that thine eyes might see his salvation.[68] Whatever judgments come in these latter days, yet whosoever shall call on the name of the Lord Jesus shall be delivered.[69]

Call upon him now, O sinner, and continue instant in prayer, till he answer thee in peace and power. Wrestle for the blessing.[70] Thy life, thy soul, is at stake. Cry mightily unto him,—Jesus, thou Son of David, have mercy upon me.[71] God be merciful unto me a sinner.[72] Lord, help me. Help my unbelief.[73] Save, or I perish.[74] Sprinkle my troubled heart. Wash me thoroughly in the fountain of thy blood; guide me by thy Spirit; sanctify me throughout, and receive me up into glory.

Now to God the Father, &c.

---

[52] Cf. Matt. 9: 2.   [53] Cf. Gal. 5: 6.   [54] Cf. 1 John 5: 4.
[55] Cf. Acts 15: 9.   [56] Cf. Matt. 17: 20; 21: 20; 1 Cor. 13: 2.   [57] Cf. Mark 9: 23.
[58] Cf. Rom. 5: 1.   [59] Cf. Titus 2: 13.   [60] 1 John 5: 10.
[61] Cf. Eph. 1: 14.   [62] Song of Songs 8: 6.   [63] 1 Cor. 15: 55.
[64] 2 Tim 1: 12.   [65] Rom. 8: 35.
[66] Charles may have intended this to be read as 'the root of all—thy unbelief'.   [67] Matt. 11: 28.
[68] Cf. Luke 2: 30.   [69] Cf. Rom. 10: 13.   [70] Cf. Gen 32: 22, 24.
[71] Mark 10: 47.   [72] Luke 18: 13.   [73] Mark 9: 24.   [74] Cf. Matt. 8: 25.

SERMON 10
JOHN 8: 1–11

INTRODUCTORY COMMENT

Charles preached his sermon on John 8: 1–11 at least three times. The first was on 20 February 1739 'at Mr Stonehouse's'. In the journal Charles wrote

> Waked full of concern for the poor harlot and began an hymn for her. At 5 call[ed] on Miss Crisp; then on Mr St[onehouse] where I expounded the woman taken in adultery.[1]

This date matches that given on the verso of leaf 1 of the later MS. It is not clear from the MS or the journal entry whether Charles used this MS on 20 February 1739 or, as was his practice, expounded the 'woman taken in adultery' extempore (which seems probable given the concern for the 'harlot' he had on that particular day) and then wrote up his thoughts some time after. Charles further records that he 'expounded' this passage on April 15, 1739[2] and 30 September 1739.[3] There are no further references to the preaching of this sermon in the journal. However, as was noted in Chapter 4, Charles 'transcribed' the sermon from MS A to MS B on 24 November 1758, which suggests that it was still in his repertoire even at that much later date.

The authenticity of this sermon is not in any doubt. Both MSS are clearly in Charles's hand and neither has any indication of his copying from any other source. The relationship between the two MSS has been discussed in detail in Chapter 4 and need not be entered into again here.[4]

Both MSS are now held at the John Rylands University Library of Manchester;[5] MS A is the better preserved of the two, though neither is in a state of disrepair. It comprises 16 leaves made up of 8 stitched folded sheets. The sermon is contained on leaves 2–14 written recto only. Leaf 1 forms the front cover, on the recto of which are written the words (in shorthand) 'transcribed November 24, 1758'. On the verso of leaf 1 the words 'Islington April 15. 1739' have been written in longhand. Leaves 15 and 16 are blank. MS B comprises 6 leaves (2 folded sheets and 2 separate leaves) which have been left loose. The leaves are written recto and verso and are numbered 1–12. These are, then, clear MSS which have

---

[1] MARC DDCW 10/2 *in loc.*; Telford, *Journal*, 223.

[2] 'At Islington [in the] vestry, the churchwardens demanded my licence. I wrote down my name; preached, with increase of power, on the woman taken in adultery. None went out. I gave the cup'; MARC DDCW 10/2 *in loc.*; Telford, *Journal*, 227–8.

[3] 'At the Hall I expounded the woman taken in adultery. Some, convicted by their own conscience, went out' (MARC DDCW 10/2 *in loc.*; Jackson, *Journal*, i. 183). The 'Hall' is Weavers Hall in Bristol. Charles preached here almost daily during September 1739 (see MARC DDCW 10/2 *in loc.*).

[4] The text printed here is that of MS A with differences between this and MS B pointed out in the notes. However, repeated minor differences such as the switch between 'you' to 'ye' and 'has' to 'hath' have not been indicated.   [5] MARC ref. CW Box 5.

been relatively well preserved. There is nothing obviously missing and little strike-through that cannot be recovered.

This sermon has been published twice before. The first publication was in the Albin-Beckerlegge edition of 1987.[6] That edition has been invaluable in preparing the form of the text printed here, though, as is made clear in the notes, it has been necessary to amend the Albin-Beckerlegge transcription and/or draw attention to ambiguity in a number of places. The second publication was in Tyson.[7] However, the numerous misprints evident in the latter make it unreliable, even as a reprint of the Albin-Beckerlegge text.

This is a sermon which exudes a soteriological confidence founded upon a deep distrust of any claim to inherent goodness in humanity. The concomitant free-flowing, all-sufficient grace of God made available through the blood of Christ is vigorously promoted. As Charles moves through the text he seeks to drive home his basic point: no one is righteous in the sight of God and the Pharisee is no better than the harlot. Indeed, the Pharisee (in either his historic or contemporary form) is in a worse state than the harlot, for the harlot at least knows her sin. (This is a theme worked out also in Sermon 12 on Luke 18: 9–14.) Both are dependent upon God's grace for salvation. Throughout Charles seeks to draw attention to the attitude of Jesus as represented in this passage to the accusers of the woman, and to encourage his audience to think of themselves in the light of the story. The typical evangelical plan is in place: tell people how wicked they are, offer them salvation in Christ and warn them of the consequences of not accepting the offer made.

In this sermon something of Charles's power as a preacher is clearly perceptible, albeit inevitably muted. There are some strong words here. One example will suffice.

> When I speak as the oracles of God, and tell you the truth as it is in Jesus, is it a small thing, think you, not to receive my testimony. Nay, but in not receiving it, in not embracing these offers of salvation by grace, you have trodden under foot the Son of God, and counted the blood of the covenant an unholy thing, and done despite unto the Spirit of grace. Ye stiff-necked and uncircumcised in heart and ears, ye do always resist the Holy Ghost. Though you are cut to the heart and gnash upon me with your teeth, yet must I warn you of this your wickedness, else you shall die in your iniquity, but your blood will God require at my hand. Wherefore in his name who hath set me a watchman unto the house of Israel, I warn you of the dreadful consequences of your having so denied the Lord that bought you; for which, unless you truly repent, you shall surely die in your iniquity, but I have delivered my own soul. Hear ye this and tremble, you who have turned your back upon a Saviour! For to you am I sent to cry aloud and spare not, to lift up my voice like a trumpet, and show you your transgressions and your sins. How shall you escape who have neglected so great salvation! Why, hitherto you have never thought about it. . . .

One can only wonder what effect such words must have had upon the audience. They are direct and sharp, perhaps even ill-mannered, and certainly potentially offensive. However, here we see Charles at his most lively. One glimpses in this extract, and more generally in the sermon as a whole, the extent to which he felt himself to be under a divine commission to preach the gospel as he saw it and to do so directly and without reference to the sensitivities of his 'stiff-necked' audience. Like Paul he is convinced of his own God-given right

---

[6] Albin and Beckerlegge, *Sermons*, 71–86.   [7] *Charles Wesley: A Reader*, 172–83.

and duty to preach Christ to the unconverted and to warn them of the consequences of their rejection of his message, and like Paul he seems to lack any concern for the potentially negative effect his words might have on his audience. Given the strength of these words and the apparent force with which they were delivered, the fact that 'None went out' when Charles preached the sermon in Islington is rather surprising. The less than fully favourable response he got from the audience in Bristol is perhaps more easily understood.

This then is a lively text and one that gives an insight into Charles's homiletic style, his theological persuasion, and his own understanding of his 'divine commission' to preach the gospel. As such it deserves careful attention.

John 8.1 etc.: Jesus went unto the Mount of Olives: and early in the morning he came again
into the Temple, and all the people came unto him: and he sat down and taught them. And
the Scribes and Pharisees brought unto him a woman taken in adultery; and when they had
set her in the midst, they say unto him, Master, this woman was taken in adultery, in the very
act. Now Moses in the law commanded us, that such should be stoned; but what sayest thou?
This they said, tempting him, that they might have to accuse him. But Jesus stooped down,
and with his finger wrote on the ground as though he heard them not. So when they contin-
ued asking him, he lift[ed][2] up himself and said unto them, he that is without sin among you,
let him first cast a stone at her. And again he stooped down and wrote on the ground. And
they which heard it, being convicted by their own conscience,[3] went out one by one, beginning
at the eldest, even unto the last. And Jesus was left alone, and the woman standing in the
midst. When Jesus had lift[ed][4] up himself, and saw none but the woman, he said unto her,
'Woman, where are those thine accusers? Hath no man condemned thee'? She said, 'No man,
Lord'. And Jesus said unto her, 'Neither do I condemn thee; go, and sin no more'.

([5]Jesus went unto the Mount of Olives, and early in the morning he came again
into the Temple). The life of Christ is[6] the life of Christians; who, if they are
Christians indeed, walk as he also walked,[7] spending their time in works of pity[8]
and[9] charity, on the Mount or with the multitude. From prayer they return with
their Lord to doing good,[10] from doing good they retire to prayer. Each fits for
other; retirement for action, and action for retirement.

(And early in the morning he came again into the Temple) leaving us an example that we should tread in his steps. A Christian therefore as such, is early at his
devotions; else he has nothing of Christ but the name.

(He came again into the Temple, and all the people came unto him.) It is into
the temple we must come, if we would find Christ. At the hours of prayer, it is here

---

[1] '*In Nomine Iesu*'; This is written in longhand.

[2] The KJV has 'lifted', which is clearly required in context and which may have been what Charles
intended and may have read. However, the shorthand in both MSS A and B is clearly 'lift' without
the normal 'ed' suffix.

[3] Albin and Beckerlegge (p. 71) have 'consciences' rather than 'conscience'. The KJV has the singular
form. The shorthand reads only 'cn' with a dot so positioned as to indicate that a major contraction has
taken place.   [4] See n. 2 above.

[5] Charles encloses words taken from his text in square brackets. Parentheses have been used here
and below to avoid confusion.   [6] MS B reads 'should be'.

[7] Cf. 1 John 2: 6.

[8] Albin and Beckerlegge (p. 4) suggest that MS B (their 'draft 1') reads 'piety' in place of 'pity' at
this point. This is possible, but unclear in the MSS: MS A (Albin and Beckerlegge's 'draft 2') has 'pti'
(which one might just read as 'purity'); MS B has 'pit'.

[9] MS B has 'or' in place of 'and' at this point.

[10] Before 'good' in MS B there appears the sign 'f/v' which has been struck out. This is probably a
simple mistake and represents the first stroke of the 'from' which follows.

alone[11] only we must look for him. Whosoever wholly[12] neglects to seek him here
shall find him nowhere else. Many indeed come to this place without meeting
him,[13] but no man can expect to meet him without coming to this place. Many miss
finding him here because they come Scribes and Pharisees; and they who[14] judge[15]
forbear[16] assembling themselves together are no followers of Christ; they are quite
out of his way; they cannot find, for they will not seek him.[17]

(All the people came unto him) All the publicans and sinners drew nigh unto
him to hear him, saith St. Luke (15.1), but have any of the rulers believed on
him?[18] No! They were too wise and too holy. But this people which is accursed,[19]
and harlots and publicans,[20] run after him, the poor have the gospel preached to
them.[21] (He sat down and taught them) for they only had ears to hear.[22] They were
not whole, but such as had need of a physician.[23] They were not righteous but sinners,[24] and utterly lost without him. Therefore they were the very persons he came
to call to repentance;[25] they were the very persons he came to seek and to save,[26]
and accordingly these outcasts of men were almost his only followers.

(He taught them) For they knew themselves ignorant: he healed them, for they
felt themselves sick: he pardoned them, for they confessed themselves sinners; he
saved them, for they owned they deserved to be damned.

(The Scribes and Pharisees brought unto him a woman taken in adultery) What
a triumph is here for the Scribes and Pharisees! A woman taken in adultery! What
a glorious occasion of setting forth their own virtues; their spotless chastity, their
zeal for justice, their abhorrence of sinners! On this only[27] occasion they can touch
sinners without being defiled, when they are dragging them to execution; and they
are never so happy as in this employment; they never shone[28] so bright as by this
comparison!

(They brought unto him) The friend of publicans and sinners![29] As they truly
called him, though he was so in a sense more glorious than their malice meant it.
Seeking to gratify their revenge no less than their pride, (they brought unto him a

---

[11] This struck-out word is omitted by Albin and Beckerlegge. It is clear enough in MS A.
[12] Albin and Beckerlegge mark this word as uncertain. Both MSS A and B read simply 'w' with a dot
so placed as to indicate an adverb.   [13] 'Him' has been inserted above the line in MS A.
[14] The stroke here is unclear. It is probably 'wo', but it is possible that it is the combined sign for
'ww', perhaps 'who would'.
[15] The word 'judge' is very unclear in the MS. The struck-out sign is probably a 'j', though this is not
certain. Albin and Beckerlegge suggest 'would' (presumably taking the struck-out sign as a 'w'), which
seems incorrect.   [16] In place of 'and they who judge forbear', MS B reads 'but they who forbear'.
[17] Cf. Matt. 7: 7 and parallel.   [18] Cf. John 7: 48.   [19] Cf. John 7: 49.
[20] Cf. Matt. 21: 31–2.   [21] Cf. Matt. 11: 5 and parallel.   [22] Cf. Matt. 11: 15.
[23] Cf. Mark 2: 17 and parallels.   [24] Cf. ibid.   [25] Cf. Mark 2: 17.
[26] Cf. Luke 19: 10.
[27] Albin and Beckerlegge mark this word as uncertain. MS A reads 'nli'; in MS B, on the other hand,
the sign 'nli' also has a dot so positioned as to suggest 'unli', which Albin and Beckerlegge take to mean
'unholy'. This is possible, but unlikely given the absence of either the 'h' or the 'o'. Probably the dot
taken by Albin and Beckerlegge as representing 'u' is slightly too far to the right and an 'o' is in fact
meant (the difference between the position of the dot for 'o' and that for 'u' is very slight).
[28] MS B reads 'shine'.   [29] Cf. Matt. 11: 19 and parallel.

woman taken in adultery). And why the woman rather, since the man's offence was equal if not greater? Perhaps they hoped for more likely matter to accuse Christ in the case of the woman than of the man, as supposing his merciful disposition might more probably incline him to compassionate[30] her wickedness, and so illegally[31] to acquit her.

(And when they had set her in the midst) Shame must make way for punishment. She had escaped too cheaply had they[32] suffered her to die without first insulting and triumphing over her. Therefore they drag her out to light, and place her in the face of the congregation. See then this miserable adulteress! How she stands confounded in the midst of that gazing and disdainful multitude! How she hides her head, and with trembling silence expects and anticipates the dreadful sentence. Not so the Scribes and Pharisees. They stand forth to accuse her. With boldness and confidence (they say unto him, Master, this woman was taken in adultery, in the very act). How plausibly do they begin! With what reverence do they accost him! With what veneration to[33] his person, and deference to his judgment! What holy, honest and conscientious men are these! Such strict lovers of justice! Such devout followers of Christ! So we should be[34] apt to think of them; but he who made and knows their hearts tells us all this is but done to tempt him. Whence we may justly infer that the highest outward profession of righteousness, the greatest seeming esteem of it, is perfectly consistent with all filthiness of spirit, and may proceed from the corrupt heart of a wholly false, hypocrite Pharisee.[35]

But what say these holy executioners? (Master this woman was taken in adultery, in the very act). This is made an aggravation of her guilt. 'She was taken!' And with a Pharisee this is all in all. It is not the guilt, but its discovery, makes the sinner. ~~Sin concealed is with them~~[36] ~~no sin at all~~[37] ~~with them at all~~[38] It is not the sin, but the scandal they are afraid of. Sin concealed is with them no sin at all; but when detected it is most abominable. If they can but preserve their reputation, all is well. If they can but hide their vices from men they think themselves as good as innocent; while only God and their own conscience knows it, they are safe enough. But alas, what shall it avail them to lurk awhile under the mask of innocence! When

---

[30] This reading is rather strange, but alternatives not easy to construct. The shorthand reads 'cmpssht'.

[31] Albin and Beckerlegge mark this word as uncertain. In both MSS A and B the sign gives 'ilegli', which seems clear enough.   [32] MS B reads 'if they had' in place of 'had they'.

[33] MS B reads 'of' in place of 'to'.   [34] MS B reads 'have been' in place of 'be'.

[35] In MS A it would appear that Charles wrote 'the corrupt heart of a wholly false hypocrite' and that he then added 'Pharisee' in the right hand margin of the text. Albin and Beckerlegge (p. 73) suggest 'hypocritical Pharisee'. In MS A there is no indication in the sign itself that 'hpoc' is meant to be taken as an adjective. However, in MS B the 'c' has been written in such a way as to suggest that the suffix 'ical' is intended.   [36] The sign for 'with them' has been inserted above the line.

[37] The sign for 'at all' has been inserted above the line.

[38] Albin and Beckerlegge indicate that this struck-out sentence is unclear. However, from the insertions and deletions, it would appear that Charles originally wrote 'sin concealed is no sin with them at all' which he changed to 'sin concealed is with them no sin at all'. Charles then struck out the sentence, only to repeat it on the line below.

the secrets of all hearts shall so soon be[39] revealed and God shall bring to light the hidden things of darkness.[40] In that day they shall find their conscience more than a thousand witnesses, and God more than a thousand consciences.

Till then they may happily pass for saints, and hide their sin under a seeming abhorrence of sin, and drown their own guilt in a clamorous cry for justice upon others. So their holy predecessors in the history before us. They accuse and loudly call for ~~justice~~ punishment against a notorious offender. (Now Moses in the law, commanded us that such should be stoned, but what sayest thou?) What a suspicious, subtle, ensnaring question! Here, they think, he cannot escape, but which way soever he answers, must give them the occasion they sought for. (For this they said tempting him, that they might have to accuse him.) Like their father the devil,[41] the tempter, the accuser! And who therefore tempts that he may accuse; like his genuine[42] children of this generation,[43] who come after the preacher, laying wait for him, and seeking to catch something out of his mouth that they may accuse him.[44] Poor miserable men, ye know not who employs you, ye consider not who sends you, or that you are the apostles of Satan. He inspires your thoughts, he speaks your words, he sets you to work, and he will pay you your wages. ~~But to return~~

(Now Moses in the law commanded us that such should be stoned, but what sayest thou?) They know Christ's inclination to mercy and compassion. Their self-righteous souls had been often grieved at seeing him eat with known sinners.[45] They had murmured at his receiving them, his dismissing one, justifying another, inviting and speaking kindly to all. Hence they hoped his pity might draw him to acquit her, whom the law condemned; and they would not have desired a better advantage than that he should[46] contradict their received lawgiver. 'We are Moses' disciples; we know God spoke to Moses',[47] and had our Lord spoken otherwise, they would have had to accuse him. It is still the aim of those that are enemies to the truth to set Christ and Moses at variance; particularly as to the use of the law. 'You make void the law through faith,'[48] say they, 'that is, through your doctrine of justification by faith only.' ~~But~~ We answer with St. Paul, 'Yea, we establish the law'.[49] Christ and Moses are two inseparable friends: each speaks for each. One confirms the other. They are subordinate[50] not opposite. Moses as the servant,

---

[39] MS B reads 'shall be soon' in place of 'shall so soon be'.   [40] Cf. 1 Cor. 4: 5.

[41] Cf. John 8.44.

[42] The shorthand stroke here in both MSS A and B gives 'gnn'; MS B has a point indicating an 'e' between the 'g' and 'n'. 'genuine' seems probable, though, as Albin and Beckelegge note, this is somewhat uncertain.   [43] Cf. Luke 16: 8. This text is the subject of Sermon 17.

[44] Luke 11: 54.   [45] Cf. Mark 2: 16; Luke 5: 30.   [46] MS B reads 'might' for 'should'.

[47] Cf. John 9: 28–9.   [48] Cf. Rom 3: 31.

[49] The words 'We answer with St. Paul, "Yea, we establish the law"' have been inserted above the line. The words are from Rom. 3: 31.

[50] The shorthand stroke in MS A has the prefix 'sub' followed by 'or' ('subor'); in MS B the stroke is fuller. Here the shorthand gives 'subordnt'. The word therefore looks reasonably certain, though Albin and Beckerlegge retain some doubts.

Christ the Son:[51] Moses as the schoolmaster;[52] Christ to supply Moses.[53] 'By him all that believe[54] are justified from all things from which they could not be justified by the law'.[55] ~~If~~ Moses brings us to Christ;[56] Christ brings us to glory. Faith does not ~~overthrow~~ destroy good works, unless the cause ~~overthrows~~ destroys the effect. Faith alone is unto[57] justification, works to[58] evidence our justification as consequents not conditions, as fruits not causes.

As vainly therefore do our Pharisees labour to make Christ contradict Moses, as ~~work~~ their predecessors of old whom we are now considering. These reasoned thus: 'Either he must clear the guilty, or condemn her. If he acquits her, where is his justice; if he condemns her, where is his mercy'? Let them extort a legal sentence, and they thereby blast the honour of his clemency.[59] Let him consent to the law, and he loses his reputation with the people, and his enemies will immediately cry, 'See here your friend of sinners! who condemns them without mercy; who inflicts the cruellest punishment; who stones them that are brought unto him!' Howsoever he answers, they gain their point;[60] he cannot escape; but they will[61] have to accuse him either of injustice or unmercifulness.

Such is the cunning folly of vain men that would hope to beguile wisdom[62] itself!

(But Jesus stooped down, and with his finger wrote on the ground as though he heard them not). Silence and neglect is their first answer; and in many cases we shall find it the best.

(As though he heard them not), his ear is not heavy that it cannot hear our calls for mercy:[63] his ear is ever open to the sinner's cry, but when devils and Pharisees cry out for justice, he becomes as a deaf man and one that heareth not. How often have our sins demanded justice against us, and he would not hear? So rich is he in goodness and forbearance and longsuffering, so slow to anger[64] and averse from punishing! which he therefore calls his strange work[65] and comes to it, as it were, with the utmost reluctance. Nay, he pauses in the very act of punishing; ~~he lays by the lifted belt~~[66] his justice lingers and relents and yields: he drops the lifted belt[67] and says[68] 'How shall I give thee up, Oh Ephraim!'[69]

---

[51] MS B reads 'Christ as the Son'.

[52] Charles may have in mind the word 'παιδαγωγὸς' from Gal. 3: 24 here, a word that can mean 'schoolmaster' (as it is translated in the KJV).   [53] Charles may have Gal. 3: 24 in mind here.

[54] MS B omits the words 'that believe' at this point.   [55] Cf. Acts 13: 39.

[56] Charles may again have Gal. 3: 24 in mind here.

[57] MS A has 'nto' at this point, which is Charles's normal shorthand for 'into' or 'unto'. MS B, however, has 'nssri to', that is, 'necessary to'.

[58] In MS A Charles wrote 'ot' for 'to', this is corrected in MS B.

[59] Albin and Beckerlegge mark this word as uncertain. The shorthand reads 'clmnsi' in MS A and in MS B a dot indicating 'e' is placed after the 'l'. 'Clemency' therefore seems highly probable.

[60] The words 'they gain their point' have been inserted above the line.

[61] MS B reads 'must' for 'will'.   [62] There is a possible echo of Matt. 11: 19 here.

[63] Cf. Isa. 59: 1.   [64] Cf. Ps. 103: 8.   [65] Cf. Isa. 28: 21.

[66] Albin and Beckerlegge have 'bolt' in place of 'belt' at this point. 'Belt' seems more appropriate in context (an act of punishment). The struck out words are omitted from MS B.

[67] Albin and Beckerlegge suggest 'bolt'.   [68] MS A reads 'cries' in place of 'says'.

[69] Cf. Hos. 11: 8.

The more unwilling he seems to give an[70] answer, the more eager are they[71] to extort one from him. And in this case we are to follow our Lord's example, when our Pharisees insist and urge us to answer, we must at last[72] reply plainly and fully. We are even[73] under a necessity of uncasing[74] them, of tearing off the mask and exposing them to the people.[75] (So when they continued asking him, he lift[ed][76] up himself and said unto them, he that is without sin, let him first cast a stone at her). He lifted up himself, as if his action had said, I was willing to let you escape, I was loth to shame you, but since you will needs have it, and by your vehemence force my justice, I must tell you there is no one of you, but is as faulty as she whom ye accuse. There is no difference; only your sin is secret, and hers notorious.[77] You have more need to make your own peace with God by a humble repentance, than to urge severity against her. Death is justly due to such horrid offences, but what then would become of you? She deserves to die; but not by your unclean hands. Your hearts know you are not honest enough to accuse.

(He that is without sin among you, let him first cast a stone at her.) How wise an answer; how worthy of him that spoke it! Here both his justice and his mercy are preserved. He takes neither part of our[78] dilemma, not condemning either Moses or the sinner. In this punishment the witnesses were first to lay their hands upon the guilty; well therefore doth our Lord check these accusers with the conscience of their so foul incompetency. He takes off these bloody hands by turning their eyes upon themselves. Innocence is justly required in the accuser. She is worthy to be stoned, but by whom? Who shall first cast the stones at her? Not Scribes and Pharisees. Ill would it become hands as guilty as her own. With what face, with what heart could they stone their own[79] sin in another person!

These Scribes and Pharisees, we know, were noted for holiness. They went beyond even our good sort of people, and in all outward appearance were most exemplary[80] saints; but God's ~~justice is not as man's justice his~~[81] thoughts are not as our thoughts.[82] These are they that justify themselves before men, but God knoweth their hearts, ~~and searcheth them out to~~[83] for that which is highly esteemed among men is abominable with him. He searcheth them out to perfection. In vain do they hope to escape that all-seeing eye which can find folly in the angels.[84] The heavens[85] are not clean in his sight; how much less they that dwell in houses of

---

[70] 'Give an' has been inserted above the line in MS A (it is integrated into the text in MS B).

[71] MS B reads 'they are'.   [72] One might read 'least' for 'last'.

[73] 'Even' has been inserted above the line in MS A (it is integrated into the text in MS B).

[74] Albin and Beckerlegge mark this word as uncertain. However, in MS A the shorthand reads 'uncsing' and in MS B 'uncasing'. The word seems appropriate in context.

[75] MS B begins a new paragraph after this full stop.   [76] See above n. 2.

[77] MS B reads 'hers is notorious'.   [78] MS B reads 'the' for 'our'.

[79] MS B omits 'their own'.

[80] In MS A the shorthand reads only 'xr'; however, 'exemplary' is confirmed by the reading in MS B, which gives 'xmplri'.   [81] The struck-out words are absent from MS B.

[82] Cf. Isa. 55: 8–9.   [83] The struck-out words are absent from MS B.   [84] Cf. Job 4: 18

[85] Albin and Beckerlegge suggest that one might read 'heavenly spirits' for 'heavens' at this point. On the basis of the shorthand alone the suggestion seems a fair one since both MSS A and B read only

clay,[86] how least of all the self-justifying Pharisees! Such as be unrighteous shall not stand in his sight;[87] and now they find it. Now indeed his eyes are as a flame of fire;[88] and out of his mouth goeth a sharp two edged sword,[89] and his countenance is as the sun shineth[90] in his strength. No wonder therefore that Pharisees cannot behold him, but are thunderstruck, astonished, confounded! The accusers are cast down, the high looks are fallen; Pharisees themselves are silent, and no longer outrageous against notorious sinners.

Perhaps these secret sins, with which our Lord now stops their clamorous mouths, had been long since forgot. They thought no more of them, and said, 'Hath not God forgotten'?[91] But all these things are noted in his book, and are now brought to[92] remembrance by their Judge. 'These things hast thou done, and I held my peace, and thou thoughtest wickedly that I am even such a one as thyself. But I will reprove thee, and set before thee the things which thou hast done.'[93] So will God speak to every lurking sinner, and[94] but if we would that he should not remember our sins, we should never forget them ourselves. Let them be ever before us[95] that he may not set them in the light of his countenance:[96] and for the time to come, let us see ourselves as[97] seen by him, and we shall not dare to offend.

(And again he stooped down and wrote on the ground), to give them an opportunity of escaping unobserved. He seems[98] to disregard them, but we all know how his medicine worked. Accordingly, we do not see them stand out in their innocence. No! Their hearts misgive them, and they feared if they had stood out,[99] he would have utterly shamed them, by displaying all their old sins, and turning their pretended saintliness inside out. This was a discovery they were not fond of, especially before the people, who began to find them out, and to beware of Scribes and Pharisees, hypocrites.[100] They see the rod held over them, ~~had just now~~ they felt the smart, and willingly spared our Lord any further explanation; going out ~~by d~~[101] one by one, that they might not seem driven away.

'hs' with a dot so positioned beneath the stroke for 'h' as to suggest that an entire word is indicated. However, Charles is here quoting from Job 15: 15, which reads, 'Behold he putteth no trust in his saints; yea, the heavens are not clean in his sight.'

[86] Cf. Job 4: 19.   [87] Charles may have in mind Ps. 5: 5 at this point.

[88] Cf. Rev. 1: 14; 2: 18; 19: 12.   [89] Cf. Rev. 1: 16.

[90] MS B reads 'shining' in place of 'shineth'; cf. Rev. 1: 16.   [91] Cf. Ps. 10: 11.

[92] MS B reads 'out to'.   [93] Cf. Ps. 50: 21.

[94] The word 'and' in MS A comes at the end of a very short line, which is left incomplete. The next line, which is not indented and hence does not begin a new paragraph, begins with 'but'. MS B does not have the word 'and' at this point.   [95] Cf. Ps. 51: 3.

[96] Cf. Ps. 90: 8.

[97] The word 'as' is not present in MS A, though it is required by context (and added by Albin and Beckerlegge). Albin and Beckerlegge also note that 'as seen by him' is found in MS B ('draft 1'), though this is incorrect; 'as' is missing also in MS B.   [98] MS B reads 'seemed'.

[99] MS A reads 'stood it out'.   [100] Cf. Matt. 23: 13 ff.

[101] The struck-out 'd' is clear in the MS and there is a dot so positioned below the stroke as to suggest that a significant contraction is indicated. However, it is unclear what the intended word was. The struck-out words are not present in MS B.

(And[102] they which heard it, being convicted by their own conscience, went out one by one, beginning at the eldest, even unto the last.) Oh irresistible truth! Oh wonderful power of conscience! Man can no more stand out against that, than that can against God. When the Almighty, whose substance[103] it is, sets it on[104] work, it has, as it were, the force of omnipotence. When that says, we are guilty, there is no denying. In vain does the world acquit us while our hearts are consumed by the worm that never dies.[105] No wicked man need seek out of himself a judge, accuser, witness, tormentor.

(And they which heard it, being convicted by their own conscience,[106] went out). How boldly did these hypocrites set upon Christ! With what insolent triumph, what diabolical subtlety, what foulness of self-righteousness! Now[107] are they thunderstruck, and drop away confounded. No sooner do they hear of their own sins from the mouth of Christ, but they are gone. He had given them a convincing proof that he was God, and as such had power to forgive sins upon earth.[108] They ought therefore to have humbly confessed their sins unto him, and earnestly prayed ~~that~~ him to forgive them their sins, and to cleanse them of all unrighteousness.[109] But you will not easily bring a Pharisee to that, to own himself a sinner that deserved[110] to be damned. No, instead of that, he turns his back upon his Saviour and hastes away.

A Pharisee cares not how little he hears, either of the power of God, or[111] the multitude of his sins. When he does hear a searching truth, which he cannot deny and will not[112] receive, he has nothing else for it but to flee as fast as he can. This, as it is a certain token of guilt, so is it an infallible mark of a Pharisee, your turning your back upon the ambassadors of Christ[113] and by despising them, despising him that sent them:[114] your going out of Church, as your predecessors out of the Temple, and thereby counting and proclaiming yourselves unworthy of eternal life. By this speechless action you cry out, like Paul in the council, 'I am a Pharisee, and the son of a Pharisee'.[115] You make the application of what is spoken to yourselves, as plainly as if you answered with an audible voice, 'I am the man![116] My conscience is my accuser! I cannot cast the first stone. I myself am a[117] secret

---

[102] MS B has a note in the margin at this point which reads, in Charles's longhand, 'omit this and the next page'. The intended omission (which is actually of the following MS page and nearly two-thirds of the one after) is further noted by Charles by means of a vertical dotted line in the left hand margin which extends to the words 'And Jesus was left alone' below.

[103] Albin and Beckerlegge mark this word as uncertain. In MS A the shorthand reads 'sst', where the initial 's' is so formed as to indicate the prefix 'sub'. The form of the 'st' suggests that the 't' could be read as 'th', but what the resulting 'substh' might indicate is unclear.

[104] 'In' would appear to be more suitable here. However, in both MSS (in MS B more obviously) the dot is quite clearly in the 'o' rather than the 'i' position.   [105] Cf. Isa. 66: 24; Mark 9: 44, 46, 48.

[106] Albin and Beckerlegge (p. 79) suggests 'consciences'.

[107] Albin and Beckerlegge begin a new paragraph at this point. There is no such division in the MSS.

[108] Cf. Mark 2: 10 and parallels.   [109] Cf. 1 John 1: 9.

[110] MS B reads 'deserves' in place of 'deserved'.   [111] MS B reads 'or of'.

[112] MS B reads 'and which he will not'.   [113] Cf. 2 Cor. 5: 20.   [114] Cf. Luke 10: 16.

[115] Cf. Acts 23: 6.   [116] Cf. 2 Sam. 12: 7.   [117] MS B reads 'I am myself'.

adulterer, an hypocritical fornicator; and come not to the light because I love darkness, and cannot bear the light because my deeds are evil.'[118]

My brethren, I wait to see which of you goes out now. If your conscience will
not let you stay, I would even favour your escape, and not see you—[119]was it not,
that by seeing you I might recommend you to the prayers of the congregation.
Indeed you need them ~~whosoever among you has~~[120] as many among[121] you as have
ever dared to go out of Church, for you are in the very gall of bitterness,[122] in the
bond of iniquity; and now you know you cannot fly from conviction, I think it my
duty to tell you so.

You that go out of Church, and yet call yourselves Christians, to you I speak,
and set before you the things which you have done. You are they that cannot
endure sound doctrine.[123] Well do you Pharisees reject the counsel of God against
yourselves, even his counsel to save lost sinners, to justify them freely when they
own they deserve to be damned. But you spurn away from[124] you so cheap[125] salvation; you will not accept of ~~Jesus~~[126] Christ upon his own so easy terms; you will
not have this man reign over you. When I speak as the oracles of God,[127] and tell
you the truth as it is in Jesus, is it a small thing, think you, not to receive my testimony. Nay, but in not receiving it, in not embracing these offers of salvation by
grace, you have trodden under foot the Son of God, and counted the blood of the
covenant an unholy thing, and done despite unto the Spirit of grace.[128] Ye stiff-
necked and uncircumcised in heart and ears, ye do always resist the Holy Ghost.[129]
Though you are cut to the heart and gnash upon me with your teeth,[130] yet must I
warn you of this your wickedness, else you shall die in your iniquity, but your
blood will God require at my hand.[131] Wherefore in his name who hath set me a
watchman unto[132] the house of Israel,[133] I warn you of the dreadful consequences
of your[134] having so denied the Lord that bought you;[135] for which, unless you truly
repent, you shall surely die in your iniquity, but I have delivered my own soul.[136]
Hear ye this and tremble, you who have turned your back upon a Saviour! For to
you am I sent to cry aloud and spare not, to lift up my voice like a trumpet, and

[118] Cf. John 3: 19.   [119] A horizontal line is present in both MSS A and B at this point.

[120] The struck-out words are not present in MS B.   [121] MS A reads 'of' in place of 'among'.

[122] In MS A 'Gall of bitterness' is 'gb' only in the shorthand. However, the reading is confirmed by
MS B which reads 'gal f bitrness' (cf. Acts 8: 23).   [123] Cf. 2 Tim. 4: 3.

[124] The word 'from' has been inserted above the line in MS A.

[125] There is a possible echo here of Heb. 2: 3; the sign here transcribed as 'cheap' is clear in both MSS
as 'chp'.

[126] In MS A the word 'Jesus' has been inserted above the line and then struck out. The word does
not appear at all in MS B.   [127] Cf. 1 Pet. 4: 11.

[128] Cf. Heb. 10: 29.   [129] Cf. Acts 7: 51.   [130] Cf. Acts 7: 54.

[131] MS B reads 'hands' in place of 'hand'; cf. Ezek. 3: 18.

[132] MS B reads 'as the watchman over'.   [133] Cf. Ezek. 3: 17; 33: 7.   [134] MS B omits 'your'.

[135] In the left hand margin of the line which begins in the MS with the words 'you; for which' there
appears a vertical dotted line similar to the one employed in MS B to note the deletion of a section.
The line extends to the end of this paragraph.   [136] Cf. Ezek. 3: 19.

show you your transgressions and your sins.[137] How shall you escape who have neglected so great salvation![138] Why, hitherto you have never thought about it . . .[139]

If I am come amongst you preaching the gospel; if it be the gospel[140] and you have rejected it, and I shake off the dust of my feet again, 'Verily, verily,' Christ saith unto you, 'it shall be more tolerable for Sodom and Gomorrah[141] in the day of judgment than for you.'[142]

Unhappy foolish men![143] What doth it profit you to flee from him? If you could run away from God it were something; but while ye move[144] in him what do ye? Where go ye? You may run from his mercy; you cannot from his justice. Nay, you must run upon his justice by fleeing from his mercy.

Repent therefore of this your wickedness, and pray God if perhaps it may be forgiven you.[145] Humble yourselves under the mighty hand of God;[146] bow your stiff necks, ye rebellious worms; ye potentates of the earth,[147]and [148] strive no longer with your maker.[149] Justify God in his saying; clear him whom ye have[150] judged, and confess you do deserve to be damned. Till you do confess it, you ~~still continue~~ are in a state of damnation still, as surely as God is true. And the man that dares tell you otherwise to say,[151] peace, peace, where there is no peace,[152] he shall bear his burden, whosoever he be. I myself shall rise up in judgment against that man: and I put all my[153] hopes of finding mercy in that day upon the truth ~~of what I know~~[154] of this report that whosoever does not ~~confess~~ from his heart believe[155] he deserves to be damned, is in a state of damnation at this very hour![156]

---

[137] Cf. Isa. 58: 1.   [138] Cf. Heb. 2: 3.

[139] As Albin and Beckerlegge note, several blank lines exist here in MS A ('draft 2' in Albin and Beckerlegge's scheme). They suggest that MS B ('draft 1') 'makes it clear that it is to be a significant rhetorical pause'. However, the reasons for suggesting this clarity in MS B are in themselves obscure; MS B has a series of dots at this point.   [140] MS B reads 'true gospel'.

[141] Before 'Gomorrah' there appears in MS B the sign for 'g'. This appears to be a mistaken start of the word 'Gomorrah' (the form it has been given is one to which it would have been impossible neatly to join the required sign for 'm') which Charles abandoned.   [142] Cf. Mark 6: 11 and parallels.

[143] 'Men' could be read as 'man'. There is no sign for the vowel in the shorthand.

[144] Albin and Beckerlegge mark this word as uncertain. The shorthand reads 'mf/v' with a dot so positioned between the consonants as to indicate either a 'u' (which seems more probable) or an 'o'.

[145] Cf. Acts 8: 22.   [146] Cf. 1 Pet. 5: 6.

[147] The words 'ye potentates of the earth' have been inserted above the line (but are inserted into the flow of the text in MS B).

[148] The word 'and' is somewhat unclear in the text. Albin and Beckerlegge omit it. However, the struck-out sign is visible.   [149] Cf. Isa. 45: 9.

[150] MS B reads 'when ye are' in place of 'have'.   [151] MS B reads 'and says'.

[152] Cf. Ezek. 13: 16.

[153] The word 'all' has been inserted above the line. The resultant reading 'my all hopes' is plainly an error. Albin and Beckerlegge note that Charles may have intended 'all my hopes' or 'all hopes'. The situation is clarified by MS B which reads 'all my hopes'.

[154] MS B reads 'of this assertion, which I once more repeat'.

[155] The words 'from his heart believe' have been inserted below the line (this is the last line on MS page 8) to replace the struck-out 'confess'. MS B reads 'confess'.

[156] The words 'at this very hour' mark the end of the section identified for omission by the dotted vertical line in the margin of MS B.

Return we now to the history[157] (And Jesus was left alone, and the woman standing in the midst). Jesus was left ~~alone~~ by the Scribes and Pharisees, but the people
and the mournful adulteress remained.[158] She still[159] stands in the midst being fastened down by her own[160] guilt, not daring to lift up her eyes, or to encourage the
faintly dawning hope of mercy. Oh how well was this sinner to be left there! Could
she be in a safer place than before the tribunal of a Saviour! Might she have
chosen her refuge, where should she have rather fled? Happy, happy are we, if
when convinced of sin we can set ourselves before ~~our~~ that judge, who is our
surety,[161] our advocate,[162] our redeemer,[163] our ransom,[164] our peace![165]

Some hope she doubtless had from her accusers being gone; but a much
stronger fear of the punishment she deserved. Divided she is, but not equally
between hope and fear, and now while she trembles in expectation of a sentence,
she hears, (Woman, where are those thine accusers?). We do not hear him railing
on her, or reviling her; he doth not say, Thou vile creature, thou execrable adulteress, thou shameless strumpet, but (Woman, where are those thine accusers?).[166]
Those who but now so importunately demanded justice against thee, who hauled
thee so triumphantly to execution? Has the Ethiopian changed his skin,[167] or the
Pharisee forgot his implacable hatred against[168] open sinners? Whence is it that
their cries for blood are suspended and they suffer the prey to be taken out of their
teeth?[169] What unnatural compassion is this which makes them drop their charge
and leave a gross sinner[170] any hope of mercy? Is it out of pity that they leave thee
unpunished? Or is it not[171] rather guilt which has driven them away, and withheld
their foul hands from inflicting a punishment they themselves deserve?[172]

(Hath no man condemned thee?) or cast the first stone at thee? Is there
then none among them[173] without sin? Is there none righteous, no not

---

[157] The words 'Return we now to the history' are absent from MS B (a point not noted by Albin and
Beckerlegge).

[158] Before 'remained' there appears another word in the text that has been so heavily struck out as to
make it largely unreadable. The word may be 'still' (see the insertion two words further on in this sentence),
but only the 's' is clear. There is no corresponding word in MS A. 'Remained' is 'remain' in MS B.

[159] The word 'still' has been inserted above the line.   [160] MS B does not have the word 'own'.

[161] Cf. Heb. 7: 22.   [162] Cf. 1 John 2: 1.   [163] Cf. inter alia Job 19: 25.

[164] Cf. Mark 10: 45 and parallel; 1 Tim. 2: 6.   [165] Cf. Eph. 2: 14.

[166] The words 'We do not hear him railing on her, or reviling her; he doth not say, Thou vile creature,
thou execrable adulteress, thou shameless strumpet, but (Woman, where are those thine accusers?)' are
absent from MS B. This would appear to be a clear case of homeoteleuton and strong evidence for the
primacy of MS A.   [167] Cf. Jer. 13: 23.

[168] 'Against' is replaced by 'of' in MS B. This change is not noted by Albin and Beckerlegge.

[169] Cf. Ps. 124: 6.

[170] 'Gross sinner' is clear in both MSS A and B (the shorthand in MS A is 'gros snr' and in MS B
'grs sinr'). Consequently Albin and Beckerlegge's suggestion that MS B (their 'draft 1') reads 'grave
sinner' at this point seems incorrect.

[171] The word 'not' is omitted from MS B. This omission is not noted by Albin and Beckerlegge.

[172] MS A reads 'deserve themselves' in place of 'themselves deserve'.

[173] Albin and Beckerlegge enclose 'them' in square brackets, suggesting that they have taken the
shorthand here transcribed as 'among them' as indicating only 'among'. This is possible, since the
stroke for the second 'm' might just be a 'g' (the two are distinguished only by the presence or absence

one,[174] even among the self-justifying Scribes and Pharisees? He seems, as it were, to triumph over these self-righteous ones, whom their flight convinces of sin far more abominable than hers.

(She said, No man, Lord). And what, though every man had condemned, if God acquitted her? (And Jesus said unto her, Neither do I condemn thee, go, and sin no more). A gracious ~~sound~~ word! A comfortable sound in the ears of a despairing sinner! (Neither do I condemn thee). I judge no man. For God sent not his Son into the world to condemn the world, but that the world through him should be saved.[175] 'As I live, saith the Lord, I have no pleasure in the death of'[176] the wicked.'[177] Man's miserable justice oft-times has;[178] but God is love,[179] and mercy rejoices[180] against judgment.[181]

It is thus in the case before us. The Pharisees thought he could not save so great a sinner; he therefore shows them he can. But these things were written for our instruction; for our sakes principally[182] he lets her go free, to convince us our sins cannot be too great for his mercy, and to show us the temper which fits us for pardon.[183]

When a notorious sinner is hauled to justice, and by men not even suffered to live, let him by the Holy Ghost call Jesus Lord,[184] and he shall know that the arm of the Lord is not shortened,[185] but that Christ is able to save to the uttermost all

of a small loop at the beginning of the stroke). However, 'mm' looks reasonably clear in the MS and hence 'among them' (or less probably 'among men') seems justified (Charles frequently uses 'm' for 'them'). The situation is clarified in MS B which reads 'm thm' as two separate signs.

[174] Cf. Rom. 3: 10.

[175] In place of 'For God sent not his Son into the world to condemn the world, but that the world through him should be saved' MS B reads at this point 'For God sent his son into the world, not to condemn the world, but that the world through him should be saved'; cf. John 3: 17.

[176] Before 'of' MS B inserts the words 'of him that dieth' (cf. Ezek. 18: 32), which have been struck out. These words are not noted by Albin and Beckerlegge.   [177] Cf. Ezek. 33: 11.

[178] MS B reads 'hath' in place of 'has' at this point in the MS.   [179] Cf. 1 John 4: 8, 16.

[180] MS B reads 'rejoiceth' in place of 'rejoices' at this point in the MS.   [181] Cf. Jas. 2: 13.

[182] Albin and Beckerlegge suggest that one might read 'brethren' here rather than 'principally'. This is possible, but seems unlikely. While there is some room for doubt, the initial stroke of the shorthand sign quite clearly suggests that a 'p' rather than a 'b' is meant and the dot placed above the 'n' looks very much as though it is intended to occupy the position indicating an adverb. The position of that dot is clearer still in MS B, where almost certainly an adverb is indicated (the whole word is written above the line in MS B). The compound stroke in MS B also includes a dot so positioned as to suggest that an 'i' follows the 'r'.

[183] Albin and Beckerlegge suggest 'for our pardon' at this point. This is possible; however, the shorthand in both MSS A and B is 'fr' written as one stroke with no vowel. This suggests 'for' rather than 'for our' since where 'for our' is meant, Charles seems generally to include the vowel 'o'. We might compare, for example, Charles's sign for 'for our' in 'for our sakes' in the line above (written in both MSS as 'for') and his sign for 'for' in 'for his mercy' just a few words before (written as 'fr').

[184] Cf. 1 Cor. 12: 3.

[185] Cf. Isa. 50: 2; 59: 1; Num. 11: 23. In the KJV the word is 'hand' rather than 'arm'. There may be no significance at all in this since Charles may have been quoting from memory, or even not been fully aware that he was quoting at all. However, one might suggest (and it is just a suggestion) that Charles, like the later translators of the RSV, knew that *yad*, the Hebrew word translated as 'hand' in the KJV, may also mean 'arm'. It is perhaps significant in this context that Charles had in his library a copy of the Hebrew Psalter (MARC MAW CW186). The volume carries a note in Charles's hand indicating that

that come unto God by him.[186] Oh that the greatest sinner now out of hell were present, that I might show unto him the way of salvation, and make him a free offer of it in the blood of Jesus! 'This is a faithful saying and worthy of all men to be received, that Christ Jesus came into the world to save sinners; of whom I am chief!'[187] This let him see and feel. Let him place himself like the miserable adulteress in the presence of his[188] judge, not daring so much as to lift up his eyes,[189] but with confusion of face,[190] and horror of heart confess that[191] all his desert is hell. Let him be as fully convinced that he deserves damnation, as the woman that she deserved a temporal punishment. Let ~~him be this~~ him stand before his judge trembling and self-condemned; let him become guilty before God, having his mouth stopped,[192] and before his eyes the sentence of eternal death. Let the greatest sinner upon earth be thus humbled, thus convinced, and to him,[193] even[194] to him, do I glory in giving encouragement. To him do I publish the glad tidings of a Saviour. And he may have a[195] strong consolation, who flies for refuge to lay hold[196] upon the hope which I set before him:[197] Jesus Christ,[198] the same yesterday, today, and forever![199] Christ Jesus,[200] the same physician of them that that [sic][201] are sick,[202] the same quickener of them that are dead in trespasses and sins,[203] the same justifier of the ungodly,[204] the same friend of publicans and sinners,[205] the same Lamb of God that taketh away the sin of the world.[206] Believe this, Oh thou chief of sinners; believe he suffered once for all, the just for the unjust;[207] he tasted death for every man;[208] he loved thee and gave himself for thee.[209] Then shalt thou feel the power of this[210] scripture: 'Hath no man condemned

---

he aquired the volume on 1 March 1733. 'J. Gambold 1730' also appears in a hand other than Charles's own (presumably that of Gambold (1711–71)). John Wesley published *A Short Hebrew Grammar* in 1751.

[186] Cf. Heb. 7: 25.   [187] Cf. 1 Tim. 1: 15.

[188] The compound sign for 'presence of his' has been altered from 'presence of our' in MS A. It is written as 'presence of his' in MS B.   [189] Cf. Luke 18: 13.

[190] Cf. Dan. 9: 8.

[191] MS B reads at this point 'but with confusion of face, and horror of heart confess that ~~he deserves to be damned~~ all his desert is hell'.   [192] Cf. Rom. 3: 19.

[193] The words 'let him become guilty before God, having his mouth stopped, and before his eyes the sentence of eternal death. Let ~~him be this~~ the greatest sinner upon earth be thus humbled, thus convinced, and to him' are absent from MS B.   [194] MS B adds 'and' before 'even' at this point.

[195] The word 'a' is omitted from MS B. The omission is not noted by Albin and Beckerlegge.

[196] The word 'hold' has been inserted above the line in MS A. It is integrated in MS B.

[197] Cf. Heb. 6: 18.

[198] MS B inserts 'even' before 'Jesus Christ'. The insertion is not noted by Albin and Beckerlegge.

[199] Cf. Heb. 13: 8.   [200] MS B has 'Jesus Christ' in the place of 'Christ Jesus' at this point.

[201] The second 'that' is omitted from MS B.

[202] Following the word 'sick' there appears in MS A an insertion mark below the line. What was to be inserted is not indicated.

[203] Cf. Eph. 2.1; Col. 2: 13. Following the compound sign here transcribed as 'trespasses and sins' ('ts' in the MS) there appears in MS A an insertion mark below the line. What was to be inserted is not indicated.   [204] Cf. Rom. 4: 5.

[205] Cf. Matt. 11: 19; Luke 7: 34; following the compound sign here transcribed as 'publicans and sinners' ('ps' in the MS) there appears in MS A an insertion mark below the line. What was to be inserted is not indicated.   [206] Cf. John 1: 29.

[207] Cf. 1 Pet. 3: 18.   [208] Cf. Heb. 2: 9.   [209] Cf. Gal. 2: 20.

[210] At this point MS B reads 'power of his resurrection of this scripture'.

thee'? . . . . . .[211] Let any, let every man upon earth, let all the devils in hell condemn thee, yea if thy heart condemn thee too,[212] and thou canst believe in him [213] in Jesus, he himself shall say,[214] (I do not condemn thee,[will Jesus say]²¹⁵ go, and sin no more.)[216]

He that believeth on the Jesus Christ[217] Son of God shall never come into condemnation,[218] but may boldly make the apostle's challenge, who shall lay anything to the charge of God's elect? It is God that justifieth; who is he that condemneth? It is Christ that died; yea rather, that is risen again; who is even at the right hand of God; who also maketh intercession for us![219] How great or many soever his sins have been, it matters not. Although we think[220] he was the first born son[221] of the devil, he had seven devils, his name was legion,[222]—but he is washed, but he is sanctified, but he is justified in the name of the Lord Jesus, and by the Spirit of our God.[223]

I know the offence this gives to Pharisees. Here therefore will I join issue with you self-righteous ones, and show you what manner of spirit ye are of.[224] This woman is my touchstone, and shall discover your counterfeit virtue. What says your holiness to an adulteress, a notorious, open sinner? Is pity the first emotion you feel at the sight of her, and do your eyes gush out with water, because she hath not kept God's law? Do you see yourself[225] in her? Do you immediately look within and say, 'I am as this adulteress! By nature I am in no wise better than she. There is no difference but that which grace hath made.' Are you ready to encourage the first divine spark[226] of grace in her, the faintest endeavours towards[227] a return? Have you compassion on her while she is yet a great way off?[228] And can you run unto her, while she is beginning to come to herself and say, I will arise and go[229] to my Father?[230] Can you put yourself upon a level with her, and take her unto

---

[211] This series of dots is present in both MSS.   [212] Cf. 1 John 3: 20.

[213] These struck-out words are not present in MS B.

[214] The words 'in Jesus, he himself shall say' have been inserted above the line to replace the struck-out words 'in him'. In MS B the words are integrated into the text.

[215] The struck-out words 'will Jesus say' are enclosed in parentheses in the MS. They are absent from MS B.   [216] The final bracket is omitted in the MS.

[217] The struck-out words are absent from MS B.   [218] Cf. John 5: 24.

[219] Cf. Rom. 8: 33–4.

[220] The words 'although we think' have been inserted above the line. They are integrated into the text in MS B.

[221] The word 'son' is omitted from MS B. This omission is not noted by Albin and Beckerlegge.

[222] Cf. Luke 8: 30; Mark 5: 9, 15.   [223] Cf. 1 Cor. 6: 11.   [224] Cf. Luke 9: 55.

[225] Albin and Beckerlegge have 'yourselves'. However, the singular reflexive suffix seems reasonably clear in the text and the singular is in any case required by 'I am as this adulteress . . .' in the next sentence. In MS B 'yourself' seems clear.

[226] The word 'spark' has been added in the right hand margin in MS A. In MS B it is integrated into the text.   [227] MS B reads 'to' in place of 'towards' at this point.

[228] Cf. Luke 15: 20.

[229] MS B inserts 'will' before 'go'. This insertion is not noted by Albin and Beckerlegge.

[230] Cf. Luke 15: 18.

your bosom,[231] and call[232] her sister the moment she looks up to the brazen serpent?[233]

Are you thus affected towards her, thus full of pity, sorrow and love, and duly humbled under a sense of your own like sinfulness? Or do you not find the contrary tempers? Are you not out of patience at the sight or mention of her? Does not the Pharisee rise within you in resentment and disdain and ~~hatred~~ [234] abhorrence and vindictiveness? Are you not like the troubled sea when it cannot rest,[235] whose waters cast up mire and dirt?[236] Have you put away from you all bitterness and wrath and anger and evil speaking?[237] Or do you exercise all these blessed tempers upon her? Dare you bring against her what Michael durst not against the devil[238] a railing accusation?[239] Do you not find a disdain and loathing of her person; and can you understand[240] that distinction of hating the sin, but loving the sinner? Deal plainly with yourself and examine whether you do not think stoning too good for her, and are you not for tearing the creature to pieces? I need not multiply these questions. If you do feel a fierceness and bitterness against sinners, a scornful disdain, an unrelenting hate, a forwardness to accuse, a readiness to condemn, a joy and triumph in their punishment,[241] however you may cloak this spirit under the mask of zeal for justice, it is the Pharisee, it is the devil in you. It is as contrary to the mind which was in Jesus,[242] as ~~light~~[243] ~~to~~[244] darkness to light, hell to heaven, you to Christians.

Fury is not in me, saith God.[245] The Lord is full of mercy and compassion, slow to anger, long-suffering, and of great kindness, and repenteth him of the evil.[246] God is love;[247] love in himself, love towards a world of sinners. He wept[248] over the bloody city, he lamented and mourned for Scribes and Pharisees,[249] he prayed for his very murderers.[250] He was brought as a lamb to the slaughter, and as a sheep before his shearers is dumb, so he opened not his mouth.[251] When he was reviled,

---

[231] There is a minor error at this point in the Albin-Beckerlegge text. They suggest that in 'draft 1' (MS B) this word appears as 'calls'. However, 'calls' is in fact an alternative reading in MS B for 'call' which appears two words later; 'bosom' is clear here in both MSS.

[232] MS B reads 'calls' rather than 'call' at this point in the text.   [233] Cf. Num. 21: 9; John 3: 14.

[234] This struck-out word is absent from MS B.

[235] MS B reads 'which cannot rest' rather than 'when it cannot rest'.   [236] Cf. Isa. 57: 20.

[237] Cf. Eph. 4: 31.   [238] MS B reads 'devil himself' at this point in the text.   [239] Cf. Jude 9.

[240] MS B reads 'comprehend' in the place of 'understand'.

[241] At this point in the text there appears an insertion mark. What was to be inserted is not indicated.

[242] Cf. Phil. 2: 5.

[243] Albin and Beckerlegge suggest 'loath'. However, 'light' appears much more appropriate in context and more obviously intended by the form of the shorthand sign (the shorthand reads 'lt' with a dot so placed as to suggest an 'i'; the same stroke is used for 't' as for 'th', though when 'th' is meant the strokes of the letters to which it is joined are normally half-size. The stroke here for 'l' is full size).

[244] These struck-out words are absent from MS B.

[245] Cf. Isa. 27: 4; MS B reads 'the Lord' in the place of 'God' at this point in the MS.

[246] Cf. Jonah 4: 2.   [247] Cf. 1 John 4: 8, 16.

[248] The formation of this word is rather unclear in the MSS, but given the context 'wept' seems highly probable.   [249] Charles may have in mind Matt. 23: 37–9.

[250] Charles may have in mind Luke 23: 34.   [251] Cf. Isa. 53: 7; Acts 8: 32.

he reviled not again;[252] when he suffered, he threatened not, but committed himself to him that judgeth righteously. And can you call yourselves followers of the meek and lowly Jesus? You that allow no mercy, no place for repentance to known sinners, but deliver them over to Satan[253] in the fullness of your own self righteousness? You who brought out nothing but threatenings against them, and think you are called, like Samuel, to hew them to pieces in the presence of the Lord?[254] Nay, you even pride yourselves on this temper, and would have your outrageousness pass for virtue. Your very vices must be countenanced, and you yourselves thought children of God for that very thing which proves you children of the devil. Saints you are indeed![255] But it is of his and the world's making.[256] For had not the god of this world blinded your eyes,[257] was [sic] you not given up to a strange delusion, you could not so believe a lie,[258] or so much as dream there is anything of [a] Christian in you.

Bring forth the meanest object of your scorn, the filthiest prostitute that walks the streets, and he that is without sin among you, let him first cast a stone at her. Tell the searcher of hearts, in whose presence ye are, that you never had any[259] lustful thought in your lives; and then, and not till then, let your hands be upon her. If you are convicted[260] by your own conscience of but one impure thought which[261] you ever entertained, then[262] consider who checked that thought, and restrained you from running into her excess of lewdness. Give God the glory, and confess[263] that you are a sinner, that you are as this harlot; whose wickedness, like yours, began with a single thought. Who maketh thee to differ from another? from a notorious sinner, from an abandoned harlot? If you think[264] you make yourself differ from her, then are you as[265] much worse than this[266] harlot as filthiness of spirit ~~flesh~~ is worse than filthiness [of flesh],[267] ~~of spirit~~ or a devil worse than a beast.

---

[252] Cf. 1 Pet. 2: 23.   [253] Cf. 1 Cor. 5: 5.   [254] Cf. 1 Sam. 15: 33.

[255] Albin and Beckerlegge omit the exclamation mark. It is clear enough in MS A, though absent from MS B.

[256] MS B reads 'but it is of the world and the devil's making' rather than 'but it is of his and the world's making' at this point.   [257] Cf. 2 Cor. 4: 4.

[258] Cf. 2 Thess. 2: 11.

[259] 'Any' is replaced by 'a' in MS B. The change is not noted by Albin and Beckerlegge.

[260] Before 'convicted' there appears another word in the text that has been heavily struck out. The shorthand appears to be 'cnvced', presumably 'convicted' that has been rewritten as 'cnvcted' in the next sign.   [261] MS B reads 'that' rather than 'which' at this point.

[262] The word 'then' has been inserted above the line in MS A. It is integrated in MS B.

[263] Cf. Josh. 7: 19.   [264] Written as 'thinkst' in MS B.

[265] 'Then are you as' reads 'then you are as' in MS B.

[266] In MS B the word 'her' has been written and struck out before 'this harlot'. This alteration is not noted by Albin and Beckerlegge.

[267] As Albin and Beckerlegge note, the context here indicates that Charles intended to insert 'of flesh' even though it does not actually appear in the manuscript. It appears that Charles originally wrote 'as filthiness of flesh is worse than filthiness of spirit', which he intended to correct to 'as filthiness of spirit is worse than filthiness of flesh'. In order to effect this, he added 'spirit' after the first 'filthiness of' ('spirit' is here on the end of the line and protrudes somewhat into the right hand margin). He then struck out 'flesh' and 'of spirit' after the second 'filthiness', but failed to insert 'of flesh' in its place.

But must notorious ~~sinners~~ offenders[268] go unpunished? Should any[269] sincere person ask the question I would answer, no, in no wise; but you are not to revenge yourselves; neither is anyone to punish, but the ruler whom God hath ordained; he beareth not the sword in vain for he is the minister of God to execute wrath upon him that doeth evil.[270] And let him follow the example of a judge of our own, who never pronounced sentence without tears. As to you, my brethren, let me earnestly warn you against that abominable abhorrence, that sinful bitterness against sinners, in which some men's righteousness altogether consists; against that spirit which rules in[271] the children of unbelief. Let me at the same time[272] recommend to you, the deepest compassion,[273] the utmost gentleness, the tenderest love, towards known sinners: towards even these worst of sinners, the Pharisees. It is my duty to warn you of these serpents, this generation of vipers,[274] that you may beware of the Scribes' and Pharisees' hypocrisy.[275] With my Lord I must rebuke them sharply that you, and if possible they, may be sound in the faith. But you and I must ~~bless and~~[276] love and pray for them, and bless them.[277] I hope,[278] my dear brethren, you can ~~heartily~~ truly say with me, '[279]I do not despise others, no, not even Pharisees. I am as other men; I am as this publican;[280] nay, I was as this Pharisee; nor can I therefore cast the first stone at him. For I have swelled with proud wrath[281] against sinners greater,[282] as I supposed, because more scandalous than myself. Though I am a sinful man myself, though I am altogether born in

This is clarified in MS B which reads, without any corrective editing on Charles's part, 'as filthiness of spirit is worse than filthiness of flesh'.

[268] The word 'offenders' has been inserted above the line to replace the struck-out 'sinners'. MS B reads 'offenders'.

[269] MS B reads 'a' rather than 'any' at this point. This change is not noted by Albin and Beckerlegge.

[270] Cf. Rom. 13: 4.

[271] Albin and Beckerlegge suggest 'rails on'. However, in MS A a dot indicating a 'u' before the 'l' appears to be visible (though the MS is not altogether clear at this point). There is no vowel point in either MS accompanying the stroke for 'n'.

[272] Albin and Beckerlegge mark 'time' as uncertain. In MS A the shorthand reads 'tst' only; however, in context 'the same time' seems very probable; 'at' is very clear. In MS B the situation is clarified. Here the words are written 'at t sm tm'.

[273] The words 'the deepest compassion' are absent from MS B.

[274] Cf. Matt. 3: 7 and parallel; 12: 34; 23: 33.

[275] As Albin and Beckerlegge note, the shorthand does not make it possible to distinguish clearly between 'hypocrisy' and 'hypocrites' (the stroke reads only 'hip' with a dot so positioned as to suggest a significant contraction). Consequently this phrase may read 'Scribes, and Pharisees, hypocrites' (cf. Matt. 23: 13, 14, 15, 23, 25, 27, 29).

[276] Following 'and' there is another word in the text that has been struck out. It is now unreadable.

[277] The words 'love and pray for them, and bless them' are altered to 'love and bless and pray for them' in MS B. This change in not noted by Albin and Beckerlegge.

[278] MS B reads 'I trust' rather than 'I hope' at this point.

[279] The quotation marks are omitted by Albin and Beckerlegge. They are clear enough in the text.

[280] Cf. Luke 18: 11.   [281] MS B reads 'pride' for 'proud wrath'.

[282] The word 'greater' has been inserted above the line in MS A. It is integrated into the text of MS B.

sin,[283] I have said to the gross sinner, Depart from me,[284] stand by thyself! But God has opened my closed[285] eyes; but God has stopped my mouth,[286] and from a Pharisee changed me into a publican.

GOD BE MERCIFUL TO[287] ME A SINNER![288]

[283] Charles may have Ps. 51: 5 in mind here.

[284] Charles appears here to be playing on the words 'Depart from me, for I am a sinful man' from Luke 5: 8.

[285] Albin and Beckerlegge mark this word as uncertain. The shorthand reads only 'c', but in context 'closed' seems entirely appropriate. MS B omits the 'c' altogether.

[286] Cf. Rom. 3: 19.   [287] MS B reads 'unto'. The change is not noted by Albin and Beckerlegge.

[288] Cf. Luke 18: 13; the shorthand for these words is in a noticeably larger form.

SERMON 11
JOHN 4: 41

INTRODUCTORY COMMENT

There is no indication on the MS of this sermon relating to where or when it was preached, though the content suggests Charles's 'post-Pentecost' period. Other extant sources provide no further illumination. Charles's journal indicates that he expounded 'the woman of Samaria' several times (15 February 1739; 11 March 1739; 27 August 1739; 14 September 1739; 19 May 1740; 24 September 1742; 27 September 1742), but the content of this sermon cannot be described as an 'exposition of the woman of Samaria'. It is reasonable to presume, however, that this and the exposition of the wider passage from John 4 may have overlapped.

The rather untidy appearance of the MS gives grounds for hope that here we have an original Charles Wesley composition and need not think in terms of Charles's copying it from some other source. There are numerous corrections and deletions, all of which are indicated in the text printed below, an indication, it seems, that Charles is composing rather than transcribing. Some of the evidence for this hypothesis has already been outlined in Chapter 4. As further slight evidence in support of the originality of this sermon we might note also that John is not known to have preached from this text.[1] Charles is unlikely, then, to have copied from that source.

The sermon has never before been published, though its existence has been noted in passing by some other scholars.[2] The text given below has been transcribed from the MS, now held at the John Rylands University Library of Manchester.[3] The MS comprises sixteen leaves, fifteen of which are written recto only. The last is written verso also, an indication, it appears, that Charles was seeking to complete the text of the sermon without the necessity of adding extra leaves to the MS. The final paragraph is in shorthand. The material in this paragraph is not sensitive; hence it is probably in shorthand simply to save space, rather than for concealment from the eyes of an unwanted public (which is probably the reason for Charles's sudden switch to shorthand in Sermon 15, on Matt. 5: 20).

The remark made on the top of the MS, apparently by 'W.P.', the probable editor of the 1816 edition, that the sermon was 'not finished' (a remark repeated by Albin),[4] seems not to be accurate. The sermon does end rather abruptly, but the physical evidence suggests that this was as a result of Charles running short of space, not time.[5] This then, unlike Sermon 13 on Acts 20: 7, is in all probability a sermon which Charles finished composing

---

[1] I am grateful to Wanda Smith for offering this information. According to her 'there is not a single instance that he [John Wesley] ever used John 4:41'.

[2] See Albin, 'Charles Wesley's Other Prose Writings', 93; Heitzenrater, 'Early Sermons of John and Charles Wesley', in *Mirror and Memory*, 161.   [3] MARC DDCW Box 5.

[4] Albin, 'Charles Wesley's Other Prose Writings', 93.

[5] As was discussed in Chapter 4, however, there is clear evidence that one leaf has gone missing from the MS as it is now found.

and represents a rounded, if not entirely complete, summary of what he wished to say regarding the importance of John 4: 41 to the theory and practice of true religion.[6]

Charles's main point about true religion is that it is marked by its spontaneity, and that enforced devotion is by definition false devotion. This is true, he says, of both inward and outward acts—we may note again the importance of 'outward acts' in his thinking. Thus, for example, the true Christian will keep the Sabbath not as a result of national laws, nor even as a result of the external authority of the fourth commandment, but as a natural result of his love for God and his seeking after him. Neither will the true Christian be satisfied with merely obeying the negative command not to work, but in addition he or she will seek the positive experience and communion of God within. External acts have an inward motive and dimension. In short, the truly religious soul will desire spiritual food, which, as Charles notes, is described as 'doing the Father's will' (John 4: 34) as naturally as the body requires physical food.

[6] It is possible that this sermon was one of a pair on this text, since in the opening section Charles says that from the text he will 'take notice' of two of the properties of true religion 'its freeness and activity'. However, he then goes on to state that 'in my following discourse I shall confine myself to the . . . former'. He may have written, or have intended to write, a second sermon dealing with the latter issue. This is, however, no more than justified speculation.

~~Serm. III~~[2]

Joh 4.41 But whosoever drinketh of the water that I shall give him shall never thirst; but the water that I shall give him shall be in him a well of water, springing up into everlasting life.

From the nature of religion I proceed to speak of its properties, contained[3] under the phrase 'springing up into everlasting life'. From which words I shall only take notice of those 2 properties of true religion, its freeness and activity. In my following discourse I shall confine myself to the ~~first of these~~ former and

I.   Explain the freeness and unconstrainedness of religion.

II.   I shall enquire into the nature,[4] causes and properties of forced devotion.

and I. as to the freeness and unconstrainedness of religion. It is a principle, and ~~acts~~ it flows and acts freely in the soul, after the manner of a fountain. And in the day of its power, makes the people a willing people[5] ~~and the soul in which it is seated~~, a free-will offering unto God.[6] The king of souls obtains an amicable conquest over the hearts of his elect,[7] and so overpowers them that they love to be his servants and to obey him. ~~Hence it is that~~ Therefore the propagation of this people is called their *flowing* unto the Lord (Is 2.2 'the mountain of the Lord's house shall be established, and all nations shall flow unto it;' and again Jer 31.12, 'they shall flow together to the goodness of the Lord'.)[8] Now this freeness of ~~godly souls~~ Christians may be explained by considering both their outward and inward acts.

1.   As to the outward acts of service which the true Christian performs, he is freely carried out towards them without any constraint or force. If he keeps himself from the evils of the place and age and company he lives in, it is not merely by

---

[1] The number '11' appears in parentheses at the top left hand corner of the MS. It is not clear whether this is the work of Charles.

[2] The words 'No date and not finished' are found in parentheses at this point in the MS, but not in Charles's hand. From the handwriting it appears that they were probably added by 'W.P.' As was argued in Chapter 4, the remark 'and not finished' is in error.

[3] At this point in the MS Charles has changed the word 'containing' to 'contained'.

[4] The word 'nature' is inserted above the line in the MS. The addition is in Charles's hand.

[5] Cf. Ps. 110: 3.   [6] Cf. Ezra 8: 28.

[7] The word 'people' has been written underneath 'elect' at this point in the MS, and has then been struck out.

[8] Charles uses square brackets rather than parentheses to mark off the quotations from Isaiah and Jeremiah. To avoid confusion to the modern reader, however, the custom of using square brackets only where an addition has been made to the text for the sake of clarity is here observed. The whole of the passage 'Hence it is . . . to the freeness of the Lord' has been struck out here in pencil by another unknown hand. This is not the only place on this MS where this unknown editor has left his mark. There are a few similar indications of editorial activity on the MSS of the sermons in the 1816 edition. These pencil marks were not, it seems, made by the editor of the 1816 edition, since they do not conform to editorial changes evident in the 1816 texts (compare for example p. 100 of DDCW 8/13 and the corresponding text as it appears on p. 38 of the 1816 edition). It appears, then, that the sermon has been read through by someone other than the editor of the 1816 edition with, perhaps, a view to publication. If so the project never came to fruition.

a restraint from without, but by a principle of holy temperance planted in his soul: it is the seed of God abiding in him that preserves him from the commission of sin (1 Joh 3.9). He is not kept back from it as a horse by a bridle,[9] but by an inward and spiritual change made in his nature.

On the other hand, if he employ himself in any external acts of moral or instituted duty, he does it freely, not of necessity. In acts of charity, he gives from a principle of love to God, and man for God's sake, and so cheerfully, not grudgingly. His alms are not wrung out of him, but proceed from him, as a stream from its fountain: therefore is he called a deviser of liberal things.[10] In acts of righteousness or temperance he is not compelled by laws, but acted upon[11] by the power of that law, which is written upon his mind. In acts of worship, he is also free, as to any constraint. Prayer is not his task, or a price[12] of penance, but the natural cry of the new-born soul. Neither does he take it up to bribe God's justice to quiet his own clamorous conscience, or to purchase favour with God or man; but he prays, because he wants and loves and believes; he wants the fuller presence of that God whom he loves, he loves that presence which he wants, he believes that he that loves him will not suffer him to want any good thing he prays for.[13] And therefore he does not limit himself penuriously to a morning and evening sacrifice, but his loving and longing soul is continually aspiring after God.

In keeping the observing Sabbaths, he is not tied up, merely by the force of a national law, no nor yet by the authority of the 4th commandment, as he is not content with barely resting from work, but presses after intimacy with God in the duties of his worship. So neither can he be content with one Sabbath in a week nor think himself absolved any day[14] from heavenly meditations; but labours to make every day a Sabbath by keeping up his heart in a holy frame, and by maintaining a constant communion with God.

As to fasts, he keeps them, not merely by virtue of a civil, no nor a divine institution, but from a principle of godly sorrow, afflicts his soul for sin, and daily endeavours more and more to be emptied of himself, which is the most excellent fasting in the world. As to thanksgiving, he does not give thanks by laws and ordinances but having in himself a law of thankfulness and an ordinance of love engraven upon his soul,[15] he delights to live unto God, and to make his heart and which is the most divine way of thank-offering, the hallelujah which the angels sing continually.[16]

The Christian is 2. free from any constraint in his inward acts. Love to God is one principal act of the gracious soul whereby it is carried out freely, and with an

---

[9] Charles may have in mind the words of Ps. 32: 9.   [10] Cf. Isa. 32: 8.

[11] The word 'upon' has been written in the margin. The addition is in Charles's hand.

[12] The word 'price' is not clear in the text.   [13] There is a possible echo of Ps. 34: 10 here.

[14] The words 'any day' are inserted above the line in the MS. It is not clear whether this is the work of Charles himself.   [15] There is a probable echo here of Jer. 31: 33.

[16] At this point in the text there is an insertion mark followed by a second unclear sign. Both have been struck out. There is a possible echo here of Rev. 4: 8.

ardent ~~lust~~ desire toward an object infinitely lovely. Love is[17] an affection that can't be extorted, like fear, and 'if a man would give all the substance of his house for love, it would utterly be contemned' (Cant. 8.7). It is not begotten by the influences of even the divine law, as a law, but as holy, just and good.[18] The spirit of love and of power more influences that godly man in his pursuit of God than any law without him; (this is as a wing to the soul, whereas outward commandments are but as guides in his way, or at most, but as goads in his side).

The same ~~we~~ may be said of holy delight in God ~~which is~~ or love grown up to its full age and stature, ~~which has no torment in it and consequently no force~~[19] of faith and hope, which are ingenuous, and natural acts of the religious soul, ~~whereby it hastens into the divine embraces, as the eagle hasteneth to the prey.~~[20] These are all the genuine offspring of religion and in their nature utterly incapable of force.

Now a little farther to explain this excellent property of true religion, we may consider the author and the object of it.

The author of this ~~noble~~ free principle is God himself, the free agent, the fountain of his own acts, who[21] hath made it a partaker of his own nature. The uncreated life and liberty hath given this privilege to the religious soul, in some sense to have life and liberty in itself. In nothing does the soul more resemble the divine essence than in this noble freedom, which ~~is~~ may therefore justly claim the free spirit for its author, (Ps 51.12; 2 Cor 3.17) or the Son of God for its original [*sic*],[22] according to that of S. Joh (8.36 'If the Son shall make you free, then shall you be free indeed').

Nor does a good man so properly[23] love God and holiness, by virtue of a command so to do, as by virtue of a new nature put into him. Being reconciled to the nature of God, he embraces all his laws not because commanded but because they are in themselves to be desired. To love the Lord our God with all our heart, and mind, and soul and strength,[24] is not only a duty, but likewise the highest privilege, honour, and happiness of the soul; which therefore with David 'chooses the way of truth'.[25] What our blessed saviour says concerning himself is also true of every Christian. It is his meat and drink to do the will of his father.[26] Now as men do not eat and drink because physicians prescribe it as a means to preserve life, but the sensual appetite is carried out toward food, because it is good and suitable; so is the spiritual appetite carried out toward spiritual food, not so much by an external

---

[17] The word 'is' is inserted above the line and replaces a word that Charles has struck out. That original word is not clear in the MS, but would appear to be 'as', perhaps a simple error.

[18] Cf. Rom. 7: 12.   [19] The word 'force' is not clear in the text.   [20] Cf. Job 9: 26.

[21] The word 'who' is not clear in the text. Charles appears to have written 'w' and added 'o', probably at a later stage, above the line.

[22] 'Original' is clear enough in the MS; however, 'origin' or 'originator' was perhaps intended.

[23] The words 'so properly' have been inserted above the line in the MS. The emendation is the work of Charles himself.   [24] Cf. Mark 12: 30 and parallel.

[25] Cf. Ps. 119: 30.   [26] Cf. John 4: 34.

precept, as by the attractive power of that higher good which it finds suitable and sufficient for it.

As for the object of this free and generous spirit, it is no other than God himself ultimately, and other things only as they are subservient to the enjoyment of him: the soul eyes God as the perfect and absolute good, attainable through Christ, and therefore fixes upon him as upon its own ~~obje~~ centre, its proper and adequate object. 'Tis overpowered indeed, but it is only with the infinite goodness of God, exercising its sovereignty over all the faculties of the soul, which overpowering is so far from straitening, that it makes it truly free and generous in its motions. Religion wings the soul, and makes it take a flight freely and swiftly toward God and eternal life or[27] ~~it is of God, and by sympathy~~[28] ~~carried the soul out after him, and into conjunction with him~~. In a word, the godly soul being loosened from self-love emptied of self-fulness, beaten[29] out of all self-satisfaction, and delivered from all self-confining lusts, wills, interests and ends, and being mightily overcome with a sense of a higher and more excellent good, goes after that freely, centres upon it firmly, grasps after it continually, and ~~had~~ would rather be that, than what itself is, as seeing the nature of the supreme good is infinitely more excellent and desirable than its own.

It must indeed be granted that some things without the soul may be motives, or encouragements to quicken it; that grace, though an inward principle and free from any constraint, may yet be stirred up by the means God has appointed, such as prayer, meditation, reading, and the like. It must likewise be contested that God ordinarily uses afflictions to make good men better, and bad men good. These may be as weights to hasten the soul's motions towards God, but they do not principally beget such motions. Thus again, temporal prosperity, may be as oil to the wheels, and ought to encourage to the study of powerful godliness, but they are not the spring of the soul's motions: they ought to be as ~~dew~~ dew[30] upon the grass, to refresh and make fruitful, but it is the root which properly gives life and growth.

Secondly, it may be granted that there is a kind of constraint and necessity lying upon the godly soul, in its most excellent motions: according to that of the apostle (2 Cor 5.14) 'the love of Christ constraineth us', and again (1 Cor 9.16) 'necessity is laid upon me' to preach the gospel. But yet it holds good that grace is a most free principle (in the soul) and *where the spirit of the Lord is, there is liberty*.[31] For the constraint the apostle speaks of, is not opposed to freedom of soul, but to not acting. Now although the soul so principled and spirited cannot but act, yet it acts freely. Those things that are according to nature, though they be done necessarily,

---

[27] At this point Charles has added a sign which appears to be the shorthand symbol 'or', perhaps as a means of smoothing the transition to the material which comes after the deletion.

[28] The word 'sympathy' is not clear in the MS and seems to make little sense in context. The other struck-out words in this section are fairly plain, though their sense (whether or not 'sympathy' is accepted) is not.   [29] The word 'beaten' is not absolutely clear in the MS, but looks probable.

[30] At this point in the MS Charles has written 'dew', struck it out and then reinserted it above the line.   [31] Cf. 2 Cor. 3: 17.

yet are they done with the greatest freedom ~~imaginable~~.[32] The water flows and the
fire burns necessarily, yet freely. Religion is a new nature in the soul, which being
touched effectually with the sense and impressed with the influences of divine
goodness, fullness and perfection, is carried indeed necessarily towards God as its
proper centre, and yet its motions are ~~pure~~ pure,[33] free, generous, and with the
greatest delight imaginable. ~~The it~~[34] The Christian cannot but love God as ~~he its~~[35]
his chief good, yet he delights in this necessity, and is exceeding ~~glad that he~~ exults
to finds [sic] his heart framed and enlarged to love him. I say enlarged, because
God is such an object as does not contract and straiten the soul, like all created
objects. The sinful soul, the more it spends itself upon the creature, the more is it
contracted, and its native freedom debased and destroyed: but grace establishes
the freedom of the soul and restores it to its primitive's [sic] perfection: so that it
is never more large, and more at liberty than when it finds itself delivered from all
self-confining creature-loves and desires, and under the most powerful influences
and constraint of infinite love and goodness.

By what has been said of the free spirit of true religion, we shall be enabled

II   To enquire into the nature of ~~o~~[36] forced devotion:

1. Into the causes
2. Into the properties of it.

1. The cause may be, men themselves, other men, or the providences of God.

and 1. A formal and unprincipled Christian may force himself not only to perform some external duties, such as hearing, praying, giving alms, and the like, but
even to imitate the more spiritual part of religion, and as it were to act over the
very temper and disposition of a son of God. ~~3~~ Three things there seem to be
which do especially force this show of devotion from him: conscience of guilt, self-
love, and false apprehensions of God. First there is in all men a natural conscience
of guilt, which though in some more quick, in others more languid, is not utterly
extinguished in any, but disturbs their security, and embitters their pleasures, fas-
tening its stings in their very souls, filling them with agony and anguish, and
haunting them with[37] dreadful apprehensions, which they can no more be rid of

[32] The word here given as 'imaginable' has been very heavily struck out in the MS and is largely
unreadable. However, this reading seems probable.

[33] At this point in the MS Charles has written 'pure', struck it out and then reinserted it above the
line.

[34] The MS is somewhat confusing at this point. However, it would appear that Charles first wrote
'the', which he then struck out and restarted with 'it' (i.e. the soul) and then continued 'cannot but love
God'. He then appears to have deleted 'it' and wrote in its place 'the Christian' to give 'the Christian
cannot but love God'.

[35] The confusion in the MS continues at this point. Charles appears to have written 'he' which he
then changed to 'its'; 'its' was in turn deleted and replaced by 'his'.

[36] At this point in the MS there is written what seems to be an 'o' that has been struck out with a
diagonal line. However, if this is the case, it should be noted that the mode of strike-out is highly
unusual (Charles generally uses a straight horizontal line). In fact the stroke here looks quite distinctly
like the Greek letter φ. If so, its meaning is not plain.

[37] The word 'with' is not clear in the MS, but seems required by the context.

than they can run away from themselves. This foundation of hell is laid in the bowels of sin itself as a preface to eternal horror. Now although some more desperate wretches force their way through these briars, yet others are so caught in them that they cannot escape, without making a composition, and entering into terms to live less scandalously. Conscience having discovered the certain reward and wages of sin, self-love will easily prompt ~~men~~ a man to do something or other to escape it. But what shall ~~they~~[38] they do? Why, religion is the only expedient, and therefore ~~they~~ they begins to think how they[39] may become friends with God; they[40] will up and be doing but how ~~comes he~~ they ~~to~~[41] run into so great mistakes about religion? Why, their gross and false apprehensions of God drive them from him, in the way of superstition and hypocrisy, instead of leading them to him in the way of sincere love and self-resignation. Self being the great Diana of every natural man, and the only standard by which he measures all things, he knows not how to judge of God himself but by this: thus he comes to fancy him as an austere, revengeful majesty, and so something must be done to appease him: but yet he imagines this angry deity to be of an impotent, mercenary temper like himself, and that consequently some cheap services and specious oblations will engage and make him a friend; a sheep, or a goat, or a bullock under the Old Testament, a prayer, or a sacrament, or an alms under the New. For it is reconciliation ~~to~~ with an angry God he aims at, not union with a good God; he seeks to be reconciled to God, not united to him, though indeed these two can never be divided.

2. Sometimes men may be forced by others to put on a vizard of holiness. And this constraint they may lay upon them by their tongues, hands and eyes. By their tongues, ~~while in the business of education, they~~ that is, by frequent and ardent exhortation and inculcating things divine and heavenly; and thus ~~a man~~ one who fears not God, may yet be overcome by the importunity of his father, friend or minister, to do some righteous acts. This seems to have been the case of Joash, the head spring[42] of whose religion was no higher than the instructions of his tutor and guardian Jehoida.[43] *By their hands,* that is, either by executing penal laws upon them or by the holy example they continually set before them. *By their eyes,* that is, by continual observing and watching their behaviour. When many eyes are upon men, they must do something to satisfy the[44] expectations of others, and purchase a reputation to themselves.

It may be said that 3. Sometimes God lays an external force upon men; as particularly by his severe judgments or thwartings, awakening, humbling, and constraining them to some kind of worship and religion. Such a forced devotion as this was the humiliation of Ahab,[45] and the supplication of Saul.[46] For God him-

---

[38] At this point in the text Charles has amended 'he' to 'they' and then struck 'they' out and written 'they' again above the line.   [39] Amended from 'he' to 'they'.

[40] Amended from 'he' to 'they'.   [41] The strike-out is not clear in the MS.

[42] After 'spring' there appears a sign in the MS that is quite unclear, but appears to be sp. Perhaps Charles began writing the word 'spring' a second time and then struck it out.

[43] Cf. 2 Chron. 24.   [44] The word 'the' has been inserted above the line.   [45] Cf. 1 Kgs. 21.

[46] Cf. 1 Sam. 13: 11–12.

self, acting upon men only from without, is far from producing a living principle of religion in the soul.

I proceed secondly to describe this forced religion by its properties

And 1. It is for the most part dry and spiritless. Fancy indeed may sometimes raise the mind into a kind of rapture and in the outward acts of religion the mechanical Christian may rise higher than the free. This seems exemplified in Jehu whose religious actions (as he would fain have them esteemed) were rather fury than zeal.[47] But commonly this artificial devotion is barren and dry, void of zeal and warmth, and drives on heavily in pursuit of God, as Pharaoh when his chariot wheels were taken off.[48]

2. It is penurious and needy. Something the slavish spirited Christian must do to appease an angry God or clamorous conscience, but it should be as little as may be. He grudges God so much of his time and strength and asks with those in the prophet, when will be the Sabbath be past and the new moon gone?[49] Not but this kind of r[eligion][50]

. . . and slow, high and low, according as they are supplied with rain.

4. It is not permanent. The motives[51] will sink down again and be choked in the earth whence they arose. Take away the weight and the motion ceases; take away Jehoida and Joash stands still.

From[52] all that has been said it will sadly appear how little we poor sinful creatures naturally know of God, or the way to serve and praise him. We talk of righteousness and pretend unto it; but alas how few are there that know and consider what it means? How easily do we mistake the affections of our nature, and I shall say the self-love, for those divine graces which alone can render us acceptable in the sight of God. It may justly grieve us to consider, that we should have wandered so long and contented ourselves so often with vain shadows and false images of piety and devotion; yet ought we to acknowledge and adore the divine goodness if it has been pleased in some measure to open our eyes, and let us see what we ought to aim at. We should rejoice to consider what mighty improvements our nature is capable of, and what a divine temper and spirit shines in those whom God is pleased to choose, and causes to approach unto himself.

---

[47] Cf. 2 Kgs. 9–10.   [48] Cf. Exod. 14: 25.   [49] Cf. Amos 8: 5.

[50] It is apparent at this point that one leaf of the MS has been lost (see the Introduction). The words 'and slow, high and low . . .' presumably complete Charles's third summary point, which is nowhere begun on the extant MS. Neither do the words 'and slow, high and low' run on from 'not but this kind of r[eligion]'.   [51] The word 'motives' is not clear in the text.

[52] The remainder of the sermon is written in shorthand.

SERMON 12
LUKE 18: 9–14

INTRODUCTORY COMMENT

This sermon exists in two drafts, one complete, the other not. Both are held at the John Rylands University Library of Manchester.[1] The incomplete MS is quite clearly only a portion of what we may presume to have been a completed whole; it ends at the bottom of page 4, the following pages being now lost. The longer, complete, MS is here referred to as 'MS B' and the shorter, incomplete, as 'MS A'.

There is no indication on either MS as to where or when the sermon was preached. However, the journal seems to be helpful on this point. The first explicit reference to Charles's preaching on this text is on Sunday, 14 August 1743, when he preached from it in West Street Chapel, London.[2] Almost five years later (28, April 1748) he 'discoursed on the Pharisee and publican' and 'the divine power and blessing made the word effectual'.[3] We cannot of course be certain that he used this sermon on either occasion, but it must be a distinct possibility. At the very least it may be presumed that there was some considerable overlap.

It is not clear which of these two drafts is the earlier. Albin and Beckerlegge think that it is MS A, and in this they are probably right. For example, we may note that the shorthand script in MS B seems more abbreviated than its counterpart in MS A. This suggests, perhaps, that as Charles became more acquainted with the text of the sermon he was able to rely less on the script before him and more upon his memory for the words he was to preach. Thus while in MS A he felt it wise to write 'fr ts t gift f gd n jc' for 'for it is the gift of God in Jesus Christ', in MS B he could rely on the letters 'fr tsgg n cj' to provide him with the framework of the same basic phrase.[4] Such examples could easily be multiplied.[5] The form of the text presented here corresponds directly to MS B, the complete MS. Differences between this and MS A are noted in the footnotes.

---

[1] MARC CW Box 5.

[2] 'At the chapel I expounded the Pharisee and the publican. The 2 edged sword slew some, I am persuaded'. MARC DDCW 10/2 *in loc.*; Jackson, *Journal*, i. 334.

[3] MARC DDCW 10/2 *in loc.*; Jackson, *Journal*, ii. 12.

[4] See MS A page 2 lines 2–3 and compare MS B page 1 lines 20–1.

[5] See for example MS A page 2 line 10, where Charles has written 'at this tm' for 'at this time'; in MS B the shorthand has been contracted further into one compound stroke of 'atst' followed by an abbreviation point. We may note also MS A page 2 line 5 where Charles has 'rpntns' for 'repentance'. In MS B (page. 2 line 2) this has become simply 'r' with the abbreviation point underneath. This is Charles's usual abbreviation for 'righteousness'; he must have felt confident that he knew the text of the sermon well enough not to misread when he stood up to preach.

The sermon is in the form of an exposition of the parable of the Pharisee and the publican (though it is Charles's view that this parable, like most of the others, is also a 'real history'). Its contents are unsurprising and not particularly imaginative. Here Charles draws out the importance of repentance and of confessing oneself as one who 'deserves to be damned'. There is no place for self-righteousness or ignorance of one's true condition.

†

Luke 18.9 etc. And he spake this parable unto certain which trusted in themselves that they were righteous and despised others. Two men went up into the temple to pray; the one a Pharisee and the other a publican. The Pharisee stood and prayed thus with himself, God, I thank thee that I am not as other men are, extortioners, unjust, adulterers, or even as this publican. I fast twice in the week, I give tithes of all that I possess. And the publican, standing afar off, would not lift up so much as his eyes unto heaven, but smote upon his breast, saying, God be merciful unto me a sinner.[1] I tell you this man went down[2] to his house justified rather than the other; for every one that exalteth himself shall be abased, and he that humbleth himself shall be exalted.

In this parable, as in a glass, may every person here present see himself; for there is no one of us who is not either a Pharisee or a publican. Indeed by nature every man is a Pharisee, being utterly blind to sin, though he is born[3] in it; being utterly senseless of his disease, though his whole head is sick, and his whole heart faint;[4] though from the sole of the foot even unto the head, there is no soundness in him, but wounds and bruises and putrefying sores, which have not been closed, neither bound up, nor[5] mollified with ointment.[6] He is no other than an eternal spirit in his passage to that God from whom he is fallen. Fallen he is indeed! For he knows it not, but boasts of light, life, health of[7] liberty in the midst of darkness and disease and chains and death.

This is the highest aggravation of his misery, the worst circumstance of his fall, that he is so dreadfully insensible of it. Many deny it in express terms; and so, in effect, does every one who does not feel himself a lost sinner. If he has not yet found himself out to be a publican, he continues a Pharisee, and trusts in himself that he is righteous. And so he must do, till that blessed spirit, whose only[8] property it is to convince of sin,[9] shine into his soul, and search out his spirit, and show him what is in his heart.

God offers to all this divine instructor.[10] The light shineth in darkness, though the darkness comprehendeth it not.[11] Yet have we a power to comprehend it; not indeed of our own, for it is the gift of God in Christ Jesus;[12] whose death restored us to a capacity of salvation. Him hath God exalted to be a prince and a Saviour, to give repentance and forgiveness of sins.[13]

Repentance in its lowest signification implies a sensible conviction or feeling of sin. It is this distinguishes the publican from the Pharisee. It is this humble consciousness of our own inherent misery, this poverty and mournfulness of spirit,

---

[1] MS A has an exclamation mark at this point.
[2] MS A omits 'down' at this point. However, 'down' appears in the KJV and hence Charles has corrected the earlier reading here.   [3] MS A reads 'altogether born'.
[4] Cf. Isa. 1: 5.   [5] MS A reads 'neither'.   [6] Isa. 1: 6.
[7] MS A reads 'and'.   [8] MS A omits 'only' at this point.   [9] Cf. John 16: 8.
[10] Charles may have in mind John 16: 13 at this point.   [11] Cf. John 1: 5.
[12] Cf. Rom. 6: 23. MS A reads 'Jesus Christ'.   [13] Cf. Acts 5: 31.

which disposes us to believe and embrace the gospel. We cannot be saved, unless[14] we believe: we cannot believe, unless we repent: we cannot repent unless we see ourselves lost. Wherefore, my brethren, let me ardently conjure you to examine yourselves by this history and see whether[15] you[16] are not at this time righteous and not sinners, Pharisees and not publicans.

([17]And he spake this parable to certain which trusted in themselves that they were righteous and despised others). This is the sure effect and infallible mark of a man's trusting in himself that he is righteous, his despising others. Whoso[18] despises another, thinks himself better than that other; but whosoever thinks himself better in himself[19] than the vilest sinner upon earth, is an open notorious convicted Pharisee.

(Two men went up into the Temple to pray, the one a Pharisee and the other a publican). Whence we may observe that going to church is no certain sign of a Christian; and yet that in so doing a man puts himself in God's way. The publican came a sinner, and went back justified. Nor is it impossible but the Pharisee[20] may come a self-justifier and return a publican.

The name and profession of a publican was most odious among the Jews. They looked upon him as no better than a heathen. 'Let him be unto thee as a heathen man and a publican' (Matt 18.17). They abhorred him as we do the meanest and most profligate thieves, the most scandalous, abominable and notorious sinner.

Of the Pharisee I need say nothing; but leave him to do what he much delights in, to give you his own character. (The Pharisee stood, and prayed thus with himself) For a man may make prayers, yea, and long prayers too, and yet be a Pharisee. He is no Christian, who is not constant in the means of grace; and yet a man may use them constantly without being a Christian. Though[21] saying our prayers be one particular duty of religion,[22] religion[23] does not stand in purely saying our prayers.

But the Pharisee goes further than this. (He stood and prayed thus with himself and said, God, I thank thee that I am not as other men are, extortioners, unjust, adulterers, or even as this publican). He loves to pray standing on the corners of the streets that he may be seen of men.[24] But here he prays with himself to God, and we must not therefore question his sincerity. Observe hence that a man may believe himself sincere, and yet be a Pharisee. Nay, he may even ascribe his righteousness to God, acknowledge it to be his working in him, give him the glory[25] and say, 'God, I thank thee'.

---

[14] MS A reads 'except'.   [15] MS A reads 'if'.   [16] MS A reads 'we'.
[17] Charles uses square brackets to mark off the portion of the text upon which he will comment. Parentheses have been used here in order to avoid any possible confusion which might be caused by the use of square brackets in a modern printed text.   [18] MS A contains the form 'whosoever'.
[19] In MS A the words 'better in himself' are underlined.
[20] MS A reads 'Nor is it impossible ~~that~~ but the ~~publican~~ Pharisee'. The fact that neither of the words struck out in MS A appear in MS B suggests that MS B is the later.
[21] MS A reads 'Although'.   [22] Or 'righteousness'.   [23] Or 'righteousness'.
[24] Matt. 6: 5.   [25] MS A reads 'glory in words'.

(I thank thee that I am not as other men are etc.[26]). A Pharisee's righteousness stands in negatives; and he that trusts to his having done no harm, to his not being the worst of people, to his having never wronged[27] any man, is a most notorious Pharisee. Whatever our good sort of people may imagine, righteousness does not altogether consist in going to church and paying every man his own. Yet how many content themselves with no higher[28] a righteousness than this.[29] 'I am not as other men are, extortioners, unjust, adulterers. I am not guilty of any[30] notorious vice; I am no cheat, no rake, no prostitute. I never committed murder or adultery. I have kept the commandments outwardly. I never did any harm in my life.'

But can the Pharisee say with truth (I am not as other men are);[31] is he really[32] better than they? No, in no wise. His plea is not only insufficient but false. He is such as other men are. All are[33] in sin. As it is written,[34] there is none righteous, no not [one].[35] There is no difference. All have sinned and come short of the glory of God.'[36] The Pharisees' sins may be more refined than the publican's. This man's filthiness may be of the flesh,[37] and that man's of the spirit,[38] but both have the same original corruption, though it shows itself differently. The fashionable sinner is as truly a sinner as the scandalous one. She that liveth in pleasures is as really dead to God,[39] and[40] she that liveth in adultery.[41] He that harbours anger or ill will against his brother is as certainly a murderer as he that sheddeth men's blood.[42]

Wherefore no man can say, 'I am not as this publican.' Or if he does, he is worse than this publican; for he is a Pharisee, and does not so much as know it. He is a Pharisee who thinks himself better than another, nay, than the vilest sinner upon

---

[26] MS A omits 'etc.'.

[27] In the place of the words 'to his not being the worst of people, to his having never wronged', MS A reads 'to his being not one of the worst of people, to his not having wronged'.

[28] Charles first wrote 'better' (as in MS A) and then altered it to read 'higher'.

[29] MS A adds an exclamation mark at this point.   [30] MS A omits 'any'.

[31] In MS B these words begin a new paragraph and are written in one continuous line. In MS A, however, Charles begins the new paragraph with the quotation, and the words 'but can the Pharisee say with truth' are written above the line in the space not taken up by the end of the previous paragraph. This again suggests that MS A is the earlier and that the rather confusing state of the MS at this point has been cleared up in the later MS B.   [32] MS A reads 'is he really by nature better than they?'

[33] MS A reads 'all are concluded in sin'.   [34] MS A reads 'it is written'.

[35] Cf. Rom. 3: 10. MS B page 3 ends at this point and the word 'one', which is plainly required by the context, has, presumably accidentally, been omitted. The word is found in MS A.

[36] Cf. Rom. 3: 22b–23. Charles has a quotation mark at this point. However, the beginning of the quotation is not marked.

[37] Charles has written a small '2' beneath the sign to indicate that it should be interchanged with 'spirit'. MS A reads 'spirit'.

[38] Charles has written a small '1' beneath the sign to indicate that it should be interchanged with 'flesh'. MS A reads 'flesh'.   [39] Cf. 1 Tim. 5: 6.

[40] MS A reads 'as' in the place of 'and' at this point. Obviously MS A is correct; MS B probably represents a minor transcription error on Charles's part.

[41] At this point in the MS Charles appears to have left a small space before the full stop. The presence of what appears to be an insertion mark below the line suggests that he may have planned to add something here in the spoken form of the sermon.   [42] Cf. Matt. 5: 21–2.

earth. He that says,[43] '[44]stand by thyself, come not near to me,[45] I am holier than thou', Isaiah 65: 5[46] is of all men the most unholy; for he is stained with spiritual pride, which is of all sins the foulest and most abominable.

But let us hear what his type and predecessor[47] has further to say for himself. (I fast twice a week, I give tithes of all that I possess) and in so doing he did well. These things ought he to have done, and not to have left undone those[48] weightier matters of the law, judgment, mercy and faith.[49] But this is as far as a Pharisee can go; to abstain from open vice, to use outward means, and do outward duties. A course of services, a model of external performances, this is his highest profession and hereby he justifies himself before men.

Turn we now our eyes to his despised companion. (And the publican standing afar off, would not lift up so much as his eyes to heaven, but smote upon his breast saying, God be merciful to me a sinner!) See here a pattern of true repentance! (The publican standing afar off). Being thoroughly oppressed with a sense of sin, and justly conscious of his own unworthiness, he durst not presume to approach the divine majesty he had so highly offended. He saw the immeasurable distance between God and sinners, and humbled himself in[50] the dust before him. (He would not so much as lift up his eyes to heaven) as knowing ~~that God was of purer eyes than to behold iniquity, and~~ that no unclean thing can stand in his sight who was of purer eyes than to behold iniquity.[51] But (he smote upon his breast) he felt the hell of his own nature, was painfully sensible that in him dwelt no good thing,[52] but that he was a motley mixture of beast and devil.[53] His gesture showed him a condemned criminal, that he had the sentence of death in himself,[54] and did from his heart believe he deserved to be damned.

But what has he to say in arrest[55] of judgment (God be merciful unto me a sinner!) His mouth is stopped,[56] and[57] he only opens it to confess himself guilty, and his damnation just. He has no merit, no works, no righteousness to plead. All he says is (God be merciful to me a sinner!) There is nothing in the case but sin and mercy. He finds nothing in himself but matter for condemnation, and therefore he goes out of himself to seek salvation in the unknown depths of the[58] divine goodness. If

---

[43] MS A reads 'said' or possibly 'saith'.
[44] Quotation marks are omitted in MS B, but present in MS A.
[45] MS A reads 'come not near me'.   [46] MS A omits 'Isaiah 65: 5'.
[47] MS A omits 'type and'.   [48] MS A reads 'the' for 'those'.   [49] Cf. Matt. 23: 3.
[50] MS A reads 'sank as unto' in place of 'humbled himself in'.   [51] Cf. Hab. 1: 13.
[52] Cf. Rom. 7: 18.
[53] As Albin and Beckerlegge note (p. 52 n. 6), this phrase originated with William Law.
[54] Cf. 2 Cor. 1: 9.
[55] This word is far from clear in the text. The sign gives only 'arst' or possibly 'erst'.
[56] Charles may have in mind Rom. 3: 19 at this point.   [57] MS A reads 'or'.
[58] MS A ends at this point. As has been argued above, MS A is almost certainly the earlier of the two and the shorthand in which it is written, while typically contracted, is not as severely abbreviated as that in MS B. For this reason the text to this point is reasonably certain. From this point on, however, the text becomes less clear since the difficulty of deciphering the shorthand is increased in proportion to the extent to which it abbreviates words (and sometimes whole phrases) into a few strokes of the pen.

he is a sinner, God, he knows, is merciful: if he is misery, God is love.[59] Here his hopes begin: and he ~~runs to[?]~~ casts himself before the throne of grace, and says in his heart with Esther, 'if I perish, I perish'.[60]

This parable, as most of the others, is a real history. Nor can we doubt there having been such a poor publican, the type of every convicted sinner, who thus condemning himself was justified by God. His only appeal was (God be merciful, (or as it is in the original, God be propitious or reconciled)[61] to me a sinner). As he spoke these words he received the atonement.[62] He looked up to him whom God hath set forth to be a propitiation through faith in his blood;[63] he believed in him that justifies the ungodly:[64] as the friend of sinners[65] himself testifies. (I tell you this man went down to his house justified rather than the other). Justified, that is forgiven and counted righteous. It is literally thus; this man went down to his house justified, and not the other. The reason whereof is very observable (for every one that exalteth himself shall be abased, and he that humbleth himself shall be exalted).[66] That is, every one that sees himself lost, shall be found in Christ, every one who will not see himself lost, shall be lost eternally. Whoso[67] condemns himself, shall be justified by God, whoso justifies himself shall be condemned by God. He that thinketh the better of himself for anything God has done by him or in him, and prefers himself to the vilest sinner, he shall be abased, shall lose the reward of all his good deeds, be counted worse than the worst sinner he despises, and see the publicans and heathen enter into the kingdom of God[68] before him.[69] While the most filthy sinner, that can feel himself such and despair of himself and confess that all his desert is hell, the most abandoned wretch that can humble himself under the mighty hand of God, and fly to the Father and Son[70] for refuge, he shall be exalted in due time. Being brought down to the gates of hell, God shall bring him up again, shall justify him freely by his grace, through the redemption that is in Jesus:[71] shall say unto his soul, 'Be of good cheer, thy sins are forgiven thee; go thy way, thy faith hath made thee whole.'[72]

The greatest sinner, who knows himself to be so, is in a fairer way than the holiest Pharisee, who trusts in himself that he is righteous. This latter is the Pharisee here described; whose pharisaism consisted in his not knowing himself to be a sinner.

---

[59] 1 John 4: 8, 16.

[60] Esther 4: 16. Charles has no quotation marks; they have been added here for the sake of clarity.

[61] Charles here has in mind the Greek words ἱλάσθητί μοι.   [62] Rom. 5: 11.

[63] Rom. 3: 25.   [64] Cf. Rom. 4: 5 and, perhaps, Rom. 5: 6.   [65] Matt. 11: 19 and parallel.

[66] Cf. Matt. 23: 12 and parallel. The closing parenthesis is not present in the text but is added here for the sake of clarity.   [67] At this point there is an unreadable sign that has been struck out.

[68] The sign for 'the kingdom of God' is 'kg'. The context requires the addition of the definite article.

[69] Cf. Matt. 21: 31. There is an insertion mark at this point in the text. However, there is no indication of what it was that Charles wished to insert.

[70] This is unclear in the text; the sign is simply 'fs'. Albin and Beckerlegge suggest 'father of spirits', but this seems a rather peculiar phrase in context. The same sign is used with the relatively clear meaning of 'father and son' in the MS sermon on Rom. 3: 23–5 page 13 line 25.   [71] Cf. Rom. 3: 24.

[72] This composite quotation appears to be based most closely on Matt. 9: 2 and Mark 10: 52, with their parallels.

His deeds were praiseworthy[73] in themselves[74] and[75] he did right in thinking good of them. Wherein then did he offend? Why, he went up to the temple to pray, and his prayer has nothing of petition in it. It is only an encomium upon himself. He asks for nothing, he wants nothing. He does not sue for mercy. No! That ~~becomes~~ is only for publicans to do. 'God be merciful to me a sinner',[76] is a fit prayer for him. As for them, he is none of your sinners; he is righteous, he is whole, and has no need of a physician![77]

Suppose a preacher, to convince him of sin, was to ask him this plain question, do you from your heart believe you deserve to be damned? How would he take it, think you? Could you easily persuade him to believe he did deserve it? ~~Or would he not rather~~ What! he deserved to be damned! He that had so long distinguished himself from the horde of vicious wretches, he that was so constantly heard praying, he that had done so much good! Put him upon a level with publicans! Rather than confess this, would he not[78] be cut to the heart and gnash upon you with his teeth?[79] I fear he would be tempted to go out of church, to turn his back upon ~~God's house and~~ the minister and house of God, and vow he would never come there again. But what would you infer from such a behaviour? That the unhappy man was yet in his sins, in the gall of bitterness and the bond of iniquity;[80] that the god of this world had blinded his eyes,[81] and still kept possession of him; that he was, my brethren, the picture of us.

(He that is a Pharisee let him declare it by departing now. Depart ye unregenerate ones, depart ye Pharisees! But remember the day will overtake you when you cannot fly from God, but must stay and hear this terrible word, depart, depart from me ye cursed, into everlasting fire, prepared for the devil and his angels.)[82]

Suppose we asked the poor publican the same question, would he be offended at it? Oh no! But he would smite upon his breast once more and say, God be merciful to me a sinner! I do, I do indeed deserve to be damned! I deserve a thousand hells; but Christ has taken my deserts and given me his. He was made sin for me, who knew no sin, that I might be made the righteousness of God in him.[83] He came to seek and to save that which was lost.[84] He is the physician of them that be sick, the friend,[85] saviour and advocate[86] of sinners. He suffered for the

---

[73] This is not clear in the text. The sign gives 'prsw' with a point so positioned beneath the 'w' as to indicate an adjective. Albin and Beckelegge (p. 92) suggest 'persuasive', which appears to be a very rare example of a sheer mistake in their work.

[74] The words 'in themselves' appear in the margin and may have been added at a later date.

[75] The signs for 'and' and 'that' are very similar in Charles's shorthand script. One might therefore read 'that' here in place of 'and'. However, the resultant reading, which is the one adopted by Albin and Beckerlegge, lacks grammatical sense.

[76] Charles does not include quotation marks; they have been added here for the sake of clarity.

[77] Cf. Mark 2: 17 and parallels.

[78] The words 'What! he deserved to be damned . . . would he not' are found at the bottom of page 7 of the MS. The point at which they were to be inserted in the text is clearly indicated by Charles.

[79] Cf. Acts 7: 54.   [80] Acts 8: 23.   [81] Cf. 2 Cor. 4: 4.

[82] Matt. 25: 41.   [83] Cf. 2 Cor. 5: 21.   [84] Luke 19: 10.

[85] Matt. 11: 19 and parallel.   [86] Charles probably has in mind 1 John 2: 1 at this point.

unjust:[87] I am unjust. He died for sinners:[88] I am a sinner! He justifies the ungodly:[89] I am ungodly! Here is the stay and anchor of my soul;[90] this is my confidence, this shall be my plea for ever. I do deserve to be damned, but Christ hath died. The Son of God loved me and gave himself for me![91] This is a faithful saying and worthy of all acceptation, that Christ Jesus came into the world to save sinners: of whom I am chief.[92] The Son of God was lifted up that whosoever believeth in him should not perish but have everlasting life.[93] Lord I believe, help thou my unbelief![94]

---

[87] Cf. 1 Pet. 3: 18.   [88] Cf. Rom. 5: 8.   [89] Cf. Rom. 4: 5 and, possibly, Rom. 5: 6.
[90] Cf. Heb. 6: 19.   [91] Gal. 2: 20.   [92] 1 Tim. 1: 15.
[93] Cf. John 3: 14–15.   [94] Mark 9: 24.

SERMON 13

ACTS 20: 7

INTRODUCTORY COMMENT

It is not altogether clear that Charles's composition on Acts 20: 7 is truly a sermon, a fact reflected in the catalogue entries relative to this text where it is described as a 'treatise' as well as a 'sermon'. This general issue has been discussed already in Chapter 4 and need not be entered into again here. The text is important in that it is perhaps the best example in this volume of Charles working systematically at a theological question. In the course of this engagement he refers to a number of early Church sources, which he quotes extensively in Greek. He also subjects a number of individual words and phrases from the Greek New Testament to careful analysis. Here, then, is a good example of his arguing a case on the basis of reason, historical evidence, and careful linguistic exegesis of the relevant biblical and extra-canonical early Christian texts. It is a work of the head not of the heart.

There is no evidence to suggest that this is anything other than an authentic Charles Wesley composition. The MS is clearly in his own hand and the general content, as well as the fairly frequent use of the first person, all suggest its origin with Charles himself. Similarly, though there are several quotations from other writers, there is nothing to suggest that the work as a whole is an abstract.[1] There is no indication on the MS of when or where Charles might have preached this sermon (if it is indeed a sermon) and neither the journal nor the letters are able to break the silence of the MS on this point.

The MS is held at the John Rylands University Library of Manchester.[2] It has been well preserved. It comprises eight leaves which have been separated and bound between hard covers. The date of the binding is unclear, but it appears to be nineteenth-century. Leaves 2–7 are written recto and verso; leaves 1 and 8 are written recto only. The number '12' appears on the MS in a hand which seems not to be Charles's, and the words 'on a weekly sacrament' and 'unfinished' appear on the recto of leaf 1 (the previous front cover) in what is unquestionably the hand of 'W.P.', though the initials 'W.P.' do not themselves appear. In another hand are written the words 'Thos. Marriott' and '2 March 1849'. The same Thomas Marriott (of City Road Chapel)[3] also seems to have been the one responsible for writing 'see C.W. journal Sep 18 1748' on the recto of leaf 1, words which have

---

[1] In this context it is worth noting in passing the existence of a very substantial MS in Charles's hand held at Wesley College in Bristol. The MS, some 40-plus pages in length, is written entirely in French and much of it appears to be from the Catholic writer Fénelon. Charles, then, did extract, but this present MS seems not to be an example.

[2] MARC DDCW 9/14 (previously catalogued as item 667 in the Lamplough Collection).

[3] On Thomas Marriott see especially George J. Stevenson, *City Road Chapel London and its Associations Historical, Biographical, and Memorial* (London, (1873)), 574–5. I owe this reference to Bowmer, *The Lord's Supper*, 223, who summarizes the material in Stevenson.

subsequently been struck out.[4] Bowmer recounts a little more of the custodial history of the MS, though the basis for this is unclear. (Perhaps it was recorded with the original MS when held at the Book Room prior to its move to Manchester.) According to Bowmer, the MS was purchased by the Revd J. Alfred Sharpe on behalf of the Methodist Book Room in 1925 from Dobell's bookseller of New Bond Street.[5]

The text of this sermon was published by Bowmer in his *Sacrament of the Lord's Supper in Early Methodism*. However, his transcription is somewhat flawed. The transcription offered below has therefore been freshly prepared from the MS itself; only major differences from the text as published by Bowmer have been noted.

The main point of this sermon is plain. It is proper, beneficial, and indeed necessary for the believer to communicate regularly. This participation in the 'weekly' sacrament is in tune, says Charles, with both the biblical and early Church testimony on the matter. After referring to the evidence from a variety of early Christian sources supporting, he claims, the view that 'the holy Eucharist is to be celebrated every Lord's Day at the least', Charles completes this section of the sermon (which in fact is the end of the document since it was left unfinished) with the words

> More authorities might have been added, both from the ancient fathers and from the oracles of God, but these, I think, are abundantly sufficient to prove what I undertook namely, that both scripture and tradition do give plain evidence for the necessity of making at best a weekly oblation of the Christian sacrifice, and of honouring every Lord's Day with a solemn public celebration of the Lord's Supper.

There are a number of individual words in this short quotation and elsewhere in the sermon that are clearly of potential significance in the context of Charles's eucharistic views. The Eucharist is, it appears, a 'Christian sacrifice'; elsewhere Charles refers to the Eucharist as 'an unbloody sacrifice'. Such terminology clearly indicates his own eucharistic thinking, which is evident also in many of his hymns on the same topic. In essence he espoused the high-church understanding of the Eucharist as being far more than simply an act of remembrance, though this was a part of the greater whole. His doctrine of the Eucharist lacks the main elements which might cause it to be labelled 'Roman': hence he speaks here of the 'monster' of transubstantiation, and generally elsewhere rejects the view that the Eucharist was a re-sacrifice of Christ. Christ has died once for all and that sacrificial death cannot be repeated. Nevertheless, Charles looks upon the Eucharist as a re-presentation (rather than a representation) of the sacrifice of Christ. In the mysteries of God time and space lose their significance. The

---

[4] Part of the entry for that day reads,

'Rose, as I lay down, in pain which confined me the whole day. I prayed God to suspend it, if it was his will I should speak an useful word at parting with his people. Went to meet them at 5, for a few minutes. The marsh was quite covered. Above 10,000, as was supposed, stood fixed in deep attention. Not a breath was heard among them all. I faintly read my text, Acts 2.42 "And they continued &c". They observed my weakness, and prayed me strong. I urged them to walk as the first followers of Christ. My words sunk into their hearts, and melted them into tears. For 2 hours we wept and rejoiced together; commended each other again and again to God' (MARC DDCW 10/2 *in loc.*; Jackson, *Journal*, ii. 34).

The link between this sermon and Charles's activities on 18 September 1748 is slight. The only point of contact is the reference in the Journal to Charles preaching on Acts 2: 42, which itself reports how some early Christians 'continued stedfastly in the apostles' doctrine and fellowship, and in breaking of bread, and in prayers'.   [5] Bowmer, *The Lord's Supper*, 223.

single act is hence eternal and as they participate in the Eucharist, so believers in all ages partake in the one great sacrificial act of Christ. Tyson has conducted some detailed work in this area and ought to be consulted.[6] Similarly, Bowmer's discussion of the eucharistic theology evident in this sermon and its place in the overall development in the eucharistic theology of the Wesleys is well worth consideration.[7]

[6] Tyson, *Charles Wesley on Sanctification*.

[7] In this context see especially Rattenbury, *The Eucharistic Hymns of John and Charles Wesley*. For an old but still valuable and authoritative survey of Eucharistic doctrine in its Anglican context up to the time of the Wesleys see further C. W. Dugmore, *Eucharistic Doctrine in England from Hooker to Waterland* (London: SPCK, 1942).

And upon the first Day of the Week

Ἐν δὲ τῇ μιᾷ τῶν σαββάτων, συνηγμένων τῶν μαθητῶν τοῦ κλάσαι ἄρτον ὁ Παῦλος διελέγετο αὐτοῖς.

Κατὰ μίαν σαββάτων ἕκαστος ὑμῶς παρ᾽ ἑαυτῷ τιθέτω, θησαυρίζων ὅ τι ἂν εὐοδῶται.[1]

Just. Mar. Apol. 1. C. 87 Καὶ τῇ τοῦ ἡλίου λεγομένῃ ἡμέρᾳ πάντων κατὰ πόλεις ἢ ἀγρούς μενόντων ἐπὶ τὸ αὐτὸ συνέλευσις τῶν προφητῶν ἀναινώσκεται μέχρις ἐγχωρεῖ. Εἶτα παυσαμένου τοῦ ἀναγινώσκοντος ὁ προεστὼς διὰ λόγου τὴν νουθεσίαν καὶ πρόκλησιν τῆς τῶν κάλων τούτων μιμήσεως ποιεῖτει. Ἔπειτα ἀνισάμεθα κοινῇ πάντες καὶ ἑυχὰς[2] πέμπομεν. Καὶ ὡς προέφημεν παυσαμένων ἡμῶν τῆς ἑυχῆς ἄρτος προσφέρεται καὶ οἶνος καὶ ὕδωρ. Καὶ ὁ προεστὼς ἑυχὰς ὁμοίως καὶ Εὐχαριστίας, ὅση δύναμις αὐτῷ, ἀναπέμπει καὶ ἡ λαὸς ἐπευφημεῖ, λέγων το Ἀμήν καὶ ἡ διάδοσις, καὶ ἡ μεταλήψις, ἀπὸ τῶν εὐχαριστηθέντων. Ἐκάστῳ γίνεται καὶ τοῖς οὐ παροῦσιν διὰ τῶν διακόνων πέμπεται.

Const. Apos.[3] 1. L.7 c. 30 τὴν ἀναστάσιμον τοῦ κυρίου ἡμέραν, τὴν κυριακὴν φάμεν, συνέρχεσθε ἀδιαλείπτως, εὐχαριστοῦντες. τῷ θεῷ καὶ ἐξομολογούμενοι ἐφ᾽ οἷς εὐηργέτησεν ὑμᾶς ὁ θεὸς διὰ Χριστοῦ.[4]

Const. Apos. 1.7. c. 36 ὡς κυριακὴ παρακελεύσεται,[5] σοι δέσποτα, τὴν ὑπὲρ πάντων εὐχαριστίαν προφέρειν.

It is the[6] Church of England's observation that there was never anything by the wit of man so well devised, or so surely established, which in continuance of time hath not been corrupted.[7] Now this observation is capable of being carried a great deal further, for it may be as truly remarked that the Catholic tradition of Christ's Church, nay and the very oracles of God[8] themselves, have escaped no better in this particular than have the devices and innovations of men. The former of these have been scandalously misrepresented or industriously[9] concealed, and the latter explained by the private glosses and unauthorised judgements[10] of particular men, till at length the interpretation hath been a stranger to the text, and borne no manner of relation to the words which it was designed to explain. By these means,

---

[1] 1 Cor. 16: 2.

[2] Here as elsewhere the breathing mark is positioned as it is in the MS.

[3] The *Apostolic Constitutions* are a collection of eight books, attributed to the twelve apostles, though that claim is now generally disputed (and indeed is here disputed by Charles himself). They comprise a manual for the Christian life. While they draw upon earlier Christian tradition (especially the *Didascalia Apostolorum* (third century) and the *Didache* (2nd century)), it is improbable that the *Constitutions* themselves were compiled much before the middle of the fourth century.

[4] At this point in the MS the quotation from the *Apostolic Constitutions* ends. Bowmer, however, continues the quotation for several more lines.   [5] In the MS this word is truncated.

[6] Bowmer has 'that' rather than 'the' at this point; 'the' is plain enough in the MS.

[7] *BCP*, Concerning the Service of the Church.   [8] cf. 1 Pet. 4: 11.

[9] Bowmer has 'industrially' in place of 'industriously' at this point. Industriously is plain enough in the MS.

[10] Bowmer has 'judgement' rather than 'judgements' at this point; 'judgements' is plain enough in the MS.

those many unhappy revolutions of the Christian Church were effected which have at length brought her down from her primitive original purity and concord[11] to that lamentable state both of corruption and division wherein we at present find her. When Christians began to depart from the pure word of God, the ground and pillar of the faith, and to deviate from that unerring rule of interpreting it, the tradition of the holy Catholic Church, and to set up human reason and private opinion as the test and standard of the truth, from that time, I say, may we fairly date the beginning of innovation, the rise of error, and the introducing of corruption. That this is fact[12] may be shown in a multitude of instances, but I choose to confine myself to that notable one of the holy sacrifice of the Eucharist. We know while the Church stuck to scripture, as interpreted by apostolical[13] tradition, as her rule of faith, while the Lord's Supper was understood in an orthodox sense and looked upon as the unbloody sacrifice of the representative body and blood of Christ, the oblation thereof made a constant part of the public service[14] of the Church. But in process of time when the speculative reasonings of the school-men and the tyrannical impositions of the popes of Rome, had made a change in this ancient Christian doctrine and raised their monster of transubstan[tia]tion upon the ruins of the primitive doctrine of the Christian sacrifice, the constant participation thereof began to decline, and was by degrees dwindled down to that scandalous infrequency which every good Christian must see and lament. And though at the Reformation Calvin and Luther and their adherents did agree in condemning the Popish transubstantiation, yet did they[15] likewise accord in rejecting the primitive doctrine and because they either wanted learning enough to examine the ancient records of the Church, or modesty enough to submit to their determination, they went through their Reformation merely upon the strength of their own judgement, and then no wonder that it was clouded with so many substantial errors and ~~notable~~[16] defects. In·this particular case of the Eucharist I cannot for my own part esteem the doctrines of either Luther or Calvin one jot less heretical than I do that of the Church of Rome. In several things they coincide with them, particularly in the doctrine of the non-necessity of constant Communion, which I believe was and is to this day universally held by them and the whole herd of their followers, whether in England or beyond the seas. We know how the case stands in our neighbouring kingdom of Scotland, where the Communion is hardly ever pretended to be administered above once or twice a year. Indeed, the Presbyterians in England I believe[17] are somewhat more moderate, but still their practice shows they are

[11] Bowmer omits 'from her primitive original purity and concord' at this point.
[12] Bowmer has 'a fact' at this point.
[13] Bowmer has 'apostolic' at this point; 'apostolical' is plain enough in the MS.
[14] Bowmer has 'services' at this point; 'service' is plain enough in the MS.
[15] Bowmer has 'they did' at this point; 'did they' is plain enough in the MS.
[16] The word 'notable' has been struck out in the MS and the word 'obvious' written in above it. This change does not appear to be the work of Charles himself.
[17] The words 'I believe' have been struck out in the MS, but the manner of strike-out is not that which Charles himself regularly uses.

tainted with the old leaven, and would God the infection had not reached even the
household of faith.[18] But alas it is but too evident that the Church of England is
blameable for infrequency of Communion, as well as her Presbyterian neighbours.
Many churches and chapels in the kingdom never have this holy feast celebrated
in them except 3 stated times in the year. And some others who are not so scandalously negligent, do still fall vastly short of their duty, contenting themselves
with administering the Eucharist every month perhaps, or it may not be so often.
But, my brethren,[19] from the beginning, it was not so, and if we examine the scriptures and the practice of the Catholic Church in this point we shall find ourselves
obliged to say with the Apostle, 'We have no such custom, neither the Churches of
God'.[20] And to prove this the more effectually, I shall first show from scripture as
well as the tradition of the Church that the Holy Communion ought necessarily to
be administered every Lord's Day at the least; secondly, I shall prove that we are
indispensably held to the same duty by the plain positive injunctions of our own
Church; and thirdly, I shall conclude with a practical application of what is said in
the foregoing heads.[21]

First, etc. A plain text of scripture we have in proof of this point in[22] that which
I have chosen for the introduction to this discourse 'On the first day of the week,
when the disciples came together to break bread'. Now on this text I shall make but
these two observations. First that the phrase, 'Breaking of Bread' does in scripture
and Christian antiquity always signify celebrating the Eucharist, which is a principle so universally allowed among the learned that the judicious Dr. Hammond
without troubling himself or his reader with a defence of his explication, thus
paraphrases the text, 'On the Lord's Day or Sunday, the Christians being met
together to receive the Sacrament, Paul spoke to them at large'.[23] 2. I would
observe that the breaking of bread or celebrating the Eucharist is by the text
expressly declared to be the end and design of the Christians meeting together.
The text does not tell us that being Sacrament Sunday, the Christians came
together, but that on the first day of the week they came together to break bread.
Which amounts to as much as if he it had said that on every first day of the week
they came together for that purpose. And it is very remarkable that though the
Christians at Troas happened that week to be blessed with the presence of S. Paul
amongst them and knew doubtless that he would preach to them on the Lord's
Day, yet the sermon is not mentioned as any part of their motive for coming to
church, but on the contrary the Apostle is represented as knowing that on every

---

[18] Cf. Gal. 6: 10.

[19] The use of 'my brethren' here should be noted. As was argued in Chapter 4 it is perhaps an indication that this text was intended by Charles to be spoken directly to a plural audience.

[20] Cf. 1 Cor. 11: 16.

[21] Only the first of these three points is actually addressed in this sermon/treatise as it now stands.

[22] Bowmer has 'is' rather than 'in' at this point; 'in' is plain enough in the MS.

[23] Henry Hammond (1605–60) *A Paraphrase and Annotations Upon all the Books of the New Testament
briefly Explaining all the Difficult Places Thereof*, 4th edn. (1675), 415 (which Charles quotes verbatim.)

Lord's Day all the Christians, both in town and country, came together to celebrate the Eucharist and therefore as taking that public opportunity solemnly to preach to them. Secondly, S. Paul in his 1 Cor 16.2 gives this[24] command, 'upon the first day of the week let every one of you lay by him in store as God hath prospered him' [1].[25] The original Greek will make this text stronger to our purpose than the English translation has done, for the meaning of the words evidently seems to be this: 'Upon the first day of the week let every one of you set apart something— offering it to the treasury according to the prosperity wherewith God hath blessed him'. Now upon this[26] text we may observe that instead of 'laying by him' the Greek says 'let every one set apart something',[27] that is to say, dedicate or conse- crate it to Almighty[28] God, as appears by the words immediately following, 'offer- ing to the treasury'. To understand which we must remember that in every church there was a public treasury into which the offerings of the people were put and there kept for the relief of the poor saints that were in want, as well as for the sup- port of the clergy, and the repairs and decent ornaments of the church. So that it is plain, here[29] is an offertory prescribed in the text on every Lord's Day, and any- one who understands at all the constitution of the primitive Church, will easily see the absurdity of supposing a weekly offertory without a weekly Communion. But indeed why should I spend the time in citing texts to prove that the Eucharist was celebrated every Lord's Day: for I may safely challenge any person[30] to produce one text of scripture where the meeting of Christians is mentioned after the descent of the Holy Ghost[31] on the Day of Pentecost where the oblation of the Eucharist is not directly specified as a solemn part of their public service. Indeed, whoever continued steadfast in the Apostles' doctrine and fellowship must likewise continue in breaking of bread, for of them 'tis recorded, Acts 2: 46, that they con- tinued daily with one accord in the Temple and breaking of bread, not 'from house to house', as it is corruptly translated, but κατ' οἶκον as the Greek expresses it, that is to say, in one of those upper rooms which were consecrated and made into Christian churches.

But though they did celebrate the Eucharist every day, yet they looked upon the Lord's Day as a time when they were more particularly obliged to administer it, as from the two forecited positive texts may abundantly appear. Indeed, if we consider

---

[24] Bowmer has 'his' in place of 'this' at this point; 'this' is plain.

[25] The significance of the number '1' in square brackets at this point is not plain, but it appears to be a referencing system, here used to signify the quotation from 1 Cor. 16: 2. Similar insertions are found before the quotations from Justin Martyr and the *Apostolic Constitutions*.

[26] Bowmer has 'the' in place of 'this' at this point; 'the' is plain enough in the MS.

[27] Charles is here discussing the word τιθέτω (τίθημι) which generally means 'to place' or 'to lay aside'.

[28] Before 'Almighty' the word 'the' (written as 'the' and not yᵉ) has been inserted above the line. The hand does not appear to be that of Charles himself.

[29] Bowmer has 'how' in place of 'here' at this point; 'here' is plain enough in the MS.

[30] Bowmer has 'persons' at this point; 'person' is plain enough in the MS.

[31] Bowmer has 'Spirit' at this point, which is probably an unintentional modernization.

the name of the Lord's Day we shall scarcely be able to assign a better reason for its being called so, than because it was constantly celebrated with the Lord's Supper which was in those early days of Christianity looked upon as the necessary distinguishing service of that day's solemnity, the omission of which was accounted the greatest profanation[32] of the holy festival that could be imagined or supposed. Thus far then I think we may take for granted that we have evident scripture on our side for the necessity of celebrating the Eucharist every Lord's Day. That we have Christian antiquity to support us in the same doctrine, I believe none of the opponents of this practice will be so hardy as to deny. However, for their[33] better satisfaction, I shall quote a few passages, all of them of the best antiquity and greatest authority. [2] S. Justin the Martyr is the first testimony which I shall mention who in his apology for the Christians offered to the Senate of Rome gives this remarkable description of the Lord's Day Service: 'on the day called Sunday, all that live either in town or country meet together in one place and the works of the evangelists or the writings of the prophets are read as long as is thought proper. After the reader has done, the bishop makes a sermon by way of admonition and exhortation to the imitation of such good works.[34] Afterward we all rise up with one consent, and pour out our supplications, and as I have before observed, when we have finished our prayers, bread and wine and water is brought and the bishop sends up prayers and thanksgivings to God with all his might[35] and the people join in them by saying Amen, and a distribution of these consecrated elements is made to every one *present* and sent[36] by the deacons to those that are absent'.[37] So far this glorious saint and blessed martyr. And of this noble testimony, we may observe that 1. Justin lived very near the age of the Apostles, that he flourished not above 40 years after the death of S. John the Evangelist and was, as he himself informs us, personally acquainted with many of his disciples, who were alive then and a considerable time after S. Justin's death. So that he must be allowed to be a credible evidence of this matter of fact, that the apostolical Churches, the principal of which he had personally been present in, did constantly celebrate the Eucharist every Lord's Day. His apology likewise being writ to the Senate of Rome, not in his own name only, but in the name of the whole body of Christians of his time, cannot but be allowed to speak the sense of them all; and therefore is a ~~notable~~ proof that the whole Christian world did at that time universally agree in this practice.

---

[32] The word 'profanation' has been struck out in the MS and the word 'neglect' written in its place. This change does not appear to be the work of Charles himself.

[33] Bowmer has 'the' rather than 'their' at this point; 'their' is plain enough in the MS.

[34] After 'works' the words 'as he specifies' have been inserted above the line. The insertion does not seem to be the work of Charles himself.

[35] The word 'might' has been struck out in the text and replaced by 'soul'. The change does not seem to be the work of Charles himself.

[36] Before 'sent' the words 'they are' have been inserted above the line. The insertion does not seem to be the work of Charles himself.   [37] Justin, *First Apology*, ch. 67.

Secondly Pliny, the younger, likewise, though a heathen writer, may be admitted as a strong testimony of this matter of fact. He lived before S. Justin's time, and was contemporary with S. John the beloved apostle. In an account which he gives his master, the Emperor Trajan, of the manners and behaviour of the Christians, he tells him among other things that they were wont upon a stated day, to meet together before it was light and to bind themselves by a sacrament not to do any ill thing (Pliny, Epis. L. 10, 1, 33).[38] Now what day can this stated day be except the first day of the week, mentioned both by S. Luke and S. Justin; or what sacrament can we suppose the Primitive Christians bound themselves by, but by the Sacrament of the Eucharist. Besides, the time 'before it was light', irrefragably proves that it must be the Eucharist, it being usual in those times of persecution to meet together before day for the celebration of the holy mystery that so the Christians might be concealed both from the cruelty and irreverence of their enemies which practice is fully proved by Tertullian who flourished about the year 192 after Christ, who expressly testifies that the holy Eucharist was commanded by our Lord to be celebrated in all Christian assemblies, even in those which were held before day (Tert. de Corona, mil. c. iii).[39]

The Apostolic Constitutions do likewise give evidence to this matter which (though I look *not* upon them as the genuine work of the Apostles) I can't[40] but esteem as most valuable records of Christian antiquity. In the 30th chapter of the seventh book of these[41] Constitutions [3] we have this direction, 'upon the day of our Lord's Resurrection, the Lord's day, as we call it, see that ye constantly meet together and offer the Eucharist to God, giving praise for all the good works which God hath done for you through Christ'.[42] And that we may be sure this passage is designed as an injunction of the weekly oblation of the Christian sacrifice, it is closed with a quotation of the famous passage in the prophet Malachi, cp. 11,[43] which all learned commentators, both ancient and modern, have universally understood as a prediction of the Christian sacrifice of the Eucharist.

These same Constitutions do likewise give further testimony of this practice in the 36th chapter of the same book, where in a Prayer of Thanksgiving,[44] appointed for the Sabbath, there is a declaration made of the superior excellency of the Lord's Day above the Sabbath, on account of the resurrection of the Lord Jesus and the completion of our redemption thereby, which the Church ever esteemed to be a mercy far surpassing even that of the creation. On this account, as the prayer testifieth, 'we are commanded to rejoice together, and solemnly to assemble

---

[38] Pliny, *Letters*, 10. 96.   [39] Tertullian, *The Chaplet*, ch. 3.

[40] The word 'can't' has been struck out and replaced by 'cannot' in the MS. The change does not appear to be the work of Charles himself.

[41] The word 'these', written 'yˢ', has been struck out in the MS and replaced by 'these' written out in full. The change does not appear to be the work of Charles himself.

[42] *Apostolic Constitutions*, 7. 30.

[43] Bowmer has '1' at this point; '11' is plain enough in the MS, though it is incorrect since Malachi has only four chapters, and Charles is clearly thinking of chapter 1.

[44] *Apostolic Constitutions*, 7: 36.

for the celebration of this festival, and we are likewise commanded to offer the Eucharist for all to thee, O Lord, on the Lord's Day. [4].' Now I would ask these two questions—first, whether these Constitutions are not ancient enough to determine whether the Church thought herself obliged to offer the Eucharist on the Lord's Day or no. Secondly whether a declaration that they did think themselves so obliged would have been made part of a solemn prayer, if in truth there had been no such obligation. Now that the Constitutions are early enough to determine the matter of fact the learned are in general pretty well agreed, who[45] hardly any of them venture to degrade them below S. Epiphanius's days; who flourished about the year 368 and himself expressly quotes the Apostolic Constitutions; and as to the latter question, any one that at all considers the great piety and zeal of the primitive Church will not be at a loss for an answer to the question whether the Christians of those days would have suffered a notorious falsity to have been so positively asserted in the body of a solemn prayer, so that I can't but look upon this evidence as the strongest that can possibly be imagined, both for the truth of the fact that the primitive Christians did celebrate the Eucharist every Lord's Day and likewise for the truth of the doctrine that they looked upon themselves as indispensably obliged to do so. The sum of the matter is this. We have the testimony of S. Luke in several passages of his Acts of the Apostle[46] [sic], of S. Paul in his first Epistle to Corinth, of Tertullian[47] S. Justin the Martyr, the Apostolic Constitutions, and lastly of the Roman Pliny to prove that the holy Eucharist is to be celebrated every Lord's Day at the least. More authorities might have been added, both from the ancient fathers and from the oracles of God,[48] but these, I think, are abundantly sufficient to prove[49] what I undertook namely, that both scripture and tradition do give plain evidence for the necessity of making at best[50] a weekly oblation of the Christian sacrifice, and of honouring every Lord's Day with a solemn public celebration of the Lord's Supper.

[45] Before 'who' there appears another letter or letters in the text that have been struck out. The letters are unclear, but appears to be 'th'.   [46] Bowmer corrects 'Apostle' to 'Apostles' at this point.

[47] The number '2' is written above the word 'Tertullian' and the number '1' above the word 'Justin', indicating that Charles intended to reverse these names in the spoken form of the discourse.

[48] Cf. 1 Pet. 4: 11.

[49] The word 'prove' has been struck out in the MS and replaced by 'demonstrate'. The change does not appear to be the work of Charles himself.

[50] The word here taken as 'best' is somewhat unclear in the MS, partially due to the fact that it has been struck out and replaced by 'least'. That change does not appear to be the work of Charles himself.

SERMON 14
LUKE 16: 10

INTRODUCTORY COMMENT

All of the sermons printed above have an excellent claim to being original Charles Wesley compositions. For some the case is indisputable, and for the remainder it is very strong. Sermons 14–23 in this volume, however, are somewhat more problematic. Most are identified by Charles himself as copies from his brother's MSS, while the origin of the others is unknown. The reasons for including such sermons in this volume have been discussed in Chapter 4.

Most problematic of all is this sermon on Luke 16: 10, for almost nothing of its history is now recoverable. There is no evidence of when or where it was preached, how extensively it was used by Charles, or any particular circumstances surrounding its original composition. It is not mentioned in the journal, nor, as far as is known, in the extant MS letters.[1] However, this should not be taken as evidence against its use by, and perhaps even origin with, Charles. The sermon on John 4: 41 is similarly absent from the record in the journal and letters, but its authenticity is almost beyond doubt.

As was stated in Chapter 4, no MS for this sermon has survived, in either John's or Charles's hand. The only form of it known is the one printed in the 1816 edition of the sermons.[2] This is also problematic for, as has been seen, it is clear from the other sermons printed in that edition that the editor has frequently deviated from the text of the MS forms, and that editorial policy has presumably left its mark here also. Allowance for this fact must be made, and those using this sermon in support of reconstructions of Charles's theology will need to exercise caution.

The lack of a MS is regrettable also in that it may well have been the case, as frequently with the others, that the MS carried some information regarding when and where the sermon was preached and whether it had been 'transcribed' from another's, perhaps John's, copy. As has been noted, there is no evidence to suggest that John ever wrote or preached a sermon on this precise text, but that he did must remain a possibility since our knowledge of John's sermon register is patchy.

The authenticity of this sermon must, then, remain open to question. However, as has been argued at length in Chapter 4, these doubts and uncertainties are not sufficient to warrant its wholesale rejection. What it reveals about Charles's own views is clearly going to be somewhat conjectural and open to dispute. However, those conjectures are worth making and the disputes worth having in the light of the better evidence afforded by the other texts which can be more confidently recovered.

---

[1] Work on the letters is at a rudimentary stage and this judgement naturally remains subject to review in the light of future findings. However, there does not appear to be any reference to this sermon in any of the letters so far catalogued from those found in MARC folios/boxes DDCW1–10.

[2] *Sermons*, 43–67.

The probability is that this is a relatively early sermon, perhaps stemming from Charles's time in America. This is so for two reasons. First, it seems likely that the editor of the 1816 edition had access to a collection of Charles's sermons from this period or shortly thereafter; all of the other sermons in it are dateable to that early period. More important, however, is the fact that the theology and style seems to be in line with that found in the early (dateable) sources. We note again Charles's insistence upon the rigour of the Christian life. It is not just in the great things of life that God demands obedience and seriousness, but even in the smallest point. He writes

> Secondly, we find in effect that the Almighty hath most rigidly extended the rule of his commandments to all our actions, and that there is not any thing we can either do, or speak, or think, wherein some of his precepts are not immediately concerned. Now, since our Creator has seen good to lay down regulations for every instance of our behaviour, are we not indispensably required to conform ourselves to his rules? Will any man doubt whether he be obliged to demean himself in a manner strictly consonant to a divine command? That be far from us to question so plain a principle as whether a creature is bound to obey his Creator!

This kind of reasoning characterizes the whole of this sermon. Charles goes on to speak of the 'reward' that is to be given to those who keep the 'least of the commandments' (drawing on Matthew 5: 19).

> No action is to be considered unimportant which will be followed by such an inconceivably great reward. The text proves evidently that the eternal God has respect to the little actions of our lives; and if they be conformable to his holy commandments, he will not fail to fulfil his gracious promise, and greatly to reward them in the next life.[3]

It is not by any means impossible that Charles wrote such words after 1738. However, when they are compared with the substance of the other sermons in this volume they seem to be more closely allied to the 'pre-Pentecost' material than to the later.

This, then, is a problematic text and many may wish to discard it altogether as a guide to Charles's own thinking. However, such an action would be over-cautious. The text must be used warily, but that it reveals something of Charles's thinking and homiletic style seems entirely probable. Here again we find an early expression of his theology of salvation, a theology which, as with several other of the sermons from this period, is characterized by works-righteousness and in which Christ is noticeable mainly by his absence.

---

[3] Consider also in particular the final paragraph of the sermon, which sums up Charles's reasoning.

He that is faithful in that which is least is faithful also in much: and he that is unjust in the least is unjust also in much (Luke xvi.10).

Christianity, from its first establishment in the world, has met with strong opposition from two different sorts of people—the persecutor and the scorner. The one has essayed by force of arms and violence to drive it out of the world; the other, by scoffs and insults to render it contemptible in it. By the mercy of God and the constancy of Christians, the former have been disappointed of their purpose, and their cruel intentions have been entirely defeated; but the latter too often have succeeded, and by their taunts and jeers, their insults and reproaches, have done more injury to Christianity, than bonds and imprisonments, racks and tortures, ever could effect. They have made people ashamed of their profession, brought religion into disrepute, and prevailed upon many of its followers to sacrifice their piety to preserve their reputation. One of the arts by which these scorners have been able most effectually to serve their master, the devil, has been to represent the several duties of the gospel as too mean for the Most High God to impose, or for man (his most excellent work) to be solicitous about.

For instance, profane jesting and loose conversation[1] are expressly forbidden by God himself; but these enemies of righteousness will boldly venture to deny their obligation to obedience in such immaterial matters; that, provided a man is honest and performs his duty in the main, he need not extend his care to a jest or a word; for that the Almighty is too great and too good to take cognizance of such things, or expect that man himself should do so.

Another (if he finds you reluctant to spend your time and money in idle diversions and recreations) will ridicule your scrupulosity, and ask you if you suppose that God can deign to concern himself respecting these trifles, or has given any precept on such unimportant subjects? In short, they have so far carried their cause, that religion is almost wholly excluded from common life, and confined to solemn times and places, to forms and modes of worship. The practice of Christianity is restricted within the bounds of the church; and he that would regulate all his behaviour and conversation by the rules of the gospel will be inevitably branded with the names of superstitious, scrupulous, and pharisaical.

It is this error which I design to combat in my present discourse, and show,

First, that no action is too trifling and insignificant to be made a part of our religion, or regulated by the rule of the gospel:

Secondly, that by neglecting to take care of what we call our little actions, we are led into great transgressions:

Thirdly, that the advantage of thus regulating the little common actions of our lives by the rule of the divine command will be greater than Christians at first may imagine.

---

[1] Charles may have in mind Eph. 5: 4 at this point, a text which he quotes directly later in this sermon.

We know there is but one rule for the Christian's behaviour in the world; and that is, that he should have a constant view to the great end of his creation in every action of his life. Now the end for which man was created and sent forth to be an inhabitant of this lower world was the glory of God and the salvation of his own soul. Accordingly we find St. Paul exhorting his Corinthians to look constantly, with a simple heart and single eye,[2] to this great end of their being; and 'whether they eat or drink, or whatever they do, to do all to the glory of God'.[3]

Now I would ask whether the doctrines of my text do not evidently and clearly prove the point we are discussing? Eating and drinking, those common necessary actions of life, are commanded to be done in such a manner as that the glory of God may be promoted. Now it is certain we should never be required to refer these actions to God, unless they were in some measure capable of advancing and promoting his glory: and surely no work can be termed trifling and insignificant, whereby so noble an end is attained; no action be deemed indifferent, which tends to promote the one design of our creation. Eating and drinking, therefore, those essential means of supporting and preserving our lives, are in this text positively declared to be subservient to the glory of God, and, as such, are expressly referred to him. And if this principle respecting these necessary actions must actuate us, it applies to every thing we do; the consequence of which is, that no action is too mean or trifling to be incorporated into our religion, or to be regulated by the strictest rules of the gospel.

Secondly, we find in effect that the Almighty hath most rigidly extended the rule of his commandments to all our actions, and that there is not any thing we can either do, or speak, or think, wherein some of his precepts are not immediately concerned. Now, since our Creator has seen good to lay down regulations for every instance of our behaviour, are we not indispensably required to conform ourselves to his rules? Will any man doubt whether he be obliged to demean himself in a manner strictly consonant to a divine command? That be far from us to question so plain a principle as whether a creature is bound to obey his Creator! All those commandments which enjoin us to love the Lord our God with all our heart, with all our mind, and with all our strength, and to serve him faithfully with all our soul,[4] do evidently extend their sense so far as to include every thought, word, and action; for what action can be lawful which cannot be referred to him, directly or indirectly? What are we at liberty to do without having a view to his service? When the Son of God in his holy gospel has particularised those several duties comprised in this saying, to obviate all objections, and silence all cavils that might have been made against his precepts as trifling and unimportant, he strengthens it with this solemn sanction, 'He that keepeth the least of these commandments, and teacheth

---

[2] Cf. Matt. 6: 22 and parallel. 'The Single Intention' (Matt. 6: 22–3) is the subject of Sermon 16.
[3] Cf. 1 Cor. 10: 31.
[4] Cf. Deut. 6: 5; 10: 12; 11: 13; 30: 6; Josh. 22: 5; Mark 12: 30 (the text of Sermon 20) and parallels.

men so to do, shall be called *great* in the kingdom of heaven; but he that breaketh the least of these sayings shall be esteemed least in the kingdom of heaven.'[5]

Now the sense of this passage is plainly this—that nothing is too insignificant to be made an instance of his laws, nor any action so inconsiderable as not to be in some measure a means of increasing our great and glorious reward in his heavenly kingdom; which suggests a third argument, namely, that

No action is to be considered unimportant which will be followed by such an inconceivably great reward. The text proves evidently that the eternal God has respect to the little actions of our lives; and if they be conformable to his holy commandments, he will not fail to fulfil his gracious promise, and greatly to reward them in the next life.

Had the prophet bid thee do some great thing, wouldst thou not have done it? And how much more when he saith, 'wash and be clean,'[6] was the reproof that Naaman's servant gave him when he rejected Elisha's advice, and refused to make use of the means he had prescribed for the recovery of his leprosy. And may not the Almighty make the application to those servants whom he hath ordered to be faithful in that which is least, and for encouragement hath promised to make *great* in the kingdom of heaven?[7] Heavy, without doubt, will be the condemnation of those who neglect to secure the mighty recompense of heaven, from not observing to fulfil the jots and tittles of the law.[8] He cannot have a due sense of the value of those good things which God hath *prepared for all who love him,*[9] who refuses any labour, or starts at any difficulty, which lies in the way of attaining them; much less who refuses to comply with easy bonds, and so light a yoke;[10] to submit to little grievances and self-denials, which are privileges to a devout Christian. Surely, if heaven be worth all our care and pains, we cannot think ourselves blameless if we do not labour in every action of our life to secure it; and if the kingdom of God is so invaluable, so beyond all that we can hope or conceive, as to deserve the struggle of 'taking it by force',[11] how can we be justified for not entering in, when encouraged by this divine promise; 'He that keepeth the least of these commandments shall be called great in the kingdom of heaven'.[12]

To evince this important truth beyond all possibility of contradiction, and to remove every doubt, whether we are obliged to refer all our actions to the glory of God, and consequently that none of them are too mean to be made a part of our religion, or to be regulated by the strict rules of the gospel, the blessed Jesus expressly assures us that, at the day of judgment, every individual action of our lives will be scanned and strictly examined.[13] Now, if not one be too insignificant to deserve the censure and cognizance of the Almighty, not one is too mean to be

---

[5] Cf. Matt. 5: 19.   [6] 2 Kgs. 5: 13.   [7] Matt. 5: 19.
[8] Cf. Matt. 5: 18.   [9] Cf. 1 Cor. 2: 9.   [10] Cf. Matt. 11: 29–30.
[11] Cf. Matt. 11: 12.   [12] Cf. Matt. 5: 19.
[13] Charles may have in mind Matt. 12: 36 at this point. The use of the phrase 'it should be done *as to the Lord*' below indicates also the influence of Matt. 25: 31 ff.

referred to his service. If we are to give an account for each, certain it is, that each should be done *as to the Lord*.[14]

Persuaded I am that no action can stand the test of this strict and solemn scrutiny, which is not begun, continued, and ended in his service; and therefore the proof of this article of our faith ought to convince us of the importance, as well as the truth, of the doctrine now under consideration, and effectually prevail upon us to do every thing we do as in the presence of our God, in the sight of our judge, who hath required it of us that himself should be the ultimate end of all our actions.

That we may not think that we shall escape unpunished in the great and terrible day of the Lord,[15] merely for the innocence, or rather the insignificance of our actions, our blessed Saviour has told us, that we shall give an account at the day of judgement even for every idle word.[16] Now, if our idle words will not escape censure, where shall he appear who has a whole train of idle actions?

Now every word and action is idle which is not done with a view proposed by our Creator in our very existence here. This interpretation is corroborated by St. Paul's well-known passage in his epistle to the Ephesians, iv. 29, 30: 'Let no corrupt communication proceed out of your mouth, but such as is good to the use of edifying, that it may minister grace to the hearers', and 'Grieve not the holy Spirit, whereby ye are sealed unto the day of redemption'.

If any ask what we mean by idle words, my answer is, the same that the apostle means by 'corrupt communication'; words that are not edifying or beneficial, such as minister no grace to the hearers. In this manner, then, we must not converse or speak, but preserve an invariable view to the great end of our being, the glory of God, and the good of others.

Now if no conversation can be vindicated, which is not sanctified, consecrated, if I may so say; if no subject, however light, be exempted from some moral tendency; I ask whether it doth not hold equally true, that no action or business we can undertake is too despicable to have a reference to religion, or to be made an offering holy and acceptable to the Most High?

Indeed, if we consider human actions simply in themselves, they are all infinitely too mean for the great majesty of heaven to regard. What are our best services to the Almighty God? Is he honoured by the bowing of our knee, or lifting up of our hands? Oh no! the high and lofty one who inhabiteth eternity need not be worshipped with man's worship, the worm of yesterday! Neither hath he respect to the *outward* actions of his creature, but to the temper and spirit with which they are performed. He, therefore, who is faithful in that which is least, is esteemed, in his sight, as faithful in much; and he that is conscientious, and fearful of doing a little thing which may offend God, will be blessed with a reward exceeding all comprehension of mortals.

---

[14] Cf. Matt. 25: 40; Col. 3: 23.   [15] Cf. Joel 2: 31.   [16] Cf. Matt. 12: 36.

We know that the two mites of the widow were accepted before the abundance which the rich cast into the treasury, because of that simplicity of heart, and fervent piety, wherewith the offering was made.[17] And is not the same spirit capable of sanctifying the meanest actions of our lives, that is, the desire to please God, and rendering every thing acceptable in his sight?

Yes; God is a spirit, and seeketh such to worship him as worship him in spirit and in truth.[18] He that hath promised that even a cup of cold water given to a disciple in the name of God shall in no wise lose its reward,[19] will doubtless have a great respect to, and will mightily bless and prosper, him who in his least action has reference to the advancement of his glory. He, therefore, who refuses to indulge himself in pleasure, who lays various restraints upon his behaviour and conversation, who is fearful of doing many things which the generality of people freely allow themselves in, if he has made God the foundation of his scrupulosity, and a desire of his glory the ground and reason of his singularity—he shall be received as *great* in the kingdom of heaven.[20]

Thus have I endeavoured to prove my first position; and, I trust, have incontrovertibly proved that there is no act of our lives too mean to be made a part of our devotion, consequently, to be laid under the strictest rules of his holy gospel.

Secondly, I have now to show the danger of not being faithful in that which is least, and to evince that, by neglecting what we call our little actions, we are often led into great and heinous transgressions.

It is the observation of the wise son of Sirach, that he who despiseth little things, shall fall by little and little;[21] and experience will attest this truth, and prove it to every attentive Christian. See we not that vice, as well as virtue, is of a progressive nature, and by degrees encroaches on the hearts of its votaries? The evil spirit is too subtle a tempter to show the heinousness of sin at the first glance, and therefore adapts his temptations to the conscience and disposition: and, knowing that mankind (until they become thoroughly reprobate) are averse from monstrous crimes, he ensnares them into little transgressions; aware that he who is once habituated to small offences will soon lose his horror at sin, shake off his tenderness of conscience, and by degrees grow hardened in vice and impiety. Therefore this enemy of our souls, when he would seduce any of the servants of God from the path of righteousness, would make the first declension from that path as small as possible, that he might ensnare them in his nets, without their even perceiving the danger, and bring them unawares from the road to heaven to the gate of destruction.[22] For instance, is drunkenness the sin to which he tempts?—his method is to conceal this frightful vice, and its dreadful consequences, under the veil of innocent mirth and social pleasure, so that his victim is beguiled, by a desire of being easy and agreeable to his companions, to weaken his understanding, till he becomes a beast, and makes shipwreck of his reason as well as conscience. Now had this man been

---

[17] Cf. Mark 12: 42 and parallel.   [18] John 4: 24.   [19] Cf. Mark 9: 41 and parallel.
[20] Cf. Matt. 5: 19.   [21] Sir. (= Ecclesiasticus) 19: 1.   [22] Cf. Matt. 7: 13.

so upon his guard as never to exceed the bounds of Christian temperance and sobriety, had he been scrupulously exact in observing the rule of the apostle, of eating and drinking only to the glory of God,[23] he would have preserved the intellects [*sic*] which the Almighty bestowed upon him, avoided the stumbling block which the evil one cast in his way, and escaped the guilt, the misery, and the punishment, which those incur who are overcharged 'with surfeiting and drunkenness'.[24]

Again:—a virtuous youth who would tremble at the sin of fornication, will be tempted to loose conversation, and 'jestings which are not convenient';[25] he will hear them amongst his irreligious companions, till he joins in them, and easily be persuaded there is no great evil in such little things, till by little and little he flings off all restraint, falls into the commission of vices which he once regarded with indignation and horror, and at last is ensnared by the strange woman whose 'house is the gate of death, and her chambers the path-way to hell'.[26] Now had this man been so obedient to his Maker, and faithful to himself, as to have 'set a watch to his words, and kept the door of his lips',[27] he had avoided this most dangerous of sins, and been preserved from the iniquity which will now in all probability bring him to destruction.

Farther, the generality of mankind, in theory, abhor gambling; though most of them allow themselves in games, and recreation is made a pretence for extravagances, and diversion becomes an inlet to profuseness and prodigality. A trifling wager may be risked and lost without injury, and a small part of our income appropriated to pleasure and chance; but alas! insignificant as these beginnings appear, they are likely to end in serious evil. The gentleman too often degenerates into the gambler; and by degrees it comes to pass that many wager away their estates, and cast the fatal die which reduces themselves and their families to beggary and want.

Now all these may serve as examples to demonstrate the direful tendency of being negligent of our little actions, and the important truth of my text, 'that he that is unjust in the least is unjust also in much': that he who places not his common ordinary actions under the restraints of religion is bringing himself under snares and temptations, blindly enters into the confines of vice, and throws himself by steps and degrees under the full power and dominion of the adversary.

And indeed a little spark will quickly kindle to a flame; a small breach in the river's bank will soon cause an inundation. He that will venture to go ever so little out of the right way ought seriously to weigh with himself where may be the end. Every step out of the path of life is a step leading to death. We have the testimony of the Holy Scriptures that the way to heaven is narrow,[28] and beset with traps and pitfalls; and, if we deviate from it, no wonder if we are entangled or dragged down to ruin and destruction. To be secure, we must go on in holiness; and to be free from danger of evil, we must constantly practise all that is good. He that can trifle himself into a *spirit of carelessness* and want of thought, deceives his own heart if he

---

[23] Cf. 1 Cor. 10: 31.   [24] Luke 21: 34.   [25] Cf. Eph. 5: 4.
[26] Cf. Prov. 7: 27.   [27] Cf. Ps. 141: 3 (which is quoted in Eccl. 22: 27).   [28] Cf. Matt. 7: 14.

fancies he is safe; and the man who suffers himself at any time, or in any degree, to relax in circumspection, exposes himself at that time, and in that degree, to all the assaults of a vigilant and subtle adversary, who seeks to destroy his immortal soul.

But, it will be said, is the Christian then secluded from mirth and diversion, pleasures and entertainments? Yes; as far as they are inconsistent with piety and innocence, with temperance and safety. Whatever pleasure may be enjoyed *consistent with these,* and is entered upon with either a mediate or immediate reference to the glory of his Creator, a Christian may delight himself in. But whatever is incompatible with these principles, whatever diversion is unlawful, either in itself or in its necessary consequences, which tends to evil, or exposes men to be an easier prey to temptation, I scruple not to say, cannot be a pleasure designed for Christians; so manifestly the reverse, that God, who seeth the evil as well as the danger, has solemnly forbidden such diversions in his holy word, by commanding us to abstain from all appearance of evil,[29] and strictly enjoining us to do nothing which may not be done as unto the Lord,[30] and be some way subservient to his honour and glory.

So much I have deemed proper to remark on the danger of not being faithful in that which is least, and established the truth I undertook to discuss; namely, that by neglecting to take care of our miscalled little actions, we are often led into great and heinous transgressions. I therefore proceed to my third head of discourse, wherein I promised to show,

Thirdly, the incalculable advantages which will arise from regulation of the little common actions of our lives by the strict rules of God's commandments.

He that would be secure must not approach the precipice of evil. The danger has been demonstrated, and the only means of avoiding it is to keep at a distance from the very appearance. He that maketh every action a point of duty will not easily be ensnared into a flagrant breach of it, and he that is circumspect in little will scarcely ever fall into great transgressions.

Tenderness of conscience is the noblest preservative from sin, and a scrupulous fear of offending the best safeguard against it. The fortress of virtue is most effectually secured, when the inlets to vice are most sedulously guarded. Constant recollection impedes attack; and he who never exposes himself to the least shadow of temptation will never be in danger of being overcome by the greatest. Were the good man of the house always on the watch, the thief could never break in and spoil his goods;[31] and if the Christian would not indulge himself in the full enjoyment of that liberty which he thinks allowed, but conscientiously abstain from *some* of those worldly good things, which he sees his brethren use intemperately, it would be as probable a means to preserve him from falling as can be conceived. Who is so likely to persevere as such a faithful servant, to whose mind the injunction of his Lord (to all Christians, as well as to his disciples) is ever present, 'What I say

---

[29] 1 Thess. 5: 22.   [30] Charles may have in mind Col. 3: 23 at this point.
[31] Cf. Mark 3: 27 and parallel.

unto you, I say unto all, *watch!*[32] Is it not one of the most awful punishments that
attend the wicked, to be given over to a reprobate mind;[33] to have their hearts hardened[34] and their consciences seared.[35] Now such as is the curse of a callous heart,
so great is the blessing of a tender conscience; and as on one hand an obdurate
resolution is a certain forerunner of eternal destruction, so on the other, a sedulous
adherence to virtue, and a nice sense of every little breach of duty, is of all others the
most powerful preservative from the guilt, as well as the punishment, of sin; and
universal conscientiousness is an invulnerable shield against the force of temptation.

Hazael, king of Syria, was offended highly at the prophet, for predicting the
evils which he should bring upon the Israelites. 'Is thy servant a dog that he should
do this great thing?'[36] was the rebuke he gave the man of God; but when he had
contemplated the splendour of a crown, and permitted his thoughts to dwell on
the pleasures of high station, his heart swelled with pride and ambition, and he
soon fulfilled the awful prognostication, slew his master, ascended his throne, and
exercised his ill-gotten power with so much tyrannic cruelty, as served to accomplish
the designs of Providence, who appointed him a scourge to the rebellious nation,
which had become traitors to their God; and has given in this narration, to all ages,
a striking instance of the deceitfulness of the human heart, and the danger of not
checking evil thoughts before they proceed to actions.

The case is plain; if we would be holy, we must use the means. The lesson of
Christian perfection is not to be learned at once; we must be well exercised in rudiments and first principles, if we ever hope to make a progress in the school of
Christ. By habituating ourselves to little restraints in the first instance, by voluntarily imposing on ourselves small crosses, we shall in time become conformed to
his death, who deemed no sacrifice too great to purchase our salvation. By abstaining
from taking the utmost liberty we lawfully may, we shall be effectually secured
from even the desire of criminal gratifications, and escape the dreadful guilt of
heinous and presumptuous sins.

The children of this world (who in their generation are wiser than the children
of light[37]) will eminently prove the advantages resulting from strict exactness, and
punctual regularity, in the most trifling things; they will tell us of the benefits
resulting from doing every thing by rule and order, neglecting no means of gain,
and ever adding to their accumulations; and why the same attention is not required
in a Christian, which experience teaches us is so useful in a tradesman's concerns,
it will be difficult to show. Christianity is an employment no less extensive than
important; its influence may reach, if we please, to every action, and render the
most insignificant of them holy and acceptable to God. Why then should not every

---

[32] Mark 13: 37.   [33] Cf. Rom. 1: 28.

[34] The theme of hardening of hearts is one that occurs several times in the Bible, most obviously in
the story of Pharaoh and the children of Israel (see Exod 4: 21 ff.). Here, however, given the general
development of the argument, Charles may be reflecting upon the thrust of the argument in Rom.
1: 21 ff., which speaks of the foolish heart being 'darkened'.   [35] Cf. 1 Tim. 4: 2.

[36] 2 Kgs. 8: 13.   [37] See Luke 16: 8, which is the subject of Sermon 17.

thing we think, and say, and do, be undertaken with this view, and wholly referred to his most sacred and adorable name?

I have shown in the first part of this discourse that all our actions are capable of being thus piously and advantageously improved; that none are too mean to be dedicated to the service of God, or instrumental in promoting his glory. Away then with this objection of their being unworthy of the Most High, and not fit to be made instances of our obedience to him, or to be regulated by the strict rules of the gospel; away with all jeering scoffs against this religious scrupulosity which I have been inculcating: and if any men there be that still continue to laugh at any such little singularities of the true disciples of Christ, let them remember it is written, 'Woe unto you that laugh now, for ye shall mourn and weep'.[38] No doubt can possibly be made, that every action of our lives may be referred to God, and there is demonstration to prove that we are thus to refer every action: for if we consider, on the one hand, the great danger which those incur who are negligent of their little actions, to what manifold and great temptations they are exposed, even to commit heinous sins; and on the other, those mighty benefits which accrue from bringing our indifferent actions to the standard and test of God's holy will and commandment—I say, whoever weighs these great truths as he ought will find the indispensable necessity of no longer living to himself, but unto God; and of doing the most insignificant action of his life with such a spirit and temper, as that it might be done unto the Lord and not to man.

This is the method to escape the punishment due to those who live for themselves, and not to God: hereby we shall assure our hearts before him, when he is constantly in our thoughts, and is set always before us. How eminent a share of glory shall they receive, who are thus perpetually concerned in promoting the glory of God? How abundantly shall they be recompensed for those pleasures from which they have voluntarily abstained for Christ's sake! Much doubtless shall be given, as well as forgiven, to those who have loved so much[39] as to make the great object of their love the end of every thing they do. We have our blessed Saviour's promise that, in consequence of their being faithful in that which is least, they shall be esteemed faithful in much, and for their tender fear of transgressing their Divine master's little commands, they shall be pronounced great in the kingdom of heaven.[40]

Blessed therefore are all they who hear these sayings and keep them![41] They shall escape the guilt and punishment of heinous transgressions, and receive a glorious recompense for their labour, an incalculable reward for their care and industry; such a recompense as fadeth not away,[42] eternal in the heavens;[43] such a reward—great as their Master's love, and extensive as the grace which enabled them to do him 'true and laudable service'.

---

[38] Luke 6: 25.   [39] Cf. Luke 7: 47.   [40] Matt 5: 19.
[41] Cf. Luke 11: 28.   [42] 1 Pet. 1: 4; 5: 4.   [43] 2 Cor. 5: 1.

Sermon 15

Matthew 5: 20

INTRODUCTORY COMMENT

The MS of this sermon provides no clear evidence regarding where or when it was preached by Charles. This said, the circumstantial evidence (and indeed the content) suggests that this is a sermon from the 'pre-Pentecost' period, and probably from Charles's time on the way to or in America. The only date on the MS is 5 January 1735, a date prior to Charles's own ordination, but upon which John preached a sermon on the same text.[1] It thus seems probable, as Albin has argued, that this is a sermon which Charles copied from one of John's MSS, though the fact that Charles has not said so raises some doubts. These issues have been discussed more fully in Chapter 4.

Even allowing for the probability that this is a sermon copied from John, however, it is still properly printed in this volume and may be taken as indicative of Charles's own view and homiletic art. As already argued, it is highly unlikely that he simply copied his brother's sermons without taking the opportunity which that process provided of pulling them fully into line with his own thinking. In this sermon there is quite strong MS evidence to suggest that this was indeed the case.

The MS is held at the John Rylands University Library of Manchester.[2] It comprises ten leaves; leaves 2–9 are written recto and verso. Leaf 1, the front cover, is written recto only, though nothing upon it appears to be in Charles's own hand, and leaf 10 is blank verso and recto. However, this simple account of the MS conceals a possibly quite complex story, though not one that can be reconstructed with any certainty. The verso of leaf 2 is clearly numbered by Charles as page '2' and the numbering is then consecutive up to and including the recto of leaf 6 (numbered as page '13'). The numbering then stops, though in fact there is material written on the verso of leaf 6 and on the recto and verso of leaf 7, which one would have expected to be numbered pages 14–16. Further, the last three lines on Charles's page 13 are written in shorthand, and that shorthand continues over the page for a further four lines. The rest of that page is then left blank and the sermon restarts on the recto of leaf 7 with a new sentence. This is a confusing state of affairs. Why would Charles have stopped numbering the pages and left such a large gap? Why would he have reverted to shorthand at one point in the MS? It may be conjectured that the reason was this: Charles was copying his brother's MS in a fairly mechanical way up to the point where the shorthand section begins. However, at this point he felt that some reference to the Quietists was appropriate, given that he had just written/copied a section relating to the relative importance of the internal and external aspects of the religious life. He thus introduced into the sermon a section of his own, written in shorthand, relating to the views of those who rejected the 'outward parts of our most holy religion'. This section continues overleaf for four more lines, at which point Charles broke off, though he left himself space to continue

---

[1] See Albin, 'Charles Wesley's other 'Prose Writings', 89.   [2] MARC CW Box 5.

with his interpolation at a later point should circumstances require it. He then returned to his brother's copy to restart at the top of the recto of leaf 9. This section actually follows on perfectly well from the section before the shorthand and struck-out longhand. He did not, however, restart the numbering of the pages, since he was aware that he might actually insert another leaf should the space available on the verso of leaf 8 prove insufficient for any further editorial additions he might wish to make.

This reconstruction is highly conjectural, but it is not inherently unlikely, and it does explain the physical evidence. The alternative hypothesis is that Charles simply went into shorthand to copy this part of his brother's MS since it dealt with a sensitive area, left 80 per cent of the verso of leaf 8 blank for no particular reason and concurrently forgot to number the pages. This is of course not impossible, but is hardly compelling.

This sermon was among those published in the 1816 edition,[3] and like the others in that volume, shows the hand of the later editor. The shorthand section referred to above is absent in its entirety, and a comparison of the material following this shorthand section in the MS itself and in the 1816 edition reveals remarkable divergence. There is no need to give a full account of those differences here, but the reader may wish to compare the last paragraph in the MS with that of the 1816 edition.

Though this sermon is not dated by Charles, it appears to be relatively early. The content reflects the pessimistic soteriological uncertainty and an emphasis upon works as leading to a potential 'reward' that characterizes the other sermons already given that can be clearly dated to the period in America. In the MS (though not in the 1816 edition) the last sentence includes the prayer that the Christian may 'attain the reward of the Lord' and this language of 'rewards' for things done is found dotted throughout the rest of the text. Christ is felt more by his absence than his presence and the blood of Jesus is not mentioned at all.[4] This is not, then, in all probability, a sermon which Charles would have preached very naturally after May 1738. The key themes of the wider evangelical revival in general, themes which find adequate echo in the evangelical sermons of Charles Wesley, of the blood of Christ and the assurance of personal salvation, are missing.

---

[3] *Sermons*, 68–80.

[4] Simple word statistics have been avoided to this point as they are a relatively poor way of latching onto Charles's conceptual framework. However, it is somewhat surprising that in this sermon 'blood' is not used at all, 'Jesus' appears but once and 'Christ' only twice.

I say unto you that except your righteousness shall exceed the righteousness of the scribes and
Pharisees, ye shall in no case enter into the kingdom of heaven.

These words are a part of that divine sermon which our blessed Lord delivered
from the mount to the people, who, having seen the mighty and wonderful works
he had done in the towns where he had preached, followed him in crowds and
pressed upon him, to see the signs he wrought and to hear the doctrine he
preached. These, therefore, he instructs in the perfection of that religion he came
into the world to establish, and shows how infinitely it exceeded all other religious
dispensations, wherewith mankind till then had been blessed. And as the people to
whom he spoke were all of them Jews, and had a high veneration for the religion
of their fathers, he chiefly compares his commands with those of Moses, to convince them how far even the law and the prophets fell short of that religion which
the Son of God himself came to establish. And as all the people of Israel were wonderfully prepossessed with the high notions of the scribes and Pharisees, whom
they supposed to be ~~excellent~~[2] exalted patterns of piety, and religious perfection
he informed them that holy and eminent as they thought those men to be yet the
meanest servant of Christ must infinitely surpass them in righteousness and
true holiness or else he could never hope to be made partaker of the kingdom of
heaven. 'For except your righteousness exceed the righteousness of the scribes and
Pharisees ye shall in no case enter into the kingdom of heaven'. In discoursing on
which words I shall

I.   Show wherein consisted the righteousness of the scribes and Pharisees.

II. Consider in what instances all Christians are obliged to exceed them and

III. Conclude with some practical inferences from the whole.

The scribes as we may learn from several passages of holy scripture, were for the
most part learned doctors and teachers of the law who sat in Moses's seat,[3] and
explained those portions of holy scripture to the people which through their blindness and weakness of understanding they would otherwise have remained ignorant
of. They are sometimes called by the name of Rabbi, which signifies master, one
that had been brought up in the schools of the prophets, and was licensed[4] to teach
a set of disciples or followers the weighty matters of the law.[5]

The Pharisees were the strictest sect of the Jews, men who obliged themselves
to the most exact observation of the things required by the law and who distinguished themselves even by laying their lives under some restraints, that were not

---

[1] The date is written in shorthand in the MS; it appears only as 'jn' with a dot so positioned over the
n as to indicate a contraction. One might read rather 'June'. However, January seems fairly secure since
on that day John Wesley preached a sermon on this very text.

[2] This mistake suggests that Charles is copying this text, read 'ex', assumed 'excellent' but then had
to correct to 'exalted'.   [3] Cf. Matt. 23: 2.

[4] This word is not entirely clear in the MS. However, 'licensed' looks probable.   [5] Matt .23: 23.

obligatory and denying themselves such liberties, as were by the law allowed to the people, and hence they derive their name from a word which signifies to distinguish or separate.[6]

Now both these sets of men, we may imagine, pretended to extraordinary degrees of piety. The very name of Pharisee implies a recluse person, or one who separated or distinguished himself from his brethren by the wonderful strictness of his life and conversation. And we can scarcely imagine those scribes, who were trusted with the education of young people, could be other than sober and ~~religious~~ moral as well as grave and learned men. And indeed we find their character to be agreeable to this. They were remarkable for leading exemplary lives and possessing strict doctrines. They observed great severity and sanctity of behaviour,[7] were regular and constant in their attendance upon the public offices of religion, fasted and prayed often and gave much alms. They were zealous for the law even to excess, and reverenced the institution thereof as divine appointments deserve to be reverenced. In short there was nothing in their outward behaviour but what was edifying and exemplary. They showed the greatest regard to God, the strictest veneration to things and persons appropriated to his service and the sharpest resentment of any profanation of them. Such was the holiness of the scribes and Pharisees which our saviour declared not to be sufficient to bring any one to the possession of his kingdom. And this brings me to my

II General Head

Wherein I am to show in which instances all Christians are required to exceed these scribes and Pharisees.

1. We see their great external regularity, ~~is such as might well be proposed to a Christian's imitation~~. Their zeal for religion, their severity of manners and their reverend and decent ~~behaviour~~ deportment are[8] such as might well be proposed to a Christian imitation. But yet they are patterns which we must not be content to equal, but we must infinitely exceed them or our righteousness will avail us nothing in the great day of accounts. True it is the Christian religion doth require an exemplary behaviour, an external reverence to God and holy things and all possible demonstration of our piety and virtue. But it stoppeth not here. Its chief residence is in the heart of its professors, and there is it designed to work the greatest change. Its principal aim is to convert the sinner, to rectify his mind and to alter the most prevailing tempers of his soul. And herein is the grand difference between the righteousness required of Christians, and that which was practised by the scribes and Pharisees. Theirs was an outside holiness; our[s] is commanded to be an holiness

---

[6] Charles is here referring to the commoly held view that the name 'Pharisee' is derived from the Hebrew root 'prsh' meaning 'separate'.

[7] These words are written 'of behaviour and sanctity' in the MS. However, the numbers '3, 4, 1, 2' have been inserted respectively, indicating that Charles would have read 'and sanctity of behaviour'.

[8] 'Are' is a correction for 'is' in the MS; it is not clear whether this correction is the work of Charles himself.

of the heart. Their virtue consisted in their sanctified actions; ours is required to proceed from upright intentions. Their works of piety were done to be seen of men, whereas ours must be performed to please our father which is in heaven.[9] In short the scribes and Pharisees looked upon external holiness as all that was required of them, whereas the Christian is taught principally to regard the state and disposition of his heart and to consider his outward behaviour only as a testimony and proof of the internal spirit and temper he is of. For instance the learned scribe and proud Pharisee would think he had sufficiently done his duty to God, by having been present at his public worship, but the humble and pious Christian knows that God will not accept a religion which is confined to time and place or has any regard to such holiness as is bounded by the walls of the Church. No! his conscience tells him that holy devotions without an answerable purity of mind are so far from being pleasing to God that they are rather an abomination in his sight. Indeed devotion, if it consist in no more than bodily worship and the prayers and thanksgivings of our lips, is a solemn mockery rather than a humble adoration of God, and therefore must be expected rather to draw down his sorest vengeance than his kindest pity[10] ~~blessing~~ upon us. In short any[11] instance of piety whose best merit consists in the decency of performing it is perhaps the piety of the scribes and Pharisees but not of Christians.

2. Another instance wherein the righteousness of Christians is to exceed that of the scribes and Pharisees is in the extrusiveness of it. Any Christian who is pious upon principle and whose virtue proceeds from the purity of his heart will quickly see the necessity he lives[12] under of letting his behaviour be all of a piece and taking care that one part of his life doth not contradict the other.[13] The scribes and Pharisees made long prayers but at the same time they devoured widows' houses.[14] They paid tithe of mint, anise and cummin, and in this they did well; but then they neglected the weightier matters of the law, judgment, justice and truth.[15] In short they were pious as far as ceremonies and modes of worship were concerned, but impious and profane in their common life. And herein is the Christian required to exceed them. He is commanded to do every action with the same spirit as he performs his devotions. The glory of God is the end that he proposes in his prayers and the same sacred purpose is to be the rule of every part of his life. We have an apostolical precept to regulate the most ordinary, as well as necessary, actions of

[9] Cf. Matt. 6: 1–5; 23: 5.

[10] The words 'pity' is not clear in the text, being partly obscured by a smudge.

[11] The word 'any' has been inserted above the line and replaces a word that has been struck out. The struck-out word is largely obscured, but appears to be 'no'. The correction does not appear to be in the hand of Charles, though this judgement is not certain.

[12] The word 'lives' is not entirely clear in the MS.

[13] The words 'letting his behaviour be all of a piece and taking care that one part of his life doth not contradict the other' have been altered in the MS in what is clearly another hand. The words of the alterations are unreadable.   [14] Cf. Mark 12: 40 and parallels.

[15] Cf. Matt. 23: 23 and parallel.

our lives by this rule[16] 'Whether ye eat or drink ~~saith~~ or whatever ye do, do all to the glory of God'[17] and therefore he must be a very loose casuist who can find an exception to this glorious rule; or point out any actions of a Christian which are not to be tried by it. And whoever thinks that he needs only to have a view to the glory of God, whilst he is in the immediate act of worshipping him, may perhaps lay claim to the righteousness of scribes and Pharisees, but has certainly no title to that of Christians. The religion which the blessed Jesus established was designed to shine forth in the lives as well as the public devotions of its professors; and therefore every one who prays to God with devotion and solemnity at church and yet at the same time lives without God everywhere else may please himself with the name of Christian, but, be assured, has nothing else to boast of. He neither feeleth the power of Christ in his soul, nor has any lot or portion in that glorious inheritance which is prepared for those who love and fear him.[18]

3. A third instance, wherein our righteousness is to exceed the righteousness of the scribes and Pharisees is the motive from whence it proceeds. They fasted and prayed and did alms to be seen of men,[19] and were pious for the sake of that reputation which they gained among their brethren for being so. They made use of their religion to be a cloak to their iniquities.[20] The end of it extended no farther than the world, their honour and their interest being the only views they proposed by it. And therefore of them doth our saviour justly say 'verily I say unto you they have their reward.'[21] But the piety of Christians is founded on a nobler principle and proceedeth not from a view of human interest, but from the pure love of God. This must be the foundation of every holy action and design, if ever we hope to be rewarded for it, the love of God must be the reason why we desire to please him, or else that our desire can never be fulfilled: for any exercise of piety, any acts of devotion, which are performed with another view lose all their excellency. For instance, should we comply with the worship of God, because it has custom and the practice of the world to recommend it; should we regulate our actions by the rules of God's commandments, for fear of growing scandalous to our neighbours; ([22]should we comply with the established modes of worship and submit to the use of the stated service of God for the sake of entitling ourselves to some place of honour or profit: I say should any of these be the motive to piety; what thanks should we deserve for our holiness? We justly condemn the gross profaneness, and monstrous hypocrisy of those dissenters, who can occasionally conform to the service of our[23] church, for the sake of enjoying the privileges and immunities of her members, and just such our sentiments ought to be of all those, who have any other motive to piety and holiness than a desire of pleasing God founded upon a

---

[16] The words 'this rule' have been struck out in the MS and replaced by one or two other now unreadable words. The hand does not appear to be that of Charles himself.   [17] 1 Cor. 10: 31.

[18] Cf. 1 Cor. 2: 9.   [19] Cf. Matt. 6: 1–5; 23: 5.

[20] This is possibly dependent upon Matt. 23: 5, 25, 28.   [21] Matt. 6: 2, 5, 16.

[22] At this point in the MS Charles has added a square bracket. See n. 24 below.

[23] The word 'our' is not clear in the MS, but seems probable.

sincere love of him).[24] This piety may be admired by the world, but it will never be accepted of him who searcheth the heart and knoweth not only the actions of men, but likewise discerneth those secret springs and motives to them, even the thoughts and intentions of the soul.[25]

I have now shown wherein the righteousness of the scribes and Pharisees consisted, and in what instances Christians are required to exceed them. It remains to draw a practical inference or two from what has been said. And

1. We have seen that great exactness and rigour wherewith the scribes and Pharisees adhered to all the outward ordinances of the law. And from hence may Christians learn the great veneration and esteem which is[26] due to the institutions of the New Testament. The ordinances of the Jewish Church were but types and figures of those of the Christians, and therefore are we more immediately concerned, not to let the Jews exceed us in the reverence they paid to[27] them. The scribes and Pharisees may in this case be admitted as patterns to Christians. For they were scrupulous in adhering to every the least jot or ceremony of the law, and so far their zeal is laudable and recommended to us by our blessed Lord himself who speaking of their tithing mint and anise and cummin, is pleased to say that these things ought to be done, but at the same time the other weightier matters were not to be left undone.[28] True it is,[29] the inward spirit of Christianity is to be principally regarded, and the greatest danger is that men will trust too much to external duties; even so far as to neglect the religion of the heart: ~~but yet we have had those among us~~[30] who[31] have dared to ridicule and pass their buffooning jests upon the outward parts of our most holy religion; reflecting not only upon the sermons but even not sparing the ordinance and sacraments, and the wanton impiety and profane scoffs of these pretenders to learning may be accounted to be a sufficient vindication of these actions, and a stronger proof of the necessity that lies upon every Christian to beware how he either superstitiously adopts the use of externals on the one hand or profanely and enthusiastically rejects them on the other.[32]

---

[24] Square bracket in the MS; Charles may have marked this section out for omission in the spoken form of the sermon. Some of the words enclosed in the brackets are present in the 1816 edition, but here, as elsewhere, the section has been heavily edited.   [25] Cf. 1 Chron. 28: 9.

[26] The word 'is' has been corrected to 'are' in the MS. The correction does not appear to be that of Charles himself.   [27] The word 'to' has been inserted above the line.

[28] Cf. Matt. 23: 23 and parallel.

[29] This sentence is somewhat ambiguous. However, if the words 'true it is' are taken as an introductory clause and the second 'is' taken as the main verb, the sentence does make sense. The insertion of 'that' after 'true it is' would perhaps clarify things.

[30] The words 'but yet we have had those among us' have been struck out in the text, though probably not by Charles himself. The words which follow this introductory phrase are in shorthand and if the shorthand is omitted the words 'but yet we have had those among us' must also be deleted from the text.

[31] From here to the end of the paragraph the MS is written in shorthand. It may well be an insertion by Charles. I am grateful to Oliver Beckerlegge for checking my transcription of this passage and offering valuable suggestions.   [32] This is the last word in the shorthand section.

Christianity is a religion designed for men and not for angels and therefore its worship is partly spiritual, partly bodily, and on this account may we see the reasonableness of that direction given to every professor of it, glorify God in your bodies as well as your spirits since they both of them are God's.[33]

2. We have seen that strict as the lives and conversation of the scribes and Pharisees were, yet they were not accepted for want of sincerity. From hence learn we the great value of that cardinal virtue and the great account it is of in the sight of God. Are we but sincere in our profession and offer to God our best services we have the strongest assurance of being accepted: but for want of this the strictest life and most perfect[34] obedience becomes of none effect and is even abominable in the sight of God. Hypocrisy is of all others the most odious sin; its baleful influence extends the farthest, and its poison is noxious enough to blast our best performances. The scribes and Pharisees were careful and vigilant in their duty. They forced themselves through the labour and difficulties of religion, and endured the toil and danger of good servants of their Lord and master. And yet are they by him rejected, because their holy services were all performed for by-ends and undertaken with sinister views. And let it[35] teach us carefully to try our ways and nicely[36] to examine the state of our own hearts, that so, we may not only see that we are religious, but approve ourselves to be so upon Christian principles, that so at length we may attain the reward of our Lord and not be condemned to those woes which are pronounced to the scribes and Pharisees, hypocrites[37] and deceivers and to all who hold the truth in unrighteousness.

---

[33] Cf. 1 Cor. 6: 20.

[34] An unreadable word has been added above the line at this point in the MS, but not in Charles's hand.

[35] The word 'it' has been inserted in the left hand margin. The insertion does not appear to be the work of Charles himself.

[36] The word 'nicely' has been struck out in the text and replaced by another word. That word is unclear, but appears to be 'accurately'. The alteration does not seem to be the work of Charles himself.

[37] Cf. Matt. 23: 13 ff.; Luke 11: 44.

SERMON 16
MATTHEW 6: 22–3

INTRODUCTORY COMMENT

This is a sermon which Charles preached several times, both in America and in England. The earliest date given is 14 March, 1736, when Charles preached it in Frederica (the date is confirmed in the journal).[1] The latest is 1 May, 1737, when he preached it in Oxford.[2] The other dates are given as 23 May, 1736 (in Savannah)[3] and 24 April, 1736 (Aston and Wickham).[4] Charles preached on the same topic on 13 March, 1746, but it is not certain that he used this MS.[5]

There is no doubt that this is a sermon which Charles copied from John. He says as much in a shorthand note at the conclusion. According to this he transcribed it on 4 February, 1736, while still on board the *Simmonds*. John had composed the sermon at sea and in the wake of a storm, but also in anticipation of a safe arrival in America.[6] The extent to which Charles altered his brother's sermon in the process of transcription cannot be ascertained. However, as is often the case, there is some textual evidence that he did do so. This is brought out more fully in the notes to the sermon itself, but we may note here in passing that Charles's numbering of the paragraphs is not consistent. For example, under the 'second head' he has points 1–3 in order. Point 4 is point 4ᵃ and what was originally listed as point 5 has been changed to point 4. These changes appear to be in the hand of Charles. There is then no point 5, one point 6 and two points 7. Of course this may be interpreted as being simply sloppiness in transcription on Charles's part, but if so it is rather uncharacteristic. Alternatively, one might suggest that Charles has omitted John's original point 5 and expanded his point 4 into two separate points (now points 4ᵃ and 4). Point 6 has been left as it was. Charles has then added his own point 7 and also left John's intact, but failed to 'correct' the original numbering. This is no more than speculation, but it is not unreasonable, and no less likely than simply assuming that Charles was sloppy, which would not itself explain his use of 4ᵃ and 4. There has also been an addition at the end of point 2 and the words to be inserted have been written on the verso of the preceding leaf. Again, this might just indicate that Charles was less than careful and had to backtrack to make a

[1] See MARC DDCW 10/2 *in loc.*; Telford, *Journal*, 11. 'I preached with boldness on singleness of intention to about 20 people among whom was Mr O[glethorpe].'

[2] There is no entry in Charles's journal for that day, but as stated above the journal makes it clear that he was in the Oxford region at this time.

[3] There is no entry in Charles's journal for that day. However, on 19 May he wrote 'According to our agreement, my brother set forward for Frederica, and I took charge of Savannah in his absence' (MARC DDCW 10/2 *in loc.*; Telford, *Journal*, 51).

[4] The date of '1736' must be an error, since he was still in America at that date. There is no entry for 24 April, 1737, but other entries make it plain that he was in the Oxford area around this time. The 'Aston' to which he refers is about 15 miles from Oxford. Wickham has not been traced.

[5] See MARC DDCW 10/2 *in loc.*; Jackson, *Journal*, i. 410. 'God confirmed the word, while I enforced the necessity of a single eye.'   [6] See further Outler (ed.), *Sermons*, iv. 371 n. 1.

correction. Alternatively, he may have re-read the sermon at some point subsequent to his original transcription and felt that it needed a few further words of comment and explanation at this point.

The MS of this sermon is held at the John Rylands University Library of Manchester.[7] It comprises ten stitch-bound leaves, mostly written recto only. The exceptions are leaf 5, which has the addition to point 2 discussed above, and leaf 1, which forms the front cover; on the verso of this is a note concerning the date and location of the sermon's delivery in America. The information is written also on the recto. The hand of 'W.P.' is clearly visible at several points on the front cover, and there has been some emendation in a hand other than Charles's in the text as well. These later changes are indicated in the notes below.

The sermon was published as sermon VIII in the 1816 edition[8] and as usual there are significant differences between the form in the MS and in that edition. No attempt is made here to indicate all of these changes or suggest possible reasons for them. We note only in passing the editor's addition of a few significant words to a sentence found on page 128 of the 1816 edition. Charles originally wrote

> The sum is this: as long as thou hast but one end in all thy thoughts, and words, and actions, to please God, or, which is all one, to improve in holiness, in the love of God and thy neighbour; so long thou shalt clearly see what conduces thereto.

In the 1816 edition these have been modified, only slightly in terms of words, but significantly in terms of theology, to

> The sum is this: so long as thou hast but one end in all thy thoughts, and words, and actions, to please God, or, which is all one, to improve in his ways of holiness, in the love of God, and of thy neighbour; so long thou shalt clearly perceive what is conducive to it.

The key difference is of course the addition of the words 'his ways of' before 'holiness'. The precise theological intention of the editor is unclear, but the addition of these words at the very least puts the emphasis upon the action of God rather than the action of the individual. The 'ways of holiness' are God's, not the individual's. Further, at the risk of over-stressing the significance of the change, one might even suggest that there is potentially quite a difference theologically between 'improving in holiness', a phrase which suggests an increase in the overcoming of sin, and 'improving in his ways of holiness', where the emphasis could be upon prayer and faith. The sermon is also printed in Outler's edition of the sermons of John Wesley.[9] The few relatively minor slips in that transcription have been corrected here.

This sermon was preached only five days after Charles's arrival in America on 9 March 1736. It is not surprising, then, that it reflects the new situation in which he and his fellow travellers found themselves. The basic point is plain: God has brought the people to the place they would be, and they must now consider the way forward from this point. Charles here urges his audience to give God the place he rightly deserves. They are to serve him with all their might. Their intention must be single, for God will not be served by halves. It is plain, then, that this is a sermon well suited to its context in the lives of the colonists. The basic message is one that Charles had preached before (see Sermon 2), but it has been adapted for the new situation.

---

[7] MARC cw Box 5 (Outler gives a reference to the Colman collection, which is in error).
[8] *Sermons*, 125–35.   [9] Outler (ed.), *Sermons*, iv. 371–7.

Sermon Register[1]

Matt. 6.22, 23—A Single Intention

Preached at Frederica in the Island of St Simon's Georgia in the forenoon March 14, 1736 1[2]

Preached, 1, at Savannah[3] in Georgia May 23, 1736 in the morning

Aston, & Wickham April 24, 1736.

Castle in O[xford] May 1, 1737[4]

I.N.D.[5]

Matthew 6: 22, 23

The light of the body is the eye: if therefore thine eye be single, thy whole body shall be full of light. But if thine eye be evil, thy whole body shall be full of darkness.

1. The good providence of God hath at length brought you all unto the haven where you would be. This is the time which you have so long wished to find; this is the place you have so long desired to see. What then ought to be your thoughts, your designs, your resolutions, now God has given you your heart's desire? Consider well what ye have to do; now choose, whether ye will serve God or not. But consider withal that if ye do serve him, ye must do it with all your might. Consider that no man can serve two masters; ye cannot serve God and mammon.[6] Either therefore ye must give God your whole heart, or none at all; he cannot, will not, be served by halves.[7] Either wholly lay aside the thoughts of pleasing him, and choose you another master, or let the pleasing him be your one view in all your thoughts, all your words, and all your actions. Believe our Lord, you can find no middle way; 'The light of the body is the eye. If therefore thine eye be single, thy whole body shall be full of light; but if thine eye be not single, but evil, thy whole body shall be full of darkness'.[8]

I am persuaded there is not one of you here, from the least even to the greatest, who will not earnestly attend while in the name of that God who hath hitherto defended us, and is now present with us, I first briefly explain these important words of our Lord, and secondly, apply them to your present circumstances.

1. And, first, may the God who spoke them enable me so to explain them that the meaning thereof may sink deep into your hearts. 'The light of the body is the

---

[1] This information is repeated inside the front cover. On the dates given here see the introduction to this sermon.

[2] This '1' is plain on the MS, both here and on the following line, but its meaning unclear.

[3] This information is given on the inside of the front cover as 'Savannah May 23, 1736'.

[4] There also appears on the front cover the number '4', not obviously in Charles's own hand. 'W.P.' has also left his familiar mark 'Exd W.P.' and several notes. These read 'Frederica March 14 1736—Savannah May 23' and 'on occasion of their arrival (local)'. In another hand the letters CW appear in large script.   [5] *In Nomine Dei*; see the note on Sermon 3.

[6] Cf. Matt. 6: 24 and parallel.   [7] A theme worked out in detail in Sermon 2.

[8] Matt. 6: 22–3.

eye;' that is, the intention is to the soul what the eye is to the body. As every part of the body is directed when and how to move by the eye, so every power of the soul is in all its motions[9] directed by the intention. As every turn of the foot or hand depends on and is governed by the bodily eye, so on this eye of the mind depends every deliberate movement of the understanding, and the affections, and consequently of whatever depends upon these, as do the very most both of our words and actions.

2. 'If therefore thine eye be single'; that is, if thy intention be not divided between two ends; if in all thy thoughts, words, and works, thou hast one only view, namely, to serve and please God: 'thy whole body shall be full of light.' This single intention will be a light in all thy paths: all darkness and doubt will vanish before it. All will be plain before thy face. Thou wilt clearly see the way wherein thou shouldst go, and steadily walk in it.

3. 'But if thine eye be evil', if thy intention be not single, if thou hast more ends than one in view; if, besides that of pleasing God, thou hast a design to please thyself, or to do thy own will; if thou aimest at anything beside the one thing needful,[10] namely, a recovery of the image of God: 'thy whole body shall be full of darkness;' thou wilt see no light, which way soever thou turnest. Thou wilt never be free from doubt and perplexity; never out of uncertainty and entanglement. As thou art continually aiming at what cannot be done, thou wilt be continually disappointed. The thick darkness of ignorance, guilt, and misery, will gather about thee more and more, nor wilt thou be able, while[11] encompassed with such a cloud, ever to recover the way of light and peace.

4. The sum is this: as long as thou hast but one end in all thy thoughts, and words, and actions, to please God, or, which is all one, to improve in holiness, in the love of God and thy neighbour;[12] so long thou shalt clearly see what conduces thereto. The God whom thou servest shall so watch over thee that light, and love, and peace, shall guide all thy ways, and shine upon all thy paths. But no sooner shalt thou divide thy heart, and aim at anything beside holiness, than the light from which thou turnest away, being withdrawn, thou shalt not know whither thou goest. Ignorance, sin, and misery shall overspread thee, till thou fall headlong into utter darkness.

II.1. To apply these words to your present circumstances was the next thing I proposed. In order to do which the more effectually I shall, by the assistance of God, first, give you some directions concerning the singleness of intention, and secondly, exhort you to practice them.

2. I would not willingly believe that any of you need to be directed to have a single eye in your religious exercises. To aim at the favour or praise of men, or indeed

---

[9] Outler has 'motion'; however, 'motions' is clear in the MS.
[10] Cf. Luke 10: 42, which is the subject of Sermon 21.
[11] The word 'while' has been inserted above the line.   [12] Cf. Mark 12: 30–1; Luke 10: 27.

at anything beside the mere pleasing of God, in communicating,[13] prayer, or any other duty of the like nature, is such an affront both to God and man that we should be very cautious of charging anyone with it, yea, even in our heart. It may be enough therefore barely to mention to you that there is no name bad enough for[14] the folly of those who, in any of these solemn offices, have any other view than to please God, and to save their own souls.

2.[15] But you are not perhaps so well aware that the same singleness of intention is full as necessary in every part of your business as it is in your devotions; and yet this is the very truth. Unless your single view therein be to please God, and to be more holy, the most lawful business becomes unlawful to you, and is an abomination in his sight. For it is no more allowed a Christian to work with any other intention than it is to pray. And a mixture of any other does as much pollute our work as it does our prayers. Everything that proceeds from and is suitable to this intention is holy, and just, and good,[16] and everything which does not proceed from this is so far wicked and unholy. This, therefore, is the second direction I would give, to keep a single intention in all your business, which indeed turns all business into religion, which ennobles every employment, and makes the meanest offices of life a reasonable sacrifice, acceptable to God through Jesus Christ.[17]

3. Nor is a single eye less necessary in our refreshments than it is in our business and our devotions. As every creature of God is good if it be sanctified by the Spirit of God and by prayer,[18] so without this sort of prayer at least, an intention to please God by using it, no creature is good, nor can be used without hurt to the user. And lest[19] we should fancy meat and drink were too little things for God to have any regard to,[20] he has been pleased to cut up this pretence by the roots by

---

[13] The word 'communicating' has been struck out in the text and replaced by the word 'sacrament'. This alteration is not in Charles's hand. Outler notes that 'communicating' has been replaced by 'the sacrament', though the definite article is not present in the MS.

[14] The words 'bad enough for' have been struck out in the MS and replaced by the words 'sufficiently expressive of'. The alteration is not in the hand of Charles (and is not noted by Outler).

[15] The paragraph is misnumbered in the MS. That misnumbering has been retained here. Outler renumbers, as can be seen in his use of square brackets, but does not explain his policy on this point. The misnumbering may be accidental. However, it is worth considering the possibility (though it is only that) that point '2' above is Charles's insertion and that the second point '2' indicates Charles's return to his brother's MS. This possibility is strengthened by the statement Charles makes in the paragraph numbered '4' below to the effect that this is the 'fourth' direction that needs to be made.

[16] Cf. Rom. 7: 12.

[17] As Outler notes, this whole sentence has been written by Charles on the verso of the preceeding leaf. Outler suggests that this may indicate that here we have an insertion by Charles himself into his brother's sermon, which is a reasonable enough point. From it comes another: once Charles is allowed an editorial foot in the door, the question must be asked 'at what other point or points has Charles left his mark?' To the question there is no unequivocal answer, but the fact that it can be raised is in itself important. Charles, as Outler notes, seems to have edited his brother's work in the process of transcription. Here then is a text which may be taken as reflective of Charles's views, even if it is built upon the earlier work of his brother. This whole topic is discussed more fully in Chapter 4.

[18] Cf. 1 Tim. 4: 4–5.   [19] Corrected from 'least' in the MS.

[20] The words 'have any' and 'to' are struck out in the MS to leave the reading 'for God to regard' (the reading given by Outler).

giving you this third direction in express terms: 'Whether ye eat or drink, or what-soever ye do, do all to the glory of God.'[21]

4. 'Whatsoever[22] ye do'? That plainly takes in our diversions[23] as well as refreshments. A fourth direction therefore equally necessary is, 'let the same singleness of intention be preserved in these, likewise: go through these too with a single[24] view to the will of God, not your own'.[25] It is his will you should use them in such a manner and measure as they prepare you for business or devotion. So far therefore as your present weakness makes them necessary to this end you are to use them, but no farther. And you will clearly see how far they are necessary to this, if this be the single end for which you use them.

5.[26] One direction more is very necessary to be given before we close this head; and that is, that you are above all concerned to keep a single eye in your conversations. Whether devotion or business be the subject thereof, or whether you converse for refreshment or diversion,[27] in all these cases you are equally obliged to do all to[28] the glory of God. Whatever conversation has not this aim cometh from the evil one. That[29] is, an idle word; or conversation, rather, as the term should be translated. And of every such idle word, our Lord plainly tells us before, we shall give an account in the day of judgment.[30]

6. I have now given you the plainest directions I could wherein this singleness of intention is to be preserved. Nothing remains but to exhort you instantly, zealously, and diligently to practise them.

7. The God of your fathers hath lately given you full proof that he hath not forsaken you or your children. Your eyes have seen that his ears are not heavy that they should not hear, neither his hand shortened that it cannot save.[31] Ye have cried unto him in your trouble, and he hath delivered you out of your distress.[32] He hath led you through the terrors of the great deep: he there made bare his mighty arm before you.[33] At his word the stormy wind arose, and lifted up the waves thereof.[34]

---

[21] Cf. 1 Cor. 10: 31.
[22] Charles originally wrote 'whatever', but inserted 'so' at an appropriate place above the line to indicate 'whatsoever'.
[23] The word 'diversions' has been struck out in the MS and replaced by 'recreations'. The change is not in Charles's hand and is not noted by Outler.
[24] The word 'single' has been struck out in the MS and replaced by 'simple'. The alteration is not in Charles's hand and is not noted by Outler.
[25] There are no quotation marks in the text; they have been added here for the sake of clarity.
[26] At this point the numbering system seems to be have been altered by another hand. The paragraph is numbered '5' in the MS (corrected to '6' by Outler), but has been changed to '4' in another hand. It appears to be the same hand that wrote 'on whatever other subjects you may converse' below.
[27] At this point in the text the words 'on whatever other subjects you may converse' have been written in at the bottom of the page. The words are not in Charles's hand and are not noted by Outler.
[28] The words 'do all to' have been struck out in the MS and replaced by 'aim at'. The change is not in Charles's hand and is not noted by Outler.
[29] The word 'that' has been struck out in the MS and replaced by the word 'it'. The change is not in Charles's hand and is not noted by Outler.   [30] Cf. Matt. 12: 36.
[31] Cf. Isa. 59: 1.   [32] Cf. Ps. 107: 13.   [33] Cf. Isa. 52: 10.
[34] Cf. Ps. 107: 25.

We reeled to and fro, and staggered like drunken men, and were at our wit's end.[35] But[36] he 'made the storm to cease, so that the waves thereof were still'.[37] 'He hath prepared a table for you[38] in the way wherein you went; even there with corn and wine hath he sustained you.'[39] Some of you he hath delivered out of sickness. To some he hath forbidden sickness to approach. To all of you, who allowed them to be any blessings at all, hath he given abundance of spiritual blessings. Yea, in these he hath been found of them that sought him not;[40] he hath spoken to the heart even of those who asked not after him.[41] And now, behold, to complete all, he hath brought you unto the haven where ye would be.[42]

7.[43] 'What reward then will ye give unto the Lord, for all the benefits he hath done unto you?'[44] What? Why, give him your hearts; love him with all your souls; serve him with all your strength.[45] Forget the things that are behind:[46] riches, honour, power; in a word, whatever does not lead to God. Behold, all things about you are become new![47] Be ye likewise new creatures! From this hour at least let your eye be single: whatever ye speak, or think, or do, let God be your aim, and God only! Let your one end be to please and love God! In all your business, all your refreshments, all your diversions, all your conversations, as well as in all those which are commonly called religious duties, let your eye look straight forward to God. He that hath ears to hear, let him hear![48] Have one design, one desire, one hope! Even that the God whom ye[49] serve may be your God and your all, in time and in eternity! O be not of a double heart! Think of nothing else! Seek nothing else! To love God, and to be beloved by him, is enough. Be your eyes fixed on this one point, and your whole bodies shall be full of light. God shall continually lift ~~you~~ up, and that more and more, the light of his countenance upon you.[50] His Holy Spirit shall dwell in you, and shine more and more upon your souls unto the perfect day.[51] He shall purify your hearts by faith from every earthly thought, every unholy affection. He shall establish your souls with so lively a hope as already lays hold on the prize of your high calling.[52] He shall fill you with peace, and joy, and love! Love, the brightness of his glory, the express image of his person![53] Love which never rest [sic],[54] never faileth, but still spreads its flame, still goeth on con-

---

[35] Cf. Ps. 107: 27.

[36] Above the word 'but' there appear another word or words in the MS that have been struck out. Those words (or word) are unclear, but appear to be 'yea it'. The change does not appear to be the work of Charles.   [37] Cf. Ps. 107: 29 (*BCP*).

[38] Cf. Ps. 23: 5.   [39] Cf. Gen. 27: 37.   [40] Cf. Rom. 10: 20 (Isa. 65.1).

[41] Cf. Isa. 65: 1.   [42] Ps. 107: 30 (*BCP*).

[43] Here again the numbering of the paragraphs is inconsistent, perhaps the result of Charles's editorial hand.   [44] Cf. Ps. 116: 11 (*BCP*).

[45] Cf. Mark 12: 30, 33 and parallel citing Deut. 6: 4. This text is the subject of Sermon 20.

[46] Cf. Phil. 3: 13.   [47] Cf. 2 Cor. 5: 17.

[48] This is a refrain used frequently in the New Testament; see for example Mark 4: 9, 23.

[49] Outler has 'we'; however, 'ye' is clear enough in the MS.   [50] Cf. Num. 6: 26; Ps. 4: 7 (*BCP*).

[51] Cf. Prov. 4: 18.   [52] The language of this sentence reflects Phil. 3: 14 and 1 Pet. 1: 3.

[53] Cf. Heb. 1: 3; Col. 1: 15.   [54] Outler corrects to 'rests'.

quering and to conquer,[55] till what was but now a weak, foolish, wavering, sinful creature, be filled with all the fullness of God![56]

From[57] my brother's copy; transcribed February 4, 1736 on board the Simmonds within sight of Carolina. D.G.[58]

[55] Cf. Rev. 6: 2.   [56] Cf. Eph. 3: 19.
[57] Charles's record of transcription is in shorthand in the MS.
[58] *Deo Gratias*—Thanks be to God.

SERMON 17
LUKE 16: 8

INTRODUCTORY COMMENT

Charles's sermon on Luke 16: 8 comes from his period in America. The MS carries annotation to the effect that it was 'preached at Frederica May 9. 1736'[1] and again at Savannah on 25 July of the same year, which was Charles's last full day in Georgia.[2] A shorthand note at the end indicates that Charles has transcribed the text, though from what source he does not say; it reads simply 'transcribed May 6. 1736 at Frederica'. There is no entry in the journal for 6 May 1736; however, as Outler notes,[3] Charles did transcribe John's sermon on John 13: 7 (Sermon 18 below) on 7 May 1736, which indicates that he was working with his brother's MSS at this time.

The fact that Charles indicates that he has transcribed this sermon clearly raises the question of authenticity. This subject has been discussed already and need not be entered into again here. Suffice it to say that even if this is a copy of another's sermon (as opposed to, perhaps, a fair copy of one of his own MSS—an hypothesis worth considering) it yet reveals something of Charles's own theological persuasion and homiletic art for, as has been argued already, there is every reason to think that he did far more than copy out word for word the texts of which he made use. In this context his use of square brackets in the MS text ought to be noted carefully. Their function is far from clear; they do not bracket off any words or phrases that seem in themselves significant. It may be that these were words that Charles felt might be omitted in the spoken form of the sermon should that seem appropriate in view of the time and the audience. Alternatively, and this also seems a perfectly plausible suggestion, they may contain Charles's own interpolations into the text from which he is transcribing.[4] Certainly these words can be omitted when reading the text with no obvious hiatus.

The MS for this sermon is held at the John Rylands University Library of Manchester.[5] It comprises sixteen leaves made from eight folded sheets. These have been stitch-bound to form a small booklet. The text of the sermon is found on leaves 2–16, which have been written recto only. Leaf 1 forms the front cover and has information written verso and recto. The MS is in a good state of repair, though leaves 1 and 16 have become detached, and there are no missing sections. There is some strike-through but it can, with one exception indicated below, be reasonably confidently recovered.

---

[1] This annotation appears in both shorthand and, immediately below it, longhand. There is no reference to the preaching of this sermon in Charles's journal entry for that day, which was a Sunday. John was in Savannah (*J&D*, xviii. 157–8) so this is not an account of his preaching of the text.

[2] There is no reference to the preaching of this sermon in Charles's journal entry for that day, which was a Sunday. It was the day upon which he resigned his post as secretary to General Oglethorpe and his last in Georgia.   [3] Outler (ed.), *Sermons*, iv. 360.

[4] See further the notes to the text itself.   [5] MARC CW Box 5.

It is something of a surprise that this sermon was not included in the 1816 edition, and the reasons for that omission can only be guessed at. It may have been that the editor did not have access to the MS. It is clear that the body of material in what is now CW Box 5 is not the same as that to which the editor of the 1816 edition had access, since there is no MS in that box for the sermon on Luke 16: 10, and yet a transcription of it appears in the 1816 edition. It may be, then, that the MS of this sermon was not available. However, it has been argued above that the editor of the 1816 edition was 'W.P.' If so, it must be noted that this same 'W.P.' has left his initials on the MS of this sermon too. If 'W.P.' was the editor, then, he did have access to the MS and must therefore have chosen not to include it in the collection. Why that should be is not clear.

This sermon was published by Outler in his edition of John Wesley's Sermons.[6] The more significant of the changes to the Outler text are indicated in the notes.

The main point is plain: those who seek to serve God and find thereby salvation must do so with their whole hearts, minds and souls (there is an obvious overlap here with Sermons 2 and 16 on 1 Kings 18: 21 and Matthew 6: 22–3). The form this argument takes is quite contrary to what one might expect, and Charles must have been confident that his audience would be able to pick up and appreciate the irony with which his argument advances. The children of this world seek the things of this world and know how to pursue this goal with integrity. They know what they want and seek wholeheartedly to achieve it. In this sense they are wiser than many professed Christians who, though they know the goal for which they must strive, do not seek it with due diligence or clarity of focus. In Charles's words

> The thing directly asserted is this, that notwithstanding their want of true wisdom (that wisdom which is from above) they are, however, wiser in their generation than the children of light. That is, that however they are befooled in the choice of their end, yet they make more prudent provisions for its attainment, and prosecute it by more apt means, and with greater cunning and diligence, than they who have chosen a better do theirs.

[6] Outler (ed.), *Sermons*, iv. 360–70.

Sermon Register[1]

VII[2]

Preached at Frederica May 9, 1736[3]
Preached at Frederica May 9, 1736[4]
at Savannah, July 25, 1736

In the sixteenth chapter of S. Luke's Gospel, at the eighth verse, it is thus written:

The children of this world are in their generation wiser than the children of light.

In these words there is something implied and something directly asserted. It is implied,

First, that there are a sort of men who are children of this world, that is, who make the good of this world their end, and seek no further for their rest and happiness. It is implied again, on the other side,

II, that there are a sort of men who are children of ~~this world~~ light, who look beyond this black vale of misery,[5] and propose to themselves the happiness of another life as their true and last end. It is implied,

III[ly], that the former of these are not absolutely wise, but only wiser in their generation.

IV. The thing directly asserted is this, that notwithstanding their want of true wisdom (that wisdom which is from above) they are, however, wiser in their generation than the children of light. That is, that however they are befooled in the choice of their end, yet they make more prudent provisions for its attainment, and prosecute it by more apt means, and with greater cunning[6] and diligence, than they who have chosen a better do theirs. Of these in their order.

And, I, it is implied, that there are a sort etc.[7] 'Tis indeed strange that there should be any such, considering that the world is no proper boundary for the soul, even in its natural capacity, much less in its spiritual: it is too cheap and

---

[1] This information is found on the inside of the front cover of the MS. On the front cover itself there appear, in Charles's hand, a reference to Luke 16: 8 followed by the words of the text 'the children of this world are in their generation wiser than the children of light' written first in longhand and then repeated in shorthand. The number (9) also appears on the front cover, though the hand does not appear to be that of Charles himself, and 'W.P.' has written '1736 at Frederica and Savannah, May 6, July 25 Ex[d] W.P.'.   [2] The meaning of this number is not clear.

[3] This entry is in shorthand. See the introduction to this sermon for this and the following date.

[4] This duplicate entry is in longhand.

[5] Before 'misery' there appears in the text another word that has been deleted. The word is unclear, but would appear to be 'va', probably indicating that Charles was mistakenly about to write again 'vale'. Cf. Ps. 84: 6 (*BCP*).

[6] The word 'cunning' is struck out in the text and replaced by 'craft'. The amendment does not appear to be the work of Charles himself and is omitted by Outler.

[7] Charles presumably intended here that the words found under 'First' above ('that there are a sort of men who are children of this world, that is, who make the good of this world their end, and seek no further for their rest and happiness') should be read again at this point.

inconsiderable a good for an immortal spirit, much more for a divine nature. And therefore, did not the commonness of the thing take off from the wonder, it would seem no doubt as great a prodigy to see a man make the world his end as to see a stone hang in the air. ⟦⁸For what is it else for a man, the weight of whose nature presses hard towards a stable and never failing center,⁹ to stop short in a fluid and yielding medium, and take up with the slender stays of vanity, and lean upon the dream of a shadow?¹⁰ I say, why is not this to be looked upon as equally strange and preternatural as a stone's hanging in the air?⟧ Is not the air as proper a boundary for a ~~soul~~ stone as the world is for a¹¹ soul? And why then is not one as strange as the other? For in the first place, one would think it next to impossible that a man who thinks at all should not frequently and thoroughly consider the vanity and emptiness of all worldly good, the shortness and uncertainty of life, the certainty of dying, and the uncertainty of the time when; the immortality of the soul, the doubtful and important issues of eternity, the terrors of damnation, and the glorious things which are spoken and which cannot be uttered of the city of God.¹² These are meditations so very obvious, so almost unavoidable, and that so block up a man's way, and besides they are so very concerning,¹³ that the wonder is how a man can think of anything else. And if a man does consider these things, one would think it yet more impossible that he should make so vain a thing as this world his end; that he should think of building tabernacles of rest on this side [of] the grave, and say, 'It is good to be here.'¹⁴

But whether it is that men do not heartily believe such a thing as a future state of happiness and misery, or do not actually and seriously consider it, we are too well assured from experience that there are such men in the world: men who going through the vale of misery use it not only as a well¹⁵ to refresh and allay, but fully to quench and satisfy their thirst; 'who mind and relish earthly things';¹⁶ who

---

⁸ This and the other struck-out square brackets in the MS are omitted by Outler. It is, however, of some possible significance. If all the material enclosed in the brackets is omitted, the text still reads well and without any obvious hiatus. Indeed, despite the fact that the section enclosed in the square brackets is a fairly long one, the words which immediately precede and follow that section seem to run together very well indeed. It would read, 'And therefore, did not the commonness of the thing take off from the wonder, it would seem no doubt as great a prodigy to see a man make the world his end as to see a stone hang in the air. [. . .] Is not the air as proper a boundary for a stone as the world is for a soul?'

It might quite reasonably be conjectured, then, that the words enclosed in square brackets are those that Charles himself has added to his brother's MS. If this is not the reason for the square brackets, they must have some other significance. Perhaps Charles, aware of the constraints of time, edited the MS in this way to indicate to himself what sections might be omitted in the interests of economy. The same is true of the other sections enclosed in square brackets at other points in the MS.

⁹ The spelling of 'center' has been corrected to 'centre', though probably not by Charles himself.

¹⁰ Pindar, *Pythian Odes*, 9. 95–6; I owe this reference to Outler (ed.), *Sermons*, iv. 362 n. 5.

¹¹ Before 'a' there appears the superscripted sign '†'. This corresponds to a note written in at the bottom of the page which reads 'an immortal soul'. The hand is clearly not that of Charles, and is omitted by Outler.   ¹² Cf. Ps. 87: 3.

¹³ The word 'concerning' has been struck out in the text and replaced by 'important'. The change does not seem to be the work of Charles himself. Outler (iv. 362) has 'important', but offers no comment on the ambiguity of the MS at this point.   ¹⁴ Cf. Mark 9: 5 and parallels.

¹⁵ Cf. Ps. 84: 6 (*BCP*).   ¹⁶ Cf. Phil. 3: 19.

make the good of this world their last aim, the sum total of their wishes, ⊦[17]the
upshot of their desires and expectations, their end; who love it as they are commanded to love God, with all their heart, soul, mind, and strength;[18] who rest and
lean upon the world with the whole stress and full weight of their being, who outdo
the curse of the serpent,[19] and whose very soul cleaves to the dust.[20]

For (I demand) is not the interest of this animal life the great governing principle
of the world?[21] Is not everything, almost, reckoned profitable only so far as it
conduces to some temporal interest, insomuch that the very name 'interest' is
almost[22] appropriated to worldly advantage? And is not this the great bias of
mankind? Do we not see men all set and intent upon the world, that lay themselves
out wholly upon it, and can relish nothing but what has relation to it; men that
seem to grow into the soil where they dwell, and to have their heads and hearts
fastened to the ground with as many cords and fibres as the root of a tree; and that
seem to be staked down and nailed fast to the earth, and that can no more be
moved from it than the earth itself can from its centre? In one word, men of whom
it may be said (without censure) that the world is their God, and its pleasures,
honours, and profit, their Trinity.

⊦To our experience we may add the attestation of scripture in proof of[23] this
low-sunk, wretched, and deplorable degeneracy of soul. So Job: 'If I have made
gold my hope, or said to the fine gold, Thou art my confidence' (Job 31.24),[24]
implying that some there were that did so. And does not the Psalmist say
(Ps 52.8),[25] 'Lo, this is the man that took not God for his strength, but trusted in
the multitude of his riches, and strengthened himself in his wickedness'? And does
not the Apostle tell us of some 'whose God is their belly' (Phil 3.19), and of others,
'whose godliness is their gain' (1 Tim 6.5)?[26] And what else does he mean when he
says of covetousness that it is idolatry,[27] than that the covetous wretch not only
delights in his possessions, but places his end and chief happiness in them, that he
falls down and adores his golden calf,[28] makes gold his hope, and[29] says to the fine
gold, 'Thou art my confidence'!⊦[30]

But the minds of men (thanks be to God)[31] are not all under this eclipse, nor is
this darkness spread over the whole face of the deep.[32] ⊦[33]Light and darkness divide

---

[17] There is no closing ']' to match this opening one. It may be that Charles simply forgot to close off
this insertion.   [18] Cf. Mark 12: 30 and parallel; this text is the subject of Sermon 20.

[19] Cf. Gen. 3: 14.   [20] Cf. Ps. 119: 25.

[21] Outler has a semicolon in the place of the question mark at this point. The question mark is clear
enough in the MS.   [22] After 'almost' Outler adds [always] to the text.

[23] Originally spelt 'off', but corrected to 'of'.

[24] This and the subsequent references in parentheses are written in the text.   [25] BCP.

[26] The reference is actually to 1 Tim. 6: 6 and the quotation is not verbatim KJV. Charles may have
been quoting from memory at this point.   [27] Cf. Col. 3: 5.

[28] Cf. Exod. 32.

[29] An ampersand has been inserted above the line and replaces a word that has been so heavily struck
out as to make it unreadable. That word appears to be 'or'. Outler has 'and' but offers no comment on
the ambiguity of the MS at this point.   [30] Job 31: 24.

[31] Outler inserts an exclamation mark following 'God'.   [32] Cf. Gen. 1: 2.

[33] The struck-out square bracket is omitted by Outler.

the moral, as well as the natural world, though with the difference of unequal proportions—the darker is here the bigger[34] side.} There are, {however}, though not many, yet there are,

II. Secondly, a sort of men who are children of light; whose minds are more enlightened, and their eye more clear and single; who look beyond the veil of the material world, the beauty of which can neither charm, nor its thickness detain their piercing sight, and propose to themselves the happiness of another life as their true and last end. This ~~many~~ all Christians[35] do in profession, and some few in reality; aiming indeed at the right mark, though all of them have not a hand steady enough to strike it.

III. But to return again to the children of this world. It is implied, in the third place, that these are not absolutely wise, but only that they are wiser in their generation. Indeed they think themselves wise, and the world for the ~~world~~ most part is of their opinion. They are generally esteemed, not only wise, but the only wise men; men of reach[36] and design, policy, and conduct. Nay, hence, and hence only, are taken the measures of wisdom and prudence, and this is made the rule and standard of all policy and discretion: a man is counted so far wise and no farther than he knows how to get[37] an estate, or raise a family, or give birth to a name, and make himself great and considerable in the world. He that can do this is a shrewd man, and he that cannot is either pitied or laughed at by those that can.

But whatever the opinion of ~~the world~~[38] men may be, we are assured by the Apostle that 'the wisdom of this world is foolishness with God.'[39] And the Psalmist, speaking of worldly-minded men that think their houses shall continue for ever, and call their lands after their own names, says expressly, 'This is their foolishness.'[40] {[41]And this censure he boldly charges upon them, how singular soever it might seem, and though not only the present generation of men should vote them wise, but even their posterity, those of more improved reasonings and more enlarged experience, should 'praise their saying'.}[42]

Thus light do these men weigh in the balance of the sanctuary: nor will they be found to be less wanting in that of reason. For how can they deserve the title of wise men who are out in the very first and leading part of wisdom, the choosing of a right end? This is such a mighty flaw as nothing that comes after can make up. When once a man has fixed [for][43] himself a wrong end, he has cut out a false

---

[34] The word 'bigger' has been struck out in the MS and replaced by 'larger'. The change does not appear to be the work of Charles himself.

[35] 'All Christians' has been written above the line to replace 'many'. The change is in the hand of Charles.

[36] The word 'reach' has been struck out in the MS. However, the mode of strike-out (here three horizontal lines) is not that generally used by Charles.

[37] The word 'get' has been struck out in the MS and replaced by 'gain'. The change is not in the hand of Charles and is not noted by Outler.   [38] These struck-out words are not noted by Outler.

[39] Cf. 1 Cor. 3: 19.   [40] Cf. Ps. 49: 11–13 (BCP).

[41] The struck-out square bracket is not noted by Outler.   [42] Cf. Ps. 49: 13 (BCP).

[43] The word 'for' has been inserted above the line. The addition does not appear to be the work of Charles himself.

channel for the whole course of his life, which must needs be ever after one constant blunder; and though he be never so ingenious afterward to compass this end, his wisdom comes too late, and does but serve to ensure and hasten his ruin. The ship indeed has good sails, there is nothing wanting in the executive part; but steering to a wrong point, it has this only advantage from them: to be dashed upon the rock with the greater speed and violence.

[44]I now proceed, in the fourth place, to the thing directly asserted in the text, which is that, notwithstanding the want of true wisdom in the children of this world, they are however wiser than the children of light. Or, in other words, that however they are befooled in the choice of their end, yet they make more prudent provisions for its attainment, and prosecute it by more agreeable means, and with more cunning and diligence, than they who have chosen a better do theirs. They come vastly short indeed of the children of light in the first part of wisdom, the choice of a right end, in which respect the child of light has as much the precedence in point of wisdom as heaven is better than earth; but then they exceed them as much in the second, the choice and application of right means.

[45]I shall first show the probability that it should be so, and then prove that it is so.

For, first, the good things of this world are present, those of the other remote and distant. ⟨How far distant we do not know, and are therefore apt to fancy the farthest remove, like travellers that think the way always longest where they are the greatest strangers.⟩ W̶ Now we know a present good has a great advantage above a far distant and late reversion. For the good that is present opens itself all at once to the soul, and acts upon it with its full and entire force; there is not so much as a ray of its light but what strikes us. But now that which is future is seen by parts and in succession, and a great deal of it is not seen at all, like the rays of a too distant object, which are too much dispersed before they come at us, and so most of them miss the eye. ⟨This makes the least present interest outweigh a very considerable reversion, since the former strikes upon us with the strong influence and warmth of the neighbouring sun, the latter with the faint and cold glimmerings of a twinkling star.⟩

Then, secondly, the good things of this world, as they are present, so do they strike upon the most tender part about us, our senses. They attempt[46] us, as the devil did Adam, in our weaker part, through the Eve of our natures. A sensible representation is the strongest of all representations. A sensible representation, even of the vanity of the world, would work more with us than the discourse of an

---

[44] Outler adds the required 'IV' at this point in the text.

[45] Outler adds '1.' to the text at this point.

[46] The word 'attempt' has been struck out in the MS and replaced with 'attack'. This change does not appear to be the work of Charles himself. Outler does not note the ambiguity at this point, though he does note that the verbal form 'to attempt' had the possible meaning of 'to attack' or 'to tempt' in eighteenth-century English (Outler (ed.), *Sermons*, iv. 366 n. 26, citing Johnson's Dictionary).

angel about it; what then shall we think of the glory of it, when so represented? How would that affect[47] and subdue us?[48]

And this the devil very well knew and considered when he was to tempt the Son of God to[49] covetousness and ambition.[50] In order to[51] this he might have entertained him with fine discourses about the wealth and glories of the terrestrial globe. But he knew his advantage better than so, and chose rather to draw a visionary landskip[52] before him, knowing by old experience how much more apt the senses are to take impression than any other faculty of man.

Now this is the great advantage that the good things of this world have: they are obvious to our senses; we see them, we hear them, we smell them; we taste them, we feel and handle them, and have the most intimate and endearing conversation with them. 'The things that are temporal are seen;' ~~it is their distinguishing character~~[53] 'but the things that are eternal are not seen,[54] but only through a glass darkly',[55] and in reference to the other world, 'we walk by faith, and not by sight.'[56]

[57]I come now in the second place to prove that the children of this world are more heartily concerned for the attainment of their end than the children of light for theirs.

And here, first, we find by experience that the men of this world do *prefer* their secular interest above all other things whatsoever, in every instant of action, in all junctures and circumstances. Though their *end* be false, yet *they* are not so, but keep true to it, and always prefer it. They will adhere to it at any rate, they will forfeit any good, and undergo any evil, to secure this their grand stake. For this will they not[58] rise early, and late take rest; drudge and toil, plot and contrive, cheat and defraud, lie and dissemble, be of any religion or of no religion, and submit to all the basenesses[59] imaginable? Will they not incur the curses of the widow and orphan, the contempt of wise men, the hatred of mankind, the censures of posterity, the displeasure of God, and even damnation itself, for the sake of their beloved mammon? They will. They will bustle through[60] all this, and will gain their point, though they lose everything besides. {And herein they are consistent with themselves; they act agreeably to their principles.}

---

[47] Outler (iv. 336) reads 'attest', but 'affect' looks more probable in the MS.

[48] Outler has an exclamation mark in place of a question mark at this point. The question mark is clear enough in the MS.

[49] Outler has 'in' in place of 'to' at this point. The word 'to' is clear enough in the MS.

[50] Cf. Matt. 4: 8 and parallel.

[51] The infinitive form 'to do' or 'to accomplish' seems intended here.

[52] i.e. 'landscape'; see Outler (ed.), *Sermons*, iv. 366 n. 28.

[53] Outler omits the struck-out words from the body of the text, but includes them in a footnote (iv. 367 n. 29). It is impossible to be certain whether Charles deleted these words himself, though the mode of striking out (a single horizontal line) is that which he normally employs.   [54] Cf. 2 Cor. 4: 18.

[55] Cf. 1 Cor. 13: 12.   [56] Cf. 2 Cor. 5: 7.   [57] Outler adds '2.' to the text at this point.

[58] The word 'not' has been struck out in the text. It is not clear whether this change has been effected by Charles himself. Outler does not note the ambiguity.

[59] Outler has 'baseness' at this point. The plural 'basenesses' is clear enough in the MS.

[60] The words 'bustle through' have been struck out in the text and replaced by 'despise'. This alteration does not appear to be the work of Charles himself and is not noted by Outler.

But will the children of light do as much for their end? Will these part with the world for heaven, as the other will part with heaven for the world? Will these do or suffer anything for the interest of their souls, as the other will for that of their bodies? Some few there are that will; and God[61] add to their number. But are there not many who have proposed to themselves heaven for their end, yet when they come to have any other considerable interest ~~come~~ brought[62] into competition with ~~that~~ it, will they not then suffer a present interruption of their former judgment, and actually undervalue what they habitually prefer? Will they not enter into a cloud of darkness and obscurity, lose the present light of their former convictions, and so act as foolishly as those that never had any better principles? Will they not prove false to their cause and to themselves, refuse to take up the crown for fear of the thorns that guard it, and choose rather to lose heaven than to be translated thither in a fiery chariot?[63] Yes, it is to be feared that most of them ~~would~~ will, and that of those many who have proposed heaven as their end, there are but few that would have the courage to be martyrs for it.

Again, secondly, the children of this world, as they will spare no pains, so will they lose no time or opportunity for the securing a temporal interest. They greedily seize upon the next minute, and make haste to be rich, though by doing so they know they shall not be innocent. They know well that the present time is the only time they are masters of, and that they may reckon upon as their own; and therefore ~~that~~ they will be sure to improve it[64] and not trust to the uncertainties of futurity. Let but a question arise about their title to their estate, and they cannot sleep till it be cleared up. Let but a place of dignity or profit fall, and with what expedition do these eagles repair to the carcase![65] They take the wings of the morning,[66] perhaps of the night too, and fly as if running for a prize or chased by an enemy.

But now are the children of light such prizers of time, and such improvers of opportunity? 'Twere well if they were. But what is more common than to see men who have set their faces Sionward, and propose heaven as their end, to put off their repentance from day to day, to delay their preparations for eternity, and to sleep securely in a doubtful, and sometimes in a damnable and irreconciled ~~shape~~ state; and all this though they know how short and uncertain their lives are, that it is but a breath, and[67] a vapour,[68] that soon passes away, and we are gone. Though they know that there is but this one time of probation, and that 'there is no work, nor device, nor knowledge, nor wisdom, in the grave' (Ecl 9: 10), though they know that 'Now is the accepted time, that now is the day of salvation' (2 Cor 6: 2).

---

[61] Before 'God' the word 'may' has been inserted above the line (and is included by Outler in his text). However, the hand does not appear to be that of Charles himself.

[62] The word 'come' has been struck out in the text and replaced by 'brought'. This change does appear to be the work of Charles himself. Outler does not note it.   [63] Cf. 2 Kgs. 2: 11.

[64] The word 'it' has been inserted above the line.

[65] These words may have been influenced by Matt. 24: 28 and parallel.   [66] Ps. 139: 9.

[67] The ampersand which appears in the text at this point has been struck out. However, the mode of strike-out (here two vertical lines) is not that employed by Charles himself. Outler does not include 'and' at this point; nor does he note the ambiguity of the text.   [68] Cf. Jas. 4: 14.

Again, thirdly, the children of this world, as they will lose no time, so neither will they let slip any other advantage of advancing their fortunes. They twist their own interest with the interest of their friends, seek out for all helps, and make early preparations for every accident. Nor do they foresee danger more suddenly than they provide against it. Thus the unjust steward, when he foresaw that he should quit his office, he made an interest with his lord's debtors, by under-rating their accounts, that so when his master should discard him, they might receive and harbour him.[69]

But ~~now~~ are the children of light so careful to make use of all helps and means that may further them in the attainment of their great end? Such as the grace of God, happiness of temper and complexion, good education, well-disposed circumstances of life, the good example of others, advice of spiritual persons, and the like? Besides, are they so frugal and forecasting for the future? Are they so careful in the day of grace to lay up in store against a spiritual famine; in the days of peace to store themselves with spiritual armour against the time of persecution?[70] In the time of life and health, to provide against the hour of sickness and death, and by a wise dispensation of the fading and unrighteous mammon to procure[71] for themselves everlasting habitations?[72] Are they? Everyone's experience may assure him that they are not.

Once more: the children of this world, as they catch at all advantages that may further their grand affair, so are they withal as careful to avoid all occasions of loss and damage; they love to tread upon firm ground, shun hazards as well as actual misfortunes, and will not so much as come within the possibility of danger.

But do the children of light take the same care to avoid all appearances of evil, all spiritual dangers, all occasions and temptations of sinning against God and their own happiness? We pray indeed that God would not lead us into temptation:[73] but do we not often lead ourselves into as bad as the worst of those we can pray against? We venture often times causelessly and rashly within reach of the devil's chain, and are not afraid to stir up and awake that roaring lion.[74] We love to play with danger, and to hazard our virtue and innocence,[75] by needless and doubtful trials. So much do the children of this world exceed the children of light in wisdom.

Thus it is, and to our shame we must confess it: we are utterly distanced in the race, and see the prize of wisdom borne[76] away before us. We have indeed in our eye a much nobler mark, but we want a steady hand. Our end is better than theirs, but our management is not so good. And what a shame is it for us that have

---

[69] Cf. Luke 16: 1–8.   [70] Cf. Eph. 6: 13.

[71] The words 'to procure for' have been deleted in the MS and are replaced by 'to lay up for'. This alteration does not appear to be the work of Charles himself and is left unnoted by Outler.

[72] Cf. Luke 16: 9; the words 'everlasting habitations' have been deleted in the MS and replaced by 'heaven', but the alteration is not in Charles's hand.   [73] Cf. Matt. 6: 13 and parallel.

[74] Cf. 1 Pet. 5: 8.

[75] The words 'virtue and innocence' have been altered in the MS by what appears to be a hand other than Charles's. The amended reading gives 'piety and virtue' with 'and innocence' being struck out.

[76] Corrected in the MS (not in Charles's hand) from 'born'.

proposed a greater and a better end, and are also more instructed in the choice of means, ⟨which are pointed out to us by God himself⟩, to be yet so far outwitted by those of lower aims, and who are fain to study and contrive their own means, and whose wisdom after all is foolishness with God![77] And yet thus it is, the Devil's scholars are better proficients than Christ's disciples; the ark falls before Dagon,[78] and light is outshone by darkness.[79]

What therefore remains, but that since we will not learn in Christ's, we should be sent to the Devil's school, and imitate the politics of the dark kingdom, and of the children of this world? Not in the choice of the end, which indeed is very poor and low, but in that wisdom, diligence, and care wherewith they prosecute it, and be as wise at least unto salvation, as they are to destruction.

Let us then be as wise as these serpents:[80] and since we have chosen the better part,[81] and are so nigh to the kingdom of God,[82] let us not, for the want of one thing, miss of being completely wise and happy. But as we have made a good choice, let us prosecute it with equal prudence; so will our wisdom be whole and entire, uniform and consistent, blameless and unreprovable; in a word, that wisdom which shall be 'justified of all her children'.[83]

Transcribed May 6. 1736 at Frederica.[84]

---

[77] Cf. 1 Cor. 3: 19.   [78] Cf. 1 Sam. 5: 4.   [79] A reversal of John 1: 5.
[80] Cf. Matt. 10: 16.   [81] Cf. Luke 10: 42. This text is the subject of Sermon 21.
[82] Cf. Mark 12: 34.   [83] Cf. Matt. 11: 19 and parallel.
[84] These words appear in shorthand. On the final page of the MS there appear also the words 'The first principles strongly and correctly inferred; and the style highly characteristic of the man'; these latter words are not in Charles's hand. They are signed 'H.M.'

SERMON 18
JOHN 13: 7

INTRODUCTORY COMMENT

In a shorthand note at the conclusion of this sermon, Charles has indicated that he transcribed the text from his brother's copy on 7 May 1736 in Frederica. This is useful in that
it gives some indication of the date of Charles's interest in the subject matter. However,
there is no indication on the MS itself regarding where or when Charles preached from this
text. To date no further information has come to light from the journal or letters. The fact
that he chose to copy this sermon, when others were presumably available to him, should
not be ignored; it indicates that the subject matter was to his liking.

The transcription is a very clean one. There are few corrections other than of obvious
slips (for example 'which' is corrected to 'why' at one point). The only disruption in paragraph numbering comes under head 3. Point 2 under this head is divided by Charles into
'2a' and '2b', which may suggest some interpolation into the text. This is discussed further
in the note to the text itself.

The MS is located at the John Rylands University Library of Manchester.[1] It comprises
seventeen[2] leaves made from eight stitch-bound folded sheets plus a front cover which has
now become detached from the booklet. This front cover may also have been originally
formed from a folded sheet; if so the back cover with which it would have been joined has
now been lost. Leaves 2–16 are written recto only. Leaf 17, however, has a brief shorthand
note written verso. This relates to John's preaching of the sermon.

It was published as sermon VI in the 1816 edition.[3] The form that it takes in that edition,
however, is as usual rather different from the MS itself. For example, following a statement
regarding the absolute inability of humankind to understand how it is that the Holy Spirit
is prepared to intervene in the life of one person in response to the prayers of another, the
editor has added several examples from the Old Testament showing that the Holy Spirit
does act in this way—examples which are not found in the MS.

Outler printed this text in his edition of John Wesley's sermons[4] and provides good information regarding the place of this sermon in the life and thought of John Wesley. He comments that the sermon was first preached by John at All Saints in Oxford on 1 November
1730. However, Charles has recorded on the recto of leaf 17 (in shorthand) that the sermon
was also preached, doubtless by John rather than himself, at Epworth and Stanton in that
year, and these two entries are written above the entry for All Saints. There is also a note
indicating that it was preached in Manchester in '5', presumably 1735. These and the few
other relatively minor transcription errors in Outler have been corrected here.

---

[1] MARC CW Box 5.
[2] Outler (ed.), *Sermons*, iv. 280 states that the MS comprises sixteen leaves, which is in error.
[3] *Sermons*, 95–113.   [4] Outler (ed.), *Sermons*, iv. 281–9.

The focal point of this sermon is the limits of human knowledge. The argument put forward is that human knowledge provides great pleasure. However, it should be realized that this knowledge is severely limited and that this is the way God has ordained it to be. There is a promise of understanding 'hereafter' but this promise is for the future not the present state of humankind. Consequently human knowledge cannot know how God works. It cannot know how the earth hangs upon nothing, or how the lights of the heavens maintain order despite the passing millennia. (This has an obvious relevance in the context of developments in eighteenth-century philosophy and science.) Neither can humankind know why God acts in certain ways, why, for example, he has permitted evil in his good creation. However, this limitation in human knowledge serves a purpose, for by limiting the extent to which humankind can know God the risk of pride is also limited—it was just such a pride that brought Lucifer down. The individual becomes dependent upon faith.

In[1] the thirteenth chapter of the Gospel according to St. John, at the seventh verse, it is thus written:

'What I do thou knowest not now, but thou shalt know hereafter.'

It is ~~not~~ easy to observe that one of the earliest principles in the soul of man is a desire of knowledge. This often attains to considerable strength before reason shakes off its infant weakness. This it is which insensibly leads us on to improve and perfect our reason, which, by the present pleasure it gives, encourages us to seek, and makes us capable of receiving more.[2]

So long as this is contained within proper bounds and directed to proper objects, there is scarce in the mind of of [*sic*] man a more delightful or more useful inclination. The pleasures it yields are without number; the field of knowledge hath no ~~bounds~~ end; and in almost every part of it springs up some plant not only pleasing to the eyes and rejoicing the heart, but of use to make one wise, to give the true wisdom, to enlighten the eyes,[3] to enlarge the heart, to make us see the all-wise, the all-merciful God in every one even of these his lowest works.

It is[4] true, this source of generous, lasting pleasure may by accident give us much pain, if our desires either fix on improper objects, on any of those parts of knowledge which, as they were not designed for man in this station, cannot be obtained by him till his removal into another, or if his desire of useful knowledge, even of knowing his Creator, be not kept within proper bounds. He who lays out his search even on the ways of God, and will not be content till he has searched them out thoroughly, will not be satisfied till he knows them all, will never be content, never satisfied on this side the grave. For what soul is that which, clogged with flesh and blood, can find out the Almighty to perfection?[5] No, it will not be; we may trust what God himself affirms of the ways of God: 'What I do thou canst not know now, but thou shalt know hereafter.'

This assertion, though uttered by our Lord upon a particular account[6] to one of his disciples, may, if well understood and duly remembered, be of great use to all his followers. Should a perplexing thought arise in any of our hearts touching any of the ways of God, or the reasons of them, should our soul be troubled because unable to comprehend them, we might[7] immediately silence it with this reflection:

[1] These are the first words of the sermon itself. However, on the front cover of the booklet, in long-hand, are written the words 'John 13.7 What I do thou knowest not now, but thou shalt know hereafter'; these are repeated in shorthand immediately below. Also on the front cover there appears the number '6' in brackets and the words (not in Charles's hand) '~~No date, 1738 at Islington, Sept 24~~ 1736 preached in America' and the familiar 'Ex. W.P.' On the date see the Introduction to this sermon.

[2] The word 'more' has been inserted above the line.   [3] Cf. Gen. 3: 6; Ps. 19: 8.

[4] Outler has ''tis' in place of 'it is' at this point. 'It is' is clear in the MS.   [5] Job 11: 7.

[6] The word 'account' has been struck out in the MS and replaced with 'occasion' (the reading given by Outler). However, this change does not appear to be in the hand of Charles himself.

[7] The word 'might' has been struck out in the MS and replaced by 'may' (the reading adopted by Outler). However, this change does not appear to be in the hand of Charles himself.

'Peace; this is an unavoidable evil. What God doth thou canst not know now. Or rather, it is no evil at all, for thou shalt know hereafter.'[8]

Man[9] cannot know now, either

I.   First, how God works in numberless cases which are daily before his eyes, or

II.   Secondly, why other things are done by him which yet he is fully sensible are done. After having mentioned a few instances of our ignorance in each of these particulars,

III.   I intend, thirdly, to offer some reasons why we may suppose this ignorance to be a[10] portion; which why[11] God has pleased to ordain that, as to most of his ways, we cannot know them till hereafter.

I.   First, we cannot know till hereafter how God works in many cases which are daily before our eyes. We know not, for instance, how it is that he holds the world in its present state, 'how he spreadeth the north over'[12] the empty space, and hangeth the earth upon nothing';[13] 'how he teacheth the sun his certain seasons, and maketh the moon to still to know his going down';[14] how he sustaineth those other great lights which continually float in the firmament of heaven; how he balances them, so that no force can shake them, and so ranges their innumerable armies that every one keeps his appointed station, and constantly runs his appointed race; that though each of them has moved so many thousands of years, with that inconceivable swiftness, yet each still preserves exactly its due rank, its due distance from all others; that amidst the infinite variety of their motions there is the most perfect regularity; no confusion, no injuring each other, but all is order, harmony, and peace.[15]

It is true, they who are too knowing to own they know nothing of it, say all this is done by a power unknown to the old philosophers; that this holds the universe together, and all the hosts of heaven keep their courses because they continually gravitate with such a determinate force towards each other. How clearly do these explain the ways of God?[16] How plentifully[17] do they declare the thing as it is! We grant all things do gravitate towards each other with a force proportioned to their quantity of matter. That this is done we know: but we ask how it is done? We ask

---

[8] Cf. John 13: 7.

[9] The word 'man' is the first word on page 3 of the MS. Before it appear the letters 'D.G.' (*Deo Gratia*).

[10] The word 'a' has been struck out in the MS and replaced by 'our' (the reading adopted by Outler). However, this change does not appear to be in the hand of Charles himself.

[11] Charles first wrote 'which', which he then changed to 'why'.

[12] The MS appears to have 'o're' at this point (perhaps 'o'er' was intended). This has been struck out and the word 'over' written in above the line. It is not clear whether this correction is the work of Charles himself.   [13] Cf. Job 26: 7.

[14] Cf. Ps. 104: 19.

[15] Charles actually wrote 'harmony, peace and order'. He then inserted the numbers '2', '3', and '1' over them to indicate that they should be reversed. This point is not noted by Outler.

[16] Outler has an exclamation mark at this point in place of the question mark. The question mark is clear in the MS.

[17] The word 'plentifully' has been struck out in the MS and replaced by 'satisfactorily' (the reading adopted by Outler). However, this change does not appear to be in the hand of Charles himself.

what this gravity is? What is this secret chain by which all parts of the universe are so firmly and durably connected![18] What is this universal spring to which all earth and heaven submit? What is this attraction, this tendency in every natural body to approach to every other? We know it is the law of nature; it is the finger of God,[19] and here our knowledge ends.

2. Not that we need go up to heaven or down to the deep for instances of man's ignorance in the ways of God; they are nigh thee, even in thy heart;[20] nay, in the most inconsiderable, the most obvious parts of thy own body. Who knoweth how God holdeth his soul in life? How he encloseth spirit in matter? How he so intimately joins two substances of so totally different natures? How he who established it at first, so still preserves that exact dependence of one on the other? Who knows how the thought of his inmost soul immediately strikes the outmost part of his body? How an impression made on the outmost part of his body immediately strikes his inmost soul? How a consciousness in the mind of having done anything amiss instantly spreads a blush over the cheek? How the prick of a needle on the hand immediately occasions a painful thought in the soul?

Man is all a mystery to himself. That God does work wonderfully in him he knows, but the manner of his working he cannot know; it is too wonderful for his present capacity. Whether he surveys his own hand or heart or head, he sees numberless footsteps of the Almighty; but vainly does he attempt to ~~search out~~ trace them up to their spring: 'clouds and darkness are round about it.'[21]

As vainly does man attempt to search out how God works in him the life of grace. The springs whence we draw spiritual life are at least as unsearchable as those of the natural. That it is the Divine Spirit 'who worketh in us both to will and to do of his good pleasure',[22] of this ~~both~~ experience, and reason, and Scripture convince every sincere enquirer. But how he worketh this in us, who shall tell? Who shall point out his particular methods of working? This indeed we know, that when the passions are laid, and our souls are calm and still, then chiefly the Spirit of God loves to move upon the face of the waters;[23] yet are we not able to explain how he moves. Darkness is upon the face of the deep.[24] 'The wind bloweth', as our Lord observes, 'where it listeth, and thou hearest the sound thereof, but canst not tell whence it cometh, nor whither it goeth.'[25]

If there be any particular work of the Holy Spirit which we can tell less of than the rest, it seems to be his influencing one person in answer to the prayers of another. That he does pour a larger measure of his blessed influence upon us at the request of those in whom he is well pleased he hath given us sufficient ground to

---

[18] The exclamation mark is clear in the MS, though a question mark would be more appropriate (and Outler supplies one).   [19] Cf. Luke 11: 20; Deut 9: 10.
[20] Cf. Deut. 30: 12–14.   [21] Cf. Ps. 97: 2.   [22] Cf. Phil. 2: 13.
[23] Cf. Gen. 1: 2.   [24] Cf. ibid.
[25] Cf. John 3: 8; Charles would of course have been aware that the text may be translated differently from the KJV. For 'wind' one might read 'spirit' ($\pi\nu\epsilon\hat{\upsilon}\mu\alpha$) and it is this link to the mysterious movement of the Spirit of God that is presumably the reason for the association of Gen. 1: 2 and John 3: 8.

believe in several places of holy scripture. That of St. James is express, 'Confess your faults one to another, and pray one for[26] another that ye may be healed. The effectual fervent prayer of a righteous man availeth much.'[27] But how it avails we cannot explain. How God acts upon us in consequence of our friends' prayers, the manner of his returning the intercession of the one into the bosom of the other, we cannot know.

II. Nor yet is the manner wherein God acts in any of these particulars more perfectly unknown to the wisest of men than are the reasons whereon he acts in others. To produce a few instances of this truth was the second thing I proposed, to mention some things of which we cannot say why they are, though we are sure they are done.

1. And first, we cannot say why God suffered evil to have a place in his creation; why he, who is so infinitely good himself, who made all things very good,[28] and who rejoices in the good of all his creatures, permitted what is so entirely contrary to his own nature, and so destructive of his noblest works. 'Why are sin and its attendant pain in the world?' has been a question ever since the world began; and the world will probably end before human understandings have answered it with any certainty.

It has indeed been well observed, that all evil is either natural, moral, or penal; that natural evil or pain is no evil at all if it be overbalanced with following pleasure; that moral evil, or sin, cannot possibly befall anyone[29] unless those who wilfully[30] embrace, who choose it; and that penal evil, or punishment, cannot possibly befall any unless they likewise choose it by choosing sin. This entirely cuts off all imputation on the justice or goodness of God, since it can never be proved that it is contrary to either of these to give his creatures liberty of embracing either good or evil, to put happiness and misery in their own hands, to leave them the choice of life and death.[31] But still this does not come up to the present question: why did God give them that choice? It is sure, in so doing he did not act contrary to any of his attributes; but can we say it would have been contrary to them to have acted in a different manner? To have determined man to God, to have tied him down to happiness, to have given him no choice of misery? It was perfectly consistent with his goodness and justice to set life and death before his creatures; but would it have been inconsistent with them to have let him know only life? Why he chose one of these paths before the other, where is the man that can determine? The all-wise could not do anything without sufficient motives, and such therefore doubtless there are. But what they are is hid from human eyes. Man cannot attain unto them. Reasons questionless he had, and such reasons as when heard will abundantly

---

[26] Outler has 'for one another'; 'one for another' is clear in the MS.   [27] Cf. Jas. 5: 16.

[28] Cf. Gen. 1: 31.

[29] The word 'one' has been inserted above the line. The insertion is in the hand of Charles.

[30] Outler has 'willingly'; 'wilfully' is clear in the MS.

[31] Charles may have Deut. 30: 15, 19 in mind at this point.

justify him to every understanding. But reasons they are which the ear of man hath not heard, nor can it yet enter into the heart to conceive them.[32]

2. Nor can we yet conceive why, among those that choose happiness, God makes the differences which we see he does. Why he appointeth[33] that such or such a person shall attain such a degree of virtue. Why he hath said to each, 'Hitherto shalt thou go, and no farther'[34]—'this be thy bound which thou canst not pass.'[35] Indeed, he hath not so bounded any of his rational creatures but that they may obtain an inconceivable degree of happiness; and more or less of it everyone doubtless will obtain in proportion to his industry. But still, some he hath chosen to such happiness as no others can attain, to such virtue as all others unsuccessfully, though not vainly, aspire to equal.

3. Why God is pleased to bestow on these persons such a measure of virtue and happiness we can no more tell than why he is pleased to bestow such a measure of suffering as he does on others. In the latter case we may, it is true, commonly trace the immediate reason of the suffering. We may commonly observe that [the][36] particular affliction under which a man labours either is pointed at the particular vice to which he naturally inclines, or is conducive to that virtue he particularly wants. But if we move one step further, we are lost again. We cannot tell why it was that he was suffered to be naturally inclined to that vice or averse from that virtue.

4. Or if it should happen, as it sometimes does, that we can give a reason for a particular fault in our natural temper, yet we only put off our ignorance one remove, and shall quickly fall into it anew. So if we should happen to see that our nature is therefore suffered to be very prone to some shameful sin, because there is no other way of bringing us to humility, without which all we do is sinful, yet the difficulty recurs: 'But why did the good God suffer me to be so prone to pride?' And here at least we must hold; here we have nothing more to do but to rest on his good pleasure, and to own that his judgements are unsearchable, and his ways past finding out![37]

Innumerable are the other particulars wherein it might be observed that man knoweth not the ways of God, that he never designed us to be of his council, or privy to the secret springs of his conduct. It might be observed that we know not why he gives to this man one endowment, to that another; why he distributes the several blessings of his Holy Spirit in those measures and at those times which he does; why—but it is vain to attempt to declare all the instances of this one branch of human ignorance, unless we could declare all 'the depths of the riches, both of the wisdom and knowledge of God'.[38] Attempt we rather to search after that part of his ways which is not past finding out—to inquire, as we proposed to do in the third place, why this ignorance is our portion.

---

[32] Cf. 1 Cor. 2: 9.   [33] Altered, in Charles's hand, from 'appointed'.   [34] Cf. Job 38: 11.
[35] Cf. Ps. 104: 9; Jer. 5: 22.
[36] The word 'the' is inserted here also by Outler. It is clearly required by the context.
[37] Cf. Rom. 11: 33.   [38] Cf. ibid.

III.1. And one great reason why God (as we may reasonably suppose) suffers this cloud to rest upon us, why he cuts our knowledge so short on every side, and shows so small a part of his ways, is that ignorance may teach us the usefullest knowledge, may lead us to humility; that, conscious how little we can know of him, we may be the more intent upon knowing ourselves; that from a due sense of our utter inability to understand either the manner or reasons of God's acting, we may seriously apply to what we are able to understand—the manner and reasons of our own.[39] Nor is anything more fit to give us a just, that is, a mean opinion of ourselves, than to have so many instances daily before us of the imperfection of our noblest endowment. If reason, boasted reason, be so imperfect, what must be the meaner parts of our frame? If thy understanding, 'if the light that is in thee be darkness, how great is that darkness'?[40]

[III.2a][41] By pride, saith the prophet, didst even thou fall from heaven, O Lucifer, son of the morning![42] Lest his next race of creatures should fall by it, too, God peculiarly guarded them against it. 'He made them lower than the[43] angels',[44] that, not having the same temptation to a high opinion of their own perfections, they might continue capable of that glory and honour wherewith he designed to crown them; that he suffered them so strangely to debase all their powers, to corrupt their will, and obscure their understanding, that he might withdraw them from this of[45] all vices; that he might at least 'hide pride from man'.[46]

[III.2b] Here then is one wise and merciful reason for the present weakness of our understanding, that God, by hiding himself from man, might teach him humility, and so bring man to himself more surely. Another reason[47] why he now hides himself from us is to fulfil his eternal purpose, that man, so[48] long as he continued upon earth, should walk by faith, not by sight.[49] His purpose was not that we should see and know, whether we would or no,[50] that all his ways are wise and

---

[39] Outler inserts 'acting' at this point.

[40] See Matt. 6: 23. Outler replaces the question mark (which is clear in the MS) with an exclamation mark. This sentence is wanting grammatically, but is clear in the MS. This may be the result of a transcription error on Charles's part.

[41] The paragraphs here numbered 2a and 2b are not numbered in the MS, though paragraph 3 is. This is potentially important in the context of seeking to assess the extent to which this sermon (and the others Charles 'transcribed' from his brother's copies) represent Charles's own views. If the text from which Charles was copying the paragraphs were numbered consistently and consecutively (which is an assumption of course), it is clear that something has happened to the text between the form it had in John's copy and the form we find in the present MS. Either Charles has split a paragraph in two, or he has added one paragraph, or he has deleted one paragraph and added two. Whichever is the case, it adds further weight to the general argument advanced in Chapter 4 above that these texts are not simply copies of John's material, but rather represent Charles's creative interaction with the pre-existent form of the text.   [42] Cf. Isa. 14: 12.

[43] Outler has 'his' rather than 'the'; 'the' is clear in the MS.   [44] Cf. Ps. 8: 5 (Heb. 2: 7, 9).

[45] Before 'of' Outler inserts 'worst'.   [46] Cf. Job 33: 17.

[47] The word 'reason' has been inserted above the line. It is not clear whether this insertion is the work of Charles himself.   [48] Outler has 'as' in place of 'so'; 'so' is clear in the MS.

[49] Cf. 2 Cor. 5: 7.

[50] The word 'no' has been altered in another hand to 'not' (the reading adopted by Outler).

good and gracious; but that we should believe this, should give an assent to it, if we gave any which was in our own[51] power; such an assent as we were free to give or withhold, as depended wholly on our choice. And this intention of our Creator is excellently served by the measure of understanding we now enjoy. It suffices for faith, but not for knowledge. We can believe in God; we cannot see him.

[III.]3.   A third reason why we are so little acquainted with his ways, why 'what God doth man cannot know', seems to be hinted at in the text itself: 'but thou shalt know hereafter'. This knowledge is therefore denied us on earth because it is an entertainment[52] for heaven. And what an entertainment?[53] To have the curtain drawn at once, and enjoy the full blaze of God's wisdom and goodness! To see clearly how the author of this visible world fastened all its parts together, by what chain both the pillars of the earth were upheld, and the armies of the sky! How he effected and maintained that amazing union between the body and the soul of man, that astonishing correspondence between spirit and matter, between perishing dust and immortal flame.[54] How the Holy Ghost, the author of the world of grace, upheld our soul in moral[55] life! How, in answer either to our own prayers or to the prayers of others, his blessed influence overshadowing us out of the darkness, storm, and confusion of our unformed natures, called forth light, and peace, and order.[56] To see why he suffered sin and pain to mingle with those works of which he had declared that they were very good.[57] What unspeakable blessings those are which owe their being to this curse; what infinite beauty arises from, and overbalances this deformity; why it was just and right, as well as merciful in God, to deal to every man his distinct measure of faith, and anoint some whom he chose before the world began[58] with the oil of gladness above their fellows;[59] why he dealt to every man his distinct measure of suffering; why particular men were naturally prone to particular vices; why the several gifts of his Spirit were distributed as they were with respect to kind, degree, time, and persons![60] What an entertainment must it be to a reasonable soul to have such a prospect displayed before him.[61] To have the eye of the mind opened, strengthened, and cleared, that he may command and enjoy it to the full! A prospect which we could not see and live, which flesh

---

[51] Outler omits the word 'own'; the word is clear in the MS.

[52] In the MS there appears a question mark after the word 'entertainment'. This appears to be a simple error. Six words later the word 'entertainment' appears again followed, properly this time, by a question mark. Charles's eye has probably slipped from one to the other in the process of transcription.

[53] Outler replaces the question mark with an exclamation mark.

[54] Outler adds an exclamation mark at this point.

[55] Outler has 'mortal' in place of 'moral'; 'moral' is clear in the MS.

[56] Outler adds an exclamation mark at this point.

[57] Cf. Gen. 1:12, 18, 21, 25, 31. Outler adds an exclamation mark at this point.

[58] Cf. 2 Tim. 1: 9.   [59] Cf. Ps. 45: 7 (Heb. 1: 9).

[60] Outler has a period in place of the exclamation mark at this point. The exclamation mark is clear in the MS.

[61] Outler has an exclamation mark at this point in the text. In the MS the punctuation is in fact a colon (which in keeping with the general editorial policy adopted throughout this edition has been modernized here to a period).

and blood could not bear; and which therefore is fitly reserved for that state wherein, being clothed with glory and immortality, we shall be like the angels now in heaven—pure and strong enough to see God! Amen.

To him who dwelleth in the light which no mortal can approach to, whom flesh and blood hath not seen nor can see, to the ever-blessed Trinity, be glory and praise, might and majesty, now and for ever!

Transcribed at Frederica May 7, 1736 from my brother's copy.[62]

---

[62] These words are written in shorthand. On the back cover the following register is found in shorthand:
Preached at Epworth
Stanton   30
L/snts Exeter
Manchester   5

For details on this register, which refers to John's preaching not Charles's, see the Introduction to this sermon.

SERMON 19

EXODUS 20: 8

INTRODUCTORY COMMENT

On the front cover of the MS there is written in what appears to be the hand of 'W.P.' a note indicating that Charles preached this sermon in Islington, on 24 September 1738. This information is not provided anywhere on the MS by Charles, nor is it apparent from the journal that he preached this precise sermon in Islington on that date. However, Charles does record that he was in Islington and that he preached there 'with great boldness'.[1] It appears, then, that the information given anonymously on the front cover may well be correct; if so it raises the interesting question of where it came from originally. There are no further references to Charles preaching this sermon in the journal.

This is a sermon that Charles copied from John. The reasons for including it in this volume of Charles's sermons have already been outlined in Chapter 4. The MS is located at the John Rylands University Library of Manchester.[2] It comprises eighteen stitch-bound leaves, written almost exclusively recto only. The exception is leaf 17 on the verso of which there appears, in shorthand, a list of places and dates that John preached the sermon. These range from Epworth in July 1730 to St Ebbe's [Oxford] in September 1733. Outler notes that these dates and places can be confirmed (and further refined) from John's diary.[3]

The sermon was published as sermon X in the 1816 edition,[4] where it appears with the note on the MS transcribed as 'Preached at Islington Church, London; 1738'.[5] As is usual, there are significant differences between the form in the 1816 edtion and the MS itself, and the reason for those differences deserves investigation, though such is not of concern here. It was also published by Outler in his edition of John's sermons.[6] The few relatively minor errors in Outler's transcriptions have been corrected and the more significant and/or debateable of these have been indicated.

As Outler has noted,[7] the sermon draws for part of its argument on Peter Heylyn's *The History of the Sabbath*.[8] Outler's sketch of the debates that surrounded the issue of Sabbath observance during the eighteenth century are well worth consideration here. Charles puts forward the view that the Sabbath[9] is to be observed as a special day for the

---

[1] MARC DDCW 10/2 *in loc.*; Telford, *Journal*, 204.   [2] MARC CW Box 5.

[3] Outler (ed.), *Sermons*, iv. 267.   [4] *Sermons*, 165–85.

[5] Outler (ed.), *Sermons*, iv. 268 has '1739', which is in error.   [6] Outler (ed.), *Sermons*, iv. 267–78.

[7] Ibid., iv. 269.

[8] Peter Heylyn, *The History of the Sabbath: In two Bookes* (1633).

[9] There is only a brief mention of the question of which day is to be kept as the Sabbath, that is, 'whether we are to keep the sabbath upon the seventh day, as was the practice of the Jews, or on the first day of the week, according to the usage of the Christian church from our Lord's resurrection to this day'. It is not surprising that Charles assumes the latter, and on occasions refers to Sunday as 'the Sabbath' in his journal—see for example 24 July, 1743 (MARC DDCW 10/2 *in loc.*; Jackson, *Journal*, i. 326).

pursuit of holiness. Work should be put to one side and special provision made for prayer and praise.[10] It is not a particularly hard line that is taken, but it does, as Outler notes, suggest a basic sympathy with a more Puritan than traditionally Anglican approach to the issue.

[10] In this context it is worth comparing Charles's poetic composition 'Come let us with our Lord arise' (*Hymns for Children* (1763; Osborn, *Poetical Works*, vi. 429–30)) the last verse of which reads, 'Honour and praise to Jesus pay | Throughout His consecrated day | Be all in Jesu's praise employ'd | Nor leave a single moment void | With utmost care the time improve | And only breathe His praise and love'.

In the twentieth chapter of Exodus, at the eighth verse, it is thus written:

Remember the sabbath day, to keep it holy

'That the sabbath was not ordained in the beginning of the world, nor ever observed from the creation till the time of Moses; that being given by Moses to the Jews, it was not observed as a moral precept, but like other ceremonies was sometimes kept and sometimes not, as public or private business gave way; that, lastly, it was for ever repealed at the destruction of the temple'[2]—these are the assertions of those who would so remember the sabbath as not to keep it holy at all.

In answer to so much of these objections as seems to require an answer, and to the conclusions drawn from them, I shall endeavour to show:

I.   That the command for keeping the sabbath holy was given for wise ends, by such an authority that none but the same which gave it can repeal it.

II. That it has not been repealed by this authority, as the ends for which it was given are still in force. And,

III. What that keeping the sabbath holy is, by which we obey this command and answer the ends of it.

The I [First] thing to be shown is that the command of keeping the sabbath holy was given for wise ends, by such an author[3] that none but the same which gave it can repeal it. I dispute not here whether or no this command was given to Adam, nor whether it was observed before Moses; nor yet whether we are to keep the sabbath upon the seventh day, as was the practice of the Jews, or on the first day of the week, according to the usage of the Christian church from our Lord's resurrection to this day. My present enquiry is only this: what authority commands us to keep one day in seven holy? And what were the chief ends for which this command was given?

1. The authority by which it was given was God's. He it was who from the holy place of Sinai spake all those words, among which are these, 'Remember the sabbath day, to keep it holy.' He it was who declared again and again, 'Verily my sabbath ye shall keep'[4] (Ex. 31.13, 14) 'It is holy unto you; everyone that defileth it shall be put to death'.

---

[1] *In Nomine Dei*; see note on Sermon 3. This inscription starts the sermon itself. However, on the front cover there appears 'Exod 20.8 Remember the Sabbath-day to keep it holy'. The number '3' also appears on the cover (not in Charles's hand) together with the words 'Islington, Sept. 24 1738, Ex^d W.P.' On this date see the Introduction to this sermon.

[2] See Outler (ed.), *Sermons*, iv. 269 n. 2 for an account of the source of this quotation. It is a summary of part of Heylyn's *The History of the Sabbath*.

[3] Outler reads 'author[ity]' at this point. This reading was probably intended (and may have been in the MS from which Charles is copying) since in point I above and in the paragraphs below it is the 'authority' by which the commandment was given that comes under scrutiny.

[4] After 'keep' there appears in the MS a superscripted 'a'. This was almost certainly a footnote reference in the MS which Charles is copying, which gave the reference to Exod. 31. Charles has raised

Now who but God hath power to repeal what God hath once established? Seeing then it was he who established this law, none but himself hath power to repeal it. Till he repeals it, it must be the duty of all men to obey it, whether the reasons for which he hath established it are known to them or no.[5] An abundantly sufficient reason for their obedience is this alone, that he gave it, if they know no other. Not that this is the case here.

2.[6] The wise reasons of this command are, or may be, known to all men; the chief ends of it are almost everywhere delivered, together with the command itself. The first we have in the second chapter of Genesis (v. 3): 'And God blessed the seventh[7] day, and sanctified it, because that in it he had rested from all his works which God created and made.' And again in the twentieth chapter of Exodus, 'In six days the Lord made heaven and earth, and all that in them is; wherefore the Lord blessed the sabbath day, and hallowed it'.[8]

In these words three things are plainly affirmed: 1, that God is the creator of this[9] world; 2, that having created it in six days he ceased from his work on the seventh; 3, that hereon he blessed the seventh day, and hallowed, or sanctified, it, ordaining that man, being made in the image and for the imitation of God, should imitate him in this, in bestowing six days on the works pertaining to this world, and resting from all these works on the seventh, to retire to a better world.

We see here the chief reason of this command, the great end for which it was given, even that man might learn to imitate God, to fulfil the purpose of his creation; that he might ever remember who it was that created himself, and heaven and earth; that like him, having finished his six days, he might on the seventh retire from this world, and ascend in heart and mind into the heaven of heavens, whither his Creator went in person before him.

2. Another end of this command God declared both on Mount Sinai and long after by his prophet Ezekiel: 'I gave them my sabbaths—that they might know that I am the Lord which sanctifieth them.'[10] That these sacred days, so often as they returned, might confirm them in that important knowledge, that God was the author of their virtue and happiness as well as of their being; that should he withdraw his sanctifying power they would as naturally sink into sin and misery as, should he withdraw his quickening power, they would fall into their native dust.

3. That as they knew how holiness was to be attained, so they actually might attain it, was a third wise end of God's commanding man to keep one day in seven

---

the note to the body of the text. The same method of footnoting is used on the following leaf of the MS to refer to Heylyn's *History of the Sabbath*.

[5] 'No' has been altered to 'not' in another hand.

[6] The intended position of this '2' is not clear in the MS. It is placed in the margin and seems to have been added later by Charles. It appears, however, that Charles intended a break at this point and hence a paragraph break has been inserted here into what is continuous in the MS. This numbering disrupts the paragraph sequence.

[7] Outler has 'sabbath' in place of 'seventh' at this point; 'seventh' is clear in the MS.

[8] Cf. Exod. 20: 11.   [9] Outler has 'the' rather than 'this'; 'this' is clear in the MS.

[10] Cf. Ezek. 20: 12.

holy. This we learn from that other declaration of God, wherein after 'Ye shall be holy, for I the Lord your God am holy,'[11] it follows in the very next verse, 'Ye shall keep my sabbaths',[12] plainly intimating that one reason why they were to keep his sabbaths was that they might be holy as God is holy; that by constantly dedicating to him one day in seven they might be enabled to spend the other six as became those who acknowledged their Creator and Sanctifier to be of purer eyes than to behold iniquity;[13] that they might ever be mindful ~~to~~ of taking him for their pattern, not only in one particular, but in the general course of their lives, which after his example should be holy, just, and good.[14]

~~Recollection~~[15] The sum of what has been hitherto observed is this: God, who hath an undoubted right to command men what he pleases, and is under no obligation of acquainting them with the reasons of his commands, was pleased to give them this command, 'Remember the Sabbath day, to keep it holy.' Nay, and was also pleased to acquaint them with several of the reasons that moved him so to do, the chief of which are these: 1, that man, by imitating one particular action of God, might retain a more lively and lasting sense of God's being the Creator of himself[16] and all things; 2, that he might constantly remember who it is that is his Sanctifier as well as Creator; 3, that he might be ever mindful that it is the business of his life to imitate him in all things; to make God's mercy, justice, and holiness the pattern of all his thoughts, words, and actions.

II. The next question, therefore, is whether this command has yet been repealed by the authority that gave it, and whether these ends for which it was given are still in force or no?[17]

1. As to the former part of the question, it is roundly affirmed that God did repeal it when he was made man; to prove which a famous manager[18] in this controversy gives us the strength of his cause in these words:

In[19] these rigid vanities by which the Pharisees had abused the sabbath, our Saviour thought it requisite to detect their follies. They taught [. . .] it was unlawful on the sabbath day either to heal the impotent, or relieve the sick, or feed the hungry; but he confutes them in them, both by his actions and by his disputations . . . Did they accuse his followers of gathering corn upon the sabbath, being an hungered? He lets them know what David did in the same extremity . . . The cures

---

[11] Cf. Lev. 19: 2.   [12] Cf. Lev. 19: 3.   [13] Cf. Hab. 1: 13.

[14] Cf. Rom. 7: 12.

[15] The word 'recollection', abbreviated in the MS to 'rec.' is found in the left hand margin. It has been deleted. The thick horizontal stroke used to effect this deletion is uncharacteristic of Charles's own mode of striking out.

[16] In the MS 'himself' is 'Himself'. However, the sense clearly requires that the antecedent of 'Himself' be 'man' and not 'God'.

[17] Outler has a period rather than a question mark at this point. The question mark is clear in the MS.

[18] After 'manager' a footnote reference is inserted in the text itself. That footnote reads 'Dr Peter Heylin's History of the Sabbath first edition p. 168'. The reference is self-explanatory.

[19] The following paragraph, as Charles notes, is from Heylyn, *History of the Sabbath*.

he did upon the sabbath, what were they more than what themselves did daily in laying salves upon those infants whom they had circumcised on the sabbath? His bidding of the impotent man to take up his bed, was it so great a toil as to lift up the ox out of the ditch? . . . Nor had God so spoke the word but that he could repeal it . . . the Son of man being Lord also of the sabbath. Nay, it is rightly remarked that he did more works of charity upon the sabbath day[20] than on all days else; and several of them when there was no extreme necessity that the cure should be performed that day, or the man perish . . . What then? Came our Saviour to destroy the law? No—but to let them understand the right meaning of it, that they might no longer be misled by the Scribes and Pharisees.

Further[21] 'that the sabbath was to be repealed is by this apparent, 1, that it was an institute of Moses; 2, that it was an institute peculiar ~~th~~ to the Jewish nation'.[22]

Thus ~~th~~ far the historian, whose numerous assertions it may be worth while to examine apart, beginning at that wherewith he ends, as being of most importance.

'The sabbath' (says he) 'was to be repealed because it was, 1, an institute[23] of Moses; 2, an institute peculiar to the Jewish nation.' Now as every institute peculiar to the Jewish nation was an institute of Moses, all we have to do is to enquire whether the sanctifying the sabbath was an institute of Moses or no.

I therefore think it was not, because it was instituted at least two thousand years before Moses was born. So saith the text in Genesis expressly: 'Thus the heavens and the earth were finished and all the host of them. And on the seventh day God ended his work which he had made; and he rested on the seventh day from all his work which he had made. And God blessed the seventh day, and sanctified it'.[24]

Indeed, so soon as it shall be proved that there is an absurdity in taking this in the plain literal sense, then we shall be forced to take it in a less plain, in a figurative sense, and to say, 'Though this is related as done at the creation, it was not done till the giving of manna in the time of Moses, four or five and twenty hundred years after the creation.' But till this absurdity be shown we have no pretence for giving up the letter. We have no pretence to interpret any Scripture figuratively but when an absurdity follows a proper interpretation. This not being the case here, we may, we must, conclude that the sabbath was instituted at the creation; therefore that it was not an institute of Moses; and consequently that from this supposition, which is manifestly false, it cannot be inferred that it was to be repealed at all.

However, that it actually was repealed is inferred from the other assertions above mentioned, which are briefly these: 1, that the Pharisees thought it unlawful to do even works of necessity or mercy on the sabbath; 2, that our Saviour proved they thought wrong therein, such works being lawful on any day; 3, that

---

[20] Outler omits 'day'. The word is clear in the MS.

[21] Outler encloses 'further' in square brackets, presumably to indicate that this one word is not from Heylyn. It is, however, in the MS sermon itself.   [22] At this point the quotation from Heylyn ends.

[23] Amended in the MS from 'institution'. It is not clear whether this amendment has been effected by Charles himself.   [24] Cf. Gen. 2: 1–3.

the Son of Man, being God,[25] could, if he pleased, set aside his own command; 4, that himself did more works both of necessity and mercy on this than on any other day; and 5, that he came, not to destroy the law but to fulfil, to teach men its right meaning.

All and every one of these five propositions we allow to be perfectly true, and would be exceeding glad to know from which of the five we are to infer the conclusion. Are we to[26] say, the Pharisees had wrong notions of the sabbath, therefore the sabbath is abolished? Or, our Lord proved their notions of it to be wrong, therefore it is disannulled? Or, God *could* if he pleased set it aside; therefore he *did* set it aside? Or, Christ did works of necessity and mercy on the sabbath, therefore we may do works that belong neither to necessity nor mercy? Or, lastly, the Son of man came to fulfil the law; therefore he destroyed this branch of it?

I hope it will not be thought an unpardonable presumption if, notwithstanding all these arguments to the contrary, I still conceive that God hath not yet repealed his command touching the sabbath; nay, and that he never will, till the Great Sabbath begins; both because he hath not done it yet, and because the reasons for which he gave it are still in full force, and must be so till the consummation of all things.

For, 1, to preserve in man a lively and constant sense of God's being the Creator of all things, this end of the sabbath must remain in full force so long as men remain upon the earth. This reason for keeping it can never be wanting so long as any of those creatures are living who, in spite of all methods used to prevent it, are so extremely apt to forget their Creator; who so readily lay hold of any pretence, nay, who are so willing without any pretence at all, if not to think that they are the work of chance or their own hands, at least[27] to act as if they did think so.

And the second end of the sabbath can no more cease than the first. That man should be constantly and deeply sensible that he can no more sanctify than he could create himself must ever[28] be of the last importance. It must ever be of the highest concern to men to remember that they are unable to help themselves; to keep the impression of this great truth ever strong upon their minds, that he who is born of a woman must be born again of God, or it is impossible he should please him.

3.[29] It must ever be of equal concern to men to remember that it is the business of their lives to imitate God. I presume no one will be so hardy as to affirm that

---

[25] The MS actually reads 'that the Son of God, being man', the reading adopted by Outler. However, beneath 'God' and 'man' Charles (the hand is almost certainly his) has written '2' and '1' respectively, indicating that the order of the words should be reversed.

[26] The word 'to' has been inserted above the line. The insertion does not appear to be in the hand of Charles himself.

[27] The MS has 'lest' with an 'a' inserted above the line. The correction does not appear to be the work of Charles himself.

[28] The word 'ever' has been amended in the MS, a clearer 'e' being written in for what appears to be a somewhat indistinct 'e' in the original. The hand is not that of Charles himself.

[29] There is no point '2' in this section of the MS, perhaps suggesting editorial activity.

this end of the sabbath has lost any of its force; that it does not hold full as strongly at this day as it did on the birthday of the creation. It being therefore clear that God hath given this command, and that he hath not repealed it, and [that it is][30] sufficiently probable that he never will, since the ends of it must ever be in full force, all that remains is to show,

III. Thirdly, what it is to keep the sabbath holy, so as to obey this command, and answer the ends of it.

To keep either a day or a place holy is plainly this, to set it apart to religious uses. This is both the proper and the common sense of the word. By saying 'This day or this place is kept holy,' both the learned and unlearned mean, it is dedicated to God, it is appropriated to his service. And to unhallow or profane a holy place or day is not to set it apart to those uses; to use it in the same manner with other things which are not dedicated to God, not appropriated to his service; to perform on the holy place or in the consecrated day[31] the works of ordinary days and unhallowed places.

To keep the sabbath day holy, as well in the proper as common sense of the word, is therefore to set it apart to religious uses, to dedicate it to the service of God. What is implied in this we shall easily see if we consider, 1, what we must; 2, what we may; and 3, what we may not do ~~of~~ on it.

1. We must, if we will obey this command at all, and answer the ends for which it was given us, employ a considerable part of this day in praying to and praising God. We must retire with him from this lower world into those regions that are above the firmament. We must employ ourselves in thinking on the various works he hath made, and on the goodness, wisdom, and power of the Maker; and in talking of his marvellous acts, in telling the memorial of his abundant kindness; that branch of his kindness, in particular, whereby he daily renews the face of the earth,[32] whereby he restores lost man to pardon and peace, and gives him the second, better life of holiness. That this his last, noblest gift may not be in vain, we must now especially work together with him; we must labour to conform ourselves to his likeness, to be holy as he is holy.[33] We must make it our peculiar business to perfect his image in our souls, to bind mercy and truth about our neck, to write them deep on the tablet of our heart.[34]

2. Not that our mind need be every moment intent upon this; that might make even devotion a burden. No—we have bodies as well as souls; and this our Lord considered, though the Pharisees did not. He therefore took away that intolerable severity wherewith their traditions had loaded the sabbath, and made it of none effect but to hinder those ends for the furthering of which it was ordained.[35] He brought it back to its original standard, to its just and natural extent. Accordingly

[30] Outler adds these words at this point. Since the context clearly requires them, Outler's suggestion has been followed here.

[31] Outler has, probably rightly, corrected this to 'perform on the holy day or in the consecrated place' adding a note to the actual MS reading.   [32] Cf. Ps. 104: 30.

[33] Cf. Lev. 19: 2; Matt. 5: 48.   [34] Prov. 3: 3.   [35] Cf. Mark 7: 13.

both his words and his actions showed that we may do works of necessity and mercy on this day; that we may do whatever cannot be done on another day, or not without manifest inconvenience, such as giving ourselves decent and proper recreation; as feeding and watering of cattle, for this is a work of necessity; that we *may* relieve our sick or hungry neighbour, for this is a work of mercy.

3. This therefore we may do. But we may not do any other work on the sabbath. We may not do any manner of work therein which neither necessity nor mercy requires. We may not do any work which can be done on another day, and done without much inconvenience, the delaying of which a day longer would not give either to ourselves or our neighbour much loss or pain.

Neither may we use any such recreation on the sabbath as does not further the ends for which it was given us. Some recreation is therefore allowed on this day, because few minds are of so firm a temper as to be able to preserve a cheerful devotion, a lively gratitude, without it. It is therefore a proper work of necessity so far as it conduces to these ends. But we may not therefore go ~~ther~~ farther; we may not use such kinds of recreation, or any in such a degree, as does not conduce to these ends, as does not enliven our devotion and quicken our gratitude. Here is a short and sure rule: all such recreation as helps devotion we may use; all such as hinders or does not help ~~it's~~ g this great end of its institution, we may not use on this day.

The case is just the same as to the day as to the house of God; and for this reason doubtless it is that God more than once mentions them together: 'Ye shall keep my sabbaths, and reverence my sanctuary.'[36] We are not to reverence the sanctuary of God so much as not to show mercy, ~~to~~ not to save life therein; we may likewise do necessary works there, such as cannot be done elsewhere, or not without great inconvenience. But we may not do common works therein, much less use common diversions. The former actions are not at all contrary to its holiness; the latter unhallow, pollute, and profane it. And when either the temple or the sabbath of God is made a day or a house of merchandise,[37] it will not be long before truth itself will pronounce the one an abomination and the other a den of thieves.[38]

~~General Recollection~~[39] If from what has been said it appears, 1, that this command, 'Keep the sabbath holy,' was given to man by God, and that for wise ends, even to keep him duly sensible that God is his Creator, his Sanctifier, and his Pattern; 2, that as God has not yet repealed this command, so the ends of it are in full force; and, lastly, that the only way of keeping the sabbath holy, of obeying this command and answering its ends, is to abstain from all[40] diversions as well as works which neither necessity nor mercy requires, that we may set apart God's day for the service of God, which alone is to sanctify ~~and~~ or keep it holy; then is the

---

[36] Cf. Lev. 19: 30; 26: 2.   [37] Cf. John 2: 16.   [38] Cf. Mark 11: 17 and parallels.

[39] The words 'General recollection', abbreviated in the MS to 'Gen. rec.' are found in the left hand margin. They have been deleted. It is not clear whether this deletion is the work of Charles himself.

[40] The word 'all', which is present in the MS itself, has been inserted for a second time above the line so that the text reads 'from all all diversions'. This insertion does not appear to be the work of Charles himself and the purpose of it is unclear.

sabbath no institution of Moses, neither is it peculiar to the Jews, but the command to observe it, as well as the reasons of that command, extend to all ages and nations. Then, if we cut away from it the additions of the latter Jews, and that one circumstance 'Let no man go out of his place on the sabbath day,'[41] wherewith God guarded it for a time from the disobedience of their stiff-necked forefathers, we may safely affirm of the Fourth Commandment, as well as of the other nine, Christ came 'not to destroy, but to fulfil it; and till heaven and earth pass away, one jot or one tittle shall in no wise pass from this law till all be fulfilled'.[42]

~~Exhortation~~[43] Brethren, let me add one word of exhortation. And be ye assured of this, that those who watch over your souls as they that must give account[44] will not wilfully lead them out of the way. So that when you and we give up our great account, it will not increase your condemnation. If there be any here who will not ~~who will not~~[45] be at the trouble of keeping the sabbath holy, who says he cannot submit to the drudgery of worshipping God; who thinks prayer and praise, meditation and pious discourse, too heavy a burden to be borne a whole day, and so resolves to spend at least a part of this day either in diversions or business; I exhort all such, all who will do one, to work rather than play. I exhort you that are parents, in particular, if ye care not to train up your children ~~in~~ to[46] devotion, when they come from church not to send them to the streets or market-place, but rather of the two, to school. As to the innocence of either, it is no matter which you do, but to do the latter looks more like prudence. If ye do not care for the other world, yet why should you neglect this too? Why should ye sell your own and your children's souls for nothing? Perhaps ye may get a little for them. As to the command of God, ye throw that out[47] of the question; that ye reject either way. Ye no more keep that day holy whereon ye play than whereon ye work. And as to the ends of it, ye destroy them alike, one way or the other. Ye are no more endeavouring to remember your Creator, to be thankful for his benefits, and conformed to his holiness, while ye unhallow his day by common diversion, than while ye do it by common work. But by the latter ye may gain something in exchange for your souls.[48] You may perhaps get some money for your conscience. If ye lift up your hand against your God in labour rather than idleness, ye may have this comfort in your rebellion, that ye did not serve the devil for naught.

Not that those who serve God, who keep his day holy both from common work and ~~common~~ diversions, have less reason to expect a reward from *their* Master, and even in the present world. For to these, who would not be wicked even to be rich,

---

[41] Cf. Exod. 16: 29 (the KJV actually has 'seventh' rather than 'sabbath'.)

[42] Cf. Matt. 5: 17–18.

[43] The word 'exhortation', abbreviated in the MS to 'Exh.', is found in the left hand margin. It has been deleted. It is not clear whether this deletion is the work of Charles himself.

[44] Cf. Heb. 13: 17.   [45] These struck-out words are not noted by Outler.

[46] The word 'to' has been inserted above the line and the word 'in' before it struck out. This appears to be the work of Charles. Outler adopts the reading 'in'.

[47] Before 'out' Outler inserts 'quite'. There is no support for such a reading in the MS.

[48] Cf. Mark 8: 37 and parallel.

who love God even better than gain, to these thus saith God: 'If thou turn away thy foot from doing thy pleasure on my holy day, and call the sabbath a delight, holy of the Lord, honourable; and shalt honour him, not doing thine own ways, nor finding thine own pleasure, nor speaking thine own words; then shalt thou delight thyself in the Lord, and I will cause thee to ride upon the high places of the earth, and feed thee with the heritage of Jacob thy father; for the mouth of the Lord hath spoken it'.[49]

Transcribed[50] from my brother's April 6, 1736.

[49] Cf. Isa. 58: 13–14.
[50] These words are in shorthand. On the verso there appears a list of places where John Wesley preached this sermon, on which see further above in the Introduction to this sermon.

SERMON 20

MARK 12: 30

INTRODUCTORY COMMENT

This is a sermon which Charles copied from his brother John, a fact that he indicated in shorthand on the title page of the small hard-bound booklet in which this and the three next sermons are found. The transcriptions were made in September 1736 'between Charles-town and Boston', that is, on the first leg of Charles's journey back to England.[1] The pages in the booklet are clearly numbered and on page 34 there appears, again in shorthand, a list of places where the sermons were preached. The entries are arranged in two columns. On the left hand side there appears a list of places and years for John's preaching of the texts (confirmed by John's own journal and diary). All these predate Charles's transcription of the sermons in 1736. However, in a much less neat format, there appears also on the right hand side a further list of places, and dates from 1737 and 1738. These appear to be dates upon which Charles preached the sermons.

In the case of this present sermon this can be confirmed beyond doubt, for he recorded in his journal for 13 November 1737 the detail that he 'preached at Bexley, on the love of God'.[2] In the register on page 34 of the sermon booklet the same information appears.[3] This pattern is repeated for Sermon 21, on Luke 10: 42; in this latter case Charles even wrote, in shorthand, 'by me' before the entries.

The link between the register on the right hand side of the page and Charles's own preaching schedule being clearly established, the earlier entry on the register indicating that he preached 'On the Love of God' at Duke Street[4] on 23 October 1737 can also be taken as a reference to his own preaching of this sermon even though there is no confirming external evidence. Thus it can be concluded that he preached this sermon on at least two occasions, both in 1737: 23 October and 13 November.

As was noted above, the sermon is copied from John. However, it has now been established that this is also a sermon which Charles himself preached. It was, then, in this sense 'his'. The MS itself is fairly neat and holds little clue as to the extent to which Charles may have edited his brother's sermon in the process of transcription. There is one place, however, where one might just detect Charles's editorial hand. In the third major section which answers 'the grand objection', there appears a sequence of numbers to paragraphs and major points that are being made. These are numbered 1, 2, 6, 7, 8. In the other two major sections in the sermon (Charles's heads 1–2) the paragraphs are numbered without a break.

---

[1] Charles set off from Savannah on 26 July 1736 and arrived in Charlestown on 31 July. He departed thence on 11 August and arrived in Boston on 24 September. He finally boarded for England on 25 October arriving on 3 December. See MARC DDCW 10.2 *in loc.*; Telford, *Journal*, 67–97 *passim*.

[2] MARC DDCW 10/2 *in loc.*; Telford, *Journal*, 130.

[3] The entry reads 'bekli 9r 13' where '9r' appears to mean 'November'.

[4] The entry reads simply 'dk strt ok 23, 1737'. There is no entry for October 1737 in the journal extract.

There are two obvious interpretations of this data. First, it may be that Charles simply forgot to copy the paragraph/point numbers 3–5 in section 3. Alternatively, he may have omitted John's points 3–5, perhaps replacing them with the unnumbered material of his own. (That interpolated section includes a lengthy quotation from Edward Young's sermons, which we know that he did have in his own library.) This is admittedly nothing more than speculation, but it is not wild. In any case, even if Charles has left the sermon much as it was as he copied it (forgetting to number points 3–5 in section 3) this was presumably because he agreed with the form, content, and style of his brother's sermon. For several reasons, then, this sermon is properly included in this collection of Charles's material; there is better reason to include it than, as some others have argued, to omit it.

It was published as sermon IX in the 1816 edition,[5] and, as is generally the case, it is plain that the editor felt free to make numerous changes. It is included also in Outler's edition of John Wesley's sermons,[6] and Outler's comments on the text in the context of John's life and theological development are well worth noting. The few inaccuracies in the Outler edition have been corrected here and those of any significance are highlighted in the notes.

The sermon contains an extensive quotation from Edward Young and another from John Norris; Outler notes also various echoes from a number of other sources including De Renty.[7] The appeal is here made to a total love of God. Outler highlights this aspect of the sermon and argues that the lack of balance here between the love of God and the love of neighbour is both obvious in the sermon and also uncharacteristic of the later John Wesley. The latter point is true, but the former seems a less than fully adequate account of a sermon which includes the paragraph

> Not that God is so to be the only object of our love as to exclude his creatures from a subordinate share of it. 'The Lord rejoiceth in his works', and consequently man, made after his likeness, not only may, but ought to imitate him therein, and with pleasure to own that 'they are very good.' Nay, the love of God constraineth those in whose hearts it is shed abroad to love what bears his image. And we cannot suppose any love forbidden by God which necessarily flows from this love of him.

Charles, like John, emphasized the two commandments of the love of God and love of man. That is reflected in this sermon, though to be sure it is the former that comes to the fore.

---

[5] *Sermons*, 136–164.   [6] Outler (ed.), *Sermons*, iv. 329–45.

[7] On this general point see further Butler, *Methodists and Papists*, 138, 143, 145–6, where Butler shows the influence of writers such as de Renty on John Wesley. Charles's transcription of a section of Fénelon's work was noted previously. That he took the trouble to copy out sections from Fénelon shows the influence of the tradition on him. So perhaps does the fact that he had a copy of A. M. Ramsay's *Histoire de la Vie et des Ouvrages de Messire Francois de Solignac de la Mothe-Fénelon* (1729) MARC MAW.CW53.

Sermon Register[1]

Duke Street, October 23, 1737[2]

Bexley November 13

Thou shalt love the Lord thy God with all thy heart, and with all thy soul, and with all thy mind, and with all thy strength.[3] *12 Mark 30.*

1. When God had formed man of the dust of the ground, and breathed into him the breath of life,[4] when he had stamped his own image[5] and superscription upon him, in his understanding, will, and affections, he gave him a law, even to love him in whose image he was made. And love, the one thing [that] his[6] Creator required in return for all his benefits, he therefore required, because it was the one thing needful[7] to perfect his creature's happiness.

2. Thou shalt love the Lord thy God, was the whole of that law which God gave to man in his original state. But when he had wilfully degraded himself from that state of happiness and perfection, by transgressing the single prohibition which was appointed for the test of his love, a more particular law became needful for him, for a remedy of those many inventions[8] he had found out, whereby, being alienated from the love of God, he was enslaved to the love of his creatures, and consequently to error and vice, to shame and misery. A more particular law was accordingly given him, by the rules whereof he was fully apprised of every avenue at which sin and pain might break in upon his soul. By this too he was directed to those several means which God had appointed for the renewal of his nature. And to complete its use, till his nature was renewed after the image of him that created him, it pointed out all those thoughts, and words, and works, by so many express injunctions, which the love of God, when that was the spring of his soul, produced without any injunction.

3. Yet we may easily observe that even in this state of man, love is still the fulfilling of the law;[9] of every law which hath proceeded out of the mouth of God,[10] at sundry times and in divers manners, and particularly of that which in these last days he hath given us by his Son.[11] Love is the end of every commandment[12] of Christ, all of which, from the least even to the greatest, are given to man, not for

---

[1] This information is found on the verso of the final leaf of this sermon. As has been noted in the Introduction to this sermon, several of the entries refer to John's preaching. However, the ones listed here are those that refer to Charles's use of the text.

[2] There is no entry in the journal for that day.

[3] The Marcan text is drawn from Deut. 6: 5, and is paralleled in Matt. 22: 37 and Luke 10: 27.

[4] Cf. Gen. 2: 7.   [5] Cf. Gen. 1: 26.

[6] Before 'his' there appears an insertion mark in the text, though what is to be inserted is not indicated. Outler supplies 'that', which is surely probable.

[7] Cf. Luke 10: 42. This text is the subject of Sermon 21.   [8] Cf. Eccl. 7: 29.

[9] Cf. Rom. 13: 10.   [10] Cf. Deut. 8: 3; Matt. 4: 4 and parallel.   [11] Cf Heb. 1: 1–2.

[12] See 1 Tim. 1: 5.

their own sakes, but purely in order to this. The negative commands, what are they but so many cautions against what estranges us from the love of God? And the positive either enjoin the use of the means of grace, which are only so many means of love, or the practice of those particular virtues which are the genuine fruits of love, and the steps whereby we ascend from strength to strength, towards a perfect obedience of the first and great commandment—that commandment which contains all, which preceded all, and which shall remain when all the rest are done away: '*Thou shalt love the Lord thy God with all thy heart, and with all thy ~~strength~~[13] soul, and with all thy mind, and with all thy strength*'.

I shall endeavour, first, to lay down a plain sense of this commandment;[14]

Secondly, to prove this sense to be the true one; and,[15]

Thirdly, to answer the grand objection against it.[16]

First, I am to lay down a plain sense of this commandment, 'Thou shalt love the Lord thy God with all thy heart, and with all thy soul, and with all thy mind, and with all thy strength.'

1. The love of God may be taken in various senses: as it is, first, for obedience to him. So St. John: 'This is the love of God, that we keep his commandments.'[17] And such a metonymy, or putting of[18] the cause for the effect, frequently occurs in the sacred writings; whereby, as the love of him is put for the outward obedience, of which it is the vital principle, so the fear of God is said to be 'the departing from evil',[19] which is the necessary effect of it.

2. By the same figure, the love of God has been sometimes taken for a desire of enjoying him. For this too immediately flows from love, and increases in the same proportion with it. Whence some eminent men have unwarily confounded the stream with the fountain, and have improperly termed the desire of enjoying God, love of desire. As if love and desire were all one, whereas *desire* is as essentially distinct from the love that produces it as is any fruit from the tree upon which it grows.

3. Love itself is, by the common consent of mankind, and agreeably to universal experience, divided into love of complacency, or delight, and love of gratitude, or benevolence. And accordingly the love of God may be divided into love of delight, and love of gratitude—the one regarding what he is in himself, the other what he is to us. The boundless perfections of his nature are an eternal ground of delight to every creature capable of apprehending them. And the numberless exertions of

[13] The word 'strength' has been struck out in the MS and replaced by 'soul'. The change has been effected by Charles himself.

[14] At this point in the MS the Roman numeral 'I' appears in the right hand margin. It is not clear whether this is the work of Charles himself.

[15] At this point in the MS the Roman numeral 'II' appears in the right hand margin. It is not clear whether this is the work of Charles himself.

[16] At this point in the MS the Roman numeral 'III' appears in the right hand margin. It is not clear whether this is the work of Charles himself.   [17] Cf. 1 John 5: 3.

[18] The word 'of' has been inserted above the line.

[19] Cf. Prov. 3: 7; Job 28: 28. Despite the quotation marks the reference is actually a rather loose application of the text.

all those perfections on our behalf lay the strongest claim to our gratitude. In the former sense, every reasonable creature is to love God, because his power, wisdom, yea, and his goodness, are infinite. In the latter, 'We love him', says the Apostle, 'because he first loved us.'[20] When these fountains have once united their streams, they flow with redoubled violence, and bear the Christian strongly forward to please and obey the All-merciful, and to be made one with the All-perfect; to love the Lord his God with all his heart, and with all his ~~mind~~[21] soul, and with all his mind, and with all his strength.

4. As to the measure of love prescribed in these words, all commentators agree that they mean at least thus much: we must not love anything more than God, we may not love the creature above the Creator.[22] Nay, that we must not love anything so much as him; that he claims of us a love of pre-eminence; that we must reserve for him the highest seat in our hearts, the largest and choicest share of our affection. They are all likewise agreed that we must entertain no love which is contrary to the love of him; that whatever affection we find, or have reason to suspect, will either prevent the kindling of this divine flame, or quench it when kindled, or any way obstruct its increase, or diminish its heat and brightness—that affection we must not give place to for a moment, but immediately resist with all our might.

5. But we must go higher than this, or we shall never rise up to the plain sense of this commandment. 'Thou shalt love the Lord thy God with all thy heart, and with all thy soul, and with all thy mind, and with all thy strength' imports in ordinary construction (to use the words of a great master of reason as well as love), 'that we love God, not only with the most and best, but with the whole of our affection; that we love him not only with every capacity, passion, and faculty, with the understanding, will, and affections, but with every degree of every power, with all the latitude of our will, with the whole possibility of our souls; that we devote to him, not only the highest degree of our love, but every degree of it; in one word, that God be not only the principal, but the only object of our love.'[23]

6. Not that God is so to be the only object of our love as to exclude his creatures from a subordinate share of it. 'The Lord rejoiceth in his works',[24] and consequently man, made after his likeness, not only may, but ought to imitate him therein, and with pleasure to own that 'they are very good.'[25] Nay, the love of God constraineth those in whose hearts it is shed abroad[26] to love what bears his image. And we cannot suppose any love forbidden by God which necessarily flows from this love of him.

7. And even that love of the creatures which does not flow from the love of God, if it lead thereto, is accepted. For this end hath he given us them to enjoy,

---

[20] Cf. 1 John 4: 19.
[21] The word 'mind' has been struck out in the text and replaced by 'soul'. The change has been effected by Charles himself.   [22] See Rom. 1: 25.
[23] At this point in the text there appears the sign '†'. It is footnoted 'Norris, Ser[mons] vol. 3 S[ermon] 1 p. 7'. See Outler (ed.), *Sermons* iv. 334 n. a, for an account of the origin of this quotation.
[24] Cf. Ps. 104: 31.   [25] Cf. Gen. 1: 4, 10, 12, 18, 21, 25, 31.   [26] Cf. Rom. 5: 5.

that by these steps we may ascend to higher enjoyments. Therefore whatever love tends to the love of God is no more forbidden than[27] that which flows from it.

8. Yet farther, there are many of the works of his hands[28] which God expressly commands us to love; and that not only with a love of gratitude or benevolence, but of complacence, too. For such surely is natural affection; such is that tenderest of all passions toward our fellow-creatures, which our blessed Redeemer does not disdain to compare to the love between himself and his church.[29] And such is the delight which we ought to have in the saints that are upon earth, and in those that excel in virtue. The contrary opinion, that we are forbid to love any creature in any degree, supposes the all-knowing God to command our love of himself, and yet to prohibit the immediate necessary effect of it. It charges the All-wise with enjoining the end, and in that very injunction forbidding the means. It blasphemes his most holy and perfect law, as notoriously contradictory to itself, as requiring elsewhere what was absolutely condemned in the very first commandment of it.

9. This therefore considered, the sense of that command is easily resolved into this: 'Thou shalt so love the Lord thy God with all thy powers, and with the whole force of all, as ever to remember that thou art bound, yea, by this very law, (1) to obey him thou lovest, and therefore to love those things which he commands thee to love, so far as he commands it; (2) to cherish that love which is the necessary effect of thus loving the Lord thy God, viz., the love of those men who are renewed after his image in righteousness and true holiness; and, (3) to use all the means which experience and reason recommend as conducive to this great end, in particular, to love all his creatures so far as it tends to the love of thy Creator.' Indeed this third rule includes both the preceding, seeing all obedience to God tends to the love of him; and seeing every other fruit of divine love increases the love from which it sprung. The full sense of the first and great commandment is therefore contained in this single sentence: 'Thou shalt love God alone for his own sake, and all things else only so far as they tend to him.'

II. That this is the mark toward which we are all to press if we would attain the prize of our high calling;[30] that none can attain it unless they press towards this mark, according to the several abilities God hath given them; that this plain sense of the great command is the true one, I am in the second place to show. And this I shall endeavour to prove, (1) from the Holy Scriptures; (2) from reason.

1. From every part of the Holy Scriptures it appears that love is the proper worship of a reasonable nature. To go no farther than the words immediately preceding the text: 'Hear, O Israel', says our Divine Teacher, 'the Lord thy God is one Lord, and thou shalt love the Lord thy God.' Thou shalt love him—Why? Because he is '*the Lord thy God*', and as such has a just claim to thy love; because love is the worship due to thy God; because it is the proper homage of a rational creature to his Creator. 'Thinkest thou that he will eat bulls' flesh, and drink the

---

[27] Incorrectly written as 'that' in the MS.   [28] Cf. Ps. 104: 24.   [29] Cf. Eph. 5: 25 ff.
[30] Cf. Phil. 3: 14.

blood of goats? Offer unto God thanksgiving, and pay thy heart to the most Highest.'[31] Without this he will not be pleased, though thou shouldst give him thousands of rams,[32] or give all thy substance to feed his poor.[33] But with love every sacrifice is accepted; in this he is always well pleased.

2. 'Hear, O Israel, God is thy Lord!'[34] Therefore shalt thou worship him. And all worship but love is an abomination before him. Therefore thou shalt love the Lord thy God. But '*the Lord thy God is one Lord*.' Therefore thou shalt love the Lord thy God with all thy heart; thou shalt not divide thy heart. He has the right to it all; thou mayst not alienate any part of it. Reserve for him, not the largest share, but the whole of thy affection. Hadst thou more lords thou mightst[35] have more loves than one; but if thou hast no other God, thou canst have no other love. 'It is written, "Thou shalt worship the Lord thy God, and him only shalt thou serve." '[36] Behold, love is the worship of thy Lord; this alone is his reasonable service. Therefore thou shalt delight in the Lord thy God, and him only shalt thou love.

3. What wonder is it, then, that the essential wisdom of the Father knew no mean between a single[37] and an evil eye! That his inspired Apostle cries out with such vehemence of affection, 'Purify your hearts, ye double-minded;'[38] that his beloved disciple, after 'This is the true God,'[39] immediately subjoins, 'Little children, keep yourselves from idols.'[40] What idols and what idolatry we are to keep ourselves from he elsewhere explicitly declares, in those well-known words, 'Love not the world, neither the things of the world: if any man love the world, the love of the Father is not in him.'[41]

4. If any farther proof from the Holy Scriptures be required of this first principle of all religion, let us hear St. Paul's words: 'Whether ye eat or drink, or whatever ye do, do all to the glory of God.'[42] It is here enjoined that whatever use we make of any power which God hath given us, whatever act of any faculty we exert, all should tend to the glory, the love, of God. And it is enjoined expressly. We need not argue from a parity of reason—'whether ye eat or drink', therefore, 'whether ye rejoice or love'. We need not argue from the less to the greater—if every bodily action, which at best profiteth but little, how much more is every movement of our soul to be subordinated to the end of our being?[43] No, we have yet a more sure word of direction; the very terms are, 'whatever ye do'. This commandment is indeed exceeding broad. Not a word of our tongue, not a thought of our heart, can

---

[31] Perhaps Ps. 50: 14 *BCP* (actually 'pay thy vows unto the most highest'). Charles may be working with the Hebrew here since the word translated as 'vows' may also mean 'votive offerings' or 'personal service'. Charles did possess a Hebrew psalter.   [32] Cf. Mic. 6: 7.

[33] Cf. 1 Cor. 13: 3.   [34] Deut. 6: 4.

[35] Written 'mightest' in the MS and changed to 'mightst' in another hand.

[36] Cf. Matt. 4: 10, citing Deut. 6: 13.

[37] Cf. Matt. 6: 22–3 and parallel. This text is the subject of Sermon 16.   [38] Cf. Jas. 4: 8.

[39] Cf. 1 John 5: 20.   [40] Cf. 1 John 5: 21.   [41] Cf. 1 John 2: 15.

[42] Cf. 1 Cor. 10: 31.

[43] Outler has an exclamation mark in place of the question mark at this point. However, the question mark is clear enough in the MS.

escape it. Do ye act, do ye speak, do ye reason, do ye love? Do all to the glory of God!

5. 'Tis true, if the literal sense of these Scriptures were absurd, and apparently contrary to reason, then we should be obliged not to interpret them according to the letter, but to look out for a looser meaning.[44] To guard those, therefore, who desire to love God even as he requires from this specious pretence for idolatry, I hasten to show that this very sense is not contrary but agreeable to the strictest reason.

6. And how reasonable is it ~~is~~ so to love the Lord our God with all our heart and with all our strength as to love nothing else but for his sake and in subordination to the love of him, may appear, first, from the general concession of all men that 'we ought to love nothing above God'. This is granted to be of the last concern. All men own that on this eternity depends. Reason, therefore, must direct to make all sure here; to run no hazard of so mighty a stake; whatever we do, to secure from all possible danger our passport into a happy eternity. But this cannot be done while we retain any love not subordinate to the love of God. For while we love any object besides God, we are never secure that we shall not love it above him. So long as the very disease of our nature is the loving the creature above the Creator, so long as the love of anything for its own sake so imperceptibly steals upon us that it is impossible to fix its bounds, and to say, 'Hitherto shalt thou come and no farther';[45] it is equally impossible that we should be safe from loving it more than God. If then reason forbid us to run any the least hazard of loving anything more than God, and if we must be in imminent hazard of doing so while we love anything without reference to him, then reason, as well as the Holy Scriptures, requires that we should so love God with all our heart as to love nothing else but for his sake, and in subordination to the love of him.

7. The same truth may be as evidently inferred from that other concession made by all men, 'that we may not entertain any love which is contrary to, or obstructive of, the love of God'. For all love which does not either directly or remotely tend to the love of God obstructs it. If it does not lessen what we have already attained, it prevents our attaining what we otherwise might attain.[46] For the force of a divided can never be equal to that of an united heart; nor is it possible that a part of our strength should carry us so far as the whole.

8. But this is not the heaviest charge against that[47] love of the creatures which is not conducive to the love of God. No; it is not only obstructive, but subversive of it; they are inconsistent and incompatible. Indeed many loves may consist in the same heart, so they be all subordinate to one. But two ultimate loves are as flat a contradiction as two firsts, or two lasts. So that when the son of Sirach says, 'Woe

---

[44] The spelling has been corrected from 'meanning' in the MS. It is not clear whether the correction is the work of Charles.   [45] Cf. Job 38: 11.

[46] The word 'attain' has been inserted above the line.

[47] Outler has 'the' rather than 'that' at this point in the text; 'that' is clear enough in the MS, although the superscripted 't' in Charles's original 'y^t' appears to have been struck out in another hand.

be to the fearful hearts, and faint hands, and the sinner that goeth two ways,'[48] he can only mean, either, [he][49] that flatters himself he goes both toward God and toward his idol, or rather, [he][50] that is unstable in his ways, sometimes walking in one, and sometimes in the other. That this is frequent, our own unhappy experience is sufficient to prove. But not the Almighty himself can make it possible for us to walk in two ways at the same time. All our habitual love must at any one time terminate either in God or in some of his creatures. And if it terminates in him, then it does not in them; if in them, then not in him. We cannot therefore have two ultimate loves; and by undeniable consequence, when we have any ultimate love but that of God, the love of God is not in us.[51]

9. Nor can it be said that there may be an unsubordinate love which yet is not an ultimate one.[52] For as every end which is subordinate to no other is itself an ultimate end, so every love which is subordinate to no other is itself an ultimate love, ultimate and subordinate being contradictory terms, between which there is no mean.

10. But who is this, touching whom we thus coldly debate whether he should wholly possess or only share our affection? Is it not the Lord—our God—the All-sufficient! The All-perfect! In whom are hid all the treasures of loveliness! Is it not he of whose faithfulness, of whose wisdom, of whose goodness, there is no number? And are we afraid of loving him too much? With too fervent, too entire an affection? Hath the love of God toward us been restrained![53] Hath he set any bounds to this ocean? Who is he that hath raised us from the dust? Who breathed into us these living souls? Who upholdeth us by the word of his power? Who protects us by his gracious providence? Who redeemed us by the blood of his Son? Who sanctifies us by the grace of his Spirit? O God, are the creatures of thy hand, the purchase of thy Son's blood, disputing whether they may not love thee too much? Whether thou art worthy of all their affection? Does not then the essential loveliness of his nature deserve, not all, but infinitely more than all our love? Is not our whole affection immeasurably less than the least of his mercies? Or if the whole mite of our love would overpay these, hath he no more? Is his hand shortened?[54] Is he not able, is he not willing, hath he not sworn, to render us a thousandfold for every particle of love we give him? Can we withhold from him one atom of the whole mass without tearing one star from our own crown? And shall it be thought unreasonable that he should demand the whole? That he should require all our love? Yea, worthy art thou, O Lord,[55] of all the love of all the creatures whom thou

[48] Cf. Sir. 2: 12.   [49] Outler's suggested clarification of the reading has been adopted here.

[50] Outler's suggested clarification of the reading has been adopted here.

[51] Cf. 1 John 3: 17, although the sentence appears to be a reflection on the text rather than a direct quotation.

[52] Outler has 'love' in place of 'one' at this point in the MS. However, 'one' is clear enough in the MS.

[53] The allusion may be to Isa. 63: 15. Outler has a question mark in place of the exclamation mark at this point in the text. The exclamation mark is, however, clear enough in the MS.

[54] Cf. Isa. 50: 2.   [55] Cf. Rev. 4: 11; 5: 9.

hast made! Especially of those whom thou hast redeemed! Whom thou now guidest by thy counsel, and wilt hereafter receive into thy glory!

III.1. The grand objection that has been frequently made against this sense of the great commandment (to which most others are easily reducible), which I proposed to consider in the third place, is this, 'that did it oblige us so to love God with all our heart as to love nothing else but for his sake, and in order to the love of him, such an obligation would be destructive of that happiness which our blessed religion was designed to establish. It would reduce us to a gloomy and melancholy state, and make the true Christian of a sad countenance.[56] It would deprive us of all the innocent pleasures of life, and reduce our enjoyments to so narrow a compass that they would not suffice for a balance to our pains, and a support under the evils to which we are exposed. So that, if in[57] this life only there were hope, we should be of all men most miserable'.[58]

2. I shall reply first to the particular branches of this objection, and then in general to the whole. And with regard to the first branch of it, be it observed that the happiness whereof it supposes the entire love of God to be destructive is a happiness that is to result from an enjoyment of the creatures, not referred to the Creator: that is, it is such a happiness as never did, nor ever will exist. 'That happiness is not, cannot be found in any creature' (to use the beautiful words of the above-cited author), 'is plain from experience, from the vanity which we find in all things, and from that restlessness and desire of change which is consequent upon it. We try one thing after another, as the searching bee wanders from flower to flower, but go off from every one with disappointment and a deluded expectation. Though almost everything promises, nothing answers; and even the succession of new enjoyments (the best remedy we have for the emptiness we find in each) amuses, but does not satisfy.' A glorious happiness this! 'Tis vexation, and pain, disappointment and loss, all over! And of this happiness it must be allowed the entire love of God is absolutely destructive.

But does it not make men gloomy and melancholy, by depriving them of the innocent pleasures of life? They who speak thus seem not to be aware how easy it is to produce a cloud of witnesses,[59] and those heathen as well as Christian, who, though they allow there are a thousand sorts of pleasure, which, considered with regard to the whole species, are neither good nor bad, yet utterly deny that any individual pleasure is barely innocent. But we need them not, since plain reason is enough to show (how strange soever it may sound to some ears) that this expression can never be used with propriety. It must import either too much or too little. For every pleasure, weighed with the circumstances that attend it, is either more or less than innocent. If it tends to the love of God, it is more; if it does not, it is less than innocent. Pleasures of all sorts, used in that proportion wherein they enliven and

---

[56] Cf. Matt. 6: 16.
[57] Outler has 'only' before 'in' at this point. No such word is, however, evident in the MS.
[58] Cf. 1 Cor. 15: 19.   [59] Cf. Heb. 12: 1.

strengthen our minds, and make us more fit for discharging the duties of our respective stations, deserve a better title than that of innocent: they are virtuous and rewardable. And pleasures of any sort, used in any other proportion, deserve not so good a title, as implying a sinful and punishable waste of time, and of the other talents which God hath lent us. If these be the innocent pleasures in the objection, we own the entire love of God does destroy them. But it deprives us of none that in any way conduce to that even cheerfulness which is both the parent and daughter of divine love, and life of virtue, and the beauty of holiness.[60]

The clearness and strength of reason with which one of our most celebrated divines confirms this important truth will excuse the repetition of his words:

Some of the heathen philosophers were of opinion that no actions (whether pleasing or not) are indifferent, but that all are positively either good or evil. Wherein they meant, not that no actions are indifferent in their own nature, but that no actions are indifferent in fact. In fact, I say, for in this state actions, besides their formal essence, include the end and intention of the doer. And in this sense they affirmed that a good man made all his indifferent actions good; and on the contrary an ill man made all his indifferent actions evil. For they laid down this for a rule, that every man ought to fix a certain general purpose and scope to all his actions, viz., to act agreeably to right reason, and that while a man held his eye upon this, so long all his actions, even those that were in themselves indifferent, were made wise and good. But on the contrary, while this was not fixed, all a man's actions, however indifferent in their own nature, became loose, irrational, and evil. And so St. Paul tells *us* that every Christian ought [to][61] have a general purpose to which all his actions should be directed. The charge runs: 'Whether ye eat, or drink, or whatever ye do, do all to the glory of God.'[62] Now 'tis certain that if we have an eye to the glory of God in all that we do, this is an aim that will sanctify all our actions, though in themselves indifferent. But on the contrary, so long as we have not an eye to this general end, all the mass of our indifferent actions become an irrational and profuse wasting of that precious time which God has given us for better uses, i.e., to devote and give it back again to himself. We should therefore be often putting the question to our soul

Dic anima, quo tendis? et in quod dirigis arcum?[63]

'Say, my soul, whither aimest thou? Whither tends this action?' Hast thou the glory of God in prospect? Or else shootest thou at rovers, and only beatest the air. This kind of reflection will consecrate the soul in all she does, and make every natural action[64] turn into religious; and make us meet God everywhere, and converse with his wisdom, goodness, providence in our walk, at our business, at our table; and render us more holy to God at our work than without this we can be at our prayers'. Dr Young's sermons vol. 2 p. 184.[65]

---

[60] Cf. 1 Chron. 16: 29.

[61] Outler has 'ought to have' here, though the word 'to', while clearly implied, is absent from the MS itself.   [62] Cf. 1 Cor. 10: 31.

[63] Cf. Persius, *Satires*, 3. 60. I owe this reference to Outler (ed.), *Sermons*, iv. 342 n. 46.

[64] The change from 'action' to 'act' appears to be the work of Charles himself.

[65] See further Outler (ed.), *Sermons*, iv. 342 n. b, for an account of the origin of this reference.

As to the last part of this objection, that such a love of God would reduce our enjoyments to so narrow a compass that they would not balance our pains, nor suffice for our support under the troubles we are daily exposed to, I answer, it was never designed they should: God hath provided far[66] other supports for us. And, in fact, who is he whom these did ever support under sharp pain, or heavy affliction? For whom did these comforts ever suffice when God wrote bitter things[67] against him? When the waters came in even unto his soul, and the floods of trouble ran over him?[68] Not one, ever since the world began—'miserable comforters are they all,'[69] utterly unable to heal the broken in heart, unfit medicines for that sickness!

6.[70] I come now to the direct and adequate answer to all the parts of this celebrated objection. The entire love of God, though it does exclude all such enjoyment of his creatures as neither directly nor remotely conduces to our enjoying him; though it does particularly prevent our leaning on those broken reeds when affliction presses down our soul; and though it does set us above what are sometimes called innocent pleasures, that is, unnecessary, untending, useless enjoyments; yet it is in no wise destructive of that happiness which our blessed religion was designed to establish. So far from it that love, entire love, is the point wherein all the lines of our holy religion centre. This is the very happiness which the great author of it lived and died to establish among us. And a happiness it is, worthy of God! Worthy of infinite goodness and wisdom[71] to bestow! A happiness not built on imagination, but real and rational; a happiness that does not play before our eyes at a distance, and vanish when we attempt to grasp it, but such as will bear the closest inspection, and the more it is tried will delight the more. In the happiness of love there is no vanity, neither any vexation of spirit.[72] No delusion, no disappointment is here; peace and joy ever dwell with love. The man who loves God feels that 'God hath given him all things richly to enjoy.'[73] He delights in his works, and surveys with joy all the creatures which God hath made. Love increases both the number of his delights, and the weight of them, a thousandfold. For in every creature he sees as in a glass[74] the glory of the great Creator. And while everything reflects to his enlightened eye the image of him whom his soul loves,[75] the sense of his presence, over and above that delight which he feels in common with other men, 'imparts such a vital joy and gladness to his heart, that, were eternity added to it, it would be heaven!'[76]

7. Here is the sufficient, and the only sufficient support under all the evils of life. Evils? Nothing is an evil to him who loves God! All things are to him very

---

[66] 'Far' is clear in the MS, though 'for' seems intended (which is the reading given by Outler).
[67] Cf. Job 13: 26.   [68] Cf. Ps. 69: 1, 2.   [69] Cf. Job 16: 2.
[70] There are no points 3–5 enumbered in the MS, which may suggest editorial activity.
[71] Outler inserts 'infinite' before 'wisdom'. This is not supported by the MS.
[72] Cf. Eccl. 2: 17.   [73] Cf. 1 Tim. 6: 17.   [74] 2 Cor. 3: 18.
[75] Cf. Song of Songs 3: 4.
[76] Cf. John Norris, *Practical Discourses upon Several Divine Subjects*, iii. 69–70, 82–3; I owe this reference to Outler (ed.), *Sermons*, iv. 344 n. 53.

good! He has but one desire—to delight in God; and God hath given him the desire of his heart. And while his spirit cleaves steadfastly to him, he is safe from the power of evil. Indeed, if his heart were not whole with God, as many things as he loved besides him, so many ways would he lie open to disappointment, and fear, and grief, and misery. But so long as he has one object of his love, and regards all things else only as they minister unto it, his heart standeth fast. For he is assured that 'neither life nor death, nor things present, nor things to come, nor height, nor depth, nor any other creature, shall be able to separate him from the love of God.'[77]

8. I shall conclude in the words of that happy and excellent man above cited, who so well practised what he taught:[78] 'Ye have heard what is the full and true extent of divine love, and the full and true import of the great commandment— which now appears to be a great commandment indeed! Both worthy of him who gave it, and worthy of that solemn mark of attention wherewith it was more than once delivered, 'Hear, O Israel!' And let all the whole creation hear, and with silence attend to this great law, which, lest any should fancy himself unconcerned in it, is expressly directed to every creature: 'Thou shalt love the Lord thy God with all thy heart, and with all thy soul, and with all thy mind, and with all thy strength.' 'My son, give me thy heart,'[79] is the language of the great God to every rational creature. 'Give me thy heart, for it was I that made it, it was I that gave it thee! It was I that gavest[80] its vital motion, and that for no other end but to direct and incline it toward me. I[81] only am thy true good: in me alone canst thou find rest for thy soul; all the springs of thy happiness are in me. Therefore, my son, give me thy heart![82] I only merit, and 'tis I alone that can reward, thy love! Let none have any share therein but me; and let me have it all!'

With angels, therefore, and archangels, and all the company of heaven,[83] having unclasped our arms from the embraces of the creation, let us love the Lord our God, and him alone. Let not God any longer divide with the creature (an unfit companion for so divine a guest) but let him reign an absolute monarch in our hearts, and engross our whole love. Yea, 'let us love the Lord our God with all our heart, and with all our mind, and with all our soul, and with all our strength!'

Unto God the Father, who first loved us, and made us accepted in the beloved;[84] unto God the Son, who loved us, and washed us from our sins in his own blood;[85]

---

[77] Cf. Rom. 8: 38–9.

[78] The following passages are from Norris, *Practical Discourses*, iii. 69–70, 82–3; I owe this reference to Outler (ed.), *Sermons*, iv. 344 nn. 56, 58.   [79] Cf. Prov. 23: 26.

[80] The word 'gavest' has been struck out in the MS and replaced by 'bestowed' (the reading given by Outler). The change does not appear to be in the hand of Charles himself.

[81] Before 'I' there is another word in the MS that has been so heavily struck out as to make it unreadable.   [82] The exclamation mark is omitted by Outler.

[83] *BCP*, Communion (the phrase is found in all six proper prefaces).   [84] Cf. Eph. 1: 6.

[85] Cf. Rev. 1: 5.

unto God the Holy Ghost, who sheddeth the love of God abroad in our hearts,[86] be all love and all glory for time and for eternity!

Transcribed[87] on board the London Galley, off Boston, September 4, 1736. From my brother's copy.

---

[86] Cf. Rom. 5: 5.   [87] These final words are in shorthand.

SERMON 21
LUKE 10: 42

INTRODUCTORY COMMENT

According to the record on the MS, Charles[1] preached this sermon some six times,[2] and further accounts of his preaching the sermon appear in the journal.[3] The entries are dates in 1737 and 1738 (see the text below for details). Clearly, then, this was a sermon Charles was happy to preach and he must therefore have been in agreement with its content. Thus, while it was copied from his brother's MS, shows no evidence of significant interruption in the order of paragraphs, and has no sections of shorthand or other obvious interpolations, it can nevertheless properly be included here as a sermon of Charles himself.

The MS is held at the John Rylands University Library of Manchester,[4] where it is one of four contained in a small bound volume (the others being Sermons 20, 22, and 23, on Mark 12: 30, Proverbs 11: 30, and Psalm 91: 11 respectively).[5] It was published as sermon V in the 1816 edition,[6] and as always there are significant differences between its form in that edition and in the MS. Outler also published the text in his edition of John's sermons.[7] The few inaccuracies in Outler's edition have been corrected here and the more significant of these are indicated in the notes.

Outler gives a good account of the way in which the reference in Luke to the 'one thing needful' was interpreted in the eighteenth century and his notes are well worth consideration at this point. There were numerous possibilities. In his *Unum Necessarium* published in 1655, Jeremy Taylor (1613–67) put forward the view that the one thing that was needful was the practice of true repentance. Other commentators had different views. Charles here makes the case that 'the one thing needful' is none other than 'the renewal of our fallen nature', that is, the restoration of the image of God.

---

[1] The record also gives details of John's preaching of the sermon; see further in the Introduction to Sermon 20.

[2] Outler counts seven, but this seems to be in error. At the very least the situation is unclear. He lists also Mickleton and Stanton as places where Charles preached the sermon, but it appears that these entries are meant by Charles to be additions to the column listing John's preaching, not Charles's. (It must be noted however that these entries cannot be confirmed from the records of John's preaching. I am grateful to Wanda Smith for assistance with this question.) Conversely, Outler omits reference to Charles preaching the sermon on 6 February 1737 'at chapel'.

[3] See the entries for 26 September 1736; 11 September 1737; 22 October 1738 (Charles preached the sermon twice on that day, the sermon record indicates only one); 26 July 1741; 5 March 1744; 29 July 1748 (it is not clear that Charles actually preached the sermon on this occasion; 22 August 1748; 11 April 1749; 24 October 1756. The relationship between the sermon as preached on these other occasions and the form it takes in this MS is not clear. (Telford, *Journal*, 82, 123, and 209; Jackson, *Journal*, i. 134, 291, 354; ii. 16, 20, 57, and 133.)   [4] MARC DDCW 8/13.

[5] On the date of the transcription see further above in the Introduction to Sermon 20.

[6] *Sermons*, 81–94.   [7] Outler (ed.), *Sermons*, iv. 351–9.

To recover our first estate, from which we are thus fallen, is the one thing now need-ful—to re-exchange the image of Satan for the image of God, bondage for freedom, sickness for health.

As is clear from the record of Charles's preaching, he continued to preach such a mes-sage even after the events of May 1738. However, the precise understanding of what that 'one thing needful' was seems to have undergone some development with the passing of the years. In 1762 Charles published a poetical comment on Luke 10: 42. He wrote

> Needful for the good of man
> One only thing there is,
> Here to live for God, and gain
> The everlasting bliss:
> Earth we soon shall leave behind,
> Our life is as a shadow gone;
> An eternal soul should mind
> Eternity alone.

> What is everything beside
> For which the world contend?
> Baits of lust, or boasts of pride,
> Which in a moment end:
> After earthly happiness
> I can no longer pant or rove,
> Need no more, who all possess
> In Jesu's heart-felt love.[8]

---

[8] Albin and Beckerlegge (eds.), *Unpublishd Poetry*, ii. 125–6; the second verse was originally published in *Short Hymns on Select Passages of the Holy Scriptures* in 1762 (Osborn, *Poetical Works*, xi. 198).

Sermon Register[1]

Chapel, February 6, 1737 afternoon[2]
Duke Street chapel 1737[3]
St Olaves, Old Jewry October 30 1737[4]
St Helen's, Bishopsgate Street October 30 1737[5]
Islington October 1738[6]
St Clement's on October 22, 1738[7]

In the tenth chapter of the Gospel according to St. Luke, at the 42 verse,
it is thus written:

One thing is needful

1. Could we suppose an intelligent being, entirely a stranger to the state of this world and its inhabitants, to take a view of their various enterprises and employments, and thence conjecture the end of their existence, he would surely conclude that these creatures were designed to be busied about many things. While he observed not only the infinite ~~distance~~ difference of the ends which different men were pursuing, but how vast a multitude of objects were successively pursued by almost every different person, he might fairly infer that for all these things were the sons of men placed upon the earth, even to gratify their several desires with sensual pleasure, or riches, or honour, or power.

2. How surprised then would he be to hear their Creator declare to all, without distinction, 'One thing is needful!'[8] But how much more when he knew that this one thing needful for men, their one business, the one end of their existence, was none of all those things which men were troubled about, none of all those ends they were pursuing, none of all those businesses wherein they were so deeply

---

[1] This information is on the verso of the final leaf of the sermon on Mark 12: 30 (Sermon 20 above) found in the same booklet as this sermon. As has been noted, several of the entries refer to John's preaching. However, those listed here refer to Charles's use of the text.

[2] After the date 'fb 6, 1737' Charles has written 'af/v' with a dot so positioned beneath the stroke as to suggest that a major contraction has been made. The journal entry for the day does not provide any confirmation of the register.

[3] The journal does not provide any evidence supportive of this entry.   [4] See the next note.

[5] See MARC DDCW 10/2 *in loc.*; Telford, *Journal*, 129. 'I preached at S. Helen's the one thing needful. In the afternoon I carried her and her brother to Mr. Chadwicks's (my usual lodgings), and thence to Ironmonger's Lane. After preaching the same sermon here, we drank tea at Mr Chadwick's.'

[6] The journal account indicates that Charles preached the sermon at Islington on 15 October of that year (MARC DDCW 10/2 *in loc.*; Jackson, *Journal*, i. 132), though the day is not recorded in the sermon register itself.

[7] This is confirmed by the journal, which indicates that Charles preached the sermon twice on that day. It reads: 'I preached one thing needful at St. Clement's, to a very large audience (many of whom stayed the communion), and again at Sir G. Wheeler's chapel.' MARC DDCW 10/2 *in loc.*; Jackson, *Journal*, i. 134.

[8] Here, and elsewhere in the MS, the spelling of 'needful' has been altered from 'needfull'. It is unclear whether this correction is the work of Charles.

engaged, which filled their hearts and employed their hands. Nay, that it was an end not only distinct from but contrary to them all—as contrary as light and darkness, heaven and hell, the kingdom of God and that of Satan.[9]

3. The only thought he could form in their favour must be, that they had a surplusage of time at their command; that they therefore trifled a few hours, because they were assured of thousands of years wherein to work. But how beyond measure would he be amazed when he heard farther that these were creatures of a day; that as they yesterday arose out of the dust,[10] so tomorrow they were to sink into it again![11] that the time they had for their great work was but a span long, a moment; and yet that they had no manner of assurance of not being snatched away in the midst of this moment, or indeed at the very beginning of it! When he saw that all men were placed on a narrow, weak, tottering bridge, whereof either end was swallowed up in eternity; that the waves and storms which went over it were continually bearing away one after another, in an hour when they looked not for it;[12] and that they who yet stood, knew not but they should plunge into the great gulf[13] the very next instant, but well knew that if they fell before they had finished their work they were lost, destroyed, undone—for ever: how would all utterance, nay, all thought, be lost! How would he express, how would he conceive the senselessness, the madness, of those creatures who, being in such a situation, could think of anything else, could talk of anything else, could do anything besides, could find time for any other design, or care, but that of[14] ensuring the one thing needful!

4. It cannot, therefore, be an improper employment for us, first, to observe what this one thing needful is; and, secondly, to consider a few of the numberless reasons that prove this to be the one thing needful.

[I]1. We may observe what this one thing is, in which, 'tis true, many things are comprised—as are all the works of our callings, all that properly belong to our several stations in the world, insomuch that whoever neglects any of these so far neglects the one thing needful. And this indeed can no otherwise be pursued than by performing all the works of our calling, but performing them in such a manner as in and by every one to advance our great work.

2. Now this great work, this one thing needful, is the renewal of a our[15] fallen nature. In the image of God was man made,[16] but a little lower than the angels.[17] His nature was perfect, angelical, divine. He was an incorruptible picture of the God of glory. He bore his stamp on every part of his soul; the brightness of his

---

[9] Outler inserts an exclamation mark at this point in the text.   [10] Cf. Gen. 3: 19.

[11] Outler replaces the exclamation mark with a semicolon at this point.

[12] Cf. Matt. 24: 50 and parallel.   [13] Luke 16: 26.

[14] The words 'that of' have been inserted above the line. The insertion does not appear to be in the hand of Charles himself.

[15] The word 'a' has been struck out in the MS and replaced by 'our'. This change appears to be the work of Charles himself.   [16] Cf. Gen. 1: 26.

[17] Ps. 8: 5.

Creator shone mightily upon him. But sin hath now effaced the image of God. He is no longer nearly allied to angels. He is sunk lower than the very beasts of the field. His soul is not only earthly and sensual, but devilish.[18] Thus is the mighty fallen![19] The glory is departed[20] from him! His brightness is swallowed up in utter darkness!

3. From the glorious liberty[21] wherein he was made he is fallen into the basest bondage. The devil, whose slave he now is, to work his will, hath him so fast in prison that he cannot get forth. He hath bound him with a thousand chains, the heavy chains of his own vile affections. For every inordinate appetite, every unholy passion, as it is the express image of the god[22] of this world, so it is the most galling yoke, the most grievous chain, that can bind a free-born spirit. And with these is every child of Adam, everyone that is born into this world, so loaded that he cannot lift up an eye, ~~and~~ a thought to heaven; that his whole soul cleaveth unto the dust![23]

4. But these chains of darkness[24] under which we groan do not only hold us in on every side,[25] but they are within us too. They enter into our soul; they pierce through its inmost substance.[26] Vile affections are not only so many chains, but likewise so many diseases. Our nature is distempered, as well as enslaved; the whole head is faint, and the whole heart sick.[27] Our body, soul, and spirit, are infected, overspread, consumed, with the most fatal leprosy. We are all over, within and without, in the eye of God, full of diseases, and wounds, and putrefying sores.[28] Every one of our brutal passions and diabolical tempers, every kind of sensuality, pride, selfishness, is one of those deadly wounds, of those loathsome sores, full of corruption, and of all uncleanness.[29]

5. To recover our first estate, from which we are thus fallen, is the one thing now needful—to re-exchange the image of Satan for the image of God, bondage for freedom, sickness for health. Our one business[30] is to rase out of our souls the likeness of our destroyer, and to be born again, to be formed anew after the likeness of our Creator. It is our one concern to shake off this servile yoke and to regain our native freedom; to throw off every chain, every passion and desire that does not suit an angelical nature. The one work we have to do is to return from the gates of death to perfect soundness; to have our diseases cured, our wounds healed, and our uncleanness done away.

II.I Let us in the second place consider a few of the numberless reasons which prove that this is the one thing needful; so needful that this alone is to be had in

---

[18] Cf. Jas. 3: 15.   [19] Cf. 2 Sam. 1: 19.   [20] 1 Sam. 4: 21–2.

[21] Rom. 8: 21.

[22] Here, as almost always in Charles's prose, he has written 'God/god' as 'GOD'. However, 'god' is clearly implied by the context. Cf. 2 Cor. 4: 4.   [23] Cf. Ps. 119: 25.

[24] Cf. 2 Pet. 2: 4.   [25] Cf. Luke 19: 43.   [26] Cf. Heb. 4: 12.

[27] Cf. Isa. 1: 5.   [28] Cf. Isa. 1: 6.   [29] Cf. Matt. 23: 27.

[30] Before 'business' Outler inserts 'great'. This word is not present in the MS, though it is found in the 1816 edition (p. 86).

view, and pursued at all times and in all places; not indeed by neglecting our temporal affairs, but by making them all minister unto it; by so conducting them all, that every step therein may be a step to this higher end.

2. Now, that the recovery of the image of God, of this glorious liberty,[31] of this perfect soundness, is the one thing needful upon earth, appears first from hence, that the enjoyment of them was the one end of our creation. For to this end was man created, to love God; and to this end alone, even to love the Lord his God with all his heart, and soul, and mind, and strength.[32] But love is the very image of God: it is the brightness of his glory.[33] By love man is not only made like God, but in some sense one with him. 'If any man love God, God loveth him, and cometh to him, and maketh his abode with him.'[34] He 'dwelleth in God, and God in him';[35] and 'he that is thus joined to the Lord is one spirit.'[36] Love is perfect freedom; as there is no fear, or pain, so there is no constraint in love.[37] Whoever acts from this principle alone, he doth whatsoever he will. All his thoughts move freely; they follow the bent of his own mind, they run after the beloved object. All his words flow easy and unconstrained; for it is the abundance of the heart that dictates.[38] All his actions are the result of pure choice: the thing he would, that he does, and that only.[39] Love is the health of the soul, the full exertion of all its powers, the perfection of all its faculties. Therefore, since the enjoyment of these was the one end of our creation, the recovering of them is the one thing now needful.

3. May not the same truth appear, secondly, from hence, that this was the one end of our redemption; of all our blessed Lord did and suffered for us; of his incarnation, his life, his death? All these miracles of love were wrought with no other view than to restore us to health and freedom. Thus himself testifies of the end of his coming into the world: 'The Spirit of the Lord is upon me; he hath sent me to heal the broken-hearted, to preach deliverance to the captives;'[40] ~~and~~ or, as the prophet expresses it, 'to preach good tidings to the meek, to bind up the broken-hearted, to proclaim liberty to the captives, and the opening of the prison to them that are bound'.[41] For this only he lived, that he might heal every disease, every spiritual sickness of our nature. For this only he died, that he might deliver those who were all their lifetime subject to bondage.[42] And it was in pursuance of the very same design that he gave us his merciful law. The end of his commandment, too, was only our health, liberty, perfection, or, to say all in one word, charity. All the parts of it centre in this one point, our renewal in the love of God; either enjoining what is necessary for our recovery thereof, or forbidding what is obstructive of it. Therefore this, being the one end of our redemption as well as creation,[43] is the one thing needful for us upon earth.

---

[31] Cf. Rom. 8: 21.   [32] Cf. Mark 12: 30 (the subject of Sermon 20) and parallel; Deut. 6: 5.
[33] Cf. Heb. 1: 3.   [34] Cf John 14: 23.   [35] Cf. 1 John 4: 12, 15, 16.
[36] Cf. 1 Cor. 6: 17.   [37] Charles appears to be reflecting on 1 John 4: 18.   [38] Matt. 12: 34.
[39] Cf. Rom. 7: 15, 19.   [40] Cf. Luke 4: 18.   [41] Cf. Isa. 61: 1, 2.
[42] Cf. Heb. 2: 15.
[43] Before 'creation' Outler inserts 'our'. The word is not in the MS, though it is found in the 1816 edition (p. 89).

4. This is the one thing needful, thirdly, because it is the one end of all God's providential dispensations. Pleasure and pain, health and sickness, riches and poverty, honour and dishonour, friends and enemies, are all bestowed by his unerring wisdom and ~~justice~~ goodness with a view to this one thing. The will of God, in allotting us our several portions of all these, is solely our sanctification; our recovery from that vile bondage, the love of his creatures, to the free love of our Creator. All his providences, be they mild or severe, point at no other end than this. They are all designed either to wean us from what is not, or to unite us to what is worthy [of] our affection. Are they pleasing? Then they are designed to lift up our hearts to the parent of all good. Are they painful? Then they are means of rooting out those passions that forcibly withhold us from him. So that all lead the[44] same way, either directly or indirectly, either by gratitude or mortification. For to those that have ears to hear,[45] every loss, especially of what was nearest and dearest to them, speaks as clearly as if it were an articulate voice from heaven, 'Little children, keep yourselves from idols.'[46] Every pain cries aloud, 'Love not the world, neither the things of the world.'[47] And every pleasure says, with a still small voice,[48] 'Thou shalt love the Lord thy God with all thy heart.'[49]

5. To the same end are all the internal dispensations of God, all the influences of his Holy Spirit. Whether he gives us joy or sorrow of heart, whether he inspires us with vigour and cheerfulness,[50] or permits us to sink into numbness of soul, into dryness and heaviness, 'tis all with the same view, viz., to restore us to health, to liberty, to holiness. These are all designed to heal those inbred diseases of our nature, self-love, and the[51] love of the world. They are all given together with the daily bread[52] of his external dispensations, to enable us to turn that into proper nourishment, and so recover his love, the health of our souls. Therefore the renewal of our nature in this love being not only the one end of our creation and our redemption, but likewise of all the providences of God over us, and all the operations of his Spirit in us, must be, as the eternal wisdom of God hath declared, the one thing needful.

[III] Exhortation[53] 1. How great reason is there, then, even in the Christian world, to resume the Apostle's exhortation, 'Awake, thou that sleepest, and arise from the dead!'[54] Hath not Christ given thee light? Why then sittest thou still in the shadow of death?[55] What slumber is this which[56] hangs on thy temples? Knowest thou not that only one thing is needful? What then are all these? Why hath any but that the least place in thy thoughts, the least share in thy affections? Is the

---

[44] Outler has 'that' in place of 'the' at this point; 'the' is clear enough in the text.

[45] Cf. Mark 4: 9, 23; Matt. 11: 15; 13: 9, 43.   [46] Cf. 1 John 5: 21.   [47] Cf. 1 John 2: 15.

[48] Cf. 1 Kgs. 19: 12.   [49] Cf. Deut. 6: 5; Matt. 22: 37 and parallel.

[50] The word is spelt 'chearfulness' in the MS and has been corrected to 'cheerfulness' in another hand.   [51] The word 'the' has been inserted above the line.

[52] Cf. Matt. 6: 11 and parallel.

[53] 'Exhortation' is written as 'exh' only in the MS, but the expansion seems certain.

[54] Eph. 5: 14. This text is the subject of Sermon 8.   [55] Cf. Luke 1: 79.

[56] 'Which' has been inserted above the line. It is not clear whether this is the work of Charles himself.

entertainment of the senses the one thing needful? Or the gratifying the imagination with uncommon, or great, or beautiful objects? Our Lord saith not so.
Saith he then that the one thing is to acquire a fortune, or to increase that thou
hast already? I tell you, Nay: these may be the thoughts of those that dream, but
they cannot [be those][57] of waking men. Is it to obtain honour, power, reputation,
or (as the phrase is) to get preferment? Is the one thing to gain a large share in
that fairest of the fruits of earth, learning? No. Though any of these may sometimes be conducive to, none of them is, the one thing needful. That is simply to
escape out of the snare of the devil, to regain an angelical nature; to recover the
image wherein we were formed; to be like the Most High. This, this alone, is the
one end of our abode here; for this alone are we placed on the earth; for this
alone did the Son of God pour out his blood; for this alone doth his Holy Spirit
watch over us. One thing we have to do, to press towards this mark of the prize
of our high calling;[58] to emerge out of chains, diseases, death, into liberty, health,
and life immortal!

2. Let us well observe, that our Lord doth not call this our main concern, our
great business, the chief thing needful, but the *one*[59] thing— all others being either
parts of this or quite foreign to the end of life. On this then let us fix our single
view, our pure unmixed intention; regarding nothing at all, small or great, but as
it stands referred to this. We must use many means; but let us ever remember we
have but one end. For as while our eye is single our whole body will be full of light,
so, should it ever cease to be single, in that moment our whole body would be full
of darkness.[60]

3. Be we then continually jealous over our souls, that there be no mixture in our
intention. Be it our one view in all our thoughts, and words, and works, to be partakers of the divine nature,[61] to regain the highest measure we can of that faith
which works by[62] love, and makes us[63] become one spirit with God. I say, the highest measure we can; for who will plead for any abatement of health, liberty, life, and
glory? Let us then labour to be made perfectly whole, to burst every bond in
sunder;[64] to attain the fullest conquest over this body of death,[65] the most entire
renovation of our nature; knowing this, that when the Son of man shall send forth
his angels to cast the double-minded into outer darkness, then shall the single of

---

[57] These words have been inserted by Outler, whose suggestion is followed here for the sake of clarity.
[58] Cf. Phil. 3: 14. This text is the subject of Sermon 1.
[59] The word 'one' is written 'One' in the MS with an apparent concern for emphasis (hence, presumably, it is underlined by Outler).
[60] Cf. Matt. 6: 22 and parallel. This text is the subject of Sermon 16.   [61] 2 Pet. 1: 4
[62] The words 'faith which works by' have been inserted above the line. The words are in Charles's
hand (cf. Gal. 5: 6).
[63] The words 'and makes us' have been inserted above the line (in Charles's hand) and replace words
that have been struck out. Those struck-out words are now almsot unreadable, but appear to be
'whereby we'.   [64] Cf. Nahum. 1: 13.
[65] Cf. Rom. 7: 24.

heart receive the one thing they sought, and shine forth as the sun[66] in the kingdom of their Father!

Now to God the Father, God the Son, and God the Holy Ghost, be ascribed all honour and glory, adoration and worship, both now and for ever. Amen

---

[66] Cf. Matt. 13: 41–3.

SERMON 22

PROVERBS 11: 30

INTRODUCTORY COMMENT

This is another sermon that Charles copied from his brother John. It is found, together with Sermons 20, 21, and 23, on Mark 12: 20, Luke 10: 42 and Psalm 91: 11, in a hard-bound volume now held at the John Rylands University Library of Manchester.[1] The transcriptions were made on board the *London Galley* in September 1736 as Charles was beginning his journey back to England.[2]

The sermon register on page 34 of the booklet is again useful here. Charles has listed a number of dates and places relevant to John's preaching of this sermon (and Outler has given a good insight into the place of this text in John's work). However, in addition Charles has also recorded that he preached the sermon at St John's on 23 October 1737, though this cannot be confirmed from the extant journal material, which makes no reference anywhere to Charles preaching on either 'The wisdom of winning souls' or Proverbs 11. Neither do other sources provide any further insight into the frequency with which Charles preached this text.

This was, then, a sermon which Charles preached, at least once, and it was in that sense 'his'. The form of the MS offers no suggestion regarding the nature and extent of any editorial emendation that he may have introduced into his brother's text. It is worth noting, however, that he appears to have left intact the initial words as they were used quite appropriately by John on the occasion of his first preaching of the sermon in Oxford: 'a place where philosophy or the love of wisdom is so universally professed and so carefully cultivated . . .' Charles must presumably have departed extempore from this opening when he preached at St John's.

It was published as sermon I in the 1816 edition, and shows signs of the editorial hand.[3] It was also published by Outler in his edition of John's sermons.[4] The few inaccuracies in the Outler edition have been corrected and the most significant are indicated in the notes.

The sermon was particularly well suited to the original audience for whom John wrote it, those who had gathered at an ordination service in Christ Church.[5] However, it obviously appealed to Charles since he took the trouble to copy it out. Just why it did so is not easy to gauge. It may well have been its uncompromising affirmation of the importance of the task of evangelism. This involves both convicting the sinner of the need of being cleansed and also the guidance of that same person in the subsequent pursuit of holy living.

As Outler notes,[6] one of the more challenging aspects of this sermon, when seen in the context of the eighteenth century, is its openness to non-ordained ministerial activity.

[1] MARC DDCW 8/13.
[2] On the date of the transcription see further above in the Introduction to Sermon 20.
[3] *Sermons*, 1–21.   [4] Outler (ed.), *Sermons*, iv. 304–17.   [5] Ibid. iv. 305.
[6] Ibid. *Sermons*, iv. 305.

Charles maintains that there is a clear line which separates the work of the ordained from those of the unordained. 'Several acts of our blessed office indeed there are which may not be performed unless by particularly commissioned officers.' However, this division of labour, it is argued in this sermon, does not extend to evangelistic activity.

Indeed, if Solomon had only said, 'The priest that winneth souls is wise,' they had some colour for saying to all who are not invested with this office, 'Ye have neither part nor lot in this wisdom; even with such sacrifices God is not pleased, when they are offered by your unhallowed hands.' But Solomon's words are universal, 'He that winneth souls is wise!' Who is he that is wiser and inspired by a better spirit? Let him stand forth and make the restriction!

The issue of the extent to which the work of God is to be carried out by those not specifically ordained thereunto was later to be the cause of some considerable dispute between the Wesley brothers. However, Charles did not fundamentally resist the involvement of the laity in the broad evangelical task. He appears not to have been against lay preaching *per se*, but against poorly qualified and ill-suited lay preachers practising the homiletic art. On such issues as presidency at the Eucharist, he was immovable, as he was on the necessity of episcopal ordination. The latter issues are not addressed in this sermon, and Charles is here fully supportive of the involvement of the laity in the spreading of the gospel and the weeding out of sin.

In the eleventh chapter of the Proverbs, at the thirtieth verse, it is written,

He that winneth souls is wise

In a place where philosophy or the love of wisdom is so universally professed and so carefully cultivated, where so many are obliged by their office to study and practise this particular sort of wisdom, and where more are designed and endeavouring to qualify themselves for the same holy function, it can't but be highly proper to make that wisdom the subject of our consideration, which so a great part of us are engaged by so peculiar ties to recommend both by our lives and doctrines; and to explain and enforce this important truth, 'He that winneth souls is wise.'

He that winneth souls, that draws them from vice to virtue, from rebellion against God to obedience, that recovers them from darkness and the shadow of death to the way of light and peace,[2] that disentangles them from that fatal snare from which they had no hope, nay, no desire, of escaping, that disappoints the lion of his prey, even when he had said, there is none to help them; he is wise indeed! As will be evident if we consider:

First, the end he proposes, and secondly, the means that lead to it.

I. First, the end he proposes, winning of souls, may be considered, first, as bringing glory to God. 'Tis true, no action of any created being can do this in a strict sense, can at all add to that essential glory wherewith his creator was clothed from eternity. Yet in a lower sense, whatsoever we do may be done to the glory of God; that is, may at least remotely tend to manifest his glory, to increase the honour paid to him by his creatures, to make us him more known and more loved.

And in this sense he that winneth souls eminently advances the glory of God, by displaying his glorious nature and attributes to the sons of men, who alone of all the visible creation are capable of contemplating them. Man alone of all the inhabitants of this world can acknowledge and praise him that made it; can raise his thoughts and affections from sensible objects to him 'whom no man hath seen nor can see'.[3] And to persuade him to make this true use of the privileges[4] he enjoys, to declare to him the wonderful works which God hath done,[5] the wisdom and goodness he hath shown in all his works, is as noble a way of advancing his glory as any creature can aspire to.

It was for this very thing that God wrought those works, that 'his eternal power and Godhead might be known'.[6] That the invisible nature of him might be seen in them, 'He spake, and they were made.'[7] With this design were 'the heavens and the

---

[1] *In Nomine Dei*; see further the note on Sermon 3. On the page facing the words 'preached before the University of Oxford' appear in the hand of 'W.P.'. This relates to John's preaching of the sermon there on 19 September 1731, see further Outler, *Sermons*, iv. 305.   [2] Cf. Luke 1: 79.
[3] 1 Tim 6: 16.
[4] Spelt 'priviledges' in the MS and corrected in what appears to be another hand.
[5] 1 Chron. 16: 12.   [6] Cf. Rom. 1: 20.   [7] Cf. Ps. 148: 5 (*BCP*).

earth created, and all the hosts of them'.[8] For this ~~end~~, God formed man of the dust of the ground and breathed into his nostrils the breath of life.[9] With the same great view he preserves what he has made, and 'upholds all things by the word of his power'.[10] With the same [view],[11] after all his other gifts, 'he withheld not from us his Son, his only Son!'[12] He gave us him, after he had freely given us all things,[13] that his name might be known and glorified.

This purpose it is which God hath uniformly pursued through our creation, preservation, and redemption.[14] And this purpose it is, seeing the glory of God is inseparably connected with the winning of souls, which the wise man we are speaking of is continually promoting; as well as its necessary consequence, with regard to which we may, in the second place, consider the end he proposes, namely, the good it brings to every person whom he wins to glorify God.

Now this is of two sorts: deliverance from misery, and advancement to happiness. Of the former we need only observe this one circumstance, that it is eternal (as indeed it must be, unless there were repentance in the grave, since endless sin implies endless misery). This alone is abundantly sufficient to show us the greatness of it. To show that if it were proposed either to save the whole world, or to save a soul, to preserve ten thousand millions from being in pain sixty years, or one man from being in pain, though but equal, to all eternity, a wise man would not pause a moment which were the nobler instance of mercy; seeing although as many men as there are stars in heaven[15] or sands on the sea-shore[16] were to be miserable for sixty years, the whole quantity of misery they sustained would bear no more proportion to the endless misery of one than finite to infinite, than time to eternity.

The same single consideration is enough to give us a general notion of that happiness, the enjoyment of which is secured to him who is rescued from endless misery. That this too is eternal we know, and so need not inquire into the particulars. Nor indeed can we tell these if we would. If it were possible for man to utter them, St. Paul doubtless, after having been in the third heaven, would have been best able to have done it.[17] But since even he was not equal to the task, well may we decline so fruitless a task an attempt. Only we are expressly told that no pain is there,[18] but inexhaustible rivers of pleasure;[19] that the hungry soul shall there be satisfied with good,[20] and no desire of his soul return empty. And that part of this happiness will be an intimate union with and enjoyment of 'the spirits of just men made perfect, of the general assembly of the church of the first-born, of an innu-

---

[8] Cf. Gen. 2: 1.   [9] Cf. Gen. 2: 7.   [10] Cf. Heb. 1.3.
[11] The word 'view' is added by Outler and seems appropriate in context.
[12] Cf. Gen. 22: 12, 16.
[13] Cf. Rom. 8: 32.
[14] As Outler notes, this phrase echoes the *BCP* 'General Thanksgiving' prayer.
[15] In place of 'in heaven', Outler has 'in the heavens'. However, 'in heaven' is clear in the MS.
[16] Cf. Gen. 22: 17.   [17] Cf. 2 Cor. 12: 2.   [18] Cf. Rev. 21: 4.
[19] Cf. Ps. 36: 8.   [20] Cf. Ps. 107: 9 (*BCP*).

merable company of angels, and lastly, of God, the judge of all, and Jesus, the mediator of the new covenant'.[21]

Here is wisdom! The pursuing such an end as this! The recovering him that was just sinking into the gulf of misery to happiness incomprehensible, eternal! To the depth of the mercies of God! This is the good which he that wins a soul brings to him whom he wins to virtue, over and above the good he brings to himself, which is thirdly to be considered.

And no small part of the good it brings to himself is the honour that necessarily attends it, the honour of answering the end of his creation, promoting at once the glory of God and the good of man; of sharing in the office of those superior natures who continually minister to the heirs of salvation;[22] of working together with God, of being a fellow-labourer with the ever blessed Spirit, and Jesus Christ the righteous! An honour which however lightly it may be esteemed by those who count zeal madness, is justly prized by those whose supposed foolishness is wiser than the wisdom of the world.[23] An honour which shall not fail to be paid them in part in the moment wherein they deserve it, if not by men, yet by those more discerning beings who disdain not to call good men their fellow-servants; and by their common master, who hath expressly declared, 'them that honour me, I will honour.'[24]

Nor can it ever be said of this honour, as is too often true of the honour of men, that it brings no advantage with it. This is never the case with regard to the honour which cometh from God.

None can be conscious of this without an immediate advantage, without such a satisfaction as words cannot express. None can resemble God in extending his mercy even to the evil and unjust,[25] without experiencing, even at that time, some degree of his happiness whose goodness he imitates. No human creature can have so little of the law of kindness written[26] in his heart as not to feel his heart burn within him[27] while he is saving a soul from death.[28]

A foretaste this of that more ample reward which shall hereafter enlarge his heart, when he, with those whom he hath been a means of saving, shall together enter into the joy of their Lord.[29] We need not dispute whether St. James touches upon this reward in those remarkable words, 'Brethren, if any of you do err from the truth, and one convert him, let him know that he which converteth a sinner from the error of his way shall save a soul from death, and hide a multitude of sins.'[30] Now supposing these be[31] only the sins of the person saved, and not the infirmities of the saver, yet how will every good man rejoice even in the joy of the

---

[21] Cf. Heb. 12: 22–4. Despite the quotation marks this is not verbatim, the clauses being in a different order.   [22] Cf. Heb. 1: 14.
[23] Cf. 1 Cor. 1: 25.   [24] 1 Sam. 2: 30.   [25] Cf. Matt. 5: 44–5.
[26] Corrected in the MS from 'writ'. It is not clear whether this correction is the work of Charles himself.
[27] Cf. Luke 24: 32.   [28] Cf. Jas. 5: 20.   [29] Cf. Matt. 25: 21, 23.
[30] Cf. Jas. 5: 20.   [31] The words 'these be' have been inserted above the line.

penitent?[32] And how eminent a share must he have in this, who was the instrument of his conversion, who has occasioned that joy in heaven, which is more over one sinner that repenteth than over ninety and nine that need no such repentance?[33] To whom, under God, it is owing that all his sins which he had committed are not once mentioned unto him,[34] that the handwriting against him is blotted out,[35] and his name written in the book of life![36]

Neither need we inquire what foundation there is for that opinion of the ancients, that the same reward awaits those who give witness to the truth by dying for it themselves, or by saving a soul from death. For whether the reward of a martyr and of a winner of souls be one or no,[37] sure we are that either is sufficient; sure we are that either is eminently glorious above that of common Christians. Neither God's word nor his attributes suffer us to doubt that different men will have different rewards in heaven; 'that as one star differeth from another star in glory, so it will be in the resurrection of the dead';[38] 'every man shall receive his own reward, according to his own labour' (1 Cor 3.8).[39] And some of the highest of these rewards are promised to the converters of sinners. All who are admitted into the presence of God will be glorious, but these shall exceed in glory. 'They that are wise shall shine as the brightness of the firmament, that[40] they that turn many to righteousness as the stars for ever and ever!'[41]

Such is the wisdom of him that winneth souls! Such is the end which he proposes! The means which lead to that end I come now, under my second general head, to consider.

II. The first of these is the regulating his understanding whom[42] he endeavours to win to virtue;[43] the freeing him from those confused apprehensions of things, those false judgments and ill-grounded conclusions which he has long been planting in himself, and which perhaps have been striking root for many years. Whether the first seeds of these were early sown by education, or afterwards by ill advice or example; whether they relate to faith or practice in general, or to any particular branch of either; whether they are errors of a whole sect of men, or peculiar to the person infected, they are carefully to be weeded out, and no root of bitterness left.[44]

---

[32] Outler has an exclamation mark in place of a question mark at this point. The question mark is clear in the MS.

[33] Cf. Luke 15: 7. Outler has an exclamation mark in place of a question mark at this point. The question mark is clear in the MS.   [34] Cf. Ezek. 18: 22.

[35] Cf. Col. 2: 14.   [36] Cf. Rev. 3: 5; 21: 27.

[37] The word 'no' has been altered to 'not' in the MS, but the change is not in Charles's hand.

[38] Cf. 1 Cor. 15: 41–2.

[39] The reference to 1 Cor. 3: 8 has been struck out in the MS. It is not clear whether this deletion is the work of Charles himself.

[40] The word 'that' has been struck out in the MS in what appears to be Charles's hand. Outler adds '[and]' at this point.   [41] Cf. Dan. 12: 3.

[42] Before 'whom' Outler inserts '[of him]'.

[43] The word 'virtue' has been struck out in the MS and replaced by 'piety'. The change is not in the hand of Charles himself.   [44] Cf. Heb. 12: 15.

In particular there is an absolute necessity of removing the confused notion which most vicious men have[45] of virtue. They apprehend religion as 'a terrible spectre looking down from heaven only to enslave the earth, standing over them with so horrible an aspect'[46] as damps the courage of all who behold it; and such a monster as this they cannot but judge to be the bane of happiness, the destroyer of pleasure, and the imposer of numberless burdens too painful to be borne; whence they naturally infer that to throw off her yoke is the surest mark of a good understanding, and that the first rule of prudence is, 'Be not righteous overmuch.'[47] He who is so, they are persuaded, destroys himself, and so at best can't be over-wise.

To make one who thinks thus wise unto salvation, he must be rescued from all these errors. And that the confused notion he has of religion, the ground of them all, may be cleared, he must be brought to fix his eye upon her, that he may perceive 'he feared where no fear was';[48] that he may see the monster of his imagination in[49] her real shape, her native loveliness; that he may know that righteousness therefore looked down from heaven[50] that mercy might flourish upon earth, that men might have a light to guide them to her, whose 'ways are ways of pleasantness, and all whose paths are peace'.[51] He is to be convinced that religion forbids no pleasure but what would deprive him of a greater, nor requires any pain to be embraced, unless in order to more than equal pleasure. The plain consequence of which, he may readily observe, is that a 'good understanding have all they that do thereafter;'[52] and that there is the very same danger of being righteous overmuch, provided a man knows what righteousness is, as of having overmuch ease and safety in this life, or overmuch happiness in the other.

But the convincing an ill man of these and the like truths is only one step towards his conversion, and often no step at all; since every conviction is not a lasting one. No, a man who has been long wedded to a mistake, if he be at last convinced it is so, will, unless great care be taken to prevent it, soon unconvince himself. Old opinions, though not quickly parted with, are quickly received into favour again; and the new, which seemed so firmly fixed that no force could make them give way, are by a prejudiced mind as easily broke through 'as a thread of tow that has touched the fire'.[53] The confirming one who is brought to a knowledge of the truth is therefore as necessary as the convincing him at first. And when this is done, when due care has been used to strengthen his understanding, then 'tis time to use the other great means of winning souls, namely, the regulating his affections.

Indeed without doing this the other can't be done throughly. He that would well enlighten the head must cleanse the heart. Otherwise the disorder of the will again disorders the understanding, and perverseness of affection will again cause an

---

[45] Outler has 'entertain' in place of 'have'. This is unsupported by the MS.
[46] See Outler (ed.), *Sermons*, iv. 311 n. 32 for the source of this quotation.   [47] Cf. Eccl. 7: 16.
[48] Cf. Ps. 53: 5 (*BCP*).
[49] The word 'in' has been inserted above the line. The insertion does not appear to be the work of Charles himself.   [50] Cf. Ps. 85: 11(*BCP*).
[51] Cf. Prov. 3: 17.   [52] Cf. Ps. 111: 10 (*BCP*).   [53] Cf. Judg. 16: 9.

equal perverseness of judgment. For whatever inclination is contrary to reason is likewise destructive of it; and whoever makes the world his god, that god will surely blind his eyes.[54]

This then is the most important work of all, namely, 'the laying the axe to the root of the tree';[55] the prevailing on a man to purify his heart, till it be holy and undefiled; to resolve upon giving up all his darling lusts which will not submit to the law of God; to stifle every inclination which is contrary to the spirit of holiness, which would either prevent his entering upon, or retard his progress in, the race set before him. To lay aside pride, malice, envy, revenge, intemperance, covetousness; indeed every passion, every habit, which would keep him 'a stranger to the covenant of promise, and alien from the commonwealth of Israel, without hope, and without God in the world'.[56]

When he has determined to renounce those[57] inclinations which are evil in themselves, the next point is to bring him to a resolution of transferring those which are not so to new objects, of 'setting these affections on things above, and not on things of the earth'.[58] On things that were designed to be the delight, and engage the desires, of rational creatures, and are accordingly adequate to their capacities, which no perishable objects are. To a resolution of seeking his happiness, not in the things that are seen, but in the things that are not seen;[59] not like the half-Christians who (to speak in the words of an excellent man[60]) 'use God, and enjoy the world', but as one who knows his privilege[61] better, 'who uses the world, but enjoys God'.

After inspiring a sinner with this generous resolution, one step more is to be taken, and that is to fix him in it, to guard him from a relapse, lest his last state should be worse than the first;[62] in spite of the arts which his old enemies will soon use to draw him from his steadfastness, to 'hold up his goings in the way, that his footsteps slip not';[63] to watch over his soul till he has fully proved the whole armour of God,[64] that he may be able to 'wrestle with principalities and powers, with the rulers of the darkness of this world, to quench every fiery dart of the wicked, and having done all, to stand'.[65] He who hath thus enlightened the understanding and regulated the will of a sinner, he hath eminently advanced the glory of God, he hath rescued a fellow-creature from destruction, he hath procured an exceeding reward for himself; he hath won a soul; he is wise.[66]

---

[54] Cf. 2 Cor. 4: 4.   [55] Cf. Luke 3: 9.   [56] Cf. Eph. 2: 12.

[57] Outler has 'these' in place of 'those'; the word is not entirely clear in the MS.

[58] Cf. Col. 3: 2.   [59] Cf. 2 Cor. 4: 18.

[60] The quotation is from Pascal. See Outler (ed.), *Sermons*, iv. 314 n. 47 for a discussion.

[61] Spelt 'priviledge' in the MS and corrected in what appears to be another hand to 'privileges'.

[62] Cf. Matt. 12: 45 and parallel.   [63] Cf. Ps. 17: 5.   [64] Cf. Eph. 6: 11.

[65] Cf. Eph. 6: 12, 13, 16.

[66] Before 'wise' the word 'truly' has been inserted above the line. The insertion is not in the hand of Charles himself.

Inf[erences]:[67] But is not this a higher degree of wisdom than anyone who was born of a woman hath yet attained to? This is the inference which a man of reflection would immediately draw from what has been said of it. 'Who is sufficient for these things?'[68] Who is equal to so vast an undertaking? We have heard indeed that it is easy for a designing man to lead others whither he pleases; to bring them into just what opinions he will, and set their affections by his own. Nay, but he who has seen how slowly a confused apprehension is cleared, or a prejudiced judgment rectified, and how unwillingly men admit a truth they have long despised, even as if it were a sword piercing through their hearts; he who has observed that an ill[69] man is almost as easily brought to cut off a right hand, or pluck out a right eye,[70] as to set his affections on things above,[71] and mortify his darling lusts; in a word, he who knows that the persuading a bad man to be happy is the persuading him out of his fancy, judgment, and inclinations, all which must take an entirely new turn, must undergo such a change as is that from death to life: he knows that the winning a soul ~~from~~ is a work of no common difficulty. He knows that, after every help of nature and art, after the nicest observations both upon things and men, after the most intense study and even the longest experience, still 'with men this is impossible.'[72]

But with God all things are possible! Here is our hold! This bids us go on and prosper! This bids us not doubt but when we have cleansed our own hearts, God will deliver others into our hands. What though we can do nothing of ourselves? 'We can do all things through Christ which strengtheneth us.'[73] What though we are not able to turn away the least captain in our enemy's army? He who is with us hath counsel and strength for the war,[74] and his power is sufficient for us.[75] His power will never forsake the duly prepared and commissioned labourers in his harvest, but as their day is, so their strength will be;[76] they shall reap, if they faint not.[77]

I would not here be understood to exclude all but these from having any share in this glorious work. No,[78] God forbid! How shall I curse whom God hath not cursed,[79] by denying them the blessing of joining with us in converting some from the error of their ways? Far be it from us, from the ministers of mercy, to be guilty of such arrogant cruelty as to condemn all who have not a part in our ministry as reprobate from God, and from the benefits of it; which we must do if we forbid their doing this work of God, so far as he hath given them ability; since our Lord himself expressly declares, 'He that gathereth not with me, scattereth.'[80] He that

---

[67] 'Inf' is written in the left hand margin of the text at this point. Outler's expansion to 'inferences' seems correct.   [68] 2 Cor. 2: 16.

[69] The words 'an ill' have been struck out in the text and replaced by 'a wicked'. The change is not in the hand of Charles himself.   [70] Cf. Mark 9: 47 and parallel.

[71] Cf. Col. 3: 2.   [72] Cf. Mark 10: 27 and parallels.

[73] Cf. Phil. 4: 13; Outler inserts an exclamation mark at this point in the text.

[74] Cf. 2 Kgs. 18: 20.   [75] Cf. 2 Cor. 12: 9; Outler adds an exclamation mark at this point.

[76] Cf. Deut. 33: 25.   [77] Cf. Gal. 6: 9.   [78] Outler inserts an exclamation mark at this point.

[79] Cf. Num. 23: 8.   [80] Cf. Matt. 12.30 and parallel.

gathers not, as he may, subjects to my kingdom, scattereth them away from it. He that is not, according to his power, an agent for God, is a factor for the devil!

Several acts of our blessed office indeed there are which may not be performed unless by particularly commissioned officers. But here a general commission is given to all the servants of Christ to tread in his steps, to do what in them lies in their several stations, to save the souls for whom Christ died. 'Tis true, we are the ambassadors of God,[81] and as such have many powers which they have not. But what Scripture[82] denies any man the power of beseeching others, for Christ's sake, to be reconciled to God?[83] Yea, God will do so to us, and more also,[84] should we thus outrage our fellow-Christians, should we thus magnify our office by speaking as from God what God hath not spoken, as to cut off any who stretch not themselves beyond their measure,[85] from the wisdom of winning souls.

Indeed, if Solomon had only said, 'The priest that winneth souls is wise,' they had some colour for saying to all who are not invested with this office, 'Ye have neither part nor lot in this wisdom;[86] even with such sacrifices God is not pleased, when they are offered by your unhallowed hands.' But Solomon's words are universal, 'He that winneth souls is wise!' Who is he that is wiser and inspired by a better spirit? Let him stand forth and make the restriction!

But is this a time for making restrictions![87] For binding the hands of any of our fellow-labourers![88] When the avowed opposers and blasphemers of our holy religion are so zealously labouring to destroy souls; when those who have themselves made shipwreck of the faith[89] so earnestly endeavour to plunge others in the same gulf; when even 'of ourselves have men arisen, speaking perverse things,'[90] and not content 'to deny the Lord that bought them'[91] themselves, unless they drew disciples after them. Is this a time for refusing any help? For driving away any that would assist us? Is this a time for turning back any soldier of Christ who offers to set himself in array against the destroyer? Rather is there not a cause that we should cry aloud, 'Who is on our side, who?'[92] Who will rise up with us against the enemy?[93] Who will stand with us in the gap[94] against these wolves, that now no longer put on sheep's clothing,[95] but go about in their own shape, seeking whom they may devour?[96] The apostles of Satan labour one and all: shall any of the servants of God stand idle? Every one of those is zealous to destroy: shall not every one of these be zealous to save? Yea, in this let the heathen teach the Christian. Let us too do something, from the least to the greatest! Now surely let us suffer even the little children to fight for Christ, and forbid them not,[97] lest it be said of us,

---

[81] Cf. 2 Cor. 5: 20.

[82] Corrected in the MS from 'scriptures'. It is not clear whether the correction is the work of Charles himself. [83] Cf. 2 Cor 5: 20.

[84] See, e.g., Ruth 1: 17.   [85] Cf. 2 Cor. 10: 14.   [86] Cf. Acts 8: 21.

[87] Outler has a question mark here. The MS is not completely clear, but an exclamation mark seems more probable.   [88] Outler has a question mark here. The exclamation mark is clear in the MS.

[89] Cf. 1 Tim. 1: 19.   [90] Cf. Acts 20: 30.   [91] Cf. 2 Pet. 2: 1.

[92] Cf. 2 Kgs. 9: 32.   [93] Cf. Ps. 94: 16.   [94] Cf. Ezek. 22: 30; Ps. 106: 23 (BCP).

[95] Cf. Matt. 7: 15.   [96] Cf. 1 Pet. 5: 8.   [97] Cf. Mark 10: 14 and parallels.

with more justice than it has been hitherto, 'Ye take too much upon you, ye sons of Levi.'[98] Let us cut off this occasion of reproach from them that seek occasion; nor let it always be true that 'the children of this world are in their generation wiser than the children of light!'[99]

[98] Cf. Num. 16: 7.   [99] Cf. Luke 16: 8. This text is the subject of Sermon 17.

SERMON 23
PSALM 91: 11

INTRODUCTORY COMMENT

This final sermon is again one which Charles copied from his brother's MS during the first leg of his journey back to England in 1736 and like the other three (Sermons 20, 21, and 22, on Mark 12: 30; Luke 10: 42 and Proverbs 11: 30) is found in a hard-back volume of sermons now held at the John Rylands University Library of Manchester.[1] Charles records that John preached the sermon on several occasions, the first being at St Michael's [Oxford] in 1726.[2] On the right hand side of the page, however, is the entry 'St John's, October 23, 1737'. This is most likely a reference to Charles's preaching of the sermon.[3] There is no entry in the journal for that day.

There is little indication in the MS itself that Charles has made any major changes to his brother's form of the sermon, and since John's copy has not survived the correlation cannot be checked. If Charles copied more or less exactly what he found it was presumably because he agreed with it, and hence the sermon may be taken as an indication of his views on the question of angelic intervention no less than John's. Certainly he was ready to see the work of such agents in his own ministry. For example, the journal entry for 10 February 1748 includes the words

> I observed the man who had knocked down J. Healey striking him on the face with his club; cried to him to stop, which drew him upon me, and probably saved our brother's life, whom another blow might have dispatched. They had gathered against our coming great heaps of stones, one of which was sufficient to beat out our brains. How we escaped them, God only knows, and our guardian angels. I had no apprehension of their hurting me, even when one struck me on the back with a large stone, which took away my breath.[4]

And again for 19 July of the same year he wrote

---

[1] MARC DDCW 8/13.

[2] This can be clarified as being on 29 September 1726. See Outler (ed.), *Sermons*, iv. 224.

[3] See the notes to the introduction to Sermon 20 for an account of the layout of the sermon register in general.

[4] See MARC DDCW 10/2 entry for 11 February 1748. Charles's MS journal is in some confusion at this point. Both he and John (*J&D*, xx. 206) indicate that 29 January 1748 was a Friday. The following Friday was 5 February, but Charles enters 'Fri. Feb 6' in his journal. The Wednesday after was 10 February, but Charles gives it as 'Wednesday Feb. 11'. Jackson corrects the dates. (MARC DDCW 10/2 *in loc.*; Jackson, *Journal*, ii. 2–3).

I set out at 4 with Mr. Gw[ynne] and Sally. At 11, in Windsor, my horse threw me with violence over his head. My companion fell upon me. The guardian angels bore us in their hands, so that neither was hurt.[5]

The sermon was published as number II in the 1816 edition,[6] and the usual level of editorial emendation to the text is apparent. Outler also published this sermon in his edition of John's sermons.[7] The minor errors in Outler's transcription have been corrected here.

The main argument of this sermon is straightforward enough: God provides guardian angels to keep 'good men' in their ways, and in particular 'when our body is threatened with pain or sickness, or our souls with violent passion or sin, then are they especially watchful over us, to ward off the approaching evil'. This they do in a number of ways. For example, they may cleanse polluted air (through increasing its current) which would otherwise cause sickness. Guardian angels, however, care not only for the bodies of the faithful but also for their souls, through, for example, 'instilling good thoughts into their hearts'. The third and final part of the sermon is perhaps the most interesting, for here the question is addressed as to why God uses guardian angels as intermediaries rather than simply acting directly in such matters himself. The reasons include the fact that, according to Charles, the angels themselves delight in such activities and hence God in his goodness allows them this pleasure. Angels are, however, part of the created order and should not be afforded worship; this is due to God alone.

---

[5] MARC DDCW 10/2 *in loc.*; Jackson, *Journal*, ii. 14. See also the entry for 25 October 1743, where Charles puts down to the work of angels his brother's escape from serious injury at the hands of an anti-Methodist mob (Jackson, *Journal*, i. 338).   [6] *Sermons*, 22–42.

[7] Outler (ed.), *Sermons*, iv. 224–35.

Sermon Register[1]

St John's October, 23 1737[2]

~~Islington October~~[3]

In the 91st Psalm at the eleventh verse it is thus written:

He shall give his angels charge over thee, to keep thee in all thy ways.

One would think it scarce possible that a man, even through the wantonness of wealth, power, or glory, should forget the very condition of his nature, that we are weak, miserable, helpless creatures, that we are by no means equal to those many and great dangers that continually surround us, and threat[en][4] not only our souls (those, men have little care for) with indelible guilt, that[5] is endless misery, but our darling bodies, too, with tedious, painful diseases, and at length with a total dissolution. The meanest object of our scorn—a beast, an insect, nay, even things that themselves have no life—are sufficient either to take away ours, or to make it a curse rather than a blessing. Pangs yet sharper than these can inflict we may often feel from the perverse injustice or malice of our brethren, encouraged therein by those wicked spirits, our fiercest enemies, who, like roaring lions, daily range in quest of prey,[6] and when they are not permitted to do it themselves, rejoice in seeing us devour one another.

'But where',[7] then will the unbeliever say, 'is the boasted goodness of your Creator, if he delivers over his impotent helpless creatures to their numerous, powerful, and cruel enemies?' God forbid that he should deliver us to them! Mercy is still over all his works![8] tis true, to humble our natural pride and self-sufficiency, he suffers them to 'hold us in on every side';[9] tis true, too, 'that we are unable of ourselves to help ourselves'.[10] Yet 'hath he not given us over as a prey unto their teeth'.[11] On the contrary he hath established a law, and ordained it shall never be broken, that unless by our own positive voluntary act they 'shall have no advantage over us'.[12] For all who do not wilfully, obstinately refuse to accept it, he hath appointed an inviolable refuge (beautifully described at large in that Psalm, part of which you

---

[1] This information is found on the verso of the final leaf of the sermon on Mark 12: 30 (Sermon 20 above), found in the same booklet as this. As has been noted, several of the entries refer to John's preaching. However, the one listed here refers to Charles's use of the text. See further the Introduction to Sermon 20. [2] There is no entry in the journal for that day.

[3] This entry is written in shorthand and is then struck out.

[4] The word is written 'threat' in the MS. Outler's expansion to 'threaten' seems correct.

[5] The word 'that' is corrected to 'which' in the MS. The correction does not appear to be in the hand of Charles himself. [6] Cf. 1 Pet. 5: 8.

[7] The word 'where' is a correction from 'why'. The change is in the hand of Charles.

[8] *BCP* Forms of Prayer to be Used at Sea, Alternative Collect of Thanksgiving.

[9] Cf. Luke 19: 43. [10] *BCP* Collect for Second Sunday in Lent. [11] Cf. Ps. 124: 6.

[12] Perhaps *BCP* The Order for the Visitation of the Sick (opening prayers) and/or 2 Cor. 2: 11.

have heard repeated). 'They may dwell in the secret place of the Most High, may abide under the shadow of the Almighty.'[13]

That while the afflictions which vex the rest of mankind increase ever more and more, while a thousand fall into various troubles at their side, and ten thousand at their right hand,[14] yet no evil shall befall[15] these, unless for good, 'no plague come nigh their dwelling',[16] we cannot doubt, if we consider what peculiar care he hath taken for their protection, that 'he hath given his angels charge over them, to keep them in all their ways.'

A stronger proof of the truth of this general proposition we cannot have than the authority of the Proposer. A clearer view of the sense of it we may have by making a particular inquiry,

I[st], when the angels of God attend this their charge; at what times they are peculiarly employed in keeping good men in their ways;

Secondly, how they attend upon it; what methods they take, as we may probably suppose, thus to keep them;

Thirdly, why this charge is assigned them; for what reasons we may presume him who is omnipresent and omnipotent not to make use of his own immediate power, but of these 'his servants to do his pleasure'.[17] To these inquiries, that they may not seem to be matter of mere speculation, an inference or two naturally resulting from them may, not unfitly, be subjoined.

First: As to the times when the holy angels attend this their charge, this in general we may be assured of, that they are always ready to assist us when we need their assistance, always present when their presence may be of service, in every circumstance of life wherein is danger of any sort, or would be if they were absent. The commission they bear plainly reaches thus far: they are 'to keep us in all our ways'; and we know when these ministers are employed here by God his will is done in earth as it is in heaven.[18]

In particular, when our body is threatened with pain or sickness, or our souls with violent passion or sin, then are they especially watchful over us, to ward off the approaching evil. And these no doubt approach often when we are sensible of no danger; which is often nearest when we apprehend it farthest off. Destruction does not always 'waste at noon-day';[19] it more frequently 'walketh in darkness'.[20] And our being delivered from it then is wholly owing to their timely interposition, though neither the attack nor the repulse falls under the notice of our imperfect senses.

Other times there are at which we are sensible of our danger, but not of the means by which we escape it, which we suppose to be either the natural work of material causes, or chance, or our own strength or wisdom. But were we left to these, and ourselves, we should soon find how little resistance we could make

---

[13] Cf. Ps. 91: 1.   [14] Cf. Ps. 91: 7.   [15] Cf. Ps. 91: 10.
[16] Cf. ibid.   [17] Cf. Ps. 103: 21 (BCP).   [18] Cf. Matt. 6: 10 and parallel.
[19] Cf. Ps. 91: 6.   [20] Cf. ibid.

against the enemies that daily besiege us, without those on our side who are more skilful to save, than these to destroy!

And doubtless they would save us whenever assaulted by any evil, whether visible or invisible, but that this exceeds the commission they have received from their and our Master. This he did not appoint, could not permit them to do, since he knew it would not benefit, but hurt us. He knows of what infinite service afflictions are to creatures in our station, and therefore that to be delivered from all while on earth would be the greatest evil that could befall us. Such an undistinguishing tenderness to the body would be an irreparable injury to the soul: if one were continually comforted here, 'tis great odds but both would hereafter be tormented.

Neither would it be kindness thus to exempt us from spiritual any more than from temporal danger; to deliver the soul from all ~~sin~~ temptation, any more than the body from all pain. Were the angels of God enjoined to do this, as we should be without vice, so we must have been without virtue, seeing we should have no choice left; and where there is no choice, there can be no virtue. But had we been without virtue, we must have been content with some lower happiness than that we now hope to partake of, which is the natural necessary result of virtue, and its genuine and inseparable fruit.

But although for these reasons (and who knows how many others the divine wisdom may have in view) the blessed angels may not always prevent sin or affliction from assaulting the soul or body, yet when either has taken hold upon us, they may prevent our being totally overthrown. They may preserve us from sinking under temporal misfortunes, from being enslaved by spiritual enemies. They may likewise recover us out of that trouble which they might not hinder us from falling into; nay, and often assist us to rise by our fall; by having been defeated, to obtain a nobler conquest.

II [Second] How it is that the angels of God do this, by what particular methods they may be supposed to keep us, I proceed under my second general head to inquire, according to the light that is given us. Little of certainty, you are sensible, can be expected on a subject of this nature, unless where there is the express warrant of his revelation who made all things,[21] and therefore knows them.

1. And, first, in general, his revelation expressly assures me that these his servants 'excel in strength';[22] which we may likewise infer from the works ascribed to them in many places of Holy Writ. That one of them shut the lion's mouth, which would otherwise have devoured Daniel;[23] that at the word of another the chains fell off St. Peter's hands, and the prison gates opened of their own accord,[24] seems little when we consider what is elsewhere related of the tasks their Sovereign had assigned them. 'I saw', saith St. John, 'four angels standing on the four corners of the earth, holding the four winds of the earth, that they should not blow.'[25] Of four others, who seem to have been of that number which probably lost much of their

---

[21] There is perhaps here an echo of John 1: 3.   [22] Ps. 103: 20.   [23] Cf. Dan. 6: 22.
[24] Cf. Acts 12: 7, 10.   [25] Cf. Rev. 7: 1.

strength with their purity,[26] the same Apostle records that they were loosed from their bonds in the River Euphrates, 'to slay the third part of men'.[27] What then cannot those do, whose strength is still entire, when they are permitted to exert it? Especially since,

2. Secondly, they excel equally in wisdom, as we have the strongest reason to believe. They, like man, were undoubtedly created upright, though with higher powers, as they are beings of an higher order. But they fell not like him, and have therefore retained them unimpaired, at least[28] ever since this[29] world began, if not many ages before. But we may be assured they neither would nor could retain them without continually improving them. At what degree, then, of knowledge and wisdom may we not suppose they are now arrived? If a creature of so confined, so depraved an understanding as man can improve it so much in threescore years, what bounds can fancy set to the understanding of an angel, which, with so vast a grasp, and so right unbiased an apprehension, hath been travelling onward toward perfection for probably many thousands of ages? Especially considering whose face they almost[30] continually behold,[31] even his, 'of whose understanding is no number';[32] and that to imitate him, as far as the noblest creature can, is both their business, and pleasure, and glory.

By these perfections, strength, and wisdom, they are well able to preserve us, either from the approach, if that be more profitable for us, or otherwise in the attack of any evil. By their wisdom they discern whatever either obstructs or promotes our real advantage: by their strength they effectually repel the one and secure a free course to the other. By the first they choose means conducive to these ends; by the second they put them in execution.

One particular method of preserving good men which we may reasonably suppose these wise beings sometimes to[33] choose, and by their strength to put in execution, is the altering some material cause that else would have a pernicious effect; the cleansing, for instance, tainted air, that would otherwise produce a contagious distemper. And this they may easily do, either by increasing the current of it, so naturally to purge off its impurity, or by mixing with it some other substance, so to correct its hurtful qualities and make it friendly to human bodies.

Another method they may be supposed to take when their commission is not so general, when they are only authorized to preserve some few persons from a common calamity. 'Tis then likely they do not alter the cause, but the subject on which it is to work; that they do not lessen the strength of the one, but increase the strength of the other. Thus, too, where they are not allowed to prevent, they may remove

---

[26] Charles may here be reflecting on Gen. 6: 2.   [27] Cf. Rev. 9: 14, 15.

[28] Corrected in another hand from 'lest' in the MS.

[29] Outler gives 'the'; 'this' is clear in the MS.

[30] The word 'almost' is omitted by Outler. It is clear in the MS.   [31] Cf. Matt. 18: 10.

[32] Cf. Isa. 40: 28; Psa 147: 5 (Charles is closer to the *BCP* than the KJV at this point).

[33] The word 'to' has been inserted above the line.

pain or sickness: thus the angel restored Daniel in a moment, 'when neither strength nor breath remained in him'.[34]

By these means, by altering either our bodies or the material causes that use to affect them, they may easily defend us from all bodily ~~pain~~ evils, so far as is expedient for us. A third method they may be conceived to take to defend us from spiritual dangers: by applying themselves immediately to our soul, to raise or allay our passions. And this province indeed seems more natural to them than either of the former. How a spiritual being can act upon matter seems more unaccountable than how it can act on spirit. That one immaterial being, by touching another, should either increase or lessen its motion, that an angel should either retard or quicken the stream wherewith the passions of an angelic substance flow, is no more to be wondered at than that one piece of matter should have the same effect on its kindred substance, that a flood-gate or other material instrument should retard or quicken the stream of a river. Rather, considering of how contagious a nature the passions are, the wonder is on the other side; not how they can affect them at all, but how they can avoid affecting them more; how they can continue so near us, who are so subject to catch them, without spreading the flames that burn in themselves.

And a plain instance of their power to allay human passions the Scriptures gives us in the case of Daniel, when he beheld that gloriously terrible minister 'whose face was as the appearance of lightning, and his eyes as lamps of fire, his arms and feet like polished brass, and his voice as the voice of a multitude' (10.6) 'His fears and sorrows were turned so strongly upon him that he was in a deep sleep',[35] void of sense and motion. Yet these turbulent passions the angel allayed in an instant; when they were hurrying on with the utmost impetuosity he stopped them short in their mid-course, so that immediately after we find him desiring the continuance of that converse which he was before utterly unable to sustain.[36] The same effect was doubtless wrought on all those to whom these superior beings, on their first appearance, used that common salutation, 'Fear not'[37]—which would have been a mere insult upon human weakness had they not with that advice given power to follow it.

Near akin to this method of affecting the passions is the last I intend to mention, by which the angels, as 'tis probable, keep good men especially in or from spiritual dangers. And this is by applying themselves to their reason, by instilling good thoughts into their hearts; either such as are good in their own nature, as tend to our improvement in virtue, or such as are contrary to those suggestions of the flesh or the devil by which we are tempted to vice. 'Tis not unlikely that we are indebted to them, not only for most of those reflections which suddenly dart across our

---

[34] Cf. Dan. 8: 15–18; 10: 8–9. (Despite the quotation marks, this is in the nature of a comment on the texts rather than a direct quotation or even a paraphrase. Charles may have been (mis)quoting from memory.)

[35] Cf. Dan. 10: 9, 16. As previously, despite the quotation marks, this is in the nature of a comment on the text rather than a direct quotation or even a paraphrase.   [36] Cf. Dan. 10: 19.

[37] Cf. e.g. Gen. 43: 23; Judg. 6: 23; Dan. 10: 12, 19; Luke 1: 13, 30; Rev. 1: 17.

minds, we know not how, having no connection with any that went before them; but for many of those, too, that seem entirely our own, and naturally consequent from the preceding.

III [third]: It were easy to show that to some of these heads all those actions are reducible which we can conceive these our guardians ever to perform in execution of this their charge. But 'tis time that we came to our third inquiry, which was, why this charge was assigned them; for what reasons we may presume he who is omnipresent and omnipotent not to make use of his own immediate power, but of these his servants, to do his pleasure.[38]

I am not ignorant that this is usually thought a 'knowledge too wonderful for us'[39]—that man cannot attain a view of these ways of God, these hidden treasures of his providence. However, it cannot be unlawful to extend our search as far as our limited faculties will permit, provided we proceed[40] with due reverence and humility, and do not contradict the analogy of our faith.

Consistently with these we may presume one reason why God assigns this charge to his holy angels to be because they delight in it, because they have an additional pleasure therein besides what always results from their being employed in his service. Seeing the more benevolent any being is, the more delight he takes in doing good; seeing that these are benevolent in the highest degree, we cannot but infer by their holding the highest rank among creatures, inasmuch as God always favours and honours them most who are most like him; but[41] 'God is love':[42] to conduct others in the paths of happiness must be a particular addition to their own.

Nor is it a barren, useless pleasure which these sons of God reap from their attendance on the children of men, but a pleasure joined with improvement. In doing good to us they do good to themselves also, and this perhaps is a second reason why the Most High hath allotted this province to them, because by exercising the goodness they have already they continually acquire more, and swiftly, too. Even we, fettered as we are in this house[43] of earth, and weighed down by original corruption, perceive the[44] more acts of virtue we perform, the stronger habit we slowly attain to. Much more swiftly must exercise improve them who have neither of these impediments: much more sensibly by the acts of benevolence they perform must they advance in that godlike virtue.

3.[45] And thirdly, as by this exercise of benevolence they are even now both more benevolent and happy, so thereby they every moment treasure up to themselves

---

[38] Outler inserts a question mark at this point. The reference is to Ps. 103: 21.

[39] Cf. Ps. 139: 6.

[40] The word 'proceed' has been struck out in the manuscript and replaced by 'approach'; the hand is not that of Charles.

[41] The word 'but' has been struck out in the manuscript and replaced by another. That word, which is virtually unreadable (Outler suggests 'for'), is not in Charles's hand.		[42] Cf. 1 John 4: 8, 16.

[43] The word 'house' has been struck out in the manuscript and replaced by 'tabernacle'. This change is not in Charles's hand. Cf. 2 Cor. 5: 1.			[44] Before 'the' Outler adds 'that'.

[45] The paragraph numbering is not consistent in the MS, perhaps suggesting editorial emendation on Charles's part (see further Chapter 4).

fresh matter of future happiness. The greater goodwill they bear to men, the greater must be their joy when these men, in the fullness of time, are received into that glory appointed for them. The more exquisitely will they sympathize with them when all their troubles are done away, when the days of sickness and pain and sin are over, are swallowed up in immortality,[46] and they are admitted to drink of 'those rivers of pleasure'[47] that flow at God's right hand for evermore![48]

4. In those days we shall plainly see a fourth reason likewise why these ministering spirits were so constantly 'sent forth' to guard 'them who were to be heirs of salvation';[49] namely, that the heirs of salvation, when entered into that inheritance, might be gratefully sensible of their benefits; that when they experienced the inestimable value of those benefits, this gratitude might ripen into love; that this love might be a means of increasing their happiness, by seeing them whom they loved, and seeing them so happy; and by reflecting that themselves, unworthy as they were, had in some degree contributed to it.

IV.I. From that little we have been able to feel out touching this one dispensation of providence, touching the time when, the manner how, and the reasons why, the blessed angels have charge to keep good men, may we not naturally infer that we should adore his goodness and wisdom who hath instituted the services both of angels and men in so wonderful an order! How great is that goodness which hath not left without defence his weak, miserable, helpless creatures! How great is that wisdom which hath so well proportioned the powers of our defenders to their office! How infinitely great is[50] that[51] wisdom and goodness which have made us serviceable to them? Which have derived such advantage from weak, miserable, helpless creatures to beings only not almighty!

2. Hence we may secondly infer the weakness of that objection which men who pretended to believe a God have often made against his providence: that 'tis beneath a being of such infinite greatness to concern himself in our little affairs. Supposing it were (though 'tis palpably absurd to suppose it of him who is omnipresent as well as omnipotent), yet what would this avail them? How would it follow that fortune governed the world, since there is a particular order of beings whose business it is to attend on this very thing; who are ready on all occasions to assist such as need and will accept of their assistance, and by the powers wherewith he hath endued them are sufficiently able (were that the will of their Master) to keep both the natural and moral world in order without his ever interposing?[52]

3. We learn hence, in the third place, to condemn the folly and impiety[53] that obtains in the Romish church; namely, the worshipping of angels, the paying to the

---

[46] Cf. 1 Cor. 15: 53–4.   [47] Cf. Ps. 36: 8.   [48] Ps. 16: 11.

[49] Cf. Heb. 1: 14.

[50] The word 'is' is corrected in the MS to 'are'. The correction does not appear to be in the hand of Charles himself.

[51] The word 'that' is corrected in the MS to 'the'. The correction does not appear to be in the hand of Charles himself.   [52] The question mark is not in the MS, but seems required by the context.

[53] The word 'impiety' has been replaced in the margin by 'error'. This alteration is not in the hand of Charles himself.

creature the incommunicable honour of the Creator. 'Let no man beguile us of our reward'[54] in this show of gratitude and humility. They keep us in all our ways, 'tis true, but we know who gives them a charge so to do. The Lord our God is but one Lord;[55] these are servants that do his pleasure.[56] And if their doing this, if their obeying his order, were a sufficient reason for us to worship them, 'fire and hail, wind and storm fulfill[ing][57] his word',[58] as well as they, would have an equal claim to our adoration.

4. 'Tis God himself, as we may fourthly collect from what has been said, to whom our praises and prayers are due, to whom we ought to return our sincerest acknowledgements, whom we should implore with the deepest humility, that we may reap the fruits of his wisdom and goodness, from the constant ministry of his servants. To him our petition should be addressed, according to the wise direction our Church has given us, 'that as his holy angels do him service in heaven, so they may succour and defend us upon earth';[59] that their general commission to inspect human affairs may affect us in particular, and secure to us such a degree of present ease as suits best with our future happiness.

Con[clusion]: Happy is the man, even now, as he can be upon earth, who is in such a case, who enjoys such a protection! Happy in having the greatest possible security that he never shall be unhappy! That even no temporal evil shall befall him, unless to clear the way for a greater good! What though he wrestles not only against inanimate enemies, but against flesh and blood, the depravity of his own nature, with the perverseness, malice, and injustice of other men; nay, and not only against flesh and blood, but against principalities, the rulers of the darkness of this world, the wicked spirits in high places?[60] They that are for him are not only more, but stronger and wiser than they that are against him![61] And are not these at least as watchful to do good as those are to do us evil? So watchful, that let him but be true to himself, let him but fix his love on their common Creator, and nothing in the creation, animate or inanimate, by design or chance, shall have power to hurt him.[62] 'In famine they shall preserve the good man from death; in war, from the hand of the sword. They shall hide thee from the scourge of the tongue. Thou shalt laugh at destruction when it cometh. The very beasts of the earth shall they make to be at peace with thee, and thou shalt be at league with the stones of the field.'[63] (Job 5.22 etc.[64])

---

[54] Cf. Col. 2: 18.   [55] Cf. Deut. 6: 4.   [56] Cf. Ps. 103: 21.

[57] Corrected to 'fulfilling' by the insertion of 'ing' above the line. It is not clear whether this correction is the work of Charles himself. (It brings the verb into exact correspondence with the KJV—an exactitude with which Charles seems generally unconcerned; the text quoted actually reads 'fire and hail . . . stormy wind fulfilling his word' in KJV.)   [58] Cf. Ps. 148: 8 (*BCP*).

[59] *BCP*, Collect for St Michael and All Angels, 29 September ('Mercifully grant, that as thy holy angels always do thee service in Heaven, so by thy appointment they may succour and defend us on earth.')   [60] Cf. Eph. 6: 12.

[61] Cf. 2 Kgs. 6: 16.   [62] Cf. Rom. 8: 35, 38–9.

[63] The closing quotation mark is not present in the MS. It has been added here for clarity.

[64] The quotation actually starts from Job 5: 20. It is not verbatim.

Wherefore to him who hath thus loved us, and given us this good consolation among the numberless evils wherewith we are surrounded, to God the Father, God the Son, and God the Holy Ghost, let us yield all praise, majesty, and dominion, now and for ever! Amen!

Bibiliography

ADAMS, CHARLES, *The Poet Preacher: A Brief Memorial of Charles Wesley, the Eminent Preacher and Poet* (Carlton and Porter, 1859)

ALBIN, THOMAS R., 'Charles Wesley's Other Prose Writings', in Kimbrough (ed.), *Charles Wesley: Poet and Theologian*, 85–94

ALBIN, THOMAS R., and BECKERLEGGE, OLIVER A.,*Charles Wesley's Earliest Evangelical Sermons: Six Shorthand Manuscript Sermons Now for the First Time Transcribed from the Original* (Ilford: Wesley Historical Society, 1987)

ANDREWS, STUART, *Methodism and Society* (London: Longman, 1970)

BAKER, E. W., *A Herald of the Evangelical Revival: A Critical Inquiry into the Relation of William Law to John Wesley and the Beginnings of Methodism* (London: Epworth, 1948)

BAKER, FRANK, 'Charles Wesley to Varanese', *Proceedings of the Wesley Historical Society* 25 (1945–6): 97–104

—— *Charles Wesley as Revealed by His Letters* (London: Epworth, 1948; rev. edn 1995)

—— *Charles Wesley's Verse: An Introduction* (London: Epworth, 1964; rev. edn. 1988)

—— *Representative Verse of Charles Wesley* (London: Epworth, 1962)

—— *William Grimshaw 1708–1763* (London: Epworth, 1963)

—— *John Wesley and the Church of England*, (Nashville, TN: Abingdon Press, 1970)

—— *Letters*, vols. xxv and xxvi in the Bicentennial Edition of the Works of John Wesley

—— 'A Poet in Love—the Courtship of Charles Wesley, 1747–1749' *Methodist History* 29 (1991) :235–47

—— Draft of a proposed bibliography of the works of John and Charles Wesley, 3 vols. A copy is held at the MARC.

—— 'Charles Wesley's Letters', in Kimbrough (ed.), *Charles Wesley: Poet and Theologian*, 72–84

BECKERLEGGE, OLIVER A., 'Charles Wesley's Shorthand', *Methodist History* 29 (1991): 225–34

—— 'Charles Wesley's Poetical Corpus', in Kimbrough (ed.), *Charles Wesley: Poet and Theologian*, 30–44

BERGER, TERESA, 'Charles Wesley: A Literary Overview', in Kimbrough, (ed.), *Charles Wesley: Poet and Theologian*, 205–21

—— 'Charles Wesley and Roman Catholicism' in Kimbrough, (ed.) *Charles Wesley Poet and Theologian*, 205–21

—— *Theology in Hymns? A Study of the Relationship of Doxology and Theology according to A Collection of Hymns for the Use of the People Called Methodists* (1780), ET by Timothy Edward Kimbrough, (Nashville, TN: Kingswood Books, 1995)

Bicentennial Edition of the Works of John Wesley; 27 vols. (Nashville, TN: Abingdon Press, 1980–)

BIRD, FREDERICK, *Charles Wesley and Methodist Hymns* (Andover: Warren F. Draper, 1864)

BOWMER, JOHN C., *The Sacrament of the Lord's Supper in Early Methodism* (London: Dacre Press, 1951)

BRAILSFORD, MABEL R., *A Tale of Two Brothers: John and Charles Wesley* (London: Rupert Hart-Davis, 1954)

BROSE, MARTIN E., *Charles Wesley (1707–1738): Tagebuch 1738* (Stuttgart: Christliches Verlagshaus, 1992)

BROWN, ROBERT W., 'Charles Wesley, Hymnwriter: Notes on Research Carried out to Establish the Location of his Residence in Bristol during the Period 1749–1771' (unpublished pamphlet, 1993; available from the New Room, Bristol)

BROWN-LAWSON, A., *John Wesley and the Anglican Evangelicals of the Eighteenth Century* (Edinburgh: Pentland Press, 1994)

BRYANT, BARRY E., 'Trinity and Hymnody: the Doctrine of the Trinity in the Hymns of Charles Wesley', *Wesleyan Theological Journal* 25 (1990): 64–73

BUTLER, DAVID, *Methodists and Papists* (London: Darton, Longman and Todd, 1993)

CALKIN, HOMER L., *Catalog of Methodist Archival and Manuscript Collections* (World Methodist Historical Society, 1985), A. 9

Catalogue of the Charles Wesley Papers ref. DDCW, 2 vols. (John Rylands University Library of Manchester, Methodist Archives and Research Centre, 1994)

Certain Sermons or Homilies Appointed to be Read in Churches in the Time of Queen Elizabeth of Famous Memory. Together with the Thirty-Nine Articles of Religion (1766)

CHRISTIE, IAN R., *Stress and Stability in Late Eighteenth-Century Britian: Reflections on the British Avoidance of Revolution* (Oxford: Clarendon, 1984)

CLARK, GLENN, 'Charles Wesley's Greatest Poem', *Methodist History* 26 (1988): 163–71

CROSS, F. L. and Livingstone, E. A., (eds.), *Oxford Dictionary of the Christian Church* (Oxford: Oxford University Press, 1997)

CURRIE, ROBERT, *Methodism Divided* (London: Faber, 1968)

DALE, JAMES, 'The Theological and Literary Qualities of the Poetry of Charles Wesley in Relation to the Standards of his Age' (Ph.D. thesis, Cambridge, 1960)

DALLIMORE, ARNOLD A., *A Heart Set Free: The Life of Charles Wesley* (Westchester, IL: Crossway Books, 1988)

DARGAN, EDWIN CHARLES, *A History of Preaching*, 2 vols. (London: Hodder and Stoughton, 1905–12)

DAVIES, RUPERT,George, A. Raymond, and Rupp, Gordon eds., *A History of the Methodist Church in Great Britain*, 4 vols. (London: Epworth, 1965–88)

DOUGHTY, W. L., 'Charles Wesley, Preacher', *LQHR* 182 (1957): 263–7

DOWNEY, JAMES, *The Eighteenth-Century Pulpit: A Study of the Sermons of Butler, Berkeley, Secker, Sterne, Whitefield and Wesley* (Oxford: Clarendon, 1969)

DUGMORE, C. W., *Eucharistic Doctrine in England from Hooker to Waterland* (London: SPCK, 1942)

EDWARDS, MALDWYN, *Family Circle: A Study of the Epworth Household in Relation to John and Charles Wesley* (London: Epworth, 1949)

—— *Sons to Samuel* (London: Epworth, 1961)

EKRUT, JAMES, 'Universal Redemption: Assurance of Salvation, and Christian Perfection in the Hymns of Charles Wesley with a Poetic Analysis and Tune Examples' (MM Thesis, South-Western Baptist Theological Seminary, 1978)

ELLIS, CHARLES, 'Charles Wesley's Prose Works: A Theological Study' (Ph.D. thesis, Liverpool, in process)

FLEMMING, RICHARD L., 'The Concept of Sacrifice in the Eucharistic Hymns of John and Charles Wesley' (Ph.D. thesis, Southern Methodist University, 1980)

FLEW R. N., *The Hymns of Charles Wesley: A Study* (London: Epworth, 1953)

FLINT, CHARLES WESLEY, *Charles Wesley and His Colleagues* (Washington: Public Affairs Press, 1957)

GALLAWAY, CRAIG, 'The Presence of Christ with the Worshipping Community: A Study in the Hymns of John and Charles Wesley' (Ph.D. thesis, Emory, 1988)

GILL, FREDERICK C., *Charles Wesley: The First Methodist* (London: Lutterworth, 1964)

HANNON, E., 'The Influence of Paradise Lost on the Hymns of Charles Wesley' (MA thesis, Columbia, 1985)

HARMON, NOLAN B. (ed.), *Encyclopedia of World Methodism*, 2 vols. (Nashville, TN: United Methodist Publishing House, 1974)

HARRISON, G. ELSIE, 'A Charles Wesley Letter', *Proceedings of the Wesley Historical Society* 25(1945–6): 17–23

HEITZENRATER, RICHARD P., 'John Wesley's Earliest Sermons', *Proceedings of the Wesley Historical Society* 37 (1969–70) 112–13

—— 'The Present State of Wesley Studies', *Methodist History* 22 (1983–4): 221–33

—— *Mirror and Memory: Reflections on Early Methodist History* (Nashville, TN: Kingswood Books, 1989)

—— Early Sermons of John and Charles Wesley; in *Mirror and Memory*

—— *Wesley and the People Called Methodists* (Nashville, TN: Abingdon Press, 1995).

—— (ed.), *Diary of an Oxford Methodist: Benjamin Ingham 1733–1734* (Durham, NC: Duke University Press, 1985)

HILDEBRANDT, FRANZ, and BECKERLEGGE, OLIVER A. (eds.), *A Collection of Hymns for the Use of the People Called Methodists* (vol. vii (1983) in the Bicentennial Edition of the Works of John Wesley)

HILL, CHRISTOPHER, 'Till the Conversion of the Jews', in Popkin, Richard H. (ed.), *Millenarianism and Messianism in English Literature and Thought 1650–1800* (Leiden: E. J. Brill, 1988), 12–36

HOOLE, ELIJAH, *Oglethorpe and the Wesleys in America* (London: 1863)

JACKSON, THOMAS, *The Journal of the Rev. Charles Wesley*, reprint (Baker Book House, 1984)

—— *The Life of the Rev Charles Wesley*, 2 vols. (London: John Mason, 1841)

JARBOE, BETTY M., *John and Charles Wesley: A Bibliography* (Metuchen, NJ, and London: Scarecrow Press, 1987)

JONES, D. M., *Charles Wesley: A Study* (London: Epworth, 1919)

KELLOCK, JOHN M., 'Charles Wesley and his Hymns', *Methodist Review* 112 (1929): 527–39

KENT, JOHN, *The Age of Disunity* (London: Epworth, 1966)

KIMBROUGH, ST, 'Charles Wesley as a Biblical Interpreter', *Methodist History* 26 (1988): 139–53

—— 'Charles Wesley as Biblical Interpreter', in Kimbrough, (ed.), *Charles Wesley: Poet and Theologian*, 106–36

—— (ed.), *Charles Wesley: Poet and Theologian* (Nashville, TN: Kingswood Books, 1992)

—— AND BECKERLEGGE, OLIVER A., (eds.), *The Unpublished Poetry of Charles Wesley*, 3 vols. (Nashville, TN: Kingswood Books, 1988–92)

KIRK, JOHN, *Charles Wesley, the Poet of Methodism: A Lecture* (London: Hamilton, Adams, and Co., 1860)

LANGFORD, THOMAS A., 'Charles Wesley as Theologian', in Kimbrough (ed.), *Charles Wesley: Poet and Theologian*, 97–105

LAWSON, JOHN, 'The Conversion of the Wesleys: 1738 Reconsidered', *Asbury Theological Journal* 43 (1988): 7–44

LEWIS, DONALD M. (ed.), *The Blackwell Dictionary of Evangelical Biography 1730–1860*, 2 vols. (Oxford: Blackwell, 1995)

LISTER, DOUGLAS G., AND TYSON, JOHN R., 'Charles Wesley, Pastor: A Glimpse inside his Shorthand Journal', *QR: The Methodist Quarterly Review* 4 (1984): 9–21

MADDOX, RANDY L. (ed.), *Rethinking John Wesley's Theology for Contemporary Methodism* (Nashville, TN : Kingswood Books, 1998)

MANNING, BERNARD, *The Hymns of Wesley and Watts* (London: Epworth, 1942)

MITCHELL, T. CRICHTON, *Charles Wesley: Man with the Dancing Heart* (Kansas: Beacon Press, 1994)

MITCHELL, WILLIAM FRASER, *English Pulpit Oratory from Andrewes to Tillotson*, 2nd edn. (London: Macmillan, 1962)

MOORE, HENRY, *The Life of the Rev John Wesley and the Rev Charles Wesley*, 2 vols. (New York: Methodist Episcopal Church, 1824–5)

MORRIS, GILBERT LESLIE, 'Imagery in the Hymns of Charles Wesley' (Ph.D. thesis, Arkansas, 1969)

MYERS, E. P., *Singer of a Thousand Songs: A Life of Charles Wesley* (London: T. Nelson, 1965)

NEWPORT, KENNETH G. C., 'Charles Wesley's Interpretation of Some Biblical Prophecies according to a Previously Unpublished Letter Dated 25 April, 1754', *Bulletin of the John Rylands University Library of Manchester* 77 (1995): 31–52

—— 'Charles Wesley and the End of the World', *Proceedings of the Charles Wesley Society* 3 (1996): 33–61

—— 'The French Prophets and Early Methodism: Some New Evidence', *Proceedings of the Wesley Historical Society* 50 (1996): 127–40

—— 'George Bell, Prophet and Enthusiast', *Methodist History* 35 (1997): 95–105

—— 'Premillennialism in the Early Writings of Charles Wesley', *Wesleyan Theological Journal* 32/1 (Spring 1997): 85–106

—— *Apocalypse and Millenium* (Cambridge: Cambridge University Press, 2000)

—— and LLOYD, GARETH, 'George Bell and Early Methodist Enthusiasm: A new Source from the Manchester Archives' *Bulletin of the John Rylands University Library of Manchester* 80 (1998): 89–101

NEWTON, JOHN A., *Susanna Wesley and the Puritan Tradition in Methodism* (London: Epworth, 1968)

NOLL, MARK A., 'Romanticism and the Hymns of Charles Wesley', *Evangelical Quarterly* 46 (1974): 195–223

NORRIS, JOHN, *Practical Discourses on Several Divine Subjects*, 4 vols. (London: 1690)

NUTTALL, GEOFFREY F., 'Charles Wesley in 1739. By Joseph Williams of Kidderminster', *Proceedings of the Wesley Historical Society* 42 (1980): 181–5

NUTTER, CHARLES SUMNER 'Charles Wesley as a Hymnist' *Methodist Review* 108 (1925): 341–57

NYE, ROBERT (ed.), *The English Sermon*, vol. iii: *1750–1850* (Cheadle Hulme, Cheshire: Carcanet Press Ltd., 1976)

OSBORN, GEORGE (ed.), *The Poetical Works of John and Charles Wesley*, 13 vols. (1868–72)

OUTLER, ALBERT C. (ed.), *Sermons*, vols. i–iv (1984–7) in the Bicentennial Edition of the Works of John Wesley

PASCAL, BLAISE, *Pensées*, ed. Louis Lafuma, trans. John Warrington (London: Dent, 1973)

POPKIN, RICHARD H. (ed.), *Millenarianism and Messianism in English Literature and Thought 1650–1800* (Leiden: E. J. Brill, 1988)

QUANTRILLE, WILMA JEAN, 'The Triune God in the Hymns of Charles Wesley' (Ph.D. thesis, Drew University, 1989)

QUILLER-COUCH, ARTHUR, *Hetty Wesley* (New York and London: Macmillan, 1903)

RATTENBURY, J. ERNEST, *The Eucharistic Hymns of John and Charles Wesley to Which is Appended Wesley's Preface Extracted from Brevint's 'Christian Sacrament and Sacrifice', Together with Hymns on the Lord's Supper* (London: Epworth, 1948)

—— *The Evangelical Doctrine of Charles Wesley's Hymns* (London: Epworth, 1941)

RENSHAW, JOHN R., 'The Atonement in the Theology of John and Charles Wesley' (Th.D. thesis, Boston, 1965)

ROGAL, SAMUEL J., 'Old Testament Prophecy in Charles Wesley's Paraphrase of Scripture', *Christian Scholar's Review* 13 (1984): 205–16

—— *A Biographical Dictionary of Eighteenth Century Methodism*, 8 vols. (Lewiston, NY: Edwin Mellen Press, 1997–)

ROTH, HERBERT JOHN, 'A Literary Study of the Calvinistic and Deistic Implications in the Hymns of Isaac Watts, Charles Wesley and William Cowper' (Ph.D. thesis, Texas Christian University, 1978)

SANGSTER, W. E., *The Craft of Sermon Construction*, reprint (London: Marshall Pickering, 1978)

Sermons by the Late Rev. Charles Wesley, A. M. Student of Christ-Church, Oxford. With a Memoir of the Author by the Editor (London: Baldwin, Cradock, and Joy, 1816)

SHEPHERD, NEVILLE, 'Charles Wesley and the Doctrine of the Atonement' (Ph.D. thesis, Bristol, 1999)

SHIELDS, KENNETH D., 'Charles Wesley as Poet', in Kimbrough (ed.), *Charles Wesley: Poet and Theologian*, 45–71

SISSON, C. H., *The English Sermon* vol. ii: *1650–1750* (Cheadle Hulme, Cheshire: Carcanet, 1976)

SMYTH, CHARLES, *The Art of Preaching: A Practical Survey of Preaching in the Church of England 1747–1939* (London: SPCK, 1940)

STEVENSON, GEORGE J., *City Road Chapel London and its Associations Historical, Biographical, and Memorial* (London (1873))

TELFORD, JOHN, *The Journal of the Rev. Charles Wesley,* (London: Robert Culley, (1910)

—— *Wesley's Veterans*, 6 vols. (London: Charles A. Kelly, 1912)

TYERMAN, LUKE, *The Life and Times of the Rev. John Wesley, M.A.*, 3 vols. (1870–1)

TYSON, JOHN R., 'Charles Wesley's Theology of the Cross: An Examination of the Theology and Method of Charles Wesley as seen in his Doctrine of the Atonement' (Ph.D. thesis, Drew University, 1983)

—— 'Charles Wesley, Evangelist: The Unpublished Newcastle Journal', *Methodist History* 25 (1986): 41–60.

—— *Charles Wesley: A Reader* (New York: Oxford University Press, 1989)

—— *Charles Wesley on Sanctification: A Biographical and Theological Study* (Salem, OH: Schmul Publishing Co. Inc., 1992)

WALLACE, CHARLES (ed.), *Susanna Wesley: The Complete Writings* (Oxford: Oxford University Press, 1997)

WARD, W. REGINALD, AND HEITZENRATER, RICHARD P. (eds.), *Journals and Diaries of John Wesley*, vols. xviii–xxiii (1988–93), in the Bicentennial Edition of the Works of John Wesley

WATERHOUSE, JOHN W., *The Bible in Charles Wesley's Hymns* (London: Epworth, 1954)

WATSON, J. RICHARD, *The English Hymn* (Oxford: Clarendon, 1997)

WHITEHEAD, JOHN, *Life of the Rev. John Wesley*, 2 vols. (1793–6)

—— *The Life of the Rev. Charles Wesley: Late Student of the [sic] Christ Church, Oxford, Collected from his Private Journal* (1805)

WISEMAN, F. L., *Charles Wesley, Evangelist and Poet* (New York: Abingdon, 1931)

The Works of John Wesley, 14 vols. (1872)

Scriptural Index

Subject Index